## THIRD EDITION

# Total Quality

# MANAGEMENT

## Text, Cases and Readings

THIRD EDITION

# Total Quality MANAGEMENT

## Text, Cases and Readings

## Joel E. Ross

with contributions by

## Susan Perry

$$S^t_L$$

St. Lucie Press
Boca Raton   London   New York   Washington, D.C.

**Library of Congress Cataloging-in-Publication Data**

Catalog information may be obtained from the Library of Congress

© 1999 by CRC Press LLC
St. Lucie Press is an imprint of CRC Press LLC

No claim to original U.S. Government works
International Standard Book Number 1-57444-266-X
Printed in the United States of America 1 2 3 4 5 6 7 8 9 0
Printed on acid-free paper

# PREFACE

Since the publication of the first and second editions of this book, interest in and acceptance of total quality management (TQM) have continued to accelerate around the world. It is now widely agreed that quality in products and services is a prerequisite for becoming a player in domestic and global markets.

The first two editions of this book have been adopted by over 200 colleges and universities for courses in the topic. Many organizations and individual managers are using the book as well. This reflects the growing recognition of the need to train and educate for quality management in all types of organizations.

This edition has been thoroughly revised, updated, and greatly expanded. Among the changes and revisions are

- A new chapter on the emerging theory of constraints (Chapter 13)
- Expanded treatment of process management
- Twelve new readings
- Twelve new cases
- Examples of TQM at 12 Baldrige Award winners
- End of chapter recommendations for further reading
- Revised and updated textual material

The Varifilm case is retained as a comprehensive study that illustrates good and not so good practices. This is a case used by the Baldrige Award organization in preparing examiners to visit and evaluate companies that apply for that award. Most chapters contain an exercise which provides the reader an opportunity to apply TQM principles to the practices illustrated in this case.

Discussion questions, exercises, examples, cases, and readings support the textual material. (The examples are based on material from the National Bureau of Standards.) Together these tools provide reinforcement so that the reader is able to understand the principles and can apply them in practice.

The book is practical yet based on sound principles. It is not about the "hard" science of statistical quality control, although this subject is treated in enough depth to provide a practical approach to the topic. Other tools, techniques, and principles are treated in sufficient depth to permit the development and implementation of a quality program. The book is an excellent text for college students as well as for organizational and management development programs directed to practitioners who are responsible for developing and implementing TQM programs in their own organizations, whether in manufacturing or service firms.

# AUTHORS

**Dr. Joel Ross** is Emeritus Professor of Management at Florida Atlantic University in Boca Raton, Florida. He graduated from Yale University and received his doctorate in business administration from George Washington University. He has been Chairman of Management and Director of the MBA Program. Prior to his academic career, Dr. Ross was a Commander in the U.S. Navy.

Dr. Ross is widely known as a platform speaker, seminar leader, consultant, and author. He has developed and conducted management development programs for over one hundred companies and organizations in the areas of general management, strategy, productivity, and quality. He has been an invited lecturer on management topics in Israel, South Africa, Venezuela, Panama, India, Ecuador, the Philippines, and Japan.

His articles have appeared in such journals as *Journal of Systems Management, Business Horizons, Long Range Planning, Industrial Management, Personnel, Management Accounting,* and *Academy of Management Review.* He is the author of thirteen books, including the landmark *Management Information Systems, People, Profits, and Productivity,* and *Total Quality Management: Text, Cases and Readings,* which has been adopted by over 200 colleges and universities.

Dr. Ross has the reputation of being able to integrate academic principle with real-world practice.

**Dr. Susan Perry** has been an adjunct faculty member in the Department of Management, International Business and Entrepreneurship at Florida Atlantic University. She graduated from the University of Florida and received her Ph.D. from Florida Atlantic University. Dr. Perry is experienced in industry and has conducted research in general management and corporate strategy.

# CONTENTS

# INTRODUCTION TO TOTAL QUALITY MANAGEMENT

*Total Quality Management (TQM) is the set of management processes and systems that create delighted customers through empowered employees, leading to higher revenue and lower cost.*

J. M. Juran, quality expert

Total quality management (TQM) is the integration of all functions and processes within an organization in order to achieve continuous improvement of the quality of goods and services. The goal is customer satisfaction.

Of all the management issues faced in the last decade, none has had the impact of or caused as much concern as quality in American products and services. A report by the Conference Board indicates that senior executives in the United States agree that the banner of total quality is essential to ensure competitiveness in global markets. Quality expert J. M. Juran calls it a major phenomenon in this age.[1] This concern for quality is not misplaced.

The interest in quality is due, in part, to foreign competition and the trade deficit.[2] Analysts estimate that the vast majority of U.S. businesses will continue to face strong competition from the Pacific Rim and the European Economic Community for the remainder of the 1990s and beyond.[3] This comes in the face of a serious erosion of corporate America's ability to compete in global markets over the past 20 years. As we come to the end of the 20th century, the competitive and trade deficit problems are compounded by the weakening situation in Asian and other global markets. To compete in these markets may require additional efforts in both cost reduction and quality.

The problem has not gone unnoticed by government officials, corporate executives, and the public at large. The concern of the president and Congress culminated in the enactment of the Malcolm Baldrige National Quality Improvement Act of 1987 (Public Law 100-107), which established an annual United States National Quality Award. The concern of business executives is reflected in their perceptions of quality. In a 1989 American Society for Quality Control (ASQC) survey, 54 percent of executives rated quality of service as extremely critical and 51 percent rated quality of product as extremely critical.[4] Seventy-four percent gave American-made products less than eight on a ten-point scale for quality. Similarly, a panel of Fortune 500 executives agreed that American products deserved no better than a grade of C+.

Public opinion regarding American-made products is somewhat less than enthusiastic. In a 1988 ASQC survey of consumer perceptions, less than one-half gave American products high marks for quality.[5] Employees also have misgivings about quality in general and, more specifically, about quality in the companies in which they work. They believe that there is a significant gap between what their companies say and what they do. More importantly, employees believe that their talents, abilities, and energies are not being fully utilized for quality improvement.[6]

Despite the pessimism reflected by these groups, progress is being made. In a 1991 survey of American owners of Japanese-made cars, 32 percent indicated that their next purchase would be a domestic model, and the reason given most often was the improved quality of cars built in the United States.[7] Ford's "Quality Is Job One" campaign may have been a contributing factor. There is also evidence that quality has become a competitive marketing strategy in the small business community, as Americans are beginning to shun mass-produced, poorly made, disposable products.

Other promising developments include the increasing acceptance of TQM as a philosophy of management and a way of company life. It is essential that this trend continue if American companies are to remain competitive in global markets. Customers are becoming more demanding and international competition more fierce. Companies that deliver quality will prosper in the next century.

## THE CONCEPT OF TQM

TQM is based on a number of ideas. It means thinking about quality in terms of all functions of the enterprise and is a start-to-finish process that integrates interrelated functions at all levels. It is a systems approach that considers every interaction between the various elements of the organization. Thus, the overall effectiveness of the system is higher than the sum of the individual outputs from the subsystems. The subsystems include all the *organizational functions* in the life cycle of a product, such as (1) design, (2) planning, (3) production, (4) distribution, and (5) field service. The *management* subsystems also require integration, including (1) strategy with a customer focus, (2) the tools of quality, and (3) employee involvement (the linking process that integrates the whole). A corollary is that any product, process, or service can be improved, and a successful organization is one that consciously seeks and exploits opportunities for improvement at all levels. The load-bearing structure is customer satisfaction. The watchword is *continuous improvement.*

The Conference Board has summarized the key issues and terminology related to TQM:

- The cost of quality as the measure of non-quality (not meeting customer requirements) and a measure of how the quality process is progressing.

- A cultural change that appreciates the primary need to meet customer requirements, implements a management philosophy that acknowledges this emphasis, encourages employee involvement, and embraces the ethic of continuous improvement.

- Enabling mechanisms of change, including training and education, communication, recognition, management behavior, teamwork, and customer satisfaction programs.

- Implementing TQM by defining the mission, identifying the output, identifying the customers, negotiating customer requirements, developing a "supplier specification" that details customer objectives, and determining the activities required to fulfill those objectives.

- Management behavior that includes acting as role models, use of quality processes and tools, encouraging communication, sponsoring feedback activities, and fostering and providing a supporting environment.[8]

## ANTECEDENTS OF MODERN QUALITY MANAGEMENT

*You [= Japan] will never be able to compete with the United States in technology, but you do make very good handkerchiefs and pajamas which you would sell very well in the USA. Why don't you export these?*

John Foster Dulles (1950)

*We are going to win and the industrial West is going to lose out; there's not much you can do about it because the reasons for your failure are within yourselves. Your firms are built on the Taylor Model. Even worse, so are your heads. With your bosses doing the thinking while the workers wield the screwdrivers, you're convinced deep down that this is the right way to run a business. For you, the essence of management is getting the ideas out of the heads of the bosses and into the hands of labor.*

Konosuke Matsushita (Matsushita)

Quality control as we know it probably had its beginnings in the factory system that developed following the Industrial Revolution. Production methods at that time were rudimentary at best. Products were made from non-standardized materials using non-standardized methods. The result was products of varying quality. The only real standards used were measures of dimensions, weight, and in some instances purity. The most common form of quality control was inspection by the purchaser, under the common-law rule of *caveat emptor*.[9]

Much later, around the turn of this century, Frederick Taylor developed his system of scientific management, which emphasized productivity at the expense of quality. Centralized inspection departments were organized to check for quality at the end of the production line. An extreme example of this approach was the Hawthorne Works at Western Electric Company, which at its peak in 1928 employed 40,000 people in the manufacturing plant, 5200 of whom were in the inspection department. The control of quality focused on final inspection of the manufactured product, and a number of techniques were developed to enhance the inspection process. Most involved visual inspection or testing of the product following manufacture. Methods of statistical quality control and quality assurance were added later. Detecting manufacturing problems was the overriding focus. Top management moved away from the idea of managing to achieve quality, and furthermore, the work force had no stake in it. The concern was limited largely to the shop floor.

Traditional quality control measures were (and still are) designed as defense mechanisms to prevent failure or eliminate defects.[10] Accountants were taught (and are still taught) that expenditures for defect prevention were justified only if they were less than the cost of failure. Of course, cost of failure was rarely computed. (Cost of quality is discussed further in Chapter 11.)[11]

Following World War II, the quality of products produced in the United States declined as manufacturers tried to keep up with the demand for non-military goods that had not been produced during the war. It was during this period that a number of pioneers began to advance a methodology of quality control in manufacturing and to develop theories and practical techniques for improved quality. The most visible of these pioneers were W. Edwards Deming, Joseph M. Juran, Armand V. Feigenbaum, and Philip Crosby.[12] It was a great loss to the quality movement when Deming died in December 1993 at the age of 93.

## THE QUALITY GURUS

*Defects are not free.*
*Somebody makes them, and gets paid for making them.*

W. Edwards Deming
*Out of the Crisis*

*In the U.S.A. about a third of what we do*
*consists of redoing work previously "done."*

J. M. Juran
*Managerial Breakthrough*

*Quality is free. It's not a gift, but it is free.*
*What costs money are the unquality things—*
*all the actions that involve not doing jobs right the first time.*

Philip Crosby
*Quality Is Free*

Deming, the best known of the "early" pioneers, is credited with popularizing quality control in Japan in the early 1950s. Today, he is regarded as a national hero in that country and is the father of the world-famous Deming Prize for Quality. He is best known for developing a system of statistical quality control, although his contribution goes substantially beyond those techniques.[13] His philosophy begins with top management but maintains that a company must adopt the 14 points of his system at all levels. He also believes that quality must be built into the product at all stages in order to achieve a high level of excellence. While it cannot be said that Deming is responsible for quality improvement in Japan or the United States, he has played a substantial role in increasing the visibility of the process and advancing an awareness of the need to improve.

Deming defines quality as a predictable degree of uniformity and dependability, at low costs and suited to the market. Deming teaches that 96 percent of variations have common causes and 4 percent have special causes. He views statistics as a management tool and relies on statistical process control as a means of managing variations in a process. Deming developed what is known as the Deming chain reaction; as quality improves, costs will decrease and productivity will increase, resulting in more jobs, greater market share, and long-term survival. Although it is the worker who will ultimately produce quality products, Deming stresses worker pride and satisfaction rather than the establishment of quantifiable goals. His overall approach focuses on improvement of the process, in that the system, rather than the worker, is the cause of process variation.

Deming's *universal 14 points* for management are summarized as follows:[14]

1. **Create consistency of purpose with a plan.**   The objective is constancy of purpose for continuous improvement. An unwavering commitment to quality must be maintained by management. Quality, not short-term profit, should be at the heart of organization purpose. Profit will follow when quality becomes the objective and purpose.

2. **Adopt the new philosophy of quality.**   The modern era demands ever-increasing quality as a means of survival and global competitiveness. Inferior material, poor workmanship, defective products, and poor service must be rejected. Reduction of defects is replaced by elimination of defects. The new culture of quality must reflect a commitment to quality and must be supported by all employees.

3. **Cease dependence on mass inspection.**   Quality cannot be inspected in; it must be built in from the start. Defects discovered during inspection cannot be avoided—it is too late; efficiency and effectiveness have been lost, as has continuous process improvement. Continuous process improvement reduces costs incurred by correcting errors that should not have been made in the first place.

4. **End the practice of choosing suppliers based on price.**   Least cost is not necessarily the best cost. Buying from a supplier based on low cost rather than a quality/cost basis defeats the need for a long-term relationship. Vendor quality can be evaluated with statistical tools.

5. **Identify problems and work continuously to improve the system.**   Continuous improvement of the system requires seeking out methods for improvement. The search for quality improvement is never-ending and results from studying the process itself, not the defects detected during inspection.

6. **Adopt modern methods of training on the job.**   Training involves teaching employees the best methods of achieving quality in their jobs and the use of tools such as statistical quality control.

7. **Change the focus from production numbers (quantity) to quality.**   The focus on volume of production instead of quality leads to defects and rework that may result in inferior products at higher costs.

8. **Drive out fear.**   Employees need to feel secure in order for quality to be achieved. Fear of asking questions, reporting problems, or making suggestions will prevent the desired climate of openness.

9. **Break down barriers between departments.**   When employees perceive themselves as specialists in one function or department without too much

regard for other areas, it tends to promote a climate of parochialism and set up barriers between departments. Quality and productivity can be improved when there is open communication and coordination based on the common organization goals.

10. **Stop requesting improved productivity without providing such methods to achieve it.** Continuous improvement as a general goal should replace motivational or inspirational slogans, signs, exhortations, and work force targets. The major cause of poor productivity and quality is the management systems, not the work force. Employees are frustrated when exhorted to achieve results that management systems prevent them from achieving.

11. **Eliminate work standards that prescribe numerical quotas.** Focus on quotas, like a focus on production, may encourage and reward people for numerical targets, frequently at the expense of quality.

12. **Remove barriers to pride of workmanship.** A major barrier to pride of workmanship is a merit or appraisal system based on targets, quotas, or some list of personal traits that have little to do with incentives related to quality. Appraisal systems that attempt to coerce performance should be replaced by systems that attempt to overcome obstacles imposed by inadequate material, equipment, or training.

13. **Institute vigorous education and retraining.** Deming emphasizes training, not only in the methods of the specific job but in the tools and techniques of quality control, as well as instruction in teamwork and the philosophy of a quality culture.

14. **Create a structure in top management that will emphasize the preceding 13 points every day.** An organization that wants to establish a culture based on quality needs to emphasize the preceding 13 points on a daily basis. This usually requires a transformation in management style and structure. The entire organization must work together to enable a quality culture to succeed.

Juran, like Deming, was invited to Japan in 1954 by the Union of Japanese Scientists and Engineers (JUSE). His lectures introduced the managerial dimensions of planning, organizing, and controlling and focused on the responsibility of management to achieve quality and the need for setting goals.[15] Juran defines quality as *fitness for use* in terms of design, conformance, availability, safety, and field use. Thus, his concept more closely incorporates the point of view of the customer. He is prepared to measure everything and relies on systems and problem-solving techniques. Unlike Deming, he focuses on top-down management and technical methods rather than worker pride and satisfaction.

Juran's ten steps to quality improvement are

1. Build awareness of opportunities to improve.
2. Set goals for improvement.
3. Organize to reach goals.
4. Provide training.
5. Carry out projects to solve problems.
6. Report progress.
7. Give recognition.
8. Communicate results.
9. Keep score.
10. Maintain momentum by making annual improvement part of the regular systems and processes of the company.

Juran is the founder of the Juran Institute in Wilton, Connecticut. He promotes a concept known as Managing Business Process Quality, which is a technique for executing cross-functional quality improvement. Juran's contribution may, over the longer term, be greater than Deming's because Juran has the broader concept, while Deming's focus on statistical process control is more technically oriented.[16]

Armand Feigenbaum, like Deming and Juran, achieved visibility through his work with the Japanese. Unlike the latter two, he used a total quality control approach that may very well be the forerunner of today's TQM. He promoted a system for integrating efforts to develop, maintain, and improve quality by the various groups in an organization. To do otherwise, according to Feigenbaum, would be to inspect for and control quality after the fact rather than build it in at an earlier stage of the process.

Philip Crosby, author of the popular book *Quality Is Free*,[17] may have achieved the greatest commercial success by promoting his views and founding the Quality College in Winter Park, Florida. He argues that poor quality in the average firm costs about 20 percent of revenues, most of which could be avoided by adopting good quality practices. His "absolutes" of quality are

- Quality is defined as conformance to requirements, not "goodness."
- The system for achieving quality is prevention, not appraisal.
- The performance standard is zero defects, not "that's close enough."
- The measurement of quality is the price of non-conformance, not indexes.[18]

Crosby stresses motivation and planning and does not dwell on statistical process control and the several problem-solving techniques of Deming and

Juran. He states that quality is free because the small costs of prevention will always be lower than the costs of detection, correction, and failure. Like Deming, Crosby has his own *14 points*:

1. **Management commitment.** Top management must become convinced of the need for quality and must clearly communicate this to the entire company by written policy, stating that each person is expected to perform according to the requirement or cause the requirement to be officially changed to what the company and the customers really need.

2. **Quality improvement team.** Form a team composed of department heads to oversee improvements in their departments and in the company as a whole.

3. **Quality measurement.** Establish measurements appropriate to every activity in order to identify areas in need of improvement.

4. **Cost of quality.** Estimate the costs of quality in order to identify areas where improvements would be profitable.

5. **Quality awareness.** Raise quality awareness among employees. They must understand the importance of product conformance and the costs of non-conformance.

6. **Corrective action.** Take corrective action as a result of steps 3 and 4.

7. **Zero defects planning.** Form a committee to plan a program appropriate to the company and its culture.

8. **Supervisor training.** All levels of management must be trained in how to implement their part of the quality improvement program.

9. **Zero defects day.** Schedule a day to signal to employees that the company has a new standard.

10. **Goal setting.** Individuals must establish improvement goals for themselves and their groups.

11. **Error cause removal.** Employees should be encouraged to inform management of any problems that prevent them from performing error-free work.

12. **Recognition.** Give public, non-financial appreciation to those who meet their quality goals or perform outstandingly.

13. **Quality councils.** Composed of quality professionals and team chairpersons, quality councils should meet regularly to share experiences, problems, and ideas.

14. **Do it all over again.** Repeat steps 1 to 13 in order to emphasize the never-ending process of quality improvement.

All of these pioneers believe that management and the system, rather than the workers, are the cause of poor quality. These and other trailblazers have largely absorbed and synthesized each other's ideas, but generally speaking they belong to two schools of thought: those who focus on technical processes and tools and those who focus on the managerial dimensions.[19] Deming provides manufacturers with methods to measure the variations in a production process in order to determine the causes of poor quality. Juran emphasizes setting specific annual goals and establishing teams to work on them. Crosby stresses a program of zero defects. Feigenbaum teaches total quality control aimed at managing by applying statistical and engineering methods throughout the company.

Despite the differences among these experts, a number of common themes arise:

1. Inspection is never the answer to quality improvement, nor is "policing."
2. Involvement of and leadership by top management are essential to the necessary culture of commitment to quality.
3. A program for quality requires organization-wide efforts and long-term commitment, accompanied by the necessary investment in training.
4. Quality is first and schedules are secondary.

Admiration for Deming's contribution is not confined to Japan. At the Yale University commencement in May 1991, Deming was awarded an honorary degree. The citation read in part:

> For the past four decades, you have been the champion of quality management. You have developed a theory of management, based on scientific and statistical principles in which people remain the least predictable and most important part. Your scholarly insights and your wisdom have revolutionized industry.[20]

## ACCELERATING USE OF TQM

The increased acceptance and use of TQM are the result of three major trends: (1) reaction to increasing domestic and global competition, (2) the pervasive need to integrate the several organizational functions for improvement of total output of the organization as well as the quality of output within each function, and (3) the acceptance of TQM in a variety of service industries.

Aside from existing competitive pressures from Japan and the Pacific Rim countries, American firms are faced with the prospect of increasing competition from members of the European Economic Community. This concern is justified by the very nature of manufacturing strategy among European firms, where quality has replaced technology as the primary consideration.

Basic to the concept of TQM is the notion that quality is essential in all functions of the business, not just manufacturing. This is justified by reason of organization synergism: the need to provide quality output to internal as well as external customers and the facilitation of a quality culture and value system throughout the organization. Companies that commit to the concept of TQM apply quality improvement techniques in almost every area of product development, manufacturing, distribution, administration, and customer service.[21] Nowhere is the philosophy of "customer is king" more prevalent than in TQM. Customers are both external (including channels) and internal (including staff functions) to the business.

The paradigm of TQM applies to all enterprises, both manufacturing and service, and many companies in manufacturing, service, and information industries have reaped the benefits. Industries as diverse as telecommunications, public utilities, and health care have applied the principles of TQM.

Most states have their own Baldrige-based award programs that have served to communicate the criteria to a broader cross-section of organizations than the national program has been able to do on its own. Baptist Hospital of Miami is one of four Florida organizations to receive the Governor's Sterling Award. In Maine, 11 winners were given the Margaret Chase Smith Maine State Quality Award. At a grass-roots level, community-based quality initiatives known as excellence councils are becoming prevalent throughout North America. In October 1998, the president signed the 1999 budget, which contains funding that will establish and manage Baldrige Awards for health care and education.

Government agencies and departments have also joined the movement, although private sector efforts have been considerably more effective.[22] According to a 1992 General Accounting Office (GAO) special report, 68 percent of the federal organizations and installations surveyed had some kind of TQM effort underway. Productivity and quality improvement programs were expected to be initiated in almost 700 federal programs in 1993.[23] Defense contractors will be particularly affected as the government moves toward requiring suppliers to adopt the TQM concept.[24] Oregon State University is the first among academic institutions to make a commitment to adopt the principles of TQM throughout the organization.[25] Others have followed.

The widespread adoption of one or more approaches or principles of TQM does not mean that results have met expectations. According to the GAO survey mentioned earlier, only 13 percent of government agency employees actively participate in the TQM efforts.[26] Human resource professionals reported a strong interest in TQM issues in 1993, ranking employee involvement, customer service, and TQM as the top three key issues.[27]

## QUALITY AND BUSINESS PERFORMANCE

The relationship among quality, profitability, and market share has been studied in depth by the Strategic Planning Institute of Cambridge, Massachusetts. The conclusion, based on performance data of about 3000 strategic business units, is unequivocal:

> One factor above all others—quality—drives market share. And when superior quality and large market share are both present, profitability is virtually guaranteed.[28]

> There is no doubt that relative perceived quality and profitability are strongly related. Whether the profit measure is return on sales or return on investment, businesses with a superior product/service offering clearly outperform those with inferior quality.[29]

Even producers of commodity or near-commodity products seek and find ways to distinguish their products through cycle time, availability, or other quality attributes.[30] In addition to profitability and market share, quality drives growth. The linkages between these correlates of quality are shown in Figure 1-1. Quality can also reduce costs. This reduction, in turn, provides an additional competitive edge. Note that Figure 1-1 includes two types of quality: customer-driven quality and conformance or internal specification quality. The latter relates to appropriate product specifications and service standards that lead to cost reduction. As will be discussed in Chapter 11, there is an inverse relationship between internal or conformance quality and costs, and thus the phrase coined by Crosby: "Quality Is Free."[31] As quality improves, so does cost, resulting in improved market share and hence profitability and growth. This, in turn, provides a means for further investment in such quality improvement areas as research and development. The cycle goes on. In summary, improving both internal (conformance) quality and external (customer-perceived) quality not only lowers cost of poor quality or "non-quality" but also serves as a driver for growth, market share, and profitability.

The rewards of higher quality are positive, substantial, and pervasive.[32] Findings indicate that attaining quality superiority produces the following organizational benefits:

1. Greater customer loyalty
2. Market share improvements
3. Higher stock prices
4. Reduced service calls

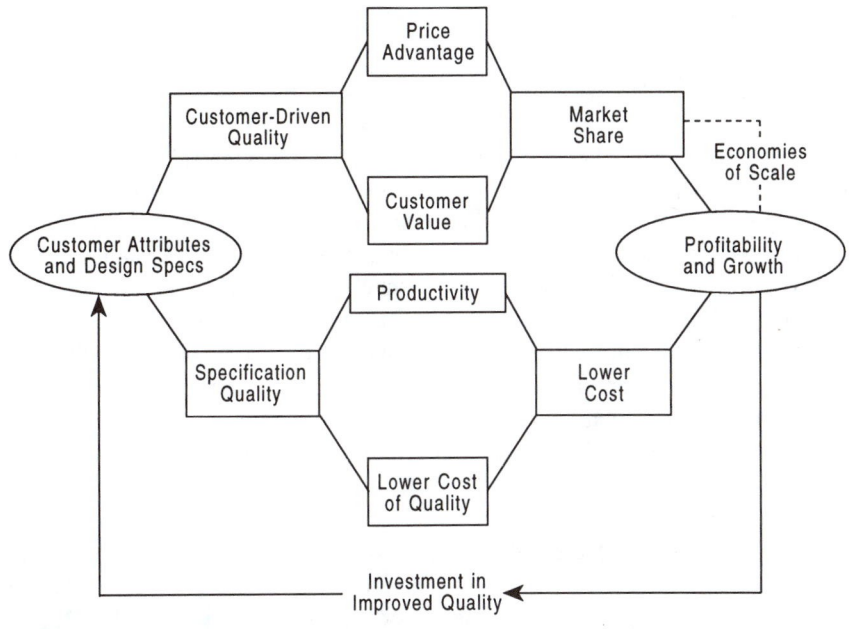

**Figure 1-1**    The Quality Circle

5. Higher prices
6. Greater productivity

## SERVICE QUALITY VS. PRODUCT QUALITY

*In the service sector, consumers expect and demand more,*
*because they know they can get more.*

Michael Hammer
*Reengineering the Corporation:*
*A Manifesto for Business Revolution*

It is paradoxical that there is more concern in the United States for product quality than there is for quality of services and service industries. Despite the fact that only 21 percent of total employment in the United States is in industries that produce goods (excluding agriculture, with approximately 3 percent),[33] the emphasis has historically been on manufacturing industries. Consider also that up to half of employment in manufacturing is in such staff or white-collar jobs as marketing, finance, or the many other activities not directly involved in physically producing products. If it is accepted that quality improvement can only be achieved through the actions of people, the conclusion emerges that possibly 90 percent or more of the potential for improvement lies in service industries and service jobs in manufacturing firms. The concept of "white-collar quality" is becoming increasingly recognized as the service sector grows.[34]

Despite this rather obvious need for quality service, people directly employed in manufacturing functions tend to focus on production first and quality second. "Get out the production" and "meet the schedule" are common cries on many shop floors. A study conducted by David Garvin of the Harvard Business School revealed that U.S. supervisors believed that a deep concern for quality was lacking among workers and that quality as an objective in manufacturing was secondary to the primary goal of meeting production schedules. This same conclusion is suggested in the experiences of over 100 companies. Supervisors almost invariably set targets related to productivity and cost reduction rather than quality improvement.[35]

This seeming manufacturing–service paradox is unusual in view of the several considerations which suggest that the emphasis on services should be substantially increased. The first of these considerations is the "bottom-line" factor. Studies have shown that companies rated highly by their customers in terms of service can charge close to 10 percent more than those rated poorly.[36] People will go out of their way and pay more for good service, which indicates the importance placed on service by customers. Conference Board reports concluded that the strongest complaints of customers were registered not for products but rather for services. Recognizing this, executives rate quality of service as a more critical issue than quality of product.[37] Tom Peters, co-author of *In Search of Excellence*, scolds U.S. manufacturers for allowing quality to deteriorate into a mindless effort to copy the Japanese and suggests that the best approach is to learn from America's leading service companies.[38]

> ■ Taking a cue from Domino's Pizza, its Michigan-based neighbor, Doctor's Hospital in Detroit, is promising to see its emergency room patients in 20 minutes or the care will be free. During the first three weeks of the offer, no patients have been treated free of charge and the number of patients has been up 30 percent.[39]

As a strategic issue, customer service can be considered a major dimension of competitiveness. In the most exhaustive study in its history, the American Management Association surveyed over 3000 international respondents;[40] 78 percent identified improving quality and service to customers as *the* key to competitive success, and 92 percent indicated that providing superior service is one of their key responsibilities, regardless of position. To say that your competitive edge is price is to admit that your products and services are commodities.

After being viewed as a manufacturing problem for most of the past decade, quality has now become a service issue as well. TQM relates not only to the product but to all the services that accompany it as well.

In many ways, defining and controlling quality of service is more difficult than quality assurance of products. Unlike manufacturing, service industries share unique characteristics that make the process of quality control less manageable but no less important. Moreover, the level of quality expected is less predictable. Service company operations are affected by several characteristics, including the intangible nature of the output and the inability to store the output. Other distinguishing characteristics include:

1. Behavior of the delivery person
2. Image of the organization
3. The customer present during the production process and performing the final inspection
4. The measure of output is difficult to define
5. Variance and acceptance ranges may not apply
6. Adjusting the control system if the customer is present[41]

However, the most significant problem with the delivery of services is that it is typically measured at the customer interface—the one-on-one, face-to-face interaction between supplier and customer. If a problem exists, it is already too late to fix it.[42]

## THE BALDRIGE AWARD

An additional impetus was provided when Congress established the Baldrige Award in 1987 as a result of Public Law 100-107. Background information on the law mentions foreign competition as the major rationale. No other business prize or development in management theory can match its impact. As evidence of this impact, over 20 states are working to develop regional quality programs.[43]

The award has set a national standard for quality, and hundreds of major corporations use the criteria in the application form as a basic management guide for quality improvement programs. Although the award has its detractors,[44] it has effectively created a new set of standards—a benchmark for quality in U.S. industry.

Applicants must address seven specific categories. These categories of examination items and their respective point values are listed in Table 1-1. The Baldrige Award framework and the dynamic relationships among the criteria are shown in Figure 1-2.

Meeting the criteria is not an easy matter. A perfect score is 1000. The distribution of scores for the 203 applicants during the first three years (1988, 1989, 1990) is shown in Table 1-2. Of the 1203 applicants, only 9 were selected for the award.

An indication of the interest in the Baldrige is the number of application guidelines requested (167,000 in 1990). In the first three years, 203 companies applied and 9 won: 6 manufacturers, 2 small companies, and 1 service company (Federal Express). Winners of the award are required to share their successful strategies with other companies. IBM's Rochester, Minnesota, site, home of the Applications System/400 and a 1990 winner, attributes the success of the divi-

**Table 1-1** 1999 Criteria for Performance Excellence—Item Listing[45]

| Categories/items | Point values |
|---|---|
| **1 Leadership** | **125** |
| The company's leadership system and senior leaders' personal leadership. How senior leaders and the leadership system address values, company directions, performance expectations, a focus on customers and other stakeholders, learning, and innovation. How the company addresses its societal responsibilities and provides support to key communities. | |
| 1.1 Organizational leadership | 85 |
| 1.2 Public responsibility and citizenship | 40 |
| **2 Strategic Planning** | **85** |
| How the company sets strategic directions and how it develops the critical strategies and action plans to support the directions. How plans are deployed and how performance is tracked. | |
| 2.1 Strategy development | 40 |
| 2.2 Strategy deployment | 45 |
| **3 Customer and Market Focus** | **85** |
| How the company determines longer term requirements, expectations, and preferences of target and/or potential customers and markets. How the company uses this information to understand and anticipate needs and to develop business opportunities. | |
| 3.1 Customer and market knowledge | 40 |
| 3.2 Customer satisfaction and relationships | 45 |

**Table 1-1 (continued)** 1999 Criteria for Performance Excellence—Item Listing[45]

| Categories/items | Point values |
|---|---|
| **4 Information and Analysis** | **85** |
| The selection, management, and effectiveness of use of information and data to support key company processes and action plans, and the company's performance management system. | |
| 4.1 Measurement of organizational performance | 40 |
| 4.2 Analysis of organizational performance | 45 |
| **5 Human Resource Focus** | **85** |
| How the company enables employees to develop and utilize their full potential, aligned with the company's objectives. The company's efforts to build and maintain a work environment and work climate conducive to performance excellence, full participation, and personal and organizational growth. | |
| 5.1 Work systems | 35 |
| 5.2 Employee education, training, and development | 25 |
| 5.3 Employee well-being and satisfaction | 25 |
| **6 Process Management** | **85** |
| The key aspects of process management, including customer-focused design, product and service delivery, support, and supplier and partnering processes involving all work units. How key processes are designed, implemented, managed, and improved to achieve better performance. | |
| 6.1 Product and service processes | 55 |
| 6.2 Support processes | 15 |
| 6.3 Supplier and partnering processes | 15 |
| **7 Business Results** | **450** |
| The company's performance and improvement in key business areas—customer satisfaction, financial and marketplace performance, human resource results, supplier and partner performance, and operational performance. Performance relative to competitors. | |
| 7.1 Customer-focused results | 115 |
| 7.2 Financial and market results | 115 |
| 7.3 Human resource results | 80 |
| 7.4 Supplier and partner results | 25 |
| 7.5 Organizational effectiveness results | 115 |
| **Total Points** | **1000** |

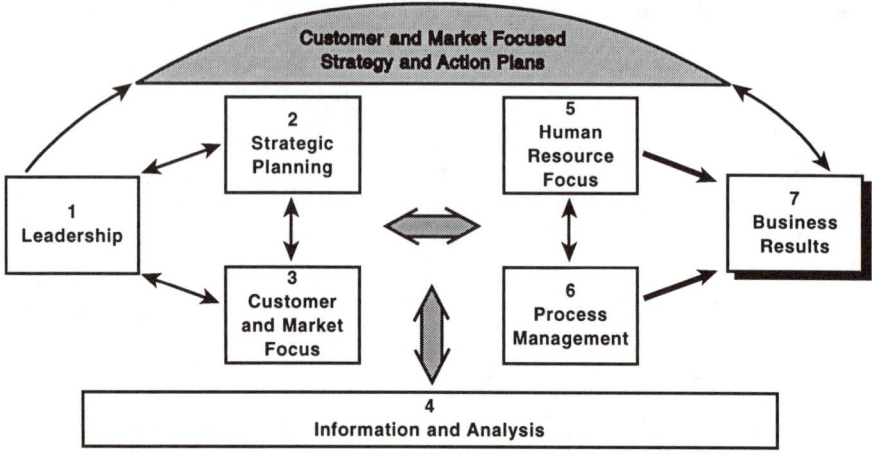

**Figure 1-2**    Baldrige Criteria for Performance Excellence Framework: A Systems Perspective

sion to the way in which it appropriated the ideas of Motorola, Xerox, and Milliken, winners in prior years. This sharing of ideas is a central purpose of the National Institute of Standards and Technology, the administering agency.[46] The sharing policy by winners ensures a multiplier effect.

Another indication of the award's leverage is the stringent criteria related to quality assurance for products and services purchased by external providers

**Table 1-2**    Distribution of Scores

| Scoring range | Number of applications | | |
| --- | --- | --- | --- |
| | 1988 | 1989 | 1990 |
| 0–125 | 0 | 0 | 0 |
| 126–250 | 0 | 1 | 7 |
| 251–400 | 1 | 8 | 18 |
| 401–600 | 31 | 15 | 51 |
| 601–750 | 23 | 12 | 19 |
| 751–875 | 11 | 4 | 2 |
| 876–1000 | 0 | 0 | 0 |
| Total | 66 | 40 | 97 |

(suppliers) of goods and services. It is clear that suppliers are a critical link in the chain of processes that constitute TQM. As a result, many companies require their suppliers to apply for the Baldrige. For example, Motorola and Westinghouse, two winners, will not do business with a supplier that has not applied for the award and does not use its criteria. Another winner, Globe Metallurgical, is certified as a supplier by Ford. Globe in turn requires certification by its suppliers. Thus, the number of firms using the Baldrige criteria may grow geometrically as first-tier suppliers certify second-tier suppliers and so on.

Award recipients attribute positive results to the use of the Baldrige criteria. Some of these results are reported by the National Institute of Standards and Technology, administrator of the National Quality Program:[47]

### ■ Globalization

**Eastman Chemical Company** (1993 Baldrige Award Recipient—Manufacturing) continues to move toward its globalization goals to increase sales outside the U.S. to 50% of total sales and to increase manufacturing assets outside the U.S. to 30%. From 1993 through 1997, sales outside the U.S. have grown from 32% to 39% of total sales, while manufacturing assets outside the U.S. have grown from 6% to 21% for the same time period.

### ■ Time to Market

**IBM Rochester's** (1990 Baldrige Award Recipient—Manufacturing) make-to-market cycle time has been reduced by 23%, and its manufacturing cycle time has been reduced 160% since 1990. This allows it to direct ship "build-to-order" AS/400 computers to customers within four days of order receipt, versus 28 days in 1990. The company's on-time shipment commitment has been improved by 63% with 1997 levels exceeding 99% on-time delivery.

### ■ New Product Sales

Over the last 10 years, **3M Dental Products Division** (1997 Baldrige Award Recipient—Manufacturing) has doubled global sales and market share, and from 1991 to 1996, it doubled its rate of profit. In addition, products introduced within the last five years now account for 45% of total annual sales, up from 12% in 1992.

### ■ Employee Involvement

**Milliken & Company's** (1989 Baldrige Award Recipient—Manufacturing) "Pursuit of Excellence" process continues to evolve after starting the journey 17 years ago. For the last six years, each associate submitted 50–60 "Opportunities for Improvement," and last year, Milliken associates participated on over 13,000 teams. Associates were formally recognized in the company's Sharing Rally. Milliken celebrated its 139th Sharing Rally this year.

■ **Customer Satisfaction**

Through its surprise and delight strategy, **Custom Research Inc.** (CRI) (1996 Baldrige Award Recipient—Small Business) exceeded clients' expectations on 73% of its projects in 1996, up from 47% in 1988. In addition, this was CRI's best year ever in sales and profits, demonstrating that "quality pays" for small firms too.

The **Ritz-Carlton Hotel Company** (1992 Baldrige Award Recipient—Service) reports that 75% of its customers would not use a competitor regardless of the offer.

■ **Return on Assets**

**Merrill Lynch Credit Corporation** (1997 Baldrige Award Recipient—Service) saw an increase in return on equity of approximately 74% between 1994 and 1996. Return on assets rose approximately 36% and net income increased 100% over the same time period.

Return on assets, a major financial indicator for **Xerox Corporation Business Products and Systems** (1989 Baldrige Award Recipient—Manufacturing), improved 47% over the past three years.

■ **Employee Productivity**

Over the past ten years, **Motorola Inc.'s** (1988 Baldrige Award Recipient—Manufacturing) employee productivity has increased 223% through robust design, continuous improvement, defect reduction, and employee education and empowerment.

■ **Research and Development**

By applying total quality management concepts to its R&D operations, **Marlow Industries, Inc.** (1991 Baldrige Award Recipient—Small Business) has been able to form a virtual lab with leading scientists and laboratories from across the world.

■ **Market Share**

By building on its total quality foundation, the **Westinghouse Commercial Nuclear Fuel Division's** (1988 Baldrige Recipient—Manufacturing) Time-Based Management strategy has helped the division to sustain its 60% U.S. and 20% worldwide market share and create value for its customers by having shorter cycle times for product development and manufacturing with a 25% reduction in 1996.

■ **Employee Empowerment**

**Trident Precision Manufacturing, Inc.** (1996 Baldrige Award Recipient—Small Business) empowers its employees to make process improvements, implementing 98% of its employees' suggestions. In fact, 95% of the improvement at Trident comes from its own resources and people. Trident received over 2200 process improvement suggestions in 1996 from its 170 employees.

### ■ Revenue

**ADAC Laboratories'** (1996 Baldrige Award Recipient—Manufacturing) revenue per employee has gone from $175,000 per employee to over $325,000 per employee in the last several years. Its U.S. market share has increased from 12% to 50%.

Since winning the Baldrige Award in 1988, **Globe Metallurgical, Inc.** (1988 Baldrige Award Recipient—Small Business) has experienced a 204% increase in revenues and a 310% increase in profits. The company set 67 new production records in 1996.

**Xerox Business Services** (1997 Baldrige Award Recipient—Service) has experienced revenue growth of over 40% for the past two years. In less than five years, XBS has grown into a $2 billion division with projections to reach $6 billion by 2000.

From 1990 through 1996, **Zytec Corporation's** (1991 Baldrige Award Recipient—Manufacturing) revenues grew 309%, and its net income grew 878%. (As of 12/29/97, Zytec Corporation merged with Computer Products and formed Artesyn Technologies.)

### ■ Product Reliability

Based on the 1997 J.D. Powers & Associates Vehicle Dependability Study, **Cadillac Motor Car Company** (1990 Baldrige Award Recipient—Manufacturing) continues to be ranked among the top automotive nameplates in initial product quality, sales and service satisfaction, and five-year dependability.

Since 1989, Lucent Technologies, Inc., Network Systems (includes what was formerly **AT&T Network Systems, Transmission Systems Business Unit**, 1992 Baldrige Award Recipient—Manufacturing) has improved productivity by 150% and product reliability by 75%.

### ■ Cycle Time

**Wainwright Industries, Inc.** (1994 Baldrige Award Recipient—Small Business) has reduced its customer reject rate by 91% and cycle time by more than 90% using the Baldrige framework to drive implementation of more than 10,000 associate quality and process improvement suggestions each year since 1994. Customer satisfaction reached an all-time high of 98% in 1997.

### ■ Cost Reduction

In the last five years, **Federal Express Corporation** (1990 Baldrige Award Recipient—Service) has increased its operating income by 147%, while reducing costs per parcel (its primary indicator of efficiency) by 20%.

The winners since the beginning of the award in 1988 are listed in Table 1-3.[48]

**Table 1-3** Award Winners: 1988 to 1998

**1998 award winners**

| | |
|---|---|
| Manufacturing | Boeing Airlift and Tanker, Long Beach, California |
| | Solar Turbines, Inc., San Diego, California |
| Small Business | Texas Nameplate Company, Dallas, Texas |

**1997 award winners**

| | |
|---|---|
| Manufacturing | 3M Dental Products Division, St. Paul, Minnesota |
| | Solectron Corporation, Milpitas, California |
| Service | Merrill Lynch Credit Corporation, Jacksonville, Florida |
| | Xerox Business Services, Rochester, New York |

**1996 award winners**

| | |
|---|---|
| Manufacturing | ADAC Laboratories, Milpitas, California |
| Service | Dana Commercial Credit Corporation, Toledo, Ohio |
| Small Business | Custom Research, Inc., Minneapolis, Minnesota |
| | Trident Precision Manufacturing, Inc., Webster, New York |

**1995 award winners**

| | |
|---|---|
| Manufacturing | Armstrong World Industries, Inc., Lancaster, Pennsylvania |
| | Corning, Inc. Telecommunications Products Division, Corning, New York |

**1994 award winners**

| | |
|---|---|
| Service | AT&T Consumer Communications Service, Baskings Ridge, New Jersey |
| | GTE Directories Corporation, Dallas/Fort Worth Airport, Dallas, Texas |
| Small Business | Wainwright Industries, St. Peters, Missouri |

**1993 award winners**

| | |
|---|---|
| Manufacturing | Eastman Chemical Company, Kingsport, Tennessee |
| Small Business | Ames Rubber Corporation, Hamburg, New Jersey |

**1992 award winners**

| | |
|---|---|
| Manufacturing | AT&T Network Systems Group, Transmission Systems Business Unit, Morristown, New Jersey |
| | Texas Instruments, Inc. Defense Systems & Electronics Group, Dallas, Texas |
| Service | AT&T Universal Card Services, Jacksonville, Florida |
| | The Ritz-Carlton Hotel Company, Atlanta, Georgia |
| Small Business | Granite Rock Company, Watsonville, California |

**1991 award winners**

| | |
|---|---|
| Manufacturing | Solectron Corporation, San Jose, California |
| | Zytec Corporation, Eden Prairie, Minnesota |
| Small Business | Marlow Industries, Dallas, Texas |

**Table 1-3 (continued)**    Award Winners: 1988 to 1998

**1990 award winners**
| | |
|---|---|
| Manufacturing | Cadillac Motor Car Company, Detroit, Michigan |
| | IBM Rochester, Rochester, Minnesota |
| Service | Federal Express Corporation, Memphis, Tennessee |
| Small Business | Wallace Company, Inc., Houston, Texas |

**1989 award winners**
| | |
|---|---|
| Manufacturing | Milliken & Company, Spartanburg, South Carolina |
| | Xerox Business Products and Systems, Stamford, Connecticut |

**1988 award winners**
| | |
|---|---|
| Manufacturing | Motorola, Inc., Schaumburg, Illinois |
| | Westinghouse Commercial Nuclear Fuel Division, Pittsburgh, Pennsylvania |
| Small Business | Globe Metallurgical, Inc., Cleveland, Ohio |

## QUESTIONS FOR DISCUSSION

**1-1** Give one or more examples of products made in Japan or Western Europe that are superior in quality to American-made products. How do you explain this difference?

**1-2** Illustrate how the TQM concept can integrate design, engineering, manufacturing, and service.

**1-3** Explain why quality should be better by following the TQM concept than in a system that depends on final inspection.

**1-4** What common elements or principles can you identify among (1) the Baldrige criteria and (2) Deming, Juran, and Crosby?

**1-5** Describe how increased market share and profitability might result from improved quality.

**1-6** Select one staff department (e.g., accounting, finance, marketing services, human resources) and describe how this department can deliver quality service to its *internal* customers.

**1-7** Compare the Baldrige Award criteria to the principles promoted by Deming and Crosby. What are the similarities and/or differences?

# ENDNOTES

1. J. M. Juran, "Strategies for World Class Quality," *Quality Progress,* March 1991, p. 81.

2. Armand V. Feigenbaum, "America on the Threshold of Quality," *Quality,* Jan. 1990, p. 16. Feigenbaum, a pioneer and current expert in quality, estimates that TQM could mean a 7 percent increase in the country's gross national product. See Armand V. Feigenbaum, "Quality: An International Imperative," *Journal for Quality and Participation,* March 1991, p. 16. Estimates from the U.S. Chamber of Commerce Department suggest that nearly 75 percent of all products manufactured in the United States are targets for strong competition from imports.

3. Ronald M. Fortuna, "The Quality Imperative," *Executive Excellence,* March 1990, p. 1. It is expected that competition from Europe may become more severe than that from Japan. Despite the surface congeniality at the G-7 meetings in London in mid-July 1991, it is apparent that the European Economic Community plans a united front against the United States. German Chancellor Helmut Kohl stated, "Europe's return to its original unity means that the '90s will be the decade of Europe, not Japan. This is Europe's hour." (Peter Truell and Philip Revzin, "A New Era Is at Hand in Global Competition: U.S. vs. United Europe," *Wall Street Journal,* July 15, 1991, p. 1.)

4. American Society for Quality Control, *Quality: Executive Priority or Afterthought?* Milwaukee: ASQC, 1989.

5. American Society for Quality Control, *'88 Gallup Survey: Consumers' Perceptions Concerning the Quality of American Products and Services,* Milwaukee: ASQC, 1988, p. iv. This survey and the survey cited in Endnote 4 were conducted by the Gallup Organization.

6. American Society for Quality Control, *Quality: Everyone's Job, Many Vacancies,* Milwaukee: ASQC, 1990. This survey was conducted by the Gallup Organization. Other findings include: (1) where quality improvement programs exist, the level of participation among employees is actually higher in small companies and service companies and (2) people who participate in quality improvement activities are more satisfied than nonparticipants with the rate of quality improvement their companies have been able to achieve.

7. A survey conducted by Integrated Automotive Resources, Wayne, Pa.

8. David Mercer, "Total Quality Management: Key Quality Issues," in *Global Perspectives on Total Quality,* New York: Conference Board, 1991, p. 11. See also Walter E. Breisch, "Employee Involvement," *Quality,* May 1990, pp. 49–51; John Hauser, "The House of Quality," *Harvard Business Review,* May/June 1988, pp. 63–73; W. F. Wheaton, "The Journey to Total Quality: A Fundamental Strategic Renewal," *Business Forum,* Spring 1989, pp. 4–7.

9. Claude S. George, Jr., *The History of Management Thought,* Englewood Cliffs, N.J.: Prentice-Hall, 1972, p. 53.

10. David A. Garvin, "Competing on the Eight Dimensions of Quality," *Harvard Business Review,* Nov./Dec. 1987, pp. 101–109. This same author has provided an excellent description of the background of quality developments in his book *Managing Quality* (New York: Free Press, 1988).

11. See Joel E. Ross and David E. Wegman, "Quality Management and the Role of the Accountant," *Industrial Management,* July/Aug. 1990, pp. 21–23.

12. Yunum Kathawala, "A Comparative Analysis of Selected Approaches to Quality," *International Journal of Quality and Reliability Management,* Vol. 6 Issue 5, 1989, pp. 7–17. Other writers and researchers with less visibility than those mentioned here have contributed to the literature. For a review of this rapidly expanding literature, see Jayant V. Saraph, P. George Benson, and Roger G. Schroeder, "An Instrument for Measuring the Critical Factors of Quality Management," *Decision Sciences,* Vol. 20, 1989. The research described in this article identified 120 prescriptions for effective quality management, which were subsequently grouped into 8 categories that are quite similar to the Baldrige Award criteria: (1) the role of management leadership and quality policy, (2) the role of the quality department, (3) training, (4) product/service design, (5) supplier quality management, (6) process management, (7) quality data and reporting, and (8) employee relations.

13. W. Edwards Deming, *Quality, Productivity, and Competitive Position,* Cambridge, Mass.: Center for Advanced Engineering Study, Massachusetts Institute of Technology, 1982. See also W. Edwards Deming, *Out of the Crisis,* Cambridge, Mass.: Center for Advanced Engineering Study, Massachusetts Institute of Technology, 1982.

14. J. A. Swift, Joel E. Ross, and Vincent K. Omachonu, *Principles of Total Quality,* 2nd ed., Boca Raton, Fla.: St. Lucie Press, 1998, pp. 8–9.

15. Juran's early approach appears in J. M. Juran, *Quality Control Handbook,* New York: McGraw-Hill, 1951. For more recent contributions, see (all by Juran) "The Quality Trilogy," *Quality Progress,* Aug. 1986, pp. 19–24; "Universal Approach to Managing Quality," *Executive Excellence,* May 1989, pp. 15–17; "Made in USA—A Quality Resurgence," *Journal for Quality and Participation,* March 1991, pp. 6–8; "Strategies for World Progress," *Quality Progress,* March 1991, pp. 81–85.

16. "Dueling Pioneers," *Business Week,* Oct. 25, 1991. This is a special report and bonus issue of *Business Week* entitled "The Quality Imperative."

17. Philip Crosby, *Quality Is Free,* New York: McGraw-Hill, 1979.

18. From *Quality,* a promotional brochure by Philip Crosby Associates, Inc.

19. Sara Jackson, "Calling in the Gurus," *Director (UK),* Oct. 1990, pp. 95–101. In this article, the author reports that in the U.K., it is not the quality gurus as much as government initiatives that have been responsible for raising quality awareness.

20. Marc Wortman, "Commencement," *Yale Alumni Magazine,* Summer 1991, p. 61. One of the authors happens to be a Yale graduate, although not of the class of '28.

21. Daniel M. Stowell, "Quality in the Marketing Process," *Quality Progress,* Oct. 1989, pp. 57–62. For the sales function, see Walt Williams, "Quality: An Old Objective but a New Strategy." For R&D, see Michael F. Wolff, "Quality in R&D—It Starts With You," *Marketing News,* Oct. 15, 1990, pp. 16–22.

22. Stanley Blacker, "Data Quality and the Environment," *Quality,* April 1990, pp. 38–42.

23. Carolyn Burstein and Kathleen Sediak, "The Federal Quality and Productivity Improvement Effort," *Quality Progress,* Oct. 1988, pp. 38–41.

24. General Dynamics and McDonnell Douglas are among the defense contractors that have achieved improvement through TQM. See Bruce Smith and William B. Scott, "Douglas Tightens Controls to Improve Performance," *Aviation Week & Space Technology,* Jan. 4, 1990, pp. 16–20. See also Glenn E. Hayes, "Three Views of TQM," *Quality,* April 1990, pp. 19–24.

25. Edwin L. Coate, "TQM at Oregon State University," *Journal for Quality and Participation,* Dec. 1990, pp. 90–101.

26. Jennifer Jordan, "Everything You Wanted to Know About TQM," *Public Manager,* Winter 1992–93, pp. 45–48.

27. Karen Matthes, "A Look Ahead for '93," *HR Focus,* Jan. 1993, pp. 1, 4. See also Richard Y. Chang, "When TQM Goes Nowhere," *Training and Development,* Jan. 1993, pp. 22–29.

28. Robert D. Buzzell and Bradley T. Gale, *The PIMS Principles: Linking Strategy to Performance,* New York: The Free Press, 1987, p. 87. PIMS is the acronym for Profit Impact of Market Strategy. A PIMS study in Canada reached a similar conclusion. See William Band, "Quality Is King for Marketers," *Sales and Marketing Management in Canada,* March 1989.

29. Robert D. Buzzell and Bradley T. Gale, *The PIMS Principles: Linking Strategy to Performance,* New York: The Free Press, 1987, p. 107.

30. A good example is the "Perdue Chicken" produced by Perdue Farms. Owner Frank Perdue set out to differentiate his chicken by color, freshness, availability, and meat-to-bone ratio. These criteria of quality, as defined by the customer, led the company to growth and improved market share and profitability. See Diane Feldman, "Building a Better Bird," *Management Review,* May 1989, pp. 10–14.

31. Tom Peters reported in *Thriving on Chaos* (New York: Knopf, 1987) that experts agree that poor quality can cost about 25 percent of the people and assets in a manufacturing firm and up to 40 percent in a service firm.

32. See Joel E. Ross and David Georgoff, "A Survey of Productivity and Quality Issues in Manufacturing: The State of the Industry," *Industrial Management,* Jan./Feb. 1991.

33. U.S. Bureau of Labor Statistics, *Monthly Labor Review,* Nov. 1989. Reported in *U.S. Statistical Abstract,* 1990, p. 395.

34. For example, Campbell USA has targeted the administrative and marketing side of the corporation in its latest quality program, "Quality Proud." See Herbert M. Baum, "White-Collar Quality Comes of Age," *Journal of Business Strategy,* March/April 1990, pp. 34–37.

35. David Garvin, "Quality Problems, Policies, and Attitudes in the United States and Japan: An Exploratory Study," *Academy of Management Journal,* Dec. 1986, pp. 653–673.

36. Frank K. Sonnenberg, "Service Quality: Forethought, Not Afterthought," *Journal of Business Strategy,* Sept./Oct. 1989, pp. 56–57.

37. American Society for Quality Control, *Quality: Executive Priority or Afterthought?* Milwaukee: ASQC, 1989, p. 8. In this survey conducted by the Gallup Organization, 57 percent of service company executives rated service quality as extremely critical (ten on a scale of one to ten), while only 50 percent of industrial company executives gave service quality the same rating.

38. Tom Peters, "Total Quality Leadership. Let's Get It Right," *Journal for Quality and Participation,* March 1991, pp. 10–15.

39. "Hospital Delivers: Emergency Room Guarantees Care in 20 Minutes," Associated Press, July 15, 1991.

40. Reported in Eric R. Greenberg, "Customer Service: The Key to Competitiveness," *Management Review,* Dec. 1990, p. 29. Reported fully in AMA Research Report, *The New Competitive Edge,* New York: American Management Association, 1991.

41. See Terrence J. Smith, "Measuring a Customer Service Culture," *Retail Control,* Oct. 1989, pp. 15–18. See also Behshid Farsad and Ahmad K. Eishennawy, "Defining Service

Quality Is Difficult for Service and Manufacturing Firms," *Industrial Engineering,* March 1989, pp. 17–19; Christian Gronroos, "Service Quality: The Six Criteria of Good Perceived Service Quality," *Review of Business,* Winter 1989, pp. 10–13; Carol King, "Service Quality Assurance Is Different," *Quality Progress,* June 1985, pp. 14–18.

42. Lawrence Holpp, "Ten Steps to Total Service Quality," *Journal for Quality and Participation,* March 1990, pp. 92–96. The major steps referred to in the title include: (1) creating an awareness and a philosophy of constant improvement, (2) making the vision of the organization a personal vision for every employee, (3) empowering employees to act, (4) surveying customers personally, (5) measuring meaningful information, and (6) adopting a performance management system that rewards teamwork, improvement, and new behaviors consistent with interdepartmental cooperation.

43. Curt W. Reimann, "America Unites Behind the Baldrige Quality Crusade," *Electronic Business,* Oct. 15, 1990, p. 63. Reimann is director of the Malcolm Baldrige National Quality Award and associate director for quality programs at the National Institute of Standards and Technology, the agency that administers the Baldrige Award program. A good summary of what it takes to compete for the Baldrige is contained in Curt Reimann, "Winning Strategies for Quality Improvement," *Business America,* March 25, 1991, pp. 8–11. See also "A Standard for All Seasons," *Executive Excellence,* March 1991, p. 9, and "The Baldrige Award: Leading the Way to Quality," *Quality Progress,* July 1989, pp. 35–39.

44. See Jeremy Main, "Is the Baldrige Overblown?" *Fortune,* July 1, 1991, pp. 62–65. Philip Crosby of *Quality Is Free* fame scorns the paperwork, thinks that customers rather than the company applying should do the nominating, and deplores the lack of financial measures. Tom Peters, co-author of *In Search of Excellence,* complains that the criteria are "strangely silent on the subject of bureaucracy." There was also a bit of sour grapes when Cadillac won the award in 1990.

45. A more detailed description is contained in Criteria for Performance Excellence, Baldrige National Quality Program, 1999 and The 1999 Application Forms and Instructions. These two documents can be obtained from U.S. Department of Commerce, Technology Administration, National Institute of Standards and Technology, Baldrige National Quality Program, Administration Building, Room A635, 100 Bureau Drive, Stop 1020, Gaithersburg, MD 20899-1020 (tel. 301-975-2036, fax 301-948-3716, e-mail nqp@nist.gov, Web address http://www.quality.nist.gov).

46. Michael Fitzgerald, "Quality: Take It to the Limit," *Computerworld,* Feb. 11, 1991, pp. 71–78.

47. NIST 9850, Technology Administration, National Institute of Standards and Technology, U.S. Department of Commerce, Gaithersburg, Md.

48. Texas Instruments is one of the several Baldrige winners that attribute their turnaround to the adoption of the principles of TQM. See *Fortune,* Nov. 30, 1992, p. 80–83. In October 1992, the Ritz-Carlton Hotel Company became the first hotel company to win the Baldrige Award. Its approach to quality relies on traditional TQM principles. Edward Watkins, "How Ritz-Carlton Won the Baldrige Award," *Lodging Hospitality,* Nov. 1992, pp. 22–24. In 1990, AT&T chairman and CEO Robert Allen created the Chairman's Quality Award, the criteria and examination process for which were taken from the Malcolm Baldrige Award. See Rick Whiting, "AT&T Started a Quality Bonfire to Learn How to Put It Out," *Electronic Business,* Oct. 1992, pp. 95–103.

# TURNAROUND AT IBM
# AFTER BALDRIGE QUEST

By 1987, the year the Baldrige Award was announced, IBM was one of America's most successful and most admired corporations. But the unchallenged leader in the huge computer industry was in trouble. Its market share and profits were eroding and the company was searching for ways to reverse the pervasive decline. Applying for the Baldrige Award, the company was put to the test by judges whose stringent standards exposed the weaknesses that were evident to the public but not so much to the people at the company's famed Rochester, Minnesota, manufacturing and development center.

Turned down for the award in 1989, the experience came as a slap in the face and served as a wake-up call for the company. From the highest levels of management on down, the demands for change were converted into action, and in 1980 IBM tried again and was successful. The rest, as they say, is history.

The "Baldrige Index" is made up of publicly traded companies that have received the Malcolm Baldrige National Quality Award during the years 1988 to 1996. For the four years ending in 1998, the "index" outperformed the S&P 500 by more than 2.7 to 1, achieving a 394.5 percent return on investment compared to a 146.9 percent return for the S&P 500.

**CASE**

# LESSONS FROM THE BEST

## Michael Verespej

In a fast-paced global world where technology and products transcend borders, it's not surprising that companies are finding that the path to world-class excellence in manufacturing increasingly depends on how well—and how often—they communicate and whether they recognize people as their most important asset. Those two themes turned up repeatedly when *Industry Week* asked the winners of its 1997 America's Best Plants competition what lessons they learned en route to striving for world-class competitiveness.

"The cornerstone of all our improvement efforts is people," says plant manager Mark Hogan as he begins to explain the success of Cooper Industries' Cooper Automotive–Wagner Lighting Products plant in Hampton, Va. "Only through the efforts of each individual on the team working toward a common goal can the goals be achieved."

Steve McGowen, plant manager for Halliburton Energy Services Inc.'s Carrollton, Tex., plant (part of its Dallas Manufacturing Center) that makes equipment for the oil and gas industries, agrees. "Empowered work teams positively impact machine utilization and prioritization of work flow and create an atmosphere favorable to constructive interaction and innovative ideas. Our most important asset is our people."

## The Other Building Block: Communication

"We believe communication is the cornerstone in executing our company's vision and values," says Darryl Miller, plant manager for Aeroquip Corp.'s New Haven, Ind., air-conditioning component plant. "If every employee does not understand the company direction, how can you get there? Communication—both formal and informal—is the key to ingraining your company philosophy and goals into each and every employee."

Reprinted from *Industry Week,* Vol. 247 No. 4, February 16, 1998, pp. 28–36, with permission of Penton Media, Inc., Cleveland, Ohio.

Whatever form communication takes within your company, make sure it is "multidirectional"—that is, up, down, and through all levels of the organization, says McGowen. "Open…lines of communication, develop trust, encourage new ideas, eliminate intimidation and skepticism, and aid in building a brighter future for employees and the company." And the Best Plants winners agree: They can never communicate too much.

"Communicate frequently, personally, and through multiple vehicles to ensure that the message gets across and that you obtain understanding," says Gary W. Bushman, manager of quality assurance and manufacturing engineering at Alcatel Network Systems Inc.'s Alcatel Telecom telecommunication equipment plant in Raleigh, N.C. Don't forget, he adds, that "listening is the more important part of communication." Adds John R. Dew, manager of mission success at Lockheed Martin Utility Services' enriched-uranium plant in Paducah, Ky., "We use group meetings, required readings, a shift newsletter, a monthly newspaper, daily electronic and hard-copy news sheets, all-hands meetings, team meetings, and even public-address announcements to keep people informed. Communication is like dairy farming—you milk the cows but they never stayed milked. It has to be a process the organization uses constantly."

The 10 Best Plants winners also did more benchmarking than the other 15 finalists. The winners conducted an average of 24.4 benchmarking studies (with a median of 22.5) compared with an average of 17.84 for all 25 finalists (and a median of 10). The highest number of benchmarking studies: 58 by Aeroquip. But what do the 25 finalists from 1997 all have in common? Each of them places a major emphasis on cycle-time reduction, continuous improvement, employee cross-training, reduction of inventory, problem-solving teams, and creating opportunities for employees to have contact with customers.

In addition, all 25 have production employees inspect their own work, give suppliers long-term contracts, and invite suppliers to contribute to cost-reduction and quality improvement efforts. And each one uses an enterprise-integration strategy to link manufacturing and engineering to their other functional and geographical locations. In 1996 only 80% had that type of information–technology link.

Here's a sampling of their accomplishments, culled from the data in *IW*'s 1997 Best Plants Statistical Profile, a detailed composite analysis of last year's winners and other finalists. (The 40-page document includes data on a variety of performance indicators that measure, among other things, quality, the efficiency of manufacturing operations, supplier partnerships, customer focus, and employee involvement.)

Sales per employee increased, on average, by 80.43% during the last five years, with a median increase of 51.6%. In hard dollars, that lifted the median level of sales per employee from $169,466 to $260,184.50. Three companies had five-year gains of 188% or better, led by a manufacturer of automotive seat assemblies and seat cushions.

The median reduction in manufacturing cost per unit shipped was 23.7%, excluding the cost of purchased materials—a two-percentage-point increase from the previous year's group of finalists.

The current median first-pass yield for all finished products for the 25 finalists is 98% with 14 of the 25 finalists at or above that threshold and all but five over 95%. Such yields go hand-in-hand with very little scrap. The current median point for scrap/rework as a percentage of sales is 0.5% with three of the finalists under one-hundredth of one percentage point. What's more, the median reductions since 1992 in scrap/rework (as a percentage of sales), in-plant product defect rates, product reject rate, and warranty costs (as a percentage of sales) ranged between 40% and 47%.

Since 1992 the 25 finalists have had a median reduction in work-in-process inventories of 37.9%. One reason: a dramatic reduction in manufacturing cycle time for the two main products at each company. The median five-year reduction since 1992 is between 70% and 71%, compared with reductions in the 50% range for the 1996 finalists. In addition, the 25 finalists store an average of 75.3% of their total parts numbers at the point of use.

Most important, these productivity and efficiency gains have reaped enormous dividends for the finalists in terms of market share and profitability gains.

Of the 25 finalists in *IW*'s 1997 competition, 21 achieved gains in domestic market share since 1992, with a median gain of seven percentage points. Six had increases of nearly or more than 20% and 10 had double-digit market-share growth. Twenty of the finalists had gains in worldwide market share, translating into a median percentage increase in export dollar volume of 96.15%.

With those types of gains, it's not surprising that the average five-year productivity increase for the 25 finalists—based on total annual sales per employee—was 80.43%, with a median increase at 51.6%.

In addition, 17 of the plants can boast of the No. 1 ranking in their primary-product markets. Eleven can brag about a 100% customer retention rate the last five years, and five more of a retention rate that's 95% or higher.

The plant-level return on assets (ROA)? Nothing short of sensational. The median ROA of the 25 finalists was 47.35%, twice as high as the 1996 group, with seven plants over 94%. And the median five-year increase in ROA was 60.5%, with seven plants having a five-year ROA increase of more than 200%.

## Where to Start?

Each of the 10 winners took its own unique path toward world-class manufacturing excellence. After all, there are as many roads to success as there are companies. But it's imperative that companies remember that whatever process they use, the process is not a program. "There is no end to this journey," says Jane Song, director of operations for the EG&G Astrophysics, Long Beach, Calif., plant that makes security X-ray screening systems and food X-ray inspection systems. "As improvements are achieved, you will be lucky to savor those achievements for a day before the journey continues."

That's why it's important to begin, as renowned management expert Stephen Covey suggests, "with the end in mind," says Aeroquip's Miller. "That is the key in understanding the desired results you wish to attain. A road map must be developed in order to achieve the results. Growth and profitability do not happen by chance."

And when beginning the journey, says Alcatel's Bushman, make sure you "focus with great urgency on critical performance issues that must be improved."

"If you don't know where to start or if you're satisfied with your performance," advises Bushman, "go ask your customer if everything is perfect. Internal and external assessments...can provide an unbiased evaluation of progress, reveal weaknesses, and raise the targets of what you must achieve. Constantly seek and respond to your customer's input—both positive and negative."

## Walk the Talk

Best Plants winners have also found that manufacturing excellence and business success require a commitment from all workers, including those in senior and middle management. But it is still up to top management to set the stage for success, they add.

"Before beginning an endeavor of such magnitude," says EG&G's Song, "ensure that top management is totally committed to the success. If top management does not walk the talk, it will be very difficult to win the confidence and commitment from all of your employees."

"Management must live up to its commitment," says Clifton Ritter, environmental and facilities manager for Tenneco Automotive's Paragould, Ark., Monroe shock absorbers and struts plant. "Employees listen to management, but they are also watching them [management] to see what they are doing." Indeed, Alcatel's Bushman says it is "vital" that top management set the example "by doing what they say they will do. Culture change is obtained from repeated shared experiences and must be reinforced daily."

"Change happens only when supported by the level of leadership that has the power to effect those changes," declares Cooper's Hogan. "The production employees are the easiest to sell on the improvement process. But without the complete cooperation and buy-in of the supervisory/management personnel, all improvements will fail for lack of support."

## Unified Goals

Above all, Hogan adds, make sure everyone is aligned to the same goals. "Alignment of common goals throughout the organization," he says, "stops turf wars, and [lets] all departments and levels of the organization focus on what is truly important to the success of the operation."

Without common goals, he says, "people find themselves concentrating their efforts on the project, not the goal of the organization." And it becomes very easy to "become entrapped in the actions required to accomplish [a task]."

That's why Tenneco Automotive formed three business centers at its Paragould, Ark., plant. Each area of a business center—production, engineering, and maintenance—shares the business center's goals, which, in turn, support the plant's goals and the company's goals. "This allowed for a common direction among all employees and fostered a teamwork environment," says Ritter.

In a similar fashion, Halliburton Energy Services' Dallas Center has a "6 Key" performance-measurement system that "provides us with a consistent method to drive performance at all levels of the organization," says McGowen. "These measurements must have balance...and goals must remain consistent and complement the company vision statement in order to succeed. [It] has resulted in more employee involvement and motivation as well as employee, department, and management 'ownership' [of issues]."

Make sure goals are understood and can be measured.

"A goal not readily understood will be ignored," says Hogan. "Measure those items that are tangible and do not change without performance improvements."

## Technology Strategies

But *IW*'s Best Plants winners advise not viewing tools for performance improvements as ends in themselves.

"Total quality management [TQM], problem-solving teams, kaizen events, statistical process control, just-in-time [JIT], Taguchi experiments, etc....are strictly tools of the performance improvement process," says Cooper's Hogan. "Without integrating each of them into the total plant, each will yield only marginal results."

Alcatel's Bushman agrees. "Concepts such as TQM and JIT must be integrated into day-to-day business processes and structures to achieve meaningful goals. [They] must be pursued in a disciplined and intentional fashion."

## Customers and Suppliers

Involvement and empowerment also are trademarks at *IW*'s Best Plants. All cross-train production employees, and more than 90% have nonmanagement team leaders, use a kaizen approach to continuous improvement, and have production workers involved in concurrent engineering and process development. Perhaps equally important, they involve their entire value chain. "We invite major suppliers…and major customers to become part of our team," says Dennis R. Smith, plant manager at Lockheed Martin's Pike County missile operations, Troy, Ala.

What's the value in that? "Supplier [and customer] partnerships create more value and competitive advantage than would have been possible by either the supplier or the customer [or us] standing alone," explains Halliburton's McGowen.

All but one of the 25 finalists involve customers in product-development efforts, and 21 have formal customer-satisfaction programs—complete with surveys—and share those results with all employees. In addition, 18 of the 25 have suppliers evaluate their performance as a customer. All but two involve suppliers early in the product-development process.

"It is very easy to focus on only the activities within the four walls of your facility for improvement and not the entire value chain," says Aeroquip's Miller. "We have driven out waste…and have driven improvement through the entire value chain" with everything from "partnering initiatives with our supply base to value-added product design and proactive 50/50 cost sharing with our customers."

Senco Products Inc.'s fastener manufacturing plant in Cincinnati has had similar success. "We have worked with all of our key suppliers on the front end of any development program in order to maximize the value proposition," says James Cauhorn, project manager for North American Manufacturing. "These savings have exceeded millions of dollars for both Senco and supplier alike and, in the process, solidified the relationships between the companies [involved]."

Working with customers up front can also simplify manufacturing and design efforts. A case in point: A Voice of the Customer (VOC) process for new-product development has made the design process easier at Varian Vacuum Products Lexington in Lexington, Mass. "We now have a way to find out what the customers want and then translate those needs into design requirements," says Michael Blanchette, quality assurance engineer.

Besides, he says, "if customers are involved in the design process, they feel a sense of ownership and are more willing to accept a product they have developed. Without any customer input, new products will have features that customers don't want."

The net effect: Varian Vacuum's sales of vacuum pumps, leak detectors, gauges and controllers, valves, and other hardware have doubled since VOC went into effect as part of its customer-satisfaction process in 1992.

## Questions for Discussions

1   Compare the actions taken by *Industry Week*'s "best" companies with the Baldrige Award 1999 criteria. Which of these criteria appear to be demonstrated by the actions of the "best" companies?

2   The report says that "all 25 companies have production employees inspect their own work, give suppliers long-term contracts, and invite suppliers to contribute to quality improvement efforts." What organizational impact might this have on (a) the quality department and (b) the administrative/staff departments of the companies?

3   Which of the actions, if any, taken by the management of the companies would be appropriate for service firms as opposed to manufacturing firms? Which would be appropriate for government organizations? Give examples.

*Transformations to Quality Organizations (TQO) is making strides in bringing the principles and applications of quality management to the research lab. Managed by the National Science Foundation and supported by the Leadership Steering Committee and the American Society for Quality, TQO partners academic researchers with organizations in business, industry, and the private sector. This article offers an update of the program and a glimpse into its future.*

# FROM THE CLASSROOM TO THE BOARDROOM

## Gary J. Huysse

In its eighth year, the Leadership Steering Committee remains true to its primary aim: to advance the knowledge and application of quality among college graduates entering both the private and public sectors.

This collaboration between academic institutions and business was started by David Kearns, former chief executive officer (CEO) of Xerox Corp., who had found that college students coming to his company were not what he considered total quality graduates. He convened a meeting of 20 of the top business school presidents and a few industry representatives to discuss the fact that college graduates, on the whole, did not meet the following five criteria:

- They did not have a focus on the customer.
- They were not proficient in collaboration and teamwork.
- They were lacking in communication skills.
- They did not think about work as a process that is continuously improving.
- They did not understand how to use and interpret data for decision making.

From *Quality Progress*, November 1997. ©1997 American Society for Quality. Reprinted with permission.

That first meeting was intended to be a one-time wake-up call to assert that this problem, if not addressed, would mean that the universities would be declared ineffective suppliers. What actually resulted, though, was the continuation of Total Quality Forums and the formation of the Leadership Steering Committee by John Pepper, CEO of Procter & Gamble. That, in turn, brought about development of the Transformations to Quality Organizations (TQO) program.

The initial idea for the TQO program was this: If interest could be generated among university professors by providing reward and recognition in the way they're accustomed to receiving it, they would learn about total quality and build it into the curriculum, which would lead to quality graduates entering the work force.

There was also a secondary objective to the research—to get some practical applications that could be used broadly in industry. The belief was that if the United States' top researchers focused their attention on quality, they would be able to accelerate its practice.

The concept of TQO is a fascinating one. The notion deals with issues that are important for the whole country, not just business. If Americans improve the value of what they do and can become more productive, they could perhaps eliminate some of the disparities that exist in society today.

Moreover, changing the nature of work (for example, through technology and globalization) will require people to be more thoughtful and aware of what it takes to get the job done in a collaborative way. These collaborations and the opportunity to open people's minds to other perspectives are important for true understanding of the use of diverse resources.

The execution of the TQO program led to partnerships with the National Science Foundation and the American Society for Quality. The desire was to create an alliance to encourage research, attract the best researchers, manage the research process, and disseminate findings broadly.

When the initial recommendation to create TQO was made, it proposed that industry take the lead in fund-raising. One of the specific roles of the Leadership Steering Committee has been to gather funds from sponsors to enable participants to do the research. To date, financial commitments exceed $12 million.

In addition, industry has been intimately involved as members of research teams, in participating in research reviews and panels, and in approving the programs, to ensure there will be a lasting benefit from the program.

One other interesting aspect of the TQO program is that companies are encouraged to be open in sharing information and experiences. This provides essential data for the academics who are helping industry representatives evaluate solutions.

## How Industry Benefits from TQO

Through the research of the TQO program, one will see improvement in the college curriculum. The program is already building some faculty who have a greater appreciation for the principles of quality and for working together.

An understanding will also emerge of the linkages and overlaps between different academic disciplines, as research is conducted across areas. This will help identify research opportunities that are not currently addressed.

Finally, there should be a tangible, usable benefit from the research for the public and private sectors. We are beginning to see interest from leading companies in some of the research that is nearing completion. It is hoped that the program will reap more benefits than anyone originally anticipated.

The TQO program can be described as a work in progress; it's certainly not done yet. The framework is there to encourage continuing partnerships between industry and academia. The program can serve as a model of how successful collaborations can work.

The hope is that industry and academia will learn to work together collaboratively in a way that values strengths and differences. This would help guide them to the leading edge of relevant research—and stimulate true breakthrough changes. If that happens, the public and private sectors will benefit.

Today, most quality study is anecdotal. But that's not how new medicines or the Internet came about. These types of advances come from researchers using the best tools, techniques, and resources available to successfully develop new approaches. It is hoped that TQO can propel the study of quality organizations into the realm of quality research.

*W. Edwards Deming is unquestionably the guru of quality and is almost solely responsible for the advancement of quality management in the United States and the industrialized world. His vision, philosophy of management, and dedication are largely responsible for the turnaround and acceptance of American products both here and abroad. The ideas of the "father of quality management" were initially ignored in the United States. Later, he began to enjoy celebrity status in America after he appeared in a 1980 NBC documentary, "If Japan Can Do It, Why Can't We?" He died in 1993 at age 93.*

## QUALITY AND THE REQUIRED STYLE OF MANAGEMENT: THE NEED FOR CHANGE

### W. Edwards Deming, Ph.D.

Better quality is necessary for the survival of industry in the Western world. American industry dominated the world from 1920 through the two decades after World War II. Now it lies in a state of slumber.

The rest of the world waited in line after World War II to buy whatever North America could produce. Why? The rest of the industrialized world lay in ruins. Everyone in the US expected the good times to continue. What happened? Why?

The answer is that the quality of most American products has been found wanting, not competitive. Emphasis in the US is still on quantity, not on quality. Devaluation of the dollar against the yen is a disappointment, as anybody could predict. Lower prices against the yen will not produce a market for goods that nobody wishes to buy. Most American products are simply not salable at any price. Devaluation of the dollar is not the road to better business. Better quality

This article first appeared in 1988 in *The Journal for Quality and Participation*. Reprinted with permission of the Association for Quality and Participation (Cincinnati, Ohio) from the December 1994 issue of *The Journal for Quality and Participation*.

is. We are in a completely different position than we were in up till around 1960. What must we do?

Better quality for international trade is the answer, not restrictions to trade, nor self-pity, nor the beggar's cup. The US has already installed more restrictions to trade than any other country, second only to France. Costs go down and productivity goes up, as improvement of quality is accomplished by better management of design, engineering, testing and by improvement of processes. Better quality at lower price has a chance to capture a market. Cutting costs without improvement of quality is futile.

**Quality and innovation**—Quality is improved in three ways: through innovation in design of a product or service, through innovation in processes, and through improvement of existing processes. Hard work will not ensure quality. Best efforts will not ensure quality, and neither will gadgets, computers or investment in machinery. A necessary ingredient for improvement of quality is the application of profound knowledge. There is no substitute for knowledge. Knowledge we have in abundance. We must learn to use it.

**Styles of management**—Wrong styles of management, with concomitant bad practices, have grown up and taken root in the Western world. They become obvious under the theory that reduction in variation improves a product. Theory of variation (statistical theory) helps to identify practices of management that induce variation, high cost, and poor quality, with consequent loss of market. The same theory points to better practices.

I have for years noted appropriate practices for management. Here I will list some of the faulty management practices.

## The Wrong Style of Management

- Management of failure (too late). It is better to work on the causes of failure. Failures are not causes; they come from causes.
- Tampering with a stable system. For example, track down anything that goes wrong with a product or service. This policy does not improve the system. It is tampering, worsening the problem.
- Compiling a list or chart to show percentages right or percentages of product or service that went wrong last month.
- Annual appraisal of performance, the so-called merit system—a destroyer of people.
- Annual rating of divisions. (A manager of a division is rewarded on the basis of the rating.)
- Campaign to reduce costs—as if costs were causes.
- Incentive pay, commissions and bonuses.

- Top management failing to understand their responsibility for quality, for innovation of product and processes and for improvement of processes. Quality starts in the boardroom.
- Short term planning and quick profits.
- Churning money.
- Competition without cooperation. Getting a bigger slice of the pie, but not making the pie bigger.
- Doing business by price tag.
- Short term contracts.
- Management by objectives (MBO) or management by the numbers.
- Investment in gadgets, computers, automation and new machinery without guidance of profound knowledge.
- Posters and slogans for the workforce.
- Work standards—quotas. They double the cost of production, rob people of pride of workmanship and are a barrier to improvement.

## Deming's Five Principles

1. The central problem in lack of quality is the failure of management to understand variation. (Everything varies. Statistics help us to predict how much it is going to vary.)
2. It is management's responsibility to know whether the problems are in the system or in the behavior of the people.
3. Teamwork should be based on knowledge, design, redesign and redesign. Constant improvement is management's responsibility. Most causes of low quality and productivity belong to the system.
4. Train people until they are in statistical control (until they are achieving as much as they can within the limits of the system you are using).
5. It is management's responsibility to give detailed specifications.

## Deming's Fourteen Points

1. Create consistency of purpose with a plan.
2. Adopt the new philosophy of quality.
3. Cease dependence on mass inspection.
4. End the practice of choosing suppliers based solely on price.
5. Identify problems and work continuously to improve the system.

6. Adopt modern methods of training on the job.

7. Change the focus from production numbers (quantity) to quality.

8. Drive out fear.

9. Break down barriers between departments.

10. Stop requesting improved productivity without providing methods to achieve it.

11. Eliminate work standards that prescribe numerical quotas.

12. Remove barriers to pride of workmanship.

13. Institute vigorous education and retraining.

14. Create a structure in top management that will emphasize the preceding thirteen points every day.

# FOR FURTHER READING

Bell, Robert and Bernard Keys, "A Conversation with Curt W. Reimann on the Background and Future of the Baldrige Award," *Organizational Dynamics,* Spring 1998, pp. 51–61.

Chong, Philip S. and Sal Kukalis, "An Evaluation of American Top Management's View of Quality and Productivity," *International Journal of Management,* Sept. 1997, pp. 326–333.

Crosby, Philip B., "Illusions about Quality," *Across the Board,* June 1996, pp. 38–41.

Deliz, Jose R., "Lessons Learned from Baldrige Winners," *Computers and Industrial Engineering,* Oct. 1997, pp. 171–174.

Hendricks, Kevin B. and Vinod R. Singhal, "Does Implementing an Effective TQM Program Actually Improve Operating Performance?" *Management Science,* Sept. 1997, pp. 1258–1274.

Pace, Larry A. and Eileen P. Kelly, "TQM at Xerox: Lessons Worth Duplicating," *International Journal of Technology Management,* Vol. 16 No. 4–6, 1998, pp. 326–335.

Saco, Roberto M., "The Criteria: A Looking Glass to America's Understanding of Quality," *Quality Progress,* Nov. 1997, pp. 89–96.

**2**

# LEADERSHIP

*Most of this book is involved with leadership. Nearly every page heretofore and hereafter states a principle of good leadership.*

W. E. Deming
*Out of the Crisis*[1]

## LEADERSHIP SYSTEM

The concept of the leadership system (criterion 1.1 of the 1999 Baldrige Award criteria) is summarized as follows. Leadership system refers to how leadership is exercised, formally and informally, throughout a company—the basis for and the way that key decisions are made, communicated, and carried out. It includes structures and mechanisms for decision making, selection and development of leaders and managers, and reinforcing values, practices, and behaviors.

An effective leadership system creates clear values that respect the capabilities and requirements of employees and other company stakeholders and sets high expectations for performance and performance improvement. It builds loyalties and teamwork based upon the values and the pursuit of shared purposes. It encourages and supports initiative and risk taking, subordinates organization to purpose and function, and avoids chains of command that require long decision paths. An effective leadership system includes mechanisms for the leaders' self-examination, receipt of feedback, and improvement.

Some principles and practices of total quality management (TQM) may differ among firms and industries, but there is unanimous agreement as to the importance of leadership by top management in implementing TQM. Such leadership is a prerequisite to all strategy and action plans. According to Juran, it cannot be delegated.[2] Those firms that have succeeded in making total quality work for them have been able to do so because of strong leadership.[3] A U.S. General Accounting Office study concluded, "Ultimately, strong visionary leaders are the most important element of a quality management approach."[4]

Dr. Curt Reimann, director of the Malcolm Baldrige National Quality Award, has reviewed hundreds of applications, including those of the award winners. His review of key excellence indicators of quality management is insightful and helpful for an award applicant or anyone using the Baldrige criteria as a benchmark to evaluate the quality of management. He summarizes the characteristics of excellent leadership as follows:[5]

> **Visible, committed, and knowledgeable.** They promote the emphasis on quality and know the details and how well the company is doing. Personal involvement in education, training and recognition. Accessible to and routine contact with employees, customers and suppliers.
>
> **A missionary zeal.** The leaders are trying to effect as much change as possible through their suppliers, through the government and through any other vehicle that promotes quality in the United States. Active in promotion of quality outside the company.
>
> **Aggressive targets.** Going beyond incremental improvements and looking at the possibility of making large gains, getting the whole work force thinking about different processes—not just improving processes.
>
> **Strong drivers.** Cycle time, zero defects, six sigma or other targets to drive improvements. Clearly defined customer satisfaction and quality improvement objectives.
>
> **Communication of values.** Effecting cultural change related to quality. Written policy, mission, guidelines and other documented statements of quality values, or other bases for clear and consistent communications.
>
> **Organization.** Flat structures that allow more authority at lower levels. Empowering employees. Managers as coaches rather than bosses. Cross-functional management processes and focus on internal as well as external customers. Interdepartmental improvement teams.
>
> **Customer contact.** CEO and all senior managers are accessible to customers.

Two of the many companies that have received a great deal of visibility for their TQM programs are Westinghouse and IBM, both with divisions that have won the Baldrige Award. Westinghouse committed significant capital resources to support the quality improvement efforts of all Westinghouse divisions, including the creation of the first corporate-sponsored Productivity and Quality Center in the United States. The company's Total Quality Model (Figure 2-1) was

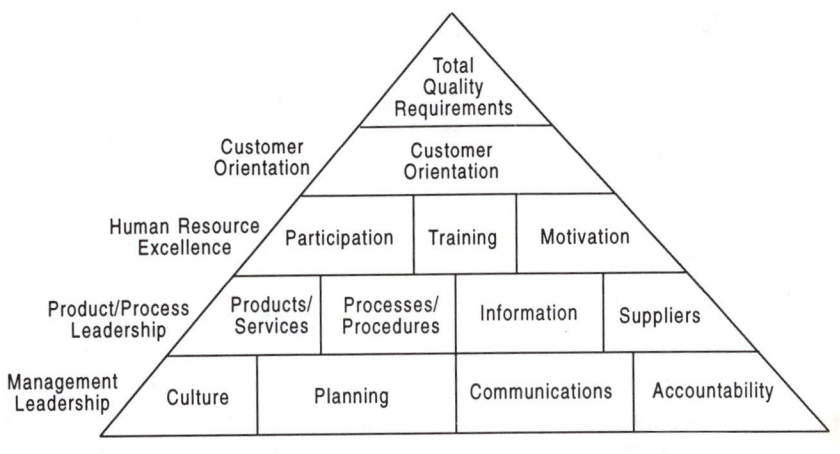

**Figure 2-1**   The Westinghouse Total Quality Model

developed for use by all division managers. Note that it is built upon a foundation of management leadership. The framework of IBM's corporate-wide quality program, called "Market Driven Quality" is shown in Figure 2-2. Again, note that the input or "driver" of the system is leadership.

David Kearns, chairman and CEO of Xerox, explains how the company's "Leadership through Quality" process achieves commitment at every level: "Training begins with our top-tier family work group—my direct reports and me. It then cascades through the organizations led by senior staff, gradually spreading worldwide to some 100,000 employees."[6] This "cascading" reflects the leverage effect of good leadership at all levels. As one executive remarked, "It goes up, down and across the organization chart."

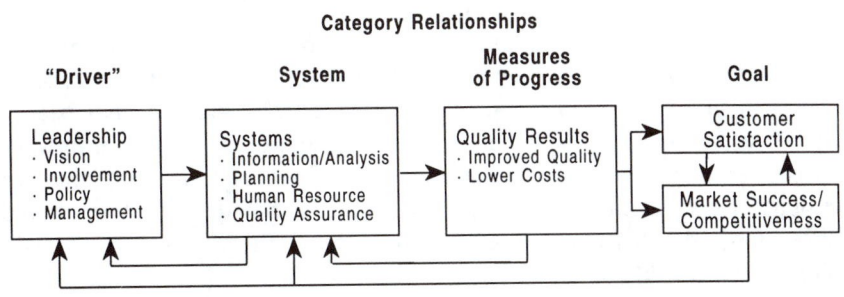

**Figure 2-2**   Framework of IBM's Market Driven Quality Program

## ATTITUDE AND INVOLVEMENT OF TOP MANAGEMENT

Over time, U.S. managers have been identified with a structured, classical, or top-down approach to leadership. Assumptions and results of this approach have been summarized as follows:[7]

| Assumptions | Results |
| --- | --- |
| People have to be controlled. Without control from the top, they will become non-productive. | An organizational caste system. Rank has its privileges. A feudal system. |
| Managers are smarter than other workers and better equipped to make decisions and issue orders. | Cynical work force. Many workers lack faith in managers. Trust and loyalty replaced by cynicism and fear. |
| People are a commodity and are seen as replaceable. "People assets" get only lip service. | Adversarial labor relationships. Each group acts to protect its own interests. |
| Organizations work best when assigned to discrete roles and responsibilities. | Bottom-line focus. Major stakeholder is shareholder. Incentives based on profit and growth. |
| Making profits is the purpose of a business. Measurement systems focus on financial results. | Disengaged work force. |

Implicit in these assumptions is the principle of delegation. While delegation is an accepted and necessary principle of organization, TQM is totally dependent on the support and involvement of the most senior group of managers. This is a case where delegation equals abdication. Deming says that quality is made in the boardroom. The job cannot be delegated. You can "install" a carpet, a new president, or a new pay plan, but not TQM.

It would not be unfair to say that there has been a tendency among U.S. managers to focus on technology and hard assets rather than soft assets such as human resources and organizational competence.[8] The tendency has been to emphasize the organizational chart and the key control points within it. Many managers place priority on the budget and the business plan (to many, these are the same) and assume that rational people will get on board and perform according to standard. This popular perception does not fit with leadership and a philosophy of quality.

It is axiomatic that organizations do not achieve quality objectives; people do. If there is a big push for quality or a new program, each employee is justifiably skeptical (the BOHICA syndrome—bend over, here it comes again).

According to A. Blanton Godfrey, chairman and CEO of the Juran Institute, top management should be prepared to answer the specific question that may be posed by each member of the organization: "What do you want me to do tomorrow that is different from what I am doing today?"[9] Thus, top managers need to be ambidextrous. They must balance the need for the *structural* dimension (e.g., hierarchy, budgets, plans, controls, procedures) on the one hand with the *behavioral* or personnel dimension on the other. The two dimensions need not be in conflict.

> ■ At 3M Company the leadership climate is proactive rather than reactive, externally focused rather than internally focused, and the quality perception views the totality of the business rather than just one aspect of it. In order to identify the gaps between its existing position and its vision of the future, 3M has developed "Quality Vision 2000" and implemented it through a process called Q90s which involves the total management system, making the process broader and deeper across the company worldwide.[10]

The commitment and involvement of management need to be demonstrated and visible. Speaking about his military experience, Dwight Eisenhower said: "They never listened to what I said, they always watch what I do."

Many managers send mixed signals. They endorse quality but reward bottom line or production. They insist on cost reduction even if it means canceling quality training. Still worse, some executives perceive the workers to be the cause of their quality problems.[11] This is hardly behavior that encourages individual involvement in decision making and personal "ownership" of the improvement process. Employee buy-in is unlikely in such a climate, where worker empowerment is talked about but not operationalized.

## COMMUNICATION

*...blocking of communications threatens all the basic needs.*[12]

Abraham Maslow

A 1998 survey of 2143 senior executives in 23 countries found that 96 percent of them identified communications between managers and workers as critical to implementing their business strategy and improving productivity. This confirms what we already know about TQM and communications. When communication fails or misguides the cause, it can usually be traced to bureaucratic barriers or a misunderstanding about what is to be done. Again, nothing can sabotage a quality movement faster than managers who are not engaged in it.

Communication is inextricably linked in the quality process, yet some executives find it difficult to tell others about the plan in a way that will be understood. An additional difficulty is filtering. As top management's vision of quality gets filtered down through the ranks, the vision and the plan can lose both clarity and momentum. Thus, top management as well as managers and supervisors at all levels serve as translators and executors of top management's directive. The ability to communicate is a valuable skill at all levels, from front-line supervisor to CEO.

Quality-conscious companies are interested in the cost of poor communication in terms of both employee productivity and customer perception of product and service quality. More important than what is written or said is the recipient's perception of the message. Limited or inaccurate facts parceled out to employees may demoralize workers and lead to rumors.[13]

According to Peter Drucker, a true guru of management thought and practice, "The communications gap within institutions and between groups in society has been widening steadily—to a point where it threatens to become an unbridgeable gulf of total misunderstanding."[14] Having said that, he provides an easily understood and simple approach to help communicate the strategy, vision, and action plans related to TQM.

Communication is defined as the *exchange of information and understanding* between two or more persons or groups. Note the emphasis on exchange and understanding. Without understanding between sender and receiver concerning the message, there is no communication. The simple model is as follows:

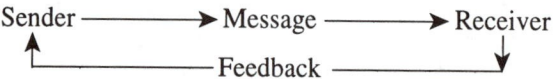

Unless sender gets feedback that receiver understands the message, no communication takes place. Yet most of us send messages with no feedback to indicate that the recipient (or percipient) has understood the message.

Despite the sorry state of communication, Drucker concludes that we do know something about communication in organizations and calls it "managerial communications." Communication is an extremely complex process. Many universities provide a doctoral program in the topic. At the risk of oversimplifying both communication theory and Drucker's approach, the essence of his principles can be paraphrased:

■ One can only communicate in terms of the recipient's language and perception, and therefore the message must be in terms of individual experience and perception. If the employee's perception of quality is "do a better job" or "keep the customer happy," it is unlikely that the message of TQM will be understood. Measures of quality are needed to ensure agreement on the meaning of the message.

■ Only the recipient can communicate—the communicator cannot. Thus, management systems (including training) should be designed from the point of view of the recipient and with a built-in mechanism for feedback. Feedback and thus the exchange of information should be based on some measure, target, benchmark, or standard.

■ All information is encoded, and prior agreement must be reached on the meaning of the code. Quality must be carefully defined and measures agreed upon.

■ Communication downward cannot work because it focuses on what one wants to say. Communication should be upward.

■ Employees should be encouraged to set measurable goals.

Larry Appley, chairman emeritus of the American Management Association, has developed a company-wide productivity improvement program that has the model in Figure 2-3 as a centerpiece. Note that the direction of communication is *upward*. Recipient (subordinate) becomes sender, and sender (boss) becomes recipient. The message is specific and measurable, and the subordinate has ownership because he or she originated the message. Both parties can henceforth communicate about a message on which there is prior agreement. The Appley approach is therefore consistent with Drucker's ideas[15] and sound principles of

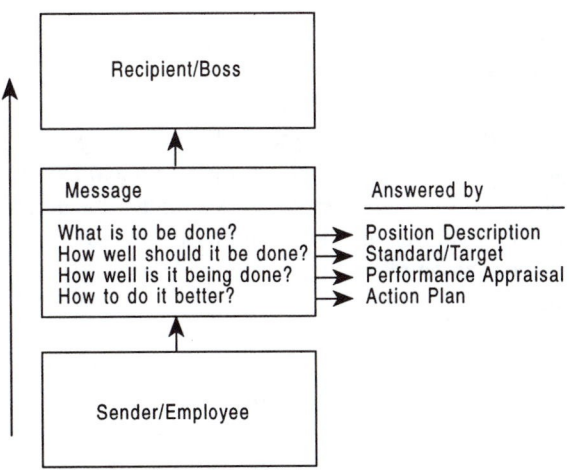

**Figure 2-3** Effective Communication

communication. A modification tailored for a specific firm may be used as a vehicle for TQM implementation.

These concepts of effective communication can provide a practical approach for communicating about quality in the organization. It only remains to encode the message(s) in terms of recipient understanding. The vehicles for communicating about quality are selected components of the TQM system:

1. Training and development for both managers and employees. Managers must understand the processes they manage as well as the basic concept of systems optimization. Employee training should focus on the integration and appropriate use of statistical tools and problem-solving methods.

2. Participation at all levels in establishing benchmarks and measures of process quality. Involvement is both vertical in the hierarchy as well as horizontal by cross-functional teams.

3. Empowerment of employees by delegating authority to make decisions regarding process improvement within individual areas of responsibility, so that the individual "owns" the particular process step.

4. Quality assurance in all organization processes, not only in manufacturing or operations but in business and supporting processes as well. The objective throughout is continuous improvement.

5. Human resource management systems that facilitate contributions at all levels (up and down and across) the organizational chart.

The Digital Switching and Customer Service Division of Northern Telecom Canada Ltd. has received awards and international recognition for its quality systems and procedures. Continually communicating the importance of quality to its 5000 employees is considered vital by division management. Three internal communications specialists generate daily newsletters, monthly newspapers, and videos.[16] One method used by Westinghouse Electric Corporation to spread the word about quality to its 118,000 employees is an annual symposium. For two days each October, more than 600 employees gather to hear colleagues' TQM success stories. The goals for the symposium are for the chairman and senior management to energize employees and to provide attendees an opportunity to talk to each other.[17]

## CULTURE

Alvin Toffler[18] of "future shock" fame describes the phenomenon as "the shattering stress and disorientation that we induce in individuals by subjecting them to too much change in too short a time." Many organizations will discover that cultural shock may accompany efforts to "install" TQM. The classical top-down organization style may no longer work. Knowledge and decisional loads need to be redistributed. Employees need to master new techniques and technologies, adapt to new organizational forms, and generate new ideas. TQM does not and will not bring results overnight. The essence of TQM is a change of culture. Unlike instant pudding, where you just add water and stir, changing the culture of an organization is a slow process and people have to want to be on board.

A dependence on posters and slogans in offices, hallways, and production sites may serve to slow the change effort. Nikita Khruschev, former chairman of the Soviet Union, concluded, "If you feed the people just with revolutionary slogans, they will listen today, they will listen tomorrow, they will listen the day after tomorrow, but on the fourth day they will say, 'To hell with you.'" Consider the following company slogans and decide whether you, as a customer or employee, are moved to action. As a customer, does the slogan induce you to buy? As an employee, can you *operationalize* it on the job?

| Company | Slogan |
| --- | --- |
| Ford (Mercury) | Where comfort and control come together |
| Korean Air Lines | We treat you as an honored guest |
| GM (Pontiac) | We build excitement |
| Eastman Kodak | You press the button, we do the rest |
| Bell Telephone | The voice with a smile |
| TWA | The things we do to make you happy |
| KMart | The quality you need at the price you want |
| JC Penney | Always first quality |
| Wal-Mart | Continuous improvement is simply the way the company does business |

Culture is the pattern of shared beliefs and values that provides the members of an organization rules of behavior or accepted norms for conducting operations. It is the philosophies, ideologies, values, assumptions, beliefs, expectations, attitudes, and norms that knit an organization together and are shared by employees.[19]

For example, IBM's basic beliefs are (1) respect for the individual, (2) best customer service, and (3) pursuit of excellence. In turn, these beliefs are operationalized in terms of strategy and customer values. In simpler terms, culture provides a framework to explain "the way things are done around here."

Other examples of basic beliefs include:

| Company | Basic belief |
|---|---|
| Ford | Quality is job one |
| Delta | A family feeling |
| 3M | Product innovation |
| Lincoln Electric | Wages proportionate to productivity |
| Caterpillar | Strong dealer support; 24-hour spare parts support around the world |
| McDonald's | Fast service, consistent quality |

Institutionalizing strategy requires a culture that supports the strategy. For most organizations, a strategy based on TQM requires a significant if not sweeping change in the way people think. Jack Welch, head of General Electric and one of the most controversial and respected executives in America, states that cultural change must be sweeping—not incremental change but "quantum." His cultural transformation at GE calls for a "boundaryless" company where internal divisions blur, everyone works as a team, and both suppliers and customers are partners. His cultural concept of change may differ from Juran, who says that, "When it comes to quality, there is no such thing as improvement in general. Any improvement is going to come about project by project and no other way."[20] The acknowledged experts agree on the need for a cultural or value system transformation:

- Deming calls for a transformation of the American management style.[21]

- Feigenbaum suggests a pervasive improvement throughout the organization.[22]

- According to Crosby, "Quality is the result of a carefully constructed culture, it has to be the fabric of the organization."[23]

It is not surprising that many executives hold the same opinions. In a Gallup Organization survey of 615 business executives, 43 percent rated a change in corporate culture as an integral part of improving quality. The needed change may be given different names in different companies. Robert Crandall, CEO of American Airlines, calls it an innovative environment,[24] while at Du Pont it is "The Way People Think"[25] and at Allied Signal "Workers' attitudes had to change."[26] Xerox specified a five-year cultural change strategy called Leadership through Quality.[27] Tom Peters even adds what he calls "the dazzle factor."[28]

Successful organizations have a central core culture around which the rest of the company revolves. It is important for the organization to have a sound basis of core values into which management and other employees will be drawn.

Without this central core, the energy of members of the organization will dissipate as they develop plans, make decisions, communicate, and carry on operations without a fundamental criterion of relevance to guide them. This is particularly true in decisions related to quality. Research has shown that quality means different things to different people and levels in the organization. Employees tend to think like their peers and think differently from those at other levels. This suggests that organizations will have considerable difficulty in improving quality unless core values are embedded in the organization.[29]

Commitment to quality as a core value for planning, organizing, and control will be doubly difficult when a concern for the practice is lacking. Research has shown that many U.S. supervisors believe that a concern for quality is lacking among workers and managers.[30] Where this is the case, the perceptions of these supervisors may become a self-fulfilling prophecy.

## Embedding a Culture of Quality

It is one thing for top management to state a commitment to quality but quite another for this commitment to be accepted or embedded in the company. The basic vehicle for embedding an organizational culture is a teaching process in which desired behaviors and activities are learned through experiences, symbols, and explicit behavior. Once again, the components of the total quality system provide the vehicles for change. These components as well as other mechanisms of cultural change are summarized in Table 2-1. Above all, demonstration of commitment by top management is essential. This commitment is demonstrated by behaviors and activities that are exhibited throughout the company. Categories of behaviors include:

**Table 2-1**  Cultural Change Mechanisms

| Focus | From traditional | To quality |
|---|---|---|
| Plan | Short-range budgets | Future strategic issues |
| Organize | Hierarchy—chain of command | Participation/empowerment |
| Control | Variance reporting | Quality measures and information for self-control |
| Communication | Top down | Top down and bottom up |
| Decisions | Ad hoc/crisis management | Planned change |
| Functional management | Parochial, competitive | Cross-functional, integrative |
| Quality management | Fixing/one-shot manufacturing | Preventive/continuous, all functions and processes |

- **Signaling.** Making statements or taking actions that support the vision of quality, such as mission statements, creeds, or charters directed toward customer satisfaction. Publix supermarkets' "Where shopping is a pleasure" and JC Penney's "The customer is always right" are examples of such statements.

- **Focus.** Every employee must know the mission, his or her part in it, and what has to be done to achieve it. What management pays attention to and how management reacts to crisis are indicative of this focus. When all functions and systems are aligned and when practice supports the culture, everyone is more likely to support the vision. Johnson & Johnson's cool reaction to the Tylenol scare is such an example.

- **Employee policies.** These may be the clearest expression of culture, at least from the viewpoint of the employee. A culture of quality can be easily demonstrated in such policies as the reward and promotion system, status symbols, and other human resource actions.

Executives at all levels could learn a lesson from David T. Kearns, chairman and chief executive officer of Xerox Corporation. In an article for the academic journal *Academy of Management Executive,* he describes the change at Xerox: "At the time Leadership-Through-Quality was introduced, I told our employees that customer satisfaction would be our top priority and that it would change the culture of the company. We redefined quality as meeting the requirements of our customers. It may have been the most significant strategy Xerox ever embarked on."[31]

Among the changes brought about by the cultural change were the management style and the role of first-line management. Kearns continues: "We altered the role of first-line management from that of the traditional, dictatorial foreman to that of a supervisor functioning primarily as a coach and expediter."

Using a modification of the Ishikawa (fishbone) diagram, Xerox demonstrated (Figure 2-4) how the major component of the company's quality system was used for the transition to TQM.

## MANAGEMENT SYSTEMS

*Management systems are essential but to depend solely upon them for TQM implementation is like straightening the deck chairs on the Titanic.*

Joel Ross

No matter how comprehensive or lofty a quality strategy may be, it is not complete until it is put into action. It is only rhetoric until it has been implemented. Quality management systems are vehicles for change and should be

Total Quality Transition

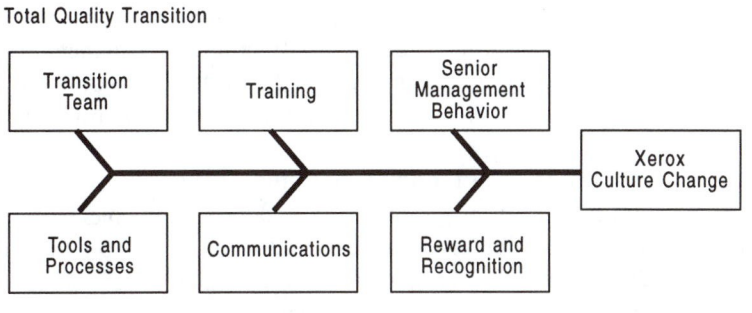

**Figure 2-4**    Transition to a Quality Culture at Xerox

designed to integrate all areas, not only the quality assurance department. They must be expanded throughout the company to include white-collar activities ranging from market research to shipping and customer service. They are directed toward achievement and commitment to purpose through four universal processes: (1) the specialization of task responsibilities through structure, (2) the provision of information systems that enable employees to know what they need to do in order to achieve goals, (3) the necessary achievement of results through action plans and projects, and (4) control through the establishment of benchmarks, standards, and feedback.

Each of these subsystems is the subject of a separate chapter in this book, but the implementation of each can only proceed from a base of clearly established goals. It is the specific task of top management to ensure that these goals are defined, disseminated, and implemented. Objectives in the areas of quality and productivity must be operationalized by establishing specific subobjectives for each function, department, or activity. Only then can courses of action be selected and plans implemented.

The problem, or conversely the opportunity, is to identify those *key* objectives and activities that are necessary in order to achieve a given strategy—in this case *quality*. The number of activities and processes in the typical organization is so large that a start-up quality management program cannot address all of them in the initial stages. Ultimately, every activity should be analyzed, its output evaluated in terms of value to both external and internal customers, and quality measures established.[32] Notwithstanding this longer term need, it is desirable to begin by setting goals only for those activities that are critical to achieving the mission statement and strategy.

What are these activities and processes that are critical to the mission of quality? The answer lies in identifying the key success factors that must be well managed if the mission or objective is to be achieved; that is, the limited number of areas in which results, if satisfactory, will ensure successful competitive performance for the organization.[33] Each activity or process can then be rated as to its importance. Advertising is a key success factor for Coca-Cola but not for McDonnell Douglas; design is critical to a hi-tech electronics firm but not to a bank.

This process can be used for any major objective, but it is also useful for providing a clear picture of things that must be done to implement a successful TQM program. Identification of key success factors emerges from three dimensions: (1) the drivers of quality such as cycle time reduction, zero defects, or six sigma; (2) operations that provide opportunities for reducing cost or improving productivity; and (3) the market side of quality, which relates to the salability of goods and services. These are converted to specific goals and targets which form the basis for subsequent programs and the universal processes identified earlier. Some U.S. managers have adopted ideas and language from Japanese companies, many of which call the process *policy deployment.*[34]

## QUESTIONS FOR DISCUSSION

2-1  List the characteristics of excellent leadership for TQM.

2-2  Describe how leadership by top management is the *driver* of quality.

2-3  How can top management communicate the need for quality throughout the organization?

2-4  Describe how setting targets for quality improvement helps to establish a culture and climate.

2-5  Give an example of a company culture as reflected in a statement of basic beliefs. Would such a statement help to institutionalize a quality culture? If so, how?

2-6  How would an organization's commitment to quality facilitate or improve the following:

- The planning process
- Organization
- Control

2-7  Choose a manufacturing company and a service company. Identify a key activity for improving quality in each.

# ENDNOTES

1. W. E. Deming, *Out of the Crisis,* Cambridge, Mass.: MIT Center for Engineering Study, 1986.

2. J. M. Juran, "Made in USA—A Quality Resurgence," *Journal for Quality and Participation,* March 1991 pp. 6–8.

3. Thomas C. Gibson, "Helping Leaders Accept Leadership of Total Quality Management," *Quality Progress,* Nov. 1990, pp. 45–47.

4. U.S. General Accounting Office, Quality Management Scoping Study, Washington, D.C.: U.S. General Accounting Office, Dec. 1990, p. 25.

5. Curt W. Reimann, "Winning Strategies for Quality Improvement," *Business America,* March 25, 1991, pp. 8–11.

6. David T. Kearns, "Leadership through Quality," *Academy of Management Executive,* Vol. 4 No. 2, 1990, p. 87.

7. Jim Beaubien, "Leadership Evolution," *Executive Excellence,* May 1998.

8. Michael Moacoby, "How to Be a Quality Leader," *Research-Technology Management,* Sept./Oct. 1990, pp. 51–52. See also Brian L. Joiner and Peter R. Scholtes, "The Quality Manager's New Job," *Quality Progress,* Oct. 1986, pp. 52–56.

9. A. Blanton Godfrey, "Strategic Quality Management," *Quality,* March 1990, pp. 17–22.

10. Doug Anderson, "The Role of Senior Management in Total Quality," *Global Perspectives on Total Quality,* Conference Board Report Number 958, New York: Conference Board, 1991, p. 17. The author is director, corporate quality services, 3M Company.

11. Lance Arrington, "Training and Commitment: Two Keys to Quality," *Chief Executive,* Sept. 1990, pp. 72–73.

12. Abraham Maslow, *Motivation and Personality,* New York: Harper & Row, 1987.

13. Dianna Booher, "Link between Corporate Communication & Quality," *Executive Excellence,* June 1990, pp. 17–18.

14. Peter Drucker, *Management: Tasks, Responsibilities, Practices,* New York: Harper & Row, 1973, p. 481.

15. The author (JR) had the pleasure and learning experience of working with Larry Appley on the development of this program, which had great success in a number of companies.

16. Bruce Van-Lane, "Good as Gold," *PEM: Plant Engineering & Maintenance (Canada),* April 1991, pp. 26–28.

17. Erika Penzer, "Spreading the Gospel about Total Quality at a Westinghouse Symposium," *Incentive,* Feb. 1991, pp. 46–49.

18. Alvin Toffler, *Future Shock,* New York: Random House, 1972.

19. Ralph H. Kilmann, Mary J. Saxton, and Roy Serpa, "Issues in Understanding and Changing Culture," *California Management Review,* Winter 1986, p. 89.

20. See "Jack Welch Reinvents General Electric—Again," *The Economist (UK),* March 30, 1991. See also Joseph M. Juran, *Juran on Leadership for Quality: An Executive Handbook,* New York: The Free Press, 1989.

21. W. Edwards Deming, "Transformation of Today's Management," *Executive Excellence,* Dec. 1987, p. 8.

22. Armand V. Feigenbaum, "Seven Keys to Constant Quality," *Journal for Quality and Participation,* March 1989, pp. 20–23.

23. Philip B. Crosby, *The Eternally Successful Organization*, New York: McGraw-Hill, 1988.

24. Aaron Sugarman, "Success through People: A New Era in the Way America Does Business," *Incentive*, May 1988, pp. 40–43.

25. Thomas C. Gibson, "The Total Quality Management Resource," *Quality Progress*, Nov. 1987, pp. 62–66.

26. Syed Shah and George Woelki, "Aerospace Industry Finds TQM Essential for TQS," *Quality*, March 1991, pp. 14–19.

27. U.S. General Accounting Office, Quality Management Scoping Study, Washington, D.C.: U.S. General Accounting Office, Dec. 1990, p. 64.

28. Tom Peters, "Total Quality Leadership: Let's Get It Right," *Journal for Quality and Participation*, March 1991, pp. 10–15.

29. Frederick Derrick, Harsha Desai, and William O'Brien, "Survey Shows Employees at Different Organizational Levels Define Quality Differently," *Industrial Engineering*, April 1989, pp. 22–26.

30. David A. Garvin, "Quality Problems, Policies, and Attitudes in the United States and Japan: An Exploratory Study," *Academy of Management Journal*, Dec. 1986, pp. 653–673.

31. David T. Kearns, "Leadership through Quality," *Academy of Management Executive*, Vol. 4 No. 2, 1990, p. 87.

32. The need to set activity output and productivity measures (productivity being the ratio of output to input) has long been recognized, but little progress was made until recently, when a method known as *activity analysis* began to emerge. It is still in the early stages of implementation in industry. The accounting profession, recognizing the need to focus not only on cost but also on quality and productivity, is now promoting a related method known as *activity-based accounting*. See H. Thomas Johnson, "A Blueprint for World-Class Management Accounting," *Management Accounting*, June 1988, pp. 23–30. A very insightful and useful treatment of the shortcomings of traditional accounting systems is contained in H. Thomas Johnson and Robert S. Kaplan, *Relevance Lost*, Boston: Harvard Business School Press, 1991. Also included are excellent prescriptions for the improvement of accounting systems for managerial decision making.

33. Joel K. Leidecker and Albert V. Bruno, "Identifying and Using Critical Success Factors," *Long Range Planning*, Vol. 17 No. 1, 1984, pp. 23–32.

34. John E. Newcomb, "Management by Policy Deployment," *Quality*, Jan. 1989, pp. 28–30.

## TRIDENT: A COMPANY WINNER DEMONSTRATES LEADERSHIP

Since Trident's foundation in 1979, when it employed only three workers and manufactured only tools and dies as a subtier supplier of major manufacturers, the company has grown into a leading manufacturer of precision sheet metal, electro/mechanical assemblies, and end item products.

In a highly competitive and dynamic market, Trident's customers demand products of the highest quality, consistently delivered in compliance with their schedules, in the most cost-effective manner. The company's achievement of its key objective—total customer satisfaction—has established Trident's reputation as an exceptionally reliable partner in the eyes of its customers.

The cornerstone of Trident's values of continuous improvement and customer satisfaction as well as its expectation of being a world-class leader is summarized in its CEO's vision statement:

> My vision for Trident is one in which each of us shares in the responsibility, growth and benefits of becoming a world-class organization.
>
> How we will, as a team, achieve this? Through quality! Not just the quality of each individual part but through Total Quality—in everything we say and do.
>
> I envision this program as an adventure. An adventure that will make us stronger as a team.
>
> Individually, you know we can do very little. As a team, we've already come a long way…As a strong team, with each headed in the same direction, we can become the unquestionable leader that our Customers, Industry and Community look up to.

Trident's executives, managers, and supervisors understand that they must take the lead in this total quality cultural transformation. They were the role models who were responsible for changing Trident from an organization where "close enough" was acceptable into an organization where meeting or exceeding customer requirements became everyone's goal. To assist them with this transition, the senior executive team defined their roles and responsibilities:

- Develop strategies consistent with our customer focus and values.
- Serve as role models for "Excellence in Motion."
- Serve on continuous improvement teams.
- Integrate quality and customer focus into strategic planning.
- Reinforce exceptional employee performance.
- Communicate customer focus and core values to employees, customers, suppliers, and community.

# MOMENTS OF TRUTH
# IN A SERVICE BUSINESS

In 1992, there were two winners of the Baldrige quality award in the service category: AT&T Universal Card Services and the Ritz-Carlton Hotel Company. The hotels of Ritz-Carlton were the envy of the industry, and many companies both within and outside of the industry traveled to Atlanta to learn how it was done. One of the visitors was Harvey Cook, owner of three full-service hotels in the coastal region of South and North Carolina. The hotels were of moderate size, ranging from 120 to 410 rooms. They were known as the Cook Hotels.

The Ritz-Carlton conducted a popular seminar in Atlanta and invited participants from various industries. The hotel was noted for all aspects of quality but principally for its training program. Before his visit to Atlanta, Cook was somewhat skeptical of the fashionable trend toward total quality management. He had always assumed that his hotels delivered quality and customer satisfaction. He had read about total quality management and how it demanded a quality culture. His response was the development of a belief in the "achievement of a total quality company" based on mutual respect, trust, and benefit. This concept formed the basis of the company's mission statement along with the pledge "to provide superior lodging, meeting and entertainment experience to our guests."

To implement his idea of the quality culture and practices, he formed teams that were guided by an executive steering committee. Each team had six to eight employees who volunteered. Overall, about 20 percent of employees were represented. Cook met with every employee to get across the point that quality is serious business.

After one year, the teams were disbanded. Barriers had arisen between team members and non-members. Employees were not sure what was expected of them. Managerial feedback was limited.

Following his visit to Atlanta, Cook returned with a renewed vow to do something about quality. His first action was to conduct a series of meetings with employees and management staff of the three hotels and announce, "The strategy of Cook Hotels will be based on quality as our competitive advantage in the market sector in which we operate. We are not Ritz-Carlton but we certainly are not Motel 6."

Realizing that the very heart of a quality strategy was customer satisfaction, he again met with employees and took every opportunity to communicate his "moments of truth" vision of customer satisfaction. He entered this statement in the company newsletter:

> A "moment of truth" can be anything that is communicated to a guest about the organization. When a guest enters your environment, there are numerous "moments of truth." Is the area clean or is there a coffee stain on the rug? Are the plants alive or are there dead leaves on the floor? Does the receptionist smile and speak pleasantly or is she a grouch? Is the guest kept waiting or is he/she met on time? "Moments of truth" add up as the minutes pass by. There can be hundreds of them from the time a guest steps off the elevator until the final check out. With each "moment of truth" the guest makes some judgement about who we are and how we treat them. This can make or break a lasting relationship.

For this second effort at a quality culture and strategy, all employees were trained in quality concepts and tools. Front-line employees actually trained their peers in customer relations, process improvement, teams, and personal action plans. Each department was involved and had the responsibility for writing its own vision/mission statement. Department managers took ownership of the challenge of making quality commitment work. There were also interdepartmental teams and cross-functional teams. No employees were excluded from the team process.

The strategy based on quality began to work. As time passed, a program of continuous improvement was implemented. A number of modifications were added. Data-based surveys of customer and employee satisfaction were conducted and the results used for setting goals for improvement. Communication was improved by adding "Quality Counts" columns to the monthly newsletter. Performance evaluations were modified to include personal development plans. Team members became involved in departmental systems and quality standards. Training was expanded to include certification and opportunities for non-technical training. Recognition and rewards were based on team, not individual, contribution.

## Questions for Discussion

1   What is your evaluation of the company's efforts to base a culture, strategy, and competitive advantage on quality?

**2**  Identify one or more "moments of truth" that you have recently encountered as a customer.

**3**  Do you think Cook has achieved a shared vision of quality? If yes, how did the following factors influence it:

- Communications
- Relationships
- Measurement
- Training

# IF IT'S TUESDAY,
# IT MUST BE ISO 9000

## Anand Sharma

The acronyms pop up everywhere—TQM, CQI, JIT. You no longer need an MBA to be a manager; you need a spelling-bee trophy. It's all one big bowl of alphabet soup. Every month, some new guru publishes a book on the latest theory of employee motivation, productivity improvement, or inventory reduction. Whoops echo up from reviewers: We're falling behind Them! (Insert the name of your favorite goblins.) We're seeking the paradigm of the future! We're returning to traditional management theories!

All this hubbub would be funny, if knowing the best way to run a plant, department or company weren't such serious business. Anxious to find that "best" approach, intelligent managers, with the best of intentions, scurry to and fro, attending seminars, subscribing to newsletters, and reading all the latest literature. But too often their efforts are doomed to failure even before they make up plans of action. Why? Because successfully implementing change requires commitment and nurturing, not a memo or a week-long indoctrination process.

A plant, shop floor, or company is a living organism with a personality, a method by which it operates, and a collective memory. Further, this organism exists as part of a larger corporate culture. Too many managers assume a memo instructing one and all on the new method of operations—the inspiration du jour—will turn everything around on a dime.

"Been there, done that," often describes the reaction of line workers when they learn of a change in plant policy. Some make bets on how long a new policy will last.

Too often, managers leave employees out of the decision-making process. Employees invest no effort in its formulation, take no public stand on its merits, and have no personal responsibility for its success or failure. They don't own the plan, and thus see no need to upset their routines by trying to make it succeed.

Reproduced, with permission, from *Manufacturing Engineering*, March 1998, p. 256.

Look at the world we live in. Technologies change, competition changes, marketing strategies and business plans change, but few people like change. When planning major changes in policy or corporate culture, you must take a step-by-step approach to developing, announcing, introducing, and ensuring acceptance of the new ways.

Implementing a new program requires a system of support, education, and motivation. Basically, a new program calls for more leadership and less management. Consensus building is crucial. Senior managers must convince mid-level managers, first-line supervisors, shop-floor supervisors, and office managers of the need for change and the value of the proposed new policies. Workers take signals from their supervisors. If they sense cynicism, doubt or lack of commitment, all will be lost. If employees believe the plan is sensible, and open to their input as well as that of management, they will be likely to support it. Also, employees know exactly what problems reduce a plant's efficiency. They can provide valuable insight.

Once you establish a consensus, and a sense of shared ownership in the new policy, you must describe the final plan to everyone, explain its rationale, and anticipate and address potential objections before they spread. Finally, you must, as a manager, inculcate the ideas of constant improvement and cooperation between line workers, floor managers, plant managers, etc.

After the initial hoopla, you must regularly promote the policy change, keep explaining the rationale behind it, and point out the benefits. Two types of resistance may arise. The first I call CAVE (Citizens Against Virtually Everything). These folks don't want to work in a changing environment. They are a nuisance. Subtler and more dangerous resistance arises from a second group of persons I call anchor-draggers, who argue by saying, "I'm all for this, but..."

Dealing with anchor-draggers requires "air cover," respected employees who believe in the new approach. For change to survive the criticisms of the anchor-draggers, you must give these people the latest data demonstrating the success of the policy shift. So armed, they can actively and aggressively rebut the criticisms of the anchor-draggers.

If your new plan was a good one, and properly supported, one and all will see the results. If you can demonstrate a record of accomplishment under the new program, achievement of targets, and solid growth for the company, the final holdouts will buckle.

Tomorrow, when you turn on CNN and hear some "expert" describe his latest theory on productivity, don't throw a shoe at the TV screen. Just remember that his or her idea, even if it's a good one, is no cure-all, only the first step in a complicated process.

**EXERCISE**

# LEADERSHIP AT VARIFILM

Compare each of the following TQM criteria to Varifilm and indicate whether the practice in the company is a *strength* (S) or *needs improvement* (I). Justify your answer.

**1.0 Leadership**                                                          S        I

■ Senior executives are personally involved in Varifilm's       ___      __
quality vision and are actively driving the quality improvement initiative.

■ Personal leadership improvement plans are developed based     ___      __
on feedback mechanisms.

■ The approach to establishing specific expectations with       ___      __
other managers and supervisors is clearly defined.

■ I-Team members are committed to spending a minimum of         ___      __
one-third of their time on quality-related activities.

■ Varifilm's quality values are clearly summarized in the       ___      __
form of goals, policies, principles, and actions and serve as
the foundation for strategic planning.

■ Senior executives are personally involved in the ongoing      ___      __
communication of customer focus and quality values.

*Additional Areas for Improvement*

_____

_____

_____

### 1.2 Management for Quality        S     I

- Key indicators are used to evaluate and improve awareness and integration of quality values.      —    —

- Unit managers are responsible for leading Varifilm's Continuous Improvement Criteria (VCIC) and High Performance Work Systems (HPWS) process and reporting annually to the I-Team.      —    —

- Customer focus and quality values are aligned through a variety of approaches and the gain-sharing process is aligned with key performance indicators.      —    —

- There is a systematic process for deploying values and principles to all units and levels.      —    —

*Additional Areas for Improvement*

_____

_____

_____

# FOR FURTHER READING

Camison, Cesar, "Total Quality Management and Cultural Change: A Model of Organizational Development," *International Journal of Technology Management,* Vol. 16 No. 4–6, 1998, pp. 479–493.

Choi, Thomas Y. and Orlando C. Behling, "Top Managers and TQM Success: One More Look After All These Years," *Academy of Management Executive,* Feb. 1997, pp. 37–47.

Fojt, Martin, "Quality Planning and the Communication Plan," *Journal of Services Marketing,* Vol. 9 No. 3, 1995, pp. 2–7.

Giordan, Judith C., "That Vision Thing—The Key to Sustainable Competitive Advantage," *Research-Technology Management,* Sept./Oct. 1995, pp. 8–9.

Krumwiede, Dennis W., Chwen Sheu, and Jerome Lavelle, "Understanding the Relationship of Top Management Personality to TQM Implementation," *Production & Inventory Management Journal,* Second Quarter 1998, pp. 6–10.

# 3

# INFORMATION AND ANALYSIS

*Organizations, as information processing systems, will tend to produce invalid information for the important, risky, threatening issues (where ironically they need valid information badly) and valid information for the unimportant, routine issues.*

Chris Argyris

Information is the critical enabler of total quality management (TQM). More and more successful companies agree that information technology and information systems serve as keys to their quality success. Conversely, this component of TQM is frequently the roadblock to improvement in many firms. In these firms, better quality and productivity may not be the issue; rather, the real issue may be better quality of information. Dr. Curt W. Reimann, director of the Malcolm Baldrige National Quality Award, suggests that the critical constraint for many companies in applying for the award is the lack of a proper information system for tracking and improving areas in the remaining award categories.[1]

The 1999 Baldrige *information and analysis* criteria for performance excellence examine the selection, management, and effectiveness of use of information and data to support key company processes and action plans and the company's performance management system.

■ **Selection and use of information and data.** The selection, management, and use of information and data to support overall business goals, with strong emphasis on process management, action plans, and performance improvement. Overall, this item represents a key foundation for a performance-oriented company that effectively utilizes non-financial and financial information and data.

■ **Selection and use of comparative information and data.** External drivers of improvement information and data related to competitive position and to best practices. Such data might have both operational and strategic value.

■ **Analysis and review of company performance.** The principal basis for guiding a company's process management toward key business results. Despite their importance, individual facts and data do not usually provide a sound basis for actions or priorities. Action depends upon understanding cause/effect relationships between processes and business result.

Selection of analyses depends upon many factors, including business type, size, and competitive position. Examples include:

How the company's product and service quality improvement correlates with key customer indicators such as customer satisfaction, customer retention, and market share

Trends in individual measures of productivity such as work force productivity

Performance trends relative to competitors on key quality attributes

Cost/revenue implications of customer-related problems and problem resolution effectiveness

Interpretation of market share changes in terms of customer gains and losses and changes in customer satisfaction

Cost trends relative to competitors

Trends in economic, market, and shareholder indicators of value

## ORGANIZATIONAL IMPLICATIONS

John Sculley, former chairman of Apple Computer, concludes that information systems and technology can no longer be regarded as staff or service functions for management. Moreover, information systems will become the most important means for companies to create distinctive quality and unique service at the lowest possible cost.[2] At a 1988 symposium in Washington, D.C. for some 175 chief executive officers of major U.S. corporations, the main topic was quality improvement and the information systems to support that effort. Designing the product, the plant configuration, and even the organizational structure is less challenging than designing the information system, which is the central component of TQM that allows the process to function.[3] It may be that the rigor of the production process is not matched by that of the information system, and the cause may lie in the increased complexity and breadth of the latter. Information is critical to *all* functions, and *all* functions need to be integrated by information.

The natural progression of information systems (used interchangeably with management information systems) in the past has frequently resulted in "band-aids" or "islands of mechanization," as applications such as inventory control, production scheduling, and sales reporting were designed without much regard for integration among each other or among other functions and activities within the organization. In recent years, additional and more sophisticated applications have emerged, such as quality function deployment, Taguchi methods, statistical process control, and just-in-time. These are now considered basic to the TQM process.[4] The challenge remains the same: to integrate these techniques and principles into a structured approach that includes related decision-making requirements across the board.

Historically, companies have automated the easy applications: payroll, financial accounting, production control, etc. Today, the concept of *reengineering* is emerging. Rather than automating tasks and isolating them into discrete departments, companies are attempting to integrate the related activities of engineering, manufacturing, marketing, and support operations. Actions proceed in parallel, rather than sequential, order. Cycle time is reduced and products get to market faster with fewer defects. In short, the process is reengineered, and computer power is applied to the new process in the form of information systems. The focus is changing from buying information technology in order to automate paperwork to a focus designed to improve the process.

## Information Technology

Systems design may be a constraint, but information technology (IT) is not. The geometric acceleration of developments is well known and can only be described as dramatic and spectacular.[5] If industry is capable of absorbing the technology, a further increase in the sophistication and importance of information will occur. Capital and direct labor will continue to be sources of value added, but the proportion contributed by intellectual and information activity will increase. Indeed, information can be considered to be a substitute for other assets because it can increase the productivity of existing capital and reduce the requirement for additional expenditures. It should be exploited.[6]

In 1990, Federal Express spent more than $243 million on IT. CEO Fred Smith stated that IT is absolutely the key to the organization's operations and that the entire quality process depends on statistical quantification, which, in turn, depends on IT. Information is generated for both employees and customers.

Unfortunately, IT could be the weak link in the TQM chain. *Forbes* magazine reports that 70 percent of IT investments are either not completed or exceed cost projections by about 200 percent. The problem is the lack of communication. Executives either do not know much about IT or they leave purchasing to information systems people, who are not generally in the loop in terms of understanding what companies are trying to achieve in the marketplace. The result is that information systems people pick out and purchase sophisticated technology and systems that provide little benefit to the company in its TQM efforts. Estimates vary, but it is known that some companies devote about 85 percent of their IT budgets to utility functions, 12 percent to productivity enhancements, and 3 percent to cutting-edge competitive advantage. Before investing in IT, three questions should be asked: (1) Can it improve performance? (2) Can it cut costs? (3) Can it generate new business opportunities? In short, applying the lessons of TQM to the use of IT will not only reduce wasteful investments in technology but will enhance its effectiveness as well.

## Decision Making

The classic tools of TQM are thinking tools. Where measurements are used, they are an aid to understanding and decision making, not an end in themselves. Consider the analogy of a modern airplane cockpit. Key indicators are monitored constantly. When an indicator, such as elevation, moves outside an acceptable range, a warning sounds. The pilot can take immediate action to correct the problem. Hundreds of indicators are monitored, yet most of them become visible to the pilot when a problem is apparent. A smaller number, such as speed, altitude, elevation, and course, are constantly visible because they show just how well the flight is going. These essential indicators are the ones that the company executive (the "pilot") must watch constantly in order to "stay on course."

The ability to make decisions quickly has always been critical to management at all levels, and information is essential to the process. It has emerged as a crucial competitive weapon.[7] Yet middle managers, who are the real change agents, spend most of their time exchanging information with subordinates, peers, or the boss, leaving little time for customers or for innovation and change. In the jargon of information systems, they need a decision support system.

## Information Systems in Japan

"Get the facts" seems to be the mantra of both U.S. and Japanese managers. Lee Iacocca, former chairman of Chrysler Corporation, advised: "I may act on my intuition—but only if my hunches are supported by the facts." Similarly, Katsuya Hosotani, of 3A Corporation in Tokyo, offers the view of the Japanese managers: "In quality control, we try as far as possible to make our various judgments based on the facts, not guesswork. Our slogan is 'speak with the facts.'"

In what continue to be customary comparisons between the United States and Japan, it is useful to examine how IT and information systems are perceived in Japan. Japanese executives believe that customer satisfaction drives the development of new services and products and that IT can be a vital means to facilitate strategies and operations to this end.[8] In true Japanese fashion, this view is apparently promoted by the national government as well. To build a foundation for future technicians and managers, the Ministry of Education has implemented national education policies for the full-scale use of computers in education.[9] There is also a national policy on software. The Ministry of International Trade and Industry has launched the Sigma Project, which calls for computerizing the software process and industrializing and computerizing software production.[10]

The Deming Prize is awarded each year to Japanese companies that demonstrate outstanding improvement in quality control. Yokogawa Hewlett-Packard, a joint venture of Hewlett-Packard and Yokogawa Electric Works, was awarded the prize for an information systems approach that yielded dramatic increases in profit, productivity, and market share.

## STRATEGIC INFORMATION SYSTEMS

The integration of management information systems (MIS) with strategic planning has been suggested as a necessary prerequisite to strategy formulation and implementation. If we assume, as we must, that the basic requirement of a strategy is environmental positioning in order to meet customer requirements and if we further assume that the ultimate purpose of each function and process within an organization is to contribute to strategy, the role of information becomes clear.

As will be discussed in Chapter 9, the value chain is a useful concept for determining the structure and processes needed by an organization in order to achieve a competitive advantage, keeping in mind that competitiveness is decided neither by the industry nor by the company, but rather by the customer.

Beginning with the customer, integration of processes and information can proceed as follows:

- Identify the market segment in which you want to compete.
- Use data collection and analysis to define the customer requirements in the chosen segment.

- Translate these requirements into major design parameters to develop, produce, deliver, and service the product that meets the customer's requirements. These are the primary functions and activities (processes) of the value chain.

- Complement the primary processes with support activities such as planning, finance and accounting, MIS, personnel, etc.

- Subdivide or "explode" the organization design parameters into the processes (functions, activities, etc.) that are necessary to achieve the quality differentiation.

- Design the information requirements necessary to manage each process and to integrate all processes horizontally.

The support activities are sometimes taken for granted and their linking potential is often overlooked. Moreover, their potential contribution to differentiation may not be realized. Marketing services, for example, when combined with the customer's expertise, can generate differentiated product and service opportunities. The customer will place high value on a supplier that delivers the right information quickly. Engineering services, usually perceived as a commodity product, can also differentiate a firm. In both cases, the information systems support is cost effective.

At Honeywell, Inc., translating long-term strategy into tactics that enhance short-term operations has resulted in new approaches that have shortened cycle time, improved quality, and reduced costs. The approach involves spreading information, standardizing, and measuring performance.

## Environmental Analysis

Strategy formulation requires an analysis of the different environments: general, industry, and competitive (see Chapter 4 for further discussion). One study found that small business owners spend over one-fourth of the day in external information search activities.[11] Competitive information is particularly valuable but is difficult to obtain.[12] In general, the minimum information needed about competitors can be related to how they stand on the key success factors for a market segment. These may differ by industry and segment but usually include the following:[13]

- Market share
- Product line breadth
- Proprietary advantages
- Age and location of facility

- Growth rate
- Distribution effectiveness
- Price competitiveness
- Capacity and productivity

- Experience curve effects
- R&D advantage and position
- Value added
- Cash throw-off

Porter has identified the information needed for positioning in an industry and in a chosen market segment, and his system is widely used. His categories are (1) intensity of rivalry, (2) bargaining power of buyers, (3) bargaining power of suppliers, (4) threat of substitution, and (5) threat of new entrants.[13] Each category includes a number of elements or subtopics that should be determined and tracked with some type of information system.

Central to all information relating to strategy formulation and implementation is the need to *define and measure* the concept of quality of product and service—as determined by the customer. This step is fundamental to positioning and subsequent follow-up.

## SHORTCOMINGS OF ACCOUNTING SYSTEMS

Financial information is perhaps the most widespread indicator of performance, and for many firms is the only indicator. Critics of accounting systems claim that they do not really support the operations and strategy of the company, two dimensions in which quality plays a dominant role. Despite the widely held conclusion that we are in the information age, management accounting would probably be labeled inadequate by managers who seek to support company operations and strategy through quality improvement. This is increasingly evident in the "new" manufacturing environment, which is characterized by the trends and implications listed in Table 3-1.

Accountant bashing is becoming increasingly popular in the management literature. The trend is symbolized by Harvard Business School Professors H. Thomas Johnson and Robert Kaplan in their popular book *Relevance Lost*.[14] They conclude that today's accounting information provides little help in reducing costs and improving quality and productivity. Indeed, they suggest that this information might even be harmful. Peter Drucker, another critic, describes some of the shortcomings that are generally recognized:[15]

1. Cost accounting is based on a 1920s reality, when direct labor was 80 percent of manufacturing costs other than raw material. Today, it is 8 to 12 percent, and in some industries (e.g., IT) it is about 3 percent.
2. Non-direct labor costs, which can run up to 90 percent, are allocated in proportion to labor costs, an arbitrary and misleading system. Benefits of a process change are allocated in the same way.

**Table 3-1** New Manufacturing Environment

| Trend | Implication for quality |
| --- | --- |
| Focus on manufacturing strategy | Quality rapidly becoming the central competitive edge of strategy |
| Production of high-quality goods | Quality directly related to market share, growth, profits |
| Reduction of inventory levels by just-in-time inventory | Reduction of costs associated with excess inventory |
| Tight schedules | Improves availability to customer, another competitive edge perceived as quality by the customer |
| Product mix and variety | Allows focus on strategy and market segmentation |
| Equipment automation | Provides justification for quality and productivity improvement |
| Shortened product life cycle | Provides opportunity to expedite market shifts and incorporate new technologies into the product, but imposes additional stress on the quality management program |
| Organizational changes | Responsibility for quality delegated to strategic business units and product managers |
| Information technology | Allows greater control of cost of quality, quality management, and cross-functional integration |

3. The cost system ignores the costs of *non-producing,* whether this be downtime, stockouts, defects, or other costs of non-quality.

4. The system cannot measure, predict, or justify change or innovation in product or process. In other words, accounting measures direct or real costs and not benefits.

5. Accounting-generated information does not recognize linkages between functions, activities, or processes.

6. Manufacturing decisions cannot be made as *business* decisions based on the information provided by accounting. The system confines itself to measurable and objective decisions and does not address the intangibles.

Efforts are underway to make accounting a true management and business system. For example, Computer-Aided Manufacturing-International (CAM-I) is a cooperative effort by automation producers, multinational manufacturers, and accountants to develop a new cost accounting system. Even internal auditors are examining their new role in TQM.[16]

## ORGANIZATIONAL LINKAGES

The importance of data linkages is illustrated by data on service calls, a primary source of measuring product field performance. These are an important source of information for design, engineering, manufacturing, sales, and service. One research study[17] reported that in some cases among air-conditioner manufacturers, the aggregate data on failure rates was of little use because of organization barriers.

■ The *service tracking report* at American Express monitors performance for all centers worldwide. For the credit card division, for example, performance is measured against 100 service measures, including how long it takes to process an application, authorize charges, bill card members, and answer customer billing inquiries. Each measure is based on customer expectations, the competition, the economy, and legislation. Application processing time has been reduced by 50 percent and the bottom line has been increased by $70 million.

This example illustrates the widespread need for organization linkages and cross-functional MIS and the need to track a process on a continuous basis. Figure 3-1 shows how each step in the life cycle of a product involves related processes as cross-functional lines.

Each step in the product life cycle involves a number of processes at these cross-functional lines in a continuous flow from design to preproduction planning to vendor management to incoming material to in-process control to fin-

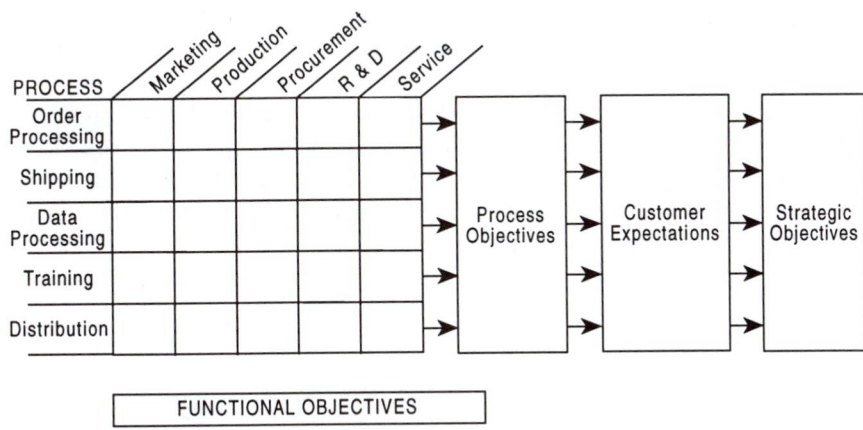

**Figure 3-1**  Cross-Functional Lines in the Life Cycle of a Product

ished goods to customer service. The steps along the flow should be accompanied by appropriate information.[18] Thus, the linkage concept may focus on internal customers (those who use products in a later step of the process) as well as external customers.

■ Federal Express, the first service sector company to earn the Baldrige Award, integrates a variety of internal measurement systems into the core of its business. The objective is "zero service defects." The system, SQI (service quality indicators), measures 12 critical points at which failure can occur in the service process and continually reinforces how employees are doing compared to their goals.

## ADVANCED PROCESSES/SYSTEMS

SPC...QFD...CAD...CIM...MRP—one gets the impression of "alphabet management." These and other basic applications represent the major systems of TQM. None stands alone and there are overlaps among them. Some advocates promote one or more as the "total system." Most, if not all, of these processes depend upon IT and a sophisticated information system design. Because systems design begins with the objective of the process, it is useful to list the objective of the major processes (Table 3-2).

At Motorola's Automotive and Industrial Electronics Group in Arcade, New York, over 1000 employees were trained in statistical process control. Operators then began doing their own inspections and plotting hourly control charts to control their own projects. Quality control inspectors were transferred out. Improvements included (1) achieving 10:1 goal of improvement, (2) significant increases in yields, and (3) reduction in scrap. The facility received the Q1 quality award as a supplier to Ford.

Donald Bell, general manager of Monsanto's Fibers Division, envisioned the "Plant of the 1990s." The scheme is a three-tiered approach encompassing human resources planning, total quality concepts, and computer-integrated manufacturing. Productivity gains of 40 to 50 percent have already been achieved. The program emphasizes the needs of internal customers—those who use products in a later step of the manufacturing process. Computer training has enabled greater acceptance of these concepts.[20]

## INFORMATION AND THE CUSTOMER

According to examiners who visit companies that apply for the Baldrige Award, most companies lack the processes that ensure efficient flow of informa-

**Table 3-2**   Objectives of Major Processes in Systems Design

| Process/system | Objective |
| --- | --- |
| Statistical quality control | Build in the control limits of a process that spot and identify causes of variations |
| Statistical process control | Provide information on how productivity and quality can be *continuously improved* through problem identification (it has been estimated that U.S. firms invest 20 to 25 percent of their operating budgets in finding and fixing mistakes[19]) |
| Just-in-time | Reduce inventory cost, production time, and space requirements |
| Computer-integrated manufacturing | Lower cost, shorten lead time, and improve quality based on information sharing by linking management and financial information systems, departmental computing, process management systems, and factory systems for controlling machinery and manufacturing processes |
| Quality function deployment | Integrate the three dimensions of (1) company-wide quality, (2) focus on customer requirements, and (3) translation of quality perceptions into product characteristics and then into the manufacturing process |

tion on customer demands and related information throughout the organization.[21] In other words, most companies do not devote the same attention to the customer that they do to the internal processes of shipping, inventory, just-in-time, manufacturing, etc. This is unfortunate because the operating processes cannot be managed according to the principles of TQM unless the loop is closed with customer feedback. Information systems should be extended beyond the plant into the marketplace. Some companies tend to define quality in terms of customer satisfaction or some other non-specific term and then relax after shipment is made, overlooking the competitive success that accompanies after-the-sale service, spare parts, or distribution.[22]

Why do information systems directly related to customer satisfaction frequently take a back seat to what otherwise might be acceptable or excellent information systems in support of quality and process control? The answer may be that it is difficult to specify information needs for an elusive system to measure customer requirements and satisfaction, which in themselves are difficult to define. Or it may be that the pressures of crisis management and internal information exchange leave little time for the customer.[23] Whatever the cause, it is a good idea to design a system that measures the pulse of the market and the customer base. It is estimated that failure to do so will cost twice as much as poor internal quality.[24]

■ The First National Bank of Chicago found that quality can be the difference between acquiring and keeping customers. Because competitive pricing varies by only a few pennies, the customer must be enlightened as to the benefits of strong quality. The bank measures customer satisfaction by how often inaccurate information is given. In 1982, the error rate was 1 in 4000 transactions; in 1990, it dropped to 1 in 810,000 transactions.

## Information Needs

After the objective of an information system is established, the next step is to determine the information needs. This is the most difficult step in designing an MIS for customer satisfaction. Everything else is detail and technique. Manager/user involvement is essential here.

If there is one fundamental principle of TQM, it is that *quality is what the buyer defines it as,* and not what the company defines it to be. Ford learned this lesson in the late 1970s, when the company definition of DQR (durability, quality, and reliability) was found to be presented in terms (engineering design tolerances and specifications) understandable only within the company, rather than in terms that represented quality to the customer. Only after reassessing quality in terms understandable to the customer was Ford able to adopt a policy called "Ford Total Quality Excellence" and achieve organization-wide commitment to continuous improvement and customer focus.

The first step, then, is to define quality as perceived by the customer by viewing it *externally* from the customer's perspective. By profiling how customers make purchase decisions, it is possible to determine which product attributes are most important and to determine how customers rate each attribute. As will be discussed in Chapter 8, this process forms the basis of *benchmarking.*[25]

Market research methods ranging from focus groups to shopper surveys are means for profiling customers and defining quality as perceived by customers. The information system can then be designed to provide the input for decisions regarding the operating plan, organizational implications, and follow-up control.

## SYSTEMS DESIGN

After reviewing hundreds of applications for the Baldrige Award, Curt Reimann, director of the award, concluded that the area of information and analysis represents a serious national problem.[26] Many firms have failed to design individual applications to fit an overall master plan. The result has been a "band-aid" solution with little integration between functions and activities.

A master plan should be centered around corporate goals and the critical success factors and cost-performance drivers related to these goals. In a manufacturing firm, data from engineering, production, and field service are used to improve product design and manufacturing techniques. If reducing cycle time in bringing a product to market is a critical success factor (as it is), a good deal of this information will flow sideways and across departmental lines, rather than upward and vertically as in the traditional model.

The individual manager/user has the job of designing his or her own system requirements and fitting these into the overall master plan. This is not easy. In discussions with dozens of system analysts, they almost always report that their number one difficulty in system design is the inability or unwillingness of the user to define information needs. This definition is not the job of the analyst— it is the job of the individual user. Before design can proceed, two critical steps must be taken: define *system objectives* and *information needs.*

Surprisingly, many users cannot define an objective. They will define it as "having the right part at the right place at the right time" or "preparing a field service report." Statements such as these are elusive, not quantifiable, and unsuitable for conversion to information needs. On the other hand, when objectives are stated in more specific terms (such as "reduce final inspection in the production process to the point of elimination" or "reduce throughput time to six days"), the designer has a benchmark from which to proceed.

The next step is to define *information needs,* another requirement that users have difficulty defining. The question is: "What information do I need to achieve the objective?" If performance measures are established, the determination of both objective and information needs will become more apparent. Successful companies benchmark their performance against world-class quality leaders. For example, Xerox measured its performance in about 240 key areas of product, service, and business performance. This process is discussed further in Chapter 8.

## QUESTIONS FOR DISCUSSION

**3-1** Describe how lack of information can be a roadblock to implementing one or more TQM actions.

**3-2** How do traditional accounting systems provide inadequate information for control of processes in an industry with low labor content?

**3-3** Choose two functions or activities (market research, R&D, design, production planning, procurement, human resources) and show how information can serve to integrate them across functional lines.

**3-4** How does information technology affect organizational structure? Give an example of how information technology can facilitate TQM.

**3-5** How would you go about designing a management information system for getting customer input for quality improvement?

**3-6** How does market segmentation influence information needs?

## ENDNOTES

1. Telephone interview with Curt W. Reimann.
2. John Sculley, "The Human Use of Information," *Journal for Quality and Participation,* Jan./Feb. 1990, pp. 10–13.
3. Elizabeth A. Haas, "Breakthrough Manufacturing," *Harvard Business Review,* March/April 1987, pp. 75–81. It is estimated here that companies adopting integrated strategies may succeed in increasing productivity by 10 or 15 percent annually. See also Julian W. Riehl, "Planning for Total Quality: The Information Technology Component," *Advanced Management Journal,* Autumn 1988, pp. 13–19.
4. Nael A. Aly, Venetta J. Maytubby, and Ahmad K. Elshennawy, "Total Quality Management: An Approach & A Case Study," *Computers and Industrial Engineering,* Issues 1–4, 1990, pp. 111–116.
5. For a description of what lies ahead, see Robb Wilmot, "Computer Integrated Management—The Next Competitive Breakthrough," *Long Range Planning,* Vol. 21 No. 6, 1988, pp. 65–70.
6. James Heskett, "Lessons in the Service Sector," *Harvard Business Review,* March/April 1987, pp. 118–126.
7. Kathleen M. Eisenhardt, "Speed and Strategic Choice: How Managers Accelerate Decision Making," *California Management Review,* Spring 1990, pp. 39–54.
8. Dennis Normile, "Japan Inc. Bows to the Customer," *CIO,* Aug. 1990, pp. 91–93. A major benefit of information systems is increasing the speed from product concept to marketing, an improvement that translates into customer satisfaction.
9. Takashi Yamagiwa, "Computer Use in the Japanese Educational System," *Business Japan,* March 1988, pp. 38–39.
10. Ryozo Hayashi, "National Policy on the Information Service Industry," *Business Japan,* March 1990, pp. 49–61.
11. J. Lynn Johnson and Ralph Kuehn, "The Small Business Owner/Manager's Search for External Information," *Journal of Small Business Management,* July 1987, pp. 53–60.
12. The pioneering book is Frank J. Aguilar, *Scanning the Business Environment,* New York: Macmillan, 1967.
13. For a comprehensive treatment of competitive information and its sources, see Michael E. Porter, *Competitive Advantage,* New York: The Free Press, 1985. Based on research

data collected from more than 3000 strategic business units, The Strategic Planning Institute, through its PIMS program, has identified the following characteristics of the most profitable companies in an industry: (1) higher market share, (2) higher quality, (3) higher labor productivity, (4) higher capacity utilization, (5) newer plant and equipment, (6) lower investment intensity per sales dollar, and (7) lower direct cost per unit. See Robert D. Buzzell and Bradley T. Gale, *The PIMS Principles: Linking Strategy to Performance,* New York: The Free Press, 1987.

14. H. Thomas Johnson and Robert S. Kaplan, *Relevance Lost: The Rise and Fall of Management Accounting,* Boston: Harvard Business School Press, 1991.

15. Peter Drucker, "The Emerging Theory of Manufacturing," *Harvard Business Review,* May/June 1990, pp. 94–102. See also Robert S. Kaplan, "The Four Stage Model of Cost Systems Design," *Management Accounting,* Feb. 1990, pp. 22–26; James M. Reeve, "TQM and Cost Management: New Definitions for Cost Accounting," *Survey of Business,* Summer 1989, pp. 26–30.

16. Fred J. Newton, "A 1990s Agenda for Auditors," *Internal Auditor,* Dec. 1990, pp. 33–39.

17. David A. Garvin, *Managing Quality,* New York: The Free Press, 1988, pp. 167–169. In this study, the best plants maintained sophisticated systems to track data and report it back to interested departments and functions.

18. See Raymond G. Ernst, "Why Automating Isn't Enough," *Journal of Business Strategy,* May/June 1989, pp. 38–42. The author argues that companies too often attempt to improve manufacturing by making large investments in automation without improving their business processes. He estimates that the savings of 10 to 20 percent that can be derived from automating can be increased to 70 percent when improvements are made to existing business processes as well. The processes can be achieved through a product-information flow.

19. Otis Port, "The Push for Quality," *Business Week,* June 8, 1987, pp. 130–135.

20. For an excellent description of how quality function deployment is implemented, see John R. Hauser and Don Clausing, "The House of Quality," *Harvard Business Review,* May/June 1988, pp. 63–73. See also Chia-Hao Chang, "Quality Function Deployment (QFD): Processes in an Integrated Quality Information System," *Computers and Industrial Engineering,* Vol. 17 Issues 1–4, 1989, pp. 311–316.

21. Peter Burrows, "Commitment to Quality: Five Lessons You Can Learn from Award Entrants," *Electronic Business,* Oct. 15, 1990, pp. 56–58.

22. Morris A. Cohen and Hau L. Lee, "Out of Touch with Customer Needs? Spare Parts and After Sales Service," *Sloan Management Review,* Winter 1990, pp. 55–66.

23. Robert W. Wilmot, "Computer Integrated Management—The Next Competitive Breakthrough," *Long Range Planning,* Dec. 1988, pp. 65–70. This author has found that typical middle managers spend less than 10 percent of their time with customers and a tiny fraction sponsoring innovation and orchestrating change.

24. John Goodman and Cynthia J. Grimm, "A Quantified Case for Improving Quality Now," *Journal for Quality and Participation,* March 1990, pp. 50–55.

25. Bradley T. Gale and Robert D. Buzzel, "Market Perceived Quality: Key Strategic Concept," *Planning Review,* March/April 1989, pp. 6–15.

26. Curt W. Reimann, "Winning Strategies for Quality Improvement," *Business America,* March 25, 1991, pp. 8–11.

# INFORMATION AND ANALYSIS AT 3M

3M is known throughout the world as a leader in innovation and is admired for its extraordinary ability to take existing technologies and materials used by one area and apply this expertise to new products and markets—which is how 3M got into the dental products business. 3M Dental was created in 1964 with the introduction of 3M Addent Anterior Restorative, the first commercial resin composite dental restorative. This product combined two 3M technologies—polymers and ceramics—and launched a new era in dental product manufacturing that would emphasize improved aesthetics and healthier, stronger restored teeth.

## Company Information and Data

**Selection and use.**   3M Dental, leveraging successful programs established by 3M Corporate, selects data and information linked to business drivers and goals that (1) monitor business performance for alignment with strategic plans, (2) identify improvement opportunities, (3) initiate and drive corrective action, and (4) feed back into the strategic planning process.

**Customer information system.**   One major source of data for employees is the customer information system that contains dentist data. The database tracks (1) purchases of 3M Dental and competitive products, (2) contact activity, (3) complaints by market segment, and (4) complaints by dentists.

**Competitive data.**   3M Dental used competitive comparisons and benchmarking to improve operational performance and compare its level of performance to industry and world-class business leaders. Knowledge gained from competitive comparisons and benchmarks supports the strategic planning process and prioritizes projects.

## Company Performance Analysis and Review

**Business process management matrix.**   3M Dental developed the business process management matrix based upon performance management, an approach developed ten years ago to quantify an organization's activities and outcomes to support continuous improvement. It is this unique process that sets 3M apart from most businesses. Matrices are constantly monitored and evaluated to gauge the relationship between continuous business improvements and business results.

The process uses a matrix format where scores, on a scale from one to ten, are assigned to each outcome and activity, then weighted for comparative importance with other components of the specific index.

3M Dental's business process management matrix measures the company's performance in all key areas, such as business drivers, goals, functional groups, and the strategic business process, against prior year performance, current year goals, and stretch goals. For example, a score of 1000 points would indicate all stretch goals were achieved, 700 to 800 would indicate major goals were accomplished, and 300 would mean performance equal to the previous year.

This major 3M Dental process, which has been refined 12 times since its inception in 1995, has been featured in *Performance Management* magazine (Winter 1996) as an example of quality excellence.

# INFORMATION SYSTEMS AT
# LAKE CITY MACHINE TOOL

Lake City Machine Tool, Inc. is a family-owned company founded in 1962 by Henry (Hank) Pierce, who at the time of the company's founding was employed as a production supervisor at one of the country's leading machine tool manufacturers. Hank knew that the reject, rework, and return rates at the plant were excessive and felt that he could do a much better job with the same or similar equipment. When one of the company's major customers offered to help finance Hank, he quit his job and leased the necessary plant and equipment to make a product line very similar to that at his previous job.

For 20 years, Lake City Machine Tool prospered and grew. Demand for the company's high-speed drills remained approximately level but began to decline in the late 1980s as new materials, technology, and methods emerged. The company's drills took on the characteristics of a commodity product, differentiated only by price. Notwithstanding these developments, Hank Pierce managed to maintain market share as he competed on quality and delivery and with his old friends in the industry.

Following the end of the Cold War and the collapse of communism in the former Soviet Union, the competitive situation began to worsen. In addition to growing imports from Japan and Western Europe, the Eastern bloc countries entered the U.S. market. In addition, the emergence of automated equipment eliminated many of the skills normally required in the manufacture of machine tools. As sales slowed, Lake City purchased an injection molding plastics company that made commodity products such as clothes hangers and plastic bowls for freezer storage. Following this acquisition, Hank reorganized the company, appointing two product managers, one for machine tools and one for plastic products.

By 1991, the situation had reached crisis proportions, particularly in the machine tool product line. Although sales were fairly level, cash flow and profitability had eroded. Hank Pierce blamed continuing price cutting by competitors. He debated what to do and considered two alternatives. He could quit the manufacture of machine tools and become a marketing company, selling the products of other manufacturers. Alternatively, he could reduce costs to the point where he could compete successfully with others in the industry. He decided to explore the second alternative.

The two plants of the machine tool operation were located at the company's site in Lake City. Production was organized by process: cutting, grinding, and milling in plant #1 and finishing, testing, and warehousing in plant #2. Considerable costs in transportation and labor were incurred in transferring work in process between plants. Testing was accomplished by a sampling method devised by Hank Pierce. No labor standards existed, and products were not costed by either process or product line. Plastic products were located across town in another site.

Production for finished goods inventory was based on an annual sales forecast but was interrupted frequently for special orders and revised forecasts. The company sold to a network of distributors and to end-use customers. The product line consisted of about 7500 standard products and many specials involving a limited production run.

Much of the time of the sales force was taken up with special requirements of customers. The sales force suspected that the company was losing money on a significant fraction of its customers, but information was not available to identify and classify them. Suppliers of raw material were generally selected on price. It was fairly common for one or more suppliers to be late in delivery, to ship an incorrect amount, or to fail to pass Lake City's inspection of incoming material.

The turnover among the two product managers (machine tools and plastics) had become a problem. They complained that they had little control over their results. They had profit and loss (P&L) responsibility but had no P&Ls with which to manage. They were under constant pressure from customers to lower prices, and these pressures were passed on to manufacturing. Because no data or information was available on costs of products or group of products, pricing decisions were made using "ballpark" estimates.

Proper information systems were almost non-existent. About the only financial information available was an overall P&L statement and a balance sheet. No reports were available to identify product line profitability, inventory turn, variance analysis, or efficiency.

Hank Pierce felt at a loss to make operational plans or develop a long-term strategy. He was frustrated by the lack of proper information systems.

## Questions for Discussion

1 Given the commodity nature of the company's machine tool products, what action(s) could the company take to differentiate its product and provide quality to the customer?

2 What action(s) would you recommend to Hank Pierce?

3 Identify the major information needs of the company.

*Peter Drucker is truly one of the great pioneers and global management schol-ars. His writings are known and admired around the world. He has long been a champion of management in a knowledge worker environment; that is to say, the information environment. In the following article, he encourages the reader to ask the question: "What information do I need to do my job and in what form?" He then demonstrates how the answer integrates with customer satisfaction, the load-bearing component of total quality management.*

## WHAT DOES IT ALL MEAN?

**Peter F. Drucker**

> *Information we have plenty of, but what's really necessary to your work, and what form should it take? Don't expect an "information specialist" to tell you.*

Our relationship to information—and its tool, the computer—is changing. Most of us continue to use computers primarily to crunch numbers, but attitudes and applications are changing fast, and we are moving rapidly toward the informa-tion-based organization. Today, the big thing to learn is not how to use the computer, or even how to organize information, but how to take information responsibility.

Information responsibility means making information a tool of understand-ing, which in turn is the basis for common action. This idea is something that we are just starting to nibble on. I know a few places where it's taken seriously, but frankly, I don't know a single place where it's yet done. We are now only beginning to ask the question: What does information mean, both for my work and for other people's work?

---

Reprinted with permission from *Across the Board,* December 1991, pp. 12–14.

The first step in taking information responsibility is to ask the question: "What information do I need, and in what form?" Most of my friends, not just in industry but in all organizations, still believe that information specialists can tell them what information they need. This approach is like asking the traffic cop, "Where should I be going?" Executives and others will have to learn that information is their tool. They must think through the kind of information they need and make sure that the people on whom they depend to deliver it understand their needs.

The next question people have to learn to ask is: "How is this information important to people in other departments?" They have to consider the meaning of, for example, a piece of engineering information for the marketing people or a piece of marketing information for the engineers. And to figure this out, they must learn not just to guess but to go and ask.

Today, we are simply providing data and leaving the interpretation to the users, who are notoriously poor interpreters. Instead, we need to look at the information from our own area of activity and ask, "What should this mean to people in other areas? What implications for action are there?" For example, if I receive information from market research about changes in distribution systems—which are changing faster today than anything else, much faster than technology—I need to think about what this means for the design of the product, the service of the product, and other efforts that are not within my area but that nonetheless have a direct effect on how well I can do my job. We have a long way to go in this area. Executives who understand their work in terms of a flow of information are still a very small minority.

Another challenge for managers in the information-based organization is to make sure that the information on hand does not become misleading. Most of the information capacity a company has is internal. In fact, fundamentally, the only data base it has is internal. External data are very poor, very abstract, and very late. Outside data will always remain unsatisfactory for the simple reason that the important things that happen outside the business happen at the margin. They are qualitative changes, so they are not expressed in figures until it's too late.

How do you tell whether a given qualitative change is meaningful or purely anecdotal? I've been struggling with this for 40 years, and I'm not the only one. The problem is that early qualitative changes have no solid geometry that can tell you whether they are significant or not. You cannot easily convert a qualitative change—say, an incipient change in a distribution system—into quantities. By the time you get outside quantitative information, it's obsolete, or at least it's so late that you are running behind the parade.

Basically, we have become internally focused, and that's very dangerous. Our new data-processing capacity, though not the cause of this imbalance, aggravates it by giving people the illusion that they have information, when, in fact, crucial pieces are missing. To balance the increasing accessibility of and increasing dependence on information from the inside, we will have to increase our experience and exposure to the outside.

Last year, for example, I worked on productivity and quality issues with the joint productivity committees of two large automobile manufacturers and the United Auto Workers. The committees consist of very able people working very hard—but their results are not terribly impressive. The reason for that is simple. They cannot see that what they mean by quality means nothing to the customer. They are manufacturing people, and they love to show you figures that demonstrate that the American-made car when it leaves the factory now has fewer defects than the Japanese-made car. (This is not true of all American models, but of quite a few.) Yet customers are deserting American car manufacturers in droves, switching to the likes of Honda, Nissan, Toyota, and Mazda.

What the engineers mean by quality and what the customer means are two different things. I live in southern California. Once a year, my wife and I drive the 1,300 miles to our summer home in Colorado. One year our car broke down in Delta, Colorado. What we mean by quality is not the shape the car was in when it came out of the factory, but the service we get in Delta, Colorado. No automotive manufacturer understands that because they're not out there listening to their customers.

In the 1930s, Alfred Sloan, who ran General Motors, would disappear from Detroit once every six weeks. The next morning he would walk into a dealership in Cincinnati or Kansas City and say, "I am Mr. Sloan from Detroit. Would you allow me to work for two days as your assistant service manager?" When he left, customers always asked, "Who was that incompetent clunk?" but that wasn't the point of the exercise.

Sloan would also pop into the dealership in Albany, New York. I know about this from the Albany dealer, who complained about it volubly. Sloan showed up one day and said, "Mr. Yeager, do you mind if I work for you as a salesman for three days? I don't want any commission." Afterward, Mr. Yeager said, "Alfred Sloan cost me more sales than I can possibly tell you." The point is that when Alfred Sloan went back to Detroit from these forays, he knew customers. Since World War II, nobody in Detroit has done that. But two weeks after I took my Japanese-made car in for its routine inspection, I got a telephone call from Nissan, asking, "Were you satisfied?" That has never happened with my Oldsmobile.

I have not been able to get the idea of knowing customers across to people, even people who have been my friends for 40 years. They don't get it because not one of them has gone to work as an assistant service manager for two days. Instead, they look at statistics. Their data show them that cars are complex. There are 38,000 parts, more or less, and something has got to go wrong. What matters to the customer is, "Do I get it fixed, and do they care?" That's customer service—not insuring that the car was in perfect shape when it left the factory. It's irrelevant to the customer what caused the problem—whether it was a pebble from the road that knocked the pipe galley west, or whether the bolt wasn't fastened.

We will have to learn to balance the increasing amount of hard information with meaningful market experience, especially as distribution channels continue to change quickly. Real market experience is the only way to get the critical information that is embodied in attitudes, expectations, and events.

The need for critical but unquantifiable information applies not only to markets but to technologies, which are changing just as fast and are becoming equally unstructured. It's no longer adequate for people in the paper industry, for example, to know all about paper chemistry and paper mechanics. Their industry will be affected by discoveries in solid-state physics that no paper-maker has ever heard of. Businesses need information on technologies that are being developed far beyond their narrow areas, and in most cases, they don't know how to get it.

Some companies are better at getting technology information than marketing information. Quite a few companies no longer subscribe to the belief that "only what goes on in our lab is technology; the rest is not relevant to us." But determining what is relevant to a company is not easy. So the next step is to define information. Information is not what the computer delivers but what executives need to take effective action.

One branch of the U.S. Armed Services, for example, recently faced a serious supply problem when the workers in a critical plant went on strike. The strike came as a shock to senior managers because they had been looking at personnel data over the whole system of plants, and they were very happy. Absenteeism was low, as was turnover. But the aggregated data failed to reveal that one of their smallest plants had absenteeism rates of 80 percent and extremely high turnover. This was a grotesquely mismanaged plant, and senior management had no inkling of that fact because the information that would have revealed years of neglect was masked by the wrong presentation of data.

So a key part of the job is to make sure that data are presented in the form in which they are capable of giving information. One has to ask not just, "Are the data reliable?" but, "Is this the right way of presenting them?"

In that light, you must also take into consideration the recipient of your information. The human race is split three ways: Some people can take in information by looking at figures, some by looking at graphs, and a third group only by touching it, feeling it, or writing it.

I learned a very valuable lesson about presenting information in 1942, when I was working for the Pentagon. I made my first appearance before a congressional committee, which was headed by an obscure politician named Harry

Truman. He cut me into tiny little pieces and fed me to the fish. And then he became a kind old gentleman and invited me to his chambers. I am not a drinker, but he poured a bottle of bourbon into me without noticeable effect. And when I thought I would survive—though I didn't yet enjoy the prospect—he said, "Sonny, don't you ever do again what you did today." And I asked, "Sir, what did I do?" He said, "You quoted fractions to Senators. If we understood fractions, what would we be doing in the Senate?" And then he said, "Go back to that so-and-so general of yours and tell him never to do again what he did." I asked, "What did General Jones do, sir?" He said, "He did something that needs to be explained; there is nothing you can explain to a U.S. Senator." From that moment on I was the first Truman booster. He was absolutely right. This is wisdom.

So you need to know in what form your people can receive information. If you talk to me, for example, don't give me graphs covered with little colored men or I crawl up the wall. Give me solid black numbers, and don't carry them out to the seventh decimal place, because I'm better than you at forging and faking figures, and I know that the less reliable the information, the more decimals. Give me numbers and let me work through them, because I like doing that. Most executives are not yet thinking about the form in which they convey information because they have not yet addressed the problem of marketing their output, which always starts with the customer, not the product.

Information responsibility, then, begins with correctly identifying the information you need to effectively carry out your job, and extends to insuring that the information flows to people in other areas who stand to benefit from it, and in a form in which those people will readily understand it. Learning to exercise this responsibility will doubtless be a slow and difficult process, as forging new ground always is. Increasingly, however, the measure of the executive will not be his ability to interpret data, but his ability to define and exploit information.

# INFORMATION SYSTEMS
# AND ANALYSIS AT VARIFILM

Compare each of the following TQM criteria to Varifilm and indicate whether the practice in the company is a *strength* (S) or *needs improvement* (I). Justify your answer.

| | | | S | I |
|---|---|---|---|---|
| **2.1 Scope and Management of Quality and Performance Data and Information** | | | | |

■ The criteria for selecting types of data and information used in quality and operational performance improvement are described. Selection factors include data related to customer satisfaction and data required for performance analysis, among others.                                    _____  _____

■ A wide range of customer-related, product and service performance, internal operations and performance, supplier performance, and cost and financial data and information is used by Varifilm to improve quality and operational performance.                                    _____  _____

■ Key indicators used to evaluate and improve the alignment of data and information with process improvement plans are clearly defined.                                    _____  _____

■ Evidence is provided to determine how Varifilm ensures data reliability.                                    _____  _____

■ A variety of methods are used to ensure rapid and accurate data transfer throughout the company, including automated laboratory data entry at all manufacturing sites, electronic data interchange (EDI) with customers and suppliers, and electronic mail.                                    _____  _____

■ Principal roles for each type of data and information used to improve quality and operational performance are provided.                                    _____  _____

|                                                                                                                                                                                                              | S | I |
|---|---|---|
| ■ Improvements in the scope and management of data are made through the assessment process, customer input, and the process management system (PMS). In addition, the use of EDI, electronic mail, and common databases has helped to reduce cycle time. | — | — |

*Additional Areas for Improvement*

_____

_____

_____

**2.3  Analysis and Uses of Company-Level Data**    S    I

■ Varifilm performs correlation analyses which compare performance indicators to customer performance. This allows the company to improve its ability to predict how products perform during end-use applications.    —    —

■ Performance in each of five customer satisfaction requirements is tracked against actual customer satisfaction and is used as a determinant of customer actions.    —    —

■ Each functional organization performs its own data and operational analysis for the business plan development process.    —    —

■ The analysis and priority-setting process considers "revenue at risk" when prioritizing needs improvement.    —    —

■ A process exists for aggregating customer-related data with other key data to set priorities.    —    —

■ The company aggregates performance data and results with other key data to determine operations-related trends and improvement requirements.    —    —

■ A method is in place to evaluate and improve data analysis and capabilities.    —    —

*Additional Areas for Improvement*

_____

_____

_____

# FOR FURTHER READING

Forza, Cipriano, "The Impact of Information Systems on Quality Performance: An Empirical Study," *International Journal of Operations and Production,* Vol. 15 No. 6, 1995, pp. 69–83.

Foster, William F., "TQM for Information Systems Management: Quality Practices for Continuous Improvement," *Quality Progress,* May 1996, pp. 164–166.

Myers, Barry L., Leon A. Kappelman, and Victor R. Frybutok, "A Comprehensive Model for Assessing the Quality and Productivity of the Information Systems Function: Toward a Theory for Information Systems Assessment," *Information Resources Management Journal,* Winter 1997, pp. 6–25.

Pearson, J. Michael, Cynthia S. McCahon, and Ross T. Hightower, "Total Quality Management—Are Information Systems Managers Ready?" *Information & Management,* Nov. 1995, pp. 251–263.

Zeffane, Rachid, Bruce Cheek, and Paul Meredith, "Does User Involvement During Information Systems Development Improve Data Quality?" *Human Systems Management,* Vol. 17 No. 2, 1998, pp. 115–121.

# 4

# STRATEGIC PLANNING

*Strategic planning—It's back!*
*Reengineering? Cost cutting? Been there, done that.*
*Now, strategy is king as corporate America searches for real growth.*

Business Week
August 26, 1996

The 1999 Baldrige criteria for performance excellence* include strategic planning, which addresses strategic and business planning and deployment of plans. This includes effective development and deployment of business, customer, and operational performance requirements derived from strategy. The category stresses that customer-driven quality and operational performance excellence are key strategic business issues that need to be an integral part of overall company planning. Specifically:

- Customer-driven quality is a strategic view of quality. The focus is on the drivers of customer satisfaction, customer retention, new markets, and market share—key factors in competitiveness, profitability, and business success.

- Operational performance improvement contributes to short-term and long-term productivity growth and cost/price competitiveness. Building operational capability, including speed, responsiveness, and flexibility, represents an investment in strengthening competitive fitness.

---

* This description is abridged from the more detailed discussion and comments contained in the 1999 criteria.

Ford's slogan, "Quality Is Job 1," has caught on with increasing segments of the car-buying public. The company's North American Automobile Group is gaining market share among U.S. manufacturers and has a higher net income than General Motors with only two-thirds the amount of sales.[1] Things were not always this way. Between 1978 and 1982, market share slipped to 16.6 percent and sales fell by 49 percent, with a cumulative loss in excess of $3 billion. Ford was losing $1000 on every car it sold. The company sought advice from W. Edwards Deming. Reports John Betti, at that time a senior executive at Ford, "I distinctly remember some of Dr. Deming's first visits. We wanted to talk about quality, improvement tools, and which programs work. He wanted to talk to us about management, cultural change, and senior management's vision for the company. It took time for us to understand the profound cultural transformation he was proposing."[2] The company's subsequent turnaround is a classic example of the results that can be obtained from a strategic change based on quality. The major changes responsible for reversing the company's fortune were as follows:

- Emphasize quality and review new product planning and design.
- Keep investing in new products and processes.
- Make employee relations a source of competitive advantage.[3]

3M's approach to quality is so highly regarded that executives from leading U.S. companies travel to St. Paul to attend monthly briefings sponsored by 3M. In *Thriving on Chaos*,[4] Tom Peters described 3M as the only truly excellent company today. *Forbes* chose 3M as one of America's three most highly regarded companies. Its total quality management (TQM) implementation strategy includes:

- Defining 3M's quality vision
- Changing management perceptions through specialized training
- Empowering employees to focus on and satisfy customer expectations
- Sustaining the process through an ongoing culture change

One executive of the company explained it as follows: "How do you meet such a wide variety of expectations in a coherent way? I think you do it with a corporate philosophy on what constitutes a total quality process...a philosophy that you can apply across the company...to all your operations."[5]

These comments reflect the importance that successful companies place on the strategy issue. In the American Management Association's survey of over 3000 international managers, the key to competitive success was defined as the improvement of quality. There is little doubt that a strategy based on quality begins with strategic planning and is implemented through program and action planning.[6]

The public sector is equally immersed in strategic planning. Strategic management and TQM have become watchwords of public administration. Administrators have been asked to "improve government performance through strategic and quality management."[7]

## STRATEGY AND THE STRATEGIC PLANNING PROCESS

*Cheshire cat: "Where are you going Alice?"*

*Alice: "I don't really know."*

*Cheshire cat: "If you don't know where you're going there's no way you can get there."*

*Alice in Wonderland*

Companies that know where they want to go typically develop strategic plans to serve as road maps. Yet, amazingly, in many large and sophisticated companies, these are complex, incomprehensible plans that fill thick binders and are never shared with the people who are responsible for implementing them. (After all, this stuff is "sensitive, confidential information.")

What is strategy and what is the strategic planning process? The answers to these questions are important because evidence suggests that those companies with strategies based on TQM have achieved stunning successes.[8]

Most of these successful companies will attribute their progress to a quality-based strategy that was developed through a formal structured approach to planning. The Commercial Nuclear Fuel Division of Westinghouse, another Baldrige winner, has discovered that the total quality concept must be viewed as a pervasive operating strategy for managing a business every day:

> Total Quality begins with a *strategic decision*—a decision that can only be made by top management—and that decision, simply put, is the decision to compete as a world-class company. Total Quality concentrates on quality performance—in every facet of the business—and the primary strategy to achieve and maintain competitive advantage. It requires taking a systematic look at an organization—looking at how each part interrelates to the whole process. In addition, it demands continuous improvement as a "way of life."[9]

Major contributors to the development of the strategic concept and to the planning process include Professors Andrews, Christensen, and others in the Policy group at the Harvard Business School.[10] In its highly regarded text on the subject,[11] the group defines strategy in terms of a pattern of decisions that determine the company's purpose and objectives. Following that step, strategy produces policies and plans for achieving goals and objectives. Strategy also defines the business the company intends to be in, the kind of economic and human organization it intends to be, and the nature of the contribution it intends to make to its shareholders.

Michael Porter is perhaps the most highly regarded and certainly the most popular writer on the subject of strategy.[12] He describes the development of a competitive strategy as "a broad formula for how a business is going to compete, what its goals should be, and what policies will be needed to carry out those goals."

A truly focused plan can be communicated in about five or six pages and understood by everyone from hourly workers to the board of directors. Key questions the plan should answer include: What business are you in? How big is the market? How fast is it growing—and in what directions? What is your niche, the market segment you hope to carve out? What will be your differentiation, your competitive edge? What is the competitive situation? What are the key success factors in the market and how do you stack up vis-à-vis the competition?

## STRATEGIC QUALITY MANAGEMENT

This pattern of goals, policies, plans, and human organization is not something to be taken lightly. It is likely to be in place over a long period of time and therefore affects the organization in many different ways. The culture that guides members of the organization and other stakeholders, the position that it will occupy in an industry and market segments, and determining particular objectives and allocating resources to achieve them all follow from the decision processes determined by strategy. It is easy to see how pervasive a strategy based on quality can become. It provides the basis upon which plans are developed and communications achieved. A basic rule of strategic planning is that *structure follows strategy*. Although the process of formulation and implementation may require staff input, the ultimate decision is fundamental to the job of the chairman or CEO. It cannot be delegated.

The pervasive role that quality plays in strategic planning can best be understood by examining the components of a strategy:

- Mission
- Product/market scope
- Competitive edge (differentiation)
- Supporting policies

■   Objectives

■   Organizational culture

These components are developed through a process of strategy formulation, the outline of which is shown in Figure 4-1. Note that the process involves positioning yourself against forces in the environment in such a way that action plans can minimize your weaknesses and take advantage of your strengths relative to the competition. Quality is the means of differentiation for the satisfaction of customer needs. Research that includes over 300 U.S. companies indicates that firms with superior quality address quality offensively, as a distinct competitive advantage, while firms with inferior quality treat it defensively (e.g., eliminate defects, lower cost of product failure).[13]

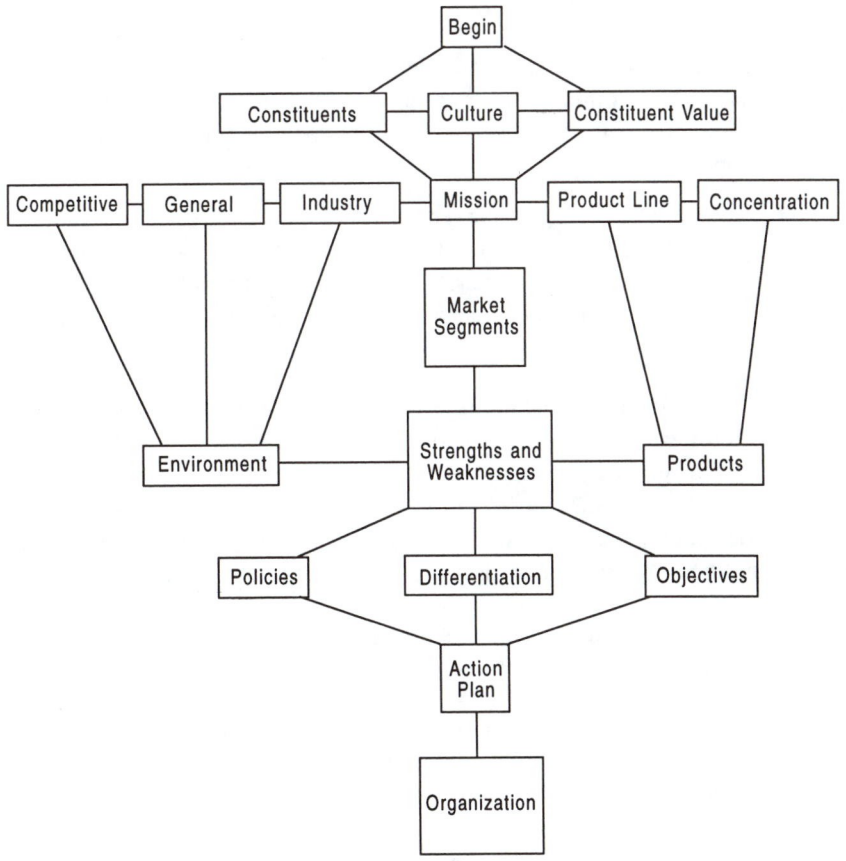

**Figure 4-1**   Strategic Planning

## Mission

To implement TQM, the CEO must create a stretch vision, make it plausible, and then convey to the whole company that this is not just another slogan but the new way of running the company. That's not easy. When Philip Caldwell announced that quality would be Job No. 1 at Ford, that was just talk and not much happened, but two years later, when he closed an assembly plant notorious for poor quality in Mahwah, New Jersey, that showed a commitment to match the vision, and things began to happen. Ford was one of the first companies to get its quality processes right. It is the painful decisions, rather than the words, that make people believe the mission and/or the vision.[14]

The mission is the primary overall purpose of an organization and its expressed reason for existence. The simplest statement of mission might be "to meet the needs/values of constituents."

■ The mission of NCR is stated simply: "Create Value for Our Stakeholders." Stakeholders are identified as employees, shareholders, suppliers, communities, and customers.[15] The mission can be operationalized by statements of how it will be implemented for each stakeholder.

■ At Goodyear, every employee carries a credit-card-sized mission statement: "Our mission is constant improvement in products and services to meet our customers' needs. This is the only means to business success for Goodyear and prosperity for its investors and employees."[16]

The mission statement includes the value that is being added and the direction in which the company intends to move. Because a mission can only be achieved by the people in an organization, it should have the commitment of the entire organization. Deming's first and what he considers his most important point of management obligation is to "create constancy of purpose for improvement of product and service with a plan to become competitive and stay in business."

This consistency must be achieved by a mission that can be operationalized and implemented. Consider the following examples:

■ All employees at Motorola consistently strive for a six sigma target. Robert Galvin, CEO of Motorola, set what seemed like an impossible goal of reducing defects to one-tenth of their existing levels in five years. When he saw that achieving that rate was not fast enough, he asked for another tenfold improvement and yet another. Then the company set its now famous six sigma goal of reducing the overall defect rate to 3.4 parts per million—an enormous improvement over the defect rate of 6 percent that prevailed a decade earlier.

■ 3M's mission focuses on innovation. To ensure consistency of purpose, the company established a requirement that 25 percent of each profit center's sales must come from products less than five years old.

## Environment

The major determinant of a mission is the environment in which the firm plans to operate: the general environment, the industry environment, and the competitive environment. Strategy is essentially the process of positioning oneself in that environment as trends and changes unfold. Thus, it is necessary to identify trends in the environment and how they affect the strategy of the firm. Figure 4-2 illustrates how a major U.S. manufacturer of computer equipment and software documented the major changes in that industry. The impact on strategy, as these issues relate to quality, is illustrated in Figure 4-3.

Both the internal and external change are inevitable, and each is difficult and threatening, which may explain why people prefer to maintain the status quo. Yet anticipating and accommodating change in a proactive mode are critical to success. Indeed, the only sustainable competitive advantage today is the ability to change, adapt, and evolve—to do it better than the competition. That is unlikely without a clearly defined and deployed strategy.

**Information Industry Shift**

**Technology**
- Predictable Cycles → · Fast Paced
- Custom Design → · Off-the-Shelf
- Proprietary → · Open Architecture

**Customers**
- DP Professionals → · End Users, Consumers
- Large Companies → · All Sizes
- Mostly U.S. → · International

**Offerings**
- Individual Products → · Complete Business Solutions
- Hardware → · Software/Services

**Competitors**
- Few, Large U.S. Fully Integrated → · Many, Diverse, Global Specialized
- Independent → · Alliances

**Figure 4-2**   Defining the Environment

**Re-Balancing for the '90s**

| Technology-Driven | | Market-Driven |
|---|---|---|
| The Product | Focus | The Customer |
| Creating Demand | Approach | Providing Solutions |
| Price and Product Function | Marketing Strategy | Customer's Hearts and Minds |
| Product Volumes Revenue Profit | Measure of Performance | Customer Satisfaction Market Share Financial Returns |

**Figure 4-3**   Impact of Changes in the Environment on Strategy

One example of change and complexity is the globalization of the world economy and the chaotic state of the world's major financial markets following the meltdown of Asian economies and the depreciation of the Japanese yen in 1998. Many experts believe that recognizing one's core competency is the key to survival and growth in an environment of change and complexity.[17]

## Product/Market Scope

This answers two questions: What am I selling and to whom am I selling it? The answers are more complex than they appear. What is Domino's Pizza selling: dough and tomato sauce or reliable delivery? What is a physician selling: surgery and diagnosis or patient involvement? Wal-Mart and Bloomingdale's are both in the retail business, but are their products simply what is on the shelves and racks in their stores? A company does not simply sell shoes or soap or banking services. It sells value to a particular segment of the market. The answers to these questions should be clear, as well as the role of quality in customer value.

What is value? It is, of course, what the customer—not the company—says it is. Timex sells watches, but does Rolex sell jewelry and prestige? Canada Dry sells sparkling water, but does Perrier sell snob appeal? Thom-McCann sells loafers, but what does Gucci sell? This does not mean that Timex, Canada Dry, and Thom-McCann do not sell on the basis of quality. Indeed, they do.

However, quality is defined differently for a different segment of the market. Each company must define its market segment and customer value in that segment. Ford's product mix includes the Lincoln Town Car and the Escort, but each is targeted at a different market segment, and quality (value) is different for each segment.

Every purchase decision is a function of price and quality. Price is generally known, but quality is in the mind of the individual customer. General Electric is aware of this and has broadened its perspective from "product quality" to "total customer satisfaction." The "product" is now defined by the customer.[18] It only remains to define customer satisfaction, perception, or expectation.

To repeat, in today's heightened competitive environment, a product or service is not simply sold to anyone who will buy it. To be effective, value must be sold to a particular market or customer segment. Strategic planning involves the determination of these strategy components, and quality plays a major role in this process.

## Differentiation

Differentiation, frequently called the competitive edge, answers the question: Why should I buy from you? Michael Porter, in his landmark book *Competitive Strategy,* identified two generic competitive strategies: (1) overall cost leadership and (2) differentiation.[19] Cost leadership in turn can be broad in market scope (e.g., Ivory Soap, Emerson Electric, Black & Decker) or market segment focused (e.g., La Quinta Motels, Porter Paint). The second strategy involves differentiating the product or service by creating something that is perceived by the buyer as unique. Differentiation can also be broad in scope (American Airlines in on-time service, Caterpillar for spare parts support) or focused (e.g., Godiva chocolates, Mercedes automobiles). Thus, there are four generic strategies, but each depends on something different—something unique or distinguishing. Even an effective cost leadership strategy must start with a good product.

Selecting a strategy and recognizing quality as the competitive dimension is important for strategic purposes. Product and service quality has become widely recognized as a major force in the competitive marketplace and in international trade.[20]

Research indicates that eight out of ten customers consider quality to be equal to or more important than price in their purchase decisions.[21] This is a doubling of buyer emphasis in ten years, and the trend is expected to continue. The message here is that whether a cost leadership or differentiation strategy is chosen, quality must be a competitive consideration in either case.

Differentiation can command a premium price or allow increased sales at a given price. Moreover, differentiation is one of two types of competitive advantage, the other being price. Price, however, should not be the sole basis of differentiation unless the product is perceived to be a commodity. Even if the product is a commodity or near commodity, it can still be differentiated by such service characteristics as availability or cycle time.

The several sources of differentiation are not well understood. Many managers perceive their uniqueness in terms of the physical product or in their marketing practices rather than in terms of value to the customer. They may waste money because their uniqueness does not provide real value to the buyer. Why spend money on extra tellers or checkout lines to reduce waiting time to one minute if the customers are willing to wait two minutes? On the other hand, buyers frequently have difficulty estimating value and how a particular firm can provide it. This incomplete knowledge can become an opportunity if the firm can adopt a new form of differentiation and educate the buyers to value it.

Many (if not most) companies try to compete based on price alone. This is characteristic of commodities such as corn and potatoes as well as the ultimate commodity—money. How are organizations in the commodity business (e.g., banks) going to differentiate? Most people probably do their banking at the bank located closest to their job or on their way to work. There is little to differentiate one bank from another. Left with no distinctive competence, banks promote universal "service" or "quality" as a reason to buy their product or service. When pressed to define these terms, few can do so, particularly staff members who are the front-line contact with customers.

If you differentiate on the basis of price alone, it is an admission that you are in the commodity business. Why do so many people buy Sony products or Coca-Cola? How can Disney stand alone in its ability to leverage the Disney name? The answer lies in the brand advantage, but an advantage derived over time by the customers' perception of quality.

Some companies attempt to build brand recognition and image through advertising. That's a good idea—except when the advertising is better than the product. The potential for erosion of the brand is greatest in the case of service industries, where the employees are the brand. When consumers come in contact with the people who work in an organization and the experience is at odds with what the brand's communications have led them to expect, irreparable damage may be done to consumer confidence in the product or service. And who can blame the employees if they have been kept in the dark about company differentiation intentions or their role in it.

McDonald's has a simple philosophy: "Marketing is everything and everything is marketing." The company knows that every employee—from cleaner to cashier to vice-president—is capable of molding consumer perceptions of the McDonald's brand name and as such is part of the company's total marketing effort. The "McDonald's way" is taught at the company's Hamburger University.

## DEFINITION OF QUALITY

*Quality is fitness for use.*

J. M. Juran

*Quality is conformance to requirements.*

Philip Crosby

*Quality means best for certain customer conditions. These conditions are (a) the actual use and (b) the selling price of the product.*

Armand V. Feigenbaum

*Quality is to give the customers what they want.*

Sam Walton

The concept and vocabulary of quality are elusive. Different people interpret quality differently. Few can define quality in measurable terms that can be operationalized. When asked what differentiates their product or service, the banker will answer "service," the health care worker will answer "quality health care," the hotel or restaurant employee will answer "customer satisfaction," and the manufacturer will simply answer "quality product." When pressed to provide a specific definition and measurement, few can do so.[22] There is an old maxim in management which says, "If you can't measure it, you can't manage it," and so it is with quality. If the strategic management system and the competitive advantage are to be based on quality, every member of the organization should be clear about its concept, definition, and measurement as it applies to his or her job. As will be discussed, it may be entirely appropriate for quality to be defined or perceived differently in the same company depending on the particular phase of the product life cycle.

Harvard Professor David Garvin, in his book *Managing Quality,*[23] summarized five principal approaches to defining quality: transcendent, product based, user based, manufacturing based, and value based.

People from around the world travel to view the Mona Lisa or Michaelangelo's David, and most would agree that these works of art represent quality. But can they define it? Those who hold the *transcendental* view would say, "I can't define it, but I know it when I see it." Advertisers are fond of promoting products in these terms. "Where shopping is a pleasure" (supermarket), "We love to fly and it shows" (airline), "The great American beauty...It's elegant" (automobile), and "It means beautiful eyes" (cosmetics) are examples. Television and print media are awash with such undefinable claims, and therein lies the problem: quality is difficult to define or to operationalize. It thus becomes elusive when using the approach as a basis for competitive advantage. Moreover, the functions of design, production, and service may find it difficult to use the definition as a basis for quality management.

**Product-based** definitions are different. Quality is viewed as a quantifiable or measurable characteristic or attribute. For example, durability or reliability can be measured (e.g., mean time between failure, fit and finish), and the engineer can design to that benchmark. Quality is determined objectively. Although this approach has many benefits, it has limitations as well. Where quality is based on individual taste or preference, the benchmark for measurement may be misleading.

**User-based** definitions are based on the idea that quality is an individual matter, and products that best satisfy their preferences (i.e., perceived quality) are those with the highest quality. This is a rational approach but leads to two problems. First, consumer preferences vary widely, and it is difficult to aggregate these preferences into products with wide appeal. This leads to the choice between a niche strategy (see later) or a market aggregation approach which tries to identify those product attributes that meet the needs of the largest number of consumers.

Another problem concerns the answer to the question: Are quality and customer satisfaction the same? The answer is probably not. One may admit that a Lincoln Continental has many quality attributes, but satisfaction may be better achieved with an Escort. One has only to recall the box office success of recent motion pictures that suffer from poor quality but are evidently preferred by the majority of moviegoers. *Blair witch project.*

**Manufacturing-based** definitions are concerned primarily with engineering and manufacturing practices and use the universal definition of "conformance to requirements." Requirements, or specifications, are established by design, and any deviation implies a reduction in quality. The concept applies to services as well as products. Excellence in quality is not necessarily in the eye of the beholder but rather in the standards set by the organization. Thus, both Cadillac and Cavalier possess quality, as do Zayre and Bloomingdale's, as long as the product or service "conforms to requirements."

This approach has a serious weakness. The consumer's perception of quality is equated with conformance and hence is internally focused. Emphasis on reliability in design and manufacturing tends to address cost reduction as the objective, and cost reduction is perceived in a limited way—invest in design and manufacturing improvement until these incremental costs equal the costs of non-quality such as rework and scrap. This approach violates Crosby's concept of "quality is free" and is examined further in Chapter 11.

**Value-based** quality is defined in terms of costs and prices as well as a number of other attributes.[24] Thus, the consumer's purchase decision is based on quality (however it is defined) at an acceptable price. This approach is reflected in the popular *Consumer Reports* magazine, which ranks products and services based on two criteria: quality and value. The highest quality product is not usually the best value. That designation is assigned to the "best-buy" product or service.

## Which Approach(es)?

Which definition or concept of quality should be adopted? If each function or department in the company is allowed to pursue its own concept, potential conflicts may occur:

| Function | Quality concerns |
| --- | --- |
| Marketing | Performance, features, service, focus on customer concerns<br>User-based concerns that raise costs |
| Engineering | Specifications<br>Product-based concerns |
| Manufacturing | Conformance to specifications<br>Cost reduction |

Adopting a single approach could lead to cost increases as well as customer dissatisfaction. Each function has a role to play, but it cannot be played in isolation. A blend is needed to coordinate meeting each of the concerns listed.

## Market Segmentation (Niche) Quality

Quality means different things to different people. In terms of strategic quality management, this means that the firm must define that segment of the industry, that generic strategy, and that particular customer group which it intends to pursue. This can be called a segmented quality strategy. The Big Three automobile manufacturers have wide product lines, each of which is marketed to a different part of the market and each with differing quality attributes.

Recent efforts to codify the concepts of quality and provide baselines for measurement have yielded the characteristics listed in Table 4-1. None of these dimensions stands alone. Differentiation may depend on one or more or a combination, but the point is that when differentiating based on quality, quality must be defined in terms that meet customer expectations, even if this is only what the customer perceives as quality.

A survey of purchasers of consumer products by the American Society for Quality Control summarized the factors influencing decisions to purchase (on a scale of one to ten) (Table 4-2).

**Table 4-1**    Measurement of Quality

| Category | Example |
|---|---|
| Performance | On-time departure of aircraft<br>Acceleration speed of automobile |
| Features | Remote control for stereo<br>Double coupons at the supermarket |
| Reliability | Absence of repair during warranty<br>Thirty-minute pizza delivery |
| Conformance | Supplier conforms to specifications<br>Cost of performance failures |
| Durability | Maytag's ten-year transmission warranty<br>Mean time between failures |
| Serviceability | Consumer "hot line" for repair information<br>Time to answer the telephone for reservation or complaint |
| Aesthetics | Restaurant ambiance<br>Perfume fragrance |
| Perceived quality | Japanese vs. American automobiles<br>Doctor A is better than Doctor B |

## Objectives

Management statesman Peter Drucker has said, "A company has but one objective: to create a customer." Following this statement, he proceeded to popularize the concept of management by objectives and identified eight key areas for which objectives must be set:[25] (1) marketing, (2) innovation, (3) human organization, (4) financial resources, (5) physical resources, (6) productivity, (7) social responsibility, and (8) profit requirements. These areas have been widely adopted by industry.

Within these eight broad areas, a company can set more specific objectives to identify the ends it hopes to achieve by implementing a strategy. Marketing becomes market share, innovation becomes new products, financial resources becomes capital structure, productivity becomes output per employee, profitability becomes return on investment or earnings per share, and so on.

Here, the question of quality becomes blurred. Is it a mission or an objective? It hardly matters if it is woven into the fabric of company strategy. If quality is chosen as central to a mission, other objectives begin to fall into place. For example, cycle time reduction, cost reduction, competitive standing, and return to shareholders can be related to the central mission.

**Table 4-2**  Factors in
Decisions to Purchase

| Factor | Mean |
| --- | --- |
| Performance | 9.37 |
| Lasts a long time | 9.03 |
| Easy to repair | 8.80 |
| Service | 8.62 |
| Warranty | 8.13 |
| Price | 8.11 |
| Ease of use | 8.09 |
| Appearance | 7.54 |
| Brand name | 6.09 |

■ Digital Equipment Corporation launched a TQM program in order to tie together various efforts scattered throughout the company. The goal is to have a consistent company vision and language. Included is a six sigma program motivated by a desire to improve competitive position.[26]

Many quality improvement programs were started in the 1980s and 1990s in reaction to the increasing importance of quality and the need to compete for market share. Many companies failed, often because they had no action plan for implementing a strategy that was based on objectives, a prerequisite for follow-on operational planning.[27]

## Supporting Policies

Policies are guidelines for action and decision making that facilitate the attainment of objectives. Taken together, a company's policies delineate its strategy fairly well. Tell me your policies and I can tell you your strategy.

The role of policies as a critical element of strategy is displayed in Figure 4-4, which can be called the *policy wheel*. In the center are the mission (the purpose of the organization), the differentiation (how to compete in the market), and the key objectives of the business. The spokes of the wheel represent the functions of the business. Each function requires supporting policies (functional strategies) to achieve the *hub*. If the firm's strategy calls for competing on quality, then this becomes the impetus for policy determination. Each functional

**Figure 4-4**   Policy Wheel

policy supports this central strategy and the objectives that are determined during the planning process.

A firm's policy choices are essential as drivers of differentiation. They determine what activities to perform and how to perform them. Grey Poupon's advertising policy for its premium mustard sets the product apart. Bic Pen's manufacturing policy of low-cost automation supports its low price. Avon's door-to-door distribution policy sets it apart. McDonald's policy of strict franchisee training and control allows it to retain its quality image. An airline's policy of "answering the phone on the third ring" reinforces a competitive edge of service.

### Testing for Consistency of Policies

Assuming that the company has decided to make quality the central focus of its strategy, objectives are then set for profitability, growth, market share, innovation, productivity, etc. The test for consistency of supporting policies for a hypothetical firm is provided in Table 4-3. Of course, each policy is related to the hub and radiates from it. Like a wheel, the spokes must be connected.

## CONTROL

The propensity of the American manager to focus on short-term financial goals is well known. In its simplest and most prevalent form, the control system

**Table 4-3**  Consistency of Supporting Policies

| Function | Illustration of policy |
|---|---|
| Target market | Map the industry and seek out those segments where we have the advantage |
| Product line | Product line breadth is confined to those products where our value chain is appropriate for focus segment |
| Marketing | Market research to be directed toward defining customer expectations |
| Sales | Sales force hired and trained to promote our competitive edge |
| Distribution | Select distributors that complement our quality edge |
| Manufacturing | Invest in automation for improvement of quality and productivity |
| Supplier | Select suppliers that have applied for Baldrige Award<br>Make life contracts |
| Human resources | Require skill and experience level for new hires<br>Partnership relations with union |
| Research and development | Percentage of budget devoted to quality improvement<br>Products designed for ease of repair |
| Finance | Service procedures in billing activity<br>Financial arrangements with suppliers |

consists of setting financial standards (the budget), getting historical feedback on performance (the variance report), and trying to meet targets after deviations have occurred.

Much has been written about the shortcomings of this approach. The major problem is the lack of focus on productivity (absolute, not financial measures), quality, and other strategic issues.

A system to control quality objectives, as distinct from quality on the shop floor, requires measures and standards designed for that purpose. Indeed, Juran suggests that the traditional control process may be put on hold while increasing the emphasis on quality planning and improvement.[28] Thus, planning and control of quality come together in an integrated system. The focus is on quality improvement set out in the planning process. The difference between traditional dollar accounting budgeting and the control of quality objectives is the participation of those who set standards and targets. Each function, department, or individual sets targets and provides real-time feedback as operations unfold.

## SERVICE QUALITY

The differences between service and product quality were discussed in Chapter 1. This topic will be examined further in Chapter 7 (Customer and Market Focus). It is both more difficult and yet simpler to plan and control service quality than it is to plan and control product quality. It is more difficult because measurement is elusive and production is frequently one on one. Like product quality, service quality should live up to expectation, but this can be a pitfall if too much service is promised.

Service quality may be more easily planned, provided objectives are defined and people committed. In any case, the payoff can be years away, and no service can overcome other weaknesses in a business.[29] The system for quality service also requires new approaches, such as restructuring incentives. In any case, a good beginning approach can be based on the Baldrige Award criteria, which are the same for both product and service. Process control in service industries is discussed further in Chapter 6.

## SUMMARY

Quality has taken center stage as the main issue in both national and corporate competitive strategies. Those organizations that adopt quality as a differentiation and a way of organizational life will, over the longer term, pull ahead of competition. Achieving this goal is not easy. It is more than just issuing pronouncements and engaging in company promotion.

When an organization chooses to make quality a major competitive edge, it becomes the central issue in strategic planning—from mission to supporting policies. An essential idea is that the product is customer value rather than a physical product or service. Another concept that is basic to the process is the need to develop an organizational culture based on quality. Finally, no strategy or plan can be effective unless it is carefully implemented.

## QUESTIONS FOR DISCUSSION

**4-1** Assume that an airline, a hotel, and a hospital have chosen quality for differentiation. Identify two or more measures of quality for a firm in each of these industries.

**4-2** Illustrate a definition of:

■ *Transcendental* quality

- Product-based quality
- User-based quality
- Value-based quality

**4-3** Choose an industry and a product or service within that industry and show how quality may differ for different segments or customer groups within that industry.

**4-4** Is the objective of cost reduction in conflict with quality improvement? If so, illustrate how.

**4-5** How can quality be reflected in the following:
- Distribution policy
- Human resources
- Sales
- Suppliers

**4-6** Illustrate how trends in an industry can change a company's strategy.

## ENDNOTES

1. U.S. General Accounting Office, Quality Management: Scoping Study, Washington, D.C.: U.S. General Accounting Office, Dec. 1990, p. 67.
2. U.S. General Accounting Office, Quality Management: Scoping Study, Washington, D.C.: U.S. General Accounting Office, Dec. 1990, p. 15.
3. The details of Ford's transformation are contained in HBS Case 390-083, available from HBR Publications, Harvard Business School, Boston, MA 02163. See also Richard T. Pascale, *Managing on the Edge,* New York: Simon & Schuster, 1990.
4. Tom Peters, *Thriving on Chaos: Handbook for a Management Revolution,* New York: Knopf, 1987.
5. Remarks of A. F. Jacobson at the Conference Board Quality Conference in Dallas, April 2, 1990.
6. Eric Rolf Greenberg, "Customer Service: The Key to Competitiveness," *Management Review,* Dec. 1990, pp. 29–31.
7. Theodore Poister and Gregory Streib, "Strategic Management in the Public Sector," *Public Productivity and Management Review,* March 1999, pp. 308–325.
8. J. M. Juran, "Made in USA—A Quality Resurgence," *Journal for Quality and Participation,* March 1991, pp. 6–8.
9. "Performance Leadership through Total Quality," a presentation made to the Conference Board Quality Conference, April 2, 1990. Two other Westinghouse divisions were runners-up for the Baldrige Award in 1989 and 1990.
10. Kenneth R. Andrews, *The Concept of Corporate Strategy,* New York: Dow Jones–Irwin, 1971.

11. Joseph L. Bower, Christopher A. Bartlett, C. Roland Christensen, Andrall E. Pearson, and Kenneth R. Andrews, *Business Policy: Text and Cases,* 7th ed., Homewood, Ill.: Irwin, 1991, p. 9.

12. Michael Porter, *Competitive Strategy: Techniques for Analyzing Industries and Competitors,* New York: The Free Press, 1980. See also his *Competitive Advantage: Creating and Sustaining Superior Performance,* New York: The Free Press, 1985, and *The Competitive Advantage of Nations,* New York: The Free Press, 1990.

13. Joel Ross and David Georgoff, "A Survey of Quality Issues in Manufacturing: The State of the Industry," *Industrial Management,* Jan./Feb. 1991.

14. Jeremy M. Main, "Fixing the CEO's Quality Vision," *Executive Excellence,* July 1995, p. 8.

15. Company brochure entitled "NCR Mission."

16. U.S. General Accounting Office, Quality Management: Scoping Study, Washington, D.C.: U.S. General Accounting Office, Dec. 1990, p. 23. T. Boone Pickens, the quintessential LBO raider, was not very charitable to Goodyear. In a speech to the Strategic Planning Institute in Boston on October 23, 1989, he used Chairman Robert Mercer as an example of corporate America in the early 1980s: "bloated, uncompetitive, bureaucratic and barely accountable to anyone...what I call the BUBBA syndrome."

17. Louisa Wah, "Making Sense of Global Chaos," *Management Review,* Sept. 1998, p. 31.

18. Elyse Allan, "Measuring Quality Costs: A Shifting Perspective," a presentation made to the Conference Board Quality Conference, April 2, 1990. *Global Perspectives on Total Quality,* Report Number 958, New York: The Conference Board, 1990, p. 35.

19. Michael Porter, *Competitive Strategy: Techniques for Analyzing Industries and Competitors,* New York: The Free Press, 1980, pp. 35–37.

20. J. M. Juran, "Strategies for World-Class Quality," *Quality Progress,* March 1991, pp. 81–85.

21. Armand V. Feigenbaum, "How to Implement Total Quality," *Executive Excellence,* Nov. 1989, pp. 15–16.

22. Y. K. Shetty and Joel Ross, "Quality and Its Management in Service Businesses," *Industrial Management,* Nov./Dec. 1985, pp. 7–12; Joel Ross and Y. K. Shetty, "Making Quality a Fundamental Part of Strategy," *Long Range Planning (UK),* Feb. 1985, pp. 53–58.

23. David A. Garvin, *Managing Quality,* New York: The Free Press, 1988, pp. 40–46.

24. In a survey of consumers' purchasing decisions conducted by the Gallup Organization, consumers were asked to rank (on a scale of one to ten) the importance of selected factors in the decision to purchase; 42 percent ranked price as ten. Other factors ranked as ten were performance (72 percent), lasts a long time (58 percent), easily repaired (52 percent), service (50 percent), warranty (48 percent), ease of use (37 percent), appearance (28 percent), and brand name (15 percent). See *'88 Gallup Survey of Consumers' Perceptions Concerning the Quality of American Products and Services,* Milwaukee: American Society for Quality Control, 1988, p. 9.

25. Peter F. Drucker, *Management: Tasks, Responsibilities, Practices,* New York: Harper & Row, 1973, p. 100.

26. Rick Whiting, "Digital Strives for a Consistent Vision of Quality," *Electronic Business,* Nov. 26, 1990, pp. 55–56.

27. A. Blanton Godfrey, "Strategic Quality Management," *Quality,* March 1990, pp. 17–22.

28. J. M. Juran, "Universal Approach to Managing for Quality," *Executive Excellence,* May 1989, pp. 15–17. See also Bradley Gale and Donald J. Swmre, "Business Strategies that Create Wealth," *Planning Review,* March/April 1988, pp. 6–13. Traditional strategic planning based on financial measures is being called into question because they do not look beyond more important measures such as quality.

29. David Eva, "The Myth of Customer Service," *Canadian Business,* March 1991, pp. 34–39.

## STRATEGY DEPLOYMENT
## AT RAYTHEON

Raytheon TI Systems (RTIS) (formerly Texas Instruments Systems Division) defines the three main areas of its total quality strategy as customer focus, continuous improvement, and people involvement. Competitive advantage is built around the following subsystems:

- Six sigma
- Cycle time
- Teaming with suppliers
- Stretch goals
- Performance metrics
- Catchball

The last of these is catchball, which is part of the annual planning cycle. It is a policy deployment process that aligns and mobilizes work groups, teams, and individuals toward a common set of strategic goals. RTIS leaders use business and benchmarking results to establish recommended goals. The goals are passed from the divisions to the departments and then to the individual work teams. Then, teams either accept the goals and pass them back up the chain or they modify the goals with a list of barriers to overcome before the goals can be achieved. Catchball focuses everyone on the goals that are important to the customers.

# AMEX LOOKS BEYOND
# SATISFACTION, SEES GROWTH

## Jan P. Murphy

Don't tell the researchers at American Express that customer satisfaction is important to business success—they know it is. But there's another factor the company rates as even more important.

"It's behavior that counts," said Doug Filak, senior director, marketing research for American Express Travel Related Services, the New York–based retail card-services division. Filak spoke recently at the ninth annual Customer Satisfaction & Quality Measurement Conference, sponsored by the AMA and the American Society for Quality Control.

"I don't know about your business, but in ours, what really matters is how we improve the bottom line," he said. "You have to look beyond satisfaction to what is happening in your business overall. A focus on improving customer satisfaction is critical, but by focusing on satisfaction, we learned more about our products' other dimensions."

Satisfaction research led the company to a better understanding of what customers wanted from the Amex cards in their pockets and purses. And that understanding was the added benefit in a new quality strategy that helped American Express develop new products and direct the positioning and promotion of its flagship charge card.

Before 1992, Filak said, American Express had no uniform method for customer satisfaction and quality measurement. Although the company had copious amounts of data on customers' card ownership and use—from who they were to what they bought—measurement programs "were ad hoc at best," Filak said. Because methodologies differed from division to division, conflicting findings would appear. There was no way to share information. And satisfaction studies often focused on how Amex could improve internal processes, rather than looking to customers for information on their needs.

Reprinted with permission from *Marketing News,* published by the American Marketing Association, Vol. 31 No. 10, May 12, 1997, pp. 6, 22.

To change that, the company developed a total quality management program, American Express Quality Leadership (AEQL). Based on criteria set by the Malcolm Baldrige quality award, AEQL recognized that Amex had three constituencies that it must satisfy: employees, customers, and shareholders.

Satisfying shareholders depended on demonstrable improvements in business performance, profit and share value, and these depended on general excellence. American Express started improving from within. "Satisfied employees work harder, and produce better business results," Filak said. "We've seen strong links between employee satisfaction and overall satisfaction." The company then began to study its relationships with two more traditional customer segments, American Express cardholders and service establishments. The goal? To define "moments of truth," or MOTs: crucial service points that made customers choose Amex over another card, or another card over Amex.

"We didn't really care about MasterCard or Visa as organizations," Filak said. "What we cared about was why you pull out that other card sometimes, and why you use American Express at other times. What we were really talking about was customer behavior."

Using primary customer research and a transaction-based survey sampling system, the company identified a number of quality attributes, out of which the MOTs grew. For instance, the accuracy, timeliness, and readability of a monthly statement made up a comprehensive "billing" MOT.

The nine final MOTs (customer service, billing, benefits, acceptance, advertising, fees, flexibility, rewards, and value) were incorporated into a relationship model as drivers of overall satisfaction for American Express cards. Overall satisfaction, in turn, was expected to be the force behind market behaviors such as card retention, share of spending, and actual spending.

More than a few attributes, however, proved to be strong enough factors in customer use that they affected retention and spending directly. American Express discovered that its original card's fees were a sticking point among both cardmembers and service establishments, discouraging its use despite a reputation for "great service, great billing, great everything else," Filak said.

The company also asked customers to rate competing cards on service MOTs, and used that information to develop a new product. The company had not yet offered a rewards card like Visa's American Airlines AAdvantage and United MileagePlus cards. Today it has two, including the popular Delta SkyMiles Optima, an indirect result of its comparative satisfaction research.

"It led us to spend a lot more time working on a rewards-based product," Filak said. "Some of the major airline rewards cards were really not up to the service level that our customers expect, so their programs' satisfaction was actually very low. But card use was still high because of the rewards. It was an important piece of information for us in the development of our strategy."

The research helped identify the most important card attributes for new customer segments, permitting the company to differentiate and target individual card products. "Original card customers pay the annual fee and in return expect status," Filak said. "For the Optima card, acceptance is more important, and we positioned it for retail use."

Amex continues to use AEQL research to back up strategic decisions. Using a one-point change chart, the company predicts the impact of any shift in customer satisfaction in a given quality attribute. For example, if certain cardmembers' satisfaction in customer service improves 1%, spending should go up approximately 8.5%.

"We've really been able to prove the linkage between improving customer satisfaction and business results," Filak said. "We've also shown that there are many components of a business that drive satisfaction of a product. But we couldn't look at satisfaction alone; we had to extend it to behavior."

And consumer behavior has improved, he said. "We had a small share increase for the first time in 1996, and in our industry, one point is worth $1 billion in revenues. To American Express, these are big stakes."

## Questions for Discussion

1   What industry trend(s) caused Amex to enter the market with the Optima card?

2   How does the Amex card's market niche (segment) differ from Visa, MasterCard, etc.? Are the "moments of truth" different?

3   How did "moments of truth" increase satisfaction for stakeholders: (a) customers, (b) employees, and (c) shareholders?

4   What competitive advantage, if any, does Amex have over Visa and MasterCard?

5   What is the linkage between customer satisfaction and (a) customer behavior and (b) financial results?

*The author addresses two dimensions of strategy. The first is the basic "givens" in support of total quality management principles. These are common to all firms that expect to compete successfully in the future. In addition, ten driving forces are identified and matched with the same number of types of firms depending on which strategic area drives the business.*

## QUALITY AND THE ROLE OF STRATEGY

### Roger Handley

Quality and process improvement are recognized major strategic issues for those who want to compete successfully through the 1990s and on into the next millennium. All businesses have "givens" by which they must excel—the membership fees to the elite club of success stories of the future. Decision Processes International's (DPI) clients often identify their own specific givens, but there are generic ones too, and to survive all companies must recognize them. They must

- Have a continuing process of quality improvement
- Have a programme of low-cost manufacturing
- Continually improve customer service
- Be sensitive to customer requirements
- Make a profit

DPI has been involved in strategy since the mid-1970s, when an explosion of literature started us browsing through a variety of material to find out what

Reprinted with permission from *Managing Service Quality,* Vol. 5 No. 5, 1995, pp. 53–56.
Copyright MCB University.

strategy meant. But we became more confused than enlightened because authors used the word differently. Some said that strategy was the goal or objective, and that tactics were the means. Others maintained that the objective was the goal and that the strategy was the means. Most of the literature was written by professors in business schools who had not even been out to talk to companies. Their formulas were developed by trying to recreate the magic recipe that a particular company had followed to achieve success. However, at DPI, we started interviewing CEOs in a variety of different industries and in different sized companies, eventually participating in the sessions these CEOs were having with their key people.

Our first observation was that the people who run companies have a vision of how their firms will be in the future. They employ and deploy the assets and resources of their organization in pursuit of that vision. Strategic thinking then translates the vision into a profile of what they want the organization to become. This profile is the target for all corporate decisions and plans.

Another way to look at this concept is to separate the activities of the executive team into "what" and "how." Although both types of thinking take place in any organization, they do so with different levels of proficiency. Some corporations, however, are proficient at both. Management has a clearly articulated strategy which is well communicated and understood, and the day-to-day operations are managed well; they are proficient at both "what" and "how." Other firms are very good at managing business operations, but do not always know where the business is heading. They cannot describe what the business will look like in the future. Still other firms know exactly what they are trying to become, but their difficulty lies in making it happen. Finally, there is the worst of both worlds—firms which do not know what they are trying to become or how to get there.

The profile or look of an organization is determined by the nature of its products, customers, market segments and geographic markets. If management wants to guide the direction of the organization and influence its eventual profile, it must determine, in advance, which products, customers, market segments and geographic markets it will pursue as well as those that it will not pursue. Management directs the organization. First, it allocates resources, giving more resources to the strategic areas it wishes to emphasize. Second, it identifies which opportunities the organization should be pursuing. The profile or vision becomes the ultimate test-bed for all decisions made in the organization.

How do we determine the line of demarcation between the items that will receive more emphasis and those that will receive less emphasis in the future? The answer to this gives rise to the most important concept of strategic thinking. The true test to determine whether an organization has a strategy is to watch management when it is faced with the decision of whether to pursue an opportunity. Management must decide whether there is a fit between the products, customers, and markets that the opportunity brings and one key component of the business. In other words, one part of the business seems to be strategically more important. If management finds a good fit, it will pursue that opportunity. If it does not find a good fit, it will not.

In each company, then, there seems to be something that is at the root of the firm's existence, pushing, propelling or driving it forward. One component of the business seems to dominate management thinking. Exploring this concept further, we find that there are basically ten components. For management to understand clearly which strategic area drives the business and serves as its heartbeat is fundamental to its ability to make intelligent choices about future products, customers, market segments and geographic markets. Failure to understand this will lead to strategic ineffectiveness and dissatisfied customers.

These ten components are:

1. A product/service-driven company is locked into a product concept whose function and profile does not change must over time. Future products are adaptations, modifications or extensions of the current product. The future product offerings are derivatives of the existing product, and the existing product is a "generic" derivative of the original product. The automobile industry is a good example.

2. The market-driven company has deliberately anchored its business to a describable category of market, the only one it serves. The firm's strategy is to scrutinize the market continuously to identify related needs. Once these needs are found, then appropriate products, which may otherwise be unrelated to each other, are made. NHS Hospital Supplies responds to a variety of needs, and its product scope ranges from bedpans to sutures and from gauze pads to electronic imaging systems. While these products are unrelated to each other, they are all used in a hospital.

3. The user/customer-driven company's strategy is similar to a market-category-driven firm except that this company has anchored its business to a discrete class of end-user. For example, Johnson & Johnson's strategy of making products for "doctors, nurses patients and mothers," or SAGA's insurance and holiday products for the over 55s.

4. A production capacity/capability-driven company strategy is usually pursued by a company which has a substantial investment in its production facility, and the thrust is to keep that facility operating at maximum capacity. The drive is to look for opportunities that can utilize whatever the production capacity can handle. Paper companies, because of the enormous capital tied up in their mills, are examples of organizations which usually pursue a capacity-driven strategy. These companies will get into newsprint,

fine paper, toilet tissue, disposable nappies, paper towels, etc., to optimize production capacity.

5. A technology/know-how-driven company invents or acquires hard or soft technology or know-how. It then looks for applications. The company becomes involved in a broad array of products, all of which stem from the particular technology, and it will serve a broad array of customers and market segments. Du Pont and 3M are good examples.

6. A sales/marketing-driven company has a unique way of attracting orders from its customers. Such a company will only offer products and pursue customers that can be brought together through that selling method. Consider door-to-door companies, party plan companies such as Amway, Tupperware and Avon Cosmetics and catalogue companies.

7. The distribution-driven company pursues an opposite strategy from that of the sales/marketing-driven firm. This company has a unique distribution method to get products to the customer. All products or services offered must use that distribution method or else they will not be offered. Telephone operating companies, with their vast networks, are good examples. Department stores are another. They push through any product to any customer that they can match with a merchandising policy.

8. Natural resource-driven company. When pursuit of, or access to, natural resources becomes the strategic drive for an organization, such a company can be perceived as pursuing a resource-driven strategy, i.e., Shell, BP, Esso, and RTZ.

9. A size/growth-driven company has only one criterion: an appetite for size and growth, i.e., conglomerates such as Hanson.

10. Return/profit-driven companies also only have one criterion, i.e., ITT, under Geneen.

Which driving force is currently acting as the heartbeat of your business? Which do you think each of your key subordinates would say drives your company? Our experience shows that there will be as many responses to these questions as there are people. Different people have different views as to which area of the business is propelling it forward and is the key determinant of the company's products, customers and markets. Unfortunately, if there is lack of consensus and clarity, the organization will zigzag its way forward. However, once management is in agreement about the driving force (not an easy task) there are a number of other questions which must be asked:

- What should drive the business in the future?
- Should we continue with the same driving force?

- If we explore a new one, which should it be?
- What implications will it have?
- What will the company look like if we change the driving force?

A company's driving force is more important than any other consideration; it is a tool which allows management to identify which area of the business is at the root of the company's products, customers and markets. However, it is also a tool which allows management to articulate its concept of doing business in that mode.

While the chosen driving force will make for different business concepts and strategies, companies which have the same driving force will also have different concepts and move in different directions. Good examples are Volvo, BMW, Mercedes and Volkswagen, all of which can be said to be product-driven. However, each of these companies has a very different concept of its product: Volvo makes "safe and durable cars," Mercedes makes the "best engineered car," and so on. As a result, each of these companies goes in a slightly different direction and seldom competes with any other even though they all make a similar product.

As we have watched companies over the years, we have seen that there are some that perpetuate their strategy successfully over long periods of time, like IBM or Daimler-Benz. Others have great difficulty doing this and their performance level resembles that of a yo-yo. A company's strategy can, like a person, become stronger and healthier or weaken and become ill. In our opinion, the determining factors are the areas of excellence that are deliberately cultivated to keep the strategy strong and healthy and to give it an edge in the marketplace. It is excellence in these two or three key areas that keeps the strategy alive and working.

If a company is product-driven, it must have the best product on the market for its strategy to work. Therefore, it must excel at product development and product servicing. Of all the things this company needs to do well, it must perform these two tasks better than well, and better than any competitor. However, a user-driven company must excel at different skills. Because it has anchored its business on a specific class of user, it must know that user better than anyone else if its strategy is to succeed. Therefore, user research becomes a required area of excellence to detect shifting needs in that user.

Why is this concept an integral part of strategic thinking? The reason is simple: No company has the resources to develop skills equally in all strategic areas that accompany each driving force. Therefore, strategic decision making relies on management's ability to identify those two or three skills that are critical to the success of its strategy and give those areas preferential resources. In good times, these areas receive additional resources; in bad times, they are the last to be cut. 3M, which can be considered a technology-driven company, clearly recognizes this. It set out to improve its profitability. It asked all division heads to cut expenses by as much as 35 percent, but R&D was spared. In fact, R&D expenditure was increased from 4.5 percent of sales to 6.6 percent. Research is a required area of excellence for a technology-driven company.

Often, when a CEO changes the strategy and direction of a company, he or she does not take the time to think through the implications of that change. As a result, CEOs end up reacting to these changes as they encounter them. Every change in strategy—even a minor one—will bring about implications of one kind or another. If you want your strategy to succeed, you must devote time and thought to identifying the issues that stand in the way of making your strategy work. What are all the changes that need to be addressed in order for the strategy to work? These changes become what we call strategic critical issues. They are management's agenda, and each one is assigned to a specific person who is responsible and accountable for it.

Strategic thinking is the most important skill required of a CEO and leader. People generally do not follow leaders blindly, and unless a leader can articulate the vision and get the commitment of followers to it, he or she will forge ahead alone. A survey conducted to identify some common characteristics of leaders across cultures and organizations found that leaders have four basic traits, irrespective of organization or country. The leader has:

1. A clear vision for the organization
2. The ability to communicate this vision to others
3. The ability to motivate others to work towards the vision
4. The ability to "work the system" to get things done

Although we agree with this, our experience shows that leaders have great difficulty articulating their strategy and vision to others. Thus it becomes imperative for the leader to understand the process of strategic thinking in order to involve others in the development of the strategy. This is how motivation, commitment, and successful implementation will result. Check the following questions to assess the strategic quotient of your organization:

- Could your colleagues articulate your vision of the company?
- Do your colleagues agree and share "buy in" with your strategy?
- Are they good strategic thinkers?
- Do they consider the strategy before making operational decisions?
- Can your colleagues describe the shape of your business in terms of the products that you will be pursuing and equally the products that you will not be pursuing?

- Could they also do this to explain the profile of your markets and your customers?
- Do you have a simple and logical filter that all management can use for deciding how budget resources are allocated and future opportunities pursued?
- Can your colleagues describe your strategic capabilities (your edge against competitors)?
- Do you have a proactive strategy against your competitors?
- Does your strategy reflect your competitive environment?
- Are your people totally positive when faced with change?
- Do your people see change as an opportunity to innovate?
- Are you continually assessing the environmental factors both inside and outside the business in order to check the validity of the present strategy?
- Is your strategy being successfully implemented?

You will have gathered by this stage that the more no answers that you feel are appropriate the more probable it is that it is time to revisit the strategy.

**EXERCISE**

# STRATEGIC PLANNING AT VARIFILM

Compare each of the following TQM criteria to Varifilm and indicate whether the practice in the company is a *strength* (S) or *needs improvement* (I). Justify your answer.

**3.1 Strategic Quality and Company Performance Planning Process**   S   I

■ An integrated strategic quality planning process (SQPP) exists, which incorporates a wide variety of internal and external information sources, including customer, competitive, environmental, supplier, co-worker, and society data.   —   —

■ The process to determine resource commitments to meet the plan requirements is made clear.   —   —

■ Productivity improvement is considered when developing operational performance improvement plans.   —   —

■ A partnership process has been developed to facilitate process analysis and redesign within work units.   —   —

■ Each work unit develops implementation action plans based on critical operating tasks presented by business leaders.   —   —

■ Each business develops a portfolio that includes an assessment of financial performance and strategies, key indicators, and the total VCIC assessment score and goal. This information is reviewed by the I-Team to verify alignment with company vision and mission, as well as to authorize resource plans.   —   —

■ Human resource development requirements are considered during the planning process.   —   —

*Additional Areas for Improvement*

---

---

---

### 3.2 Quality and Performance Plans      S     I

- ■ Key quality factors and requirements to achieve leadership include product quality, on-time delivery, partnership, responsiveness to and understanding of customer requirements, commitment to the customer's industry, and new product development.    —  —

- ■ Specific short-term and longer term quality and performance goals, including a goal to achieve substantial improvement in key indicators, have been set.    —  —

- ■ Longer term plans are committed for such expenditures as plant modernization, research, and training.    —  —

- ■ Key quality factors and requirements to achieve leadership have been deployed to all work units.    —  —

- ■ Longer term goals have been set and requirements on how to achieve them have been addressed.    —  —

- ■ Projected quality and operational performance of key competitors have been addressed.    —  —

*Additional Areas for Improvement*

---

---

---

# FOR FURTHER READING

Lederer, Albert L. and Vijay Sethi, "Seven Guidelines for Strategic Information Systems Planning," *Information Strategy: The Executive's Journal,* Fall 1998, pp. 23–28.

Luthans, Fred, Richard M. Hodgetts, and Brett C. Luthans, "The Role of HRM in Sustaining Competitive Advantage into the 21st Century," *National Productivity Review,* Winter 1997, pp. 73–81.

Porter, Michael E., "What Is Strategy?" *Harvard Business Review,* Nov.–Dec. 1996, pp. 61–78.

Vasilash, Gary S., "The Continuous Improvement Strategy," *Automotive Manufacturing & Production,* Oct. 1998, pp. 44–45.

Villeneuve, Francois, "Competitive Advantage Through People: Unleashing the Power of the Work Force," *Industrial Relations—Quebec,* Spring 1997, pp. 463–466.

Vinzant, Janet and Douglas Vinzant, "Strategic Management and Total Quality Management: Challenges and Choices," *Public Administration Quarterly,* Summer 1996, pp. 201–219.

# 5

# HUMAN RESOURCE FOCUS

*Most managers would agree that the effectiveness of their organizations would be at least doubled if they could discover how to tap the unrealized potential present in their human resources.*

Douglas McGregor
*The Human Side of Enterprise*[1]

The *human resource focus* of the Baldrige 1999 criteria for performance excellence is abridged as follows:

How the company enables employees to develop and utilize their full potential, aligned with the company's objectives. Also, the company's efforts to build and maintain a work environment and work climate conducive to performance excellence, full participation, and personal and organizational growth. Subcategories include:

■ **Work Systems.** How all employees contribute to achieving the company's performance and learning objectives, through the company's work design, and compensation and recognition approaches.

■ **Employee Education, Training, and Development.** How the company's education and training support the accomplishment of key company action plans. Company needs, including building knowledge, skills, and capabilities, and contributing to improved employee performance and development.

■ **Employee Well-Being and Satisfaction.** How the company maintains a work environment and work climate that supports the well-being, satisfaction, and motivation of employees.

The total quality management (TQM) approach offers a substantial potential for improvement if accompanied by an appropriate human resources effort. Indeed, it is becoming a maxim of good management that *human factors* are the most important dimension in quality and productivity improvement. People really do make quality happen.

Chief executive officers of some of America's most quality-conscious companies are quick to point out that the best way to achieve organization success is by involving and empowering employees at all levels. Some even say that employee empowerment is a revolution that will turn top-down companies into democratic workplaces.

> *The whole employee involvement process springs from*
> *asking all your workers the simple question, "What do you think?"*
>
> Donald Peterson
> Former Chairman of Ford

> *Empowerment is all about letting go so that others can get going. To get*
> *every worker to have a new idea every day is the route to winning in the '90s.*
>
> John Welch, Chairman
> General Electric

> *The teams at Goodyear are now telling the boss how to run things.*
> *And I must say, I'm not doing a half-bad job because of it.*
>
> Stanley Gault
> Chairman

Recall W. Edwards Deming's 14 points discussed in Chapter 1. The basis of his philosophy is contained in the following principles: (1) institute training on the job, (2) break down barriers between departments to build teamwork, (3) drive fear out in the workplace, (4) eliminate quotas on the shop floor, (5) create conditions that allow employees to have pride in their workmanship and abolish annual reviews and merit ratings, and (6) institute a program of education and self-improvement.

TQM has far-reaching implications for the management of human resources. It emphasizes self-control, autonomy, and creativity among employees and calls for greater active cooperation rather than just compliance.

The *Industry Week* magazine[2] 1997 Best Plant competition selected ten plants for world-class manufacturing excellence. The following is characteristic of all plants:

- Require commitment from all workers, including those in senior and middle management.
- Involvement and empowerment are trademarks of best plants.
- All cross-train production employees and have non-management team leaders.
- Use a kaizen approach to continuous improvement.
- Have production workers involved in concurrent engineering and process development.

## INVOLVEMENT:
## A CENTRAL IDEA OF HUMAN RESOURCE UTILIZATION

- Back in 1987, the Ames Rubber Corporation decided to adopt a TQM strategy as a major change for implementing its determination to become more competitive. The executive committee identified its best and brightest managers and asked them to reorganize around functional processes. By 1992, every employee was assigned to an *involvement* group or team.

The human resource professional magazine *HR Focus* asked over 1000 readers to rate the key issues they faced in 1993. Employee involvement was rated as one of the top three concerns by 46 percent of the respondents. Customer service followed with 39 percent and TQM with 34 percent.[3]

At the heart of TQM is the concept of intrinsic motivation–involvement in decision making. Employee involvement is a process for *empowering* members of an organization to make decisions and to solve problems appropriate to their levels in the organization. The logic is that the people closest to a problem or opportunity are in the best position to make decisions for improvement if they have ownership of the improvement process. Empowerment is equally effective in service industries, where most frequently the customer's perception of quality stands or falls based on the action of the employee in a one-on-one relationship with the customer.

At Federal Express the driver represents the company. He or she *is* the company and must deal directly with customer problems. Quality in an airline is represented not by CEOs and pilots but by counter personnel and flight attendants.

- One of the more successful efforts to *empower* employees was the Astronautics Groups at Martin Marietta's Denver, Colorado, operation (MMAG). The group instituted a TQM process. To build employee support, the group dropped its pyramid hierarchy of management in favor of a flatter structure and a more participative management approach. High-performance work teams were organized to empower people closest to the work to make decisions about how the work is performed. Aside from the substantial production area savings, less tangible benefits included improved morale.

Quality improvement can result from a reduction in cost or cycle time, an increase in throughput, or a decrease in variation within the process. In the past, the focus in achieving such improvement was frequently the *system*—traditional techniques and methods of quality control. Such a focus may overlook the fact that operation of the system depends on people, and no system will work with disinterested or poorly trained employees. The solution is simple: coordinate the system and the people.

Contrast two production management styles in manufacturing industries. The "buffered" approach is characterized by large stocks of inventory and narrowly specialized workers. "Lean" systems, utilizing just-in-time (JIT) techniques, operate with small inventory stocks, multiskilled workers, and a team approach to work organization. Lean plants are more productive because they do not have valuable resources tied up in idle inventory. Plants are smaller and more efficient, with increased communication among departments, and workers tend to have a view of the organization as a whole.

Two examples of the lean approach involving worker participation are General Motors' New United Motor Manufacturing (NUMMI) plant (a joint venture with Toyota) and Dynatech's automotive test division. In both companies, *internalization* of the JIT philosophy and worker participation have increased worker pride and involvement on the shop floor. At GM, productivity levels are 40 percent higher than typical GM plants, and the plant has the highest quality levels GM has ever known. At Dynatech, cycle time was reduced by as much as 90 percent and setup by 67 to 100 percent.

Not all of the organizations that attempt TQM implementation have the success of companies mentioned in this chapter. Indeed, even for the successful ones, the human costs are often substantial and under certain circumstances may be largely unavoidable. Excessive costs, if incurred, are probably a direct consequence of middle managers' egos and fears, employee motivations, trivial employee participation, and the coercive nature of team structures.

## TRAINING AND DEVELOPMENT

*The skills of the work force are going to be
the key competitive weapon in the twenty-first century.*

Lester Thurow

> *Training, training, retraining, then more training,*
> *and if I have to say it again then you just don't get it.*
>
> Tom Peters
> *Thriving on Chaos*

What do employees think about training? A major DDI/Gallup/Training study, titled "Employees Speak Out on Training," finds that those on the receiving end of company-sponsored training do, indeed, value it. It finds workers saying that training makes a difference not only on the job but in the way they view their employer and how inclined they might be to jump to another company. Asked whether there are areas where additional training would be useful to them, fully 99 percent of the survey respondents said yes.

Increased involvement means more responsibility, which in turn requires a greater level of skill. This must be achieved through training. Baldrige Award winners place a great deal of emphasis on training and support it with appropriate provision of resources. Motorola allocates about 2.5 percent of payroll costs or $120 million annually to training, 40 percent of which goes to quality training. The company calculates the training return at about $29 for each $1 invested. Additional benefits include (1) improved communications, (2) change in corporate culture, and (3) demonstration of management's commitment to quality. (Xerox has extended quality training to 30,000 supplier personnel.)

> ■ Since the early 1980s, Hughes Aircraft has made quality one of its chief operating philosophies. The cornerstone of the company's TQM thrust is continuous measurable improvement (CMI). Recently, the firm has championed a unique "trickle-down" training system to sustain its quality and productivity improvements. Under CMI (Cascaded Training Program), the managers responsible for achieving improvement teach the philosophy and principles of CMI leadership throughout the organization.[4]

Although the type of training depends on the needs of the particular company and may or may not extend to technical areas, the one area that should be common to all organization training programs is *problem solving.* Problem solving should be institutionalized and internalized in many, if not most, companies. This would be a prerequisite to widespread empowerment.

Training usually falls into one of three categories: (1) reinforcement of the quality message[5] and basic skill remediation, (2) job skill requirements, and (3) knowledge about principles of TQM. The latter typically covers problem-solving techniques, problem analysis, statistical process control, and quality measurement—areas that go beyond typical job skills. If groups or teams are utilized, training in the group process and group decision making is included. According to a survey conducted by the Conference Board, top companies commonly address the following topics in quality training curricula:

- Quality awareness
- Quality measurement (performance measures/quality cost benchmarking, data analysis)
- Process management and defect prevention
- Team building and quality circle training
- Focus on customers and markets
- Statistics and statistical methods
- Taguchi methods

> - Research Testing Laboratories, Inc., a TQM company providing clinical research services, encourages employees to make changes in processes in order to minimize and eliminate errors early in the work process. The goal is 100 percent customer satisfaction. To achieve this goal, employees are provided with a 25-hour training program in which they learn (1) effective interactive skills, (2) the problem-solving process, and (3) the quality improvement process.

*Managerial* training may take the form of the third item above (TQM principles). In addition, programs often are directed toward sensitizing individuals to the strategic importance of quality, the cost of poor quality, and their role in influencing the quality of products and services.

The International Quality Study was conducted among 584 companies representing four industries. The use of quality tools in the American auto industry is expected to increase 1.5- to 6-fold over the next three years. Quality training was found to have the greatest impact when coupled with other practices, such as measurement and reward systems.[6]

Common problems with different types of training include:

- **Quality concept training.** These types of survey or "overview" courses are meant to get people thinking about quality, but the "one-size-fits-all" approach does not go very far in company-specific applications. They are probably not meant for lower level employees.

- **Quality tools training.** Here, employees learn what tools are available and when to use them, but they often do not get enough practice using the tools to master them and do not learn how to apply them to problems in their work.

- **Leadership training.** Managers need ongoing feedback to know if they are using their training effectively.

In manufacturing companies, it is understandable that training would be more technical (e.g., process control, quality tools, statistical process control), but do not overlook training for employees in service industries and service departments in manufacturing companies. In these situations, the company's single most important point of contact is the moment the customer purchases the product. Such training might include such topics as customer service, hospitality, dress codes, and staff motivation.

## SELECTION

Selection is choosing from a group of potential employees (or placement from existing employees) the specific person to perform a given job. In theory, the process is simple: decide what the job involves and what abilities are necessary, and then use established selection techniques (ability tests, personality tests, interviews, assessment centers) as indicators of how the candidate will perform.

The process is not so simple, however, when TQM enters the picture. The job requirements for a typist, a machinist, or even a manager can be determined by job analysis, and the qualifications of a candidate can be compared to these requirements. When a company commits to TQM, an entirely new dimension is introduced. The skills and abilities required for a specific job can usually easily be identified and then matched with an individual. People well suited for operating in a quality climate may require additional characteristics, such as attitude, values, personality type, and analytical ability.

Persons working in a quality environment need sharp problem-solving ability in order to perform the quantitative work demanded by statistical process control, Pareto analysis, etc. Because of the emphasis on teams and group process, personnel must function well in group settings. Motorola shows applicants videotapes of problem-solving groups in action and asks them how they would respond to a particular quality issue. Presumably, this technique encourages *self-selection.*

What is perhaps different in the selection process in a TQM environment is the emphasis on a *quality-oriented organization culture* as the desired outcome of the selection process.[7]

## PERFORMANCE APPRAISAL

Performance appraisal may be the Achilles' heel of TQM. Ken Blanchard, a popular author and management consultant, comments: "Somewhere in every organization's literature, it says that its people are the most important resource. And yet, when I ask people how they like the way their performance is evaluated, everybody laughs."

What is clear is that old measurement, appraisal, and reward systems do not work for TQM. Given how people experience and cover performance error, it appears that neither performance appraisal supporters nor TQM gurus have invented a methodology for completely installing performance appraisal that meets TQM requirements. The trend appears to suggest that there is no need for performance appraisal if a company has implemented an honest TQM system. The assumption is that employee performance improves through profound knowledge, daily motivation, good supervisory coaching, and pride in a quality product.

More specifically, the human resource department/function can take the following actions to become a major contributor to company-wide TQM:

1. Jump-start the TQM process by becoming a role model for customer service. This means that the department must perceive other departments in the organization as its customer groups.

2. Demonstrate the commitment to TQM principles by soliciting feedback from its internal customers and otherwise modeling specific principles.

3. Serve as a beachhead for the TQM process throughout the company and thereby acting as senior management's tool in implementing the process.

4. Take the TQM process company-wide by developing and delivering the training and development necessary for the major culture shift that is required.

5. Utilize department strengths in recruitment, selection, appraisal, and reward system development to institutionalize a quality-first orientation.

The purpose of performance appraisal is to serve as a diagnostic tool and review process for development of the individual, team, and organization. Appraisals are used to determine reward levels, validate tests, aid career development, improve communication, and facilitate understanding of job duties.[8]

Deming cites *traditional* employee evaluation systems as one of seven deadly diseases confronting U.S. industry. He states that *individual* performance evaluations encourage short-term goals rather than long-term planning. They undermine teamwork and encourage competition among people for the same rewards. Moreover, the overwhelming cause of non-quality is not the employee but the system; by focusing on individuals, attention is diverted from the root cause of poor quality: the system.

Many TQM proponents, like Deming, argue that traditional performance appraisal methods are attempts by management to pin the blame for poor organization performance on lower level employees, rather than focusing attention on the system, for which upper management is primarily responsible.

Should individual performance appraisal be eliminated, as Deming suggests?[9] This is unlikely in view of the historical and widespread use of this human resource management tool. What, then, can be done to relate individual and group performance to a total quality strategy?

Performance appraisals are most effective when they focus on the objectives of the company and therefore of the individual or group. Because the eventual outcome of all work is quality and customer satisfaction, it follows that appraisal should somehow relate to this outcome—to the objectives of the company, the group, and the individual. In other words, a performance appraisal system should be aligned with the principle of shared responsibility for quality. This can be accomplished by focusing on development of the skills and abilities necessary to perform well and, as such, directly support collective responsibility.

■ In a model used by the Hay Group (a consulting organization), individuals are evaluated for base pay on such variables as ability to communicate, customer focus, and ability to work as a team. Managers are rated on employee development, group productivity, and leadership. Variable pay for both is based on what is accomplished. Because customer focus is a critical part of any TQM effort, a three-category rating system that involves (1) not meeting customer expectations, (2) meeting them, and (3) far exceeding them is easy to implement.[10]

Answering Deming and the other critics is not easy. The integration of total quality and performance appraisal is necessary. One should reinforce the other. One approach might be to modify existing systems in accordance with the following principles:

■ Customer expectations, not the job description, generate the individual's job expectation.

■ Results expectations meet different criteria than management-by-objectives statements.

■ Performance expectations include behavioral skills that make the real difference in achieving quality performance and total customer satisfaction.

■ The rating scale reflects actual performance, not a "grading curve."

■ Employees are active participants in the process, not merely "drawn in."

Regardless of which specific system is adopted, there seems to be little question that performance management practices need to be in line with and supportive of TQM.

# COMPENSATION SYSTEMS

This may be one of the most elusive and controversial of all systems that support TQM. Historically, compensation systems have been based on (1) pay for performance or (2) pay for responsibility (a job description). Each of these is based on individual performance, which creates a competitive atmosphere among employees. In contrast, the TQM philosophy emphasizes flexibility, lateral communication, group effectiveness, and responsibility for an entire process that has the ultimate outcome of customer satisfaction. No wonder research and writing have offered little in the way of new approaches that are more in tune with the needs of TQM.

■ Shawnee Mission (Kansas) Medical Center attempted to set up an infrastructure to push TQM ideals throughout the organization. In 1992, the center operationalized its new evaluation system based on personal development, education, and teamwork. Everyone receives the same raise.

Both training and performance appraisal are desirable components of a TQM implementation strategy, but compensation is an equally necessary dimension. Employees may perceive the system as a reflection of the company's commitment to quality.

## Individual or Team Compensation?

A company's infrastructure, specifically its reward and compensation systems, provides an accurate picture of its strategic goals. If compensation criteria are focused exclusively on individual performance, a company will find that initiatives promoting teamwork may fail. A TQM vision and the principles supporting it are unlikely to take hold unless the values on which they are based are built into the underlying structure.

■ Target Stores is among the growing number of companies in the retail industry that are going beyond logistics-specific performance measures and are tying pay to the effectiveness of TQM programs. Throughout the logistics field, pay for performance and pay for quality appear to becoming more entrenched.

There is no lack of compensation plans in U.S. industry. Gain sharing, profit sharing, and stock ownership are among the systems designed to create a financial incentive for employees to be involved in performance improvements. Gain sharing is one of the most rapidly growing compensation and involvement systems in U.S. industry. It is a system of management in which an organization seeks higher levels of performance through the involvement and participation of its people. Employees share financially in the gain when performance improves. The approach is a team effort in which employees are eligible for bonuses at regular intervals on an operational basis. Gain sharing reinforces TQM, partially because it contains common components, such as involvement and commitment.[11]

The jury is still out on the effectiveness of these plans, but evidence suggests that effectiveness is a function of strong communication programs and widespread employee involvement.

### Summary

Many reasons have been offered as the cause of poor performance in organizations: (1) system failure; (2) misunderstanding of job expectations; (3) lack of awareness about performance; (4) lack of time, tools, or resources to succeed; (5) lack of necessary knowledge or skills; (6) lack of appropriate consequences for performance; and (7) bad fit for the job. Although a compensation system supportive of TQM is not the only remedy, combined with other human resource management systems it will go a long way toward improvement of performance and development among individuals, groups, and the organization.

## TOTAL-QUALITY-ORIENTED HUMAN RESOURCE MANAGEMENT

Human resource executives are faced with both a challenge and an opportunity. They are not generally perceived with the same regard as line managers. Philip Crosby describes the human resource department as behind the times and the human resource executive as his or her own worst enemy. On the other hand, the department can play a critical role in the implementation of a holistic quality environment in support of a strategic initiative. To accomplish this role, the function should not only be designed to support TQM throughout the organization but should make sure that good quality management practices are followed within the processes of the function itself. This means continuous improvement as a way of department life. Bowen and Lawler suggest putting the following principles of TQM to work *within* the human resource department:[12]

1. Quality work the first time
2. Focus on the customer
3. Strategic holistic approach to improvement

4. Continuous improvement as a way of life

5. Mutual respect and teamwork

It is evident that some modification of traditional human resource management practices is required if the function is to support the TQM program throughout the company. Planning is the first step. The 1993 Baldrige Award criteria describe human resource planning:[13]

> Human resource plans might include the following: mechanisms for promoting cooperation such as internal customer/supplier techniques or other internal partnerships; initiatives to promote labor–management cooperation, such as partnerships with unions; creation and/or modification of recognition systems; mechanisms for increasing or broadening employee responsibilities; creating opportunities for employees to learn and use skills that go beyond current job assignments through redesign of processes; creation of high performance work teams; and education and training initiatives. Plans might also include forming partnerships with educational institutions to develop employees or to help ensure the future supply of well-prepared employees.

## QUESTIONS FOR DISCUSSION

**5-1** Would a quality improvement program based on process control be more appropriate for employee involvement than a system based on traditional production methods? If so, explain why.

**5-2** What effect does employee involvement have on motivation? Explain the effect in terms of motivational theory.

**5-3** Contrast the benefits of the different types of small groups or teams. Which would be more appropriate for achieving integration across organizational functions or departments?

**5-4** A Deming principle advises to "create conditions that allow employees to have pride in their workmanship." What are these conditions and how can they be implemented?

**5-5** Assume that a company has just committed to change from a traditional style of management to one based on TQM. What topics would you include for:

- ■ Shop floor employees

■ Front-line supervisors

■ Middle-level managers

**5-6** Describe how training in problem solving would improve:

■ Process control

■ Employee motivation

## ENDNOTES

1. Douglas McGregor, *The Human Side of Enterprise,* 25th anniversary printing, New York: McGraw-Hill, 1985.
2. Michael Verespect, "Lessons from the Best," *Industry Week,* Feb. 16, 1988, pp. 28–36.
3. *HR Focus,* Jan. 1993, pp. 1, 4.
4. Judy Rice, "Cascaded Training at Hughes Aircraft Helps Ensure Continuous Measurable Improvement," *National Productivity Review,* Winter 1992/1993, pp. 111–116.
5. Bernie Knill, "The Nitty-Gritty of Quality Manufacturing," *Materials Handling Engineering,* July 1992, pp. 40–42. In a Conference Board survey, training is first used to reinforce the quality message and then to build skills. Another finding of the survey is that leaders link TQM to performance review and compensation.
6. Trace E. Benson, "When Less Is More," *Industry Week,* Sept. 7, 1992, pp. 68–77.
7. David E. Bowen and Edward E. Lawler III, "Total Quality-Oriented Human Resource Management," *Organization Dynamics,* Spring 1992, pp. 29–41.
8. David E. Bowen and Edward E. Lawler III, "Total Quality-Oriented Human Resource Management," *Organization Dynamics,* Spring 1992, p. 36.
9. Some recent articles that treat performance appraisal in a TQM context include Kathleen A. Guinn, "Successfully Integrating Total Quality Management and Performance Appraisal," *Human Resource Professional,* Spring 1992, pp. 19–25; Mike Deblieux, "Performance Reviews Support the Quest for Quality," *HR Focus,* Nov. 1991, pp. 3–4; Jean B. Ferketish and John W. Hayden, "HRD & Quality: The Chicken or the Egg?" Jan. 1992, pp. 38–42.
10. Linda Thornburg, "Pay for Performance: What You Should Know (Part 1)," *HR Magazine,* June 1992, pp. 58–61.
11. Robert L. Masternak, "Gainsharing at B.F. Goodrich: Succeeding Together Achieves Rewards," *Tapping the Network Journal,* Fall/Winter 1991, pp. 13–16.
12. David Bowen and Edward Lawler, "Total Quality-Oriented Human Resource Management," *Organizational Dynamics,* Spring 1992, p. 29.
13. Malcolm Baldrige National Quality Award, 1993 Award Criteria, Gaithersburg, Md.: National Institute of Standards and Technology, U.S. Department of Commerce, 1993, p. 21.

# XEROX FOCUSES ON HUMAN RESOURCES

Xerox Business Services (XBS) is the document outsourcing services and solutions business of "The Document Company," Xerox. Document outsourcing, such as on-site management of mail rooms and print shops, accounts for 80 percent of revenues. The remainder is derived from "document solutions"—customized services designed to meet customers' specialized requirements for creating, producing, distributing, and storing paper and digital documents.

Customer satisfaction is XBS's number one priority, and the company has made knowing the current and future requirements of existing and prospective customers its business. Empowered employees are at the heart of XBS's customer-focused culture. Jobs, work processes, and work environments are designed by individuals and work groups to help ensure that they can satisfy the unique requirements of their customers.

Next to customer satisfaction, employee satisfaction is XBS's top priority. Xerox and XBS are consistently acknowledged as a leader in improving the workplace. *Money* magazine rated Xerox number one in providing for the well-being, satisfaction, and development of its people. XBS is continuously striving for new levels of employee satisfaction. Its annual Employee Motivation and Satisfaction Survey identifies employee concerns and issues by asking XBS people to rank a series of factors that influence their individual motivation and satisfaction. The following are the top five that employees have identified:

- Trust
- Responsible freedom
- Teamwork
- Valuing people
- Learning

XBS invests more than $10 million annually for training, and it continually is searching for innovative learning approaches. Examples are mini-camps, designed to help employees contemplate and prepare for future changes in the way they work and in how XBS addresses evolving customer requirements, and each employee's personal learning plan that is regularly reviewed by assigned "coaches."

XBS management believes that every employee has the potential to affect the bottom line. Through compensation and recognition systems aligned with division objectives, all XBS employees have a direct stake in the success of the business.

# QUALITY DRIVES
# TRIDENT'S SUCCESS

## Jennifer J. Laabs

In 1987, Trident Precision Manufacturing, Inc. in Webster, New York, was a good, profitable little operation that was humming along quite well at about $5 million in revenue a year. Trident had started as a three-person operation back in 1979, and by the late '80s, Trident had become a fast-growing, precision sheet-metal fabricator and electromechanical assembly business, with such big-name clients as Xerox, Kodak and IBM.

On the surface, Trident's customers were happy with its products, which ranged from simple brackets to machines that sort X-rays. Business was in the black.

But below the surface, problems were firing up. Turnover was clocked at a staggering 41 percent with many workers quitting within only a few months of starting their jobs. And because the firm had no particular quality process, products often got to the end of the assembly line with major defects and had to be completely redone. The company's informal motto was: "We make it nice because we make it twice."

Even so, products were getting made, customers were buying them and the company was profitable. But seeing operations from the inside, the company's owner, president and CEO, Nicholas "Nick" Juskiw, knew there must be a better way to do business. So he set out to find a solution and eventually headed his company down a path of total quality management (TQM). Trident senior managers decided to focus on workers, not products, yet the products improved. It turned out to be a visionary HR move and also a formula for financial success.

Ten years later, the company has more than quadrupled its annual revenue to more than $19 million, lowered its product defects from 3 percent in 1988 to virtually defect-free in 1997 (99.993 percent) and celebrates its revenue per employee at 73 percent. (The company didn't measure revenue per employee

Reprinted from *Workforce*, Vol. 77 No. 2, February 1998, pp. 44–45, with permission from ACC Communications, Inc.

before 1988.) And two years ago, Trident won the Malcolm Baldrige National Quality Award. This year, it wins a *Workforce* Magazine Optimas Award in the Financial Impact category.

The key to Trident's success story is that the company didn't just embark on a run-of-the-mill TQM process. The privately held firm proactively focused on improving its human resources practices in a TQM environment that translated directly into customer satisfaction. The journey started with a clear vision.

## Visioning Quality

In 1988, Juskiw attended a presentation on quality management at Stamford, Connecticut–based Xerox Corp. called "Leadership Through Quality." Juskiw came back to Trident with a new management vision—TQM. He pulled his senior team aside for nearly three days to discuss whether managers thought it was a good direction for Trident. They did. But they realized a big part of their problem was that they needed to value workers. So, the senior management team of 10 people (now 17) spent 14 months developing an entirely new management strategy to revamp company operations, which included everything from over-hauling their training initiatives to changing the company culture to be more people-oriented. They called the new plan Excellence in Motion, and the strategy has guided their actions ever since. The plan focuses on five key business drivers: supplier partnerships, operational performance, customer satisfaction, share-holder value and, last but not least, employee satisfaction.

Interestingly, April V. Lusk, the company's total quality administrator in the HR department, explains that at Trident, she's responsible for "Big Q"—the quality of the people and the environment. Lusk's associate, Joe Conchelos, vice president of quality administration, is responsible for "Little Q." It's unusual for a company to put workers before products. But that's where Trident started.

Worker issues were primary concerns. "In 1988, we actually [were proud] that we had 41 percent turnover [because it] was lower than the industry standard of 52 percent," says Lusk. "The irony of it all was that our people were leaving for as little as a nickel [more] down the street." Lusk explains that the industry was famous for not listening to employees' ideas or rewarding them for good work. Trident wanted to change this scenario.

Senior managers asked an employee team to investigate the problem, identify the root cause and help develop a corrective action. The team's answer was direct: Managers didn't care whom they hired so long as they were breathing and could do the job. The team members suggested the firm revise its hiring practices.

So, Trident's small HR department did just that—and much more. Now, instead of hiring just anyone, candidates are interviewed first by HR, then by the hiring manager and finally by members of the team with which the candidate would be working. "It's a lengthy process, but we feel we've been able to hire better people by having more input," says Margery Haywood, Trident's HR manager, who has seen the turnover rate drop to 3.5 percent in the past 10 years. (Turnover in 1997 was 1.2 percent among employees with five years' tenure or more.) Of course, winning the Baldrige has helped the flow of resumes to this small business located in a suburb of Rochester, New York. Adds Lusk: "We try to get as many perspectives as possible. We want new employees to come on board and immediately feel part of the family atmosphere we've created."

Corporate culture was another big issue to tackle. In 1987, employees at Trident weren't especially happy and weren't particularly team-oriented. Now employees are completely empowered. They can—and do—halt production for the smallest of flaws. Instead of passing problems to the next person on the line, workers own the problems and fix them. In 1990 for example, 8.9 percent of employees' time was spent reworking nonconforming products. In 1997, they spent only 1 percent of their time "making things twice." But the first step to employee ownership was education, with HR standing diligently at the blackboard.

## Empowerment Through Training

One of the first things the HR department did to move the company toward its goals was to implement a 25-hour training course on TQM tools for each employee. The education included basics on problem solving, quality improvements, just-in-time manufacturing and even interpersonal communications skills. Each year, employees receive at least 15 hours of TQM refresher courses along with information on such topics as safety and customer negotiations.

"We teach workers to read blueprints, [to do] trigonometry and [to learn] English as a second language," Juskiw said in a *USA Today* article (October 17, 1996) when his company won the Baldrige. Before 1987, most workers received no formal training. The only exception was for workers with technical jobs, who always have received technical training offsite.

Since 1987, the company has spent an astounding 4.7 percent of payroll on training each year. According to the latest research at the Saratoga Institute, an HR consulting firm in Santa Clara, California, most companies spend just over 1 percent of payroll on training. The average in Trident's industry is 1.5 percent.

The training has made a huge difference. Not only are workers empowered to shut down the line for problems, they also proactively improve their work processes through participation in a number of processes including the Total Quality Roundtable. In 1997 alone, employees made more than 2,200 process improvement suggestions. In the past several years, 98 percent of employees' suggestions have been implemented in daily work routines. "We tell people: 'You own it. Fix it,'" says Lusk. Clearly, they mean it. And they reward employees generously for their efforts.

## Say Thank You

Each year, the average Trident employee receives special recognition from the company 10.6 times. In fiscal year 1997, company supervisors and managers handed out more than 1,700 items—from hockey tickets to gift certificates for dinners for two—to say thank you for a job well done. It's a rare company that tracks its recognition efforts this closely. But to Trident managers, individual recognition is an extremely important part of Trident's strategy to keep employees happy, productive and working. And it was a big key to moving toward the more family-oriented culture they were striving for.

The HR team believes employees need to know their work is appreciated often. "If you want to change your culture, start thanking people," says Lusk. "[And] don't wait until the end of the year." Trident's HR managers haven't left their recognition efforts—or the measurement of their progress in each of the five major business drivers—to chance.

## Measure Your Progress

The lesson for all HR professionals is: HR can and should measure progress. If you don't track results, it's difficult to learn from your efforts.

In addition to tracking things like turnover and retention, HR at Trident measures employee satisfaction and customer satisfaction twice a year. In 1997, employee satisfaction ranked at a whopping 94 percent. Company managers also measure many other aspects of the firm's five key business drivers as well.

And while it isn't uncommon for a company to measure business results, it is unusual for a company to push the envelope on business measurement so diligently. You might say it's Trident's way of climbing the quality mountain— one HR track at a time.

## Questions for Discussion

1   The concept of "you own it, you fix it" reflects the degree to which employees are empowered. Given this degree of empowerment and delegation of responsibility, a question that might be asked is: Who needs a vice president of quality administration and quality administrators in the human resources department? Would you eliminate those jobs? Why or why not?

**2**   How would company training in problem solving and interpersonal communications be of benefit to quality improvement?

**3**   Explain how the driver of employee satisfaction results in customer satisfaction and vice versa.

**4**   Do hockey tickets and dinners for two motivate employees for productivity and quality? Explain.

**5**   No performance appraisal system was mentioned in Trident's case study. Would you develop and implement one? If you would, what would the measures be for front-line supervisors? If not, what would be the consequences?

## PLUGGING INTO THE POWER OF LEADERSHIP TEAMS

### Billie R. Day and Michael Moore

The previous management style at Plant Hammond served the utility business well. But then a watershed development occurred in the early 1990s—the move toward deregulation.

When the top management group at Georgia Power Company's Plant Hammond decided to become a team, everyone was quite sure that they were already a team and worked pretty well together. After all, wasn't that really all that a team amounted to?

The top leadership group in early 1995 was ten people from three management levels and two individual contributors. The management style was much the same as they had been using for many years in the utility industry and was characterized by an emphasis on the chain of command for most decisions—with the important ones made by one or two people. Information and business results were communicated on a "need to know" basis. For the most part, each department operated and made decisions independently.

This management style served the utility business well, given its business requirements. The business was relatively predictable and structured with a regulated rate of return, regional market protection, and 100 percent control of access to its own distribution facilities.

A watershed development, however, occurred in the early 1990s—a move toward deregulation.

As of today, the exact details of this deregulation are being formulated on a state-by-state basis. However, future suppliers of electricity will be those who can provide reliable power at the lowest price.

These fundamental business changes demanded fundamental changes in the way Plant Hammond operated and managed its resources.

Reprinted with permission of The Association for Quality and Participation (Cincinnati, Ohio) from the May/June 1998 issue of *The Journal for Quality and Participation.*

## Organizational Transformation

In the early 1990s, the plant had reduced the number of employees by about one third, resulting in fewer management levels and fewer managers in those levels. In early 1995, the parent organization, Southern Company, implemented a transformation process to improve the plant's ability to compete. This transformation process required an emphasis on business results at all levels and creation of an organization culture that could deal with uncertainty and competition—in other words: improvements in cost and culture. A series of initiatives provided guidance as to the outcomes of the transformation process. Plant Hammond set about implementing these initiatives in ways that made sense for its operation.

## The Top Management Team

As the plant manager considered the requirements for the future, he determined that the structure, processes, and culture of the plant would need to change. Therefore, top management must change how it operated, broadening capabilities at all levels. Processes were needed to manage decision-making risk and gain consensus on direction. A new organizational structure was one of the early steps in their transformation. The structure provided an "outside in" focus—identifying the operations function as the primary internal customer—and grouped plant activities into several functional areas.

However, plant management knew that simply changing the boxes on an organization chart was not sufficient for real change. In the summer of 1995, the plant manager and nine other employees took their first step toward becoming a team when they came together at a facilitated off-site meeting. They clarified individual roles and responsibilities on this new team and began developing team relationships. They agreed that the role of each leadership-team member should be one of "shared responsibilities with a functional focus." Top managers at the plant could no longer make decisions from only their own departments' view. In fact, managers were required to consider the impact of their decisions—not only on the total plant, but also on the total operating system of the Southern Company.

Each member took on the responsibility to champion specific transformation activities for the leadership team. The team began to have regular one-day session meetings where they discussed and made decisions on strategic and operational issues.

## Development of the Leadership Team

This management team took a key developmental step in 1996 by setting expectations for their behavior and presenting them to their organizations during reviews of the 1996 plant strategic plan. Putting these expectations "on the record" built incentives to act accordingly.

The team found several tools to be helpful in its operation and development. One was a common work plan that served multiple purposes: 1) to ensure integration of their efforts and to track team results; 2) to establish member accountability; 3) to facilitate the delegation of traditional plant manager tasks; and 4) as a catalyst to surface strategic issues. Each team member—or members—took responsibility for the accomplishment of particular parts of the work plan.

The team also used various assessment instruments to understand and deal with the different individual styles of team members. Each team member discussed his or her assessment in an open forum. As a result, members made commitments for change and support. Each team member also formulated his or her own development plan based on these and other assessments.

Since one of the plant's strategies was to improve the capabilities of the management team, the team worked with an outside consultant to identify strengths and weaknesses. The consultant observed each of the team members in work situations and provided specific personal feedback and suggestions over an extended period of time. Each team member reviewed his or her assessment with the group and asked for reactions and recommendations. The consultant also provided feedback on group processes and worked in concert with an internal consultant to improve teamwork processes.

## Concurrent Changes

The leadership team was also implementing other changes to achieve the plant's cost and culture goals, such as high-involvement work teams in the plant to give employees more of a voice in decisions that affect how they carry out their jobs. Team leaders were charged with more responsibility for the operations and maintenance of the plant and with coordinating their actions when required, particularly in the areas of personnel management and labor relations.

Special project teams redesigned and implemented some of the plant's major processes (work-order system, maintenance planning and scheduling, training, and document control). It was important that the major processes be supportive of the new plant direction. Any group, to become a real team, must meet certain expected team behaviors: no hidden agendas, no covert competition, constant support of team decisions made with the organization, and honesty at all times.

## Lessons About Top Management Teams

Implementing a team at the top management level resulted in a few important lessons for the management team. For one thing, it required a significant upfront investment in time and energy on the part of the team members.

A top management team was a confusing concept for the plant. Employees did not understand the role sharing and joint focus of leadership team members. All of their past experience at the plant told them to rely on the next person in the chain of command for information and guidance.

Perhaps the most difficult challenges were personal ones. The managers on the leadership team had to resist their temptation to defer to the boss. The plant manager had to resist the temptation to make all the decisions. Team members had to learn to openly discuss their own weaknesses and to make commitments to someone other than their direct boss. The team also had to work to assure corporate oversight functions that shared responsibility did not compromise management controls.

Plant Hammond also learned that the size of the team really does matter. During the last two years, the team has changed from ten members to six. The makeup of the members has changed as well. As the group became smaller, the individual differences in style were more obvious and required continuous effort to keep the candor levels high enough to confront differences.

The challenges of forming a top management team are similar to forming a team at any level. It is complicated, however, by the fishbowl environment in which these managers must operate. By their nature, top management teams deal with strategic issues. The team should be careful not to allow a desire to be a team to overcome the requirement for a high quality decision. They must be willing to identify those items that do not call for consensus. The Plant Hammond team identified two specific areas in advance where the final decision was retained by the plant manager: changes in the organization structure and staffing of exempt positions.

## Success Factors

Certain conditions are necessary for management teams to become "real teams" and not just a grouping of independent functional managers who report to a single executive and cooperate with each other.

- Business situation requires integration of efforts, a systems perspective, and sharing of power. This results in the team having actual work to do.
- Teams should not be used at any level where there is no business reason to do so.
- Commitment by all managers involved, particularly the plant manager, that this is the best way to manage.
- Visible and vocal support for team decisions.
- High levels of trust within the management team.

- Use of an "outside-in" focus as a unifying force.
- Willingness to question and to be questioned about methods, results, and reasoning behind actions.
- Rewards that support team behavior, including any incentive programs.
- Regular assessment of performance as a group.
- Willingness to use constructive tension and deal with conflict and different opinions.
- Adequate time to meet.
- Recognition of team boundaries and specific descriptions of any items to be retained by the top manager in the facility.

Some significant advantages to using a team concept at top management levels have occurred at Plant Hammond. Actions within individual departments have become more tightly linked to the plant's strategies. Critical decisions have been improved as the team has increased understanding and commitment to important decisions. The team structure has resulted in less dependence on the plant manager.

Most important, the leadership of Plant Hammond believes that having a management team at the top will improve its ability to meet the challenges of its business.

This project was done in collaboration with Wilts Alexander III of Alexander Scott and Associates in Atlanta, Georgia. Use of processes developed by Alexander and Abe Raab, of Abe Raab and Associates, Cherry Hill, Pennsylvania, is gratefully acknowledged.

# HUMAN RESOURCES AT VARIFILM

Compare each of the following TQM criteria to Varifilm and indicate whether the practice in the company is a *strength* (S) or *needs improvement* (I). Justify your answer.

## EMPLOYEE INVOLVEMENT

**4.1 Human Resource Development and Management**  S  I

- Plans have been established that address education and training, empowerment, recognition, and recruitment.  ___  ___

- Employee satisfaction factors are used to reduce adverse human resource indicators.  ___  ___

- Key performance indicators are used for human resource processes and practices.  ___  ___

- Key diversity goals have been established for achieving a workplace diversity balance.  ___  ___

- Reductions in cycle time have been achieved in bonus delivery, flexible benefits, travel expense reimbursement, and benefits.  ___  ___

- Third-party co-worker climate surveys that monitor key indicators have been administered and appropriate improvement actions identified.  ___  ___

- Short-term plans have been distinguished from longer term plans.  ___  ___

## 4.2 Employee Involvement

- A wide variety of teams are used to promote ongoing co-worker contributions.  ___  ___

- Involvement goals are established for all employees, based on the most important requirements.  ___  ___

|  | S | I |
|---|---|---|

■ Evidence is maintained to show how involvement is linked to key quality and operational performance improvement results. — —

■ All categories of employees are linked to empowerment through the business objectives. — —

■ Co-worker entrepreneurship is encouraged by cash grants or other means. — —

■ Co-worker involvement is evaluated by such means as self-managed team participation, co-worker climate survey, and participation in a suggestion system. — —

*Additional Areas for Improvement*

_____

_____

_____

## HUMAN RESOURCES DEVELOPMENT AND MANAGEMENT

### 4.3 Employee Education and Training     S     I

■ Adequate training for both new plant workers and non-plant workers should include orientation about policy, principles and values, self-managed team training, and safety. Quality training comprises a significant portion of the overall training. — —

■ Training and course effectiveness are evaluated and improved through the use of skill testing and participant feedback. — —

■ Trend data regarding the effectiveness of training and key indicators of effectiveness are maintained. — —

■ Training is regularly delivered and reinforced. — —

■ Acceptable methods of determining the "soft skill" training needs for management are used. — —

### 4.4 Employee Performance and Recognition

■ Key indicators are used to evaluate and improve recognition approaches. — —

|                                                                                                                  | S | I |
|------------------------------------------------------------------------------------------------------------------|---|---|
| ■ The objectivity of any quality award process is ensured.                                                       | — | — |
| ■ A wide and appropriate variety of reward and recognition methods are used for both teams and individuals.      | — | — |
| ■ A worker climate survey or other means is used to obtain feedback on how workers rate the recognition program. | — | — |
| ■ Recognition processes ensure that quality is reinforced relative to short-term financial considerations.       | — | — |

**4.5 Employee Well-Being and Satisfaction**

| | S | I |
|---|---|---|
| ■ Periodic audits are conducted to determine employee well-being and satisfaction. Other methods are used as well. | — | — |
| ■ Improvement goals are set for important factors. | — | — |
| ■ Key indicators are used and tracked. | — | — |

*Additional Areas for Improvement*

_____

_____

_____


# FOR FURTHER READING

Blackburn, Richard and Benson Rosen, "Does HRM Walk the TQM Talk?" *HR Magazine,* July 1995, pp. 69–72.

Clinton, Roy J., Stan Williamson, and Art L. Bethke, "Implementing Total Quality Management: The Role of Human Resource Management," *Advanced Management Journal,* Spring 1994, pp. 10–16.

Connor, Patrick E., "Total Quality Management: A Selective Commentary on Its Human Dimensions, With Special Reference to Its Downside," *Public Administration Review,* Nov./Dec. 1997, pp. 501–509.

Kappelman, Leon and Victor Prybutok, "Empowerment, Motivation, Training, and TQM Program Implementation Success," *Industrial Management,* May/June 1995, pp. 12–15.

Marcum, James, "TQM: Quality Training Practices," *National Productivity Review,* Spring 1994, pp. 312–313.

Weaver, Timothy W., "Linking Performance Reviews to Productivity and Quality," *HR Magazine,* Vol. 41 No. 11, Nov. 1996, pp. 93–98.

# PROCESS MANAGEMENT

*Quality improvement will result from people improving
their processes and from management improving the system.*

Peter Drucker

The need for top management to display leadership in setting the climate and culture for total quality management (TQM) was outlined in Chapter 2. Climate and culture, however, are not enough. It is unlikely that exhortations and slogans will be effective unless accompanied by action planning and implementation. A statement such as "We Are the Quality Company" convinces no one—not the employees and not the customers. The company should be organized for quality assurance in the context of modern quality management.

Assume that the criteria of the Baldrige Award fairly represent what is generally accepted as the national standard for management of process quality:

■ **6.1 Management of Product and Service Processes.** How the company designs, introduces, produces, delivers, and improves its products and services. How production/delivery processes are designed, managed, and improved. Important to the management of these processes is the trouble-free introduction of new products and services. This requires effective coordination, starting early in the product and service design phase. Also, organizational learning, through a focus on how learnings in one process or company unit are replicated and added to the knowledge base of other projects or company units.

■ **6.2 Management of Support Processes.** How the company designs, implements, manages and improves its support processes. Support processes are those that support the company's product and/ or service delivery, but are not usually designed in detail with the products and services themselves, because their requirements usually do not depend a great deal upon product and service characteristics. Support process design requirements usually depend significantly upon internal requirements and must be coordinated and integrated to ensure efficient and effective performance. Support processes might include finance and accounting, software services, sales, marketing, public relations, information services, supplies, personnel, legal services, plant and facilities management, research and development, and secretarial and other administrative services.

Everything is a process, whether it is processing a customer order, purchasing supplies, opening an account, or shipping a product. There are dozens of activities in an organization and each activity may have several processes. Hence there are hundreds of processes in a company. Each of these processes is interconnected into a total system that transforms inputs into outputs. Every process has customers (those who depend on it or are affected by it) and suppliers (those who provide the necessary input for that process). Consequently, everyone in an organization performs a transformation function (inputs into outputs), serves a customer (external or internal), or serves someone who is serving a customer.

It is apparent that this concept is directly related to how well the *processes* are managed—*all* of the processes in the organization that contribute directly or indirectly to quality as the customer defines it. The concept is illustrated in Figure 6-1. Note that the control component (quality assurance) has moved from measuring output (the traditional control system) to controlling the *continuous improvement of the process.* The feedback loop is closed.

The traditional approach to quality control was inspection of the final product, and this approach is still practiced by many firms. In this chapter, methods and techniques will be introduced that are significantly more advanced and more effective than the practice of "final inspection," which has been used for so long. Although the concepts in this chapter are not the last word in modern TQM, they represent substantial potential for improving quality, cost, and productivity in almost any company.

One of the primary objectives of TQM is to create processes in which individuals or groups will "do it right the first time" and "do the right things right." As suggested in Figure 6-2, individuals or groups can do the right things right or wrong and the wrong things right or wrong. The manner in which individuals do their work (process) can also be right or wrong. The following examples illustrate each of the four quadrants in Figure 6-2:[1]

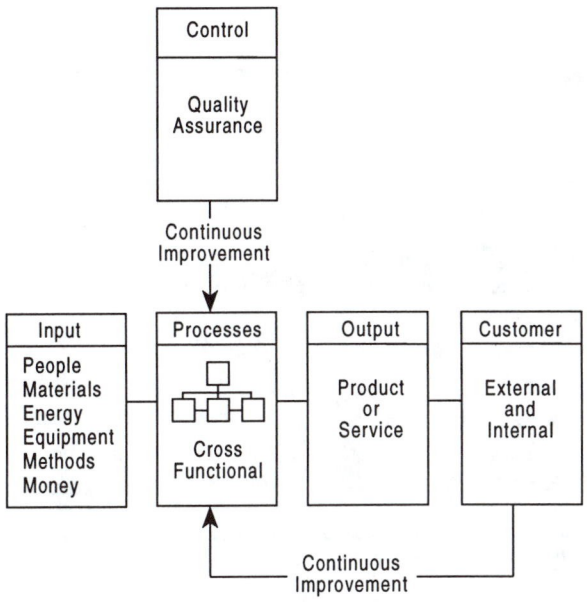

**Figure 6-1**    Management System

1. **Doing the right things wrong**
   - You have filled out the correct form, but the information is inaccurate.
   - Using the right equipment but not operating it correctly.
   - A nurse provides the necessary explanation to a sick patient, but in an unprofessional manner.

2. **Doing the wrong things wrong**
   - The accounts department sends an invoice to the wrong customer, and the calculations are incorrect (two processes are affected here—the billing process and the costing process).
   - Filling out the wrong expense reimbursement form and filling it out incorrectly.
   - Picking up the wrong work order and performing the work incorrectly.
   - Purchasing department orders the wrong parts and orders them several weeks late.

3. **Doing the wrong things right**
   Using the examples in #2 above:
   - The accounts department sends an invoice to the wrong customer, but the calculations are right.
   - Filling out the wrong expense reimbursement form, but filling it out correctly.

**HOW YOU DO IT**

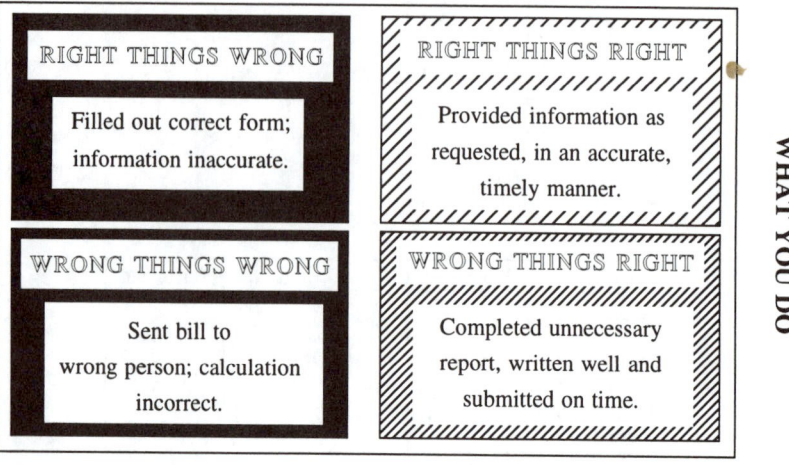

**Figure 6-2**    The Quality Grid

- Violating the optimal job sequence by picking up the wrong work order, but performing the work correctly.
- Completing an unnecessary report that is well written and submitted on time.

4. **Doing the right things right**
   - Providing the information as requested, in an accurate and timely manner.
   - Ordering the right parts in the right quantity, from the right vendor, within the lead time allowed.

The right things done right means meeting or exceeding the expectations of customers, both internal and external. It also means the elimination of waste, rework, and defects and conformance to valid requirements.

## A BRIEF HISTORY OF QUALITY CONTROL

Concern for product quality and process control is nothing new. Historians have traced the concept as far back as 3000 B.C. in Babylonia. Among the references to quality from the Code of Hammurabi, ruler of Babylonia, is the following excerpt: "The mason who builds a house which falls down and kills the inmate shall be put to death." This law reflects a concern for quality in antiquity.[2] Process control is a concept that may have begun with the pyramids of Egypt, when a system of standards for quarrying and dressing of stone was designed. One has only to examine the pyramids at Cheops to appreciate this remarkable achievement. Later, Greek architecture would surpass Egyptian architecture in the area of military applications. Centuries later, the shipbuilding operations in Venice introduced rudimentary production control and standardization.

Following the Industrial Revolution and the resulting factory system, quality and process control began to take on some of the characteristics that we know today. Specialization of labor in the factory demanded it. Interchangeability of parts was introduced by Eli Whitney when he manufactured 15,000 muskets for the federal government. This event was representative of the emerging era of mass production, when inspection by a skilled craftsman at a workbench was replaced by the specialized function of inspection conducted by individuals not directly involved in the production process.

Specialization of labor and quality assurance took a giant step forward in 1911 with the publication of Frederick W. Taylor's book *Principles of Scientific Management*.[3] This pioneering work had a profound effect on management thought and practice. Taylor's philosophy was one of extreme functional specialization, and he suggested eight functional bosses for the shop floor, one of whom was assigned the task of inspection:

> The inspector is responsible for the quality of the work, and both the workmen and the speed bosses must see that the work is finished to suit him. This man can, of course, do his work best if he is a master of the art of finishing work both well and quickly.[4]

Taylor later conceded that extreme functional specialization has its disadvantages, but his notion of process analysis and quality control by inspection of the final product still lives on in many firms today. Statistical quality control (SQC), the forerunner of today's TQM or total quality control, had its beginnings in the mid-1920s at the Western Electric plant of the Bell System. Walter Shewhart, a Bell Laboratories physicist, designed the original version of SQC for the zero-defects mass production of complex telephone exchanges and telephone sets. In 1931, Shewhart published his landmark book *Economic Control of Quality of Manufactured Product*.[5] This book provided a precise and measurable definition of quality control and developed statistical techniques for evaluating production and improving quality. During World War II, W. Edwards Deming and Joseph Juran, both former members of Shewhart's group, separately developed the versions used today.

It is generally accepted today that the Japanese owe their product leadership partly to adopting the precepts of Deming and Juran. According to Peter Drucker, U.S. industry ignored their contributions for 40 years and is only now converting to SQC.[6]

■ The Willimatic Division of Rogers Corporation, an IBM supplier, uses just-in-time techniques along with X-bar and R charts for key product attributes to achieve statistical process control. Rework is reduced by 40 percent, scrap by 50 percent, and productivity is increased by 14 percent.[7]

## PRODUCT INSPECTION VS. PROCESS CONTROL

*Structure follows strategy.*

*Nothing happens until a sale is made.*

*If you can't measure it, you can't manage it.*

These statements are typical of the popular catchphrases adopted by particular functions (e.g., planning, sales, accounting) within the business. The popularity of the expression usually means that there is a measure of truth behind it. Truisms in the field of quality management include "don't inspect the product, inspect the process" and "you can't inspect it in, you've got to build it in."

There is sound thinking behind these two statements. In the previous discussion of the control process, the point was made that controlling the output of the system *after the fact* was historical action, and nothing could be done to correct the variation after it had already occurred. This is feedback control. The same is true of inspecting the product. The variation or the defect has already occurred. What is needed is a feedforward system that will prevent defects and variations. Better yet is a system that will improve the process. This is the idea behind process control (Figure 6-1).

What is the process? Does it begin with material inspection at the receiving dock and end with final inspection, or does it begin with design and end with delivery to the customer? Does it begin with market research and end with after-sale service? If we take the broader view, the process might begin with the concept of the product idea and extend through the life cycle of the product to ultimate maturity and phaseout. This definition matches the concept of TQM.

It is clear that in the philosophy of TQM, most (if not all) business functions and activities (i.e., processes) are interrelated and none stands alone—not purchasing, engineering, shipping, order processing, or manufacturing. Key business objectives and organization success are dependent on cross-functional processes. Moreover, these processes must change as environments change. The conclusion emerges that true process optimization requires the application of tools and methods in all activities, not just manufacturing.

Historically, there have been two major barriers to effective process control. The first has been the tendency to focus on volume of output rather than quality of output. Volume of production has been the major objective in the mistaken notion that more units of output means lower unit cost. Another barrier is the quality control system that measures products or service against a set of internal conformance specifications that may or may not relate to customer expectations. The result in many cases has been inferior quality products that are reworked or scrapped or, worse, products that customers *did not buy*. As will be discussed in Chapter 11, the cost of poor quality can amount to 25 to 30 percent of sales revenues. The profit potential in quality improvement is greater than simply improved production of inferior quality.

> ■ Bytex Corporation manufactures electronic matrix switches for Citicorp, MasterCard, American Express, and others. The company has focused on understanding the process, concentrating on eliminating non-value-added transactions. Cycle time is down by 60 percent, inventory down by 43 percent, final assembly time down by 52 percent, and floor space down by 30 percent. The resulting product is superb.[8]

## MOVING FROM INSPECTION TO PROCESS CONTROL

Process control may still require measurement that is determined by inspection, but the activity of inspection is now transformed into a diagnostic role. The objective is not merely to discover defects, but rather to identify and remove the cause(s) of defects or variations. Process control now becomes problem solving for *continuous improvement*. Moving from inspection to process control takes place in steps or phases:

| Step | Action |
| --- | --- |
| 1 | Process characterization<br>Definition of process requirements and identification of key variables |
| 2 | Develop standards and measures of output<br>Involve work force |
| 3 | Monitor compliance to standards and review for better control<br>Identify any additional variables that affect quality |
| 4 | Identify and remove cause(s) of defects or variations (this requires a step-by-step documentation of the process and process control charting) |
| 5 | Achievement of process control with improved stability and reduced variation |

## STATISTICAL QUALITY CONTROL

This is the oldest and most widely known of the several process control methods. It involves the use of statistical techniques, such as control charts, to analyze a work process or its outputs. The data can be used to identify variations and to take appropriate actions in order to achieve and maintain a state of statistical control (predetermined upper and lower limits) and to improve the capability of the process. It is the best-known innovation among Deming's ideas.

Rigorously applied, SQC can virtually eliminate the production of defective parts.[9] By identifying the quality that can be expected from a given production process, control can be built into the process itself. Moreover, the method can spot the causes of variations—incoming materials, machine calibration, temperature of soldering iron, or whatever.

Despite the maturity of the method and its proven benefit, many firms do not take full advantage of it. One survey found that 49 percent of responding electronics manufacturers reported using SQC techniques, but 75 percent of them also continued to use traditional 100 percent inspection. This is in an industry where quality in the manufacturing process is essential.

> ■ At Motorola, SQC has been integrated into the corporate culture and is being applied in all areas of the plant. Steps to place a process under statistical control include (1) characterizing the process, (2) controlling it, and (3) adjusting the process when non-random deviations are observed. Six sigma is the goal.

The term *statistical process control* (SPC) can be misleading because it is so frequently confined to manufacturing processes, whereas the methods can be useful for improving results in other non-manufacturing areas such as sales and staff activities. Moreover, the methods can be used in many of the activities and functions of service industries. It is also worth noting that the only universal technique for SQC is logical reasoning applied to the improvement of a process. Thus it is a systematic way of problem solving.

A *process* is a set of causes and conditions and a set of steps comprising an activity that transforms inputs into outputs. Consider the number of processes involved in the airline industry: the process of taking and confirming a reservation, of baggage handling, of loading passengers, of meal service, etc. The process is any set of people, equipment, procedures, and conditions that work together to produce a result—an output.

The process is expected to add value to the inputs in order to produce an output. The ratio of output to input is called productivity, and the objectives are to (1) increase the ratio of output to input and (2) reduce the variation in the output of the process. If the variation is too small or insignificant to have any effect on the usefulness of the product or service, the output is said to be within tolerance. Should the output fall outside the desired tolerance, the process can be improved and returned to tolerance by defining the cause of the change (the problem) and taking action to make sure that the cause does not recur.

SPC is a method of monitoring, controlling, and improving a process through statistical analysis. It consists of four steps: measuring the process, eliminating variances in the process, monitoring the process to ensure adherence to parameters, and improving the process.[10]

SQC and its companion SPC were developed in the United States in the 1930s and 1940s by W. A. Shewhart, W. E. Deming, J. M. Juran, and others. These techniques (some call them philosophies) have been used for decades by some American firms and many Japanese companies. Despite the proven effectiveness of the techniques, many U.S. firms are reluctant to use them.[11]

The approach is designed to identify underlying causes of problems which cause process variations that are outside predetermined tolerances and to implement controls to fix the problem. The basic approach contains the following steps:

1. Awareness that a problem exists.
2. Determine the specific problem to be solved.
3. Diagnose the causes of the problem.
4. Determine and implement remedies to solve the problem.
5. Implement controls to hold the gains achieved by solving the problem.

## TOOLS FOR STATISTICAL QUALITY CONTROL

Process improvement depends to a large extent on the gathering and analysis of data which are abundant in any organization that is involved in process problems. The basic techniques are (1) data collection, (2) data display, and (3) problem analysis.

■ To illustrate the use of these SQC tools, consider the case of the National Machine Tool Company, a manufacturer of chuck jaws for the metals-working industry. The company is experiencing rejects and reworked jobs due to unknown causes. A chuck jaw is made from metal bar stock (grinding, drilling, cutting, etc.) and is a holding device used on a machine for metal turning and indexing.

## Data Collection

A **check sheet** is an aid used in assembling and compiling data concerning a problem. It is used to collect data on a process in order to determine whether any unusual or unwanted elements are present. The functions of a check sheet are

- Production process distribution checks
- Defective item checks
- Defect location checks
- Defect cause checks
- Checkup confirmation checks

  ■ At the National Machine Tool Company (discussed earlier), a team (quality circle) identified the problem as "loss of time due to reworked jobs" and agreed that in order to determine the cause(s) of the problems it would be necessary to find out which department(s) were experiencing excessive rework. As a result, data were collected and recorded on the check sheet shown in Figure 6-3. It was evident from this check sheet that department number 55 has excessive rework.

## Data Display

After data are collected, they can be converted into a variety of forms for *display* and *analysis*. The most common forms are shown in Figure 6-4.

A **control chart** reflects the ongoing control of a process and signals an alarm when the process exceeds the control limits. When the line moves beyond the control limit (dotted line in Figure 6-4a), it can signal a problem. Once set

Weeks

| Department | No. 1 | No. 2 | No. 3 | No. 4 | No. 5 | No. 6 | No. 7 | No. 8 | TOTAL |
|---|---|---|---|---|---|---|---|---|---|
| 11 | | I | | II | | I | | | 4 |
| 66 | I | | I | | II | | II | I | 7 |
| 55 | III | I | II | II | I | HH | II | IIII | 20 |
| 22 | I | II | | III | II | | I | I | 10 |
| Other | | | I | | I | | II | | 4 |

**Figure 6-3**   Check Sheet of Reworked Jobs

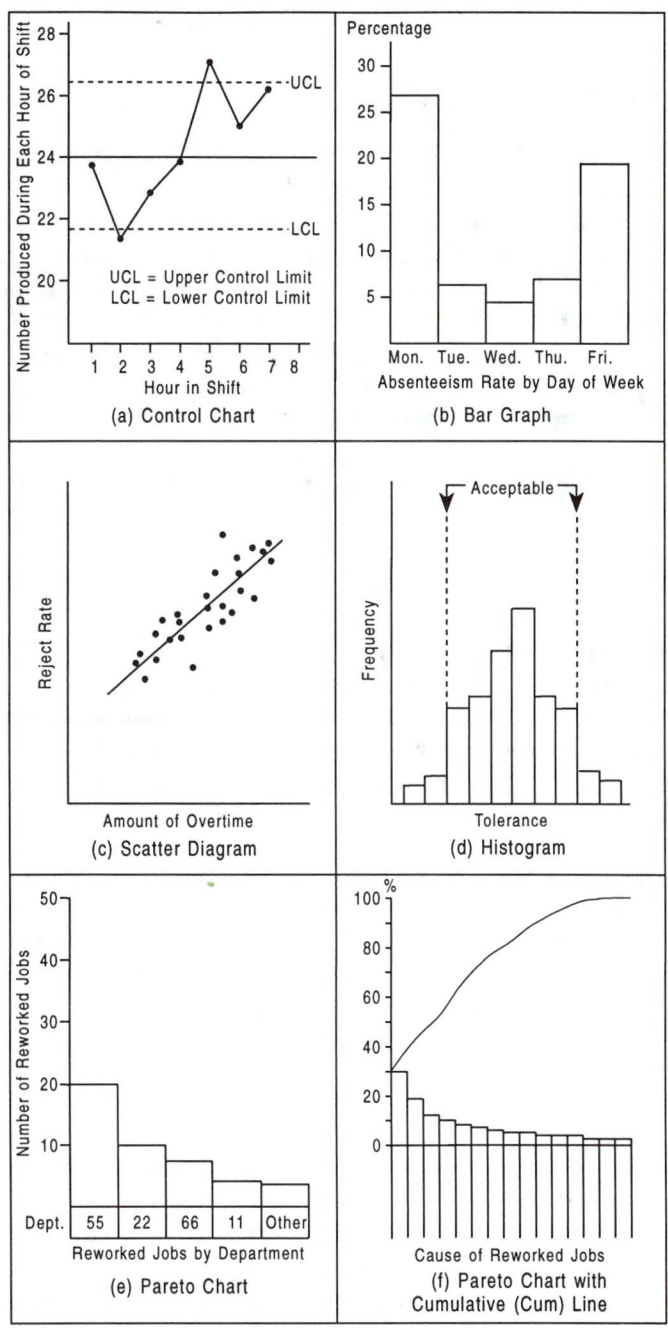

(a) Control Chart

(b) Bar Graph

(c) Scatter Diagram

(d) Histogram

(e) Pareto Chart

(f) Pareto Chart with Cumulative (Cum) Line

**Figure 6-4**    Methods of Displaying Data

up, it is an effective tool for day-to-day monitoring and management of a process.

A **bar graph** (Figure 6-4b), or column graph, summarizes and presents data in an easily understood manner.

A **scatter diagram** (Figure 6-4c) depicts the relationship between two kinds of data, and the relationship forms a pattern.

A **histogram** (Figure 6-4d) is a vertical bar graph showing the distribution of data in terms of the frequency of occurrence for specific values of data.

A **Pareto diagram** (Figure 6-4e) is the most widely used statistical tool in problem analysis. Indeed, it is almost universal in process control problem solving. It is a graphic way of summarizing data in order to focus attention on the main reason(s) why some result is occurring and to produce a cause-and-effect relationship. The *cumulative distribution line,* or "cum" line (Figure 6-4f), is an additional dimension of the Pareto diagram. The "cum" line displays the cumulative distribution of events by percentage. The total of all events is 100 percent.

## PROBLEM ANALYSIS

The **cause-and-effect diagram**, sometimes known as the "fishbone" or Ishikawa diagram, was developed and named by Professor Kaoru Ishikawa of the University of Tokyo in 1950. It is an excellent tool for organizing and documenting potential causes of problems in all areas and at all levels in the organization. As a *brainstorming* device, it is a good way to stimulate ideas during problem-solving meetings.[12]

■ Returning to the case of the National Machine Tool Company, the fishbone diagram was used to brainstorm about possible causes of excess reworked jobs. The result of the brainstorming session is shown in Figure 6-5, which also illustrates the construction and use of the cause-and-effect (fishbone) diagram.

This technique, as demonstrated in the National Machine Tool case, consists of defining an *effect* (reworked jobs) and then determining its contributing factors (*causes*).

Cause-and-effect diagrams are drawn to clearly illustrate the various factors that affect product quality and productivity by sorting out and relating the causes of problems. In a brainstorming session, the causes identified by group members or the team can be listed on a blackboard or flip chart and later transferred to a cause-and-effect diagram. A more experienced group might prepare the diagram directly as the causes are given. Reasons for using the cause-and-effect diagram include:

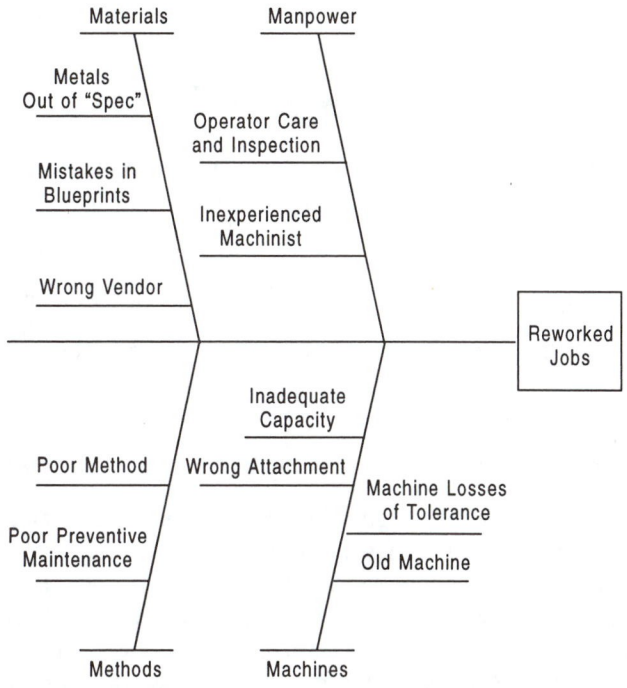

**Figure 6-5**   Cause-and-Effect Diagram

1. The diagram is a guide for discussion and focuses on the subject at hand. It serves as a measure of progress and indicates how far the discussion has progressed.

2. By encouraging group members to participate, it becomes an educational tool. Knowledge is also shared.

3. It encourages data gathering. Examination of the causes of problems leads to the gathering of additional data in order to support and validate the causes.

## PARETO ANALYSIS

Dr. J. M. Juran popularized the term "the Pareto principle" while teaching quality control methods to the Japanese following World War II. This process is derived from *Pareto's law,* named for the Italian economist Alfredo Pareto (1848–1923). The concept of this law is that any cause that results from a multiplicity of effects is primarily the result of the impact of a minor percentage of all the causes. Conversely, a majority of the causative factors play a minor role in the observed effect. In his study of the distribution of wealth and income, he observed that wealth was concentrated in the hands of the few, while the great majority of the population was poor.

This technique is similar to the "80–20" rule:

1. 80 percent of inventory value is in 20 percent of the inventory items
2. 80 percent of sales volume comes from 20 percent of the customers
3. 80 percent of overdue accounts are owed by 20 percent of the customers

Some examples where Pareto analysis is a universal tool include:

1. A problem in inventory reduction where there are large numbers of separate items
2. An analysis of sales volume by product
3. A breakdown of accounts receivable by dollar amount and customer

Dr. Juran, in his book *Managerial Breakthrough,* stated it succinctly: "The vital few are everywhere, but masquerading under a variety of aliases. In their more benevolent forms they are known by such names as key accounts or star salesmen. In their weak moments they are known as the bottlenecks, chronic clinkers, deadbeats, most wanted criminals, critical components." Thus, this separation of the *vital few* from the *trivial many* has universal application in identifying the important problems and establishing priorities.

■   In the case of the National Machine Tool Company, the data from the check sheet (Figure 6-3) were transcribed and converted to the Pareto chart shown in Figure 6-6. It becomes evident that the major problem can be traced to department 55.

## The Case of the Printing Company

The more sophisticated problem of sorting a conglomerate mixture into the vital few and the trivial many is illustrated by a cause-and-effect diagram (Figure 6-7) and a subsequent Pareto analysis (Figure 6-8) for a specific case involving a company using plastics for printing and packaging materials. The company was concerned about the number of defects coming off the machine production line, such as misprints, print out of register, warpage, etc.

Team members selected this as a project and through brainstorming prepared a cause-and-effect diagram, as shown in Figure 6-7. After a thorough study of the causes and the effect, the team agreed that a monitor would be appointed to check the causes of all defects over a four-week period. From the information collected during this period, with the use of a check sheet, a Pareto chart was developed for the circle meeting (Figure 6-8).

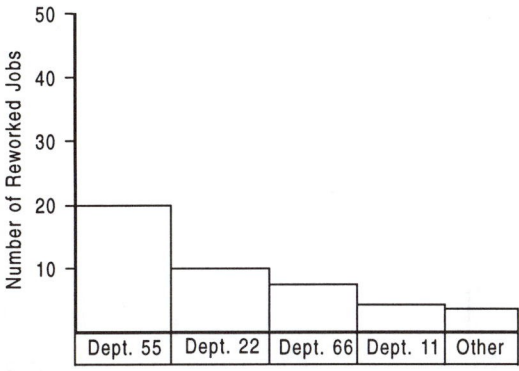

**Figure 6-6**   Pareto Chart of Reworked Jobs

As can be seen from the Pareto chart in Figure 6-8, the vital few (e.g., "tension material" and "tracking") made up 46 percent of the causes for defects. This graphically illustrates the major areas that need attention.

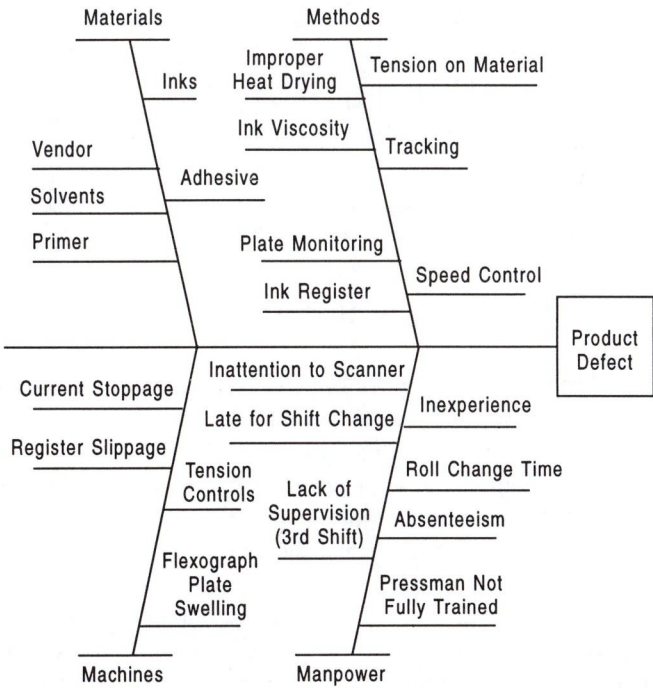

**Figure 6-7**   Cause-and-Effect Diagram

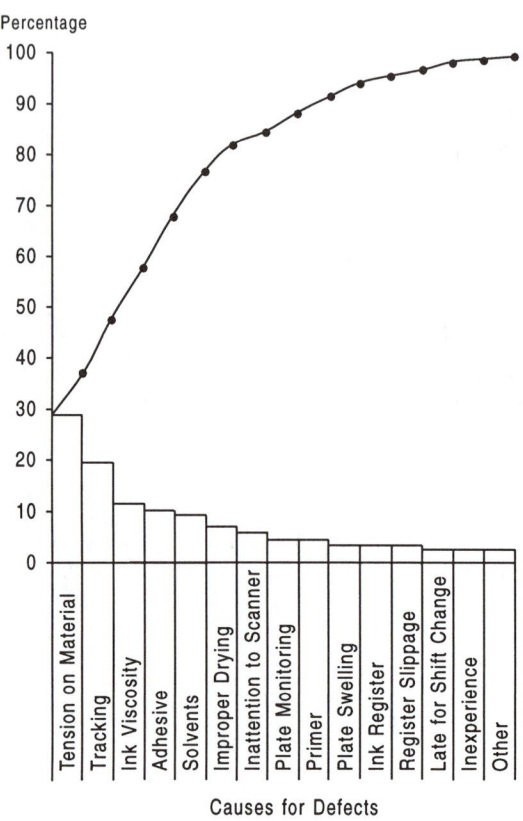

**Figure 6-8** Pareto Chart with Cumulative Total

## CONTROL CHARTS[13]

A control chart is a special type of run chart with limits. It shows the amount and nature of variation in the process over time. It also enables pattern interpretation and detection of changes in the process.

There are three main reasons for using a control chart. First, it is used to monitor a process in order to determine if the process is operating with only chance causes of variation. If it is, then the process is said to be in statistical control. If it is not, then the process is said to be out-of-control. If the process is out-of-control, then the control chart can be used to help identify the assignable causes of variation and correct the process. Second, control charts are used to estimate the parameters of a process. Third, control charts are used in reducing the variability of a process.

The type of control chart depends on the type of data used in its construction. If the data are based on measurements (such as pounds, inches, etc.), then the data are said to be **continuous** and a variables control chart is used. If the data are based on counting (such as the number of defects in a product), then the data are said to be **discrete** and an attributes control chart is used. There are two types of variables control charts. One, based on averages, is called the X-bar ($\overline{X}$) chart. An $\overline{X}$ chart is accompanied by either a range (R) chart or a standard deviation (S) chart. The second type of variables control chart is based on the individual measurements and is called an X chart. It is accompanied by a moving range (MR) chart. There are four types of control charts for attributes: the p chart, np chart, c chart, and u chart. The p chart plots the fraction non-conforming. The np chart plots the number non-conforming. The c chart plots the number of non-conformities. The u chart plots the number of non-conformities per unit.

## Uses of Control Charts

There are three basic uses of control charts. First, they are used to monitor a given process. Because a control chart shows the degree and nature of variation over time, it can be used to determine whether a process is in a state of statistical control or is out-of-control. If it is out-of-control, the chart aids in quickly finding the assignable causes of the out-of-control condition, which enables taking corrective action before too many bad products can be produced. If a process is in-control, continued monitoring allows for quicker detection of process changes. It also allows for process improvement.

Second, control charts are used to estimate the parameters (mean, variation) of a process. By knowing the parameters of a process, the output and the variability of the output can be predicted.

Third, control charts are used to improve a process. Once a process is in a state of statistical control, efforts to reduce process variability can begin. By reducing the variability of the process, the overall quality of the final product increases, which reduces scrap and rework and increases profits.

In short, the emphasis in using control charts is on the early detection and prevention of problems. By preventing problems from occurring, productivity and profits increase.

The two types of charts in common use are **variables** control charts and control charts for **attributes**. Variables charts are used to monitor measurable quality characteristics of a process. Measurable quality characteristics include weight, temperature, viscosity, etc. Anything that can be measured can be monitored using a variables chart. It monitors the mean value (the center line on the chart) and the variability of the quality characteristic being studied. The mean value is monitored by an X-bar ($\overline{X}$) chart or an individuals (X) chart. Variability is measured via a range (R) or moving range (MR) chart or a standard deviation (S) chart. A detailed treatment of the construction and use of these charts is beyond the scope of this book.[14] For purposes of illustration, the $\overline{X}$ and R charts will be used.

## Example: $\overline{X}$ and R Charts

A line foreman wants to establish statistical control on shaft lengths being cut. He decides to use $\overline{X}$ and R charts. The foreman collects 25 samples, each of size 5. The data collected are shown in Table 6-1.

**Table 6-1**  Shaft Length Measurements (Inches)

| Sample # | Sample observations | | | | | $\overline{X}$ | R |
|---|---|---|---|---|---|---|---|
| 1 | 9.26 | 10.44 | 10.39 | 9.87 | 10.26 | 10.04 | 1.18 |
| 2 | 10.92 | 10.08 | 9.97 | 10.16 | 9.30 | 10.09 | 1.62 |
| 3 | 10.10 | 10.61 | 8.62 | 10.24 | 10.17 | 9.95 | 1.99 |
| 4 | 10.17 | 9.24 | 10.60 | 10.08 | 10.51 | 10.12 | 1.35 |
| 5 | 10.29 | 10.36 | 10.39 | 10.58 | 9.96 | 10.32 | 0.63 |
| 6 | 9.84 | 9.52 | 10.11 | 9.65 | 10.18 | 9.86 | 0.66 |
| 7 | 9.84 | 9.77 | 10.47 | 10.25 | 10.28 | 10.12 | 0.70 |
| 8 | 9.94 | 9.35 | 9.61 | 9.09 | 10.09 | 9.62 | 0.99 |
| 9 | 10.18 | 11.18 | 10.16 | 10.68 | 10.80 | 10.60 | 1.02 |
| 10 | 9.46 | 10.15 | 10.80 | 9.57 | 9.20 | 9.84 | 1.61 |
| 11 | 9.64 | 9.71 | 10.38 | 10.23 | 9.92 | 9.98 | 0.74 |
| 12 | 10.54 | 10.76 | 10.83 | 9.97 | 9.91 | 10.40 | 0.92 |
| 13 | 10.41 | 9.67 | 9.88 | 10.28 | 9.77 | 10.00 | 0.75 |
| 14 | 9.72 | 8.70 | 9.81 | 9.39 | 9.68 | 9.46 | 1.12 |
| 15 | 9.35 | 10.28 | 10.86 | 11.11 | 10.05 | 10.33 | 1.76 |
| 16 | 9.11 | 10.22 | 9.50 | 9.82 | 9.65 | 9.66 | 1.11 |
| 17 | 9.53 | 10.12 | 10.03 | 9.71 | 9.72 | 9.82 | 0.60 |
| 18 | 10.14 | 8.98 | 9.84 | 9.74 | 9.68 | 9.68 | 1.16 |
| 19 | 9.81 | 10.18 | 9.95 | 10.40 | 9.71 | 10.01 | 0.69 |
| 20 | 10.12 | 10.01 | 10.01 | 9.75 | 9.25 | 9.83 | 0.87 |
| 21 | 10.30 | 9.95 | 9.55 | 9.84 | 10.46 | 10.02 | 0.91 |
| 22 | 10.73 | 9.78 | 9.27 | 11.03 | 9.99 | 10.16 | 1.76 |
| 23 | 9.89 | 9.82 | 9.40 | 10.67 | 9.43 | 9.84 | 1.27 |
| 24 | 9.99 | 10.20 | 9.37 | 9.05 | 10.27 | 9.78 | 1.21 |
| 25 | 10.10 | 10.25 | 9.51 | 9.16 | 10.17 | 9.84 | 1.09 |
| | | | | | **Total** | 249.35 | 27.70 |

$$\overline{\overline{X}} = 9.97 \qquad \overline{R} = 1.11$$

When setting up the $\overline{X}$ and R charts, begin with the R chart to ensure that the variability within samples is in-control. Using the data in Table 6-1, we find that the center line for the R chart is

$$\overline{R} = \frac{27.70}{25} = 1.11$$

For samples of size 5, the values for $D_3$ and $D_4$ are found from Appendix A to be 0.00 and 2.114, respectively. Therefore, the control limits for the R chart can be determined from the equations in Table 6-2:

$$UCL = \overline{R}D_4 = (1.11)(2.114) = 2.35$$

$$LCL = \overline{R}D_3 = (1.11)(0.00) = 0.00$$

where UCL = upper control limit and LCL = lower control limit. The R chart is shown in Figure 6-9. As can be seen, there is no indication of any out-of-control conditions. Since the within-sample variability is in-control, the $\overline{X}$ chart can now be constructed. From Table 6-1, the center line for the $\overline{X}$ chart is

**Table 6-2**    Control Chart Formula Summary[a]

| Chart | $3\sigma$ control limits | Center line |
|---|---|---|
| X | $\overline{X} \pm \dfrac{3\overline{MR}}{d_2}$ | $\overline{X}$ |
| $\overline{X}$ (using R) | $\overline{\overline{X}} \pm A_2\overline{R}$ | $\overline{\overline{X}}$ |
| $\overline{X}$ (using S) | $\overline{\overline{X}} \pm A_3\overline{S}$ | $\overline{\overline{X}}$ |
| R | $UCL = D_4\overline{R}$ <br> $LCL = D_3\overline{R}$ | $\overline{R}$ |
| MR | $UCL = D_4\overline{MR}$ <br> $LCL = D_3\overline{MR}$ | $\overline{MR}$ |
| S | $UCL = B_4\overline{S}$ <br> $LCL = B_3\overline{S}$ | $\overline{S}$ |

[a] For statistical development of these formulas, refer to J. A. Swift, *Introduction to Modern Statistical Quality Control and Management,* Boca Raton, Fla.: St. Lucie Press, 1995.

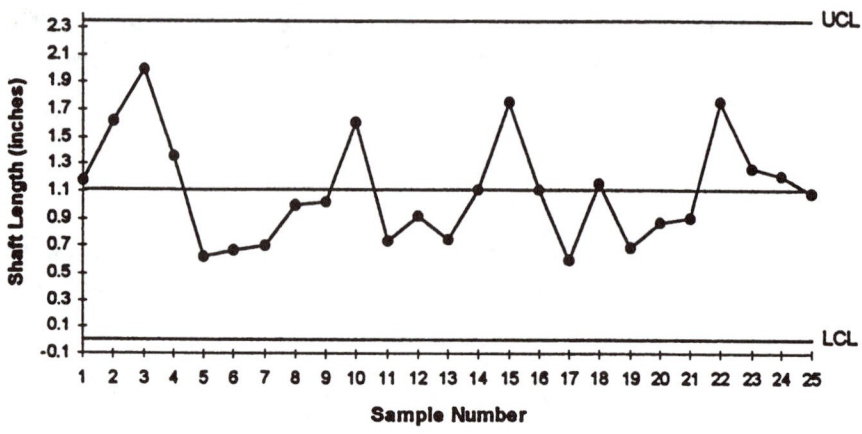

**Figure 6-9**    R Chart for Example

$$\bar{\bar{X}} = \frac{249.35}{25} = 9.97$$

From Appendix A, the value of $A_2$ is found to be 0.577 for a sample size of 5. Using the equations from Table 6-2, the control limits can be determined:

$$UCL = \bar{\bar{X}} + A_2\bar{R} = 9.97 + (0.577)(1.11) = 10.61$$

$$LCL = \bar{\bar{X}} - A_2\bar{R} = 9.97 - (0.577)(1.11) = 9.33$$

The $\bar{X}$ chart is shown in Figure 6-10. The chart shows no indication of an out-of-control condition. Therefore, both the R chart and the $\bar{X}$ chart indicate that the process is in-control.

## Control Chart for Attributes

It is often inconvenient, impractical, or impossible to take numerical measurements of the type necessary to set up variables control charts. In these cases, the quality characteristic of a unit is judged, or classified, as either conforming or non-conforming based on whether or not it has certain attributes (leaks/does not leak, works/does not work, etc.). Another means of judging the item is to count the number of non-conformities that appear on the unit (number of scratches, dents, holes, etc.). These types of quality characteristics are referred to as **attributes**. Attribute data can have only two values, such as pass/fail, conforming/non-conforming, present/absent, etc. Even though attribute data cannot be

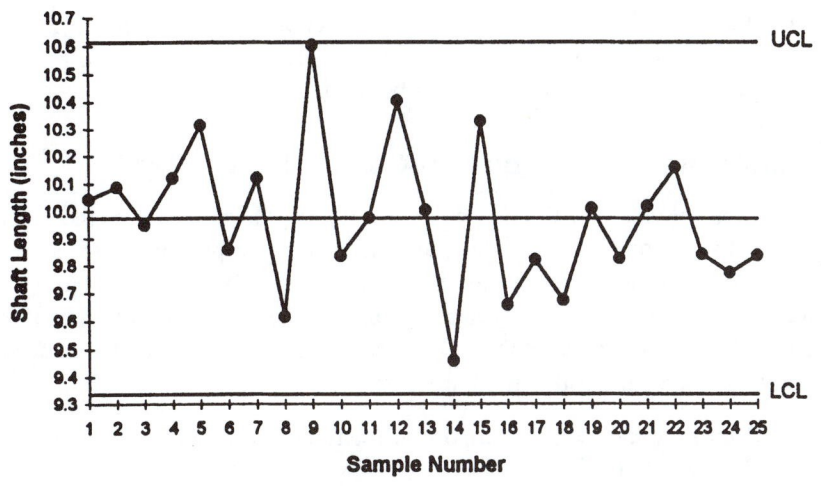

**Figure 6-10**    $\overline{X}$ Chart for Example

measured, they can be counted. There are four special control charts for analyz-ing attribute data:

- **p chart.**  Plots the fraction non-conforming per sample
- **np chart.**  Plots the number non-conforming per sample
- **c chart.**  Plots the number of non-conformities per inspection unit
- **u chart.**  Plots the average number of non-conformities per inspection unit

The following are several basic terms that are used in connection with attributes charts. It is important to understand them.

- **Non-conformity.**  A characteristic that does not meet requirements or speci-fication. Non-conformities provide reasons for not accepting (rejecting) the unit. A non-conformity is also called a **defect**.
- **Non-conforming.**  A unit that is rejected. A non-conforming unit contains more than the allowable number of non-conformities. However, in many cases, the allowable number of non-conformities is one. A non-conforming unit is also called a **defective** unit.

One advantage of using attributes charts is that they can handle multiple characteristics. Therefore, attributes charts typically require more inspection. The inspection is less precise (no measurements to be taken and recorded) and is usually cheaper (no special training needed).

Again, a detailed treatment of the construction and use of these charts is beyond the scope of this book. For purposes of illustration, the control chart for fraction non-conforming (p chart) will be used.

## Control Chart for Fraction Non-Conforming (p Chart)

The control chart for fraction non-conforming is also known as the p chart. The "p" stands for proportion because it measures the proportion of non-conforming units in a group of units being inspected. The p chart monitors the fraction non-conforming of a process by plotting sample fraction non-conforming over time. The p chart is the most versatile and widely used attribute chart. It can be used for the following purposes:

1. To determine the average proportion (or fraction) of non-conforming units over a given time span
2. To signal a change in the average fraction non-conforming
3. To identify out-of-control points that call for immediate action
4. To suggest places to implement $\overline{X}$ and R charts

The p chart is based on the **binomial distribution**. The binomial distribution assumes that:

1. For every trial, there are only two possible outcomes (e.g., pass/fail, conforming/non-conforming).
2. The same trial is repeated any number of times.
3. The repeated trials are independent of one another. For example, the outcome of the second trial is not affected by (or dependent on) the first trial, and the outcome of trial $n$ is not affected by the outcomes of trial 1 through trial $n - 1$.
4. The probability of a specific outcome remains constant from trial to trial.

The p chart plots the fraction non-conforming per sample. This means that the unit either conforms or does not conform. There are only two possible outcomes. The probability of pass/fail of each item remains constant from unit to unit. Also, the probability of a unit passing/failing is independent of how previous units tested. Therefore, the binomial distribution describes the p chart.

Typically, $p$ is not known. It is estimated from:

$$\overline{p} = \frac{\sum_{i=1}^{m} D_i}{\sum_{i=1}^{m} n_i} \qquad (6\text{-}1)$$

where $D_i$ = number of non-conforming units in sample $i$, $n_i$ = number of units in sample $i$, and $m$ = number of samples. This allows the control limits for the p chart to be determined from:

$$\text{center line} = \bar{p} \tag{6-2a}$$

$$\text{UCL} = \bar{p} + 3\sqrt{\frac{\bar{p}(1 - \bar{p})}{n}} \tag{6-2b}$$

$$\text{LCL} = \bar{p} - 3\sqrt{\frac{\bar{p}(1 - \bar{p})}{n}} \tag{6-2c}$$

Equation 6-2c may give a value less than zero for the lower control limit. Whenever this occurs, a lower control limit of zero is used.

### Example

A manager wants to keep track of the number of non-conforming circuit testers being produced. There are six types of defects which can cause a circuit tester to be considered defective or non-conforming:

1. Mechanical defect
2. Short
3. Open
4. Peak inverse voltage (PIV)
5. Voltage forward (VF)
6. Reverse polarity (RP)

The manager sets up a data collection sheet and begins to collect the information on the defective circuit testers being produced. The manager sets the sample size at 2000. The data collected for a period of 23 days are given in Table 6-3. The average fraction non-conforming can be determined using Equation 6-1:

$$\bar{p} = \frac{\displaystyle\sum_{i=1}^{m} D_i}{\displaystyle\sum_{i=1}^{m} n_i} = \frac{5851}{46,000} = 0.1272$$

**Table 6-3** Data Collected on Non-Conforming Circuit Testers

| Day | Mechanical defect | Short | Open | PIV | VF | RP | Total defective | Total inspected | Fraction non-conforming |
|-----|------|------|------|------|------|------|------|------|------|
| 1  | 38 | 50 | 67 | 78  | 7  | 1 | 241 | 2000 | 12.05 |
| 2  | 47 | 61 | 78 | 90  | 3  | 2 | 281 | 2000 | 14.05 |
| 3  | 42 | 51 | 89 | 99  | 5  | 0 | 286 | 2000 | 14.30 |
| 4  | 50 | 50 | 76 | 103 | 4  | 0 | 283 | 2000 | 14.15 |
| 5  | 12 | 47 | 72 | 98  | 2  | 1 | 232 | 2000 | 11.60 |
| 6  | 11 | 64 | 88 | 87  | 8  | 0 | 258 | 2000 | 12.90 |
| 7  | 5  | 49 | 71 | 93  | 12 | 1 | 231 | 2000 | 11.55 |
| 8  | 15 | 52 | 69 | 92  | 14 | 2 | 244 | 2000 | 12.20 |
| 9  | 13 | 63 | 70 | 98  | 7  | 3 | 254 | 2000 | 12.70 |
| 10 | 9  | 72 | 76 | 87  | 9  | 5 | 258 | 2000 | 12.90 |
| 11 | 8  | 67 | 77 | 86  | 13 | 0 | 251 | 2000 | 12.55 |
| 12 | 12 | 59 | 71 | 80  | 11 | 0 | 233 | 2000 | 11.65 |
| 13 | 22 | 62 | 74 | 82  | 9  | 1 | 250 | 2000 | 12.50 |
| 14 | 9  | 61 | 63 | 90  | 6  | 2 | 231 | 2000 | 11.55 |
| 15 | 17 | 83 | 64 | 97  | 8  | 1 | 270 | 2000 | 13.50 |
| 16 | 19 | 65 | 68 | 98  | 7  | 1 | 258 | 2000 | 12.90 |
| 17 | 18 | 50 | 79 | 104 | 4  | 0 | 255 | 2000 | 12.75 |
| 18 | 14 | 51 | 64 | 118 | 3  | 1 | 251 | 2000 | 12.55 |
| 19 | 20 | 57 | 77 | 96  | 7  | 0 | 257 | 2000 | 12.85 |
| 20 | 17 | 60 | 63 | 98  | 5  | 0 | 243 | 2000 | 12.15 |
| 21 | 16 | 68 | 79 | 114 | 3  | 1 | 281 | 2000 | 14.05 |
| 22 | 14 | 61 | 71 | 92  | 11 | 0 | 249 | 2000 | 12.45 |
| 23 | 10 | 68 | 78 | 89  | 8  | 1 | 254 | 2000 | 12.70 |

The control limits for the p chart can be found from Equations 6-2b and 6-2c:

$$\text{UCL} = \bar{p} + 3\sqrt{\frac{\bar{p}(1 - \bar{p})}{n}} = 0.1272 + 3\sqrt{\frac{0.1272(1 - 0.1272)}{2000}} = 0.1496$$

$$\text{LCL} = \bar{p} - 3\sqrt{\frac{\bar{p}(1 - \bar{p})}{n}} = 0.1272 - 3\sqrt{\frac{0.1272(1 - 0.1272)}{2000}} = 0.1048$$

The p chart for the fraction non-conforming is displayed in Figure 6-11. The process appears to be in-control, and the average fraction non-conforming is 12.72 percent.

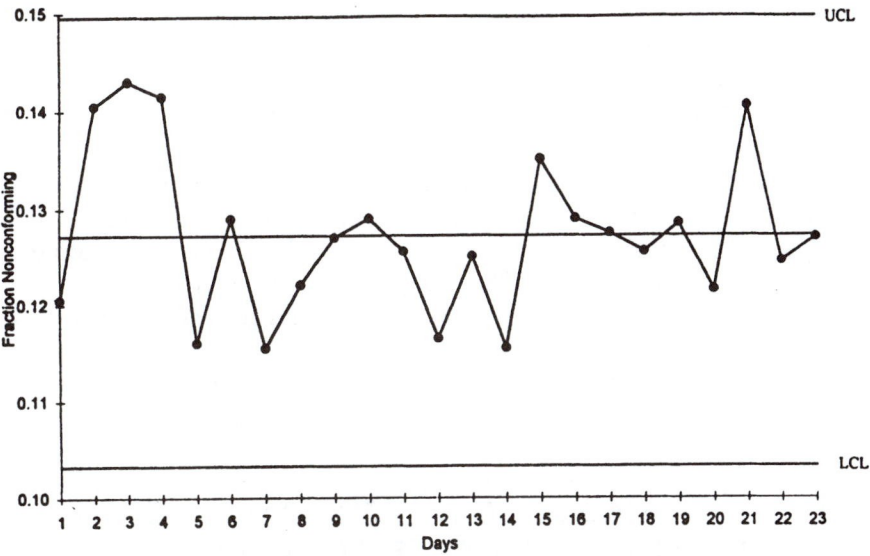

**Figure 6-11**    p Chart for Circuit Testers

## The Limits of Statistical Process Control

*To survive in today's competitive era of rapidly changing product models (some factories seldom make the same products two months in a row), factories must adopt wide-variety, small-lot production. This kind of production only runs smoothly with an accelerated cycle of discovering problems, finding causes, implementing countermeasures, and revising standards.*

Shigeru Nakamura[15]

In the early 1980s, the Big Three automakers and other manufacturers struggled to keep abreast of Japanese imports, products whose quality was clearly superior. How were these levels achieved? Japanese quality was explained, at first, by their work ethic and attitude as well as their use of consensus decision making and worker involvement. Unable to quickly adapt these characteristics in U.S. companies, the Big Three automakers turned to the use of statistical tools.

Due, in part, to the emergence of other tools and techniques (e.g., organization development, team involvement, quality function deployment, theory of constraints, kaizen, reengineering, just-in-time inventory systems), SPC has lost some of its luster. Other reasons include the manufacturing changes required to meet customer demands for more features and options and more customization of products. The result has been more part numbers, manufacturing complexity, and a progression of characteristics that require control. Henry Ford's motto, "You can have any color you want as long as it's black," no longer applies.

*Quality Progress*[16] reports a situation in which engineers had identified 72 different characteristics to be controlled with control charts. Each characteristic had an X and range (R) chart associated with it. This meant there were 144 different graphs to maintain. The enormous quantity of data necessitated a separate meeting room in which to hang all the control charts. The result was data overload. The amazing thing was that the 72 different characteristics, 144 graphs, and dedicated display room were for a single part. The data represented only one of hundreds of items manufactured at the facility.

Fortunately, quality professionals are designing new techniques and modifications of the old in order to make SPC the quality tool that it has been.

## MANUFACTURING TO SPECIFICATION VS. MANUFACTURING TO REDUCE VARIATIONS

Among production managers who manufacture to specifications or those who depend upon final inspection, the common problem can be traced to the control loop. Defect statistics are generated by inspection, but appropriate action is not taken to define problems, determine cause(s), and correct variations. Companies continue to live with a reject rate that is considered to be "normal," as typified by statements such as "We can live with $X$ percent defectives" or "That's fairly common in the industry."

The benefit of manufacturing to reduce variations (process control) is generally recognized.[17] It is the purpose of SQC to *identify* and *reduce* variations from standard and *continuously improve* the process until a theoretical condition of "zero defects" is achieved.[18] The causes of variations are many and vary from industry to industry. Common sources include (1) material balance disturbances, (2) energy balance changes, (3) process instabilities, (4) equipment failure and wear, and (5) poor control loop performance.[19] SQC is used to develop control limits for each step within the process. Measuring sample parts and graphing trends lead to identification of the cause(s) of any erratic (non-random) behavior in the process.

The objective of process control is not only production of quality output but reduction of costs as well. Quality is defined as the total acceptable variation divided by the total actual variation or $C_p$ index. When used alone, this measure may be misleading because it assumes acceptable quality product design.[20] This, of course, is not always the case and suggests the need for the cross-functional process control mentioned earlier.

Data acquisition and monitoring is an essential step if the process is to remain in-control. This tracking is generally accomplished by the operator concerned. In more sophisticated plants, particularly in unattended manufacturing, the goal is to have in-process measurement and correction in real time through the use of sensors or other measuring devices.[21] Devices such as bar code readers, vision systems, and counters are some of the tools available for collection of data. Of course, data alone is not enough. Data must be organized in such a way that process decisions can be made.

## PROCESS CONTROL IN SERVICE INDUSTRIES

Examination of the U.S. Government Standards Industrial Classification of Industries suggests many industries in which the use of SPC would be appropriate. Use of the techniques is spreading to such industries as transportation,[22] health care, and banking.[23]

To some extent, the service process is more difficult to control than manufacturing because quality is typically measured at the customer interface, when it is already too late to fix the problem. Hence, "final inspection" will always be a part of the process; the customer serves as the inspector.

Service failures are analogous to bad parts in manufacturing, and measures of service may be compared to manufacturing tolerances or standards. SPC can be used to measure consistency of service and determine causes of deterioration from prescribed standards and the cause(s) of variations. In transportation, the cause may be missed appointments, refusals, or weekend closures.[24] At the First National Bank of Chicago, a number of processes are checked weekly against over 500 customer-sensitive measures.[25]

■ L.L. Bean, a mail order company in Freeport, Maine, is known worldwide for its outstanding distribution system. It is the ideal company to benchmark for that function. The company analyzed all key activities and processes, including benchmarking competitors. It is ranked number one in virtually every product category in which it is evaluated by outside sources.[26]

### Customer Defections: The Measure of Service Process Quality

Measures of output, as the customer defines them, are not too difficult to identify in service firms. An airline can measure on-time departures and the time it takes to make a reservation. A bank can measure the ratio of ATM downtime to total number of ATM minutes available and so on. Measures such as these are necessary, but the most important measure is *customer defections* or customers lost to the competition.

What is the cost of a customer defection? Conversely, what is the value of a customer retention? Defections have a substantial effect on profits and cost, more so than market share, economies of scale, or unit costs. Simply put, losing a customer costs money and retaining one makes money.

The initial cost of acquiring a new customer involves a number of one-time costs for prospecting, advertising, records, and such. Banks, attorneys, mutual funds, and credit card companies are examples of firms that spend to recruit a customer and establish an account. However, once a relationship is established, the marginal cost of each additional dollar of sales *diminishes*—provided the customer does not defect.

Improving the processes and reducing the process variations that reduce customer defections can be perceived not as a cost but as an investment. Consider the following examples:

- Taco Bell calculates that the lifetime value of a retained customer is $11,000.

- An auto dealer believes that the lifetime value of retaining a customer is $300,000 in sales.

- MBNA America, a credit card company, has found that a 5 percent improvement in defection rates increases its average customer value by 125 percent.

## PROCESS CONTROL FOR INTERNAL SERVICES

- Until it moved to Raleigh, North Carolina, IBM's personal computer assembly operation was located at its plant in Boca Raton, Florida. The general manager was committed to internal as well as external quality. In support of this commitment, the following policy was adopted, widely disseminated, and implemented through "Excellent Plus" groups:

### Excellence Plus Commitment

IBM Boca Raton will deliver defect-free, competitive products and services, on time, to all customers. Quality will be the primary consideration in all decisions related to cost and delivery. *Likewise, each department will provide defect-free work to the next user of its output or service* (emphasis added).

An inventory of the many functions and activities in an organization will reveal that each activity is responsible for the operations of one or more processes where the customer is an *internal* user of its output or service. Many, if not most, of these processes lend themselves to process control methods.

AT&T's support services organization in Chicago is responsible for word processing and reprographics. Through SPC, a fivefold improvement in typing accuracy and a halving of turnaround time in reprographics were achieved. Most of the gain was attributed to better communications with customers.[27]

## QUALITY FUNCTION DEPLOYMENT

A team of scientists and researchers at Battelle, a research and development organization, has compiled a list of the ten most important technological challenges that will face industry during the next decade.[28] These are market-driven challenges, and topping the list is

■ **Personalized consumer products.** Consumers are increasingly better informed and harder to please. They will buy products that satisfy their own tastes, rather than accept whatever stores present. Products in the future will have to be almost as varied as individual customers. This means that companies will have to be even more consumer driven in designing and marketing their products.

Quality function deployment (QFD) is an important tool for capturing the "voice of the customer" in the very early stages of concept and design. This will help the redesign and rework that are so common. Companies can be both engineering and market driven.

For centuries, and even today, navies have built ships in the same process sequence:

Design → Build hull and launch → Outfit →

Trial run → Return to shipyard → Rework →

Operational check → Return → Fix → Operational

This sequence in modern construction of ships and other weapon systems almost always results in time and cost overruns and subsequent operational deficiencies. The same sequence is frequently followed by providers of most consumer and industrial products. A method is needed to (1) obtain customer input in the very early stages and (2) reduce cycle time from product concept to operational status.

It is generally agreed that maybe nine out of ten new product developments end up as a design, manufacturing, or marketing failure. These failures may be more the fault of the organization than the market. Many firms lack a system to integrate the market demands with the organization processes. Most applicants for the Baldrige Award, according to examiners, lack management processes that ensure the efficient flow of customer demands throughout the organization.[29]

If quality definition (customer expectation) is not introduced early in the concept or design stage, there is the risk (indeed, the probability) that design errors and product defects will only be discovered at later stages of production or final inspection. The worst scenario is discovery by the customer in the marketplace. Motorola estimates that whereas design accounts for only 5 percent of product cost, it accounts for 70 percent of the influence on manufacturing cost.

The major functions of the organization and the matching activities/processes are shown in Figure 6-12. Each is necessary throughout the life cycle of the product, but if the beginning of each process or activity must wait for the end of the preceding one, the time to market is lengthened and the product may be obsolete or overtaken by competition midway through the processes. A method is needed to integrate all processes and relate them to the customer.

Every chief executive officer would welcome a TQM system that would:

- Implement strategic quality management, including market segment differentiation based on customer expectations
- Communicate a culture of quality throughout the organization
- Translate technical requirements into process requirements and then to production planning
- Organize the potential for world-class competition
- *Integrate*
  1. The special interest functions of the company
  2. The stream of processes and provide a basis for process design and control

| Marketing | Design | Production | Usage |
|-----------|--------|------------|-------|
| Marketing | Design | Planning | Shipping |
| R & D | Trial Production | Purchase | Usage |
| Planning | Evaluation | Production | Service |
| | | Inspection | |

**Figure 6-12**   Quality Function Deployment Chart

3. Suppliers and customers
4. Everyone in the process while promoting a team culture with interfunctional teams

This is a lot to ask of any method, but proponents of QFD suggest that this method has the potential to achieve many of these requirements. It has proven so effective as a competitive advantage in some companies (e.g., Ford, Digital Equipment, Black & Decker, Budd, Kelsey Hayes, GM, Chrysler, AT&T, Procter & Gamble, ITT, Hewlett-Packard) that they are unwilling to talk about it.[30] In Japan, where the method was first used, companies have achieved dramatic improvement in the design-development process.[31]

One of the very early users of QFD in Japan was Toyota Autobody. Between January 1977 and April 1984, the company introduced four new van-type vehicles. Using 1977 as a base, Toyota reported a 20 percent reduction in start-up costs on the launch of the new van in October 1979, a 38 percent reduction in November 1982, and a cumulative 61 percent reduction in April 1984. During this period, the product development cycle (time to market) was reduced by one-third, with a corresponding improvement in quality because of a reduction in the number of engineering changes.

The first recorded case studies in QFD were in 1986. Kelsey Hayes used QFD to develop a coolant sensor that fulfilled critical customer requirements like "easy to add coolant," "easy to identify unit," and "provide cap removal instructions."

QFD is a group of techniques for planning and communicating that coordinate the activities within an organization. It is a dynamic, iterative method performed by interfunctional teams from marketing, design, engineering, manufacturing engineering, manufacturing, quality, purchasing, and accounting and in some cases suppliers and customers as well. Thus, a common quality focus is achieved across all functions: quality function deployment. The basic premise is that products should be designed to reflect the desires and tastes of customers. An additional benefit is improvement of the company's management processes.[32]

QFD unfolds in the following steps:

Step 1  **Product planning.** This begins with customer requirements, defined by specific and detailed phrases that the customers in their own words use to describe desired product characteristics.

■ Eaton Corporation, a supplier to the automobile industry, selected a control device for a QFD pilot process. A matrix chart was prepared that related desired product features to part quality characteristics. Each quality characteristic was ranked. Through QFD, selling price and engineering expenses were reduced by 50 percent.[33]

Step 2 **Prioritize** and **weight** the relative importance that customers have assigned to each characteristic. This can be done on a scale (e.g., one to five) or in terms of percentages that sum to 100 percent.[34]

Step 3 **Competitive evaluation.** For those who want to be world-class or meet or beat the competition, it is essential to know how their products compare. Specifically, will the characteristics identified in steps 1 and 2 provide a strategic competitive advantage? (See Chapter 8 for further information on benchmarking.)

Step 4 **The design process.** This is where the customer's product characteristics meet the *measurable* engineering characteristics that directly affect customer perceptions.

Step 5 **Design** (continued). The central relationship matrix indicates the degree to which each engineering characteristic affects the customer's characteristics. Strengths of relationships are entered.

Step 6 **Design** (continued). The roof of the "house" matrix encourages creativity by allowing changes between steps 4 and 5 in order to judge potential trade-offs between engineering and customer characteristics.

Step 7 **Process planning.** Output from the design process goes to process planning, where the key processes (e.g., cutting, stamping, welding, painting, assembly, etc.) are determined. This step may have its own matrix.

Step 8 **Process control.** Output from step 7 goes to process control, where the necessary process flows and controls are designed.

The entire QFD process is "deployed" as illustrated in Figure 6-13. The "hows" of one step become the "whats" of the next. Many of the statistical techniques mentioned previously can be used. Market research has particular methods for that function.

The concept of QFD is based on the following four key documents or components:

1. **Overall customer requirements planning matrix.** Translates the general customer requirements drawn from market surveys into specified final product control characteristics.

2. **Final product characteristic development matrix.** Translates the output of the planning matrix into critical component characteristics.

3. **Process plan and quality control charts.** Identify critical product and process parameters and develop checkpoints and controls for these parameters.

4. **Operating instructions.** Identify operations to be performed by plant personnel to ensure that important parameters are achieved.

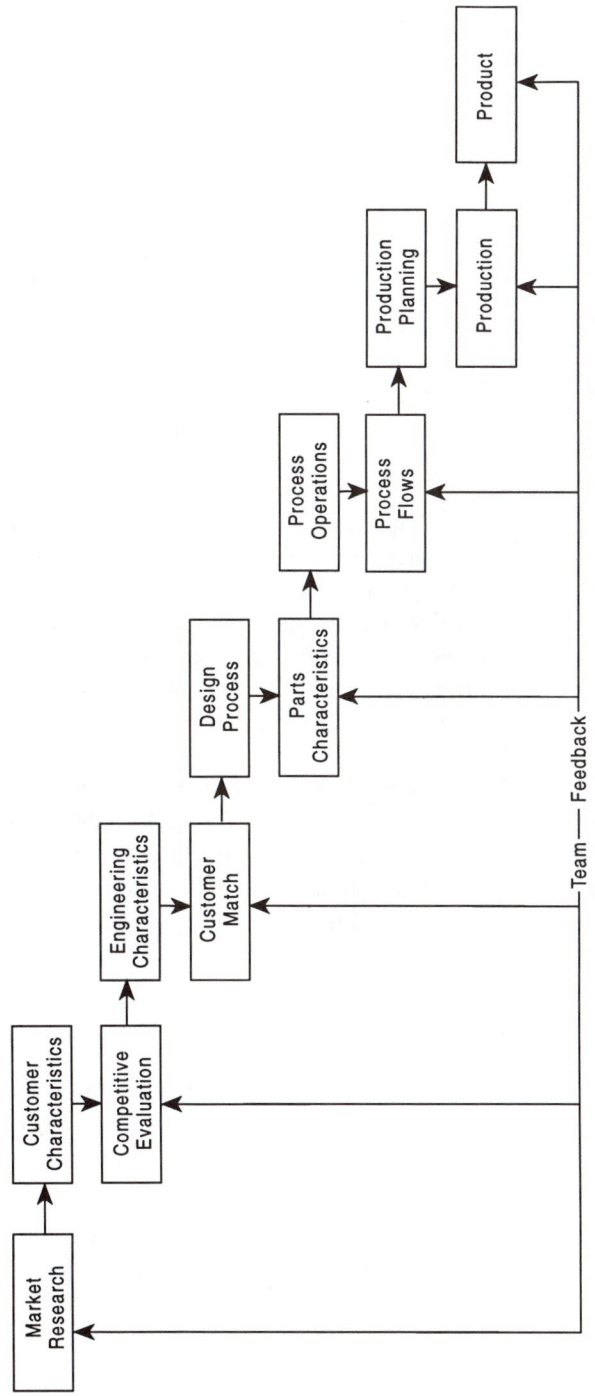

**Figure 6-13**  Quality Function Deployment

The planning matrix translates the "voice of the customer" into specific final product/service control characteristics. The deployment matrix takes the final product/service control characteristics and translates them into critical part characteristics, thus moving the customer requirements deeper into the design process. The process plan and quality control charts identify the critical product, service, and process parameters that are vital to meeting the critical part characteristics. They also identify checkpoints for each of the critical parameters. The operating instructions constitute the entire set of procedures and practices that will be performed by all personnel to ensure that the critical parameters are achieved. The main purpose of these documents is to translate and deploy the customer's requirements throughout the product/service design, development, and production process of an organization. The customer's requirements are ultimately addressed by the operational personnel who produce the product and deliver the services. The flow and relationship of these documents are illustrated in Figure 6-14.

In all cases, the interfunctional teams are involved. This is necessary to avoid rework and redesign as well as overruns in cost and time. Questions need to be answered along the way: What does the customer really want? Can we design it? Can we make it? Is it competitive? Can we sell it at a profit? Do the processes support it? Hewlett-Packard estimates that quality programs have saved the company $400 million in warranty costs. Prior to implementing QFD and quality programs, the company estimated that non-quality costs added up to 25 to 30 percent of sales dollars.[35]

The essential prerequisite for QFD is the determination of customer requirements that are defined by specific and detailed phrases that customers in their own words use to describe desired product characteristics. To achieve this degree of specificity, it may be necessary to communicate with customers one on one or in focus groups. A less desirable method is to use surveys or other means.

## JUST-IN-TIME

■ By the third year of just-in-time (JIT) implementation, Isuzu (a Japanese company) had reduced the number of employees from 15,000 to 9900, reduced work in process from 35 billion yen to 11 billion yen, and decreased the defect rate by two-thirds.[36]

■ Hewlett-Packard has spread JIT to all areas, including cost accounting, procurement, and engineering. At one plant where 290 pieces of equipment are hand assembled, product reliability has improved sixfold and productivity is up considerably.[37]

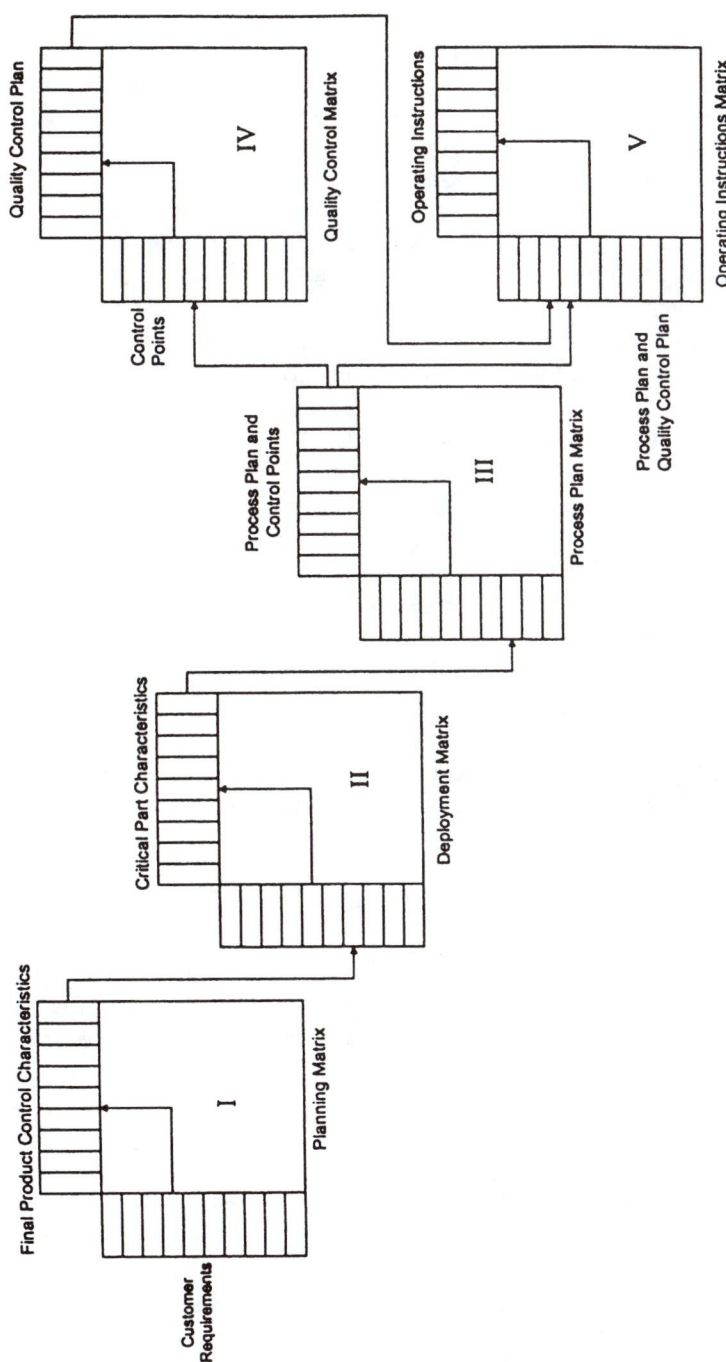

**Figure 6-14**  Flow and Relationship of the Quality Function Deployment Documents

■ As part of its conversion to JIT, Westinghouse Electric's Asheville, North Carolina, plant was run as a number of mini-plants. Cycle time has been reduced two to four times, on-time performance is up over 90 percent, and shop productivity is up by 70 percent. Employees are trained to perform multiple functions, and each will end up knowing how to build the complete product.

U.S. manufacturing has been characterized by mass production, high-volume output, and machine capacities that are pushed to the limit. This is changing as American managers begin to discover a production method called JIT. Proponents say that it is more than a manufacturing system; they call it a philosophy and a way of approaching business goals that incorporates (1) producing what is needed when it is needed, (2) minimizing problems, and (3) eliminating production processes that make safety stocks necessary.[38]

Prior to the 1960s, the goal of production planning was cost optimization. In the early 1970s, it became requirements planning, and the technique of materials requirements planning (MRP) computed material needs to meet a sales forecast and production plan. MRP was, and is, an effort to balance the sometimes conflicting demands of safety stocks, inventory carrying costs, economic order quantity, and risk factors related to possible stockouts. Today, the modern corporation is turning to manufacturing as a crucial strategic resource and is adopting JIT as a basic component of manufacturing strategy. The view is that the expense and risk of maintaining inventory can be reduced so that lower costs becomes a way of improving both productivity and quality. Of course, inventory is not the only consideration of JIT. It involves all functions and all processes.

## JUST-IN-TIME OR JUST-IN-CASE

JIT infers that "less is best," while just-in-case involves the use of buffer or safety stocks. Conventional reasons given to explain the need for buffer stock include avoiding risks of stockouts or failure of suppliers, getting a better price for volume purchasing, and avoiding an anticipated price increase. The presence of such "excess" inventory increased the risk of obsolescence and deterioration, increased the need for warehouse and shop floor space, and by "pushing" parts through the assembly process encouraged a number of wasteful practices. Operators were unconcerned with workstations other than their own. The attitude became, "There's plenty more where that came from." If a defective part was discovered, the tendency was to blame it on a previous operation or assume that it would be corrected later in the process or at the rework area.

Shigeo Shingo, who is credited with designing Toyota's JIT production system, believes that the "push" process used in the United States generates process–yield imbalances and interprocess delays.[39] *Kanban,* as JIT is called in Japan, means "visible record." It is a means of pulling parts through the assembly process; production is initiated only when a worker receives a visible cue that assembly is needed for the next step in the process. The worker orders the product from the previous operation so that it arrives just when needed. If one of the key processes fails to produce a quality part, the production line stops. Individual operators are their own inspectors and are cross-trained for a number of tasks. The system is continuously being fine-tuned.

### Benefits of Just-in-Time[40]

JIT is not just an inventory control method. It is a system of factory production that interrelates with all functions and activities. The benefits include:

- Reduction of direct and indirect labor by eliminating extraneous activities
- Reduction of floor space and warehouse space per unit of output
- Reduction of setup time and schedule delays as the factory becomes a continuous production process
- Reduction of waste, rejects, and rework by detecting errors at the source
- Reduction of lead time due to small lot sizes, so that downstream work centers provide feedback on quality problems
- Better utilization of machines and facilities
- Better relations with suppliers
- Better plant layout
- Better integration of and communication between functions such as marketing, purchasing, design, and production
- Quality control built into the process

## THE HUMAN SIDE OF PROCESS CONTROL

One study found that a very small percentage of employees could define quality or could relate what their companies were doing to improve it.[41]

The problems of managing streams of processes are both methodological and organizational. Peter Drucker concludes that SQC has its greatest impact on the factory's social organization.[42] The essence of his argument relates to the way that the use of statistical tools in the production process places information and hence accountability in the hands of the machine operator rather than non-operators such as inspectors, expediters, repair crews, and supervisors. Each operator becomes his or her own inspector. Operators "own" the machines, which allows them to spot malfunctions and correct problems. The concept is known as "workstation ownership" at IBM, where each employee is responsible for an entire operation in the production line.[43]

If Drucker is right, as he probably is, the potential exists for significant improvement in quality, cost, and productivity. However, there is a downside. Strict adherence to rigid methods and procedures means that workers and teams may lose the autonomy they previously enjoyed, only to have it replaced by the regimentation necessitated by process control. By their very nature, SPC and JIT require a focus on the process as a whole, an environment that may be strange to an operator accustomed to the segmented approach previously in effect.[44]

It is probably almost universally accepted that control of any process rests upon measuring against some standard, measure, benchmark, or target. Yet in many organizations, workers and managers operate with two different sets of goals and in two different cultures. It becomes an "us versus them" split culture. As we move from inspection to process control, it is essential that control measures become the property of the workers. SPC and JIT achieve this. Workers are involved in measures over which they have some control in monitoring continuous improvements. Control of measures alone, however, may not be enough. Understanding of and involvement in the system would enhance job satisfaction, which is a necessary dimension. Moreover, like any process or system, the people with hands-on involvement are a valuable resource for refinement and improvement.

Attention to the human resource dimension provides a basis for significant improvements in job development, job satisfaction, training, and morale. Suggested actions to improve the changes include:

- Like all major change, top management support is essential.
- Change the focus from production volume to quality, from speed to flow, from execution to task design, from performing to learning.
- Invest in training, a necessary prerequisite.

## QUESTIONS FOR DISCUSSION

**6-1**  Explain the difference between feedforward and feedback (final inspection) control. Why is feedforward more appropriate for TQM?

**6-2**  What are the steps in moving from a system of final inspection to process control?

**6-3**  Choose a non-manufacturing (service) process and show how statistical quality control would be appropriate.

**6-4** How would a *sequential* approach to product design and introduction result in overruns in time, cost, and quality? How would quality function deployment improve the system?

**6-5** Are customer defections a measure of service quality? If so, how can the measure be used to reduce customer defections?

**6-6** Explain the benefits of just-in-time.

## ENDNOTES

1. J. A. Swift, Joel E. Ross, and Vincent K. Omachonu, *Principles of Total Quality,* 2nd ed., Boca Raton, Fla.: St. Lucie Press, 1998, pp. 224–226.

2. Claude S. George, Jr., *The History of Management Thought,* Englewood Cliffs, N.J.: Prentice-Hall, 1972, p. 10. For an excellent summary of sources that have traced the history of the quality movement, see David A. Garvin, *Managing Quality,* New York: The Free Press, 1988, p. 251.

3. Frederick W. Taylor, *Principles of Scientific Management,* New York: Harper & Row, 1911.

4. Frederick W. Taylor, *Shop Management,* New York: Harper & Row, 1919, p. 101.

5. W. A. Shewhart, *Economic Control of Quality of Manufactured Product,* New York: E. Van Nostrand Company, 1931.

6. Peter Drucker, "The Emerging Theory of Manufacturing," *Harvard Business Review,* May/June 1990, p. 95.

7. Harry W. Kenworthy and Angela George, "Quality and Cost Efficiency Go Hand in Hand," *Quality Progress,* Oct. 1989, pp. 40–41.

8. Barbara Dutton, "Switching to Quality Excellence," *Manufacturing Systems,* March 1990, pp. 51–53.

9. Bob Johnstone, "Prophet with Honor," *Far Eastern Economic Review (Hong Kong),* Dec. 27, 1990, p. 50. A survey of Japanese automobile parts suppliers showed that 93 percent used SPC in their operations.

10. For a detailed treatment of SQC and SPC, see Kaoru Ishikawa, *Guide to Quality Control,* rev. ed., 1982 (available in the United States from UNIPUB [tel. 800-274-4888]). See also J. M. Juran, *Quality Control Handbook,* 3rd ed., New York: McGraw-Hill, 1974. For application of process control charts, see such standard texts as J. M. Juran and Frank Gryna, Jr., *Quality Planning and Analysis,* New York: McGraw-Hill, 1980, and E. L. Grant and R. S. Leavenworth, *Statistical Quality Control,* 5th ed., New York: McGraw-Hill, 1980.

11. One research study of over 300 U.S. firms found that less than half believed that they had a state-of-the-art quality control program that included SQC and SPC and utilized a computer support system. Joel E. Ross and David Georgoff, "A Survey of Productivity and Quality Issues in Manufacturing: The State of the Industry," *Industrial Management,* Jan./Feb. 1991.

12. For a summary discussion of the various techniques used in brainstorming, see Ron Zemke, "In Search of...Good Ideas," *Training,* Jan. 1993, pp. 46–52.

13. Part of the discussion of control charts is adapted from J. A. Swift, Joel E. Ross, and Vincent K. Omachonu, *Principles of Total Quality,* 2nd ed., Boca Raton, Fla.: St. Lucie Press, 1998.

14. More detailed treatment can be found in J. A. Swift, Joel E. Ross, and Vincent K. Omachonu, *Principles of Total Quality,* 2nd ed., Boca Raton, Fla.: St. Lucie Press, 1998.

15. Shigeru Nakamura, *The New Standardization: Keystone of Continuous Improvement in Manufacturing,* Portland, Ore.: Productivity Press, 1993.

16. Stephen Wise, "The Control Chart Dilemma," *Quality Progress,* Feb. 1998, pp. 66–71.

17. Ken Jones, "High Performance Manufacturing: A Break with Tradition," *Industrial Management (Canada),* June 1988, pp. 30–32.

18. Genichi Taguchi and Don Clausing, "Robust Quality," *Harvard Business Review,* Jan./Feb. 1990, pp. 65–75. This article provides a summary of the collection now known as Taguchi methods, a popular approach that is opposed to the zero defects concept, based on the conclusion that the concept promotes quality in terms of acceptable deviation from targets rather than a consistent effort to hit them. Zero defects, according to Taguchi, fixes design before the effects of the quality program are felt.

19. Kenneth E. Kirby and Charles F. Moore, "Process Control and Quality in the Continuous Process Industries," *Survey of Business,* Summer 1989, pp. 62–66.

20. Larry H. Anderson, "Controlling Process Variation Is Key to Manufacturing Success," *Quality Progress,* Aug. 1990, pp. 91–93.

21. Chester Placek, "CMMs in Automation," *Quality,* March 1990, pp. 28–38.

22. Ray A. Mundy, Russel Passarella, and Jay Morse, "Applying SPC in Service Industries," *Survey of Business,* Spring 1986, pp. 24–29.

23. Aleta Holub, "The Added Value of the Customer–Provider Partnership," in *Making Total Quality Happen,* Research Report No. 937, New York: The Conference Board, 1990, pp. 60–63.

24. John E. Tyworth, Pat Lemons, and Bruce Ferrin, "Improving LTL Delivery Service Quality with Statistical Process Control," *Transportation Journal,* Spring 1989, pp. 4–12.

25. Aleta Holub, Endnote 23.

26. Thomas C. Day, "Value-Driven Business = Long-Term Success," in *Total Quality Performance,* Research Report No. 909, New York: The Conference Board, 1988, pp. 27–29.

27. Laurence C. Seifert, "AT&T's Full-Stream Quality Architecture," in *Total Quality Performance,* Research Report No. 909, New York: The Conference Board, 1988, pp. 47–49.

28. "Customer Opinion Critical in the Next 10 Years," *Quality,* April 1997, pp. 12–16.

29. Peter Burrows, "Commitment to Quality: Five Lessons You Can Learn from Award Entrants," *Electronic Business,* Oct. 15, 1990, pp. 56–58.

30. Gary S. Vasilash, "Hearing the Voice of the Customer," *Production,* Feb. 1989, pp. 66–68.

31. Ronald Fortuna, "Beyond Quality: Taking SPC Upstream," *Quality Progress,* June 1988, pp. 23–28. The author is manager of the Chicago office of Ernst & Young and observes that the control charts of SPC are considered one of the "Seven Old Tools" in Japan, along with Pareto analysis, cause-and-effect diagrams, data stratification, histograms, and scatter diagrams.

32. William Band and Richard Huot, "Quality & Functionality Equal Satisfaction," *Sales and Marketing Management in Canada (Canada),* March 1990, pp. 4–5.

33. Dennis De Vera et al., "An Automotive Case Study," *Quality Progress,* June 1988, pp. 35–38.

34. At a Conference Board Quality Conference on April 2, 1990, A. F. Jacobson of 3M described how the Commercial Office Supply division brings customer expectations into the design process: "Let's say, they're going to develop an improved tape of some kind. They don't wait until the product is finished...or nearly finished...to take it to their customers. They take the idea to customers right at the beginning of the process. They ask customers what they want from a particular tape. Very often, they'll hear things like: 'Don't make it too sticky.' 'I want to be able to pull it off the roll easily.' and, 'It's no good unless I can write on it.' Now, collecting opinions is the easy part of the process. The tough part is converting these soft expectations into technical requirements. This is done on a matrix *before* the development process gets very far. These soft expectations are converted into technical specifications for, say, adhesion, roughness and reflectance."

35. Robert Haavind, "Hewlett-Packard Unravels the Mysteries of Quality," *Electronic Business,* Oct. 16, 1989, pp. 101–105.

36. Ronald M. Fortuna, "The Quality Imperative," *Executive Excellence,* March 1990, p. 1.

37. Steve Kaufman, "Quest for Quality," *Business Month,* May 1989, pp. 60–65.

38. Jack Byrd, Jr. and Mark D. Carter, "A Just-in-Time Implementation Strategy at Work," *Industrial Management,* March/April 1988, pp. 8–10. See also Ira P. Krespchin, "What Do You Mean by Just-in-Time?" *Modern Materials Handling,* Aug. 1986, pp. 93–95.

39. John H. Sheridan, "World-Class Manufacturing: Lessons from the Gurus," *Industry Week,* Aug. 6, 1990, pp. 35–41. Shingo also believes that JIT extends to plant maintenance, and with a participative environment operators will protect their own equipment.

40. There are a number of references that point out the benefits as well as the pitfalls of JIT. These sources also contain suggestions for implementation. See the following: Bruce D. Henderson, "The Logic of Kanban," *Journal of Business Strategy,* Winter 1986, pp. 6–12. The author describes how the technique can provide a competitive advantage. The need to rethink traditional practices is discussed in Lynne Perry, "Simplified Manufacturing Is Best," *Industrial Management,* July/Aug. 1986, pp. 29–30. The way that small manufacturers can adapt the technique is described in Byron Finch, "Japanese Management Techniques in Small Manufacturing Companies," *Production & Inventory Management,* Vol. 27 Issue 3, 3rd Quarter 1986, pp. 30–38. The need for continued quality control and other requirements is outlined in Mark R. Jamrog, "Just-in-Time Manufacturing: Just in Time for U.S. Manufacturers," *Price Waterhouse Review,* Vol. 32 Issue 1, 1988, pp. 17–29. The interface with other functions of the company is provided by R. Natarajan and Donald Weinrauch, "JIT and the Marketing Interface," *Production & Inventory Management Journal,* Vol. 31 Issue 3, 3rd Quarter 1990, pp. 42–46.

41. Joel E. Ross and Lawrence A. Klatt, "Quality: The Competitive Edge," *Management Decision (UK),* Vol. 24 Issue 5, 1986, pp. 12–16.

42. Peter Drucker, "The Emerging Theory of Manufacturing," *Harvard Business Review,* May/June 1990, p. 95.

43. James J. Webster, "Pulling—Not Pushing—For Higher Productivity," *Mechanical Engineering,* April 1988, pp. 42–44.

44. Gervase R. Bushe, "Cultural Contradictions of Statistical Process Control in American Manufacturing Corporations," *Journal of Management,* March 1988, pp. 19–31.

## Appendix A

| $n$ | Factors for $\bar{X}$ charts | | | Factors for R charts | | | | | Factors for S charts | | | | Factors for center line | | $n$ |
|---|---|---|---|---|---|---|---|---|---|---|---|---|---|---|---|
| | $A$ | $A_2$ | $A_3$ | $D_1$ | $D_2$ | $D_3$ | $D_4$ | $d_3$ | $B_3$ | $B_4$ | $B_5$ | $B_6$ | $c_4$ | $d_2$ | |
| 2 | 2.121 | 1.880 | 2.659 | 0.000 | 3.686 | 0.000 | 3.267 | 0.853 | 0.000 | 3.267 | 0.000 | 2.606 | 0.7979 | 1.128 | 2 |
| 3 | 1.732 | 1.023 | 1.954 | 0.000 | 4.358 | 0.000 | 2.574 | 0.888 | 0.000 | 2.568 | 0.000 | 2.276 | 0.8862 | 1.693 | 3 |
| 4 | 1.500 | 0.729 | 1.628 | 0.000 | 4.698 | 0.000 | 2.282 | 0.880 | 0.000 | 2.266 | 0.000 | 2.088 | 0.9213 | 2.059 | 4 |
| 5 | 1.342 | 0.577 | 1.427 | 0.000 | 4.918 | 0.000 | 2.114 | 0.864 | 0.000 | 2.089 | 0.000 | 1.964 | 0.9400 | 2.326 | 5 |
| 6 | 1.225 | 0.483 | 1.287 | 0.000 | 5.078 | 0.000 | 2.004 | 0.848 | 0.030 | 1.970 | 0.029 | 1.874 | 0.9515 | 2.534 | 6 |
| 7 | 1.134 | 0.419 | 1.182 | 0.204 | 5.204 | 0.076 | 1.924 | 0.833 | 0.118 | 1.882 | 0.113 | 1.806 | 0.9594 | 2.704 | 7 |
| 8 | 1.061 | 0.373 | 1.099 | 0.388 | 5.306 | 0.136 | 1.864 | 0.820 | 0.185 | 1.815 | 0.179 | 1.751 | 0.9650 | 2.847 | 8 |
| 9 | 1.000 | 0.337 | 1.032 | 0.547 | 5.393 | 0.184 | 1.816 | 0.808 | 0.239 | 1.761 | 0.232 | 1.707 | 0.9693 | 2.970 | 9 |
| 10 | 0.949 | 0.308 | 0.975 | 0.687 | 5.469 | 0.223 | 1.777 | 0.797 | 0.284 | 1.716 | 0.276 | 1.669 | 0.9727 | 3.078 | 10 |
| 11 | 0.905 | 0.285 | 0.927 | 0.811 | 5.535 | 0.256 | 1.744 | 0.787 | 0.321 | 1.679 | 0.313 | 1.637 | 0.9754 | 3.173 | 11 |
| 12 | 0.866 | 0.266 | 0.886 | 0.922 | 5.594 | 0.283 | 1.717 | 0.778 | 0.354 | 1.646 | 0.346 | 1.610 | 0.9776 | 3.258 | 12 |

# PROCESS MANAGEMENT AT MLCC

Merrill Lynch Credit Corporation (MLCC), a wholly owned subsidiary of Merrill Lynch & Company, offers real-estate- and securities-based consumer credit products—including home financing, personal credit, investment financing, and commercial real-estate financing—to primarily affluent individuals. With a host of competitors, including major banks and investment firms, MLCC distinguishes itself with a comprehensive line of innovative products.

MLCC segments its market into several categories of current and potential customers, stratified by their asset levels and age. Working with its parent company, MLCC uses in-depth research to target and deliver appropriate products and services. Its "Voice of the Client" process spells out customer satisfaction drivers for each client segment and for each of its credit categories. These priority requirements provide the basis for aligning the company's processes and work groups and for identifying indicators and key performance measures for each of its eight core processes.

The company utilizes process management to ensure alignment of *core and support processes* with client requirements. Support processes are aligned with core processes and managed through quality indicators developed from internal customer requirements. Core processes are "owned" as shown below.

| Core process | Owner | Support processes |
|---|---|---|
| Design | Business development | Technology information systems |
| Market | Marketing | Human resources |
| Preorigination | Client services | Administrative services |
| Order | Lending support service | Legal |
| Underwrite | Underwriting | Business processes |
| Approve | Lending services | Business services |
| Audit/fund | Postclosing/secondary marketing | Finance |
| Setup service | Loan administration | |

# QUALITY FUNCTION DEPLOYMENT:
# A CASE STUDY

QFD is an integrative, four-phase process which links together customer needs, product and parts design requirements, process planning, and manufacturing specifications during product development. Various tools and mechanisms are used to operationalize the QFD concept. For example, design for manufacturing and assembly (DFMA) is often used as a part of the QFD process. QFD can also help identify consistent performance measures for the different stages in the product design–process design–manufacturing–customer chain.

## QFD Benefits

The benefits of QFD are:

- Better customer satisfaction resulting from improved quality of design
- Shorter lead times due to fewer and earlier engineering changes
- Better linkages between various design and manufacturing stages
- A reduction in the number of product components
- An improved work atmosphere through the horizontal integration of functions

Also, QFD provides a structure for benchmarking competitors' designs. Japanese automakers attribute tangible benefits, such as low product cost, high quality, and short development lead times, to QFD. Engineering changes are fewer and take place earlier, resulting in reduced product lead times.

The purpose of this study was to gain insights into the use of the QFD process through its examination in a live organization. By examining the QFD process in practice, valuable lessons can be learned which may help facilitate future QFD

Reprinted with permission of APICS—The Educational Society for Resource Management, *Production & Inventory Management Journal,* Second Quarter 1995, pp. 56–60.

adoptions by other organizations. Given the exploratory nature of this study, it may also be used as a basis for future empirical QFD research.

## Research Methodology

Since the central purpose of this research was to study the QFD process, a qualitative research methodology was adopted. We conducted a detailed case study of the QFD process applied to two different vehicle programs within Chrysler Motors Corporation.

The Chrysler study included ten semi-structured interviews with program managers, design and manufacturing engineers, QFD team leaders, QFD specialists and facilitators, and DFMA specialists. Each of these interviews lasted one to three hours. In addition, we had extensive discussions with the QFD planning group at Chrysler. Of great benefit was the close interaction we had with active QFD teams. Chrysler engineers motivated us to "live" the QFD process in order to get a better feel for the working philosophy. We participated in the weekly meetings of one of the QFD Phase 1 teams. In addition, we attended meetings of a QFD Phase 3 team comprised of program management, design, advanced engineering, logistics, and plant management representatives.

Another source of information for the case study was company data. Documents pertaining to product policy, supplier meetings, and market feedback were reviewed. Chrysler also shared company manuals, QFD charts, and information on past QFD teams. We also benefited from attending Chrysler-sponsored QFD training sessions.

## Case Study: Chrysler Motors Corporation

QFD was formally launched at Chrysler in September 1986, though the first application started in June 1986. Initially, only a few of the cross-functional design teams embraced the QFD concept. Later, some of the product managers recognized the potential of QFD and implemented it for their vehicle programs. After the reorganization of Chrysler's product design function into design platforms several years ago, QFD received more support from senior managers.

The American Supplier Institute (ASI) provided QFD training for Chrysler during the first few years. This role has been taken over by Chrysler's quality planning group. During the early years of QFD adoption, the company also sought the help of well-known Japanese quality, design, and QFD experts such as Akashi Fukuhara (assistant director, Central Japan Quality Control Association).

### Adoption of QFD

The first-time implementation of QFD procedures within a Chrysler vehicle program is viewed as a four-stage process: spreading awareness; developing successful case studies and examples to motivate subsequent teams; companywide training and education on QFD techniques and philosophy; and adoption of QFD as a business philosophy.

Although our research confirmed the use of a four-stage process by Chrysler for QFD adoption, our interviews with design engineers in one vehicle platform revealed that QFD was not fully accepted as the preferred design methodology. Since QFD was not considered an integral part of the overall design process by this vehicle platform, the QFD process was perceived as requiring additional time and effort. Such opinions led to organizational and perceptual barriers regarding the successful implementation of QFD.

### The QFD Process

At Chrysler, the QFD process began at concept generation. At the business planning stage, the concept generation is implemented by initially starting with a program management-level team that sets overall guidelines and allocates responsibility to different design groups for different systems. These design groups then set up QFD teams which begin by determining system-level needs. Once these requirements are established, the team breaks up into smaller groups that focus on the various components comprising the system. The system-level QFD team, however, still maintains overall responsibility for the system. At the same time, progress is made on the sequential phases of the QFD process.

### QFD Software

In order to keep track of the QFD teams' activities, responsibilities, and progress, some QFD teams at Chrysler used a commercially available QFD software package. The software has the capability of constructing and analyzing the "house of quality" and other QFD matrices. The use of such software was not widespread in the product groups we visited. Often, it was the responsibility of the QFD facilitators/coordinators to maintain QFD charts and other information.

### Making Design Trade-offs

What happens when customer requirements lead to conflicting design requirements? Although such conflicts may occur during any of the four QFD phases, they are most likely detected during the product planning phase as negative correlations in the roof of the "house of quality." Engineers at later design stages must be made aware of such conflicts—managing information transfer and communication is the key to resolving such conflicts.

Two kinds of solutions to such trade-offs normally occur. The first uses the approach suggested by the Pugh concept selection method. In this approach, alternatives are generated, and the best alternatives are chosen based on previously set cost, quality, weight, and investment constraints and objectives. Failure mode and effects analysis (FMEA) is used to challenge the best design alternatives to expose their weaknesses and to find potential problems. However, the best alternatives may still not be very attractive. The second approach may be useful in such cases. The Taguchi design of experiments can be used to "optimize" the design by isolating controllable variables. By determining the effect of these variables on the design requirements, it is possible to determine optimum levels for controllable parameters. By understanding the behavior of certain design outcomes as a function of these controllable parameters, mathematical optimization (such as linear/nonlinear programming) can be used to determine optimal parameter settings and design outcomes. Chrysler employed both approaches in making design trade-offs.

Since QFD brings together a multifunctional team and helps challenge traditional design objectives and targets, the researchers expected an increase in design innovations resulting from the need to make such design trade-offs. A few examples did exist. For example, the cruise-control device on the new LH midsize cars is an improved version resulting from conflicting design objectives. However, discussions with several QFD design teams revealed that such innovations have not yet become common. We hypothesized that the lack of increasing levels of design innovation was due to the use of QFD primarily as a design tool. This hypothesis was confirmed through discussions with several design engineers and managers.

### Getting Data for QFD

Due to various resource constraints, Chrysler management was sometimes unable to authorize first-hand customer research for determining customer requirements. In such cases, teams were encouraged to document what they knew based on their experience. Thus, the teams would only research product areas where they did not know the customers' requirements, or felt that there was a risk of misinterpreting customers' needs. Often, team members simulated customers by actually evaluating competing vehicles and reviewing customer ratings. The teams also relied on secondary data derived from private reports or warranty information.

### Strategic Role of QFD

Our research revealed strategic benefits for Chrysler in the launch of their LH platform for mid-size cars (e.g., the 1993 Dodge Vision). The total product design cycle took approximately 36 months, versus historical cycles ranging from 62 to 54 months. LH prototypes were ready 95 weeks before the scheduled start of production, compared to the traditional 60 weeks. The program required only 740 people, compared to historical involvement levels of 1,600 people. Also, by focusing on customer requirements instead of only cost, Chrysler made significant design changes that are gaining acceptance in the marketplace.

### Performance Evaluation Systems for QFD

Our interviews with Chrysler managers revealed that records relating to QFD and project performance were rarely kept. One reason for this void was the lack of an established evaluation system suited to QFD. Another reason was the evaluation of design engineers was not always consistent with QFD objectives. A senior program executive mentioned that establishing merit and reward systems consistent with QFD and other team-based programs has been a challenge. Creating a performance measurement system that is consistent with organizational and program objectives is clearly difficult. However, the success of any program depends on measuring performance and using this to provide constructive feedback.

## Conclusions

Upon examining the case study data, we offer the following "lessons learned" concerning the use of the QFD process.

### Lesson 1: QFD Is More than a Product Design Tool

The adoption of innovations or new technologies has been described as a four-stage process composed of the following elements: identification, transfer, amplification, and acceptance. The identification stage focuses on educating the organization on the benefits of the innovation. The transfer stage consists of training a selected group in the use of the innovation and demonstrating its successful application via pilot projects. After successfully demonstrating how the innovation can provide benefits, total adoption begins in the amplification stage through: (1) company-wide training and education on the use of the innovation and (2) company-wide information sharing on how the innovation has benefited the firm. However, total adoption does not occur until the innovation is directly linked to the firm's philosophies and strategies during the acceptance stage.

QFD can be viewed as a process innovation for developing products. The adoption of QFD, therefore, requires a process analogous to the one described above. Although Chrysler had a similar implementation process, QFD was still viewed by some design teams as a "tool" unrelated to the firm's business strategy or design philosophy. To avoid this situation, QFD-related performance measures are needed which link design team actions to the firm's strategy. These measures should provide the basis for performance evaluations and rewards. A QFD performance measurement system is needed to monitor and control the product development process.

### Lesson 2: QFD Can Provide Firms with a Competitive Advantage

The benefits of QFD outlined previously can provide firms with a competitive advantage in the marketplace. Chrysler's results of using QFD in the development of its LH platform for mid-size cars illustrate the potential strategic impact of the QFD process.

### Lesson 3: The Four Phases of the QFD Product Development Cycle Are Dynamic and Must Be Adapted to the Organization's Culture and Needs

In our study, we found that the design teams used a four-step approach as a framework, but often improvised within the theoretical approach. Thus, a more fluid approach to using the QFD process may be more suitable for some organizations.

The QFD process provides a means for firms to design products which result in "customer delight." Further research in actual organizations adopting QFD is needed to understand how to most effectively operationalize the QFD process. Theoretical foundations for QFD have already been established in the literature and must now be validated to assist practitioners in its proper application.

*The Taguchi Method for design of experiments is a tool used to reduce the inherent variability in a product or process. The concept of process variation is introduced and expanded, and the use of the Taguchi Method in statistical process control is explained. A good introduction to and explanation of the basics of statistical process control are provided.*

# REDUCING VARIABILITY—
# KEY TO CONTINUOUS
# QUALITY IMPROVEMENT

### Gregg D. Stocker

In recent years, quality has undoubtedly become a strategic focus of companies expecting to do business in the 1990s and beyond. In the summer of 1988, the Department of Defense released the Total Quality Management (TQM) Master Plan to achieve continuous improvement of products and services offered and used by the department. A major component of this philosophy is the concept of variability reduction. As a result of DoD's move, many organizations are beginning to understand that reducing the variability of a process results in improved quality and reduced costs.

The concept of variability reduction has its origins in the 1920s with Dr. Walter Shewhart of Bell Laboratories. It has been expanded through the works of W. Edwards Deming, J. A. Juran, Armand Feigenbaum and Genichi Taguchi. Although variability reduction is only one of many components in a continuous improvement process, it is one whose importance calls for further examination.

### The Concept of Variation

Understanding variability reduction requires an understanding of basic statistics. This fundamental requirement has apparently frightened a number of people

Reprinted by permission of *Manufacturing Systems*, March 1990.

away from employing many proven quality improvement techniques. Fortunately, the level of statistical knowledge required to understand the underlying philosophies for quality improvement is not great.

Statistically every process experiences variation in one form or another. It is this variation that leads to quality problems. Methods employed to reduce the amount of variation will, therefore, improve quality and reduce cost.

The philosophy of variability reduction is based on the fact that there is a "best" value for a product's function, fit and appearance. This value is the target that must be achieved to ensure the highest level of quality. To address the existence of variation in a process, traditionally engineering and manufacturing have relied on tolerance or specification limits. This approach must be changed because although parts produced within the specification limits may be functional, their quality decreases and cost increases as the process varies from the target. And this variability can lose business. The company that best meets the needs of the customers within a specific market will gain the greatest share of the market.

Variability is illustrated by the normal distribution, also known as the bell-shaped curve. Figure 1 presents the output of a process that drills holes to a target value of one inch. The normal distribution states that, as long as the process is operating in a statistical state of control, most of the holes will be drilled at exactly one inch. The curve also shows that an equal portion of parts will vary above and below the one inch target, called the "spread."

Figure 2 presents a comparison of distribution of three different processes. Process A produced a greater amount of variation than process B or C, as shown by the wider and flatter curve. In terms of variability, therefore, process C is the best of the three processes for this particular part, i.e., it is the most centered around the target value.

Process A will produce parts that will be scrapped or require rework. Although process B produces virtually every piece within the tolerance limits, the increased variability over process C could result in increased assembly time or possible tolerance stackup problems.

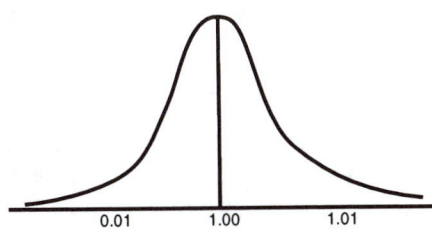

|        | 0.01  | 1.00  | 1.01  |

**Figure 1**   Distribution of a Drilling Operation

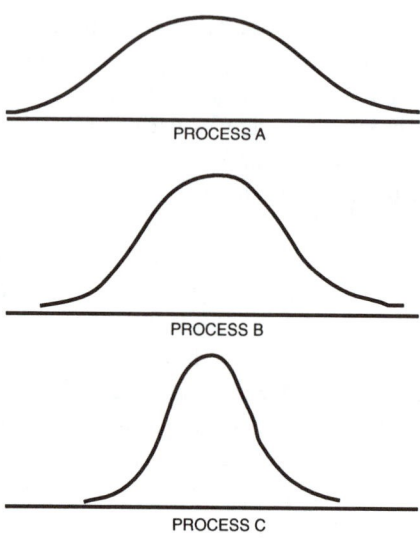

**Figure 2**    Comparison of Three Processes

The principles relating to variability of quality and cost are represented by the Quality Loss Function (QLF) which was developed by Taguchi and is discussed later in this article under "Taguchi Methods."

## Statistical Process Control (SPC)

SPC is a tool used to measure the variability of a process and determine its capability to produce a particular part. The method was developed by Shewhart in 1924 and was used extensively by government contractors during World War II.

A process consistently and predictably producing parts within three standard deviations of the average is considered in a state of statistical control. This means all the special causes of variation within the process have been removed.

A process in a state of statistical control refers *only* to the ability to predict the amount of inherent variation. It does not make any reference to the capability of the process to produce high quality parts on a consistent basis.

Figure 3 presents a process in a state of control, but only able to produce acceptable parts 60 percent of the time. This is because the spread of variation inherent in the process carries outside-the-product specification limits. The measure used to determine if the process can produce acceptable parts on a consistent basis is the process capability ($C_p$) index.

The $C_p$ index is a measure of the variation of a process with respect to the acceptable tolerance limits for an item. The formula for $C_p$ is: [Tolerance/Process

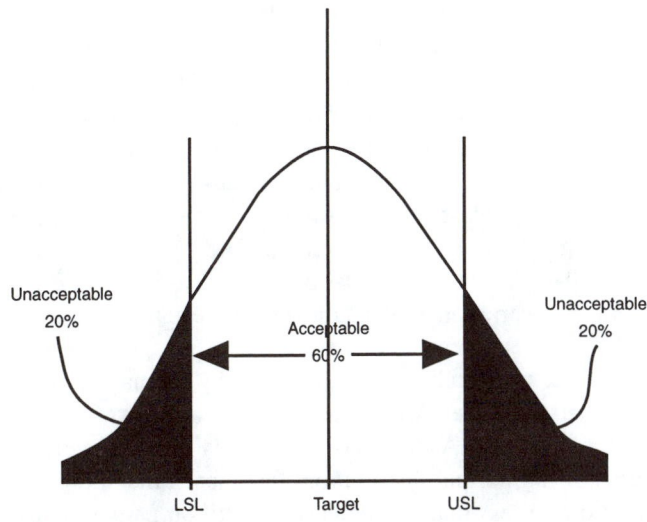

**Figure 3**  Distribution 60% Acceptable

Spread]. The higher the $C_p$ index, the smaller the variation within the process in relation to the tolerance specifications. As a general rule, any $C_p$ greater than 1.33 is considered acceptable—although statistically the process will continue to produce 66 defects per million.

The problem with the $C_p$ index is that it does not take into account the process average. The process variability may be shifted to one side or the other of the specification limits which will result in a greater number of rejected items than the measure indicates. This situation has led to the development of the $C_{pk}$ index, which is a measure of the process in relation to the item's target value and specification limits. $C_{pk}$ is calculated as the lower of:

$$\frac{(\text{Upper Spec Limit}) - (\text{Process Average})}{\text{Process Spread}}$$

$$\frac{-(\text{Lower Spec Limit}) - (\text{Process Average})}{\text{Process Spread}}$$

The process spread is calculated as 3 sigma. As with the $C_p$ index, the general rule is to consider any process capable that has a value of 1.33 or greater. The higher the $C_{pk}$ value, the less variation inherent in the process, or the larger the specification limits.

As mentioned earlier, any item produced that exhibits a value outside the 3 sigma limit for that process identifies a *special* cause of variation. Statistically, this refers to a problem not attributable to the natural variation causes that can be identified and eliminated on the shop floor by the production worker.

The problems associated with the natural variation within the process are referred to as *common* causes. The common causes, resulting in a flatter and wider curve for the process, can only be eliminated by management action through improvements in the overall system. The philosophy of TQM is based on the premise that the variation must be reduced to improve quality and that a reduction in this variation will automatically result in lower costs for the company.

Companies that use quality levels denoted by sigma are referring to the capabilities of their processes. Motorola, one of the winners of the 1988 Malcolm Baldrige National Quality Award, has targeted its quality level at 6 sigma by 1991. In terms of the normal distribution, this means they are improving their processes to produce less than 3.4 defects per million parts produced.

It is important to note that SPC is only a tool to monitor the process and identify the special causes. Although it is a very important tool for quality improvement, it is not useful in reducing the natural variation inherent within the process.

Figure 4 presents a simple example of the control chart developed by Shewhart. The chart is basically the same as the normal curve except it is presented

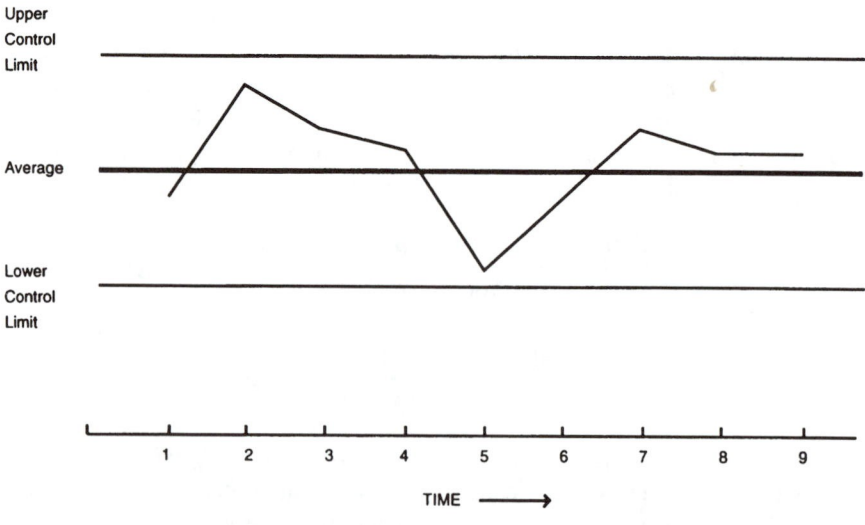

**Figure 4**   Shewhart Control Chart

horizontally and includes a time element. The sample measurements are plotted on the chart, and the process average and control limits (average ± 3 standard deviations) are calculated and drawn as straight lines. This chart does not refer to the specification limits in any way. It is hoped that the specifications of the items to be manufactured within that process are well outside the control limits. If not, the process is not considered capable of producing the item(s) in question.

Any point outside the control limits identifies a special cause of variation that can be corrected by the operator. If the part specifications are well outside the control limits the special causes can be identified and corrected before unacceptable parts are produced.

Other signals to special causes of variation include:

- Seven consecutive points on the same side of the centerline;
- Seven consecutive points that increase or decrease;
- Two out of three consecutive points on the same side of the centerline outside the ±2 sigma zone;
- Other *non-random* patterns—trends, cycles, etc.

Any efforts to bring the control limits closer to the mean need to address the (common) causes of natural variation. One method proven very successful in the reduction of the natural process variation was developed by Taguchi.

## Taguchi Methods

The Taguchi Method for design of experiments is a tool used to reduce the inherent variability in a product or process. It combines engineering and statistics to directly address the process variability problem. The tool is employed primarily in product and process engineering to identify and optimize conflicting inputs (factors) to enable improved quality and reduced cost. Developed by Taguchi, it has enabled him to win the coveted Deming Prize in Japan four times.

The factors in product and process design are defined by Taguchi as controllable and uncontrollable. The interaction of these factors has a direct impact on the performance variation inherent in the product. By concentrating solely on the controllable factors, and their resultant effect on variation, the engineer can design a product or process that minimizes variation, thereby increasing quality and reducing cost.

## Definition of Quality

The Taguchi philosophy is based on the premise that cost can be reduced by improving quality and that quality will automatically improve by reducing variation. This philosophy strongly disagrees with Philip Crosby's statements that quality is solely *conformance to specifications.*

Taguchi believes that tolerance limits are defined to cover up problems in design of the product or process. Minimal variation around the target value is the only true way to achieve high levels of quality. Taguchi states that the difference between an item that is barely within specification and one that is barely out of specification is very little; yet one is considered good and the other is considered bad. Following this philosophy, Taguchi defines quality as *"the loss a product causes to society after being shipped, other than any losses caused by its intrinsic functions."* Any product characteristic that varies from its intended value causes a loss to society, hence poor quality.

To quantify his definition of quality, Taguchi has developed the Quality Loss Function (QLF). The QLF is a graphic representation of the loss to society caused by product/process variation. The graph is a parabola in which the lowest point represents the minimal loss (expressed in monetary terms) to the customer and company. As the target value is missed in either direction, the cost to society increases. Deviations from the target can also represent an over-designed product—heavier, larger, less efficient, etc. The QLF is a tool to be used during the early stages of design, thereby enabling changes to be made as quickly and efficiently as possible (see Figure 5).

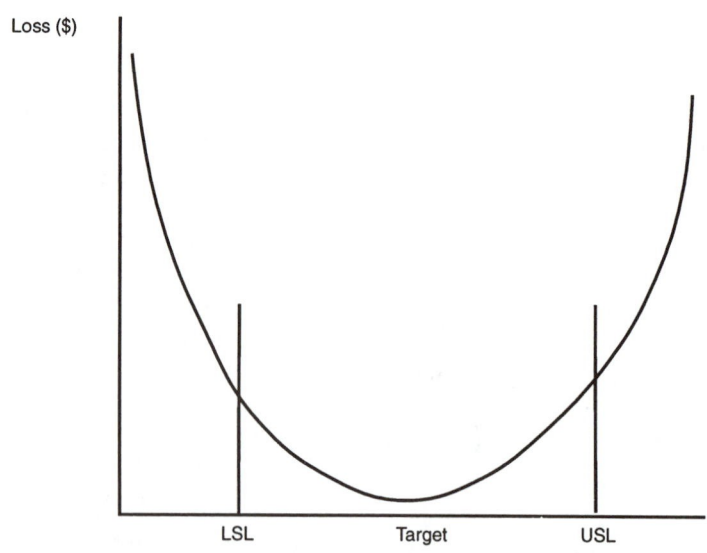

**Figure 5**    Taguchi Loss Function

By emphasizing a long-term focus on the customer's and society's needs and continuous improvement, Taguchi's philosophy closely follows the teachings of Deming and Juran. In particular, Taguchi's practice of designing a product or process that is insensitive to noise will enable the final product to be of consistent quality, thereby reducing the dependence on inspection as a means to achieve quality.

Within his method, Taguchi differentiates between the controllable and uncontrollable (noise) factors. These factors consist of any design characteristic that can cause variation in the product's performance. Examples of design factors include tubing wall thickness, screw thread length, wire diameter, cooling method and coating material. Definitions of the two types of design characteristics are as follows:

- **Control Factors:** Factors affecting product/process performance that can be easily controlled during the production of a product.

- **Noise Factors:** Factors affecting product/process performance that are impossible or too expensive to control, i.e., environmental conditions. There are three types of noise factors: external (environmental), internal (wear, shrinkage, etc.), and product-to-product (resulting from part-to-part variation).

The objective of the Taguchi Method is to reduce the effect of noise factors on variation by concentrating on their interaction with the control factors. Therefore, the control factors are the only factors that can be changed.

## Design Process

In accordance with the TQM concept, Taguchi has made improvements in product/process design by concentrating on the process itself. He has formalized the design process by defining three distinct stages for all products and processes:

- **System Design:** Determine the product's intended function and build a prototype to accomplish objectives. Tentative parameters are defined to construct a prototype.

- **Parameter Design:** Determine the factors affecting product performance and distinguish between controllable and uncontrollable. The objective is to determine the combination of factors least sensitive to changes in the noise factors through design of experiments.

- **Tolerance Design:** If the reduced variation determined through parameter design is not acceptable, design changes are made to attempt to achieve objectives. This usually involves increasing manufacturing and purchase costs, i.e., improved grades of material, tighter tolerances, etc.

## Signal-to-Noise Ratio

The effect of a specific noise factor on the quality of the design is described by its signal-to-noise (S/N) ratio. The S/N ratio refers to statistical measurement of the stability of a quality characteristic's performance. The S/N ratio objective is usually determined by the QLF, and is the target for the parameter design stage. The larger the S/N ratio, the more *robust* the design, i.e., the less sensitive performance will be to noise. If the actual S/N ratio is less than the target value, tolerance design will need to be performed.

Taguchi uses orthogonal arrays to simulate the results of different factor combinations to greatly reduce the number of experiments needed to complete the design. Statistical analysis, utilizing the arrays, quickly aids the engineer in eliminating the factors that will not affect the quality of the design.

## Results

Taguchi Methods are slowly gaining popularity in the United States. In a book published by the American Supplier Institute—the U.S. Center for Taguchi Methods—it was estimated that approximately 5,000 Taguchi Methods case studies are completed annually in the U.S. Although this number sounds impressive, estimates of the method's use in Japan exceed 100,000. Akashi Fukuhara, one person credited with the implementation of TQC at Toyota, stated that the use of Taguchi Methods is the single most important quality improvement tool used by the company.

# PROCESS QUALITY AT VARIFILM

Compare each of the following criteria to Varifilm and indicate whether the situation in the company is a *strength* (S) or *needs improvement* (I). Justify your answer.

## PROCESS MANAGEMENT

### 5.2 Process Management: Product and Service Processes

|  | S | I |
|---|---|---|
| ■ Key indicators are used to evaluate quality and operational performance. | — | — |
| ■ The process management system provides for a controlled process for each product through documentation and standard systems. | — | — |
| ■ A controlled operating system incorporates equipment specifications, production orders, controlled operations, controlled processing procedures, and measurement test methods. | — | — |
| ■ Documentation is available on how to handle out-of-control occurrences for automated processes. | — | — |
| ■ Customer input is reviewed to determine how quality, cycle time, and overall performance can be improved. | — | — |

### 5.3 Process Management: Business Processes and Support Services

| | | |
|---|---|---|
| ■ Internal and external customer requirements are determined through customer discussions, benchmark studies, and internal and external audits. | — | — |
| ■ Support service functions need key indicators with formal charts and regular reviews. | — | — |
| ■ A systematic approach is required for gathering and considering information from customers of the business processes and support services. | — | — |

|  | S | I |
|---|---|---|

■ Information concerning business and support services leads to corrective actions and documentation. ___ ___

■ Support services are prioritized according to importance (e.g., finance and accounting, MIS, human resources, facilities, etc.). ___ ___

■ Business processes are improved through the application of statistical analysis of process data and statistically designed experiments. In addition, benchmarking, process mapping, and process simplification are used. ___ ___

## SUPPLIER QUALITY AND QUALITY ASSESSMENT

### 5.4 Supplier Quality

■ Supplier quality requirements are defined, including product quality, value added, service, and capability and technology. Key indicators for each requirement are also defined. ___ ___

■ A system of supplier certification is in place, as well as a supplier recognition process. ___ ___

■ Supplier input is sought for improvement in supplier specifications, which in turn improves company specifications. ___ ___

■ Specific methods are used for gathering data from suppliers so that procurement activities can be improved. ___ ___

■ Supplier benchmarks are used to improve supplier quality. ___ ___

### 5.5 Quality Assessment

■ Internal audits, TQM fitness reviews, customer surveys, and supplier audits are among the methods for assessing systems and processes. ___ ___

■ Assessment findings lead to specific improvement actions. ___ ___

■ Who assesses the systems and processes, what is assessed, and how often the assessment takes place are clearly defined. ___ ___

*Additional Areas for Improvement*

_____

_____

_____

# FOR FURTHER READING

Cheng, Peter, C. H. Dawson, and D. Samuel, " A Study of Statistical Process Control: Practice, Problems and Training Needs," *Total Quality Management,* Feb. 1998, pp. 3–20.

Coate, Charles J. and Karen J. Frey, "Theory of Constraints: It Doesn't Mean Good-Bye to Variances," *Management Accounting—London,* Nov. 1998, pp. 31–33.

Dale, Barrie, Ruth Boaden, and Mark McQuarter, "The Use of Quality Management Techniques and Tools," *International Journal of Technology Management,* Vol. 16 No. 4–6, 1998, pp. 305–325.

Graves, Chris and Bruce Gurd, "Throughput Accounting: A Revolution in the Making?" *Australian CPA,* Aug. 1998, pp. 36–38.

Hewitt, Stephen, "Strategic Advantages Emerge from Tactical TQM Tools," *Quality Progress,* Oct. 1994, pp. 57–59.

# 7

# CUSTOMER AND MARKET FOCUS

*There is only one valid definition of business purpose:*
*To Create a Customer.*

Peter Drucker[1]

Customer and market focus is the third performance criterion of the 1999 Baldrige Award criteria:

■ **Customer and Market Knowledge.** How the company determines longer term requirements, expectations, and preferences of target and/or potential customers and markets. Also how the company uses this information to understand and anticipate needs and to develop business opportunities.

■ **Customer Satisfaction and Relationship Enhancement.** How the company determines and enhances the satisfaction of its customers to build relationships, to improve current offerings, and to support customer- and market-related planning. The following areas are addressed:
   a. Accessibility and complaint management
   b. Customer satisfaction determination
   c. Relationship building[2]

   The principles discussed in this chapter and in the entire book apply equally to both service and manufacturing firms. Judging from what is known about U.S.

manufacturing and service firms, not many companies would receive a grade of "A" for customer focus. A comprehensive study of 584 companies by the consulting firm Ernst & Young found that customer complaints were of "major or primary" importance in identifying new products and services among only 19 percent of banks and 26 percent of hospitals.

The widespread tendency to ignore complaints or track them and identify the cause(s) can have very serious consequences. This is particularly true in services, where it is estimated that for every complaint a business receives, there are 26 other customers who feel the same way but do not air their feelings to the company.[3]

Failure to identify the root cause of complaints means that reduction of variation in the causative process is more difficult. A customer unable to get through to a sales representative is evidence of a malfunction in the telephone procedure (process) or the sales and marketing function. Thus, it becomes necessary to tie the customer to the process.

Evidence indicates that part of the cause of this failure to close the customer–process loop is inadequate support from top management for the total quality management (TQM) infrastructure and a continued focus on the techniques of TQM, particularly statistical process control (SPC).

The Ernst & Young study mentioned previously found that quality-performance measures such as defect rates and customer satisfaction levels play a key role in determining pay for senior managers in only fewer than one in five companies. *Profitability* is still king. There is, of course, nothing wrong with a focus on cash flow and short-term profits, but long-term profit and market share require a base of satisfied customers that are retained by a focus on satisfaction. Some top executives may not like to believe the level or severity of customer complaints or may be offended by them. When Amtrak was criticized in the *Wall Street Journal* by a transportation analyst (Lind), the president of Amtrak responded (in the same paper):

> ■ My own conclusion is that this [comment] is based on hopelessly incorrect assumptions about Amtrak and the railroad industry, and that Mr. Lind would be well advised to limit his comments and suggestions to the streetcar and transit business with which he is familiar and to avoid getting over his depth.[4]

While it may be true that the president of Amtrak is correct in this case, such an attitude expressed publicly could very well pervade the work force, who might perceive the message as justification for continuing the existing level of service.

Another reason for the lack of customer focus is the tendency of many firms to emphasize the techniques of TQM such as SPC and other outcome-oriented methods such as productivity and cost reduction. Again, these are desirable and necessary, but a singular emphasis on these areas is to put the cart before the horse.

The customer is not really interested in the sophistication of a company's process control, its training program, or its culture. The bottom line for the customer is whether he or she obtains the desired product or service. This truism is recognized by Deming, Juran, and Crosby.

Some companies indicate a commitment to customer and market focus by adopting and publicizing a mission statement. The following is a sample of customer service mission statements:

- Focus on customers and uncover innovative ways to service their product needs.

- The consumer is our boss, quality is our work and value for money is our goal.

- Customers are the focus of everything we do—Our work must be done with our customers in mind, providing better products and services than our competition.

## PROCESS VS. CUSTOMER

Chapter 6 described the steps and methods for process analysis and design for manufacturing processes. There is no reason why similar steps and methods would not apply for design, delivery, and follow-up of service processes. Consider, for example, the processes involved in the delivery of health care.[5] Excellent service is achieved by having explicit standards with measurable targets and outcomes. Employment of process analysis methodology looks for ways of simplifying the patient flow through the service with its many subtrails, thereby reducing such costly procedures as duplication of assessments, multiple tests on separate days, and unnecessary bed days predischarge. The insurance industry is representative of a growing number of service industries that are utilizing process analysis to improve the quality of the service while reducing costs.[6]

Customer complaints are analogous to process variation. Both are undesirable and must be addressed. In both cases, the optimum output must be compared against an objective, a standard, or a benchmark. Both are integral parts of the quality improvement process. The integration of the customer and the process is shown conceptually in Figure 7-1.

From the company's point of view, customer satisfaction is the result of a three-part system: (1) company processes (operations), (2) company employees

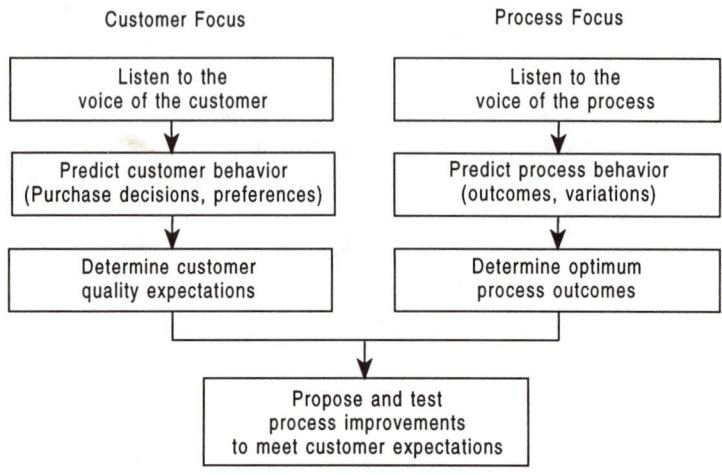

Customer Focus | Process Focus

Listen to the voice of the customer → Predict customer behavior (Purchase decisions, preferences) → Determine customer quality expectations

Listen to the voice of the process → Predict process behavior (outcomes, variations) → Determine optimum process outcomes

Propose and test process improvements to meet customer expectations

**Figure 7-1** Integration of Customer and Process (Adapted from Dean E. Headley and Bob Choi, "Achieving Service Quality through Gap Analysis and a Basic Statistical Approach," *Journal of Services Marketing,* Winter 1992, p. 7.)

who deliver the product, and service that is consistent with (3) customer expectations. Thus, the effectiveness of the three-part system is a function of how well these three factors are integrated.

This concept is shown in Figure 7-2. The overlap (shaded area) represents the extent to which customer satisfaction is achieved. The objective is to make this area as large as possible and ultimately to make all three circles converge into an integrated system. The extent to which this condition is achieved depends on the effectiveness of (1) the process, (2) employees, and (3) determination of what constitutes "satisfaction." Like any system, control is necessary.

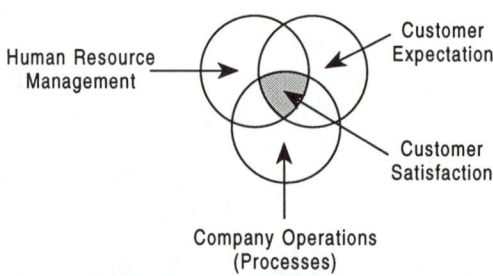

Human Resource Management — Customer Expectation — Customer Satisfaction — Company Operations (Processes)

**Figure 7-2** Customer Satisfaction: Three-Part System

Thus, standards are set, performance is measured, and variation, if any, is corrected.

■ Ritz-Carlton Hotel Company won the Baldrige Award in 1992. Many people thought that no hotel could do this because service in this industry is so difficult to measure and to deliver. The company meticulously gathers data on every aspect of the guest's stay to determine if the hotels are meeting customer expectations. Key to the research are the daily quality production reports that identify all problems and defects reported in each of 720 work areas. The data compiled range from the time it takes for housekeepers to clean a room to the number of guests who must wait in line to check in.[7]

## INTERNAL CUSTOMER CONFLICT

*The next process is your customer.*

Kaoru Ishikawa[8]

Internal customers are also important in a TQM program. These are the people, the activities, and the functions within the company that are the customers of other people, activities, or functions. Hence, manufacturing is the customer of design, and several departments may be customers of data processing.

Conflict frequently arises between the needs of internal and external customers. In many cases, processes are designed to meet the needs of internal customers. Any "customer" who has been admitted to a hospital or outpatient service understands this. The registration process is designed to meet the needs of the admitting department, business office, or medical records. The result is a long wait to give information that will be provided again and again to personnel who represent admitting, the laboratory, finance, social work, and medicine. Who is the customer? Who is the beneficiary? Who is the recipient of the output? The patient gets the impression that he or she is a piece of raw material being moved along an amorphous assembly line known as health care.

It is not too difficult to identify other examples in both the private and public sectors. How about a university? It has been said that if you want to find out what kind of organization you are about to do business with, call on the phone!

A balance needs to be struck between the needs of these two customer groups. The solution is to determine the real needs of each and design the process to meet both.

Historically, banks have designed their service quality programs using the traditional definition of a customer as someone who has one account with the bank. Provident Bank of Maryland realized that it was time to think about that view and in so doing decided that the traditional definition was too narrow. The bank recognized that the quality of service it provides to its external customers depends greatly on the quality of service that exists between departments. Service quality begins with the bank's employees. Based on this view, Provident embarked on a double-patch service quality program, with specific programs aimed at both sets of customers.

## DEFINING QUALITY

*A customer is the most important person ever in this office—in person or by mail.*
*A customer is not dependent on us, we are dependent on him or her.*
*A customer is not an interruption of our work, he is the purpose of it.*
*We are not doing him a favor by serving him, he is doing us a favor...*

L.L. Bean (poster)

In 1997, *Consumer Reports* magazine surveyed over 30,000 readers with more than 55,000 shopping experiences to find out how consumers rated clothing stores in overall satisfaction (service, quality, value). Of 34 department stores rated, only one (Nordstrom's) scored five pluses for service, only one (Nordstrom's) scored five pluses for quality, and only one (Steinmart) scored five points for value.[9] Of eight mass merchandisers, seven off-price chains, and two warehouse clubs, none scored above one plus for either service or quality. (The rating system rated satisfaction with from one to five plus [+] marks.) These results seem to indicate that consumers tend to define quality as a balance among service, quality, and value (price). The results also suggest the elusive problem of defining quality or the customer's perception of quality.

Supreme Court Justice Potter Stewart once said that while he could not define "obscenity," he knew it when he saw it. Wrestling with a definition of quality is almost as difficult, but necessary nevertheless. You cannot manage what you cannot measure.

The several dimensions of quality (performance, features, reliability, etc.) were discussed in a previous section.[10] However, the shortfall regarding product quality is that the services connected with it are so frequently overlooked. Good packaging, timely and accurate shipping, and the ability to meet deadlines matter as much as the quality of the product itself. Customers define quality in terms of their total experience with the company. Many companies approach customer satisfaction in a narrow way by confining quality considerations to the product alone.[11]

## A QUALITY FOCUS

It is impossible to avoid the constant bombardment of "quality" and "satisfaction" messages in advertising on television and radio and in print media. Much of this advertising, and the actions to deliver the product or service, is little more than vague rhetoric. Even the popular phrases "satisfaction guaranteed" or "low price guaranteed" do not state what the customer is supposed to get for his or her purchase.

Some companies have attempted to improve this rhetoric by supplementing the message with additional definitions of satisfaction. McDonald's guarantees customer satisfaction with the pledge: "If you are not satisfied, we'll make it right or the next meal is on us." What does the phrase *make it right* mean? The question is whether this guarantee relates to product quality and customer satisfaction or is merely a promotion. Perhaps the slogan should be changed to "enjoyment guaranteed."

Many firms back up a satisfaction guarantee with promises of a reward if they fail to meet their own standards or those of the customer. Hampton Inns refunds your money. At Pizza Hut, you get it free if not served in five minutes. Some firms give you a $5 bill. Delta Dental Plans of Massachusetts sends you a check for $50 if you get transferred from phone to phone while seeking an answer to an insurance question. Automobile dealers and manufacturers are fond of promoting "quality service" without defining just what this is. Some back it up with such specifics as towing service, a free ride to work, or a loaner car when the customer's car is kept overnight.

There are two advantages to backing up a guarantee with some penalty for failure to deliver. It can cure employee apathy and bring quality to the attention of employees on a personal basis. It also may leave the buyer with a perception of dedication and thereby serve to retain what otherwise may have been a lost customer. These customers may say to themselves and others: "Well, my pizza was ten minutes late but they gave me a free one, so that proves they are serious about quality." Retaining this customer, who now has a better perception and higher expectation, may be worth the cost of the pizza and the foregone sale.

It should be remembered that any effort to tie the message of satisfaction to a failure-to-deliver penalty is ineffective if the variation or failure is not traced back to process improvement and the cause of the variation. Why was the pizza delivered late? Why was the customer shifted from phone to phone? Why did the dealer keep the car overnight? The variation–cause connection is identified by problem solving and the process improvement through process control.

## Break Points

The need to improve customer satisfaction in *measurable* amounts is well known. But what is the measure and how much improvement is needed? If a customer is willing to stand in line for two minutes but finds five minutes unacceptable, anything between is merely satisfactory. Zero to one minute is outstanding. On-time delivery below 90 percent may be judged by customers as unacceptable, while over 98 percent is considered outstanding. Improvement programs should be geared toward reaching either a two-minute or five-minute range for standing in line and either 90 or 98 percent for delivery times. These are the market *break points,* where improving performance will change customer behavior, resulting in higher prices or sales volume. Forget the improvement program that targets one minute waiting in line or the delivery program that targets between 90 and 98 percent.

## A Central Theme

Although individuals and teams may have targets that are directed at process improvement in their specific activities, a common theme or focus may integrate the many individual or group efforts that may have their own priority. At Motorola, the theme is *six sigma*; at Hewlett-Packard, it is a *tenfold reduction in warranty expense.* At General Electric, no part will be produced that cannot meet a *one-part-in-a-million* defect rate. At MBNA of America (a credit card company), the target is *customer retention.* In other companies, it can be a reduction in defects or cycle time. Such a theme tends to be pervasive because so many individuals can relate their activities to it. It can serve to mobilize employees around an overall quality culture.

## THE DRIVER OF CUSTOMER SATISFACTION

The benefits of having customers who are satisfied is well known and was outlined in Chapter 1. The issues in building customer satisfaction are to acquire satisfied customers, know when you have them, and keep them.[12]

The obvious way to determine what makes customers satisfied is simply to ask them. Before or concurrently with a customer survey, an audit of the company's TQM infrastructure needs to be made. IBM is one company that has identified the key excellence indicators for customer satisfaction. These key indicators are listed in Table 7-1.[13]

Despite the obvious need for customer input in determining new product/ service offerings and improving existing ones, the widespread tendency is to

**Table 7-1**    Key Excellence Indicators for Customer Satisfaction

- Service standards derived from customer requirements
- Understanding customer requirements
  - Thoroughness/objectivity
  - Customer types
  - Product/service features
- Front-line empowerment (resolution)
- Strategic infrastructure support for front-line employees
- Attention to hiring, training, attitude, morale for front-line employees
- High levels of satisfaction—customer awards
- Proactive customer service systems
- Proactive management of relationships with customer
- Use of all listening posts
  - Surveys
  - Product/service follow-ups
  - Complaints
  - Turnover of customers
  - Employees
- Quality requirements of market segments
  - Surveys go beyond current customers
  - Commitment to customer (trust/confidence/making good on word)

determine perceived quality and perceived customer satisfaction based almost solely on in-house surveys.[14] Even when the company does attempt to get input, the survey may suffer from methodology shortcomings. Mailed questionnaires lose control over who responds, and respondents are less likely to reply if they are dissatisfied or if the name of the company or product is indicated. Just what is satisfaction? If the customer's expectation is low, satisfaction may be acceptable, but perception will not improve. If perception is low but satisfaction is acceptable, how is this determined and what can be done? Suppose that 95 percent of respondents indicate satisfaction but do not perceive the product as one of the best. Survey results can be misconstrued and lead to complacency.[15]

- The hotel chain Ritz-Carlton, a Baldrige winner, relies on technology to keep comprehensive computerized guest history profiles on the likes and dislikes of more than 240,000 repeat guests. Researchers survey more than 25,000 guests each year to find ways in which the chain can improve delivery of its service.[16]

## HANDLING SERVICE COMPLAINTS

Many companies consider investment in handling of complaints as a means of increasing customer commitment and building customer loyalty. According to the Technical Assistance Research Programs Institute, 91 percent of unhappy customers will never again purchase goods from a company with which they have an unresolved complaint. The same research shows that up to 70 percent of complainers will return to a business if the complaint is resolved; 95 percent will return if it is resolved quickly.[17]

Effective complaint handling can have a dramatic impact on customer retention rates, deflect the spread of damaging word of mouth, and improve bottom-line performance. The Hampton Inn hotel chain, for example, recently realized $11 million in additional annual revenue and achieved the highest customer retention rate in the industry from implementation of its service guarantee, part of a strategy to ensure that customer problems are dealt with effectively.[18]

Reporting in the *Journal of Marketing,* three researchers maintain an ongoing "complaint call scorecard" of complaint handling by restaurant chains based on four criteria: how long they wait, manners, follow-up times, and what remunerations were received.

In this self-serve era of the "select-from-the-following-menu" phone call, it is difficult to speak to a real person or a customer service representative. It is hard to feel like a valued customer when a listless representative reads from a script, as did the ones from Burger King and Pizza Hut. Pizza Hut defended its scripted plan: "If we have a certain corporate policy a person doesn't agree with, we don't want the person on the phone debating the policy." Want to register a complaint with Subway? Then be prepared to face "Automated Attendant." First, you will be asked to enter your zip code (which the authors did, only to be asked to do it twice more). Pressing zero for an operator only starts the recording from the top. After a few moments of silence, a voice announces that "Automated Attendant is hanging up now."

While most of the 15 chains called followed up by letter within three or four days, three (Bob Evans, Burger King, and Wendy's) took about a week and a half. Only four managed calls back. Most responses were form letters. The form letter from Denny's didn't even state the problem. The letter from Wendy's contained a terse apology and then launched into a promotion of the chain's new stuffed pita line. (During the initial complaint call, the authors were asked how many times they ate at a Wendy's and how much was spent on average.)

While receiving coupons and/or the promise of reimbursement for a meal was common (10 of 15 chains did so), Jack In The Box sent a handwritten letter, two meal coupons, and a smiley-faced antenna ball.

## GETTING EMPLOYEE INPUT

Employee input can be solicited concurrent with customer research. It can help identify barriers and solutions to service and product problems, as well as serve as a customer–company interface.[19] Such surveys can help identify changes that may be necessary for quality improvement. In addition to customer-related considerations, employee surveys can measure (1) TQM effectiveness, (2) skills and behaviors that need improvement, (3) the effectiveness of the team problem-solving process, (4) the outcomes of training programs, and (5) needs of internal customers.[20]

> ■ Corning Inc., a leader in the glassware industry, asked line and staff groups worldwide to assess themselves using the Baldrige criteria. Each group was to develop a few quality strategies that would address the most critical elements identified in the assessment. Measures, referred to a Key Result Indicators, that focused on evidence of customer deliverables and process outcomes were required.[21]

## MEASUREMENT OF CUSTOMER SATISFACTION

The accelerating interest in the measurement of customer satisfaction is reflected in the over 170 consulting firms that specialize in this activity.[22] Some firms use the "squeaky wheel" or "if it ain't broke, don't fix it" approach and measure customer satisfaction based on the level of complaints. This has a number of disadvantages. First, it focuses on the negative aspects by measuring dissatisfaction rather than satisfaction. Second, the measure is based on the complaints of a vocal few and may cause costly or unneeded changes in a process. As indicated at the beginning of this chapter, for every complaint, there are 26 others who feel the same way but do not air their feelings.

There are two basic steps in a measurement system: (1) develop key indicators that drive customer satisfaction and (2) collect data regarding the perceptions of quality received by customers.[23]

Key indicators of customer satisfaction are what the company has chosen to represent quality in its products and services and the way in which these are delivered. The building blocks that the system is designed to track are (1) expectations of the customer and (2) company perceptions of customer expectations.

In Chapter 1, a number of indicators for the physical product (e.g., reliability, aesthetics, adaptability, etc.) were identified. For service businesses or for services that accompany a product, the range of indicators depends on the nature of the service. One authority[24] has suggested that some important areas to consider are outcome, timeliness of the service, satisfaction, dependability, reputation of the provider, friendliness/courteousness of employees, safety/risk of the service, billing/invoicing procedures, responsiveness to requests, competence, appearance of the physical facilities, approachability of the service provider, location and access, respect for customer feelings/rights, willingness to listen to the customer, honesty, and an ability to communicate in clear language. These indicators, if appropriate and addressable, are converted to action items that reflect specific delivery systems where the product or service meets the customer. For example, customer needs and systems in a bank would combine to deliver short teller lines, friendly and courteous staff, ATMs that work, and low fees on accounts.

Data collection is required in order to identify the needs of customers and the related problems of process delivery. The data-gathering process surveys both customers and employees. By including employees, customer needs and barriers to service can be identified, as well as recommendations for process improvement. Different orientations are emphasized for customers and employees; the former are asked for *their* expectations, and the latter are asked what they think *customers* expect.

## THE ROLE OF MARKETING AND SALES

Marketing and sales are the functions charged with gathering customer input, but in many firms the people in these functions are unfamiliar with quality improvement.[25] Shortcomings in marketing as identified by critics include:[26]

- Partnering arrangements with dealers and distribution channels
- Focusing on the physical characteristics of products and overlooking the related services
- Losing a sense of customer price sensitivity
- Not measuring or certifying suppliers such as advertisers
- Failing to perform cost/benefit analyses on promotion costs
- Losing markets to generics and house brands

  - According to one source, Motorola is a world-class producer of products but is less than world-class in marketing. Historically, the company has been oriented toward engineering and technology. Its six sigma quality is well known. The publisher of *Technologic Com-*

*puter Letter* says, "With many product lines Motorola has an extremely compelling story to tell but it is used to hiding its light under a bushel and does not make its advantages heard."[27]

Quality and customer satisfaction have not played an important role in the sales function (*process*). Consider the stereotype of a salesperson. He or she is detail (rather than process) oriented and trained in technical product knowledge (rather than customer knowledge). Salespeople are feature oriented: "We've got six models, four colors, and it comes with a money-back guarantee." They are trained and rewarded for getting new customers, as opposed to retaining existing ones.

## THE SALES PROCESS

According to Hiroshi Osada of the Union of Japanese Scientists and Engineers (JUSE), TQM needs to begin with the salespeople.[28] Yet TQM has migrated to the sales force in only a few companies.[29] Even fewer perceive sales as a *process* that lends itself to analysis and improvement for customer satisfaction. To repeat a previous caveat, "If you can't measure it, you can't manage it." Another can be added: "You can't measure it if it's not a process." Both of these cliches are as true for sales and marketing as for any other process. The objective is quality outcomes. In order for TQM to become a part of sales and marketing, managers and employees must move toward a deeper understanding of its processes—selling, advertising, promoting, innovating, distribution, pricing, and packaging—*as they relate to customer satisfaction.*

Marketing applications need not be confined to the marketing department. Other functions can borrow these techniques to improve the satisfaction of external and internal customers. A brokerage firm should not only care about sending accurate statements on time but should also be concerned with whether the statement format fits the customer's needs. In an issue of *Marketing News,* Research Professor Eugene H. Fram of the Rochester Institute of Technology suggests the following types of non-traditional marketing extensions:[30]

- **Adapted** marketing refers to a non-marketing function that adapts traditional techniques. Relationship selling is an example. If a human resource department sends the same recruiter each year to a campus, this person can use principles of relationship selling to further company goals. This type of selling can also be used within the organization and between departments. The classic conflict between production (cost) and sales (delivery) can be reduced.

- **Morale** marketing can improve morale. Consider what the terms "Team Taurus" or "Team Xerox" did for morale in those companies.

- **Sensitivity** marketing borrows from the basic marketing principle which says that one must understand the customer's needs in order to fulfill them and to build long-term relationships. In a marketing sense, individuals, groups, and departments are better able to achieve quality and productivity if they are sensitive to the needs, concerns, and priorities of both internal and external customers.

## SERVICE QUALITY AND CUSTOMER RETENTION

Customer defection is a problem and customer retention an opportunity in both manufacturing and service firms. Manufacturers have generally been good about measuring satisfaction with products, but now they are moving into service areas. The publicity surrounding the Baldrige Award accounts for much of this. Other reasons relate to the size and growth of service industries and the growing importance of service as a means of strategically competing in the marketplace.

Service industries are playing an increasingly important role in a nation's economy. Over 75 percent of the working population in the United States is employed in the service sector, and the percentage is growing. When this employment is combined with service jobs in the manufacturing sector, it becomes evident that the importance of services is increasing. Many executives feel that the management of services is one of the most important problems they face today. Yet most of us know from personal experience that the quality of services is declining, despite the efforts of some companies to improve it.

Because so many services are intangible, the interaction between employees and customers is critical. Chase Manhattan Bank realizes that an employee's ability to meet or exceed customer expectations when conducting a routine transaction influences the customer's satisfaction with the organization. In fact, this interaction influences satisfaction more than the actual product or service obtained. The one-on-one or face-to-face contact between the customer and the deliverer of the service (nurse, flight attendant, retail clerk, restaurant server) is extremely important.

Manufacturers are careful to measure material yield, waste scrap, rework, returns, and other costs of poor quality processes. Service companies also have these costs, which are reflected in the cost of customers who will not come back because of poor service. These are customer defections, and they have a substantial impact on cost and profits. Indeed, it is estimated that customer defections can have a greater impact than economies of scale, market share, or unit cost.[31]

Despite this, many companies fail to *measure* defections, determine the *cause* of defections, and improve the *process* to reduce defections.

## CUSTOMER RETENTION AND PROFITABILITY

What is the ultimate desired outcome of customer focus and satisfaction? Is it achieving profit in the private sector or productivity in the public or non-profit sectors? The answer must be yes. Oddly enough, however, an accurate cause-and-effect relationship has yet to be established between profit and customer satisfaction. This is due, in part, to the difficulty of measuring satisfaction and relating it to profit. However, there is a proven relationship between *customer retention and profit.*

One way to put a value on customer retention is to assign or estimate a "lifetime retention value," the additional sales that would result if the customer were retained. Taco Bell calculates the lifetime value of a retained customer as $11,000. An automobile dealer believes that the lifetime value of retaining a customer is $300,000 in sales.[32] Conversely, MBNA America (a credit card company) has found that a 5 percent improvement in customer *defections* increases its average customer value by 125 percent.

The system for improving *customer retention* and profit is illustrated in Figure 7-3. The drivers are *employee satisfaction* and *employee retention*. The system components are

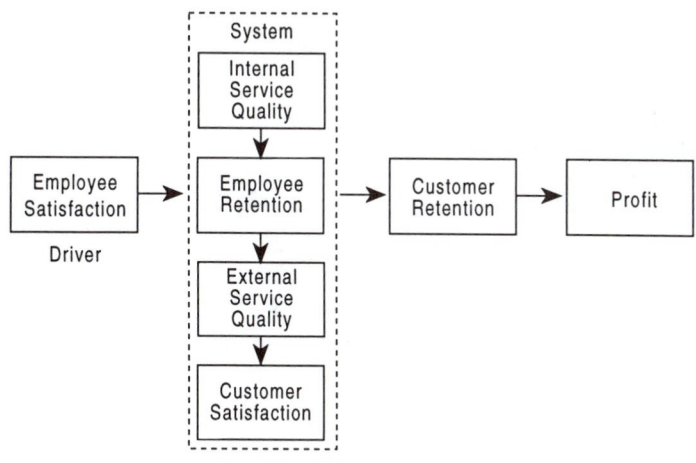

**Figure 7-3**   Profitability and Customer Retention

- **Internal service quality,** which establishes and reinforces a climate and organization culture directed toward quality.

- **Employee retention,** which is achieved through good human resource management practices and organization development methods such as teams, job development, and empowerment. Employee retention depends on employee satisfaction, which in turn can be related to external service and customer satisfaction.

- **External service quality,** which is delivered through the organization's quality infrastructure.

- **Customer satisfaction** and follow-up, in order to reduce customer defections and improve retention.

To reiterate, there is a proven relationship between customer retention and profit.

## BUYER–SUPPLIER RELATIONSHIPS

Almost every company purchases products, supplies, or services in an amount that frequently equals around 50 percent of its sales. Traditionally, many of these companies have followed the "lowest bidder" practice, where price is the critical criterion. The focus on price, even for commodity products, is changing as companies realize that careful concentration of purchases, together with long-term supplier–buyer relationships, will reduce costs and improve profits.[33] Deming realized this and suggested that a long-term relationship between purchaser and supplier is necessary for best economy.[34] If a buyer has to rework, repair, inspect, or otherwise expend time and cost on a supplier's product, the buyer is involved in a "value/quality-added" operation, which is not the purpose of having a reliable supplier. In that never-never land of the perfect buyer–supplier relationship, no rework or inspection is necessary.

A partnership arrangement is emerging between a growing number of manufacturers and suppliers. At Eastman Kodak, the Quality Leadership Process (QLP) has improved the company's production processes, reduced overall manufacturing costs, and improved quality by transforming traditional manufacturer–supplier roles. Because one-half of all components used in manufacturing are supplied by outside vendors, realignment of the supplier base has become a central strategy of QLP.[35]

- Motorola has advanced the supplier–customer relationship further than most companies. The system is based on a basic economic principle: whenever someone buys from someone else, there is a mutually beneficial transaction and pleasing both sides is important.

With this in mind, Motorola has begun to market itself as a customer. The company's director of materials and purchasing says, "If the sauce is good for the goose, it should be good for the gander, and we are genuinely trying to cooperate, collaborate and do some strategic things with our suppliers. Our goal is to become a world-class customer and that means that it is important for us to learn what the buyer needs to do in order for suppliers to see us as a world-class customer."[36]

Several guidelines will help both the supplier and customer benefit from a long-term partnering relationship:

- **Implementation of TQM by both supplier and customer.** Many customers (e.g., Motorola, Ford, Xerox) are requiring suppliers to operationalize the basic principles of TQM. Some have even required the supplier to apply for the Baldrige Award. This joint effort provides a common language and builds confidence between both parties.

- **Long-term commitment to TQM and to the partnering relationship between the parties.** This may mean a "life cycle" relationship that carries partnering through the life cycle of the product, from market research and design through production and service.

- **Reduction in the supplier base.** One or more automobile companies have reduced the number of suppliers from thousands to hundreds. Why have ten suppliers for a part when the top two will do a better job and avoid problems?

- **Get suppliers involved in the early stages of research, development, and design.** Such involvement generates additional ideas for cost and quality improvement and prevents problems at a later stage of the product life cycle.

- **Benchmarking.** Both customer and supplier can seek out and agree on the best-in-class products and processes.

How does one become a quality supplier? This, of course, depends on the criteria of the buyer, but it is reasonably safe to assume that if the following criteria are met, a company can reasonably expect to be classified in the quality category. The following criteria are required to be certified as *quality* in the automobile industry:

1. *Management philosophy* of the CEO should support TQM
2. Techniques of *quality control* should be in place (SPC, etc.)
3. Desire for a long-term *life cycle relationship*
4. Best-in-class *inventory and purchasing systems*
5. *Facilities* should be up to TQM standards

6. *Automation* level should meet quality standards
7. *R&D and design* should support customer expectations
8. Willing to *share costs*

## QUESTIONS FOR DISCUSSION

**7-1** Describe how a program directed toward customer focus and satisfaction interacts with:

- The information and analysis component of the TQM approach
- Strategic quality planning
- Human resource development and management
- Management of process quality

**7-2** Select a function or activity (e.g., design, order processing, accounting, data processing, engineering, market research) and identify a measure of quality that you would expect if you were an *internal* customer of that function or activity.

**7-3** Choose a specific product or service in a particular industry and devise an action plan for obtaining customer input and feedback. How would the information generated by such a plan be used for process improvement?

**7-4** Illustrate how a firm might focus on *internal* product or service specifications rather than customer expectations and desires.

**7-5** Choose a product or service and list four or five characteristics that you as a customer would want and expect. Based on your experience, do you think that the firm will deliver?

**7-6** How would you establish a system to measure customer satisfaction?

## ENDNOTES

1. Peter Drucker, *The Age of Discontinuity: Guidelines to Our Changing Society,* New York: Harper & Row, 1969.
2. Malcolm Baldrige National Quality Award Criteria—1999, Washington, D.C.: National Institute of Standards and Technology, U.S. Department of Commerce, 1999, p. 29.
3. "Satisfaction-Action," *Marketing News,* Feb. 4, 1991, p. 4.
4. "Management: Quality Programs Show Shoddy Results," *Wall Street Journal,* May 14, 1992, Section B, p. 1.

5. Hugh Koch, "Making the Process Responsive to the Customer," *International Journal of Health Care Quality Assurance,* Vol. 8 No. 5, 1995, p. 3.

6. Ralph Mohney, "Reengineering the New Business Process: Lessons Learned from Refocusing on the Customer," *Journal of the American Society of CLU,ChFC,* Vol. 49 No. 5, Sept. 1995, pp. 90–94.

7. Edward Watkins, "How Ritz-Carlton Won the Baldrige Award," *Lodging Hospitality,* Nov. 1992, p. 23.

8. Kaoru Ishikawa, *Guide to Quality Control,* Tokyo: Asian Productivity Organization, 1992.

9. "Sorting Out the Stores," *Consumer Reports,* Nov. 1998, pp. 12–17.

10. See David A. Garvin, *Managing Quality,* New York: The Free Press, 1988, pp. 49–59. Garvin has defined the eight dimensions of quality as performance, features, reliability, conformance, durability, serviceability, aesthetics, and perceived quality. Computer-maker NCR goes to great expense to define quality as appropriateness, reliability, aesthetics, and usability. Industrial designers have given the company a silver medal for design. For a comprehensive report on how product design enhances profits and market share, see a special report, "Hot Products: How Good Design Pays Off" (cover story), *Business Week,* June 7, 1993, pp. 54–78.

11. Oren Harari, "Quality Is a Good Bit-Box," *Management Review,* Dec. 1992, p. 8.

12. Gerald O. Cavallo and Joel Perelmuth, "Building Customer Satisfaction, Strategically," *Bottomline,* Jan. 1989, p. 29.

13. These indicators are taken from class material in an IBM in-house workshop, "MDQ (Market Driven Quality) Workshop." The company was kind enough to share this class material with the authors and several other professors from the College of Business, Florida Atlantic University. For this, we thank them.

14. It was found, for example, that in the hospital industry fewer than 5 percent of referring physicians play a prominent role in identifying new service opportunities. Nearly 40 percent of U.S. hospitals indicate that senior management "always or almost always" takes the dominant role in identifying new services." U.S. hospitals seek minimal input from patients. *The International Quality Study, Healthcare Industry Report,* American Quality Foundation and Ernst & Young, 1992.

15. For some ideas on getting customer input, see Joel E. Ross and David Georgoff, "A Survey of Productivity and Quality Issues in Manufacturing: The State of the Industry," *Industrial Management,* Jan./Feb. 1991.

16. Edward Watkins, "How Ritz-Carlton Won the Baldrige Award," *Lodging Hospitality,* Nov. 1992, p. 24.

17. Robert Klara, "Press 1 to Gripe," *Restaurant Business,* May 15, 1998, pp. 96–102.

18. Stephen S. Tax, Stephen W. Brown, and Murali Chandrashekaran, "Customer Evaluations of Service Complaint Experiences: Implications for Relationship Marketing," *Journal of Marketing,* April 1998, pp. 60–76.

19. Luane Kohnke, "Designing a Customer Satisfaction Measurement Program," *Bank Marketing,* July 1990, p. 29.

20. Kate Ludeman, "Using Employee Surveys to Revitalize TQM," *Training,* Dec. 1992, pp. 51–57.

21. David Luther, "Advanced TQM: Measurements, Missteps, and Progress through Key Result Indicators at Corning," *National Productivity Review,* Winter 1992/1993, pp. 23–36.

22. Lynn G. Coleman, "Learning What Customers Like," *Marketing News,* March 2, 1992, pp. CSM-1–CSM-11. This article contains a directory of 170 customer satisfaction measurement firms.

23. For a more detailed description of how to establish a measurement system, see J. Joseph Cronin, Jr. and Steven A. Taylor, "Measuring Service Quality: A Reexamination and Extension," *Journal of Marketing,* July 1992, pp. 55–68. See also Luane Kohnke, "Designing a Customer Measurement Program," *Bank Marketing,* July 1990, pp. 28–30; Gerald O. Cavallo and Joel Perelmuth, "Building Customer Satisfaction, Strategically," *Bottomline,* Jan. 1989, pp. 29–33.

24. Dean E. Headley and Bob Choi, "Achieving Service Quality through Gap Analysis and a Basic Statistical Approach," *Journal of Services Marketing,* Winter 1992, pp. 5–14. This is a good primer on gap analysis and the use of basic statistical techniques.

25. Joe M. Inguanzo, "Taking a Serious Look at Patient Expectations," *Hospitals,* Sept. 5, 1992, p. 68. This article points out that there is very little employee involvement in measuring satisfaction and practically none from patients.

26. Allan J. Magrath, "Marching to a Different Drummer," *Across the Board,* June 1992, pp. 53–54.

27. B. G. Yovovich, "Becoming a World-Class Customer," *Business Marketing,* Sept. 1991, p. 16.

28. Dick Schaaf, "Selling Quality," *Training,* June 1992, pp. 53–59.

29. John Franco, president of Learning International in Stamford, Connecticut, has conducted a series of round table discussions with sales executives. He reported: "When we ask participants how many of them are from companies that have a quality movement underway, we find about half do. But when we ask them whether that effort has migrated to the sales force, fewer than 10 percent say it has." Dick Schaaf, "Selling Quality," *Training,* June 1992, pp. 53–59.

30. Eugene H. Fram and Martin L. Presberg, "TQM Is a Catalyst for New Marketing Applications," *Marketing News,* Nov. 9, 1992.

31. Frederick F. Reicheld and W. Earl Sasser, Jr., "Zero Defections: Quality Comes to Services," *Harvard Business Review,* Sept./Oct. 1990, pp. 105–111. Reprint No. 90508.

32. Harvard Business School video series, "Achieving Breakthrough Service," Boston: Harvard Business School, 1992.

33. Robert D. Buzzell and Bradley Gale, *The PIMS Principles,* New York: The Free Press, 1987, p. 62. The data from over 3000 strategic business units show that concentrating purchases *improves* profitability, at least up to a point. "The positive net effect of a moderate degree of purchase concentration suggests that the efficiency gains that can be achieved via this approach to procurement are usually big enough to offset the disadvantages that might be expected as a results of an inferior bargaining position."

34. W. Edwards Deming, *Out of the Crisis,* Cambridge, Mass.: Center for Advanced Engineering Study, Massachusetts Institute of Technology, 1986, p. 35.

35. Joseph P. Aleo, Jr., "Redefining the Manufacturer–Supplier Relationship," *Journal of Business Strategy,* Sept./Oct. 1992, pp. 10–14.

36. B. G. Yovovich, "Becoming a World-Class Customer," *Business Marketing,* Sept. 1991, p. 29.

# CUSTOMER FOCUS AT SOLECTRON

Solectron Corporation is a worldwide provider of electronics design, manufacturing, and support services to leading original equipment manufacturers. It offers a broad range of premanufacturing, manufacturing, and postmanufacturing solutions. It also oversees materials logistics, managing customers' supply chains to meet product schedules.

Solectron is currently the only company to have received the Baldrige Award twice. The company attributes its success partly to its focus on its customers. For more than ten years, Solectron has tracked customer satisfaction on a weekly basis, with an 80 to 90 percent survey response rate. Scores for delivery, quality, and service are at or near the 90 percent satisfaction level. This level of satisfaction is particularly noteworthy given the company's stringent rating scale in which a "C" receives a score of 0 and a "D" receives a score of minus 100. Grades of "B–" or lower trigger Solectron's Customer Complaint Resolution Process. Within 24 hours, the account's program manager contacts the customer to acknowledge the issue and to gain additional information, and within 72 hours, a corrective action plan is submitted to the customer.

Through an annual third-party survey of executives at customer companies, Solectron again evaluates satisfaction levels and gathers information on customers' future business plans and manufacturing requirements. Respondents also are asked to rate Solectron relative to its competitors in the areas of quality, delivery, service, technical capability, material management, and overall satisfaction.

Survey results point the way to improvements in manufacturing and service capabilities that Solectron must make to meet future expectations and build new business. An example of customer-driven improvements is the newly added capability for automating exchange of customers' computer-aided designs. The technology has reduced the start-up time for new products by a factor of five. Another is greater emphasis on electronic data interchange (EDI) to link suppliers and improve on-time delivery rates. Use of EDI has yielded savings ranging between $25 and $260 per transaction.

*You may have come up with what you think customers want from your company's product or service. But how do you compare your processes with customer needs to ensure a quality fit? This company has an approach that works.*

# HEWLETT-PACKARD COMPANY

Have you ever sat down with other people at your company to look for a better way to meet customers' quality needs, only to have been disappointed with the results? The reason for your disappointment may be that one important element was missing from the equation: your customers themselves. Listening to them is what provides real insight into meeting their quality requirements.

While Hewlett-Packard Company's Northwest Integrated Circuit Division (Corvallis, OR) is in business to sell chips to other divisions inside Hewlett-Packard (HP), it also serves customers outside of HP. The problem that it faced about five years ago, however, was that many employees either didn't know who their customers were or actually believed that the customers were interfering with them as they performed their work.

Fortunately, management saw the obvious need to address these problems. "We wanted our people to become very familiar with our customers and realize that they were here to serve those customers," says Casey Collett, Ph.D., Total Quality Control manager. "Our goal was to become so responsive to our customers that we would be the only supplier with which they would want to do business."

## A Four-Step Process

To meet that goal, the Division launched its Total Quality Control effort in 1983. Collett says it involves four steps:

**Step #1** On your own, identify what you feel your major business processes are.

**Step #2** On your own, determine how you are being measured by your customers.

**Step #3** Go out and verify these two perceptions with your major customers.

**Step #4** Develop a program to improve these processes.

To execute these four steps, division management created a small group of TQC experts, who currently report directly to the division manager and work closely with a steering committee of top managers. TQC members have expertise in manufacturing, teaching, statistics, and group facilitation. Together, the division quality and TQC departments attack customer satisfaction and internal process improvement issues, respectively.

The Division has also created a three-point TQC model, which has expanded to a seven-point model over the years. (See Figure 1.)

## HP'S 10-Step Planning Process

The key to achieving TQC from the customer's point of view at HP is a 10-step business planning process pioneered by planning expert Scott Feamster. This process requires the division to understand and analyze each of the following:

1. Purpose
2. Objectives
3. Customers and distribution channels
4. Competition
5. Necessary products and services
6. Plans for necessary products and services (research, manufacturing, financial, and marketing plans)
7. Financial analysis
8. Potential problem analysis
9. Recommendations
10. Next year's tactical plan

The 10-step business planning process, then, is a systematic way of:

- Understanding the business you're proposing to be in;
- Understanding your customers' needs;

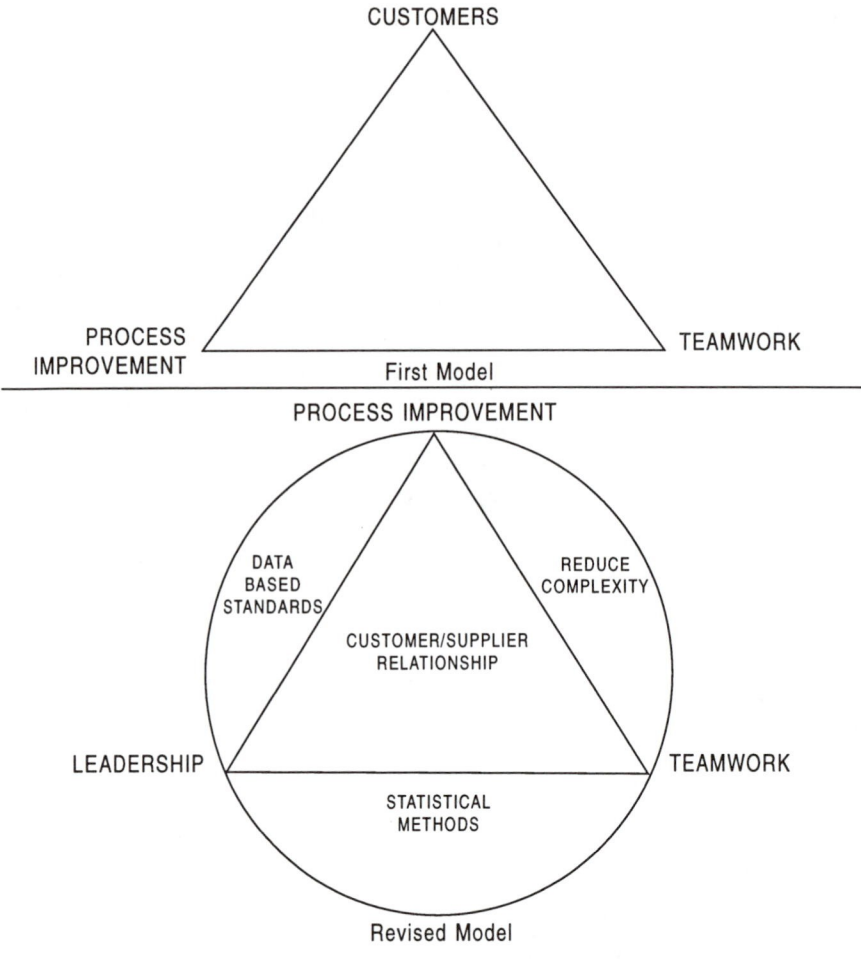

**Figure 1** The *customer/supplier relationship* is central to the model. *Process improvements* occur through quality *leadership* and *teamwork. Reducing complexity,* setting *data-based (meaningful) standards,* and using appropriate *statistical methods* are the tools used to achieve the process improvements.

- Understanding the market and competitive environment you're entering, and as a result of these understandings
- Making solid, well-thought-out plans to meet your objectives.

"When you have developed your strategy, you should have an objective, methodical business plan that looks at what customers need and what you are going to do about those needs," says Collett. "Then you can take this document back to the customer and verify its accuracy."

A crucial element of making the 10-step business planning process work is what John Doyle, HP executive vice president for Systems Technology, calls "imaginative understanding of users' needs" (IUUN). "IUUN is becoming an integral part of how HP does business," Collett reports, adding that the philosophy of IUUN is to hear what customers say their needs are, and apply the creativity and knowledge you have to create solutions for customers.

## Quality Function Deployment

While IUUN is critical to the success of the business planning process, Quality Function Deployment (QFD) is critical to the success of IUUN. QFD is the philosophy of designing your processes in response to customer needs.

"Before QFD, we didn't always realize the importance of understanding customer needs," says Collett. "As a result, we often invented products that we thought people such as ourselves would want, instead of asking our customers what they wanted."

Currently, the Division uses QFD in its R&D and marketing areas. "It helps us find out what our customers need so that we can build these needs into the next generation of our products."

## QFD's Planning Matrix

One of the most important tools in QFD is the Planning Matrix. Once you know what your customers' requirements are, the next step is to translate these data into product development plans. The Planning Matrix plots customer requirements on one axis and business processes and their measures or product features on the other axis. The idea is to be able to determine the fit between customer needs and product features. "The Planning Matrix puts a lot more objectivity into the product development process," notes Collett.

### Here's How It Works

Down the left side of the matrix are rows of user needs. Across the top of the matrix are columns of product features. With the matrix, you can see where a row intersects with a column and, in that cell, ask yourself if there is a strong relationship, a weak relationship, or no relationship between what the customer requires and what your company is doing.

If you find no relationship on a highly rated need as ranked by the customer, then you need to look at your product design plan and address the problem, since the customer considers it important. Conversely, if you are building in steps in the design process that have no bearing on customer needs, you may be able to eliminate them. For example, you may be doing test procedures on something that the customer doesn't care about.

R&D then creates another matrix of customer needs by process control characteristics (or internal manufacturing control characteristics) that will have to be met in order to give customers the features that they want. In short, the system translates raw customer data into focused activities for helping Marketing, R&D, Manufacturing, and Quality to make the desired product a reality.

## Two More Tools for Success

HP uses two other tools to ensure that it is responding to the quality requirements of customers:

- **Customer Quality Engineers** are electrical engineers who work with Marketing to gather customer data, and with R&D and Manufacturing to make sure customer issues are addressed. The task is not always easy. "Clients ask questions in their own terms," says Collett. Customer quality engineers thus need to translate these terms so that answers to their real, often unarticulated problems can be found. Then they need to translate the solutions developed by the Division back into language that the customers will be able to understand and utilize.

- **Process Improvement Teams** attack customer issues throughout the Division's team concept. "A few of these teams interface so closely with customer divisions that they ask the customers to be on one of our teams," says Collett. "This certainly gives teams direct feedback from customers."

The teams solve customer problems and then return to customer locations to show them what they have accomplished. "The concept works well, because customers essentially drive the improvement process," she adds.

## Focus on the Future

Things have been improving. "Our quality is better, our planning processes are improving, and teams are busy with improvement projects," says Collett. "Sales are up, but we never take customer satisfaction for granted. On an annual basis, we verify with our customers that our processes and the way we are measuring ourselves reflect customer satisfaction. We refine the measures more and more over time to make sure that they accurately reflect what the customer wants."

## Questions for Discussion

**1** Why is it important to understand a company's basic business processes in order to deliver customer satisfaction? Illustrate your answer.

**2** How do you determine customers' perceptions of your product or service?

**3** What are the basic differences between the first model and the revised model in Figure 1?

**4** Explain the necessity for steps 3 and 4 of Hewlett-Packard's 10-step planning process.

**5** How would you verify that customers are satisfied? What key result indicators might be used?

## OVERVIEW: CUSTOMER SATISFACTION RESEARCH

### Linda Wengel

Banks are increasingly aware that assessing their customers' satisfaction with the quality of service they are receiving is a key ingredient in customer retention. Below, we examine briefly the several methods of measuring customer satisfaction to help determine which method is most suitable for your institution.

Customer satisfaction measurement tools can include mail surveys, telephone surveys, closed-account surveys, one-on-one interviews, focus groups, advisory panels, mystery shopping, suggestion forms, even unsolicited letters to branch managers and other bank officers. The annual ABA Retail Banking Report details percentages of banks' use of various measurement techniques. The most common, surveys, focus groups, and mystery shopping, require considerable preplanning and skill to assure reliable results. Experts suggest that banks not limit themselves to a single or periodic study, but maintain some avenue for ongoing analysis.

### Surveys

Before conducting a customer survey, banks should consider the following steps suggested by Daniel Kanouse, of Take Charge Consultants: know your objectives, identify the survey population, verify your database, assemble the best-qualified team, develop a strategic plan and timeline, collect data on a timely basis, turn survey results into actionable items and carry them through (*Bank News,* December 1997). Another consultant, Rick Swindlehurst of Questar, suggests providing feedback on the results of the survey to the participants—something few companies do (*The Service Edge,* May 1994).

Surveys administered to several hundred respondents produce quantitative data that identify similarities and differences among various groups of respon-

Reprinted with permission from *Bank Marketing* magazine (Washington, D.C.), September 1998, pp. 16–19.

dents. Once you determine which group or groups of customers to measure, a representative sample of that universe must be selected using statistically acceptable standards. Sample design also requires a firm grasp of statistical theory. Once the sample and design are determined, several methods can be employed to conduct the survey: personal interviews, self-administered questionnaires, telephone interviews.

Each approach has strengths and weaknesses. People are largely more responsive to face-to-face interviewers than telephone pollsters, but these are more expensive and subject to interviewer bias. Self-administered questionnaires are the least expensive, eliminate the bias or cheating possibility, and can reach more people. However, they are the least likely to be completed, results may take long coming back, and control over the sample is sometimes lost. Telephone interviewing reduces selection bias and is faster than other interview methods, but this process gleans the least amount of information. Researchers need to consider specific circumstances, cost, time and complexity of the information sought before deciding which survey method to employ (Marketing Financial Services; Mary Ann Pezzullo, American Bankers Association, 1998).

## Focus Groups

Focus groups are one way to collect qualitative data from a bank's customers. Assembling a small group of bank customers for a couple of hours (perhaps along with a few customers from competing banks) and using a skilled moderator can elicit both positive and negative perceptions of a bank's service. While focus groups can be used as an endpoint in the research process, the narrowness of their approach, both in size and issues covered, makes them better suited for identifying issues to be researched via a survey or a mystery shopping program.

An effective moderator is the key here—one who will get the participants to open up and define impressions in terms of service behavior, not just adjectives. For example, the moderator should have group members define what they mean by "friendly," "nice," "attentive" in specifics such as "thanks me for waiting," "calls me by name," "shakes my hand." Noting specific behavior provides more useful feedback to employees, which is an important goal of any customer satisfaction measurement method. It is useful to convene focus groups periodically, sometimes using the same group, sometimes varying the participants to compare reactions. At the conclusion of the focus group, a report needs to be written and disseminated to the departments covered.

## Mystery Shopping

Several professionals believe the best way to measure the quality of service at a bank is through a carefully designed mystery shopping program conducted over an extended period of time. Mystery shopping programs can be carried out by professionals, though some banks use customers to carry out these programs. Shoppers go to the bank and perform routine and other bank transactions and complete a report grading the bank employee on a number of predefined service characteristics. Customer-based shopping systems, a relatively new twist on the traditional method, use actual bank customers to provide the information. This is an effective process because interactions are real situations between employees and familiar customers (*Bank Marketing,* November 1997).

Using customers to do mystery shopping has other advantages. Customers tell it like it is; they understand the culture of the community, as well as how your bank compares with the competition. Customers are less obvious than professional shoppers and are much more affordable. The program can be repeated several times for verification, and this method builds customer loyalty. Because of the lower expense—customer shoppers receive a small compensation for each shop—several hundred customers can be used year-round. A mystery shopping program should reinforce a bank's training program, and it is one method that provides quantitative and qualitative information to be used bank-wide (*Northwestern Financial Review,* May 18, 1996).

These are the most commonly used methods for measuring customer satisfaction. Banks can use any or all of them, as well as some simple, ongoing techniques. Mini-surveys or questionnaires that accompany a thank-you note from a bank officer for a new service purchase will provide important feedback. You could also have a branch manager stand in the lobby and ask customers about the service they just received, or display comment cards near a drop-in box (*Credit Union Times,* March 20, 1996).

No matter how a bank does it, measuring customer satisfaction is an essential ingredient in retaining your customers. However, making good use of research findings to improve service and employee training is essential.

# CUSTOMER FOCUS AT VARIFILM

Compare each of the following TQM criteria to Varifilm and indicate whether the practice in the company is a *strength* (S) or *needs improvement* (I). Justify your answer.

### 7.1 Customer Expectations: Current and Future      S      I

- Surveys, partner feedback, complaints, gains and losses of customers, and trade literature are among the approaches to understanding customer requirements and expectations.

- Third-party telephone surveys are conducted and reviewed periodically.

- Selected methods can be used to project the relative importance of key future product and service features.

- Cross-functional teams conduct post-mortem and root cause analysis to determine why projects are not on target.

- Different product requirements are considered for different market segments.

- A systematic improvement approach to evaluating and improving the process for determining customer requirements is in place.

### 7.2 Customer Relationship Management

- Specific service standards are deployed to all customer contact personnel and evaluated for service quality.

- A customer satisfaction survey is used to evaluate the effectiveness of relationship management and customer contact performance.

- Complaint data are systematically used to set priorities for improvement projects.

|  | S | I |
|---|---|---|
| ■ Customer contact personnel maintain partnerships with strategic customers through meetings and TQM fitness reviews. | — | — |
| ■ Response time standards are maintained for customer inquiries and followed up on. | — | — |
| ■ A variety of customer contact approaches are used to provide easy access for customers. | — | — |

*Additional Areas for Improvement*

_____

_____

_____

### 7.3 Commitment to Customers

|  | S | I |
|---|---|---|
| ■ Warranties and commitments to customers are compared to those made by key competitors. | — | — |
| ■ Commitments extend beyond direct customers to the consumer. Methods include warranties and a toll-free number. | — | — |
| ■ Determination of whether the customers understand and value commitments is made by customer contact personnel. | — | — |
| ■ Whether or not company commitments address the principal concerns of customers is the subject of surveys and analysis. | — | — |
| ■ Commitments such as warranties and guarantees are incorporated into every order and customer invoice along with the toll-free number. | — | — |

### 7.4 Customer Satisfaction Determination

| | | |
|---|---|---|
| ■ Key customer satisfaction requirements include product quality, on-time delivery, ease of access, price, and worker knowledge. Actual satisfaction is determined through personal contact, third-party surveys, and fitness reviews. | — | — |

| | S | I |
|---|---|---|

■ Future market behavior is determined by interviewing key customer decision makers in functions such as R&D or purchasing.      __ __

■ Competitive position relative to competitors on some appropriate index is conducted by a third-party survey.      __ __

■ Customer satisfaction data are used to improve those processes where key indicators suggest improvement.      __ __

*Additional Areas for Improvement*

---

---

---

### 7.5 Customer Satisfaction Results      S    I

■ The five key measures of customer satisfaction show overall improvement trends. The company appears to be performing at or better than the best competitor.      __ __

■ The three key measures of customer dissatisfaction show overall improvement trends.      __ __

■ The number of awards received from customers has increased.      __ __

■ Trend data by business segment are not presented.      __ __

■ Little evidence is provided to determine whether or not the key indicator measures for customer dissatisfaction address the principal concern of customers.      __ __

### 7.6 Customer Satisfaction Comparison

■ When compared to key competitors on an overall customer satisfaction rating, customers rated Varifilm higher than the average of all competitors.      __ __

■ The Customer Assessment Index shows that Varifilm became the industry leader.      __ __

■ Gains in market share relative to competitors have shown improvement during the past two years.      __ __

|  | S | I |
|---|---|---|
| ■ It is not clear how many customers were included in the overall customer satisfaction comparison rating. | — | — |
| ■ Trend data in gaining and losing customers or customer accounts to competitors are not provided. | — | — |

*Additional Areas for Improvement*

_____

_____

_____

# FOR FURTHER READING

Bartram, Peter, "The Customer Conundrum," *Director,* Sept. 1998, pp. 60–63.

Comeau-Kirschner, Cheryl, "Making Retention Work," *Management Review,* Nov. 1998, pp. 7–8.

Geller, Lois, "Customer Retention Begins with the Basics," *Direct Marketing,* Sept. 1997, pp. 58–62.

Jacobs, Fred A. and Claire Kamm Lee, "The Relationship of Customer Satisfaction to Strategic Decisions," *Journal of Managerial Issues,* Summer 1998, pp. 165–182.

McCollum, Tim, "Tools for Targeting Customer Service," *Nation's Business,* Nov. 1998, pp. 49–51.

Thompson, Harvey, "What Do Your Customers Really Want?" *Journal of Business Strategy,* July/Aug. 1998, pp. 16–21.

# 8

# BENCHMARKING

*Benchmarking is the difference between teaching yourself
how to hit a golf ball and taking lessons from Jack Nicklaus.*

Steven George[1]

In Joseph Juran's 1964 book *Managerial Breakthrough,* he asked the question: "What is it that organizations do that gets results so much better than ours?" The answer to this question opens the door to *benchmarking,* an approach that is accelerating among U.S. firms that have adopted the total quality management (TQM) philosophy.

Benchmarking is alive and well at major U.S. corporations.[2] Estimates indicate that from 45 to 60 percent[3] of U.S. companies have adopted the technique and philosophy.

The essence of benchmarking is the continuous process of comparing a company's strategy, products, and processes with those of world leaders and best-in-class organizations in order to learn how they achieved excellence, and then setting out to match and even surpass it. For many companies, benchmarking has become a key component of their TQM programs. The justification lies partly in the question: Why reinvent the wheel if I can learn from someone who has already done it? C. Jackson Grayson, Jr., chairman of the Houston-based American Productivity and Quality Center, which offers training in benchmarking and consulting services, reports an incredible amount of interest in benchmarking. Some of that interest may be explained by the criteria for the Malcolm Baldrige Award, which includes "competitive comparisons and benchmarks."[4]

# THE EVOLUTION OF BENCHMARKING

The method may have evolved in the 1950s, when W. Edwards Deming taught the Japanese the idea of quality control. Other American management innovations followed. However, the method was rarely used in the United States until the early 1980s, when IBM, Motorola, and Xerox became the pioneers. The latter company became the best-known example of the use of benchmarking.

## Xerox

The company invented the photocopier in 1959 and maintained a virtual monopoly for many year thereafter. Like "Coke" or "Kleenex," "Xerox" became a generic name for all photocopiers. By 1981, however, the company's market share shrank to 35 percent as IBM and Kodak developed high-end machines and Canon, Ricoh, and Savin dominated the low-end segment of the market. The Xerox vice-president of copier manufacturing remarked: "We were horrified to find that the Japanese were selling their machines at what it cost us to make ours...we had been benchmarking against ourselves. We weren't looking outside." The company was suffering from the "not invented here" syndrome, as Xerox managers did not want to admit that they were not the best.

The company instituted the benchmarking process, but it met with resistance at first. People did not believe that someone else could do it better. When faced with the facts, reaction went from denial to dismay to frustration and finally to action. Once the process began, the company benchmarked virtually every function and task for productivity, cost, and quality. Comparisons were made for companies both in and outside the industry. For example, the distribution function was compared to L.L. Bean, the Freeport, Maine, catalog seller of outdoor equipment and clothing and everyone's model of distribution effectiveness.

By the company's own admission, it would probably not be in the copier business today if it were not for benchmarking. Results were dramatic:

- Suppliers were reduced from 5000 to 300.
- "Concurrent engineering" was practiced. Each product development group has input from design, manufacturing, and service from the initial stages of the project.
- Commonality of parts increased from about 20 percent to 60 to 70 percent.
- Hierarchical organization structure was reduced, and the use of cross-functional "Teams Xerox" was established.
- Results included:
  - Quality problems cut by two-thirds
  - Manufacturing costs cut in half

- Development time cut by two-thirds
- Direct labor cut by 50 percent and corporate staff cut by 35 percent while increasing volume

It should be noted that all of these improvements were not the direct result of benchmarking. What happened at Xerox (and what happens at most companies) is that in adopting the process, the climate for change and continuous improvement followed as a natural result. In other words, benchmarking can be a very good intervention technique for positive change.

## Ford

The entire automobile industry may have undergone substantial change as a result of Ford's Taurus and Sable model cars. Operating performance and reliability were significantly improved, and the gains were recognized by U.S. car buyers as well as others in the industry. "Team Taurus," a cross-functional group of employees, was empowered to bring the car to market and was given considerable authority to act outside of the normal company bureaucracy.

The team defined 400 different areas that were considered important to the success of a mid-size car. A best-in-class competition was chosen for each area. Fifty different mid-size car models were chosen. Few were Ford models. Based on the 400 benchmarks, specific teams were assigned responsibility to meet or beat the best-in-class for each area of performance, and 300 features were "copied" and incorporated into the car design. Target dates were set for beating the remaining features. "Quality Is Job One" became the fight song for Ford employees.

The Taurus was, and is, a resounding success. Some auto analysts credit the Taurus experience with the partial resurgence of quality in the U.S. automobile industry. The benchmarking process provided additional benefits. During the examination of competitors' features, valuable insights into the design process were gained. Cycle time was reduced. Buyer–supplier relationship was improved as supplier input was solicited for the design. All manufacturing processes were improved as a by-product of the benchmarking process.

## Motorola

In the early 1980s, the company set a goal of improving a set of basic quality attributes *tenfold* in five years. Based on *internal* benchmarking, the goal was reached in three years. The company then began to look outside, sending teams to visit competitor plants in Japan. To their chagrin, the teams found that Motorola would have to improve its tenfold improvement level another two to three times just to match the competition.

Borrowing process benchmarks from companies as diverse as Wal-Mart, Benetton, and Domino's Pizza, the company now routinely fields benchmarking requests from those same Japanese companies it toured the first time around.[5]

An example of a benchmarking application at Motorola is the major flaws uncovered in the ordering process:

- Defects in writing up an order by sales representative
- The lack of quality with regard to a customer's knowledge and ability to answer a customer inquiry
- The cost of error, both internally and externally
- Long delays in implementing the customers' orders into the release/manufacturing cycle, due to bureaucratic policies
- Lack of involvement from operational and local management, due to the current process being divorced from operational objectives

As a result of these findings, improvement initiatives were launched, including new automated systems and human empowerment. Every defect made by a representative was edited and rectified. Training and education were introduced to ensure increased knowledge by all sales representatives. This translated into quality responses for the customer, which in turn translated into improved customer satisfaction. The results of the implementation showed a 70 percent improvement in both quality and cycle time. The time it actually takes to process a customer's order was reduced from 15 days to 3 hours.[6]

## THE ESSENCE OF BENCHMARKING

The process is more than a means of gathering data on how well a company performs against others both in and outside the industry. It is a method of identifying new ideas and new ways of improving processes and hence meeting customer expectations. Cycle time reduction and cost cutting are but two process improvements that can result. The traditional approach of measuring defect rates is not enough. The ultimate objective is *process improvement* that meets the attributes of customer expectation. This improvement, of course, should meet both strategic and operational needs.

A properly designed and implemented benchmarking program will take a total system approach by examining the company's role in the supply chain, looking upstream at the suppliers and downstream at distribution channels. How competitive are suppliers in the world market and how well are they integrated into the company's own core business processes—product design, demand forecasting, product planning, and order fulfillment?[7]

## BENCHMARKING AND THE BOTTOM LINE

There are two basic points of view regarding how to get started in benchmarking. One minority view maintains that an *initial* action plan that tries to match the techniques used by world-class performance may actually make things worse by doing too much too soon. A three-year study of 580 global companies conducted by the management consulting firm Ernst & Young concluded that it may be best to start measuring existing financial performance measures. Two key measures are return on assets (which is simply after-tax income divided by total assets) and value added per employee. Value added is sales minus the costs of materials, supplies, and work done by outside contractors. Labor and administrative costs are not subtracted from sales to arrive at value added.[8]

The focus on financial results is not recommended by the majority of executives familiar with the benefits of benchmarking. Some believe that it is easy to be fooled by financial indicators that lull the company into thinking that it is doing well when what in reality occurs is a transitory financial phenomenon that may not hold up over the longer term. A more important payoff is quality processes that lead to a quality product.

Although there is a cost involved, most companies report a positive financial return from benchmarking activities. According to a Conference Board survey of 225 companies, the application of benchmarking within the information technology function is rated as successful by almost 75 of companies that practice it.[9] In the public sector, the Department of Energy confirms that a savings of 15 to 25 percent on processes and activities can be expected.

Robert C. Camp headed up the now-famous study at Xerox in which the buzzword "benchmarking" was coined in 1980. When asked whether the best work practices necessarily improve the bottom line, he replied: "The full definition of benchmarking is finding and implementing best practices in our business, practices that meet customer requirements. So the flywheel on finding the very best is, 'Does this meet customer requirements?' There is a cost of quality that exceeds customer requirements. The basic objective is satisfying the customer, so that is the limiter."[10]

## THE BENEFITS OF BENCHMARKING

Given the considerable effort and expense required for effective benchmarking, why would an organization embark on such an effort? The answer is justified by three sets of benefits.

## Cultural Change

Benchmarking allows organizations to set realistic, rigorous new performance targets, and this process helps convince people of the credibility of these targets. This tends to overcome the "not invented here" syndrome and the "we're different" justification for the status quo. The emphasis on looking to other companies for ideas and solutions is antithetical to the traditional U.S. business culture of individualism. Robert Camp, the former Xerox guru quoted earlier, indicates that the most difficult part for a company that is starting the process is getting people to understand that there may be people out there who do things better than they do. According to Camp, overcoming that myopia is extremely important.

## Performance Improvement

Benchmarking allows the organization to define specific gaps in performance and to select the processes to improve. It provides a vehicle whereby products and services are redesigned to achieve outcomes that meet or exceed customer expectations. The gaps in performance that are discovered can provide objectives and action plans for improvement at all levels of the organization and promote improved performance for individual and group participants.

## Human Resources

Benchmarking provides a basis for training. Employees begin to see the gap between what they are doing and what best-in-class companies are doing. Closing the gap points out the need for personnel to be involved in techniques of problem solving and process improvement. Moreover, the synergy between organization activities is improved through cross-functional cooperation.

## TYPES OF BENCHMARKING

There are three basic types of benchmarking: internal, competitive, and universal.[11] **Internal benchmarking** is measuring one part of the organization against another. For example, a company that has several warehouses may benchmark one against another. One advantage of internal benchmarking is that it can help identify best practices within an organization—in other words, proven methods that work within that organization's culture and environment. It is also less expensive and less time-consuming than other forms of benchmarking. However, internal benchmarking will not reveal where a company stands relative to other companies in a given process. It also limits the potential insights to those that already exist within the organization. This type of benchmarking is most effective when a company has many operating units or divisions that perform the same processes.

**Competitive benchmarking** involves assessing a company's performance against that of its competitors. It is the type of study that most people think of when they hear about benchmarking, but its problems often outweigh the results. For obvious reasons, competitors can be very hesitant about sharing information. Legal issues often arise before, during, and after such studies. Qualitative information is often lacking or insufficient—the participants find out where they stand from a metrics standpoint, but not how they can improve.

Xerox, a very early user of benchmarking, learned some tough lessons while introducing it. The first lesson concerned the competition. Although you must focus strongly on the competition, according to Xerox, if that is the sole objective, playing catch-up is the best you can do. Watching the competition does not tell you how to outdistance them. In the early days, Xerox spent 80 percent of its time looking at the competition. Today, it spends 80 percent of that time outside the industry, because it has found innovative ideas from businesses in other industries.[12]

**Universal benchmarking** offers the richest source of insight and is much preferred over competitive benchmarking. The goal is to improve your product or service to be the best-practice company. As a minimum, however, you need to be better than your competitors. Your competitors are not usually interested in helping you improve your business.

Universal benchmarking allows organizations to focus on the best performers, regardless of industry. They can obtain insights that allow them to leap ahead of competitors, instead of merely keeping pace. The value of universal benchmarking is no secret. Every year, companies like Motorola and Xerox receive literally thousands of requests for benchmarking visits—and all those requests do not come from electronics companies!

Sharing only internal knowledge and practices can lead to myopia and the self-delusion that you are the best. Universal benchmarking scours across sectors and industries for excellence, causing goals to be set much higher. Organizations can gain not 5 to 7 percent but 30 to 50 percent.[13] Over the last five years, there has been a dramatic acceptance of benchmarking as a legitimate way to speed improvement and change. In 1998, the American Productivity and Quality Center's International Benchmarking Clearinghouse had almost 500 blue-member organizations. Xerox, Chevron, Texas Instruments, Kodak, IBM, Citibank, GE, Amgen, GTE, AT&T, and the U.S. Postal Service are fanatic about the need to overcome the not-invented-here syndrome and adopt best practices.[13]

When the customers of Remington Arms asked for smoother, shinier ammunition shells, the company targeted the cosmetics industry, which makes smooth and shiny lipstick containers, and turned to Maybelline and incorporated some of that company's practices. When Xerox was having trouble with order picking, it turned to L.L. Bean, which picked its orders three times faster.

## STRATEGIC BENCHMARKING

Strategic benchmarking is an extension of traditional benchmarking specifically designed to direct strategic action and organizational change for achieving competitive advantage. Benchmarking assessments are performed against the trio of strategic elements that are most related to competitive advantage: customers, competitors, and core competencies.[14] The vice-president of quality, office document products division of Xerox clarifies the issues of strategic benchmarking as "building core competencies that will help to sustain competitive advantage; targeting a specific shift in strategy, such as entering new markets or developing new products; developing a new line of business or making an acquisition; and creating an organization that is more capable of learning how to respond in an uncertain future because it has increased its acceptance of change."[15]

It is paradoxical that two AT&T divisions (AT&T Network Systems Group, Transmission Systems Business Unit and AT&T Universal Card Services) were 1992 winners of the Baldrige Award. Like several other winners, the company has turned this win into an advantage and organized a separate operation to market this expertise. Training is the product offered by the AT&T Benchmarking Group of Warren, New Jersey.[16] The process is illustrated in Figure 8-1.

The paradox is that ten years earlier, in 1983, AT&T was convinced that it could be a major player in the computer industry. The company owned Bell

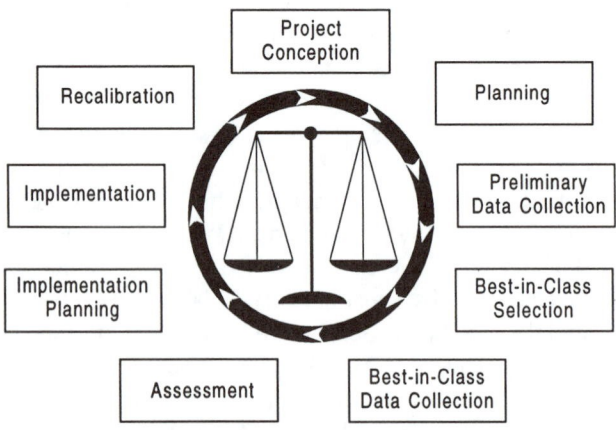

**Figure 8-1**    AT&T Benchmarking Process

Laboratories, the largest R&D facility in the world, and had extensive experience in the manufacture of telecommunications equipment, a related product.

Five years after entering the industry and after losing billions of dollars, the company was still trying to be a significant player in the market. The near disaster could be traced directly to the company's failure to (1) realize that the key success factors in the industry included sales, distribution, and service (functions with which AT&T had very little experience) and (2) conduct *strategic benchmarking* against such best-in-class competitors as IBM and Compaq. Moreover, the company apparently failed to define its market segment, the criteria used for customer purchasing decisions, and how the company's product could be differentiated in the chosen segment. If, for example, IBM, Compaq, or AT&T wanted to benchmark NCR, they would find that NCR has gone to great expense to define the criteria of product quality as "usability, aesthetics, reliability, functionality, innovation and appropriateness."[17]

One way to determine how well you are prepared to compete in a segment and to help define a best-in-class competitor is to construct a key success factor matrix similar to the one shown in Figure 8-2. Following this determination, a matrix such as the hypothetical one shown in Figure 8-3 can be constructed to measure market differentiation criteria against competitors. Note that the criteria for comparison are based on the customer's purchase decision. This type of strategic analysis can be followed by one involving specific processes—operational benchmarking. Strategy drives performance and hence quality. Indeed, quality can and should become the central theme of strategy. Note that Figures 8-2 and 8-3 can be used to benchmark best-in-class *outside* an industry.[18]

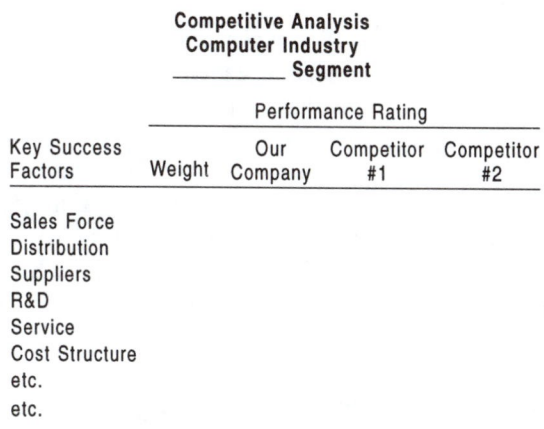

**Competitive Analysis**
**Computer Industry**
_____ **Segment**

| Key Success Factors | Weight | Performance Rating | | |
|---|---|---|---|---|
| | | Our Company | Competitor #1 | Competitor #2 |
| Sales Force | | | | |
| Distribution | | | | |
| Suppliers | | | | |
| R&D | | | | |
| Service | | | | |
| Cost Structure | | | | |
| etc. | | | | |
| etc. | | | | |

**Figure 8-2**   Key Success Factor Matrix

**Computer Industry**
_____ **Segment**
**Customer's Purchase Decision**

| | | Performance Rating | | | |
|---|---|---|---|---|---|
| Criteria | Weight | Our Company | Competitor #1 | Competitor #2 | etc. |
| Reliability | | | | | |
| Performance | | | | | |
| Features | | | | | |
| Durability | | | | | |
| Service | | | | | |
| Software | | | | | |
| etc. | | | | | |
| etc. | | | | | |

**Figure 8-3**  Measuring Market Differentiation Criteria Against Competitors

## THE BENCHMARKING PROCESS

What processes and/or functions should be benchmarked? The initial plan at Xerox identified 67 business processes, beginning with those that affected customer satisfaction the most. A number of organizations have developed classification schemes. For example, the Arthur Andersen organization has identified over 200 processes and grouped them into 13 categories.[11] By selecting from this "menu," a company could develop its own master plan for process benchmarking. Table 8-1 lists the categories and one example of each category. Note that the number of processes exceeds 200. Of course, all processes may not apply to a given organization, and few companies would choose to benchmark all of them. By using such a scheme, a company can benchmark any other company that also uses it. Thus, both have a common understanding of what a process or category of processes entails, which permits an "apples to apples" comparison.

There is no standard or commonly accepted approach to the benchmarking process. Each consulting group[19] and each company[20] uses its own method. Whatever method is used, the major steps involve (1) measuring the performance of best-in-class relative to critical performance variables, (2) determining how the levels of performance are achieved, and (3) using the information to develop and implement a plan for improvement. These steps are discussed in further detail in the following sections.

### Determine the Functions/Processes to Benchmark

Those functions or processes that will benefit the most should be targeted for benchmarking. It is wise to choose those that absorb the highest percent of cost

**Table 8-1**    Examples of Benchmarking Processes

| Process category | Number of processes | Example |
|---|---|---|
| **Operating processes** | | |
| 1. Understand markets and consumers | 10 | Determine customer reactions to competitive offerings |
| 2. Develop vision and strategy | 13 | Develop and set organization goals |
| 3. Design products and services | 15 | Plan and deploy quality targets |
| 4. Market and sell | 10 | Process customer orders |
| 5. Produce and deliver products and services | 15 | Schedule resources to meet service requirements |
| 6. Produce and deliver for service | 10 | Purchase materials and supplies |
| 7. Invoice and service customers | 7 | Manage customer complaints |
| **Management and support processes** | | |
| 8. Develop and manage human resources | 38 | Define requirements |
| 9. Manage information resources | 26 | Establish databases |
| 10. Manage financial and physical resources | 24 | Develop budget |
| 11. Execute environmental management program | 10 | Implement pollution prevention program |
| 12. Manage external relationships | 7 | Communicate with shareholders |
| 13. Manage improvement and change | 18 | Develop benchmark capability |

and contribute the greatest role in differentiation, always thinking in terms of process improvements that will have a positive impact on the customer's purchasing decision. Because no company can excel at everything, it is necessary to delineate targets. Benchmarking "manufacturing," for example, is much too broad and the subject is too ill-defined. If the elements to be benchmarked cannot be framed, data gathering is not focused and subsequent actions may be destructive.

Many companies focus their efforts on product comparisons. In manufacturing industries, this may mean product tear-downs (e.g., Ford, Xerox) and re-engineering of design standards and assembly processes. This approach should take second place to improving time to market, first-time quality of design, and design for purchasing effectiveness, which are the primary drivers of both quality and cost. Of course, these actions should be undertaken after customer satisfaction has been defined with customer input.

■   The health care industry provides an example of the potential for cost and quality improvement. For one procedure alone, coronary artery bypass grafts (CABGs, DRGs 106-7), Americans paid more than 130,000 in 1991. Of the patients treated, 6033 died. Ancillary charges alone reached $2.67 billion. Baxter Healthcare Corporation of Deerfield, Illinois, which benchmarked CABGs in ten hospitals, calculated that $1.57 billion in ancillary charges alone could be saved if all hospitals benchmarked the processes of the benchmarked ten.[21]

## Select Key Performance Variables

Functions, activities, and processes can be measured in terms of specific output measures of operations and performance. In general, these measures fall into four broad categories.

**Cost and productivity, such as overhead costs and labor efficiency.**   Total dollars per unit or per ton is a starting point in manufacturing. Other variables might include production yield of raw material, direct labor per unit produced, etc. Unless the project team begins with total costs before it breaks them down by process or activity, some very important overhead charges may be neglected when benchmarked against firms with different accounting systems. See Chapter 10 (Productivity, Quality, and Reengineering) for additional measures.

Comparing one company's financial statements and cost breakdowns against those of another would be a good method for a "me-too" strategy *if* access were available to the detailed statements of a competitor or the best-in-class and *if* they were based on similar accounting methodology. These are two big "ifs." A better way is to identify the underlying cost *drivers* of the many functions and activities that, when combined, make up total costs. For example, raw material costs may be driven by sales, purchase volume, source, or freight; direct labor by wage and benefit rates, skilled vs. unskilled, or union vs. non-union; indirect labor by the ratio of direct to indirect and salary levels; and so on.

■   A team at Mercy Hospital in San Diego decided to benchmark medical records because the activity represented the largest portion of clinical support. The team left a benchmarking visit to a sister hospital empty-handed because it found that the two hospitals were quite different in this activity. A team member commented: "They weren't equivalent to us at all. It didn't do the functions we did, it wasn't open 24 hours a day like us, and it was more decentralized— a lot of what we do, they do in various other departments and clinics."

**Timeliness.**   Often overlooked, timeliness is a major factor in internal processes as well as customer satisfaction. The measure is frequently expressed in cycle time or turnaround time, such as time to fill an order or time to answer the phone. Some manufacturing executives have been known to visit automobile races to measure pit stops as benchmarks for setup time or line changeover time.

**Differentiation and quality.** Measures of differentiation and quality are needed for both processes and product. Quality measures should capture the errors, defects, and waste attributable to an entire process and express them relative to the total output achieved. Defects tend to cascade down a chain of processes, becoming increasingly expensive to correct.

Differentiation and quality of product are essentially the same, because quality is what differentiates a product. The variables should include any factors that affect a customer's purchasing decision (see, for example, Figure 8-3).

**Business processes.** These are the processes not directly related to product design, production, sales, and service. They include the many staff and internal service activities that are costed under general and administrative (G&A) expense. One has only to look at the organizational chart to identify areas for cost reduction and for improvement of productivity and quality. Human resources, data processing, accounts receivable, marketing services, maintenance, security, data center, warehousing, public relations...the list goes on. Many companies have had severe cash flow and profit problems due to a failure to control the cost and output of these business or support processes. Whereas direct labor and material costs may make up the largest segment of total costs in a manufacturing firm and can be benchmarked more easily, G&A costs are more elusive and more difficult to measure; however, they represent fertile ground for improvement. Another area is internal quality and internal customers. A good place to start may be to use the techniques of activity analysis and activity-based costing.

## IDENTIFY THE BEST-IN-CLASS

This is a major step in the benchmark analysis. The objective is to identify companies whose operations are superior, the so-called best-in-class, so that the company's own operations can be targeted.

The quickest way to identify excellent performers is simply to visit some companies that have won the Baldrige Award. A lot could be learned in a hurry, but these companies may not have the time or may not have similar processes. Other sources include (1) available databases, (2), sharing agreements between companies, and (3) out-of-industry companies.

**Databases** are an expanding source of comparison information. The most current and most comprehensive of these is maintained by the Houston-based American Productivity & Quality Center (AP&QC). Some of the chief difficulties that organizations encounter are identifying top-performing companies in specific functions and finding companies that have already conducted studies in specific areas. Helping others overcome these difficulties is the role of the AP&QC. It serves as a central networking source and has the support of top benchmarkers.

The cost of membership in the AP&QC ranges from $6000 to $12,500, depending on the number of employees. Dissemination of benchmarking information is through face-to-face networking meetings, electronic bulletin boards, and on-line access to abstracts of company benchmark studies.[22]

As the popularity of benchmarking accelerates, so does the number of consortium efforts among industry peer groups. For example, a number of hospitals have formed the MECON-PEER database to provide information and analysis software for examining individual operations and compare them with similar operations nationwide. Some of the participants have discovered an additional use for the database: putting muscle into a budget squeeze and justifying additional resources based on benchmarking activities of peers.

Even universities are emerging as benchmarkers. Oregon State University pioneered the process in the academic world, and its success led to the creation of NACUBO, a database of the National Association of College and University Business Officers.

A number of companies are also developing *in-house* databases. This is particularly effective in large multidivision companies, where economies of scale in data sharing can be achieved. One such company is AT&T. The extent of the competitive benchmarking data maintained by the Network Systems Group for use by all company divisions is shown in Table 8-1 (see earlier).[23]

**Cooperative sharing agreements** between companies is another source of best-in-class identification. Members of the agreement may or may not be competitors and may or may not be in the same industry. DEC, Xerox, Motorola, and Boeing joined forces to standardize benchmarking procedures in training.

**Out-of-industry** companies may be the best source of information for many firms in the early or intermediate stages of project implementation. A benchmark planner at Johnson & Johnson suggests that 90 percent of all opportunities for breakthrough improvement lie in studying practices outside the industry. Perishable food companies often teach other manufacturers about supply–demand balancing, demand forecasting, production scheduling, and distribution management. Pharmaceutical companies are quite knowledgeable in production record keeping, quality assurance, and batch traceability.

Although many companies are mistakenly paranoid about sharing strategic and operating information, many others are not. Most Baldrige winners and applicants and people from many best-in-class companies are just regular people and are proud of what they have accomplished.

■ When Mid-Columbia Medical Center of The Dalles, Oregon, got serious about TQM and benchmarking, it formed the "MCMC University." The director, dubbed "Professor," decided to benchmark the training function and spent five days taking notes at Disney University, and then went on to attend Ritz-Carlton's training session for a week. "They were flattered," the "Professor" said. "We were the only people who had ever asked them if we could attend." Training videos were supplied by Northwest Tool & Die Company, Disney, Harley-Davidson, and Johnson Sausage.

Table 8-2 contains a selected list of companies noted for their best practices in the functions indicated.

## MEASURE YOUR OWN PERFORMANCE

At this step in the process, your own performance should have been premeasured; otherwise, there is nothing to compare against the benchmarking data. Moreover, data analysis of best-in-class may proceed aimlessly unless the benchmarker understands what information is being sought.

Having determined with some degree of accuracy the performance of the target firm and the extent of your own performance, it follows that an analysis of the *gap* between the two is necessary. The trickiest part of the process is to compare internal and external data on an equivalent basis. This does not mean that both sets of data must be comparable in the same exact form.

Performing a "gap analysis" of the variation with the benchmarked process involves the problem-solving process treated in Chapter 6. This analysis will reveal:

■ The extent, the size, and the frequency of the gap

■ Causes of the gap; why it exists

■ Available methods for closing the gap and reaching the performance level of the benchmarked process

## ACTIONS TO CLOSE THE GAP

Once the *cause(s)* of the gap is determined through problem analysis, alternative courses of action to close the gap become evident. Selecting the right alternative course of action is a matter of rational decision making. Among the criteria for weighing the courses of action are time, cost, technical specifications, and, of course, quality. It should be added here that the best source of information

**Table 8-2**  Selected Best-Practice Companies

| Company | Function |
|---|---|
| American Airlines | Information systems (long line) |
| American Express (Travel Services) | Billing |
| AMP | Supplier management |
| Benetton | Advertising |
| Disney World | Optimum customer experience |
| Domino's Pizza | Cycle time (order and delivery) |
| Dow Chemical | Safety |
| Emerson Electric | Asset management |
| Federal Express | Delivery time |
| General Electric | Management processes |
| GTE | Fleet management |
| Herman Miller | Compensation and benefits |
| Hewlett-Packard | Order fulfillment |
| Honda | New product development |
| IBM | Productivity |
| L.L. Bean | Distribution |
| 3M | Technology transfer |
| Marion Merrell Dow | Sales management |
| Marriott | Admissions |
| MBNA America | Customer retention |
| Merck | Employee training |
| Milliken | Cross-functional processes |
| Motorola | Flexible manufacturing |
| NEXT | Manufacturing excellence |
| Ritz-Carlton | Training |
| Travelers | Health care management |
| US Sprint | Customer relations |
| Wal-Mart | Information systems |
| Xerox | Benchmarking |

on closing the gap may be the best-in-class, because that company has already experienced what the benchmarking organization is going through.

The action plan lists each action step, the time of completion, the person responsible, and the cost, if appropriate. The results expected from each action step should also be listed in order to provide a measure of whether the objective or output of each step is achieved.

The action plan itself represents a process and lends itself to the basics of process control. Hence, monitoring, feedback, and recalibration are required.

## PITFALLS OF BENCHMARKING

Curt W. Reimann, who heads the Baldrige Award program at the National Institute of Standards and Technology, finds that a lot of people think benchmarking is "instant pudding." It will not improve performance if the proper infrastructure of a total quality program is not in place. Indeed, there is significant evidence that it can be harmful. Unless a corporate culture of quality and the basic components of TQM (such as information systems, process control, and human resource programs) are in place, trying to imitate the best-in-class may very well disrupt operations.

Other potential pitfalls include the failure to:

- Involve the employees who will ultimately use the information and improve the process. Participation can lead to enthusiasm.
- Relate process improvement to strategy and competitive positioning. Design to factors that affect the customer's purchasing decision.
- Define your own process before gathering data, or you will be overwhelmed and will not have the data to compare your own process.
- Perceive benchmarking as an ongoing process. It is not a one-time project with a finite start and complete date.
- Expand the scope of the companies studied. Confining the benchmarking firms to your own area or industry or to competitors is probably too narrow an approach in identifying excellent performers that are appropriate for your processes.
- Perceive benchmarking as a means to process improvement, rather than an end in itself.
- Set goals for closing the gap between what is (existing performance) and what can be (benchmark).
- Empower employees to achieve improvements that they identify and for which they solve problems and develop action plans.
- Maintain momentum by avoiding the temptation to put study results and action plans on the back burner. Credibility is achieved by quick and enthusiastic action.

## QUESTIONS FOR DISCUSSION

**8-1** What benefits can be gained from benchmarking?

**8-2** Identify two or three functions or activities, other than product characteristics, that could be benchmarked by:

- A manufacturer
- A service company

**8-3** How can benchmarking become an intervention technique for organizational change?

**8-4** Summarize some actions taken by Xerox, Ford, and Motorola while implementing their benchmarking programs.

**8-5** What are the pros and cons of benchmarking based on financial performance?

**8-6** Select an industry and list three or four key success factors (e.g., advertising, distribution, engineering, sales) for that industry. Which firm(s), in your opinion, would be appropriate to benchmark?

## ENDNOTES

1. Steven George, *The Baldrige Quality System: The Do-It-Yourself Way to Transform Your Business,* New York: John Wiley & Sons, 1992.
2. Leigh Ann Klaus, "Benchmarking Still a Useful Quality Tool," *Quality Progress,* Nov. 1997, p. 13.
3. "Benchmarking Being Embraced," *Quality,* Aug. 1998.
4. Rick Whiting, "Benchmarking: Lessons from the Best-in-Class," *Electronic Business,* Oct. 7, 1991, pp. 128–134. This article provides a good justification for benchmarking and the principles behind it.
5. Bob Gift and Doug Mosel, "Benchmarking: Tales from the Front," *Healthcare Forum,* Jan./Feb. 1993, pp. 37–51.
6. Graham Smith, "Benchmarking Success Demonstrated at Motorola," *CMA Magazine,* March 1993, pp. 32–33.
7. A. Steven Walleck, "Manager's Journal: A Backstage View of World-Class Performers," *Wall Street Journal,* Aug. 26, 1991, Section A, p. 10. This article contains good examples of benchmarking applications in several companies.
8. See "Quality," a special report in *Business Week,* Nov. 30, 1992, p. 66. This report suggests various benchmarking measures for three types of firms: the novice, the journeyman, and the master.
9. "Benchmarking Improves the Bottom Line in Industries," *Industrial Engineering,* May 1994, pp. 9–10.

10.  Adrienne Linsenmeyer, "Fad or Fundamental?" *Financial World,* Sept. 17, 1991, p. 34.

11.  The categories and descriptions used here are supplied by the firm of Arthur Andersen at http://www.arthurandersen.com/GBP/defsourc.asp.

12.  Robert C. Camp, "A Bible for Benchmarking, by Xerox," *Financial Executive,* July/ Aug. 1993, pp. 23–27.

13.  C. Jackson Grayson, "Back to the Basics of Benchmarking," *Quality,* Vol. 33 No. 5, May 1994, p. 20.

14.  Kenneth Jennings and Frederick Westfall, "Benchmarking for Strategic Action," *Journal of Business Strategy,* May/June 1992, pp. 22–25.

15.  "Strategic Benchmarking," *Sloan Management Review,* Summer 1993, p. 100.

16.  The address of the group is 10 Independence Blvd., Warren, NJ 07059. Florida Power & Light Company, the only U.S. winner of the Japanese Deming Prize, formed Qualtec, a consulting group offering services in quality management.

17.  *Wall Street Journal,* May 26, 1992, Section C, p. 15.

18.  Perhaps the largest *strategic* database is the PIMS (Profit Impact of Marketing Strategy) collection maintained at the Strategic Planning Institute in Cambridge, Massachusetts. The database contains the strategic and financial results of over 3000 strategic business units. A member firm can search for strategic "look-alike" firms and benchmark the determinants of good or not so good performance. See Robert D. Buzzell and Bradley T. Gale, *The PIMS Principles,* New York: The Free Press, 1987. See also Bradley T. Gale and Robert D. Buzzell, "Market Perceived Quality: Key Strategic Concept," *Planning Review,* March/April 1989, pp. 6–48.

19.  For example, Kaiser Associates, Inc. has a seven-step process which is outlined in a company publication, *Beating the Competition: A Practical Guide to Benchmarking,* Vienna, Va.: Kaiser Associates, 1988.

20.  For example, Alcoa's steps include (1) deciding what to benchmark, (2) planning the benchmarking project, (3) understanding your own performance, (4) studying others, (5) learning from the data, and (6) using the findings. See Alexandra Biesada, "Benchmarking," *Financial World,* Sept. 17, 1991, p. 31.

21.  Bob Gift and Doug Mosel, "Benchmarking: Tales from the Front," *Healthcare Forum,* Jan./Feb. 1993, p. 38.

22.  David Altany, "Benchmarkers Unite," *Industry Week,* Feb. 3, 1992, p. 25.

23.  Taken from a company brochure entitled "A Summary of AT&T Transmission Systems: Malcolm Baldrige National Quality Award Application." AT&T's database contains data from over 100 companies and over 250 benchmarking activities for key processes such as hardware and software development, manufacturing, financial planning and budgeting, international billing, and service delivery. Over 20,000 entries describe benchmarking trips or visits with internal and external customers. Sources of competitive benchmarking information include customers, visits to other companies, trade shows and journals, professional societies, standards committees, product brochures, outside consultants, and installation data.

## BENCHMARKING FOR CONTINUOUS IMPROVEMENT

Continuous improvement is one of the three essential areas of Raytheon TI Systems' (RTIS) total quality strategy; the other two are customer focus and people involvement. The company feels that continuous improvement relies on its ability to manage the wealth of knowledge it has and to build on that knowledge. Two knowledge management tools are used: *best-practice sharing* and *benchmarking*.

Best-practice sharing (BPS) is a knowledge management tool that encourages reuse of proven solutions. BPS enables the company to achieve business excellence by providing access to knowledge across RTIS. By adapting and adopting best practices from both internal and external sources, RTIS avoids "reinventing the wheel." The resulting reduction in the learning cycle time frees resources that can be used to create innovative products and processes.

Benchmarking is another important knowledge management tool used by RTIS. Benchmarking is used to measure products, services, and processes against the toughest competitors and other best-in-class companies. Successful benchmarking requires a complete understanding of the business processes before any attempt at comparisons. By answering the question "Who is the best and what do they do?" RTIS can identify benchmarking partners and establish a vision of business excellence.

Benchmarking and BPS are supported by a benchmarking/BPS core team. This team is made up of individuals who represent key processes throughout the company. They also coach process owners, managers, teams, and individuals who want to determine benchmarks, set stretch goals, and discover best practices. The team promotes benchmarking and the sharing of best practices throughout the business.

CASE

# CAN BENCHMARKING GIVE YOU A COMPETITIVE EDGE?

## Mary Ann Murray, Raymond A. Zimmerman, and Daniel J. Flaherty

Benchmarking is a process used by companies to target key areas for improvement within their operations so they can increase their productivity, competitiveness, and quality. It involves comparing their financial and operational performance against a competitor's performance or comparing the performance of various internal departments against each other. Internal comparisons allow best practices within a company to be identified so departments that aren't performing up to speed can find out why and adopt the new standards. External comparisons let companies see how they stack up in the marketplace and discover areas in which they can improve.

The benchmarking process usually consists of four steps. Step one is to analyze your company's practices, procedures, and performance in a given process and to set forth its goals and objectives for improving them. Analysis of the company's practices and procedures is crucial because the practices of other firms will not prove very revealing unless you have determined your own company's strengths and weaknesses.

Step two involves the selection of a benchmark or benchmarks. These benchmarks can be departments within your company or competing companies that perform the process under analysis optimally. This step is critical as selection of the wrong benchmarks can result in your identifying inappropriate procedures and unrealistic goals for your firm.

In step three, detailed information on your benchmarks' practices and procedures for that process must be collected and shared. While collection of such data on competing companies may prove difficult, there are various sources that offer it, which we will discuss later.

Reprinted from *Management Accounting,* August 1997, pp. 46–50, with permission of the Institute of Management Accountants.

For the final step, your company must analyze carefully the data collected in step three to determine which of the policies and procedures used by your benchmarks can be employed best by your own benchmarking division. Here it is important to make your assessment points and goals specific enough to be applicable yet not so numerous and constraining as to be unmanageable.

## Internal vs. External Comparisons

The standards of comparison used for benchmarking can be based on the performance of departments or divisions within your own company or on appropriate departments from other companies.

When using internal units as your benchmark, you can begin by identifying the best performing units within your firm, then analyze their strategies and practices for performance. Once you have determined and quantified these approaches, you can encourage the less effective departments within your company to adopt the practices of the more successful units.

A drawback to internal comparisons alone, however, is that they may foster complacency and not afford a realistic picture of your potential within the industry. For example, it is easy to assume that a growth rate of 4% a year is satisfactory, yet if outside competitors are realizing growth rates of 8%, clearly there is great room for improvement.

A second approach to benchmarking is to compare your company against top competitors Some experts believe that this approach is the most relevant point of comparison for both services and products. Internal comparisons can be limited because of one's inability to recognize one's own shortcomings or faults. Also, although one department within a company may outperform other departments substantially, that fact is not indicative of the relative performance to the industry as a whole. In essence, while the department may be outperforming other units within the company it may be falling short of the performance yields found in other, similar companies. A major stumbling block here though is that it may be difficult to obtain the necessary data for an effective comparison. This type of analysis—peer group benchmarking—is beneficial because it not only allows a company to compare itself to another company with a similar set of attributes, but it also may afford a more invigorating view of what is possible within the industry. Thus, to the extent that key result measurement ratios of individual companies can be compared with averages of a select group of companies with generally similar attributes, this examination can be quite revealing.

A third form of benchmarking is to compare your company with the best-in-class. This approach entails comparing your company with top-performing firms sharing comparable functions or philosophies, although they may not be in your same industry. The advantage of this type of cross-industry comparison is that practices and procedures followed in other industries may prove very beneficial to your company even though the practice or procedure has not been used previously in your industry. It brings new ideas, new thoughts, and even new concepts to your industry. On the downside, however, the introduction of new concepts is somewhat speculative. There is risk whenever one adapts a new concept or procedure. Because a process performs well in one industry does not mean it can be carried over effectively to a different industry. This limitation has to be considered before implementing any new ideas. As an example, consider the possibility of a CPA firm using the same type of television advertising for its services that one occasionally observes law firms using.

## Collecting the Data

It is crucial—although not always easy—to choose an appropriate benchmark and to obtain accurate data on that company's practices and operations. A good starting place is university libraries, which usually have data suitable for serving as a benchmark. Another option is to purchase the data from groups that are in the business of providing such information. These benchmark clearinghouses, which can be found in most cities, begin by matching the client with what they feel is an appropriate benchmark firm, then supplying the data necessary for comparison. In general, they make their benchmark determination by such characteristics as company size, geographical location, the type of services or products supplied, and similar traits that help define the firm or organization. The fee for this information varies according to the client's needs and requests.

Consulting firms also can prove to be valuable sources of data on competing businesses because they can act as a neutral third party. Their customary procedure is to approach potential participants, negotiate a common format, collect and collate the information, and supply the data in a manner that keeps a company's identity concealed. This attention to confidentiality also helps ensure more forthright information from the benchmark and, hence, greater detail and accuracy.

Several other reliable resources for benchmark information are trade associations and professional organizations because they often collect and publish data that can serve as effective benchmarks. For instance, in the public accounting arena, many state societies sponsor or participate in surveys of their membership to establish standards of performance. An example is a book titled *The Public Accounting Profession in California,* published by the California Bureau of Business and Economic Research and the Public Accountancy Research Program. This book provides a detailed analysis of many of the practice characteristics of California accountants.

Another such resource is "The Annual Management of Accounting Practice Survey," sponsored by the Texas Society of CPAs. Conducted annually, this survey is directed at nonnational firms and has more than 2,000 participants nationwide. Every participating accounting firm is categorized into one of four peer groups based on firm size, service mix, and geographic mix. Performance measures based on financial characteristics, sources of fees, marketing activities, administrative policies, and fringe benefits are calculated and averaged for each peer group. For example, all small firms (multi-owner companies with revenues less than $350,000) can compare their individual company performance to others in their peer group. In general, this comparison is likely to be more pertinent than a comparison with the industry overall because it focuses on realistic parameters for that size of company.

## How to Get the Most Out of Benchmarking

Benchmarking can be used most effectively by a company within a top-down strategic business plan framework.

The following example demonstrates how to integrate benchmarking into the strategic planning process effectively.

**Phase 1: Identification of issues.** In this phase, the company must identify and summarize the major challenges, opportunities, and threats it anticipates over the next three to five years. This assessment requires a thorough evaluation of key internal and external issues, such as:

- Financial characteristics, including a peer group analysis and financial position review that addresses average net income, the number of charged hours per person, the number of employees, the amount paid in salaries, and similar considerations.

- Sources of fees or revenues.

- Marketing efforts, including identification of primary and secondary markets, an analysis of the target markets' demographics, and a competitive profile.

- Organizational issues encompassing an analysis of the firm's current structure, evaluation of the span of control, and review of salary administration and training.

- Operational issues, including information systems support and quality service analysis.

**Phase 2: Strategic planning.** Here, a summary of the goals, objectives, and strategies necessary to position a company competitively and profitably must be developed. Service companies also should devise a mission statement.

**Phase 3: Tactical planning.** Now the strategic plan must be broken down into pieces for follow-up actions with responsibilities delegated to key individuals. These tactical or action plans should be developed for one or more of the following areas: information systems, service mix, market positioning, fee structure, and fringe benefits structure.

Throughout this entire strategic analysis, your company's practices and results should be compared with those of the group benchmark. Take a service firm, for example. Your analysis may suggest that your company's fees derived from various service categories are low compared with the benchmark you are using. In such a situation, you would analyze your service categories, fee schedules, and work responsibilities, such as fees lost when a professional partner serves as a day-to-day administrator. If your analysis demonstrates that a significant amount of time (and therefore fees) is lost because of, say, a professional partner spending time on administrative work rather than on providing services, your company should consider hiring an administrator. In this case, comparing your benchmark's administrative policies with your own company's would afford you the advantage of determining this course of action objectively.

If all the phases are carried out properly, benchmarking can be a practical tool for enhancing your company's prosperity. The most successful companies in the immediate and long-term future will be those willing to learn from their peers. Benchmarking can serve as the catalyst for continuous improvement.

## Questions for Discussion

1   What are the disadvantages of relying solely on internal benchmarking?

2   What role would key success factors play in the development of strategy? In benchmarking?

3   Select a company or organization of your own choosing and complete the competitive analysis in Figure 8-2 of the text. For competitor #1 and competitor #2, choose (a) the number one competitor and (b) the best-in-class. Remember, best-in-class does not necessarily have to be in the same industry.

4   Do the same for Figure 8-3 of the text.

# REDUCE VARIATION AND SAVE MONEY

## Edmund S. Fine

Analysis will show if a process improvement is worthwhile.

It almost goes without saying that you have to spend money to make money. But managers sometimes resist the idea of spending money to save money. Here's a way of deciding whether an investment in cutting cost by reducing variation will pay off.

Assume that a company operates on a six-sigma philosophy—a stable process must qualify to a Cpk (process capability index) of at least 2, and the continually monitored process is permitted to have a mean drift of 1.5 standard deviations before corrective action is taken to adjust the process.

This operating mode yields a long-term defective rate of no more than 3.4 parts per million (ppm) and often has a performance far superior to that.

Assume further that one of the company's products is a packaged bulk item, finely divided and fairly uniform (ground coffee or soap powder for example).

The product is shipped in 500-gram packages and the long-term (stable) standard deviation of the filling process has been found to be 4 grams.

By the six-sigma rules, the nominal weight must be set at 524 grams. In doing so, the company is giving away a long-term average of 4.8% (24/500) "free" product in each container.

A new engineer is hired. He examines the process and is amazed that the company has been shipping almost 5% more product than the nominal. Through experimentation and a few process improvements, he finds that the long-term standard deviation of the filling process could be reduced to 1 gram.

This would enable the company to set the nominal weight at 506 grams and to reduce the amount of free product to a long-term average of 1.2% (6/500).

From *Quality Progress,* Vol. 32 No. 3, March 1999, p. 128. ©1999 American Society for Quality. Reprinted with permission.

However, these process modifications and improvements are not free; to both reduce variation and save money, the economics of the situation must be examined.

The process modifications could save an average of 18 grams per package. The savings would have to be multiplied by the number of packages produced per month to obtain the dollars per month that the company would be saving. The savings must be balanced against the cost of the process improvements, which usually accumulate in the first month.

Various books on engineering economics have different and often complex criteria for making such decisions, but the following guideline usually works.

If you can recoup the cost of process improvements within a year, proceed with the project. If, however, the cost of the process improvements will not be recouped within two years, don't do it—there are too many uncertainties beyond that time frame.

If the cost of the process improvements will be recouped in one to two years, a detailed engineering economic analysis is probably necessary.

This analysis will take into account factors such as market forecasts, variabilities in the cost of raw materials used to make the product, projections of possible further improvements to the production machinery, and so forth.

At this level of complexity of an engineering economic analysis, it is necessary also to factor in the time value of money. Such analysis usually is not necessary for very rapid or slow paybacks; those decisions become self-evident without it.

Thus, the paradox of reducing variation and saving money can be seen at work, but it is not a cure-all. A quick economic analysis will show if a process improvement is truly worthwhile.

- Saving money through variation reduction
- Finished product costs $0.002 per gram.
- Shipments average 100,000 boxes per month.
- Shipments contain an average of 24 grams free product per box.
- Process improvements would reduce this to 6 grams of free product per box.
- Saving 18 grams per box yields a savings of $18 \times 0.002 \times 100,000 = \$3,600$ per month.
- The cost of the process improvements is $25,000 (with no charge in process operating costs after the improvements are made.

The process improvements to reduce variation would pay for themselves in less than seven months, making this project a go.

## BENCHMARKING AT VARIFILM

Compare each of the following TQM criteria to Varifilm and indicate whether the practice in the company is a *strength* (S) or *needs improvement* (I). Justify your answer.

### 2.2 Competitive Comparisons and Benchmarking

|  | S | I |
|---|---|---|
| ■ A systematic approach is used for evaluating and improving the process for selecting competitive comparisons and benchmarking information. | ___ | ___ |
| ■ Competitive and benchmarking information and data are used to establish "stretch" improvement objectives. | ___ | ___ |
| ■ Benchmarking information and data are integrated into the improvement of existing processes and/or the development of new processes. | ___ | ___ |
| ■ There exists a defined approach for determining specific benchmarking needs and priorities. | ___ | ___ |
| ■ A global competitive intelligence database is collected and used to estimate a variety of competitive indices, including sales, capacity, and cost. | ___ | ___ |
| ■ Competitive data are used to create strategies for market, product, manufacturing, technical, environmental, and resource developments. | ___ | ___ |
| ■ An overall rating is needed for suppliers, but specific benchmarks are used to compare against other companies. | ___ | ___ |

*Additional Areas for Improvement*

_____

_____

_____

# FOR FURTHER READING

Bisp, Soren, Elin Sorensen, and Klaus G. Grunert, "Using the Key Success Factors Concept in Competitor Intelligence and Benchmarking," *Competitive Intelligence Review,* July–Sept. 1998, pp. 55–67.

Blackiston, G. Howland, "Juran Institute: A Barometer of Trends in Quality," *National Productivity Review,* Winter 1996, pp. 15–23.

Elmuti, Dean, "The Perceived Impact of the Benchmarking Process on Organizational Effectiveness," *Production & Inventory Management Journal,* Third Quarter 1998, pp. 6–11.

Rogers, Hank, "Benchmarking Your Plant Against TQM Best-Practices," *Quality Progress,* June 1998, pp. 51–55.

van de Vliet, Anita, "To Beat the Best," *Management Today,* Jan. 1996, pp. 56–60.

Yi, Hyong U., "Benchmarking Best Practices: Lessons from Baseball," *Public Manager,* Summer 1998, pp. 59–62.

# 9

# ORGANIZING FOR TOTAL QUALITY MANAGEMENT

*There is a lack of congruence between the needs of
healthy individuals and the demands of the formal organizations.*

Chris Argyris[1]

Total quality management (TQM) has been attempted with varying degrees of success since it became the management buzzword in the late 1980s and early 1990s. By applying the philosophy and principles of TQM, many companies (e.g., Xerox, Motorola, IBM, Baldrige winners) have improved both competitiveness and profitability. Others have not had such success. Indeed, it appears that substantially less than half have either stalled or fallen short of delivering real improvements.[2] Many reasons have been advanced to explain this failure and near failure on the part of so many firms.[3]

If *organization* is broadly perceived as structure, processes, and people, the argument can be made that perhaps the problem, and the solution, lies in *organizing.* Many, if not most, managers, when asked to describe the reason for organizational change, would probably answer "efficiency" or "cost reduction" or "lean production." No one would argue against these *efficiency* outcomes, but it is not a strategy for sustained competitive advantage. Only an organization and strategy framed in terms of customer satisfaction will provide long-term growth and profitability. Focusing on efficiency alone (i.e., price and cost of production) will lead to management of the firm as though it were in the commodity business, producing a product or service differentiated only by price.

Fundamental to success in the use of TQM is a culture of continuous improvement and an organization that focuses on customer satisfaction. The following are examples of what can happen when the customer's values are sacrificed to "efficiency":[4]

■ A company expends a great deal of time and effort to increase on-time delivery from 42 percent to 92 percent only to lose market share because the on-time focus left little time for employees to return customer calls and explain the product.

■ An airline considers on-time departure essential to customer satisfaction and goes to great lengths to leave on time only to discover that customers considered food quality and flight status information much more important.

■ An insurance company expends a lot of effort to process claims on time only to find that most of its customers consider clarity of claim explanation to be more important.

■ On average, it takes about 22 days to process an insurance application, but the real time spent on processing is only 17 minutes.

Based on a survey of management consultants Boston Consulting Group, it was concluded that 95 to 99 percent of the internal activities of U.S. businesses have little or no relevance to the customer.[5]

It is not logical to conclude that a better alternative to efficiency and cost containment as a guide to organizational change should be customer value—how well their needs are met. Stated more simply, it means providing the outcome the customers seek, not the product or service they purchase. This view can provide the basis for how organizations are structured, operated, and managed.

Synthesizing quality values and policies into every person's job and every operation is a complex task that must be supported by an appropriate organizational infrastructure. Management texts universally define organizing as a variation of a statement such as "the process of creating a structure for the organization that will enable its people to work together effectively toward its objectives."[6] Thus, the process recognizes a structural as well as a behavioral or "people" dimension.

This chapter is concerned with the macro dimension of organization: the overall approach the company might take to establish a quality infrastructure. The micro dimension (organizing the "quality department" or the duties of the "top quality manager") is technical in nature and beyond the scope of this book. Both Deming[7] and Crosby[8] treat this in some detail.

Historically, organizations have tended to focus on the classical principles of specialization of labor, delegation of authority, span of control (a limited number of subordinates), and unity of command (no one works for two bosses). The result in many cases was the traditional pyramidal organization chart, cast in stone and accompanied by budgets, rules, procedures, and the chain-of-command hierarchy. Task specialization was extreme in some cases. The classic bureaucracy thus emerged.

Prior to the current emergence of TQM in the early 1980s, responsibility for quality was vague and confusing. Executive management grew detached from the idea of managing to achieve quality. The general work force had no stake in increasing the quality of its products and services. Quality had become the business of specialists—product specification engineers and process control statisticians who determined acceptable levels of product variability and performed quality control inspection on the factory floor.

Today, it is generally recognized that there are two prerequisites for a TQM organization. The first is a quality attitude that pervades the entire organization. Quality is not just a special activity supervised by a high-ranking quality director.[9] This attitude (culture, vision) was examined in Chapter 2 and is largely a challenge for top management. The second prerequisite is an organizational infrastructure to support the pervasive attitude. Companies must have the means and the structure to set goals, assign them to appropriate people, and convert them to action plans. People must be aware of the importance of quality and trained to accomplish the necessary tasks.

## ORGANIZING FOR TQM: THE SYSTEMS APPROACH

Boeing Aircraft Company reported a 1997 loss of $178 million based on revenue of $45.8 billion. The production line is based on the World War II B-17 bomber line—established in 1942. The company has over 400 separate computer systems—which are not linked.[10] This is hardly integration, nor does it reflect a systems approach to organization.

When Allied Signal began its TQM effort, there were 41 separate autonomous strategic business units. Now there are 32 units acting as one company.[11] Lawrence Bassidy, chairman and CEO, said, "We continue to break down internal barriers and simplify our organization. Customers are the reason we exist. We used to manage by means of hierarchical, vertical layers. Now we are solving problems and revamping processes through horizontal, cross-functional teams from many disciplines. These teams discovered inherent synergies within the operating companies."

Since the Taylorism of the early part of this century, and even today, the overwhelming form of organization structure was based on labor specialization and a hierarchy of authority delegation. The result has been a form of organizational "chimneys" where departments and functions, each "box" of the organizational chart, were analogous to a chimney, separate and unconnected to other functions and other boxes. The job of each function was to minimize cost and maximize output without too much regard for customers, either external or internal. As one chief executive said, "Production can't make what design designs and sales can't sell what production makes." Advice to the CEO: let everyone talk to the customer and to each other. Take a systems approach to organization. Integrate components, activities, and processes by focusing on the customer followed by an organization culture based on quality.

A system can be defined as an entity composed of interdependent components that are integrated for achievement of an objective. The organization is a social system comprised of a number of components such as marketing, production, finance, research, and so on. These organizational components are activities that may or may not be integrated, and they do not necessarily have objectives or operate toward achievement of an objective. Thus, synergism, a necessary attribute of a well-organized system, may be lacking as each activity takes a parochial view or operates independently of the others. This lack of synergism cannot continue under the TQM approach to strategic management because interdependency across functions and departments is a necessary precondition.

The concept of an organizational system is shown in Figure 9-1. Inputs to the system are converted by organization activities into an output. Indeed, the sole reason for the existence of the organization and each activity within it is to add value to inputs and produce an output with greater value. A measure of this conversion of inputs into outputs is known as productivity, and the ratio of output to input must be a positive number if the system is to survive in the long run.

The activities of the organization are subsystems of the whole, but are also individual systems with inputs and outputs that provide input to other systems

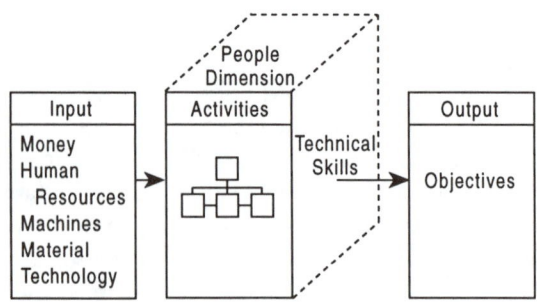

**Figure 9-1**   The Organization System

such as customers and other internal activities. This *chain* of input/output operations is depicted in Figure 9-2.

Despite the simplicity of the concept, it most often fails in practice. Activity supervisors and individuals within activities do not understand the objective or results of their "subsystem," nor can they define their output in measurable terms. When asked to define the output of their jobs, they will answer: "I am responsible for maintenance," or "I work in finance," or "My job is to ship the product." In each case, these are statements of activity and not output, objective, or results expected. *Quality* output is stated in such vague terms as "do a good job" or "keep the customer happy." People can describe what they do (activity), but not what they are supposed to get done (objective or result). They may be very efficient at doing things right but ineffective in doing the right things. This failure is critical to organization output as well as structure.

Michael Porter, in his excellent book *Competitive Advantage,*[12] has taken the systems theory a major practical step forward with his concept of the *value chain.* He suggests that "competitive advantage (in this case quality) cannot be understood by looking at a firm as a whole. It stems from the many discrete activities a firm performs in designing, producing, marketing, delivering, and supporting its product." While Porter's concept is expanded to include any of the many sources of competitive advantage, the value chain concept will be used here to focus on the organizational structure for TQM.

The discrete activities of an organization can be represented using the generic value chain shown in Figure 9-3. Note that the activities or organizational functions are comprised of primary and support activities, which may or may not be changed from those listed in Figure 9-3 depending on the firm's industry and its particular strategy. Selected examples of chain activities from Porter's book are summarized in Table 9-1.

Customers, channels, and suppliers also have value chains, and the firm's output of product or service becomes an input to the customer's value chain. The firm's differentiation and its competitive advantage depend on how the activities in its value chain relate to the needs of the customer, channel, or supplier. If quality has been chosen as a competitive advantage, it now remains to determine the customer's value chain and how the product or service can add value to the customer's system. Following this determination, the value chain should be organized into the required discrete activities, each one of which can improve the quality of the output for the purpose of meeting the customer's expectations. Before asking what you can do for the customer, ask what the customer expects to accomplish. The answer forms the basis for a quality organization. In this regard, it should be kept in mind that there are linkages between a firm's value chain and those of its customers, as well as downstream linkages with channels and suppliers. An excellent example of this is Wal-Mart, where a key competitive

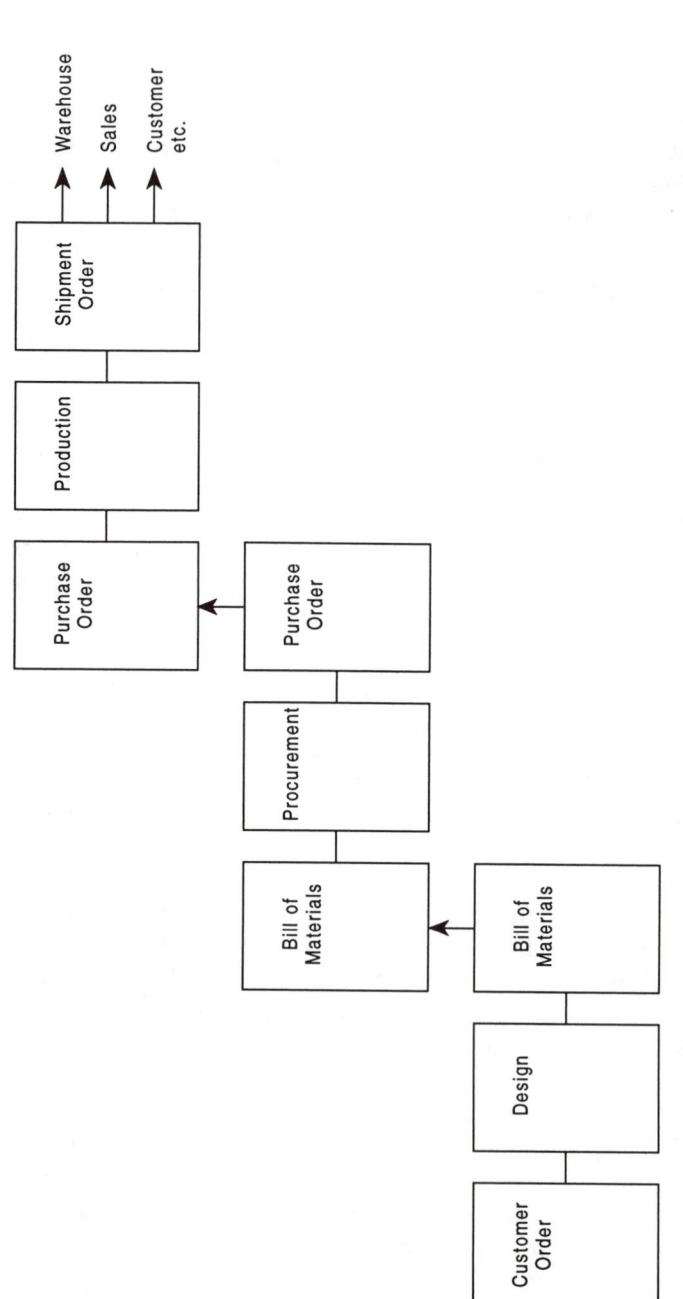

**Figure 9-2**   Chain of Subsystems

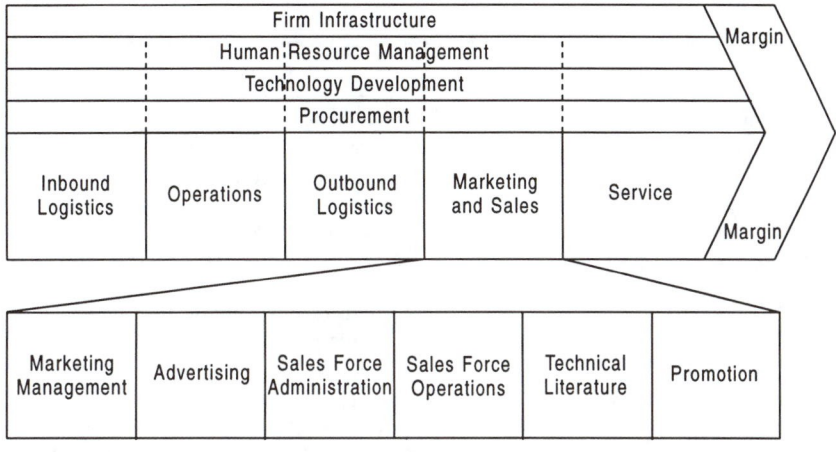

**Figure 9-3**    Subdividing a Generic Value Chain

advantage was achieved through the value chain activity of technology development; in Wal-Mart's case, it was the sophisticated computer-based information system that improved the output of many other activities such as distribution, purchasing, and warehousing.

■ A spokesperson for Winnebago Industries, manufacturer of motor homes, concludes, "You must pick the right distribution network. In our case, it is our dealers. We believe we are only as strong as our dealer network. They are our first, last, primary, and most critical link to our end customers."[13]

■ Globe Metallurgical of Cleveland, the first small company to win the Baldrige Award, realized the importance of suppliers in its own value chain. Globe's management determined that the most effective method of assuring compliance with statistical process control and quality approaches in the suppliers' facilities would be to visit each supplier location with a quality improvement team and to train the hourly employees at each location. The program is a vital aspect of Globe's quality system.[14]

■ BSQ Group, an architectural firm in Tulsa, Oklahoma, designs and constructs stores for Wal-Mart. Although the firm's immediate customer is Wal-Mart, it organizes its value chain to go downstream with linkages to Wal-Mart's customer: "Many people believe that quality is generally in the eyes of the beholder. Well, in the case of

**Table 9-1**  Chain Activities

| Primary activities | Support activities |
|---|---|
| **Inbound logistics** | **Procurement** |
| Materials handling | Dispersion of the procurement function |
| Warehousing | throughout the firm |
| Inventory control | |
| Vehicle scheduling | **Technology development** |
| Returns to suppliers | Efforts to improve products and processes |
| **Operations** | **Human resource management** |
| Machining | Recruiting |
| **Management** | Hiring |
| Packaging | Training |
| Assembly | Development |
| Maintenance | Compensation |
| Testing | |
| **Outbound logistics** | **Firm infrastructure** |
| Material handling | Supports entire chain |
| Order processing | General management |
| Scheduling | Planning |
| Finished goods warehouse | Finance, accounting |
| **Marketing and sales** | Quality management |
| Advertising | |
| Promotion | |
| Sales force | |
| Pricing | |
| **Service** | |
| Installation | |
| Repair | |
| Training | |
| Parts supply | |

Wal-Mart, that beholder is the store's customer. They are the ones that are helping us define the quality standards that we currently strive to present and it's with them in mind that we begin our study."[15]

## ORGANIZING FOR QUALITY IMPLEMENTATION

The traditional approach to organization sees the process as a mechanical assemblage of functions and activities without a great deal of attention to strategy and desired results. The process takes the product as given and groups the necessary skills and activities into homogeneous functions and departments. This approach to building an organization structure has been criticized by Peter Drucker: "What we need to know are not all the activities that might conceivably have to be housed in the organization structure. What we need to know are the load-bearing parts of the structure, the *key activities.*"[16]

Key activities will differ depending on the nature of the organization, its products, and its strategy. What is a key activity in one may not be in another. Advertising may be a key activity in the value chain of Coca-Cola, but not in Boeing Aircraft, where design is the key activity. Back-office activity may be a key activity in Merrill Lynch, but not in McDonald's. Firms frequently fail to prioritize or identify key activities in the value chain because of a tendency to organize around the chart of accounts. Some firms focus on those activities where cost, rather than quality or other sources of differentiation, is the major consideration.

The value chain concept provides a systematic way to identify the key activities necessary for quality differentiation and a way to group them into homogeneous departments and functions. Indeed, an organization structure that corresponds to the value chain is the most economic and effective way to deliver quality and therefore achieve a competitive advantage.

It should be noted that the quality assurance department is generally not the load-bearing key activity when organizing for TQM. Quality assurance activities can be found in nearly every function of the company if these functions are viewed as links in the value chain. Any activity or function is a potential source of quality differentiation. The ill-defined or elusive word "quality" may be too narrow if it focuses on product or service alone. Moreover, such limited focus may exclude the many other activities that impact the customer's value chain. Not only those functions normally classified as "line" but a variety of "staff" functions as well can be the source of quality in the organization structure. Consider the following sample activities:

| Activity | Value to customer |
|---|---|
| Purchasing | Improved cost and quality of product |
| Engineering and design characteristics | Unique product |
| Manufacturing | Product reliability |
| Order processing | Response time |
| Service | Customer installation |
| Scheduling | Response time |
| Inspection | Defect-free product |
| Spare parts | Maintenance |
| Human resources | Customer training |

By listing the activities of the organization and comparing them to a value chain such as Figure 9-3, one can see the many potential ways that quality differentiation can be achieved. It should also be noted that these activities can lower customer costs as well.

Production of quality does not stop when the product leaves the factory. Distribution and service are part of the production process. Careful identification of customer value will reveal a number of other opportunities for quality differentiation. For example, buyers and potential customers frequently perceive value in ways they do not understand or because of incomplete knowledge. Scanning a daily newspaper or magazine quickly reveals the many ways that both manufacturers and service firms signal subjective, qualitative measures of quality. Do you buy Pepsi-Cola for taste or brand image? Do you contemplate the purchase of a Volvo for performance or long life and safety? Consulting and accounting firms signal quality by the appearance and presumed professionalism of employees. Banks are known to build impressive facilities to indicate quality. Charles Revson, formerly of Revlon, once said, "I'm not selling cosmetics, I'm selling hope." The several criteria that the buyer may use to make a buying decision mean that there may be an equal number of activities that become *key* activities in the creation of customer value. Porter provides several illustrative signaling criteria,[17] to which firm examples and organization activities that become key in delivery of the criteria have been added here:

| Criteria | Firm example | Activity involved |
| --- | --- | --- |
| Reputation | Appliances | Advertising |
| Appearance | Apparel | Design |
| Label | Athletic shoes | Graphics |
| Facilities | Bank | Maintenance |
| Time in business | Whiskey | Distribution |
| Customer list | Magazine publisher | Marketing |
| Visibility of top management | Consumer products | Hot line |

Of course, having signaled a particular criterion to buyers and potential buyers, it is necessary to deliver as promised, measure the effectiveness of the criterion, and keep customer feedback communication lines open to ensure satisfaction.

Delivery of quality products or services depends on how well the many activities of the company are organized and integrated. The measurement of effectiveness is fundamental to the TQM process (see Chapter 7). It now remains to organize for customer feedback, another *key activity* that impacts other functions and activities throughout the organization.

Measuring customer satisfaction, or dissatisfaction, is an essential but often overlooked activity. What happens when a customer chooses a bank's trust department based on the criterion of experienced personnel, only to be shunted off to a recent college graduate or ignored by a "customer representative"? Research indicates that customers who are satisfied with a bank's quality will tell, on the average, three other people, while those who are dissatisfied will tell eight or nine others about poor quality.[18] How does a customer feel when returning an item under warranty only to be patronized by a retail clerk? One survey found that for every problem incident reported to corporate headquarters, there are at least 19 other similar incidents which simply were not reported or which were handled by the retailer or the front line without being recorded. Most companies spend 95 percent of their resources handling complaints and less than 5 percent analyzing them.

There is a strong correlation between consumer satisfaction with response to problems or questions and the likelihood of purchasing another product from the same company.[19] Yet few customers bother to complain, and of those who do, only a small fraction reach top management. What is needed is the institutionalization of customer service throughout the organization as a key activity to be performed by everyone. Despite this evident need, many companies have neither the activities nor the supporting policies. For many that do, there is a conflict between organization and policies that may have an opposite effect. Covertly measuring quality by using mystery shoppers, holding motivational meetings which employees perceive as paternalistic and patronizing, and paying for sales rather than service are among those policies that may conflict with the need to provide quality products and service.[20] It may be difficult for employees to be quality conscious in the face of policies that discourage this attitude.

## THE PEOPLE DIMENSION: MAKING THE TRANSITION FROM A TRADITIONAL TO A TQM ORGANIZATION

The typical company (Figure 9-4a) operates with a vertical, functional organizational structure based on reporting relationships, budgeting procedures, and specific and detailed job classifications.[21] Departmentation is by function, and communication, rewards, and loyalties are functionally oriented. Processes are forced to flow vertically from the top down, creating costly barriers to process flow.

The systems approach to organizing suggests three significant changes, one conceptual and two requiring organizational realignment:

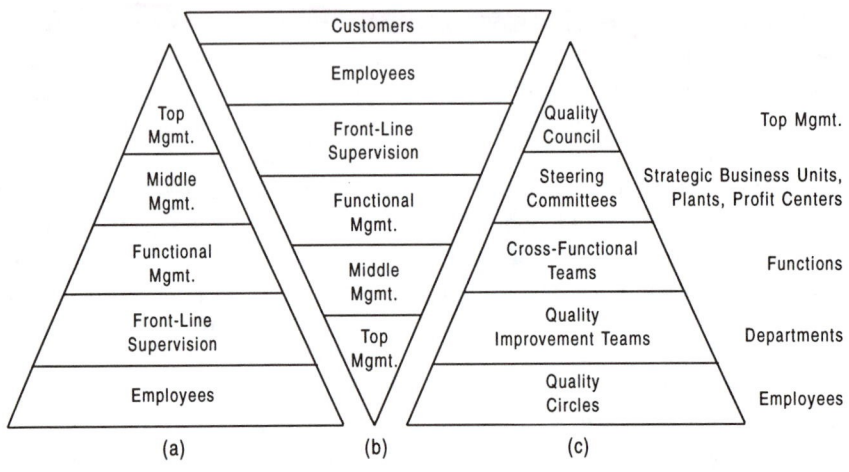

**Figure 9-4** Transition from Traditional to TQM Organization

- The concept of the inverted organizational chart
- A system of intracompany internal quality
- Horizontal and vertical integration of functions and activities

## The Inverted Organizational Chart

If you've seen one organizational chart, you've seen them all: the symmetrical pyramid with the chairman at the top and the cascading of authority to successive levels (14 at General Motors) until the functions are shown near the bottom of the chart. Front-line supervisors are rarely shown and non-supervisory personnel almost never appear.

Where are the front-line supervisor and the employees? These are the people who deliver quality to the customer. In the eyes of the customer, they *are* the company. The sports fan cares not for the owner or the manager. The players deliver the quality. And so it is with the flight attendant, the bank teller, the auto mechanic, the salesperson explaining a product, the person answering the telephone...even the college professor.

Perhaps it is time to put first things first. To make the transition from traditional to TQM management, it may be desirable to *conceptualize* a new organizational chart. Invert the existing one (Figure 9-4b) and put the customer at the top, followed by the employees and front-line supervisors. These are the deliverers of quality. This concept does not change the hierarchy and flow of authority, but the boss is no longer the boss in the old-fashioned sense. He or she is now a facilitator, a coach, and an integrator, whose job is to remove barriers that prevent subordinates from doing their jobs. The same role now falls on middle and top management. Quality is now the responsibility of everyone and not just the quality assurance department.

## Internal Quality

The Juran Institute of Wilton, Connecticut, delivers a program called "Managing Business Process Quality," which is a technique for executing cross-functional quality improvement among intracompany functions and activities.[22] A key factor in this approach is an organization-wide focus on the customer, including both *internal* and *external* customers. An enlarged definition of quality should be used to embrace all business processes, rather than just manufacturing.

The systems approach, by definition, requires the integration of organizational activities for achievement of a common goal. This goal, under the TQM form of organization, remains the satisfaction of customer requirements, but customers are now considered to be both outside as well as within the organization.[23] The process applies whether relating to a final customer or an internal customer; it is a participative process involving supplier and customer in an active dialogue. Examples include:

■ Metropolitan Life Insurance Company has made a major commitment to improve quality by implementing a *horizontal management* approach that is built on management commitment, employee involvement, and knowledge of internal suppliers.[24]

■ Campbell USA has aimed its latest quality emphasis, its "Quality Proud" program, at the administrative and marketing activities of the company. Job descriptions, promotions, pay, and bonuses for all employees are linked to the results of the new program.[25]

As a major step in its transformation to a total quality organization, DEC asked each of its 125,000 employees to answer in writing the following questions:

1. What business process are you involved in?
2. Who are your customers (that is, the next step in the processes you are involved in)?
3. Who are your suppliers (that is, the preceding step in the processes you are involved in)?
4. Are you meeting the expectations of your customers?

5. Are your suppliers meeting your expectations?

6. How can the processes be simplified and waste eliminated?[26]

■ DEC reported that this simple survey had a massive impact. In the short run, countless redundant activities were discovered and eliminated. In the long run, DEC employees now think in terms of meeting both internal and external customer expectations. (This concept is also illustrated in Figure 9-2.)

Aside from the obvious benefits of improvements in quality, productivity, and cost, a system of internal customer quality is important for a number of other reasons:

■ External customer satisfaction cannot increase unless internal customer satisfaction does.

■ No quality improvement effort can succeed without employee buy-in and proactive participation.

■ Focus on internal quality promotes a quality and entrepreneurial culture.

■ An understanding of internal quality policy is an aid in communication and decision making.

■ It is a significant criterion in the Malcolm Baldrige National Quality Award (Section 5.6).

## THE PRACTICE OF MANAGEMENT

One of the best, and essential, ways to change and embed a culture of quality is to change the concept of management as it is practiced. The focus should move from the traditional approach to one that is focused on quality.

| Management process | Traditional approach | Quality approach |
|---|---|---|
| Planning | Short-range budgets | Strategic planning followed by operational plans focused on customer |
| Organize | Hierarchical authority | Empowerment and participation |
| Control | Historical variance reports | Quality measures and information for self-control |
| Communication | Top-down | All directions |

| Management process | Traditional approach | Quality approach |
|---|---|---|
| Decision making | Ad hoc/reactive | Rational, based on planned change |
| Functional management | Parochial, competitive, internally directed | Cross-functional, integrative |
| Quality management | Problem solving, reduce defects | Continuous improvement of all processes |

## ROLES IN ORGANIZATIONAL TRANSITION TO TQM

Members of a successful organization need a sound understanding of their roles during the transition to a TQM program. People at all levels require orientation as to how they will be impacted under the new philosophy of employee involvement. The improvement process involves a group of complementary activities that provide an environment conducive to improvement of performance for both employees and managers. Each level has a role to play.

The role of **top management** is critical. Many of the most successful companies launched their programs by creating a quality council or steering committee (Figure 9-4c) whose members comprise the top management team. Some multidivision companies encourage a council in each division or strategic business unit. The council provides a good vehicle for management to demonstrate its leadership in the quality initiative. At Motorola, the CEO, who is also the chief quality officer of the corporation, chairs the Operating and Policy Committee in all-day meetings twice each quarter.[27]

Opinions differ as to who should lead or coordinate the TQM effort. One source suggests a new role similar to that of a financial controller, a role that is justified on the basis that quality is now a strategic business planning and management function.[28] Others disagree and suggest that the company should avoid setting up a quality bureaucracy headed by a high-profile quality director. There is general agreement that it should not be headed by a staff department such as personnel or quality assurance. The process should be line led and given back to the business managers who implement it on a daily basis. To reiterate, quality should not be led by a non-line manager.

The major changes are strategic and organizational and have been outlined in this and previous chapters. It now remains for top management to manage the transition.[29]

The role of **middle managers** has traditionally been an integrative one. They are the drivers of quality and the information funnel for change both vertically and horizontally—the go-between for top management and front-line employees. They implement the strategy devised by top management by linking unit goals to strategic objectives. They develop personnel, make continuous improvement possible, and accept responsibility for performance deficiencies.[30]

**Front-line supervision** has been called the missing link in TQM.[31] At Federal Express, a Baldrige winner, the communication effort is focused on the front-line supervisors because most employees report directly to them. The company realizes that the real purveyors of quality are the employees, and a basic quality concept is candid, open, two-way communication.

Supervisors can make or break a quality improvement effort. They are called upon to provide support to employee involvement teams and create a climate that builds high levels of commitment in groups and individuals.

**Quality assurance and the quality professional** are faced with good news and bad news as TQM emerges as the load-bearing concern of company strategy. On the one hand, the accelerating emphasis on quality has given them more visibility, and in some cases the reporting relationships have moved to higher levels in the organization. On the other hand, they may now be perceived as a staff support function as quality becomes more widespread and led by line managers.

Philip Crosby indicates that the quality professional must become more knowledgeable about the process of management.[32] The limited tools of inspection techniques and statistical process control have become less important as the more sophisticated approaches of TQM begin to pervade all functions and activities, rather than just manufacturing.

## SMALL GROUPS AND EMPLOYEE INVOLVEMENT

In a *Harvard Business Review* article, David Gumpert described a small "microbrewery" where the head of the company attributed their success to a loyal, small, and involved work force. He found that keeping the operation small strengthened employee cohesiveness and gave them a feeling of responsibility and pride.[33]

This anecdote tells a lot about small groups (hereafter called teams) and how they can impact motivation, productivity, and quality. If quality is the objective, employee involvement in small groups and teams will greatly facilitate the result because of two reasons: motivation and productivity.

The theory of motivation, but not necessarily its practice, is fairly mature, and there is substantial proof that it can work. By oversimplifying a complex theory, it can be shown why team membership is an effective motivational device that can lead to improved quality.[34]

**Table 9-2**    Team Membership and Motivation

| Motivating factors | Team membership |
|---|---|
| Job development (the work) | |
|    Vertical loading | Provides responsibility |
|    Job closure | Team members see results |
|    Feedback | Self-established goals |
| Achievement | Targets set by teams |
| Growth/self-development | Training, more responsibility |
| Recognition | By peers and supervisors |
| Communication | Team is vehicle for communication (see Chapter 3) |

Teams improve productivity as a result of greater motivation (Table 9-2) and reduced overlap and lack of communication in a functionally based classical structure characterized by territorial battles and parochial outlooks. There is always the danger that functional specialists, if left to their own devices, may pursue their own interests with little regard for the overall company mission. Team membership, particularly a cross-functional team, reduces many of these barriers and encourages an integrative systems approach to achievement of common objectives, those that are common to both the company and the team. There are many success stories. To cite a few:

■ Globe Metallurgical, Inc., the first small company to win the Baldrige Award, had a 380 percent increase in productivity which was attributed primarily to self-managed work teams.[35]

■ The partnering concept requires a new corporate culture of participative management and teamwork throughout the entire organization. Ford increased productivity 28 percent by using the team concept with the same workers and equipment.[36]

■ Harleysville Insurance Company's Discovery program provides synergism resulting from the team approach. The program produced a cost saving of $3.5 million, along with enthusiasm and involvement among employees.[37]

■ At Decision Data Computer Corporation, middle management is trained to support "Pride Team."[38]

■ Martin Marietta Electronics and Missiles Group has achieved success with performance measurement teams.[39]

■ Publishers Press has achieved significant productivity improvements and attitude change from the company's process improvement teams.[40]

■ PQ Corporation, a mid-size chemical company that employs 2000 people, embarked on a TQM visioning process. The company's mission was redefined, its culture formalized, and 17 core values articulated. One is that the company would conduct business on a total quality basis. This message is conveyed in the company's vision, annual planning process, monthly workshops, monthly town meetings, and conversations "in all parts of the company at all times throughout the world."

## TEAMS FOR TQM

The several subsystems or components of a TQM approach were examined in previous chapters. The most critical of these components is employee involvement, and it is the one around which the management system of TQM should be based. It is the most important of the components of TQM and also the most complex. Consider the analogy of an iceberg. Approximately 10 percent of an iceberg is visible, while 90 percent is hidden from view. Imagine that the organizational chart is an iceberg. The visible 10 percent is top management and functional management. The 90 percent, where the true potential for quality exists, is comprised of front-line supervision and non-management employees. Does it not make good sense to tap into the 90 percent which represents a reservoir of ideas for quality and productivity improvements? The vehicle for doing this is some form of *team.*

A 1989 General Accounting Office study found that over 80 percent of all companies had implemented some form of employee involvement.[41] However, the statistic is misleading because responding companies considered a suggestion system as an employee involvement program, which is hardly a systems approach or a linking vehicle. Moreover, the methods most likely to have enduring effects are those that covered the smallest percentage of employees.

### Quality Circles

The most widespread form of an employee involvement team is the quality circle, defined as "a small group of employees doing similar or related work who meet regularly to identify, analyze, and solve product-quality and production problems and to improve general operations."[42] Although the concept has had some success in white-collar operations, the major impact has been among "direct labor" employees in manufacturing, where concerns are primarily with quality, cost, specifications, productivity, and schedules. By their very nature, quality circles were limited to concerns of the small group of members and few cross-functional problems were considered.

The major growth of the circles occurred in the late 1970s and early 1980s, as thousands of companies adopted the concept. Like so many previous movements (e.g., management by objectives, value analysis, zero-based budgeting), however, the concept never met expectations, and widespread abandonment resulted. As many as 50 percent of Fortune 500 companies disbanded their circles in the 1980s.[43] The major reason for failure was a general lack of commitment to the concept of participation and the lack of interest and participation by management.[44] From a TQM perspective, quality circles lack the prerequisites of integration with strategy, company goals, and management systems. Organizations can go beyond using quality circles by creating task forces, work teams, and cross-functional teams.[45]

**Task teams** are a modification of the quality circle. The major differences are that task teams can exist at any level and the goal or topic for discussion is given, whereas in quality circles members are generally free to choose the problems they will solve. Task teams with the best chance for success are those that represent an extension of a pre-existing, successful quality circle program.[46]

**Self-managing work teams** are an extension of quality circles but differ in one major respect: members are empowered to exercise control over their jobs and optimize the efficiency and effectiveness of the total process rather than the individual steps within it. Team members perform all the necessary tasks to complete an entire job, setting up work schedules and making assignments to individual team members. Peer evaluation is another characteristic.[47]

A number of common elements are characteristic of self-managed teams:

- **Job design and structure.** The team redesigns the work before implementation and controls the entire job.
- **Supervision.** Traditional supervisors could be absent altogether. Leadership may be assigned according to talent and preference.
- **Quality.** In addition to quality, the teams may become involved in the entire job, including planning, cost, scheduling, and even sales and distribution.
- **Decisions.** Decisions are not confined to quality but may involve all areas that affect the teams. Some may become involved in appraisal, pay, and selection.
- **Customers.** Internal customers are perceived as partners for the purpose of meeting needs of external customers. The primary focus is the external customer.

■ **Authority.** If given complete responsibility for the actions of their areas, the teams may have authority and responsibility for growth and profitability.

## Cross-Functional Teams

■ Computer manufacturer DEC has integrated a range of proven TQM techniques into its program, including cross-functional process improvement teams. One element is strictly home-grown. DELTA (DEC Employees Leveraged Team Activities) is a sophisticated, closed-loop suggestion system designed to discover and address problems. Under DELTA, only an employee who makes a suggestion can dispose of it. He or she also has the responsibility of working with other employees to implement or reshape the suggestion in order to determine whether it is feasible. Thus, DELTA empowers employees and promotes team building, two essential elements of quality management.[48]

The centuries-old hierarchical form of organization with a vertical chain of command was the norm until recently, when organizational complexity demanded horizontal as well as vertical coordination in order to plan and control processes that flowed laterally. If no lateral coordination is achieved, the organization becomes a collection of islands of specialization without integration, a requirement of the systems approach. Linking business process improvement (billing, procurement, recruiting, record keeping, design, sales, etc.) to the key business objectives of the organization is necessary if quality is to become real and relevant. There is widespread agreement that cross-functional teams provide the best vehicle for linking these activities and processes. The concept of linkages is shown in Figure 9-5. Note that a cross-functional approach achieves the objectives of:

■ Customers

■ Functions

■ Processes

■ The organization

Team expert Michael Donovan summarizes a number of trends that will shape the structure and process of employee involvement efforts in the future:[49]

| From | To |
|---|---|
| Perception of employee involvement as a program | Perception as an ongoing process |

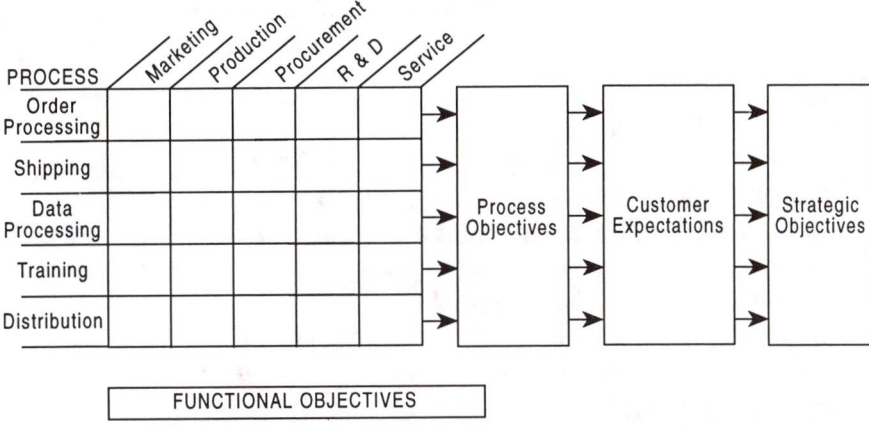

**Figure 9-5**   Cross-Functional Linkages

| From | To |
| --- | --- |
| Voluntary participation | Participation by all members as a natural work team |
| Quality circles | Several types of teams at many levels |
| Project focus | Goal focus |
| Limited management involvement | Active management involvement |
| Functional management skills | Building participative leadership and facilitation skills into management roles |
| Employee participation in operating problems | Employee participation in broader issues |

## SUMMARY: SOME PREREQUISITES FOR TQM SUCCESS

The following are some of the more important requirements for a successful TQM effort:

- **Top management commitment** is the single biggest obstacle to quality improvement. Do not even begin without it.

- **Customer focus** is the raison d'être of TQM, the justification for its existence. It is the driver of the vision and culture.

- **Vision** provides direction (the plans) and order (the organization and systems) as well as the impetus for a cultural change.

- **Organizational structure** that removes bureaucratic impediments and implements flat structure, cross-disciplinary communication, and empowerment.

- **A lean TQM organization** that avoids the tendency to build a bureaucracy within a bureaucracy.

- **Cost and benefit analysis** that measures the potential benefits of quality improvements as well as the costs of poor quality.

- **Accounting systems** that generate the true costs of products and quality and do not distort those costs through misallocation and failure to reflect the impact of quality on the bottom line.

- **Personnel training** focused on results and improvements in each person's job so that everyone can relate to the vision of quality.

- **Rewards and recognition** supported by performance measures that communicate the company's strategy and help make quality improvements real.

## QUESTIONS FOR DISCUSSION

**9-1** How does an organizational structure that is focused on classical principles (specialization of labor, unity of command, span of management, delegation of authority) tend to inhibit the implementation of TQM?

**9-2** Define the concept of *synergism*. How does organizing around the principles of TQM tend to integrate the organization and achieve synergism?

**9-3** What is the concept of the *value chain*? How can it be useful in building an organizational structure?

**9-4** In organizing for customer satisfaction, what would be a key activity for:
- A brokerage firm
- An aircraft manufacturer
- A retail store

**9-5** Explain the concept of the inverted organizational chart.

**9-6** Explain how membership in a small group might lead to improved motivation and hence improved quality.

# ENDNOTES

1. Chris Argyris, *Management and Organizational Development,* New York: McGraw-Hill, 1971.

2. See, for example, R. H. Schaffer and H. Thompson, "Successful Change Programs Begin with Results," *Harvard Business Review,* Jan./Feb. 1992, pp. 80–89. Also see "The Cracks in Quality," *The Economist,* April 18, 1992, pp. 67–68; R. Poe and C. L. Counter, "Fast Forward," *Across the Board,* June 1992, p. 5.

3. Tim Davis, "Breakdown in Total Quality," *International Journal of Management,* March 1997, pp. 13–22.

4. Lakshmi Tatikonda and Rao Tatikonda, "Top Ten Reasons Your TQM Effort Is Failing to Improve Profit," *Production and Inventory Management Journal,* Third Quarter 1996, pp. 5–9.

5. A. B. Godfrey, *Total Quality Management: Critical Issues on Planning, Measurement and Implementation,* Wilton, CT: Juran Institute, 1993.

6. For example, Michael H. Mescon, Michael Albert, and Franklin Khedouri, *Management,* New York: Harper & Row, 1988, p. 323.

7. W. Edwards Deming, *Out of the Crisis,* Cambridge, Mass.: Center for Advanced Engineering Study, Massachusetts Institute of Technology, 1982, pp. 465–474.

8. Philip B. Crosby, *Quality Is Free,* New York: McGraw-Hill, 1979, pp. 69–70.

9. The Conference Board, *Global Perspectives on Total Quality,* New York: The Conference Board, 1991, p. 9.

10. "America's Best Technology Users," *Forbes ASAP,* Aug. 24, 1998, pp. 63–86.

11. Susan Fry Bovet, "CEO Serves as Chief Communicator of TQM Program," *Public Relations Journal,* June/July 1994, pp. 16–17.

12. Michael Porter, *Competitive Advantage: Creating and Sustaining Superior Performance,* New York: The Free Press, 1985.

13. Presentation at the Total Quality Service Management Conference, Dallas, May 21–23, 1990.

14. Kenneth Leach, Vice-President, Administration of Globe Metallurgical, Inc. at the Third Annual Quality Conference, June 22, 1990.

15. Presentation at the Total Quality Service Management Conference, Dallas, May 21–23, 1990.

16. Peter Drucker, *Management: Tasks, Responsibilities, Practices,* New York: Harper & Row, 1974, p. 530.

17. Michael Porter, *Competitive Advantage: Creating and Sustaining Superior Performance,* New York: The Free Press, 1985, p. 144. Signals of value are those factors that buyers use to infer the values a firm creates.

18. Keith Brinksman, "Banking and the Baldrige Award," *Bank Marketing,* April 1991, pp. 30–32.

19. American Society for Quality Control, *'88 Gallup Survey of Consumers' Perceptions Concerning the Quality of American Products and Services,* Milwaukee: ASQC, 1988.

20. Mark Graham Brown, "How to Guarantee Poor Quality Service," *Journal for Quality and Participation,* Dec. 1990, pp. 6–11.

21. In 1981, Cleveland Twist Drill, a Cleveland-based manufacturer of cutting tools with $400 million in sales, had over 500 job classifications in a direct labor force that

numbered fewer than indirect labor. Joseph L. Bower et al., *Business Policy*, Homewood, Ill.: Irwin, 1991, p. 588.

22. "How to Profit from Managing Business Process Quality," presentation at the Total Quality Service Management Conference, Dallas, May 21–23, 1990.

23. David Mercer, "Key Quality Issues," in *Global Perspectives on Total Quality*, New York: The Conference Board, 1991, p. 11. Mercer is the project director of the European Council on Quality of The Conference Board Europe.

24. Keith D. Denton, "Horizontal Management," *SAM Advanced Management Journal*, Winter 1991, pp. 35–41.

25. Herbert M. Baum, "White-Collar Quality Comes of Age," *Journal of Business Strategy*, March/April 1990, pp. 34–37.

26. U.S. General Accounting Office, Quality Management Scoping Study, Washington, D.C.: General Accounting Office, 1991, p. 23.

27. A company handout entitled "The Motorola Story," written by Bill Smith, Senior Quality Assurance Manager, Communications Sector. The committee's meetings are described: "The Chief Quality Officer of the corporation opens the meetings with an update on key initiatives of the Quality Program. This includes results of management visits to customers, results of Quality System Reviews (QSR's) of major parts of the company, cost of poor quality reports, supplier–Motorola activity, and a review of quality breakthroughs and shortfalls. This is followed by a report by a major business manager on the current status of his/her particular quality initiative. This covers progress against plans, successes, failures, and what he projects to do to close the gap on deficient results, all pointed at achieving Six Sigma capability by 1992." Discussion follows among the leaders concerning all of these agenda items.

28. Al P. Staneas, "The Metamorphosis of the Quality Function," *Quality Progress*, Nov. 1987, pp. 30–33.

29. There are a number of good sources that provide suggestions for managing change. See, for example, Tom Peters, "Making It Happen," *Journal for Quality and Participation*, March 1989, pp. 6–11; Nina Fishman, "Playing the Transition Game Successfully," *Journal for Quality and Participation*, June 1990, pp. 52–56; John Herzog, "People: The Critical Factor in Managing Change," *Journal of Systems Management*, March 1991, pp. 6–11; Ronald Elliott, "The Challenge of Managing Change," *Personnel Journal*, March 1990, pp. 40–49; Edmund Metz, "Managing Change: Implementing Productivity and Quality Improvements," *National Productivity Review*, Summer 1984, pp. 303–314; and Richard Sparks and James Dorris, "Organizational Transformation," *Advanced Management Journal*, Summer 1990, pp. 13–18.

30. G. Harlan Carothers, Jr., "Future Organizations of Change," *Survey of Business*, Spring 1986, pp. 16–17.

31. Nina Fishman and Lee Kavanaugh, "Searching for Your Missing Quality Link," *Journal for Quality and Participation*, Dec. 1989, pp. 28–32.

32. Nancy Karabatsos, "Quality in Transition: Part One," *Quality Progress*, Dec. 1989, pp. 22–26.

33. David E. Gumpert, "The Joys of Keeping the Company Small," *Harvard Business Review*, July/Aug. 1986, pp. 6–14.

34. With apologies to Maslow and Herzberg, who have provided what is probably the most practical approach to motivation. See Abraham Maslow, "A Theory of Human Motiva-

tion," *Psychological Review,* No. 50, 1943, pp. 370–396; Frederick Herzberg, "One More Time: How Do You Motivate Employees?" *Harvard Business Review,* Jan./Feb. 1968, pp. 56–57. A complete review and summary of the writings of both of these theorists can be found in almost any principles of management textbook. For example, see Michael Mescon, Michael Albert, and Franklin Khedouri, *Management,* New York: Harper & Row, 1988.

35.   James H. Harrington, "Worklife in the Year 2000," *Journal for Quality and Participation,* March 1990, pp. 56–57.

36.   John Simmons, "Partnering Pulls Everything Together," *Journal for Quality and Participation,* June 1989, pp. 12–16.

37.   Rick L. Lansing, "The Power of Teams," *Supervisory Management,* Feb. 1989, pp. 39–43.

38.   Larry Gerhard and Walter T. Sparrow, "Pride Teams, A Quality Circle that Works," *Journal for Quality and Participation,* June 1988, pp. 32–36.

39.   Vladimir J. Mandl, "Team Up for Performance," *Manufacturing Systems,* June 1990, pp. 34–41.

40.   Gary Ferguson, "Printer Incorporates Deming—Reduces Errors, Increases Productivity," *Industrial Engineering,* Aug. 1990, pp. 32–34.

41.   As reported in Brian Usilaner and John Leitch, "Miles to Go...Or Unity at Last," *Journal for Quality and Participation,* June 1989, pp. 60–67.

42.   Joel E. Ross and William C. Ross, *Japanese Quality Circles and Productivity,* Reston, Va.: Reston Publishing, 1982, p. 6. For those contemplating the establishment of quality circles or other quality improvement teams, this book provides an action plan for the process.

43.   James H. Harrington and Wayne S. Rieker, "The End of Slavery: Quality Control Circles," *Journal for Quality and Participation,* March 1988, pp. 16–20. For an example of how the Avco division of Textron revitalized its quality circles with management support, see Peggy S. Tollison, "Managers Are People Too: A Case Study on Developing Middle Management Support," *Quality Circles Journal,* March 1987, pp. 12–15.

44.   Rick Lansing, "The Power of Teams," *Supervisory Management,* Feb. 1989, pp. 39–43.

45.   Edward E. Lawler and Susan A. Mohrman, "Quality Circles: After the Honeymoon," *Organizational Dynamics,* Spring 1987, pp. 42–54.

46.   Carol Gabor, "Special Project Task Teams: An Extension of a Successful Quality Circle Program," *Quality Circles Journal,* Sept. 1986, pp. 40–43.

47.   Michael J. Donovan, "Self-Managing Work Teams—Extending the Quality Circle Concept," *Quality Circles Journal,* Sept. 1986, pp. 15–20.

48.   U.S. General Accounting Office, Quality Management Scoping Study, Washington, D.C.: General Accounting Office, 1991, p. 22.

49.   Michael Donovan, "The Future of Excellence and Quality," *Journal for Quality and Participation,* March 1988, pp. 22–24.

## ORGANIZING WITH TEAMS AT
## EASTMAN CHEMICAL COMPANY

Founded in 1920, Eastman Chemical Company is a $5 billion company that manufactures and markets over 400 chemicals, fibers, and plastics for 5300 customers around the world. Eastman's products show up in a wide variety of consumer goods such as beverage bottles, bread and other foods, coatings for flooring materials, window cleaners, aspirin, computer diskettes, and hundreds more.

Meeting customers' needs with high-quality products and services has always been important to Eastman. In the late 1970s, however, the company lost market share of a major product and began searching for a new way of doing business. Starting in 1982 with a renewed focus on customers, Eastman gradually developed its quality management values and processes. Along the way, it used Baldrige Award criteria for self-assessment and sought advice from quality management experts and Baldrige Award winners.

Today, quality management principles and techniques are woven throughout the company's business activities. Teams are well established at Eastman and are viewed by executives and employees alike as the most effective means to execute the company's quality strategy. A network of "interlocking" teams, led by managers and supervisors, involves virtually all employees in the team and quality improvement processes. Each team uses the company's quality management process to understand and anticipate needs of both internal and external customers, to define key processes and measures, and to continually improve. Other teams are formed to improve processes, tackle projects, or build long-term relationships with suppliers and customers.

Eastman encourages innovation and provides a structured way to link ideas for new products with corporate business plans. Through the Eastman Innovation Process, a team of employees from various areas, such as business, sales, research, engineering, and manufacturing, shepherds a product idea from inception to market. Customer needs are considered early and then validated and revalidated.

In 1995, Eastman averaged 23 percent of sales from new products commercialized within the last five years.

Through the Eastman Supplier Excellence Program, joint teams with key suppliers improve quality and value of purchased materials, equipment, and services. Focused on maintaining exceptional performance levels and helping suppliers improve their performance for Eastman, the program now has approximately 70 supplier teams including suppliers of raw materials, mechanical suppliers, transportation suppliers, and service companies. Key suppliers with exceptional performance records are recognized annually.

## CASE

# ORGANIZING FOR
# NEW PRODUCT DEVELOPMENT

Ryobi Outdoor Products (ROP), an Arizona-based subsidiary of The Ryobi Group of Japan, has locations in Indiana and South Carolina. The largest volume product of ROP is gasoline string trimmers. The company has been a low-cost producer/assembler in the outdoor power equipment industry and has historically held between 15 and 20 percent share of the U.S. consumer market.

ROP was established in 1974 as the first U.S. venture of Ryobi Ltd. The company's Web site (www.Ryobi.com) describes the situation regarding the gasoline string trimmer:

> If you own a gas-powered string trimmer, there is a good chance that it was made by Ryobi Outdoor Products. We make nearly one of every four gas trimmers sold in the U.S. today. Whether gas or electric, we are dedicated to making environmentally-friendly lawn and garden tools. Take our 4-stroke engine. Until 1994, the standard for hand-held gas trimmers and blowers was the 2-stroke engine, even though they tend to produce excessive exhaust pollution. The industry recognized that 4-stroke engines ran cleaner than 2-strokes, but no one knew how to make one small enough and economical enough for lawn and garden use. So we assembled an international team to design the world's first practical hand-held 4-stroke engine. The result? A 4-stroke trimmer engine, now on the market, that can already meet turn-of-the-century exhaust standards.

### Emission Concerns

The design and manufacture of a 4-stroke gasoline engine can be traced to the late 1990s, when a number of state and federal agencies began to focus on the emissions of hand-held gasoline engines produced by outdoor equipment manu-

---

The material presented in this case is based on information from the company Web site and industry sources. For technical details, see James G. Conley, "The Ryobi 'Air-Clean' 4-Cycle Engine: A Case Study in Engineering and Manufacturing Management," *Engineering Management Journal*, Vol. 10 No. 2, June 1998, pp. 23–31.

facturers. A large portion of these power plants were simple 2-cycle devices that burned a mixture of gas and oil. The undesirable pollutants attributable to these products led some regulatory agencies to set targets for emissions reductions.

Inertia Dynamics Corporation (IDC), predecessor to ROP, saw an opportunity to innovate and bring a new technology to market. Due to the price competitiveness of lawn trimmers, any new technology would have to be developed within the constraints of cost and the new emission standards.

The U.S. company pursued the idea of adapting a small 4-cycle engine to a string trimmer and brought the concept prototypes to Japan for consideration by engineers of the parent company. This group determined that the initial prototype built in the United States could be modified to meet the exhaust gas emission standards that were due to be effective in 1994 and again in 1999.

In the fall of 1991, the project was given a high priority by management at both the Japanese parent and the U.S. subsidiary. Introduction of functioning models was targeted for the International Lawn and Garden Exposition in Louisville in July of 1993. Production launch was to be timed for the spring 1994 retail sales season.

## The Design and Manufacturing Challenge

The design and manufacturing processes for the new engine required substantial innovation and creativity. The main component processes included:

1. Component size. In most cases, the know-how for making the small individual parts for such an engine did not exist.
2. Gearing had to be designed to meet area noise control ordinances.
3. Miniaturized piston rings capable of running against a hard chrome-coated cylinder bore would be required.
4. Overall engine tribology. The engine running conditions for the target string trimmer were closer to Indy-class racing engines and were an engine-life limiting factor.
5. Heat control. The 4-cycle engine would have to accommodate a much hotter combustion cycle.
6. Engine sealing. All flanged surfaces and assembly interfaces must be completely sealed against seepage of combustion gases.
7. The 4-cycle engine requires that enough weight be designed out of the package to supplant the present 2-cycle trimmer.

All of these requirements had to be achieved within a design for assembly and design for manufacturability framework that would minimize direct labor and material costs.

## Getting Organized

Although a quality assurance activity existed within the company, it had very little time to develop, implement, or champion the organization, systems, or processes demanded by total quality management. The organization structure was a traditional form of functions with few provisions for cross-functional integration. Functions tended to act independently of each other, as evidenced by engineering and manufacturing, a relationship that was described as disconnected. Pressures for new product development forced the engineering function to "throw new designs over the wall" to the manufacturing engineers; then the back-and-forth iterations would begin. Sometimes design and manufacturing flaws were not discovered until final inspection. Ryobi management understood that this unfavorable work environment would have to be modified to bring about successful and timely development of the new engine.

In the fall of 1991, top management recognized that a well-developed plan would be required in order to orchestrate and manage the development teams operating on both sides of the Pacific. A sort of cross-Pacific team structure was established. The chief of manufacturing at ROP was put in charge of the project, a logical choice since both engineering and manufacturing reported to him. It was expected that this assignment would avoid the disconnects that typically arise when engineering hands off a new product to manufacturing. The project/team leader had the dual objectives of compliance with emission standards and meeting the 1994 market introduction of the finished product.

The initial step in planning the program was to sequence and organize engineering tasks in a way that charted the course for developing the production version of the engine. This plan became known as the AC project flow plan. The objectives and the flow plan were superimposed on a time line to create the planned AC clean air project master schedule. Once agreed to by all team members and management, this schedule became the yardstick by which progress was measured.

Compared to the sequential product development schemes previously used, the AC plan allowed minimal time slacks or buffers for unforeseen setbacks. This type of concurrent scheduling did not allow the various functions to act independently, as they had in the past. The team composition for the project needed to be cross-functional. Key personnel from management, product design, cost accounting, procurement, quality assurance, manufacturing, sales, and marketing functions were required to accomplish all tasks on time and to avoid organizational disconnects. In order to determine just how the team should be composed, an idea was borrowed from the original Team Taurus philosophy of the Ford Motor Company. The Team Taurus approach assigned responsibility for overall project direction, design, development, control, and final approval to the team members and representatives from top management. The only major difference between Team Taurus and the AC team at ROP was the absence of key supplier involvement at ROP. This was because the skills and knowledge necessary for such an engineering challenge were not available among the company's traditional low-cost supplier base.

To avoid the organizational disconnects described above and to develop a group of engineers with a comprehensive knowledge of the new product and the processes by which it was designed and manufactured, the guiding principles for the team were quality first, customer focus, employee involvement, supplier partnership, cost containment and reduction, and continuous improvement.

## Schedule Slippage

As the project began to unfold, the program schedule began to slide. To rectify the situation, the program managers formed a number of groups in support of the core team. In addition to expanding the core team, the following three support groups were formed:

- The Production Ready Team, whose job was to follow up on any and all issues that directly affect the ability to manufacture the product (e.g., tooling releases, bills of material, component releases, etc.).
- The Final Adjustment Team, composed of engineers and quality personnel responsible for identifying design- and tooling-related issues, to assign individual responsibility to resolve, and to assure follow through on all open items.
- The Value Improvement Process Team, whose mission was to identify specific cost control and cost reduction, product improvement, and enhancement opportunities. The team was also responsible for developing a system for continuous process improvement throughout the product life cycle.

These new teams were initially received with suspicion by the core team. They resented the program manager forming new groups of non-engineers whose main job was to bring the project "back on schedule."

## TQM Management Methods

One of the guiding principles of the project was customer focus. The last change to integrate the voice of the customer was in the design process. To map this voice into design specifications, the quality function deployment (QFD, see Chapter 6) methodology was attempted by the core team. Preliminary tabulations were compiled and undesirable feature interactions were investigated by examining couplings in the House of Quality roof matrix. The approach took an inordinate amount of time and resources, but no clear definition of the product specifications emerged. In frustration, the core team created its own method for capturing the voice of the customer, which in this case was considered to be the Ryobi sales and marketing companies. A "wish list" of product features was submitted by these customers, and a matrix was constructed by the core team. This imperfect analysis helped to prioritize the desired product features and saved all concerned a huge amount of time. The simplified QFD methodology was quick and painless and was considered appropriate for this project. It was estimated that a rigorous House of Quality analysis would be overkill.

Several of the component/assembly dimensions were designed by product engineers to be statistically controlled. ROP had little experience with this kind of process control and the computer numerically controlled equipment. The many samples and dimensional inspections that were required to determine the process capability of each fixture station proved to be very time consuming. This frustrated the manufacturing engineers, and they went after product engineering in an effort to get them to ease up on tolerances. The product engineers responded by describing the manufacturing engineers as "whiners."

Similar to the QFD situation, the rigorous application of statistical process control was found to be time consuming and, at times, of limited value. In most circumstances, however, statistical process control proved to be valuable provided the quality function was given the time to perform a thorough analysis.

The scenario between the two engineering groups was repeated frequently whenever representatives from a number of functions were making decisions without adequate knowledge of the new manufacturing technology. As a conflict resolution device, the weekly meetings of teams and team members became important forums for surfacing issues and making decisions.

Throughout the project, the core team worked on solving a number of design issues that required interaction with the new and existing partner suppliers. This time-consuming activity often conflicted with the labor hours required to complete engineering tasks.

## Summary

Unanswered questions about end product performance caused the project to slip by one month. As a by-product of the project effort, a number of technology breakthroughs and achievements were realized.

The AC engine was a smashing success at the Louisville Lawn and Garden Show. The Ryobi marketing function came back from the show with order volumes that exceeded all expectations. Based on the successful introduction, the marketing group made numerous promises to customers that were very difficult to satisfy. The group was located in South Carolina and due to the distance involved did not attend many of the AC team weekly meetings. The group was not aware that the first year's production was limited to 30,000 units, 70,000 short of its projected volume of 100,000 engines.

This factor combined with simple job burnout caused nearly all members of the core AC team to eventually leave the Ryobi Group. The knowledge of 4-cycle engine design and volume production that Ryobi acquired during the AC engine development program left with the core team members. As a result of this talent exodus, the initial design launched in 1994 was still in production in 1998.

With the reputation for innovation that resulted from the AC project, Ryobi has improved its market share to approximately 30 percent of the hand-held engine equipment market.

## Questions for Discussion

1 Evaluate the management methods used by Ryobi to bring the AC engine from concept to market acceptance.

2 Was the company justified in its quality function deployment and statistical process control actions?

3 Did the company meet the organizational requirements for team operation and empowerment?

4 What recommendations would you make to the top management of Ryobi?

# ORGANIZING BY PROCESS

Electric Motor Supply (EMS), located in Greenville, South Carolina, had been making and assembling electric motors for over 35 years. The company's motto was "You need it, we build it." Over the years, its business had grown as users of electric motors had begun to purchase motors from a supplier rather than assemble their own. Customers included a variety of manufacturers and assemblers ranging from the automobile industry to makers of portable hand tools. The company was proud of its technology and engineering focus.

EMS was organized around the traditional functions of marketing and sales, engineering and manufacturing, finance and accounting, and the typical support/ staff activities such as personnel and data processing. Performance appraisal and compensation were based on the management by objectives program, which tended to encourage productivity and quality within each activity but ignore the needs between and among activities. This "disconnect" between activities resulted in excessive cycle time and cost. Moreover, most individual objectives were focused on volume of output and cost rather than customer needs.

Top management realized that a change was needed. Members of top management attended a four-day total quality management seminar and were impressed with the attention given to the process approach to quality and organization. Following their return to the company, they decided that some organizational changes were necessary.

The first change was the formulation of concurrent engineering teams, whose membership included personnel from staff activities, such as accounting, order entry, and purchasing. The most drastic change, however, was the change from a functional to a process form of organization structure. The primary processes were

- **Customer process** that included all activity from the first sales contact to the placement of the purchase order.
- **Manufacturing process** from creation of the bill of materials to shipment of finished goods. The vendor selection process was also included from initial evaluation to contracting with a supplier.

■ **Product development process** from feasibility studies to design and prototyping.

Each primary process was subdivided into several other subprocesses. This allowed the output of the process to be defined and calculated and output to be tracked over time. For example, purchasing is a subprocess of the manufacturing process which can track information about incoming materials, such as delivery lead times as well as the quality of parts coming into the plant. Changes and deviations affect the assembly process and can be used as inputs to forecasts and production scheduling.

In addition to cycle time and cost reductions, it was expected that this profound organizational change would have additional benefits. Among these would be improved communications between and among activities and processes. Also, it was expected that this change would bring a culture improvement, one that would focus on the customer.

## Questions for Discussion

1   How would these organizational changes:
   ■   Improve customer focus
   ■   Reduce cycle time
   ■   Reduce costs

   Give an example of each.

2   Why would management by objectives tend to "disconnect" people and activities?

3   In what way would these changes improve the culture to one that "focuses on the customer"?

4   What actions do you recommend for facilitating these changes?

# FOR FURTHER READING

Dervitsiotis, Kostas N., "The Challenge of Managing Organizational Change: Exploring the Relationship of Re-engineering, Developing Learning Organizations and Total Quality Management," *Total Quality Management,* Feb. 1998, pp. 109–122.

Elgamal, Mahmoud A., "An Examination of Organization and Suborganization Readiness for Total Quality Management," *International Journal of Technology Management,* Vol. 16 No. 4–6, 1998, pp. 556–569.

Hellinghausen, Mary Ann and Jim Myers, "Empowered Employees: A New Team Concept," *Industrial Management,* Sept./Oct. 1998, pp. 21–23.

Kolodny, Harvey, "Building a Foundation for High Performance," *International Journal of Technology Management,* Vol. 16 No. 1–3, 1998, p. 1.

Schiemann, William, "Organizational Change Starts with a Strategic Focus," *Journal of Business Strategy,* Jan./Feb. 1993, pp. 43–48.

# 10

# PRODUCTIVITY, QUALITY, AND REENGINEERING

*To find out how to improve productivity, quality and performance—
ask the people who do the work.*

*Harvard Business Review*

The automotive industry is no stranger to productivity. Henry Ford invented the assembly line, and the Japanese automobile industry improved on it with such recent methods as kaizen and just-in-time. Production per worker increased dramatically, quality increased, and cycle time was reduced. Ultimately, the methods were adopted by others in the supply chain as suppliers and suppliers to suppliers were required to reduce costs and deliver quality products on time.

During the mid-1980s, the President's Council for Management Improvement wrestled with the productivity process mandated by Ronald Reagan. However, corporate chief executives encouraged the president to get away from processes that stressed productivity and instead to focus on quality. These events led to the creation of the Malcolm Baldrige Award and the subsequent popularity of total quality management (TQM) in U.S. industry.

The relationship among quality, market share, and profitability was examined in Chapter 1, and it was shown that higher quality leads to both increased profits and greater market share. The following questions now arise: Are productivity and quality related? Are they two sides of the same coin? Can you have both? The answer, of course, is *yes*.

**323**

Despite a growing body of evidence that indicates a positive correlation, the misconception exists that productivity and cost must be sacrificed if quality is to be improved. In an annual survey of its members in 1990, the Institute of Industrial Engineers found the general opinion to be that only when productivity and quality are considered together can competitiveness be enhanced.[1]

There may be some justification for the belief that increased quality means decreased productivity, but it seems to be the view of those who rank production ahead of quality as the top priority. It is argued that a program to improve quality causes disruptions and delays that result in reduced output. While this may be the case in the short run, it generally is not true over a longer time period. As will be discussed in Chapter 11 (The Cost of Quality), such an argument usually fails when the costs associated with poor quality are considered.

The argument for a positive relationship was made by Deming, who based it on the reduced productivity that is caused by quality defects, rework, and scrap. He concluded, "Improvement of quality transfers waste of man-hours and of machine-time into the manufacture of good products and better service."[2] Feigenbaum maintains that a certain "hidden" and non-productive plant exists to rework and repair defects and returns, and if quality is improved, this hidden plant would be available for increased productivity.[3] These arguments are straightforward; any quality improvement that reduces defects is, by definition, an improvement in productivity. The same can be said, of course, for services and for those firms in service businesses. The cost of quality improvement rarely exceeds the savings from increased productivity.

To build a case for or against quality improvement based on output or defect reduction alone is to oversimplify. A more convincing case can be built around the proven benefits of TQM. When the broader picture is considered, it can be shown that increasing quality also increases productivity, and the two are mutually reinforcing.[4] Productivity has come to mean more output for the same or less cost. TQM embraces a broader concept and can be perceived as *including* the benefits of productivity when properly implemented. Productivity has become a tactical short-term approach associated with cost reduction, greater efficiency, better use of resources, and organizational restructuring. TQM is longer term and more comprehensive and as such is concerned with cultural change and creating visions, mission, and values.

Examples of productivity improvements resulting from TQM abound:

- ■ Under Joseph Juran's guidance, the Internal Revenue Service's processing center in Ogden, Utah, adopted quality as a core value, but also achieved productivity increases of $11.3 million from team and management initiatives.

- ■ NASA's Productivity Improvement and Quality Enhancement program has evolved into a multiprogram approach incorporating

TQM in the agency and in the contractor work force, which comprises about 60 percent of NASA's total.[5]

■ The introduction of computer-integrated manufacturing, combined with TQM and self-directed work teams, resulted in a 50 percent increase in productivity at Monsanto Chemical's Fibers Division.[6]

## THE LEVERAGE OF PRODUCTIVITY AND QUALITY

If quality has a leverage effect on market share and profitability (as pointed out here and in Chapter 1), what are the bottom-line consequences of productivity improvement?

Confining the illustration to the question of profitability leverage, three hypothetical income statements will demonstrate how small (10 percent) increases in productivity will yield much greater results than a similar increase in sales:

| | I | II | III |
| --- | --- | --- | --- |
| | | Sales | Productivity |
| | Before | up 10 percent | improved 10 percent |
| Sales | $100 | $110 | $100 |
| Variable costs | 70 | 77 | 63 |
| Fixed costs | 20 | 20 | 20 |
| Profit | $10 | $13 (+30%) | $17 (+70%) |

In situation I, sales are $100, variable costs $70, and fixed costs $20, yielding a profit of $10. In situation II, a sales increase of 10 percent yields a 30 percent profit increase, while situation III shows a 70 percent profit increase with *no increase in sales.* The leverage is even more dramatic if a smaller and more realistic return on sales is used. There are also potential additional companion benefits that can be achieved in quality. Again, the answer lies in TQM and the continuous improvement of all processes.

## MANAGEMENT SYSTEMS VS. TECHNOLOGY

Since the time of Adam Smith's historic 18th century book *The Wealth of Nations,* we have been taught to believe that labor specialization accompanied by mechanization was the answer to economic growth and productivity. The Industrial Revolution proved this to be so. Even today, the conventional wisdom of economists tells us that the rate of productivity growth is largely a function of changes in real capital relative to labor.

There is a continuing debate in Washington regarding the "reindustrialization of U.S. industry" or "supply-side economics" as it is came to be known in the Reagan and Bush administrations. The primary domestic objective of these administrations was the improvement of the productivity of American industry by encouraging greater savings and thus investment in capital stock. Competitiveness, it was said, required an overhaul of U.S. technology. It is generally believed that Japan's quality and productivity advantage comes from advanced technology.

It would be a mistake to attribute Japan's success to technology alone and a bigger mistake to consider technology to be the only answer to improved U.S. quality and productivity. It is not labor replacement that is needed but rather improved processes. Why, for example, would a company invest in advanced computer equipment to improve an information system that is flawed or a manufacturing process that is antiquated? In the first case, the technology will provide bad information more quickly so that poor decisions can be made faster. In the second case, process labor may be replaced only to find an increase in lead time, inventory turn, or cost of quality.

Many people think of technology as automation and mechanization, machines and computers, and semiconductors and new inventions, but the term has a much broader meaning. It is a means of transforming inputs into outputs. Thus, technology includes methods, procedures, and techniques which enable this transformation. It includes both machines and methods. This is worth repeating: technology includes methods that improve processes to improve the output/input ratio. Company after company has achieved remarkable increases in both quality and productivity with little or no investment in the hardware side of technology.

No one can argue convincingly against the use of the hardware side of technology to improve both quality and productivity. The problem is that automation and machines require time and money, both of which are in short supply. Management systems take little of either and may be equally or more effective. The solution is to improve the system—the process—before introducing technology. General Motors has spent more on automation than the gross national product of many countries, yet the excessive cycle time from market research to manufacture resulted in the production of cars that were not competitive. While GM was taking eight years to produce a Saturn, Honda took half as long to market a more competitive car. Honda accomplished this by controlling cycle time and processes.

The general tendency is to focus on technology to reduce labor cost and to overlook the improved quality that can be achieved through improvement of related processes and tapping the potential of the work force. Good companies buy technology to improve processes, reduce lead times, boost quality, and increase flexibility.

Capital spending in service industries has exploded, but there has been very little increase in productivity or quality. Jonathan M. Tisch, president and CEO of Loews Hotels, remarked: "Productivity in manufacturing is advancing five times as fast as in the service sector. In the late 1950s we needed roughly one employee for every four occupied rooms and that was the average across the industry. Today's average, nationwide, is one employee for every two rooms. In other words, productivity is half what it used to be. Despite the advent of the computer and the introduction of many so called labor-saving devices."[7] The focus in both manufacturing and service industries has been on labor productivity, but for most businesses, capital intensity does not improve labor productivity enough to keep return on investment above the cost of capital. For those businesses that become more capital intensive relative to sales, a decline in return on investment is the result, even if a normal increase in productivity is achieved.[8]

## PRODUCTIVITY IN THE UNITED STATES

The U.S. productivity record has not been good when compared to Japan and the leading industrialized nations of Western Europe. American capital-intensive industries—home of industrial engineering and the assembly line, production planning, and the computer—continue to compare unfavorably with the rest of the industrialized world.[9]

Table 10-1 shows U.S. private business sector productivity for the period 1986–96. For a more recent period, Table 10-2 shows the percent change in manufacturing productivity in 13 countries for the period 1996–97. These and other productivity statistics indicate a definite slowdown in worldwide productivity. What are the causes?

### Reasons for Slow Growth[10]

When it comes to identifying causes for what has been called the "productivity crisis," every economist, industrialist, and government official seems to have a favorite culprit. Among the most popular explanations are the following issues.

**Management inattention.**   U.S. Secretary of Commerce Malcolm Baldrige (who died in 1987 and for whom the Baldrige Award is named) stated: "Between our own complacency and the rise of management expertise around the world, we now too often do a second-rate job of management, compared to our foreign competitors." One survey by A. T. Kearney, Inc. (management consultants) concluded that the key to productivity is better management and not continued

**Table 10-1**  U.S. Private Business Sector Productivity

| | Index 1992 = 100 | | |
| Year | Output per hour of all persons | Output per unit of capital | Multifactor productivity |
| --- | --- | --- | --- |
| 1986 | 94.0 | 102.7 | 99.6 |
| 1987 | 94.0 | 102.4 | 99.3 |
| 1988 | 94.6 | 103.3 | 99.4 |
| 1989 | 95.4 | 103.9 | 99.9 |
| 1990 | 96.1 | 102.1 | 99.5 |
| 1991 | 96.7 | 98.6 | 98.1 |
| 1992 | 100.0 | 100.0 | 100.0 |
| 1993 | 100.2 | 100.7 | 100.2 |
| 1994 | 100.5 | 102.3 | 100.6 |
| 1995 | 100.5 | 101.5 | 100.3 |
| 1996 | 102.6 | 101.3 | 101.3 |

Source: Bureau of Labor Statistics.

**Table 10-2**  Percent Change in Manufacturing Productivity

| Country | Output per hour (percent change) |
| --- | --- |
| United States | 4.6 |
| Canada | 2.7 |
| Japan | 6.1 |
| Korea | NA |
| Taiwan | NA |
| Belgium | 5.6 |
| Denmark | NA |
| France | 6.8 |
| Former West Germany | 5.9 |
| Italy | 2.7 |
| Norway | 0.6 |
| Sweden | 6.5 |
| United Kingdom | 0.9 |

Source: Bureau of Labor Statistics.

efforts to produce more pounds of automobile per worker. The decade of the 1980s is noted for top management's diversion from productivity, quality, and growth to leveraged buyouts, restructuring, downsizing, and in many case executive perks and golden parachutes.[11]

**Short-term gain.** The trend has been to focus on short-term financial ratios while failing to take action to ensure long-term growth and productivity.[12] While no one would recommend overlooking financial data, this type of information suffers from the shortcomings of all accounting data. Moreover, financial figures tend to favor the productivity of capital while overlooking the other inputs of labor, material, and energy.

**Direct labor.** Focus on direct labor has historically been the one variable cost around which financial control systems are designed. Today, the direct labor share of total production costs is down to 8 to 12 percent on average.[13] Some firms fold these costs into overhead or general and administrative expenses, categories that are frequently overlooked when searching for ideas to improve productivity and quality.

**Capital.** Capital stock formation is largely dependent on savings. Yet Americans appear to be spending more and saving less, leaving fewer dollars for capital formation.[14] The net savings ratios for the major industrialized nations of the world[15] are as follows:

|  | Average 1980–89 | 1990 | 1991 |
|---|---|---|---|
| United States | 6.0 | 4.6 | 4.3 |
| Japan | 16.0 | 14.3 | 14.5 |
| Germany | 12.5 | 13.4 | 12.8 |
| Three other major European countries (France, Italy, U.K.) | 14.1 | 12.0 | 12.2 |

**Research and development.** Expenditures for research and development in the United States surpass every other nation, yet overseas rivals are outpacing the United States in spending growth. Opinion is mixed as to the impact of R&D on productivity. Some evidence indicates that spending is directed toward product improvement rather than productivity improvement. This is good and is expected. However, as previously suggested, many quality investments also improve productivity. An R&D "peace dividend" may be expected from political events in the former Soviet Union and Eastern Europe as R&D dollars move from defense to programs in industry.

**Inflation.** Is inflation the cause of productivity decline or is inflation the result of the decline?[16] It is almost certain that lower productivity combined with higher wages does result in inflation. To the extent that inflation results in increased relative cost of plant and equipment as compared to labor and the relative cost of operating capital, there can be little doubt that these are investment *disincentives.*

Government regulation, the shift to a service economy, and the lack of goals and programs are among other reasons that have been advanced for the poor record of U.S. productivity. The cumulative effect, although significant, is difficult to estimate.

## MEASURING PRODUCTIVITY

Productivity is a scientific concept, in the sense that it can be logically defined and empirically observed. It can be measured in absolute or relative terms:

- **Absolute** productivity is the quantity of physical work produced by a unit of labor directly engaged in its production; for example, items assembled per work hour, invoices produced per work hour, and so on.

- **Relative** productivity is the ratio of the quantity of physical work produced by a unit of labor to the quantity of the same work produced by a unit of labor on a standard; for example, actual unit rate by standard unit rate.

These definitions are micro in the sense that they apply to a single business unit. Macro (economic system) measures are somewhat more complicated.[17]

Measuring productivity is somewhat easier than measuring quality because the latter is determined by the customer and may be fragmented and elusive. On the other hand, productivity can also be difficult to measure because it is measured by the output of many functions or activities, many of which are also difficult to define.[18] What is the *measurable* output of design, market research, training, or quality assurance?

Despite these difficulties, measures are needed for each activity and in most cases for each individual front-line supervisor. Standards are needed for comparison against past performance, the experience of competitors, and as a basis for action plans to improve.

Carl G. Thor, president of the American Productivity and Quality Center in Houston, is a pioneer in the productivity measurement process and has worked for many years on the development of a measurement system. His principles of measurement for both productivity and quality include:[19]

- Meet the customer's need—that person who plans to use it. The customer may be external or internal.

- Emphasize feedback directly to the workers in the process that is being measured.

- The main performance measure should measure what is important. This may not be the case with the traditional cost control report.

- Measures should be controllable and understandable by those being measured. This principle may be enhanced by the participation of those being measured.

- Base measures on available data. If not available, apply cost benefit analysis before generating new data. Information is rarely worth more than the cost of obtaining it.

Measurements are the primary method of accounting for the results of actions being taken within an organization. Measurements not only gauge results of actions, however; they also have a huge influence on the actions the average worker chooses to take in the first place. Because measurements are usually tied in some way to performance evaluation, workers tend to try to do more of whatever has a positive impact on the measurements and less of whatever has a negative impact.

## BASIC MEASURES OF PRODUCTIVITY: RATIO OF OUTPUT TO INPUT

**Total factor** is the broadest measure of output to input and can be expressed as:

$$\frac{\text{Total output}}{\text{Labor + Materials + Energy + Capital}}$$

This measure is not only concerned with how many units are produced or how many letters are typed but also considers all aspects of producing goods and services. Hence, this measure is concerned with the efficiency of the entire plant or company.

**Partial factor** measures are established by developing ratios of total output (e.g., number of automobiles, patients, depositors, students, widgets, etc.) to one or more input categories and are expressed as follows for the partial factor of labor:

$$\frac{\text{Total output}}{\text{Labor input}}$$

The same applies to material, capital, and energy. All measures are ratios of quantities. Although some ratios can be expressed in quantitative terms such as units produced per man-hour, others must combine unlike quantities of inputs, such as tons and gallons of products, employee hours, pounds, kilowatt-hours, etc. To solve this problem, a set of weights representative of the relative importance of the various items can be used to combine unlike quantities. Base period prices are the recommended weights to be used for calculating total productivity, although other weighting systems such as "man-hour equivalents" can be used.

**Functional and departmental measures** are more likely to benefit the company than an effort to apply comprehensive, company-wide coverage. Most firms rely largely on budgetary dollar accounting data to analyze their operations, even though these data include the effects of inflation, taxes, depreciation, and the arbitrary accounting cost allocations previously mentioned. Because these accounting figures are frequently not significantly related to the activity or process under study, it is desirable to develop measures that reflect output and input in more realistic terms. Where financial measures are used, it is appropriate to deflate them to a base benchmark.

It is important to establish function and activity measures because these organizational entities are where productivity and quality are delivered and where processes are improved. It is here where process design and control happens. A sampling of illustrative measures is provided in Table 10-3.

**Individual measures** provide the individual supervisor and worker with the basic target for improvement of both quality and productivity through individual action planning. Improvement can only occur if measured against some benchmark (target, yardstick, standard, objective, or result expected).

The simplest and most effective way to set a standard is to list the responsibility of the job on a piece of paper and then list the measures (results expected) that would indicate that the job is being performed satisfactorily. This provides a benchmark from which improvement can proceed. For example:

**Table 10-3**    Function and Activity Measures

| Function/activity | Measure |
| --- | --- |
| Customer support | Cost per field technician, cost per warranty callback |
| Data processing | Operations employees per systems design employees |
| Quality assurance | Units returned for warranty repair as percentage of units shipped |
| Order processing | Orders processed per employee, sales per order-processing employee |
| Production control | Order cycle time, inventory turn, machine utilization, total production to production schedule |
| Shipping | Orders shipped on time, packing expense to total shipping expense |
| Testing | Man-hours per run-hour, test expense to rework expense |

| Responsibility | Measure |
|---|---|
| Maintenance | Maintain an uptime machine rate of 95 percent |
| Assembly | Assemble 32 units per man-hour of direct labor |
| Accounts receivable | Maintain an accounts receivable level of 42 days |

Having established these measures, or standards, the individual can then write a *productivity or quality improvement objective* (results expected). Taking the examples above, these improvement objectives could be written:

*My productivity (or quality) improvement objective is*

| Action verb | Results expected | Time | Cost |
|---|---|---|---|
| Improve | Machine uptime from 94 percent to 97 percent | By June 30 | At no increase in man-hours or preventive maintenance costs |
| Increase | Actual production from 90 percent of schedule to 95 percent | Commencing this quarter | At the same cost of manufacture |

**Industry and competitive measures** are important for benchmarking against the competition, best-in-class, and others in the industry. These are examined in Chapter 8 on benchmarking.

Many companies set measures of total factor productivity such as output per labor hour, material usage rates, ratio of direct to indirect labor, etc., but such macro measures provide little in the way of functional or departmental measures from which an improvement plan can be developed. Unlike return on investment (a measure of capital productivity), which can be broken down into each of its determinants, broad macro measures mean little to those lower in the hierarchy who need specific objectives in order to develop an action plan.

## WHITE-COLLAR PRODUCTIVITY

Productivity of white-collar workers is no less important than that of direct labor or manufacturing employees. Indeed, in terms of numbers and expense, staff and non-production employees outnumber production employees by a wide margin. Yet the problem of measurement of output is more elusive. Measuring the units assembled per man-hour is not too difficult, but how many reports should an accountant prepare, not to mention the most difficult of all measures—managerial productivity? Peter Drucker tells us that it is "usually the least known, least analyzed, least managed of all factors of productivity."[20] Research has shown that white-collar employees are productive only about 50 percent of the time. The remainder is non-productive time and can be traced to personal delays (15 percent) and improper management (35 percent). Causes of wasted time include:

- Poor scheduling
- Slack start and quit times
- Lack of communication between functions
- Information overload

- Poor staffing
- Inadequate communication of assignments
- Unproductive meetings and telephone conversations

## Measuring the Service Activity

Although the manufacturing worker (one who physically alters the product) has been measured for decades by time standards, time studies, and work sampling, it is not as easy to set standards for the non-manufacturing employee or the service activity. It is unlikely that measurement can be achieved in the same way as is done for the manufacturing worker. Nevertheless, a system can be devised to describe the productivity of an *activity* at a point in time and then provide a baseline for judging continuous improvement over time. The system is particularly appropriate for multiplant or multidivisional companies with similar products or services and for individual companies within an industry.

The basis for a system of measurement starts with the existing functions and activities of the organization. Each activity is a subset of a particular function. For example, the *activity* of recruiting is a part of the human resource *function,* accounts receivable is a part of the accounting function, and so on. The typical organization may identify a hundred or more activities that can be grouped into ten or more functions. This concept is shown in Figure 10-1.

The next step is to identify the *output indicators* that "drive" the activities or cause work in the activities. In other words, if it were not for the work caused by

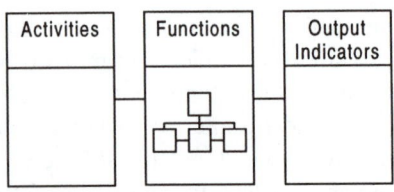

**Figure 10-1**   Measuring White-Collar (Indirect) Activity

or resulting from the *indicators,* there would be little need for the *activities.* If, for example, there were no personnel employed, there would be no need for employee relations. If there were no purchasing, there would be no need for vendor invoicing. The resources utilized in the activity of vendor invoicing are therefore a dependent variable of the purchasing function. In other words, if activities are the "input" in the productivity ratio of output to input, then the indicators are the "output."

## IMPROVING PRODUCTIVITY (AND QUALITY)

Improvement means increasing the ratio of the output of goods and services produced divided by the input used to produce them. Hence, the ratio can be increased by either increasing the output, reducing the input, or both. This concept is illustrated in Figure 10-2, along with a sampling of actions and techniques for improving the productivity ratio. This might be called the productivity wheel.

Historically, productivity improvement has focused on technology and capital equipment to reduce the input of labor cost. Improved output was generally thought to be subject to obtaining more production by applying industrial engineering techniques such as methods analysis, work flow, etc. Both of these approaches are still appropriate, but the current trend is toward better use of the potential available through human resources. Each worker can be his or her own industrial engineer—a mini-manager, so to speak. This potential can be tapped by allowing and encouraging people to innovate in one or more of the five ways described in the next section. Employee ideas can improve productivity, and in most cases this is accompanied by an improvement in quality as well.

### Five Ways to Improve Productivity (and Quality) (see Figure 10-3)

**Cost reduction** is the traditional and most widely used approach to productivity improvement and is an appropriate route to improvement if implemented correctly. However, many companies maintain a somewhat outdated "across-the-board" mentality that directs each department to "cut costs by 10 percent." Staff services are slashed and training reduced, and the result is an inefficient sales force, reduced advertising, and diminished R&D. Maintenance is delayed and machine downtime is increased. The results may be a non-competitive product and loss of market share.

Under this "management by drive" approach, people are perceived as a direct expense, and the immediate route to cost reduction is seen as cutting this expense

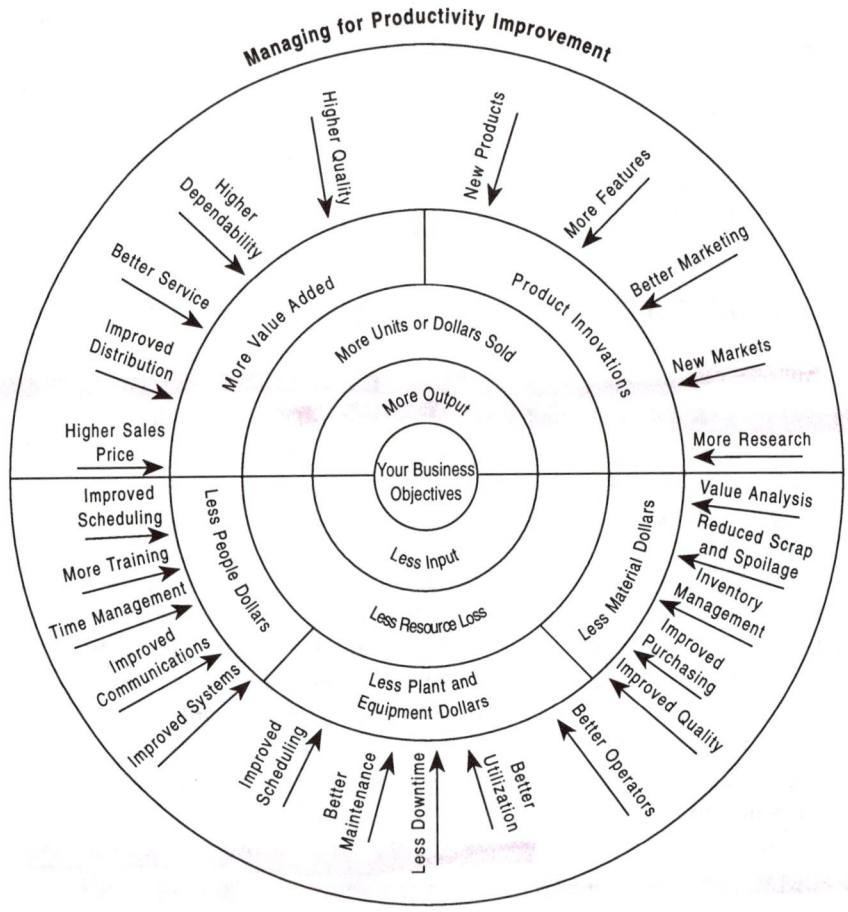

**Figure 10-2**  Productivity Wheel

as much as possible. This policy usually leads to employee resentment and is frequently counterproductive. It may result in trading today's headache for tomorrow's upset stomach.

**Managing growth** is a more positive approach, but growth without productivity improvement is *fat*. The improvement may suggest an investment or cost addition, but the investment must return more than the cost, thus increasing the ratio. Capital and technological improvements, systems design, training, organization design, and development are among the many ways to manage growth while improving productivity and quality. The approach does not necessarily mean additional investment in capital improvement. It can also mean reducing

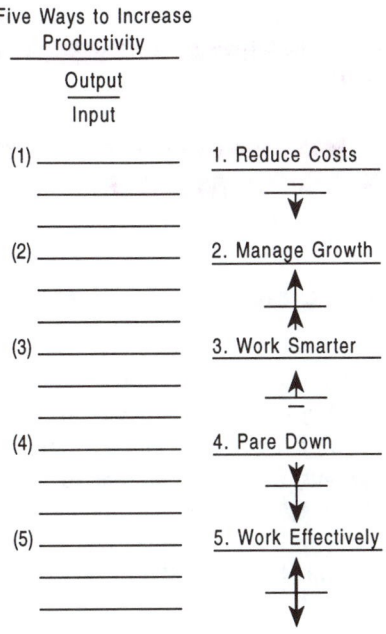

**Figure 10-3** Productivity Improvement

the amount of input per unit of output during the growth period. This may be termed *cost avoidance.*

**Working smarter** means more output from the same input, thus allowing increases in sales or production with the same gross input and lower unit cost. Many companies think that working smarter means putting a "freeze" on budgets while expecting a higher level of output. Although this may be necessary as a stopgap measure, it is hardly a rational course of action to improve productivity over the longer term. Better ways of improving this ratio might be getting more output by reducing manufacturing cost through product design, improving processes, or getting more production from the same level of raw materials by increasing inventory turnover.

**Paring down** is similar to cost reduction, except that as sales or production is off, input should be reduced by a proportionately larger amount, thus increasing the ratio. This productivity improvement can frequently be achieved through "sloughing off." In many organizations, there are many more opportunities than are generally realized to reduce marginal or unproductive facilities, employees, customers, products, or activities. Peter Drucker puts it this way: "Most plans concern themselves only with the new and additional things that have to be done—new products, new processes, new markets, and so on. But the key to doing something different tomorrow is getting rid of the no longer productive, the obsolescent, the obsolete." This "sloughing off" could apply to customers as well. Remember the 80–20 rule.

**Working effectively** is the best route to productivity and quality improvement; simply stated, you can get more for less. Some ways in which this can be accomplished are suggested in Figure 10-2.

## Examples of Increasing Productivity While Improving Quality

Experience has shown that front-line supervisors and employees have a wealth of innovative ideas for productivity and quality improvement. They have only to be asked. In workshops and seminars conducted for hundreds of participants, there has been a high degree of enthusiasm for setting improvement objectives, defining problems, and organizing action plans for improvement. A few that were converted to action plans and resulted in substantial cost reduction as well as improved productivity and quality are presented here as illustrative examples. Each improvement objective will improve the output/input ratio in one or more of the five ways outlined earlier.

- Improve assembly output by 30 percent by reducing the excessive number and types of fasteners
- Reduce repetitive machine downtime by problem solving
- Set material standards and reduce rework by 10 percent
- Decrease work in process from 45 to 30 days by improved scheduling and shop floor layout
- Improve clerical costs by 30 percent by avoiding duplication with adequate work procedures
- Set standards for setup and improve setup time by 10 percent
- Improve tool revision cost by 50 percent by decreasing lead time from design
- Improve process flow and get 30 percent increased output of presses
- Improve flow of finished goods by improving warehouse layout
- Reduce labor cost by training technicians to replace engineers
- Get more output with less input by cross-training and reduction of specialization
- Get more output with same input by better production planning
- Improve bill of materials by reducing custom parts
- Reduce assembly hours by using modular assembly

■ Improve reliability by simplified design and design for customer maintainability

## CAPITAL EQUIPMENT VS. MANAGEMENT SYSTEMS

Information technology (IT) in the service sector and in the administrative functions of manufacturing organizations demonstrates how technology may not have delivered productivity as promised. Personal and mainframe computers, desktop publishing, laser printers, and fax machines are examples of the many kinds of technology designed to get the product or service to the consumer faster, cheaper, and more efficiently. Yet there is evidence that without major restructuring, the introduction of IT may not produce savings needed to justify the investment.[21]

Peter Drucker, in an article for *Forbes,* says that the information revolution continues to focus on the "T" in IT and not the information needs of management—the collection and organization of *outside*-focused information. All the data we have so far, says Drucker, focus inward on costs. "But inside an enterprise there are only costs. Results are only on the outside. But as regards the outside (customers and, equally important, non-customers; competitors and, equally important, non-competitors; technologies other than those already in place in one's own industry; currencies; economies; and so on), we have virtually no data.[22]

Improvements in both productivity and quality have been slowed by two traditional management systems. The first has been the tendency to look to capital equipment as a solution to the problem of labor productivity. In the age of "high-tech," additions to capital have been viewed as the answer to boosting output. There is nothing wrong with this approach. Indeed, as pointed out previously, remarkable gains have been made in mechanization and automation since the Industrial Revolution. However, there are a number of arguments against depending on technology alone. It costs money and takes time, neither of which is an abundant resource.[23] Moreover, direct labor, the focus of capital equipment, is in the range of 8 to 12 percent of total cost of manufacturing. Technology has yet to make significant inroads in the productivity of indirect labor and service industries. Finally, high-tech must be accompanied by low-tech—the way workers, supervisors, and managers interact in adapting to new systems.

A basic principle of Economics 101 is illustrated in Figure 10-4. As additional increments of capital are used, productivity increases up to the point where benefits and cost are equal. This is classical economics at its best and reflects Washington thinking about U.S. industrial policy. Figure 10-4 also demonstrates

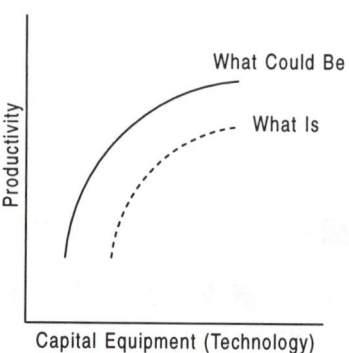

**Figure 10-4**    Productivity Curve

how the productivity curve can be shifted upward by means of improved management systems. This approach costs little and is available immediately. As discussed in earlier chapters, process control and related methods can improve both quality and productivity.

Another shortcoming of the capital investment argument as the primary or sole source of productivity and quality improvement relates to the historical focus on cost reduction. As discussed in Chapter 11, the traditional cost-accounting methods of the past provide inadequate information for decision making in the 1990s. Today, decisions on capital expenditures must be based on overall productivity, improving quality, cutting cycle time, reducing inventory, and adding flexibility. Activity analysis is a first step and it is fundamental to improving *management systems*.

## ACTIVITY ANALYSIS

Measurement of an activity output is not sufficient. Questions still remain: (1) Is the output/input ratio a positive number? (2) Can this ratio be improved? Most importantly, (3) does the *value added* by the activity contribute to the goal of the organization and the external or internal customer? The overwhelming majority of people in an organization cannot answer either of these questions, except in general and non-measurable terms. They define their activities in terms of what they are doing, not what they want to get done or whether the output is worth more than the input.

People characterized as *input* supervisors or employees are recognized by their dedication to collecting voluminous data for variance reports or closely examining the details of an expense account. The emphasis is on paperwork and the maintenance of records. They are the guardians of company rules and procedures, but are unconcerned about the value of their service to external or internal customers. The means becomes the end. Emphasis is on form and administration (doing things right) rather than process and results (doing the right things). They confuse *efficiency* with *effectiveness.* The design department is efficient at making repeated modifications to the product without regard for the impact on production. The sales force is efficient at calling on the wrong customers with the wrong product. Staff departments are efficient at providing services to internal customers who place no value on the service because they do not have to pay for it. The focus is on the budget rather than results.

*Activity*-focused supervisors and employees are intent on what they are doing, as opposed to what should be done. The accountant focuses on preparing the cost report rather than reducing overhead costs. The engineer is concerned only with the technical specifications of design without regard to cost, value analysis, or competitive considerations. When asked to define the results of their jobs, these people will reply with such platitudes as "improve the operations," "keep maintenance costs down," or "stay within the budget." It can be said of bureaucracy that focus on activity rather than results seems perfectly logical to those who are trapped within it. The activity may seem logical to the individual performing it, but to an outsider or a customer it is obviously wasteful.

The historical attention that is paid to budgets and cost control has encouraged a focus on activity rather than non-financial measures that plan and monitor sources of competitive value and *strategic* cost information. For most white-collar and service activities, the purpose of the output is to provide input to another downstream activity that can be viewed as the *internal* customer. A good starting point, therefore, is to determine whether the internal customer's expectation is met by the value provided by the upstream activity. The analysis of these activities begins by charting the flow throughout the organization and identifying sources of customer value in each. The central questions to be asked are what the value added by the activity is and what the output is worth to the supplier and receiver.

The major steps in conducting an activity analysis program include:

- Each unit, function, or activity develops a baseline budget that includes a breakdown of one year's costs.
- Set a cost, productivity, or quality target.
- Develop a mission statement for each unit that answers the question: "Why does it exist?"
- Identify each activity that supports the mission and the end products or services that result from that activity.

- Allocate end-product cost that equals the baseline budget.
- Identify receivers (customers) of the end product or service.
- Develop and implement ideas for improvement.[24]

# REENGINEERING

It has been suggested that in order to reinvent their companies, U.S. managers need to abandon the organizational and operational principles and procedures they are now using and create entirely new ones. These new ones can be combined into an emerging idea called **business reengineering**. Michael Hammer and James Champy, authors of *Reengineering the Corporation: A Manifesto for Business Revolution,*[25] call it the next revolution of business and compare its impact with that of Adam Smith's concept of labor specialization.

This managerial idea fits right in with the twin concepts of quality and productivity. Indeed, reengineering, also called process redesign, holds promise for improving quality and productivity: doing more for less—less investment, less time, and fewer people—and also doing it with better quality.

In Chapter 9 (Organizing for Total Quality Management), the classical principles of organization, which focused on structure and activity rather than outcome, were described. It is true that many, if not most, organizations remain committed to the classical principles of labor specialization and bureaucratic structure. The work is specialized and fragmented. Work is passed from one person or process to another. Workers never complete a job, nor do they understand their contribution to the whole; they just perform piecemeal tasks. Traditional process evaluation has focused on *fixing* the process. Business reengineering means starting all over—starting from scratch. **Reorganizing is out: reengineering is in.**

Reengineering a process is confusing and frustrating to some managers. They can identify a process but perceive it as one among "islands of processes" which, when combined, make up the organization. The connection between and integration among processes is elusive. More importantly, they focus on tasks, on jobs, on people, and on structure rather than on outcomes. Order processing is viewed as a series of individual tasks in a process—receiving an order form, picking up goods from the warehouse, and so forth—losing sight of the larger objective, which is to get the goods into the hands of the customer who ordered them. The tasks that make up the process are important, but the customer could care less about them. The customer only wants to know if the process works.

Consider the following scenario at IBM Credit's operations. When a salesperson sold a computer and called to get credit approval, it was important to get the approval rapidly, not only because lending money is a profitable business but also because a delay in approval gave the customer a chance to change his or her mind or get credit elsewhere. The salesperson's call was received by one of 14 clerical operators who entered the request on a piece of paper. This was the first of *five* steps involving five departments that bounced the request around for periods ranging from six days to two weeks. Ninety percent of that time involved work sitting in someone's in or out basket. When the salesperson would call to learn the status of the customer's financial deal, the information could not be furnished because the request was lost somewhere in the five-step chain.

When one manager took a financing request and walked it through all five steps, it was learned that the actual work took a total of only *90 minutes*. The remaining six days or so was consumed as the request languished in a queue on a desk awaiting movement to the next desk in the process. After reengineering the process, instead of moving the request from office to office, from desk to desk, from pile to pile, one person (called a deal structurer) now processes the entire application from start to finish. There are no handoffs. The result is that the number of requests handled has increased *100 times*.

Reengineering is not reorganizing. It is not new wine in old bottles. It is a rejection of the classical concept of labor specialization and the engineering of tasks. It is the reinvention of the organization through process redesign.

Michael Hammer, the "inventor/promoter" of reengineering, has been named (along with Peter Drucker, Malcolm Baldrige, and W. Edwards Deming) as one of "25 visionaries who shaped today's workplace."[26] Business process reengineering (BPR) has its antecedents in TQM, but its takeoff can be traced back to Hammer and Champy's book, which offered the definition of BPR as "the fundamental rethinking and radical redesign of business processes to achieve dramatic improvements in critical contemporary measures of performance."[27] They point the finger at traditional functionally organized structures as "castles surrounded by moats," preventing cross-organizational understanding.[28] They define process "as a group of interrelated activities that together create customer value."

Chapter 6 summarized process control, but not in the reengineering sense, as the three concepts outlined below demonstrate. To distinguish the three concepts associated with BPR, imagine a continuum:[29]

| Process improvement | Process redesign | Business reengineering |
|---|---|---|

**Process improvement** (Chapter 6) focuses on the individual process, function, or activity and does not include the entire value chain from suppliers as input and customers as output. Problem solving, process control, and root cause analysis are used for improving the process.

**Process redesign** or BPR goes beyond the process level to include the entire value chain and is output or results driven. The focus is always on customer value. In process improvement, the process is usually improved, changed, or modified, but the basic operation is the same. In process redesign (BPR), the process can be eliminated if the output is not valued by the customer. The initial tool can be a blank piece of paper.

**Business reengineering** is strategic in its concept and focuses on the enterprise level of the organization. It is vision driven and embraces strategic management principles.

## Principles of Reengineering

Creating new rules tailored to the modern environment ultimately requires a new conceptualization of the business process. However, according to Hammer,[30] reengineering need not be haphazard. Some of the principles that companies have already discovered while reengineering their business processes can help jump-start the effort for others.

**Organize around outcomes, not tasks.** This principle calls for the use of one person to perform all the steps in a process. Design that person's job around an objective or outcome instead of a single task. The following is an example of an electronics company that had separate organizations performing each of the five steps between selling and installing equipment.

- One group determined customer requirements, another translated those requirements into internal product codes, a third conveyed that information to various plants and warehouses, a fourth received and assembled the components, and a fifth delivered and installed the equipment. The customer order moved systematically from step to step, but this sequential processing caused problems. The people getting the information from the customer in step 1 had to get all the data needed throughout the process, even if it was not needed until step 5. In addition, the many handoffs were responsible for many errors. Finally, any complaints from customers were referred all the way back to step 1, which caused inordinate delays in customer service. When the company ultimately reengineered, the assembly line approach was eliminated. Responsibility for the various steps was compressed and assigned to one person, the customer service representative. This person would oversee the entire process. The customer service representative expedites and coordinates the process, much like a general contractor.

**Have those who use the output of the process perform the process.** In an effort to capitalize on the benefits of specialization and scale, many organizations established specialized departments to handle specialized processes. Computer-based data and expertise are now more readily available, enabling departments, units, and individuals to do more for themselves. Opportunities exist to reengineer processes so that individuals who need the result of a process can perform it themselves. When people closest to the process perform it, there is little need for the overhead associated with managing it. Interfaces and liaisons can be eliminated, as can the mechanisms used to coordinate those who perform the process with those who use it. Moreover, the problem of capacity planning for those who perform the process is greatly reduced.

**Subsume information processing work into the real work that produces the information.** The previous two principles were used to compress linear processes. This principle suggests moving work from one person or department to another. Most companies establish units that do nothing but collect and process information created by other departments. This arrangement reflects the old rule about specialized labor and the belief that people at lower levels are incapable of acting on information they generate. An accounts payable department collects information from purchasing and receiving and reconciles it with data provided by the vendor. Quality assurance gathers and analyzes information received from production. Redesigning the accounts payable process embodies the new rule, wherein receiving (which produces the information about the goods received) processes this information instead of sending it to accounts payable. The new system can easily compare the delivery with an order and initiate appropriate action.

**Treat geographically dispersed resources as though they were centralized.** The conflict between centralization and decentralization is that decentralizing a resource gives better service to those who use it, but at the cost of abundance and missed economies of scale. Companies no longer have to make such trade-offs. They can use databases, telecommunication networks, and standard processing systems to realize the benefits of scale and coordination while maintaining the benefits of flexibility of service.

**Link parallel activities instead of integrating their results.** This principle seeks to forge the links between functions and to coordinate them while their activities are in process rather than after they have been completed. Communication networks, shared databases, and teleconferencing can bring independent groups together so that coordination is ongoing.

**Put the decision point where the work is performed, and build control into the process.** In most organizations, those who do the work are distinguished from those who monitor the work and make decisions about it. The tacit assumption is that the people actually doing the work have neither the time nor the inclination to monitor and control the work and therefore lack the knowledge and scope to make decisions about it. The entire hierarchical management structure is built on this assumption. Accountants, auditors, and supervisors check, record, and monitor work. Managers handle any exceptions. The new principle suggests that the people who do the work should make decisions and that the process itself can have built-in controls. Pyramidal management layers can therefore be compressed and the organization flattened.

**Capture information once and at the source.** This last rule is simple. When information was difficult to transmit, it made sense to collect it repeatedly. Each person, department, or unit had its own requirements and forms. Companies simply had to live with the associated delays, entry errors, and costly overhead. However, by integrating and connecting these systems, the company was able to eliminate this redundant data entry, along with the attendant checking functions and the seemingly inevitable errors.

## QUESTIONS FOR DISCUSSION

**10-1**   Give an example of how improving quality can also increase productivity.

**10-2**   Illustrate how productivity improvement may be more effective than increased sales in improving profitability.

**10-3**   How can improved management be as effective as technology and capital equipment in improving productivity?

**10-4**   Why has the rate of productivity increase been low in the United States?

**10-5**   Choose four or five functions or activities in staff or white-collar jobs and indicate a measure of productivity for each.

**10-6**   List three of the five ways to improve the productivity rate of input to output, and identify a specific action that could be taken to achieve the improvement.

## ENDNOTES

1.   Institute of Industrial Engineers, "Productivity and Quality in the USA Today," *Management Services (UK)*, Jan. 1990, pp. 27–31.
2.   W. Edwards Deming, *Quality, Productivity, and Competitive Position,* Cambridge, Mass.: Center for Advanced Engineering Study, Massachusetts Institute of Technology, 1982, pp. 1–2.
3.   A. V. Feigenbaum, "Quality and Productivity," *Quality Progress,* Nov. 1977, p. 21.
4.   This conclusion is suggested by the Profit Impact of Market Strategies (PIMS) database referred to in Chapter 1. The studies suggest that higher conformance and total quality

costs are inversely related and better manufacturing-based quality results in higher output without a corresponding increase in costs. See K. E. Maani, "Productivity and Profitability through Quality: Myth and Reality," *International Journal of Quality & Reliability (UK)*, Vol. 6 Issue 3, 1989, pp. 11–23. One empirical study concludes that improvements in quality level may be related to productivity increases. See Daniel G. Hotard, "Quality and Productivity: An Examination of Some Relationships," *Engineering Management International (Netherlands)*, Jan. 1988, pp. 259–266. In one Conference Board research study of 62 firms that attempted to measure the results of quality on profitability, 47 indicated that profits have increased noticeably because of lower costs and/or increased market share. See Francis J. Walsh, Jr., *Current Practices in Measuring Quality*, New York: The Conference Board, 1989, p. 3. See also Colin Scurr, "Total Quality Management and Productivity," *Management Services*, Oct. 1991, pp. 28–30.

5.  Joyce R. Jarrett, "Long Term Strategy…A Commitment to Excellence," *Journal for Quality and Participation*, July/Aug. 1990, pp. 28–33.

6.  Raymond C. Cole and Lee H. Hales, "How Monsanto Justified Automation," *Management Accounting*, Jan. 1992, pp. 39–43.

7.  At the Third National Productivity Conference in Dallas on May 21, 1990.

8.  Robert D. Buzzell and Bradley T. Gale, *The PIMS Principles*, New York: The Free Press, 1987, pp. 10–11.

9.  Slow productivity growth is not characteristic of all U.S. industries. It has been especially high in the manufacture of computers and television sets, but negative growth has been the case in petroleum refining and retailing.

10.  For a more detailed examination of the reasons for slow productivity growth in the United States, see Joel E. Ross *Productivity, People, & Profits*, Englewood Cliffs, N.J.: Prentice-Hall, 1981; Joel E. Ross and William C. Ross, *Japanese Quality Circles & Productivity*, Englewood Cliffs, N.J.: Prentice-Hall, 1982.

11.  For one popular view of the unwillingness of managers to manage, see Robert H. Hayes and William J. Abernathy, "Managing Our Way to Decline," *Harvard Business Review*, July–Aug. 1989, pp. 67–77.

12.  "Productivity and Quality in the 90's," *Management Services (UK)*, June 1990, pp. 28–33. This article reports on a survey of British managers, the majority of whom believe that managers are more interested in short-term financial gain than in long-term productivity. Similar surveys in the United States have had similar results.

13.  "The Productivity Paradox," *Business Week*, June 6, 1988, p. 103.

14.  National Center for Productivity and Quality of Work Life, Improving Productivity in the Changing World of the 1980s, Washington, D.C.: U.S. Government Printing Office, 1978.

15.  OECD, *Economic Outlook*, July 1991, p. 3.

16.  Nobel laureate economist Milton Friedman stated that higher wages and the price–wage spiral are an *effect* of inflation, not a *cause*. Milton Friedman and Rose Friedman, *Free to Choose: A Personal Statement*, New York: Harcourt Brace Jovanovich, 1980.

17.  The categories of productivity measures published by the Bureau of Labor Statistics are described in Roy H. Webb, "National Productivity Statistics," *Economic Quarterly*, Vol. 8, Winter 1998, pp. 45–64.

18.  Coopers & Lybrand conducted a survey to determine what federal executives know and think about quality management. About half of the respondents said that the lack of

dependable ways to measure quality is a major obstacle. The same could be said of productivity measures. David Carr and Ian Littman, "Quality in the Federal Government," *Quality Progress,* Sept. 1990, pp. 49–52.

19. See Carl G. Thor, "How to Measure Organizational Productivity," *CMA Magazine,* March 1991, pp. 17–19. A company-wide system for measuring productivity is quite complex. The American Productivity and Quality Center conducts a three-day seminar on the topic. See also Brain Maskell, "Performance Measurement for World Class Manufacturing," *Management Accounting (UK),* July/Aug. 1989, pp. 48–50. This article identifies seven common characteristics used by world-class manufacturing firms: (1) performance measures are directly related to the manufacturing strategy, (2) primarily non-financial measures are used, (3) the measures vary among locations, (4) the measures change over time as needs change, (5) the measures are simple and easy to use, (6) the measures provide rapid feedback to operators and managers, and (7) the measures are meant to foster improvement instead of only monitoring.

20. Peter Drucker, *Management,* New York: Harper & Row, 1974, p. 70.

21. Levent T. Orman, "A Model Management Approach to Business Process Reengineering," *Journal of Management Information Systems,* Summer 1998, pp. 187–212.

22. Peter Drucker, "The Next Information Revolution," *Forbes ASAP,* Aug. 24, 1998, pp. 47–58.

23. Carl Thor, president of the American Productivity and Quality Center in Houston, favors management systems. Regarding high-tech additions, he says: "You need a decade's worth of that kind of investment to have an effect." See a special report entitled "The Productivity Paradox," *Business Week,* June 6, 1988, pp. 100–112.

24. For additional ideas on activity analysis, see Thomas H. Johnson, "Activity-Based Information: A Blueprint for World-Class Management Accounting," *Management Accounting,* June 1988, pp. 23–30. See also Philip Janson and Murray E. Bovarnick, "How to Conduct a Diagnostic Activity Analysis: Five Steps to a More Effective Organization," *National Productivity Review,* Spring 1988, pp. 152–160; Paul L. Brown, "Quality Improvement through Activity Analysis," *Journal of Organizational Behavior Management,* Vol. 10 Issue 1, 1989, pp. 169–179. For a more detailed program for implementing an organization-wide productivity improvement program, see Joel E. Ross, *Productivity, People & Profits,* Englewood Cliffs, N.J.: Prentice-Hall, 1981.

25. Michael Hammer and James Champy, *Reengineering the Corporation: A Manifesto for Business Revolution,* New York: HarperCollins, May 1993.

26. Samuel Greengard, "25 Visionaries Who Shaped Today's Workplace," *Workforce,* Jan. 1997, pp. 50–59.

27. D. Webster and M. Black, "Business Process Re-engineering: A Case Study of a Developmental Approach," *Total Quality Management,* May 1998, pp. 369–378.

28. Ann Mahoney, "Reengineering for Results," *Association Management,* Aug. 1997, pp. 133–138.

29. Ronald J. Recardo and David J. Jones, "A Report Card on Reengineering," *Production & Inventory Management Journal,* Vol. 38 No. 3, Third Quarter 1997, pp. 51–56.

30. M. Hammer, "Reengineering Work: Don't Automate, Obliterate," *Harvard Business Review,* July–Aug. 1990, pp. 104–112.

## WAINWRIGHT INDUSTRIES: REENGINEERING AT A SMALL COMPANY

Wainwright Industries is one of the smallest companies to win the Baldrige Award. A 47-year-old family-owned business, the company manufactures stamped and machined parts for U.S. and, increasingly, foreign customers in the automotive, aerospace, home security, and information-processing industries. The company employs about 275 associates and has sales of about $30 million.

Wainwright aims for "total customer satisfaction," a target that is tracked through extensive sets of quality measures that are aligned with five strategic indicators: safety, internal customer satisfaction, external customer satisfaction, six sigma quality, and business performance.

Indicators are supported by continuous improvement efforts that rely on reengineering for the benefit of all facets of its operations—from helping it leverage investments in computer-aided design and manufacturing equipment into new lines of business to streamlining its requisition procedures so that 95 percent of all purchase orders are processed within 24 hours of submission.

At the production end, process reengineering and simplification have enabled Wainwright to cut the lead time for making one of its principal products, drawn housings for electric motors, to 15 minutes, as compared with 8.75 days, and to reduce defect rates tenfold. For customers, the benefits translated into an on-time delivery rate of nearly 100 percent, as compared with 75 percent previously, and a 35 percent reduction in product cost.

To ensure that fully empowered associates have the knowledge and skills necessary to accomplish quality and performance objectives, the company invests up to 7 percent of its payroll in training and education. All associates take courses on quality values, communication techniques, problem solving, statistical process control, and synchronous manufacturing, a systematic method for identifying and evaluating opportunities to simplify processes and reduce waste.

**CASE**

# PRODUCTIVITY-IMPROVEMENT TEAM DOES ITS JOB

## Samantha Hoover

"That which will not kill you will make you stronger—or put some hair on your chest," reflected Stan Valencia, vice president of operations at Fielding Manufacturing, Cranston, RI. The custom injection molding company is just emerging from a four-year restructuring from a traditional, management-directed operating style to one based in total quality management (TQM). TQM places the company's processes under the leadership of the employees, who form teams to address various functions of the organization. Fielding was founded in 1962, and for 36 years functioned autocratically.

"The information flowed from top to bottom. There were a lot of layers in between," Valencia explained. "The people at the middle management [level] did not understand what upper management wanted. They were holding onto their autocratic practices. People in the rank and file did not understand what all of the fuss was about." The company has continuously tried to educate its employees in the new philosophy, with mixed results. "I don't think we've reached that stage where everybody is in a participatory mode," Valencia said.

The Productivity-Improvement Team in action is Bert Blais, vice president of finance, administration, and MIS; Stan Valencia, vice president of operations; Jerry Sherlock, tooling modernization technical coordinator; Bill Dagliesh, tooling production coordinator; and Rich Vanasse, production improvement specialist. The team examines jobs-in-progress to see how they could be changed to improve quality. Made up of a combination of middle managers, front-line supervisors, and the rank and file, the team sets up benchmarks for each manufacturing division, and then updates those benchmarks every quarter for safety, quality, and customer service.

"The Productivity-Improvement Team," Valencia explained, "looks at the performance from a weekly standpoint and meets and says, 'Look, these are the

Reprinted with permission from *Quality,* Vol. 37 No. 9, September 1998, pp. 50–52.

jobs that are running late, these are the jobs that did not meet our performance standards, these are the jobs that had quality problems.'" A champion is selected to ensure changes are implemented, but everyone on the team gets credit for improvements. "Not only do they identify areas where quality performance or production performance is lacking or needs to improve, but each team member has a part of the pie, has a part of the information."

The time from the conception of a productivity-improvement team to its success was substantial but well worth the effort. "It took us about two years to do this," Valencia said. "The first results were evident in the first six months." The company's productivity, which is measured in earned machine hours, went up 15% to 20%. Valencia attributed this success partly to the team's philosophy. "It's bad enough when we trip on one rock. It's very bad if we trip on the same rock twice. If we trip on one rock, that's good, but let's take that one rock and throw it to the side, or pulverize it, so we can improve." Fielding has also organized teams to "pulverize" problems in other areas.

A Customer-Service Team was created to ensure the timeliness of shipments. An ISO Fast-Track Team keeps the company on track in its ISO 9000 certification. All of the company's teams report to the Continuous-Improvement Council, which appoints team members. If any member sees where a change could be made in a manufacturing process, he fills out a form called a "DO IT," which has details about his idea, and then submits it to a council member, who presents the idea to the council. All of these teams might seem to have complicated things or at least bogged the system down, but instead they have reduced late shipments during some weeks to zero, streamlined whole processes, and instilled a greater sense of responsibility and importance in employees. Teams are rewarded with paid personal days and breakfasts, lunches, and dinners served by Fielding's president, Steven Fielding, and his staff.

Despite this success, some employees still drag their feet when it comes to accepting TQM and the team mentality. "There are several people who," Valencia explained, "though they think TQM is important, they don't think they're involved." Often the resistance is due to a misunderstanding of what TQM is about. In one particular instance, Valencia had to re-explain TQM to the accounting department, which felt removed from the system. "They thought TQM had something to do with some guy in quality inspecting parts," Valencia remembered. Valencia estimates that it will take at least another year for the teams and new managing system to be fully integrated and accepted by employees. "The organization is changing, and people who are not adapting to these changes are going to be sticking out like sore thumbs."

All in all, the transition has been a worthwhile and valuable experience. "In your family," Valencia observed, "sometimes it brings you closer together if you have a problem. In the '90s they call it 'bonding.' We have created some bonding by resolving the problems that we had. We became stronger, a more cohesive unit. I think we can get the answers faster, cheaper, and easier if we put all of our heads together."

## Benefits

- Productivity improved 20%
- Employee morale increased
- Processes streamlined
- Late shipments eliminated

## Questions for Discussion

1 The team(s) appear to be focused primarily in the production area. What other teams/processes/departments would you recommend for team organization?

2 Are the teams reactive or proactive? Explain.

3 Instead of "tripping on a rock," how could the rock be avoided before it becomes a tripping hazard?

4 How is productivity measured? Evaluate it.

5 What recommendations do you have for the company?

# JUST DO IT: AN INTERVIEW WITH MICHAEL HAMMER

## Christy Chapman

If you've read Michael Hammer's work, you might have the impression that he thinks internal control and internal auditing should go the way of the dinosaur. His books *Reengineering the Corporation, The Reengineering Revolution,* and *Beyond Reengineering* extol the benefits of streamlined processes with fewer hand-offs and check points—in other words, with fewer internal controls and audits. In a recent interview with *Internal Auditor,* Dr. Hammer shed a different light on his beliefs about control. In fact, he says, control and internal auditing do have a role to play in these streamlined environments; it's just not the role you might expect.

*In your message about process reengineering, you maintain that activities such as follow-up, approval, reconciliation, and checking are non-value-adding busy work that do nothing to help us provide the best product to our customers. These busy work tasks, however, have been mainstays of the control environment. Where do internal controls fit in the new process-centered company?*

Control itself is still an important corporate element, but we have to separate the mechanism of control from the goal of control. Controls don't exist to eliminate the theoretical possibility of there being any abuse, but to create a situation in which the aggregate amount of abuse is in the right ratio to the cost of preventing that abuse.

Two simple control concepts are frequently overlooked, but are becoming increasingly relevant: (1) there is no such thing as perfect control, and (2) there is no such thing as free control. Control is expensive; and almost any control system you design can be subverted. The challenge is to find the right balance. Organizations have to figure out how to achieve the best return cost ratio for their control efforts just as they do for any other organizational activity.

This article was reprinted with permission from the June 1998 issue of *Internal Auditor,* published by The Institute of Internal Auditors, Inc.

Certain traditional control mechanisms, such as audits and the segregation of responsibilities, now cost too much and often fail to deliver the required level of control. We need to find new ways to accomplish the goal of control.

*Can you give us an example?*

Consider the purchasing function. In the past, each purchase request had to go through a complex control process involving lots of paperwork, approvals, and hand-offs between individuals. When you totaled it all up, the control costs for each purchase often exceeded $100. For an item priced at $100, the control mechanism automatically doubled the cost.

Obviously, that procedure only makes sense for large-ticket items. In place of this costly process, some companies have implemented the use of procurement cards. On the surface, this strategy appears to provide a much weaker, or even absent, control environment. But in fact, control hasn't disappeared; it has just been deferred until later in the process.

Instead of every transaction being controlled to the max from the beginning, companies now search the electronic records of completed transactions for inappropriate patterns of utilization. There are also other forms of control, such as credit limits on the card. The lesson to be learned is that it is possible to sacrifice transactional level controls and still achieve adequate levels of overall control at a much lower cost. The control mechanism is different, but the goal is the same.

Such control adjustments are increasingly common, and we're beginning to see a new set of control principles emerge. The purchasing strategy I've mentioned demonstrates a shift toward exception-based controls using computer systems to recognize patterns, and from transactional level controls to aggregate controls.

*So, the notion of control as 100 percent preventative no longer works?*

That's true. In today's business environment, a better approach is to let things go on the front end, but have controls in place to make sure abuse doesn't get out of hand. Then the area can be periodically reviewed after the fact. Many organizations are beginning to recognize that this kind of exception-based control is the way to go.

*Given this new concept of control, what role can internal auditors play in today's reorganized environments?*

The audit organization should look at itself as a resource for the rest of the company. Internal auditors can play a vital role by helping management design new business processes so that the desired level of control is achieved, but in a more efficient fashion. Internal auditors should change their mission from simply one of "We conduct audits," to "We help create the processes that achieve the level of control required for organizational success."

*How can internal auditors make this change?*

What's needed is a rethinking of what we mean by controls, as well as a rethinking of the role of the internal audit organization. Internal auditors who stick too closely to classical thinking are going to go down on a sinking ship. By holding to traditional images of themselves, they cut themselves off from important things going on in the organization.

But audit groups who can make this philosophical shift will have a chance to create a very exciting new role for themselves and really be able to contribute much more to the organization. Some audit groups have already successfully navigated this change. Ameritech's audit group, for example, actively contributes to process design efforts across the company.

*You've studied and advised many large, successful organizations. Based on those experiences, how many internal audit departments have made this philosophical adjustment, and how many insist on the old "command-and-control" approach to their function?*

I think that there is reason for optimism in this area. I don't have statistical data, but I've been pleasantly surprised by what I've seen. It would be very easy for me to simply say, "All of these process reengineering ideas are heresy to internal audit organizations, and they don't want to let go." But the truth is that many of the internal audit groups I've encountered have been more flexible than I might have expected.

*Modern control frameworks emphasize the importance of "soft" controls, such as effective communication and decision-making, management philosophy, and the quality of information. What should internal audit's role be vis-à-vis these soft controls?*

This is a good example of how the internal audit function has to think of itself less as an audit organization and more as a consulting organization. I don't think that internal auditors are going to do much auditing of soft controls. But I do believe that internal auditing should play a consultative role in those difficult, but very important, soft control areas.

The audit group's role should be to help the organization shape the soft control environment. They should be process design consultants, advising management on how to create a culture in which people believe you have to be accurate and ethical in the first place. They should not, however, take on a role that enables management to think, "Well, it's up to the audit police to worry about that."

*Many auditors would respond that they've not been able to sell management on the idea of internal auditors serving as internal consultants. What advice do you have for winning management's endorsement?*

Nothing succeeds like success. In other words, do it, and then they'll believe you. It's harder to sell a concept. Find some opportunity to work with someone, and then show management what you've achieved. That achievement gives you credibility.

*Many internal auditors now include control self-assessment (CSA) facilitation in their services. Is CSA here to stay?*

CSA is more than a passing fad. It's part of two broader trends. First is the one we've already mentioned: the auditor is playing a more consultative role in the organization. Second, control is becoming a part of everyone's responsibility. Exercises like CSA are efforts to raise the organization's control consciousness. They're designed to make more people aware of areas of inadequacy and of what the consequences might be. They can then take steps on their own to try to improve the situation instead of just expecting the auditors to come out and clean up the mess.

*Do you believe that internal auditors can add value to their organizations?*

Many people in the organization—including those from finance and audit—have traditionally played bottleneck roles; but they do, in fact, have a lot to offer the organization in a consultative role. They just have to do it.

# PRODUCTIVITY AT VARIFILM

Compare the following TQM criteria to Varifilm and indicate whether the practice in the company is a *strength* (S) or *needs improvement* (I). The criteria relate to improvement in quality, operations, business processes and support, and supplier quality. It should be noted that improvement in these areas is usually followed by an improvement in productivity (see chapter text).

| | S | I |
|---|---|---|
| **6.1 Product and Service Quality Results** | | |
| ■ Key measures of film quality show overall improvement trends. Varifilm is performing better than its best competitor. | — | — |
| ■ Two key measures of on-time delivery (shipment reliability index and delivery satisfaction index) show overall improvement. Varifilm is performing better than key competitors. | — | — |
| ■ There is an overall improvement trend in the order-entry error rate. | — | — |
| **6.2 Operational Results** | | |
| ■ First-pass yield has shown an improvement trend. | — | — |
| ■ Improvement trends are shown for non-conforming product shipped, manufacturing cycle time, and order-entry cycle time. | — | — |
| ■ Improvement trends are shown for air emissions and process waste as well as return on equity, profitability, and sales per co-worker. | — | — |

*Describe how improvement in each of the preceding items should result in reduced cost as well as an increase in productivity of human resources, material, and capital.*

---

---

---

### 6.3 Business Process and Support Service Results      S    I

- An overall improvement trend has been shown for accounts receivable errors and information systems operations. Both are approaching or have exceeded the industry standard.

- Improvement trends have been shown for EDI orders and cost of purchase orders.

- An overall improvement trend has been shown for new product cycle time and has exceeded the best competitor.

- Benchmarks and industry standards against which Varifilm compares itself have been flat or have shown no change. These should be investigated to ensure that they reflect future competitive trends.

- Comparisons for key competitors and best-in-class are provided for only one measure.

### 6.4 Supplier Quality Results

- Varifilm has shown overall improvement trends for certified suppliers, supplier quality rating, and supplier quality incidents measures.

- Comparisons of key supplier quality measures to best-in-class benchmarks are provided for only one measure.

*Describe how improvement in each of the preceding items should result in reduced cost as well as an increase in productivity of human resources, material, and capital.*

---

---

---

# FOR FURTHER READING

Carlson, John B. and Mark E. Schweitzer, "Productivity Measures and the 'New Economy,'" *Economic Commentary (Federal Reserve Bank of Cleveland),* June 1998, pp. 1–4.

Chong, Philip S. and Sal Kukalis, "An Evaluation of American Top Management's View of Quality and Productivity," *International Journal of Management,* Sept. 1997, pp. 326–333.

Epelman, Michael, Derek Maher, and Dan O'Brien, "How to Fine-Tune Your Business Processes," *Quality Progress,* Oct. 1998, pp. 55–60.

Jaffe, Dennis T. and Cynthia D. Scott, "Reengineering in Practice: Where Are the People? Where Is the Learning?" *Journal of Applied Behavioral Science,* Sept. 1998, pp. 250–267.

Morris, Linda, "TQM Improves Productivity," *Training and Development,* Oct. 1993, pp. 74–75.

# 11

# THE COST OF QUALITY

*The annual national cost of nonquality to the Israeli
economy is $15 billion, which approximates
25 percent of the country's gross national product.*

Survey by the Government of Israel[1]

The survey by the Israeli government indicates just how much is being lost in time and money as a result of failure to control the cost of quality—or, more exactly, the cost of nonquality. Commenting on U.S. managers and the lack of attention paid to the problem and the potential, the chief quality systems manager at George S. May International, a consulting firm, remarked: "They usually don't have a clue what poor quality is costing them."[2]

What will it cost to improve quality? What will it cost to not improve quality? These are basic questions that managers need to ask as they focus on the bottom line and company strategic decisions. These questions about the cost of quality have served to draw attention to the quality movement. No one will deny the importance of quality, but it is the confusion surrounding the payoff and the trade-off between cost and quality that is unclear to many decision makers.

It is becoming increasingly clear that whereas the answer to the cost of poor quality may be difficult to obtain, the potential payoff from improvement is extraordinary. Hewlett-Packard estimated that the cost of not doing things right the first time was 25 to 30 percent of revenues. Travelers Insurance Company found that the figure was $1 million per hour. On a positive note, Motorola has reduced the cost of poor quality by about 5 percent of total sales, or about $480 million per year.

## COST OF QUALITY DEFINED

The cost of quality has been defined in a number of ways, some of which include:

- At 3M, quality cost equals actual cost minus no-failure cost. That is, the cost of quality is the difference between the actual cost of making and selling products and services and the cost if there were no failures during manufacture or use and no possibility of failure.[3]

- Quality costs usually are defined as costs incurred because poor quality may or does exist.[4]

- The cost of not meeting the customer's requirements—the cost of doing things wrong.[5]

- All activities that are carried out that are not needed directly to support departmental [quality] objectives are considered the cost of quality.[6]

These definitions leave unanswered the question: How much quality is enough? In theory, the answer is analogous to a principle of economics: basic marginal cost equals marginal revenue (MC = MR). That is, spend on quality improvement until the added profit equals the cost of achieving it. This is not so easy in practice. In economics, the MC and MR curves are difficult to define and more difficult to compute. The same is true of the cost/benefit curves of quality costs. What are the costs of added quality and the "hidden" costs of non-quality? What are the bottom-line benefits? Neither of these questions is easy to answer, particularly in view of the long-run strategic implications. The answer lies at the very essence of what the company is about.

## THE COST OF QUALITY

The tendency in many organizations is to think of quality costs in terms of what is visible: scrap, rework, returns, and the like. Aside from the costs of downtime and reduction in cycle time, there is the broader range of costs such as support personnel effort, inventory, equipment utilization, and procurement/reprocurement costs. The personal computer or desktop computer was promoted as a tool for improvement of quality and productivity. It may in fact be a significant contributor to the problem. Industry experts say that when these systems fail, as they frequently do, disruption costs exceed 5 percent of employee-related costs or about $300 per year per employee.[7]

A major and critical "soft" cost is the cost of customer defection (see Chapter 7). One example is provided in the *Production and Inventory Management Journal*:[8]

- The Widget (fictitious) Company, manufacturer of copying machines, sells to an average of 100,000 customers per year and estimates the average profit per customer to be $100 yearly. The company also estimates:

    - Seventy percent of its customers experience no problems and 90 percent of them will buy again.

    - Of the 30 percent that experience problems, half will report the problems and 60 percent of the reported problems will be resolved satisfactorily.

    - Eighty percent of those who have had problems resolved and 25 percent of those who have not had a problem resolved satisfactorily will buy again from the company.

    - Sixty percent of the customers that experienced a problem but did not report it will buy again from the company.

Based on this information, the estimated cost of lost profit per year will be $1,847,500. Assuming an average loyalty of five years, the potential profit lost amounts to $9,237,500. If every dissatisfied customer tells ten potential customers, the expected loss (opportunity cost) could be as high as $92,375,000.

The supply chain can be another overlooked source of quality costs. Chrysler reported that the company simply ordered its suppliers to reduce prices for services and parts when volumes increased. Today, Chrysler works with its suppliers as partners to find ways to be more efficient and to reduce costs for the company as well as its suppliers. The initiative, called SCORE (Supplier Cost Reduction Effort),[9] saved the company $2.5 billion.

The cost of quality or, more specifically, "non-quality" is a major concern to both national policymakers as well as individual firms. Because much of our national concern with competitiveness seems to be focused on Japan, it is interesting to note that some estimates of quality costs in U.S. firms indicate 25 percent of revenues, while in Japan the figure is less than 5 percent.[10] Estimates of potential savings are as high as $300 billion by nationwide application of total quality management (TQM).[11] Feigenbaum puts the estimate at 7 percent of the gross national product and suggests that this figure can be one of the tools used by policymakers in considering the quality potential of the U.S. economy in relation to the country's major competitors.[12]

The cost of poor quality in individual firms and the potential for improvement can be staggering. In *Thriving on Chaos,* Tom Peters reports that experts agree that poor quality can cost about 25 percent of the personnel and assets in a manufacturing firm and up to 40 percent in a service firm. There appears to be general agreement that the costs range between 20 and 30 percent of sales.[13]

The potential for profit improvement is very substantial. One has only to visualize a profit-and-loss statement with a net profit of 6 percent before tax and then compute what the profit would be if 20 to 30 percent of the operating budget were reduced. Add to this the additional strategic benefits and the potential is great indeed.

## THREE VIEWS OF QUALITY COSTS

Historically, business managers have assumed that increased quality is accompanied by increased cost; higher quality meant higher cost. This view was questioned by the quality pioneers. Juran examined the economics of quality and concluded that benefits outweighed costs.[14] Feigenbaum introduced "total quality control" and developed the principle that quality is everyone's job, thus expanding the notion of quality cost beyond the manufacturing function.[15] In 1979, Crosby introduced the now popular concept that "quality is free."[16] Today, the view among practitioners seems to fall into one of three categories:[17]

1. **Higher quality means higher cost.** Quality attributes such as performance and features cost more in terms of labor, material, design, and other costly resources. The additional benefits from improved quality do not compensate for the additional expense.

2. **The cost of improving quality is less than the resulting savings.** This view was originally promoted by Deming and is widely held among Japanese manufacturers. The savings result from less rework, scrap, and other *direct* expenses related to defects. This is said to account for the focus on continuous improvement of processes in Japanese firms.

3. **Quality costs are those incurred in excess of those that would have been incurred if the product were built or the service performed exactly right the first time.** This view is held by adherents of the TQM philosophy. Costs include not only those that are direct but also those resulting from lost customers, lost market share, and the many hidden costs and foregone opportunities not identified by modern cost-accounting systems.

The attention now being given to the more comprehensive view of the cost of poor quality is a fairly recent development. Even today, many companies tend to ignore or downplay this opportunity because of a continuing focus on production volume or frustration with the problem of computing the trade-off between volume and quality. This computational difficulty is compounded by accounting systems that do not recognize the expenses as manageable. More on this will be provided later in this chapter.

One survey of 94 corporate controllers found that only 31 percent of the firms regularly measured costs of quality, and even among those firms productivity was ranked higher than quality as a factor contributing to profit. Not surprisingly, the major reason for failure to measure these costs was lack of top management commitment.[18]

Philip Crosby, of "quality is free" fame, is of the firm opinion that zero defects is the absolute performance standard and the cost of quality is the price of non-conformance against that standard. His concept is catching on as more companies set goals such as parts per million, six sigma, and even zero defects. On the other hand, a goal of zero defects may be more costly than the payoff that might accrue. As one approaches zero defects, costs may begin to increase geometrically.

Another of Crosby's principles, which he calls "absolutes," is *measurement of quality:*

> The measurement of quality is the Price of Nonconformance, not indexes....Measuring quality by calculating the price of waste—wasted time, effort, material—produces a monetary figure that can be used to direct efforts to improve and measure the improvement.[19]

This monetary figure, according to Crosby, is a percentage of sales, and he suggests that the standard should be reduced to about *2 to 3 percent.* This measure has been generally accepted, and many firms use it as a target and measure of progress.

## QUALITY COSTS

The costs of quality are generally classified into four categories: (1) prevention, (2) appraisal, (3) internal failure, and (4) external failure.[20] *Prevention* costs include those activities which remove and prevent defects from occurring in the production process. Included are such activities as quality planning, production reviews, training, and engineering analysis, which are incurred to ensure that poor quality is not produced. *Appraisal* costs are those costs incurred to identify poor quality products after they occur but before shipment to customers. Inspection activity is an example.

*Failure* costs are those incurred either during the production process (*internal*) or after the product is shipped (*external*). Internal failure costs include such items as machine downtime, poor quality materials, scrap, and rework. External failure costs include returns and allowances, warranty costs, and the hidden costs of customer dissatisfaction and lost market share. Recognition of the relative importance of external failure costs has caused many companies to broaden their perspective from product quality to total consumer satisfaction as the key quality measure.

In Figure 11-1, the many costs of non-quality are classified into the four categories outlined earlier: (1) prevention, (2) appraisal, (3) internal failure, and

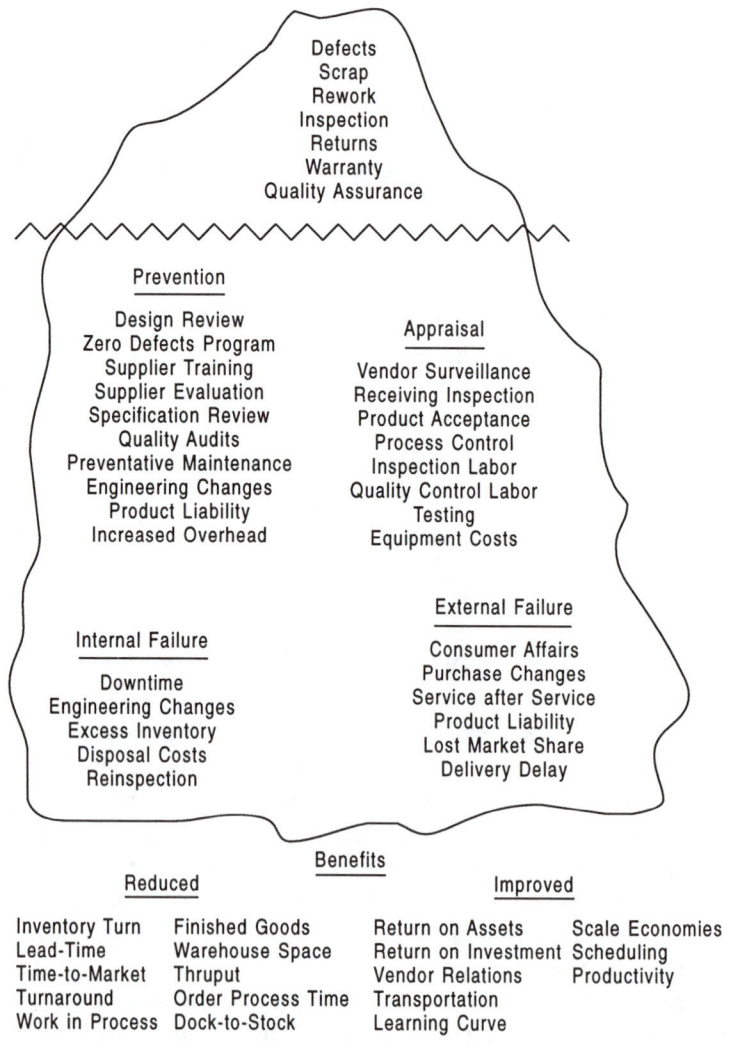

**Figure 11-1**   Benefits of Costs of Quality Control

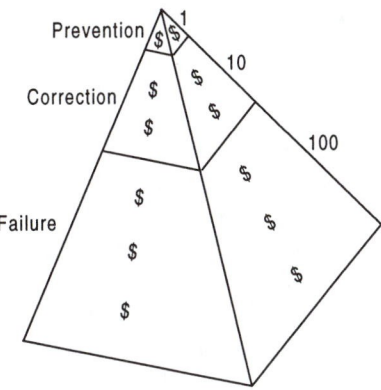

**Figure 11-2**    1-10-100 Rule

(4) external failure. The figure is an attempt to convey the idea of an iceberg, where only 10 percent is visible and 90 percent is hidden from view. The analogy is a good one because the *visible* 10 percent is comprised of such items as scrap, rework, inspection, returns under warranty, and quality assurance costs; for many companies, these comprise what they believe to be the total costs. When the *hidden* costs of quality are computed, controlled, and reduced, a firm can achieve the benefits shown at the bottom of Figure 11-1.

Of these types of costs, prevention costs should probably take priority because it is much less costly to prevent a defect than to correct one. The principle is not unlike the traditional medical axiom: "An ounce of prevention is worth a pound of cure." The relationship between these costs is reflected in the 1-10-100 rule depicted in Figure 11-2. One dollar spent on prevention will save $10 on appraisal and $100 on failure costs. As one moves along the stream of events from design to delivery or "dock-to-stock," the cost of errors escalates as failure costs become higher and the payoff from an investment in prevention becomes greater. Computer systems analysts are aware of this and understand that an hour spent on better programming or design can save up to ten hours of system retrofit and redesign. One general manager of Hewlett-Packard's Computer Systems Division observed that early prevention of a defect results in greater savings. For example, if you catch a defective two-cent resistor before it is used, you lose two cents. If it is not found until later in the production cycle, it may cost as much as $10 to repair, but if it is not discovered until it reaches the customer, it may cost hundreds of dollars. This is the 1–10–100 rule in action.[21]

When total customer satisfaction becomes the definition of a quality product or service, it creates a need to develop measures which integrate the customer perspective into a measurement system. This need moves beyond the shop floor and into the many non-product features such as delivery time, responsiveness, billing accuracy, etc. This need also leads to a search for quality, and hence quality costs, in activities not usually recognized as incurring these costs. This will change as more companies realize that all activities can contribute to total customer satisfaction. Thus, quality costs include those factors which lie behind the obvious production processes. Moreover, it becomes necessary to identify the hidden quality costs associated with foregone opportunities.

What is frequently overlooked is the unrealized potential for improved productivity and quality to be achieved by identifying and measuring the difference between no failure (parts per million, six sigma, zero defects, etc.) and actual cost. What, for example, would be the payoff from just-in-time, better process control, improved inventory turn, and reduced cycle time in the many cross-functional processes and cost interrelationships in the stream of activities during the life cycle of the product or a service? Each of these actions would improve quality, use fewer resources, and improve return on investment. How these same actions could also increase market share and profitability was previously examined in Chapter 1. To quote Feigenbaum: "Quality and cost are a sum, not a difference—complementary, not conflicting objectives."[22]

## MEASURING QUALITY COSTS

In a Conference Board survey of 149 large U.S. companies (96 manufacturing), it was found that 111 had a quality process or program. Of the 111 that had a program, 83 attempted to measure quality. The majority of the companies that attempted to measure quality costs compiled the information outside of the accounting system. The breakdown of cost categories reflected a major focus on the direct labor costs of scrap, rework, returns, and costs related to inventory including past-due receivables. There was little evidence to indicate that these costs, once collected, were used to manage processes leading to customer satisfaction quality. Rather, the systems appeared to resemble the traditional cost reduction syndrome discussed in Chapter 10.

A more recent survey by the Institute of Management Accountants found that 82 percent of respondents said their companies are currently involved in quality programs, but only 33 percent calculate the cost of quality. Of those that did, the estimate of quality costs as a percentage of revenues averaged about 6 to 10 percent.[23] This is probably on the very low side, but even if correct, the elimination of these costs would make a substantial improvement in the bottom line.

An effective cost of quality planning and control system should be directed toward the basic reason for quality improvement; that is, support of a differentiation strategy. Of course, if a company has not developed a strategy, it becomes difficult to identify those costs of quality that support differentiation of satisfaction in the minds of the customers. For a multidivision or multiproduct firm, this strategy may be different for each market segment or strategic business unit. There is little advantage to investing in equipment, overhead, or process improvements which do not add customer value. What is good for Neiman Marcus may not be good for KMart.

The cost of differentiation reflects the *cost drivers* of the value activities on which uniqueness is based.[24] Differentiation can also result from the coordination of linked value activities that may not add much cost but nevertheless provide a cost savings and a competitive edge when integrated.

The measurement and reporting of quality costs to facilitate these strategic demands need to be provided to users of the information in a form that aids in decision making. Thus, the measurement and reporting of costs of quality should meet the three-part need to (1) report quality costs, (2) identify activities where involvement is suggested, and (3) indicate interlinking activities.

Activities and functions are not independent. They form a system of interdependencies that are connected by linkages and relationships. For example, purchasing from a low-quality supplier may lead to redesign, rework, scrap, increased field service, and direct labor variance. These linkages are difficult to recognize and are often overlooked. Nor is the conventional accounting system equipped to separate the cost of quality in these linked activities. Virtually all accounting classifications group activities along functional lines and force the reporting of quality costs into several general expense categories such as salaries, depreciation, training, etc. Analyzing the accounts can produce limited estimates of quality costs, but unless the costs are designed into the system, they will be elusive for decisions and action planning.

As one of the steps in the design of a planning and control system, it is useful to identify those activities and linkages between activities where costs occur. Some form of linear or matrix organizational chart or table is useful for this purpose. Departments or activities are listed across the top and costs of quality down the left-hand side. A number (e.g., 1 for primary responsibility or 2 for coordinating responsibility) can be entered at the intersection of the cost of quality category and the activity or function involved. The chart will show overlap among activities and will therefore indicate the need for cooperation, interfunctional teams, and the like. A similar chart can be devised to present cost of quality by activity. Thus, quality costs can be presented based on both cost and activity responsibility, and this form of presentation is more likely to get the attention of top management.

A similar chart can be constructed for reporting the dollar costs of quality. The same format could be used for both budgeting and reporting. Costs can be tabulated by organization unit, by time, by cost of quality categories, or by product. Quality costs can also be normalized for volume by using one or more of the following measures: per direct labor hour, per direct labor cost, per dollar of standard manufacturing cost, per dollar of sales, or per equivalent unit of product.[25]

The most elusive category for reporting is the cost of lost opportunities, which is an external failure cost. These represent the impact of profit from lost revenues resulting from purchase of competitive products and services or from order cancellations due to customer requirements not being met. An additional problem is assigning these *estimated* costs to a quality project or action plan that may prevent recurrence. It is also elusive and difficult to compile the relationships among two or more costs that affect quality costs (i.e., prevention plus appraisal).[26]

The constant theme throughout a cost of quality system is that *costs are not incurred or allocated, but rather are caused.* Cost information does not solve quality problems, nor does it suggest specific solutions. Problems are solved by tracing the *cause* of a quality deficiency.

One manager, when asked about his quality, replied: "My quality's good, because I don't get complaints or returns." All this tells you is that what goes out the door is good. It doesn't tell you how much time you have to spend making it good. It doesn't tell you how much internal waste there is.

Some companies are using a cost-of-poor-quality report that attempts to compute the costs and bring them to everyone's attention as a basis for corrective action. One common method is to separate the quality expenses into *prevention, appraisal, internal failure, and external failure* categories. The goal is to discover how the company's time and money are spent.

One consultant suggests that if you can only look at one factor as a proxy for how effective your quality system is, you should look at how the quality assurance department personnel are spending their time. "What I see over and over again is QA departments 'fighting fires.' They're either dealing with external failures because there are customer complaints, or there are internal failures—scrap, rework, products failing their first-article inspections. It's very difficult to break that cycle."[27]

One useful method of reporting the impact of quality cost is the construction of one or more quality indices. The more common ones are

- **Labor index.**   Quality cost/labor hours
- **Cost index.**   Quality cost/manufacturing cost
- **Sales index.**   Quality cost/sales
- **Production index.**   Quality cost/units produced

**Table 11-1**   Quality Index Example

|  | 1994 | 1995 | 1996 | 1997 |
|---|---|---|---|---|
| **Quality costs** | | | | |
| Prevention | $27,000 | $41,500 | $74,600 | $112,300 |
| Appraisal | 155,000 | 122,500 | 113,400 | 107,000 |
| Internal failure | 386,400 | 469,200 | 347,800 | 219,100 |
| External failure | 242,000 | 196,000 | 103,500 | 106,000 |
| Total | $810,400 | $829,200 | $639,300 | $544,400 |
| **Accounting measures** | | | | |
| Sales | $4,360,000 | $4,450,000 | $5,050,000 | $5,190,000 |
| Manufacturing costs | 1,760,000 | 1,810,000 | 1,880,000 | 1,890,000 |

Examples of how such an index is constructed are shown in Tables 11-1 and 11-2.

## THE USE OF QUALITY COST INFORMATION[28]

Quality cost information can be used in a number of ways:

- To identify profit opportunities (every dollar saved goes to the bottom line)
- To make capital budgeting and other investment decisions (quality, as opposed to payback, is the driver of decisions to purchase new equipment or dispose of unneeded equipment; equipment for rework is not needed if the rework is eliminated or reduced)

**Table 11-2**   Quality Index

(Total quality costs $*$ 100)/sales
($810,400 $*$ 100)/4,360,000 = 18.58

|  | Quality index | |
|---|---|---|
| Year | Sales | Cost |
| 1994 | 18.58 | 46.04 |
| 1995 | 18.63 | 45.18 |
| 1996 | 12.66 | 34.00 |
| 1997 | 10.49 | 28.80 |

- To improve purchasing and supplier-related costs
- To identify waste in overhead caused by activities not required by the customer
- To identify redundant systems
- To determine whether quality costs are properly distributed
- To establish goals for budgets and profit planning
- To identify quality problems
- As a management tool for comparative measures of input–output relationships (e.g., the cost of a reliability effort versus warranty costs)
- As a tool of Pareto analysis (Chapter 6) to distinguish between the "vital few" and the "trivial many"
- As a strategic management tool to allocate resources for strategy formulation and implementation
- As an objective performance appraisal measure

General Electric's cost of quality system is increasingly emphasizing non-product features such as inquiry responsiveness, delivery times, and billing accuracy. The emphasis is on root cause analysis and process improvement: simplifying procedures and reducing cycle time and driving down quality costs while improving customer satisfaction. Internal and external systems measure performance versus customer expectations; these systems also track opportunities that have been lost by non-conformance to customer expectations.[29]

## ACCOUNTING SYSTEMS AND QUALITY MANAGEMENT[30]

The shortcomings of accounting information systems were outlined in a previous chapter, and opinions of experts who indicate that accounting information provides little help for reducing costs and improving quality and productivity were reported. The tendency is to *allocate* rather than manage costs. Moreover, the allocation is normally a function of direct labor, an item that has shrunk to 15 percent or less of manufacturing costs. Overhead, at about 55 percent, is spread across all products using the same formula. Accounting also cannot identify or account for the many non-dollar hidden costs of quality and productivity.

Critics claim that management accounting systems should be designed to support the operations and strategy of the company, two dimensions in which quality plays a dominant role. This is increasingly evident in the "new" manufacturing environment, sometimes known as advanced manufacturing technology, which is characterized by a number of emerging trends. These trends and their implications for quality management were summarized in Chapter 6. Some of the decision-making needs and how traditional accounting practices may fall short in meeting them are listed here:

| Decision needs | Traditional accounting |
| --- | --- |
| Activity management | Financial accounting |
| Investment management | Payback or ROI |
| Non-dollar measures | Dollar accounting |
| Process control | Cost allocation |
| Just-in-time | Inventory turn |
| Feedforward control | Historical control |

## ACTIVITY-BASED COSTING

The majority of companies that attempt to measure quality costs compile the information and statistics outside of the accounting system. These data are aggregated and do not reflect the true cost of quality or the activity in the process that is causing it. It is worth repeating that costs are not incurred or allocated; *they are caused*. The mere collection of data is of little use unless the data can help identify the drivers of quality costs so that problem identification leads to problem solution.

Activity-based costing (ABC), called "A Bean-Counter's Best Friend" by *Business Week,*[31] can be the system that promises to fill this gap.[32] ABC is a collection of financial and operation performance information that traces the significant activities of a firm to process, product, and quality costs. It is well suited to TQM because it encourages management to analyze activities and determine their value to the customer.

Imagine the case of a firm with excessive warranty costs. The following questions might arise: (1) What is the cost of the returns? (2) What is the cause of the returns and can the cause be traced to a specific activity? Is it the supplier, design, or one of the many activities in production? (3) How can the process(es) be improved to reduce the cost of returns? (4) What is the trade-off between cost of process revision and reduction of warranty costs? (5) What are the strategic implications? The concepts of ABC may lead to some answers.

The concepts of process control and activity analysis were described in Chapter 6 (Process Management) and Chapter 10 (Productivity, Quality, and Reengineering). ABC brings these interlinking concepts together through cross-functional analysis:

- **Process control** documents the process flow, identifies requirements of internal and external customers, defines outputs of each process step, and determines process input requirements.

- **Activity analysis** defines each activity within each process and identifies activities as value added or non-value added based on customer requirements.

Activity analysis applies to internal as well as external customers. When Rear Admiral John Kirkpatrick assumed command of the six U.S. Naval Aviation Depots, he inaugurated the use of TQM. One element of the system was that, wherever possible, the internal customer was allowed to demand only those internal products or services desired.[33] Could this be a logical extension of customer satisfaction? If it can be applied to external customers, why not internal customers as well?

The third step is to develop cause-and-effect relationships by identifying *drivers* of cost or quality. In the case of cost, the drivers are the conditions that create or "drive" the need for an activity and hence the resources consumed. If the cost driver relates to a non-value activity, it can be eliminated or reduced. It is estimated that 50 percent or more of the activities in most businesses are cost added rather than value added.[34]

ABC recognizes that activities, not products, consume resources, and process value analysis is needed to assign costs to the activities that use them. The system recognizes that costs are driven by factors other than volume or direct labor. In the case of product costing, the costs are assigned based on their consumption of activities such as order preparation, storage time, wait time, internal product movement, field maintenance, and design. The focus on the process, not the product, suggests a transition to breaking down the floor into smaller cost centers and identifying the cost drivers of each.

Cost drivers are agents that cause activity to happen. Consider an engineering change order (ECO) which causes many activities to occur, such as documentation, production schedule changes, purchase of a new machine, or change in a process. If the ECO is issued to correct excessive field maintenance costs, manufacturing will absorb additional charges, marketing's distribution costs will increase, and customer satisfaction may erode because of delays and field repairs. By using the ABC concept, the true cost of the affected product can be determined as well as its cross-functional impact on budgets and performance.

This ECO example illustrates the impact of engineering and design on product life cycle costs. Roughly 80 to 85 percent of a product's lifetime costs, including maintenance and repair expenses, are locked in at this stage. ABC might provide guidelines to help engineers design a product that meets customer expectations and can be produced and supported at a competitive cost.

## The Multiproduct Problem

■ At Rockwell International Corporation, a capital budgeting request for an $80,000 laser was denied because, at $4000 per year in labor savings, the payback would take 20 years. Further analysis showed that the process would be reduced from two weeks to ten minutes, moving shipments out faster and saving $200,000 a year in inventory holding costs.[35]

■ Tektronix, Inc. adopted ABC in a printed circuit board plant and found that one high-volume product drew on so many resources that it generated a negative margin of 46 percent and sapped profits from other products. These examples illustrate how "across the board" accounting *allocation* of costs, rather than *management* of costs, distorts the information required for good decision making.

There is great potential for inaccurate costing and control of multiproduct lines in a firm with a single overhead center, and inaccuracies in costing increase dramatically when allocation is achieved by direct labor, machine time, processing time, or some other "assignment" method. A major soft drink producer found that the costs of its array of brands varied as much as 400 percent from what traditional cost-accounting methods reported.

In summary, ABC decomposes activities, identifies the drivers of the activities, and provides measures so that costs can be traced to the activities that cause the cost.

## Strategic Planning and Activity-Based Costing

■ At a meeting of IBM's board of directors in November 1991, various restructuring proposals were considered. One option was to unburden the lines of business from general overhead expenses. For example, the company may remove from its personal computer business the burden of helping pay for research on mainframe computers. (This action was subsequently taken in 1992.)

There is a cost dimension to most strategic decisions. Product lines, channels, locations, brands, segmentation, and differentiation need to be identified, and each decision establishes a linkage between demands and spending on resources.

If costs are forecast on the arbitrary basis of some unit directly related to production, the real cost of a product or capital project may be made arbitrarily.[36] ABC can help reveal data for strategic decisions about which product lines to develop or abandon and which prices to increase or decrease. Tracing overhead to activities and then to products may also identify costs that do not contribute to quality and hence to differentiation.

ABC has leapfrogged traditional cost accounting, but it is a new and complicated system. For these reasons, the great majority of companies have not achieved a significant level of sophistication in its use. The basic concept of ABC is that costs of products and quality can be traced to the drivers of activities that consume the resources which *cause* these costs. Research reveals that there is widespread failure to compile the many prevention, appraisal, internal failure, and external failure costs that are "hidden" until identified by a cost of quality management system. If the costs are not identified, there is little chance of tracing them to the process or activity that is causing them. Only the "visible" rework, scrap, and repair/service costs are compiled by more than half of the respondents.

### Summary

Is a cost of quality program essential to a quality improvement effort? The answer may be no, but a firm cannot spend unlimited resources without regard for both strategic issues and the cost/benefit equation. Moreover, a cost of quality effort is but one of a system of interlinking efforts that comprise a management philosophy of TQM.

## QUESTIONS FOR DISCUSSION

**11-1**  Select a firm (restaurant, hotel, airline, manufacturer) and list several costs related to quality failure. Estimate these costs.

**11-2**  What is the estimated cost of poor quality in U.S. industry?

**11-3**  What is the justification for Philip Crosby's claim that "Quality Is Free"?

**11-4**  Illustrate each of the four types of costs of quality.

**11-5**  Why should prevention costs take precedence over the other three classifications?

**11-6**  What are the benefits of a cost of quality measuring system?

# ENDNOTES

1.  Avigdor Zonnenshain, Eitan Naveh, and Avner Halevyh, "A Survey of the Cost of Nonquality to a Nation's Economy: The Israeli Experience," *Quality Progress,* Oct. 1998, pp. 93–97.
2.  "Calculating Your CPQ," *Quality,* Oct. 1998, p. 39.
3.  Doug Anderson, "How to Use Cost of Quality Data," in *Global Perspectives on Total Quality,* New York: The Conference Board, 1991, p. 37.
4.  John F. Towey, "Information Please: What Are Quality Costs?" *Management Accounting,* March 1988, p. 40. Apparently this is a quasi-official definition adopted by the National Association of Accountants.
5.  Roger G. Schroeder, *Operations Management,* New York: McGraw-Hill, 1989, p. 586.
6.  J. M. Asher, "Cost of Quality in Service Industries," *International Journal of Quality & Reliability Management (UK),* Vol. 5 Issue 5, 1988, pp. 38–46.
7.  David Shaffer and Walter Dulaney, "IT Desktop Meltdown: The Next Crisis," *Chief Executive,* Oct. 1998, pp. 8–10.
8.  Lakshmi Tatikonca and J. Rao, "Measuring and Reporting the Cost of Quality," *Production & Inventory Management Journal,* Second Quarter 1996, pp. 1–7.
9.  Debra Walker, "Supply Chain Collaboration Saves Chrysler $2.5 Billion," *Automatic I.D. News,* Aug. 1998, p. 60.
10. William Band, "Marketers Need to Understand the High Cost of Poor Quality," *Sales & Marketing Management in Canada,* Nov. 1989, pp. 56–59.
11. Ned Hamson, "TQM Can Save Nearly $300 Billion for Nation," *Journal for Quality and Participation,* Dec. 1990, pp. 54–56. This potential is reflected in the quality improvement potential (QIP) index.
12. Armand V. Feigenbaum, "The Criticality of Quality and the Need to Measure It," *Financier,* Oct. 1990, pp. 33–36. This estimate reflects a national (QIP) index for the gross national product. Feigenbaum is president and chief executive officer of General Systems Company, Inc., which installs company-wide quality systems in manufacturing and service organizations.
13. Financial managers estimate the cost at 25 to 30 percent of sales. See Garrett DeYoung, "Does Quality Pay?" *CFO: The Magazine for Chief Financial Officers,* Sept. 1990, pp. 24–34. See also Lester Ravitz, "The Cost of Quality: A Different Approach to Noninterest Expenses," *Financial Manager's Statement,* March/April 1991, pp. 8–13. A 1990 study of quality in North American banks found that non-quality cost related to unnecessary rework and related factors represented 20 to 25 percent of a bank's operating budget. In Britain, the United Kingdom Institute of Management Services estimates that the cost of quality non-conformance amounts to 25 to 30 percent of sales. See John Heap and Lord Chilver, "Total Quality Management," *Management Services (UK),* June 1990, pp. 6–10.
14. J. M. Juran, Ed., *Quality Control Handbook,* New York: McGraw-Hill, 1951.
15. Armand V. Feigenbaum, *Total Quality Control,* New York: McGraw-Hill, 1961.
16. Philip Crosby, *Quality Is Free,* New York: McGraw-Hill, 1979.
17. An excellent discussion of these categories is contained in David A. Garvin, *Managing Quality,* New York: The Free Press, 1988, pp. 78–80.

18. Thomas N. Tyson, "Quality & Profitability: Have Controllers Made the Connection?" *Management Accounting,* Nov. 1987, pp. 38–42.

19. Taken from a promotional brochure by Philip Crosby Associates, Inc. of Winter Park, Florida.

20. The British Science and Engineering Research Council funded a study on quality-related costs as part of a two-year study. A literature review showed the domination of the prevention–appraisal–failure classification, a preoccupation with in-house costs, and little regard for supplier and customer-related costs. See J. J. Plunkett and B. G. Dale, "A Review of the Literature on Quality-Related Costs," *International Journal of Quality & Reliability Management (UK),* Vol. 4 Issue 1, 1987, pp. 40–52. This classification can also apply to non-manufacturing areas. Xerox is one firm that has implemented a well-defined quality program aimed at achieving quality in non-manufacturing services. A model was developed to illustrate the costs of quality based on the prevention–appraisal–failure classification. See Michael Desjardins, "Managing for Quality," *Business Quarterly (Canada),* Autumn 1989, pp. 103–107.

21. As quoted in David A. Garvin, *Managing Quality,* New York: The Free Press, 1988, p. 79.

22. Armand V. Feigenbaum, "Linking Quality Processes to International Leadership," in *Making Total Quality Happen,* New York: The Conference Board, 1990, p. 6.

23. "The Cost of Quality," *IIE Solutions,* Sept. 1996, p. 9.

24. Michael E. Porter, *Competitive Advantage,* New York: The Free Press, 1985, pp. 127–130. Although Porter does not address the specifics of cost of quality, his discussion of differentiation costs provides an excellent dimension to the topic.

25. For more detailed information on methods of compiling quality cost information, see Wayne J. Morse, Harold P. Roth, and Kay M. Poston, *Measuring, Planning, and Controlling Quality Costs,* Montvale, N.J.: National Association of Accountants, 1987. This National Association of Accountants research study provides a number of actual reporting formats used by responding companies in the survey. For the collection and reporting formats used by ITT and Xerox, see Francis J. Walsh, Jr., *Current Practices in Measuring Quality,* New York: The Conference Board, 1989 (Conference Board Research Bulletin).

26. James T. Godfrey and William R. Pasewark, "Controlling Quality Costs," *Management Accounting,* March 1988, pp. 48–51.

27. Nancy Chase, "Accounting for Quality: Counting Costs, Reaping Returns," *Quality,* Oct. 1998, pp. 38–42.

28. For sources of information regarding the use of cost of quality information, see John F. Towey, "Why Quality Costs Are Important," *Management Accounting,* March 1988, p. 40. See also James M. Reeve, "TQM and Cost Management: New Definitions for Cost Accounting," *Survey of Business,* Summer 1989, pp. 26–30; J. J. Plunkett and B. G. Dale, "A Review of the Literature on Quality-Related Costs," *International Journal of Quality & Reliability Management (UK),* Vol. 4 Issue 1, 1987, pp. 40–52; John J. Heldt, "Quality Pays," *Quality,* Nov. 1988, pp. 26–28.

29. Elyse Allan, "Measuring Quality Costs: A Shifting Perspective," in *Global Perspectives on Total Quality,* New York: The Conference Board, 1991, p. 35 (Conference Board Report Number 958).

30. H. Thomas Johnson and Robert Kaplan, *Relevance Lost: The Rise and Fall of Management Accounting,* Boston: Harvard Business School Press, 1991. Peat Marwick, one of

the Big Six accounting firms, scored a major coup by signing Kaplan to an exclusive contract in the field of activity-based cost accounting. See "A Bean-Counter's Best Friend," *Business Week/Quality 1991* (special bonus issue entitled "The Quality Imperative: What It Takes to Win in the Global Economy," Oct. 25, 1991).

31.  "A Bean-Counter's Best Friend," *Business Week*, Oct. 25, 1991, pp. 42–43 (special bonus issue entitled "The Quality Imperative: What It Takes to Win in the Global Economy").

32.  Because ABC is relatively new, there is no widespread treatment of it in the literature. Perhaps the best source of information, at least from the accountant's point of view, is *Management Accounting*. See, for example, Thomas E. Steimer, "Activity-Based Accounting for Total Quality, *Management Accounting*, Oct. 1990, pp. 39–42. See also Michael R. Ostrenga, "Activities: The Focal Point of Total Cost Management," *Management Accounting*, Feb. 1990, pp. 42–49; Norm Raffish, "How Much Does that Product Really Cost?" *Management Accounting*, March 1991, pp. 36–39. For a managerial perspective, it is suggested that a literature search be conducted for recent writings of Robert Kaplan.

33.  Michael D. Woods, "How We Changed Our Accounting," *Management Accounting*, Feb. 1989, pp. 42–45.

34.  Michael J. Stickler, "Going for the Globe. Part II: Eliminating Waste," *Production & Inventory Management Review and APICS News*, Nov. 1989, pp. 32–34.

35.  "The Productivity Paradox," *Business Week*, June 6, 1988, p. 104.

36.  Bernard C. Reimann, "Robert S. Kaplan: The ABCs of Accounting for Value Creation," *Planning Review*, July/Aug. 1990, pp. 33–34. The author reports Kaplan's contention that the "essence of strategy" is to regard all overhead expenses as variable and driven by something other than the number of units. Also, financial reporting is fine for reporting bottom-line financial performance but inadequate for strategic decisions.

## ARMSTRONG WORLD INDUSTRIES TRACKS COST OF QUALITY

At Armstrong World Industries' Building Products Operations (BPO), quality is a thing of the past. Even more clearly, however, it is the thing in BPO's present and future. Upholding a commitment to quality made more than a century ago by its corporate founder, the manufacturer of acoustical ceilings and wall panels is aligning every facet of its business with the exhaustively researched product and service requirements of its customers.

More than 250 improvement teams are operating at any given time, with the objectives ranging from correcting specific operational problems to improving key business processes that enhance the entire organization. At each of seven manufacturing plants, the quality improvement team, led by the plant's top manager, is required to develop specific action plans and set goals that will have a measurable impact on one or more of BPO's five "key business drivers": customer satisfaction, sales growth, operating profits, asset management, and high-performance organization (human resource capabilities.) Tracking "cost of quality" is common to many of these actions.

Since 1991, BPO's "cost of quality"—the company's composite indicator of the price it pays as a result of waste and non-conformance—has dropped by 37 percent, contributing $16 million in additional operating profit in 1994 alone. In 1994 overall, operating costs were reduced by $40 million while maintaining or increasing share in each of its markets.

*The following case study demonstrates how the costs of quality can be traced and reported through an activity-based approach. The purposes of the study were to make management aware of the magnitude of these costs and to provide a baseline from which continuous improvement could be measured.*

# COST-OF-QUALITY REPORTING: HOW WE SEE IT

## Richard K. Youde

Since its founding in 1979, Sola Optical, a manufacturer of ophthalmic spectacle lenses in Petaluna, Calif., has enjoyed rapid and continued growth. While management always had focused on maintaining high levels of product quality and customer service, it had no real understanding of the costs of achieving these goals nor of the opportunities for improvement. Instead, management relied on and gave credibility to traditional financial reporting and cost accounting systems because sales and profits continued to grow.

Three years ago, Sola Optical was given responsibility for the spectacle lens division of a newly acquired business. The integration of additional product lines and three geographically diverse manufacturing plants, along with the doubling of sales volume and the number of employees, added new complexity to the running of the business. Management's attention was focused on the integration process and the bottom line pressures brought with it.

Through this period, management and employees began to think about the application of world-class manufacturing (WCM) concepts such as total quality management (TQM), just-in-time (JIT) manufacturing, quality function deployment, and activity-based costing. While the company had little direct experience

Reprinted with permission from *Management Accounting,* January 1992, pp. 34–38. Copyright 1992 by Institute of Management Accountants, Montvale, N.J. 07645.

with the WCM concepts, many employees had been exposed to them through trade journals and seminars.

The company had no previous exposure to cost of (poor) quality reporting, but through the process of implementing WCM it developed a powerful new approach to cost-of-quality reporting that had a positive impact.

## TQM/JIT Implementation

Management's interest in world-class manufacturing concepts led to the hiring of a consultant to help establish an approach for its implementation. The work included development of a TQM/JIT execution plan and the calculation of cost of quality (COQ) for the divisional headquarters site, which included the division's largest factory and all marketing, administrative, and engineering support. Sola Optical's financial results, shown in Figure 1, are typical of U.S. manufacturing companies before implementing TQM, showing 20% of sales dollars being consumed by poor quality.

Management accepted the consultant's proposal for implementing Total Quality Management and Just-in-Time techniques including:

- Establishment of a TQM steering committee to oversee the implementation,
- Creation of a dedicated cross-functional TQM resource staff as a new organizational entity,
- Formation of four pilot TQM teams, and
- Contracting for the consultant's services to get the project started.

The total quality management effort initially was focused on operational effectiveness. The steering committee included the divisional president, his

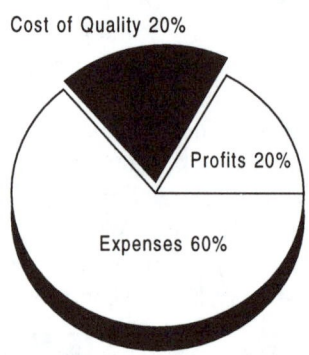

**Figure 1**   Distribution of Revenue

reporting staff, senior manufacturing managers, and TQM resource staff members who were drawn from manufacturing, marketing, quality control, research and development, and finance. The resource staff was given a charter to facilitate the implementation of TQM/JIT within Sola.

Four pilot projects with the greatest opportunity for savings were selected from the manufacturing area, and each one involved improving process yields and product quality. In a dual-track implementation role, the consulting personnel concurrently facilitated quality improvement teams, beginning with the four pilot teams, and provided training to Sola employees in TQM/JIT techniques. Special emphasis was placed on coaching the TQM resource staff who quickly assumed the responsibility of quality improvement teams.

To begin the process of cultural change, management decided to provide TQM and JIT overview training to a large number of employees. Overview/introduction classes totaling 20 hours were given to nearly every employee over a period of six months.

The pilot teams and TQM resource staff were successful, and more teams were formed in manufacturing, distribution, and administrative areas. The new teams were assisted by the consultant and TQM resource staff associates. Members often worked in areas of interest to the individual team members, however, and were not focused in the areas known to offer the most opportunity for savings. In retrospect, it was clear that many teams needed better direction, which could have been provided by better cost-of-quality information.

## Classic Cost of Quality

The initial COQ study prepared by the consultants used the classic approach and identified, through interviews with operating and financial managers and employees, costs of (poor) quality and classified them into four categories: prevention, appraisal, internal failure, and external failure.* The purpose of the COQ report was to make management aware of the magnitude of the cost and to provide a baseline against which the impact of future continuous improvement activities could be gauged.

The report demonstrated that relatively few dollars were spent on defect prevention, that appraisal costs were high (because our quality control department used final inspection to assure only good products were transferred to inventory), and that internal failure costs were extremely high. External failure costs were shown to be quite low, attributed to the high level of quality inspections performed and the corresponding high appraisal costs.

---

* Wayne Morse, Harold Roth, and Kay Poston, *Measuring, Planning, and Controlling Quality Costs,* Institute of Management Accountants, Montvale, N.J., 1987.

TQM teaches that dollars spent in preventive activities such as designing product for manufacturability, training, and development of procedures will be recovered manyfold through reduced appraisal and failure costs. By measuring over time the relative costs of prevention, appraisal, internal and external failure, management can observe whether continuous improvement activities are paying off.

## Cost-of-Quality Study

The COQ study was successful in alerting management to the magnitude of the costs and was a reasonable baseline against which to measure future performance for the site as a whole. It did not suggest specific actions that individual managers and employees could take to make improvements. Therefore, quality improvement teams did not have the information necessary to focus on the most important problems.

The lack of focus by some quality improvement teams contributed to loss of interest in the process by some employees and frustration of both management and quality improvement team members at the slow progress toward achieving real quality improvements.

## Activity-Based Approach

A method had to be devised to ensure that operating managers and quality improvement teams were focusing their activities appropriately in order to assure the success of the TQM/JIT implementation effort. Gaining management's attention and commitment is a basic requirement of world-class manufacturing concepts. Management initially supported the implementation of TQM/JIT and accepted the original cost-of-quality figures. A way was needed, however, to get its buy-in and support of specific quality improvement activities.

One of the limitations of traditional COQ reporting is its failure to associate costs with activities. Activity-based costing has shown that costs cannot be controlled. Rather, one must control activities that in turn cause costs. Relating quality costs to activities greatly enhances the usefulness of the cost-of-quality report.

The solution, in terms of cost-of-quality reporting, lies in applying techniques from world-class manufacturing, such as activity-based costing, JIT and TQM, to the development of quality costs. TQM provides simple statistical tools, such as run sheets and Pareto charts, identifying the most important problems. An activity-based cost-of-quality report works like a Pareto analysis, showing the relative costs of the most important quality-related problems along with the respective cost drivers. JIT is a philosophy promoting the elimination of waste.

Quality failures and all the activities surrounding them fall within the definition of waste.

## The Ripple Effect and Ripple Costs

At Sola Optical, we focus on "failures" in COQ reporting because we want to improve the activities that lead to failures, the major contributor to cost of quality. Besides the direct cost of failures, such as the cost of rejected product, we wanted to show the complexity the failure itself added to our processes. Thus, we coined the term "ripple effect," defined as the activities resulting from a real or potential failure. For example, the resources consumed reworking a defective product constitute the ripple effect, as do the activities associated with inspecting a product even when no defect actually exists. We also include in the cost of quality the "ripple cost" (costs of the ripple effect). Results of interviews with managers, supervisors, leads, and workers identified ripple effects of returned goods (see Figure 2).

An analysis of the chart shows that credit memos issued for customer returns result in lost gross profit on the sale. Shown next are the steps in returned goods processing (RGA processing), beginning with the receiving department, followed by the returned goods department and warehouse, and ending with the activities associated with issuing a credit memo. When large returns occur, the very complex production and inventory planning cycle is disrupted because of unplanned inventory. Finally, the chart reminds readers that there is a cost to the customer as well.

Inclusion of the ripple effect charts in the COQ report provides readers with a better understanding of their operations. The use of these charts is a powerful tool, drawing attention to opportunities for improvement. Incorporating the ripple costs, along with the direct cost of failures, in the COQ provides the same effect.

## Developing an Activity-Based COQ Report

We identified eight steps (see Table 1) in developing an activity-based COQ report.

1. **Identify cost and service problem areas:** The first step in developing an activity-based COQ report is to identify the most important cost- or service-related problems. At Sola Optical, the division president and representatives from marketing, manufacturing, materials, accounting, management information systems, and customer service were asked to identify the five most important problems/opportunities in terms of costs or customer satisfaction. Then a review of the initial COQ report, prepared by the consultants, was

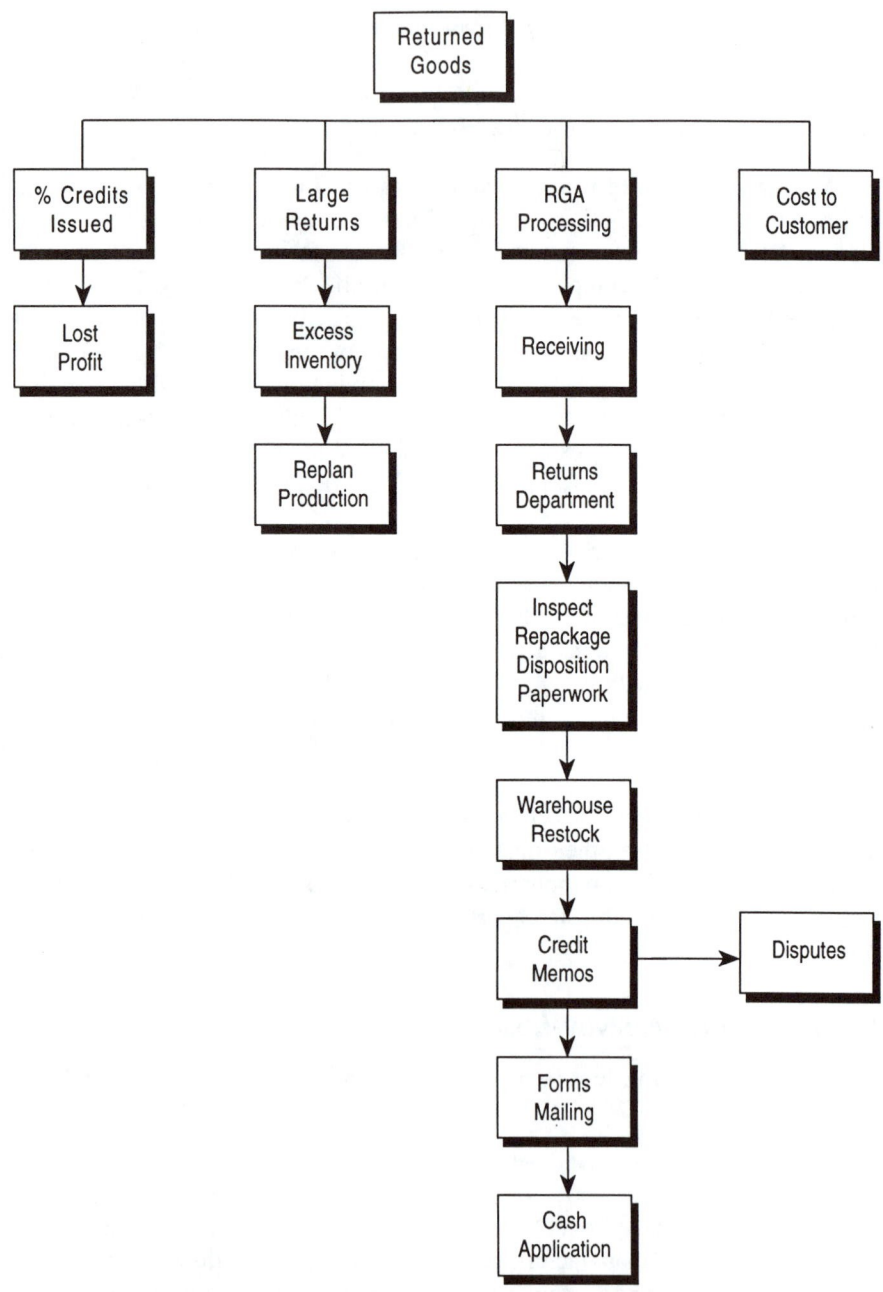

**Figure 2**   Ripple Effect of Returned Goods

**Table 1**  Steps in Developing an Activity-
Based Cost of Quality Report

- Identify cost and service problem areas.
- Summarize problems to a manageable list.
- Identify ripple effects.
- Calculate ripple costs.
- Condense the list again.
- Summarize information for presentation.
- Review with managers and steering committee.
- Publish and present to employees.

conducted to assure no important costs included in it were omitted from the list.

The list was edited to eliminate any ideas that were not related to COQ. For example, one interviewee had identified the need for employee development. But this was considered inappropriate for this purpose.

2. **Condense problems to manageable list:**  The list was summarized and ranked according to the number of responses for each idea. Then a condensed list of ideas was developed based on the number of responses and knowledge of costs and cost of quality. The ideas that remained on the list after this step were those for which data could be collected and for which the cost of quality would be high enough to warrant further consideration.

Some ideas were judged too impractical to include. For example, the cost associated with inaccurate finished goods' inventory records was dropped because of the difficulty in quantifying the costs.

Next, ripple charts were prepared and reviewed with the original interviewees to ensure their accuracy. Changes were incorporated into a final copy of the ripple chart.

3. **Calculate ripple costs:**  Several principles guided the development of costs, especially ripple costs. First, it is important to recognize that the intent of COQ reporting is to provide reasonably accurate information for use in allocating resources, not to develop a complex cost accounting system. The purpose of measurement is to tell the organization whether it is heading in the right direction.

Second, the information needs to be absolutely credible. At Sola, we wanted to avoid challenges to the whole process based on disagreements over minor elements of cost. The approach taken was to include only costs that were easily supportable. Not all ripple activities shown on the ripple charts are included in the cost. The reported cost of quality, therefore, is the minimum, and is in fact understated. But employees can recognize that the ripple chart includes other activities that contribute to cost and system complexity.

Finally, we wanted to make monthly reporting very simple. Costs that are readily available, such as the direct cost of rejected product, would be included as calculated. Costs that are not readily available, particularly those combining cross-functional activities, would be estimated on a per occurrence basis. When monthly COQ reports are prepared only the actual number of occurrences need to be collected. Calculations then are based on the per occurrence cost.

The development of yield-loss costs serves as a good example of this process. Yield loss represents the costs associated with product rejected. The direct cost of product rejected was taken from the cost accounting system and broken down by the major production processes. The cost of one major ripple effect, the quality control department (i.e., inspection), also was available from the accounting system.

The remaining ripple costs, which included disposing of product reject, record keeping, and production costs caused by a higher level of starts, were estimated on a per reject basis. The estimated costs of these activities over a six-month period were divided by the number of reject lenses produced for the same period. Ripple costs for the six areas were calculated by the same methodology.

4. **Condense the list again:** It may be necessary to condense the list again if the total costs of any of the potential areas are not significant enough to be included in the report. At Sola Optical, it was our original intent to identify 10 of the most significant COQ areas (more would tend to de-focus management attention). At this point, our list was condensed to six: yield loss (defective product), mold (tooling) loss, employee turnover, injuries, finished goods stockouts, and customer returns. Two other cost areas, excess finished goods' inventory and machine downtime, looked like strong candidates for inclusion but required more research.

5. **Summarize information for presentation:** The goal of COQ reporting is to present concise, usable information. Presenting too much detail is a sure way to lose the interest of the audience. It is the responsibility of quality improvement teams to develop and present their own detailed information.

The sequence of presentation should be adapted to the business culture. At Sola Optical, we chose to present overall costs first—shown in total, then annualized as percent of sales and as a cost per employee—followed by the individual COQ areas. Figure 3 shows an example of the total costs chart.

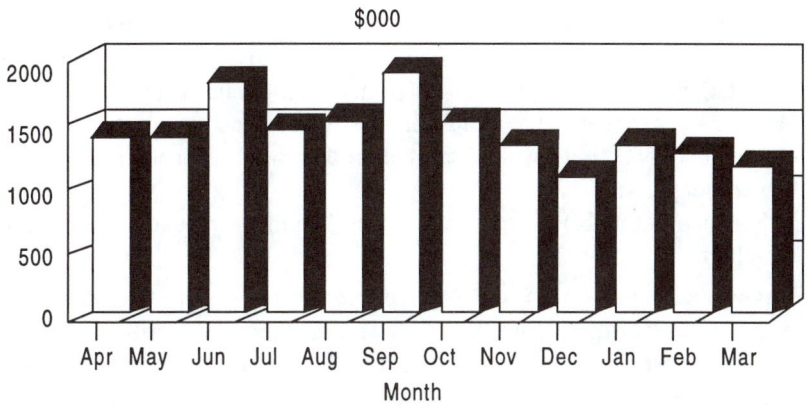

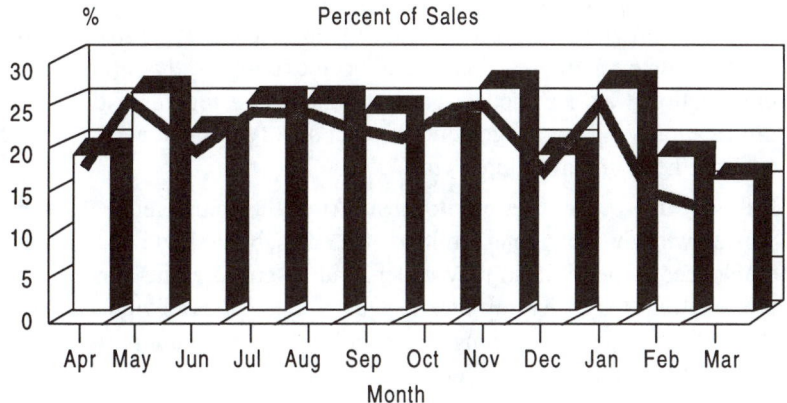

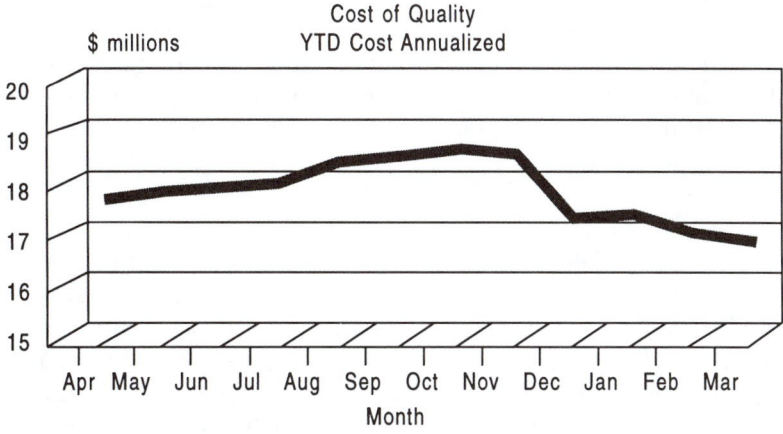

**Figure 3**  Total Cost of Quality

Individual COQ area costs then are shown together on similarly scaled graphs so that relative value of the costs is obvious. Then charts for each of the COQ areas along with their respective ripple charts are presented. For each area, the total cost per month, annualized cost, percent of the appropriate overall level of activity such as sales or production value, and the activity cost driver are shown.

For each of the COQ areas, costs are broken into direct and ripple costs on the chart.

6. **Review with managers and steering committee:** The first presentation was reviewed with key managers whose acceptance was critical to the success of the whole reporting process. If at this late date any information was to be challenged, it was better to resolve the problem individually than have the validity of the data undercut in a formal presentation.

   The next step was to present the COQ report to the TQM steering committee, whose key members already had been exposed to the information. This presentation was designed to generate discussion regarding the use of the information so that management, through quality improvement teams, could address these important problems.

7. **Publish and present to employees:** After the initial report has been reviewed with the steering committee, it is advisable to review it with as many employees as possible so they understand its purpose and contents. Formal presentations to quality improvement teams and to the individual departments within the organization, along with regularly distributed reports, were methods used to improve employee understanding.

8. **Continuously improve the report:** The COQ report is an ever-changing and improving report based on the needs of the company. As quality improvement teams achieve cost reductions, the specific cost areas being measured will change. There is a continuing need to ensure resources are being applied to the most important problems. The entire process described here should be completed each year to ensure the best information is being provided.

## A Powerful Tool

At Sola Optical, the activity-based cost-of-quality report is a powerful tool for managing quality improvement activities. Quality improvement teams are focused in the most important areas with the ripple effect concept being key to this method. Combining cross-functional costs caused by a quality failure into a single metric provides management the information needed to evaluate each type of failure relative to others and focus resources on the most important problems. The activity-based cost-of-quality approach can be applied easily in any business environment.

## Questions for Discussion

1  The article states that by relating quality costs to activities, the usefulness of the cost-of-quality report is improved. Explain why this is true and why it might improve the frustration resulting from the original cost-of-quality study.

2  Figure 2 demonstrates the "ripple effect" of returned goods. Explain why returned goods would result in costs related to disputes, excess inventory, production planning, and cash application. What additional costs not shown (e.g., redesign) might be involved?

3  Identify some cost-of-quality data that may be available from accounting records and some that are not. What is the danger of using accounting data? What role should the accounting department play in reducing cost-of-quality?

4  Choose a company or organization with which you are familiar. Refer to Figure 11-1 in the text and identify those costs that result from defects and returns. What is your estimate of the cost as a percentage of sales?

## CONTROLS AND CREATIVITY IN ORGANIZATIONS

**A. D. Amar**

To excel one needs freedom—an unbounded mind—and efficacy to do whatever one commits to do. The same is also true in an organizational setting. However, because management wants to assure that employees' ambitions concur with the organization's goals, it introduces checks and corrective actions, which we know as management controls. With the basic function of assuring compliance of work activity with the set goals, management controls are built into all stages of the firm's processes. Further, as an organization grows, management enhances and adds controls in an attempt to increase its sense of understanding of the organization. This is how eventually every aspect of the organization comes under control. The emphasis on compliance takes priority over creativity and innovation. It results in an environment that impedes change, becomes antagonistic to productivity, and becomes a ubiquitous obstacle to excellence. A large part of the organizational effort is allocated to taking care of the mundane—i.e., the organization continues to transact its business in the usual way and operates in control of all subfunctions. Performance criteria are set based on how well one works within constraints of the control. There is little emphasis on how efficiently or effectively the organization is executing its underlined function and, more than anything else, how well it is working to enhance these functions for the future.

Corporate organizational theory accepts that control is a management function, but for the greater good of encouraging innovation in contemporary organizations, it needs to be evaluated very carefully. It is somewhat ironic that organizations that thrive on innovation are more likely to fail in the presence of most of the traditional management controls than due to their lack. Theory has simply not kept pace with the practicalities of organizational change!

The obvious question is how to control or manage organizations while permitting growth and creativity.

Reprinted from *The Mid-Atlantic Journal of Business,* Vol. 34 Issue 3, June 1998, pp. 97–99, with permission of Seton Hall University, South Orange, New Jersey.

The answer to the above may lie in understanding work ethics and controls regulating those who are accomplished innovators. How were they controlled? What kinds of controls were most successful? How can we emulate these controls in an organization that hopes to germinate innovation?

In pursuit of an answer to the above we may start with transformational leaders. In an organization, these leaders include the top officers, such as the chief executive officer, chief operating officer, and some other top corporate managers. We should study the controls that regulated their behavior and gave them their work ethic, which resulted in organizational creativity, not at the expense of but to the credit of the organization.

It is often said that, typically, organizations exempt their top officers from general management controls. Organizations have one set of controls regulating top management and another regulating the rest of the employees. Organizations defend such a practice because they believe that imposition of general controls on top managers will impede effective functioning in their positions. However, the fact remains that controls hinder creativity at all levels. The difference may be dictated by what a corporation has determined to be more important, innovation or control.

It is not that the work behavior of top managers is not controlled at all. Without some type of control, they would not be able to attain the successes they actually do. However, the source of these controls is different. Understanding these controls and their underpinnings may unlock the secret to turning any organization into an innovation organization. These innovation controls may then be emulated for everyone. These are the controls that actually work. All organizations will require them since success in the future will only come through innovation emanating from all levels of the organization. The future will require creative approaches to solving all kinds of problems that organizations will face. In fact, organizations will need each member of their workforce—not just the leaders—to be innovators. This was the conundrum that Eastern European governments failed to recognize and was the chief flaw of the command-and-control system.

The new controls should focus on turning ordinarily externally controlled workers into those who feel that they are in control of their work and their work environment. The source of the new controls should be shifted from externally imposed to internally directed. Organizations should make sure that management controls do not set any one course as the course to be taken, or even convey the notion that there is one best or recommended course to be taken. The new controls should be designed based on the theme that the correct response, given a time and a situation, could be best determined only by the person who is handling the situation. Its corollary is that no one else knows exactly what to do in this case or can provide close supervision or guidance in securing effective solutions to problems. Management's sense of insecurity and/or its distrust of its employees should not be used as a guide in designing controls. If such a situation actually does exist, then that may signal a different problem that management must address separately.

The basic assumption about controls for the new work environment is that an organization will be better off without any of the management controls practiced during the twentieth century. Requirements to excel in the uncertain future environment will require totally different kinds of controls than those we have already known and which have been exercised. The challenge will be to find ways to gain operational effect of the controls without actually having to impose them overtly on employees. Any control that employees find hindering their functioning should be considered unfit for anyone in an innovation organization. The key will be to meet the desire for organizational control and function with the absolute necessity of innovation!

# FOR FURTHER READING

Chase, Nancy, "Accounting for Quality: Counting Costs, Reaping Returns," *Quality,* Oct. 1998, pp. 38–42.

Cokins, Gary, "Why Is Traditional Accounting Failing Managers?" *Hospital Material Management,* Nov. 1998, pp. 72–80.

Demmy, Steve and John Talbott, "Improve Internal Reporting with ABC and TOC," *Management Accounting,* Nov. 1998, pp. 18–24.

Rust, Kathleen G., "Measuring the Costs of Quality," *Management Accounting,* Aug. 1995, pp. 33–37.

Velocci, Anthony L., Jr., "Cost of Quality an Industry Challenge," *Aviation Week & Space Technology,* Nov. 16, 1998, p. 58.

# 12

# ISO 9000 AND ISO 14000: UNIVERSAL STANDARDS OF QUALITY

*Companies can comply with Europe's standards—or stay home*
*Business Week*

International standards had their origin in World War II when military allies needed to adopt some common units of measure and product specifications for munitions, vehicles, and military hardware. These later became known as MilSpecs. Even today, many standards are the descendants of these early standards. Industry followed the lead of the military, but industries in each country developed their own standards, and the result was incompatibility across boundaries.

With the exception of ISO 9000 and ISO 14000, the majority of ISO standards are highly specifically documented agreements that contain technical specifications of other precise criteria to be used consistently as rules, guidelines, or definitions of characteristics to ensure that material, products, processes, and services are fit for their purposes. The focus is on the product, and before ISO 9000 and ISO 14000, the ISO standards were principally of concern to engineers and other technical specialists. For example, standards for items such as bolts, nuts, screws, pins, and rivets are essential to keep products from falling apart but are of interest primarily to technical personnel.

The science of quality control emerged as the technique to ensure that standards were met, and the technique was confined almost exclusively to manufacturing. During the 1970s and 1980s, quality control evolved from reactive (inspection-dominant) to proactive (system-oriented) organizations.[1] The focus changed the end result (the product) to the process by which it was produced. The theory behind this change was that if the process used to produce the product was developed and maintained properly, the product would be consistent and the quality could be improved. This, of course, is one of the main tenets of total quality management (TQM) as described in this book. Now we have the opportunity to advance the theory even further by assimilating the practices of reengineering and the theory of constraints, which take all processes and integrate them into a system of processes.

In the ISO system, standards are developed by national delegations of experts from business, government, and other relevant organizations. They are chosen by national standards institutes participating in a specific technical committee and are required to present a consensus position based on the views of stakeholders in their countries. In 1979, a new ISO technical committee was approved: ISO/TC 176, Quality Management and Quality Assurance.[2] Today, the number of countries participating in ISO/TC 176 is more than 50.

The new committee set to work and in 1986 had completed its first published standards, known as the ISO Series 9000. Ten years later, ISO Series 14000 was published.

ISO 9000 and ISO 14000 are known as *generic management system standards* and are therefore not specific to a particular product, material, or process. Generic means that the same standards can be applied to any organization, large or small, regardless of its product—even if its "product" is actually a service— in any sector of activity and regardless of whether the organization is a business enterprise, a non-profit organization, or a government department.

ISO defines the management system as what the organization does to manage its processes or activities. To be really efficient and effective, the organization can manage its way of doing things by systematizing it. This ensures that nothing important is left out and that everyone is clear about who is responsible for doing what, when, how, why, and where. *Management system standards* provide the organization with a model to follow in setting up and operating the management system. ISO's management system standards make successful practices available to all organizations.

"Simply put, ISO 9000 has come to be the price of admission for doing business in Europe," says Robert Caine, president of the American Society for Quality Control (ASQC). "Ask any business person who has given up trying to gain entry into the European market what stopped him, and he's likely to answer in code: ISO 9000," concludes Kymberly Hockman of Du Pont's Quality Management and Technology Center. These are among the many experts who are urging U.S. firms to take the ISO Series standards seriously.

Even if a firm does not do business in Europe or does not plan to do so, it should not ignore this accelerating movement to international standards. As will be discussed, the movement is expanding into other areas of the world and into many areas of the U.S. public and private sectors as well.

ISO 9000 is a set of five worldwide standards that establish requirements for the management of quality. Unlike *product* standards, these standards are for *quality management systems.* They are being used by the 12-nation European Economic Community to provide a universal framework for quality assurance—primarily through a system of internal and external audits. The purpose is to ensure that a certified company has a quality system in place that will enable it to meet its published quality standards. The ISO standards are generic in that they apply to all functions and all industries, from banking to chemical manufacturing. They have been described as the "one-size-fits-all" standards.

## ISO AROUND THE WORLD

*It is difficult to see how you could run your business*
*without addressing the management aspects covered by ISO 9000.*

Dr. John Symonds
European-based consultant for EHSQ, Mobil

*We find ISO 9000 a very useful way to ensure*
*the entire orchestra is working from the same arrangement.*

Murray Duffin, Director TQM
SGS–Thomson Microelectronics France–Italy

*ISO 9000 is the foundation from which*
*all future quality initiatives have been developed.*

Tony Curley
Group Internal Controller, TNT, U.K.

*Each dollar invested generates*
*at least a four-fold return if the standard is implemented well.*

Robert Dore, Coordinator for Service Quality
Municipality of Saint-Augustin-de-Desmaures, Canada

The above quotes from international managers are among the many testimonials promoting the benefits of ISO 9000 certification.[3] On January 1, 1993, the European Community (EC) became the largest trading partner of the United States. More than half of the $100 billion in U.S. exports is affected by ISO 9000 standards. In Europe, more than 70,000 sites are registered for the series, which means that ISO 9000 certification is becoming like a passport or visa.

The EC consists of 12 member nations: Belgium, Denmark, France, Germany, Greece, Ireland, Italy, Luxembourg, the Netherlands, Portugal, Spain, and the United Kingdom. The goal of the EC is to create a single internal market, free of all barriers to trade. For products and services to be traded freely, there must be assurance that those products meet certain standards, whether they are produced in one of the EC nations or in a non-EC nation, such as the United States.[4] The EC is using the standards to provide a universal framework for quality assurance and to ensure the quality of goods and services across borders.

The International Organization for Standardization (ISO) is the specialized international agency for standardization and at present comprises the national standards bodies of 91 countries. The American National Standards Institute (ANSI) is the member body representing the United States. ISO is made up of approximately 180 technical committees. Each technical committee is responsible for one of many areas of specialization, ranging from asbestos to zinc. The purpose of ISO is to promote the development of standardization and related world activities in order to facilitate the international exchange of goods and services and to develop cooperation in intellectual, scientific, technological, and economic activities. The results of ISO technical work are published as international standards, and the ISO 9000 Series is a result of this process.

In 1987 (the same year the ISO 9000 Series was published), the United States adopted the ISO 9000 Series verbatim as the ANSI/ASQC Q-90 Series. Thus, the use of either of these series is equivalent to the use of the other.[5] The ISO standards are being adopted by a varying number of companies in over 50 countries around the world that have endorsed them. Many people believe that within five years, registration will be necessary to stay in business.[6]

By 1992 more than 20,000 facilities in Britain had adopted the standards and become certified.[7] Over 20,000 companies from other EC countries have registered, compared to about 620 in the United States. Japan not only has adopted the standards but also has mounted a major national effort to get its companies registered.[8]

The EC adopted ISO 9000 in 1989 to integrate the various technical norms and specifications of its member states. By 1991, ISO compliance became part of hundreds of product safety laws all over Europe, regulating everything from medical devices to telecommunications gear. Such products accounted for only about 15 percent of EC trade at that time, but the list of products is growing. Entire industries are encouraging the adoption of the standards.

One example of the impact is reflected in the requirements of Siemens, the huge German electronics firm. The company requires ISO compliance in 50 percent of its contracts and is pressing all other suppliers to conform. A major justification for this action is that it eliminates the need to test parts, which saves time and money and establishes common requirements for all markets.

Even for companies whose products are unregulated, ISO standards are becoming a de facto market requirement for doing business with other EC companies. If two suppliers are competing for a contract or an order, the one that has registered its quality systems under ISO 9000 has a clear edge.

The impact of these standards is reflected by the widespread distribution of the ISO 9000 Series, which has become the best seller in the history of the ISO, under whose auspices it was developed. ISO 9000 even outsold the universal and long-standing international weights and measurement standards. However, it is worth repeating that ISO 9000 is not standards for products but standards for operation of a *quality management system.*

## ISO 9000 IN THE UNITED STATES

*At IBM, the ISO 9000 standards have proven to be*
*a template for the creation of a sound quality system.*

Dr. Jack Small
Director ISO 9000, IBM (U.S.)[3]

*FedEx's worldwide ISO 9000 certification*
*gives us a competitive advantage in the global marketplace.*

Frederick W. Smith, Chairman and CEO
Federal Express (U.S.)[3]

As events unfold and the advantages of certification become more apparent, more and more U.S. companies are likely to get on the ISO 9000 bandwagon. U.S. companies have been slow to adopt these international standards despite the fact that 30 percent of the country's exports go to Europe. Moreover, to the extent that the standards are adopted elsewhere in the world, additional exports will be affected as well. Additional markets both within and outside the United States may be closed to those firms that ignore the requirement or fail to become certified. Du Pont, now a leader in adopting the standards, only began its ISO drive in 1989 after losing a large European order for polyester film to an ISO-certified British firm.

Some people perceive ISO 9000 as a barrier to competition and even a plot to keep U.S. firms out of Europe. This view, of course, is not the case, but a barrier can exist unless the standards are clearly understood.

Additional evidence of growing acceptance lies in the fact that the standards are being integrated into the requirements for manufacturers that make products under contract for several U.S. government agencies, including NASA, the Department of Defense, the Federal Aviation Administration, and the Food and Drug Administration.[9] To date, ISO 9000 registration is required of suppliers to the governments of Canada, Australia, and the United Kingdom.

Du Pont, Eastman Kodak, and other U.S. pioneers adopted ISO 9000 in the late 1980s to ensure that they were not locked out of European markets. They then found that the standards also helped to improve their quality. Now, Baldrige winners such as Motorola, Xerox, IBM, and others are making suppliers adopt ISO. As the movement catches on and as suppliers to suppliers are required to come on board, there may be a geometric leverage effect in the number of companies adopting the standards. This effect may give additional meaning to the often-repeated description of the market as *global* in dimension.

Despite the weight of the evidence that suggests the need to adopt ISO 9000, it appears that many U.S. firms have not done so, nor do they plan to do so. One survey of 254 mid-sized manufacturing firms conducted by the Chicago accounting firm of Grant Thornton found that only 8 percent planned to become certified by the end of 1992 and 48 percent of the senior executives never even heard of the ISO 9000 standards.[10] By 1998, these figures had improved, but many companies were still delaying the inevitable certification.

The good news is that for those firms planning to become ISO 9000 certified, the process is not all that difficult, especially if the company already has a quality effort underway. Indeed, those companies using TQM are more than halfway there. For Baldrige winners, certification would be a relatively simple process.

What is the impact of ISO 9000 for service industries and for those manufacturing firms whose products fall outside the *regulated* product areas? The answer, according to ASQC,[11] is that the impact varies from sector to sector, although, in general, the company with ISO 9000 registration may have a competitive edge. This is particularly true in aerospace, autos, electronic components, measuring and testing instruments, and so on.

Some American manufacturers have criticized the EC's adoption of ISO 9000, suggesting that the standards are inferior to those used in the United States. Moreover, it is suggested that requiring U.S. companies to conform to the standards will force them to incur larger production costs.[12]

The counterarguments are that the standards will eliminate the hodgepodge of standards that now exist around the world and that production costs will be more than offset by other savings and the increase in productivity and quality.

Criticisms and ignorance of ISO 9000 notwithstanding, there is evidence of a growing acceptance of the standards among U.S. firms.[13] It is interesting to note that the experience in Japan is similar to that in the United States. Initial resistance was largely overcome by pressure to conform to the requirements of the international marketplace.[14]

Involvement of professional and trade associations appears to be growing as firms within a particular industry band together to research how best to meet ISO requirements. The chemical industry has been a leader in this movement. Professional engineers, public utilities, software vendors, and manufacturers of information technology are among the groups with organized efforts.[15] Some have formed a network of support groups.[16]

## THE ISO 9000 AND ANSI/ASQC Q-90 SERIES STANDARDS[17]

Unlike the Baldrige, the ISO 9000 Series and its clone, the ANSI/ASQC Q-90 Series, are not awards programs. They do not require the use of any state-of-the-art system, nor do they require any prescribed method of process control. They are generic and apply to all industries.[18] As a set of requirements for quality systems, these series provide a common measuring stick for gauging quality systems. Leaving the determination of quality levels to the customer–supplier interaction, the series fill the need for a customer's guarantee that a supplier will, within defined limits, be able to deliver products and services as promised.[19] This flexibility and lack of constraining requirements mean that there is no one right way to do ISO 9000. Industries are free to find their own way and perceive this as an opportunity rather than an additional constraint. This freedom can serve as a source of both frustration as well as liberation.

The requirements for a quality system have been standardized, but most managers tend to think of their businesses as unique or different. ISO 9000 allows for the diversity of large or small companies, domestic or multinational companies, a service company, a public utility, or government administration. In other words, ISO 9000 lays down *what* requirements a quality system must meet but does not dictate *how* they should be met in an individual organization. The "family" of ISO standards provides guidance and requirements on what constitutes an effective quality management system as well as models against which this system can be audited to give an organization and its clients assurance that the system is operating effectively.

The series is produced in five parts: ISO 9000, 9001, 9002, 9003, and 9004. ISO 9000 and 9004 are guidelines, whereas ISO 9001, 9002, and 9003 are the categories for which companies may apply for certification.

ISO 9000, "Quality Management and Quality Assurance Standards—Guidelines for Selection and Use," is an advisory document. It explains how the overall standard is divided, gives guidelines to use in determining which of the three classifications (9001, 9002, 9003) is applicable to a business, and gives guidelines on how the systems may be implemented.

The three components of ISO 9000 and the 20 subclauses of the quality requirements for ISO 9001 to 9004 are shown in Figure 12-1, arranged in three major blocks. The central block of nine clauses is considered the core requirements because these relate to what happens in the operating process itself. Very broadly, this term covers input, what is done with the input (i.e., the process), and the output (i.e., what goes out to the customer). The sections in the left and right blocks have a supporting rather than a core role but are just as essential as those in the central operating process block. To meet the standard, a quality system must be shown to fulfill the requirements under Quality System Control and support activities as fully as those included under Operating Process.

The requirements of the three components of ISO 9000 (Figure 12-1)[20] are outlined below.

## Operating Process

The requirements included under Operating Process are described briefly here. Any reader who intends to design a quality system to meet ISO 9001, however, should obtain and read the actual standard.

### Contract Review

One of the fundamental aspects of quality is meeting the customer's requirements. Clearly, to meet these requirements a supplier must know what they are. Contract review is concerned with adequately defining and documenting these requirements and establishing that the resources needed to meet them are available. What should be covered in such a record of requirements and how it should be documented will vary from business to business.

In an industry in which subcontracting is the norm (e.g., printing, construction, many services), the contract review appropriately precedes any design or production activities and, therefore, fits logically as shown in Figure 12-1. However, in businesses supplying from stock, contract review would *follow* production of the product or service and would determine whether the available products met requirements. In Figure 12-1, therefore, the Contract Review inner box would be shown between 4.15 Handling, Storage, Packaging & Delivery and 4.19 Servicing.

Obviously, contract review follows drawing up the contract or offering and in effect, therefore, follows the marketing process, an activity not explicitly covered in ISO 9000. Similarly, certain other activities vital to the survival of any business are also not covered. The most obvious omission is the accounting function. This does not mean that functions such as marketing and accounting

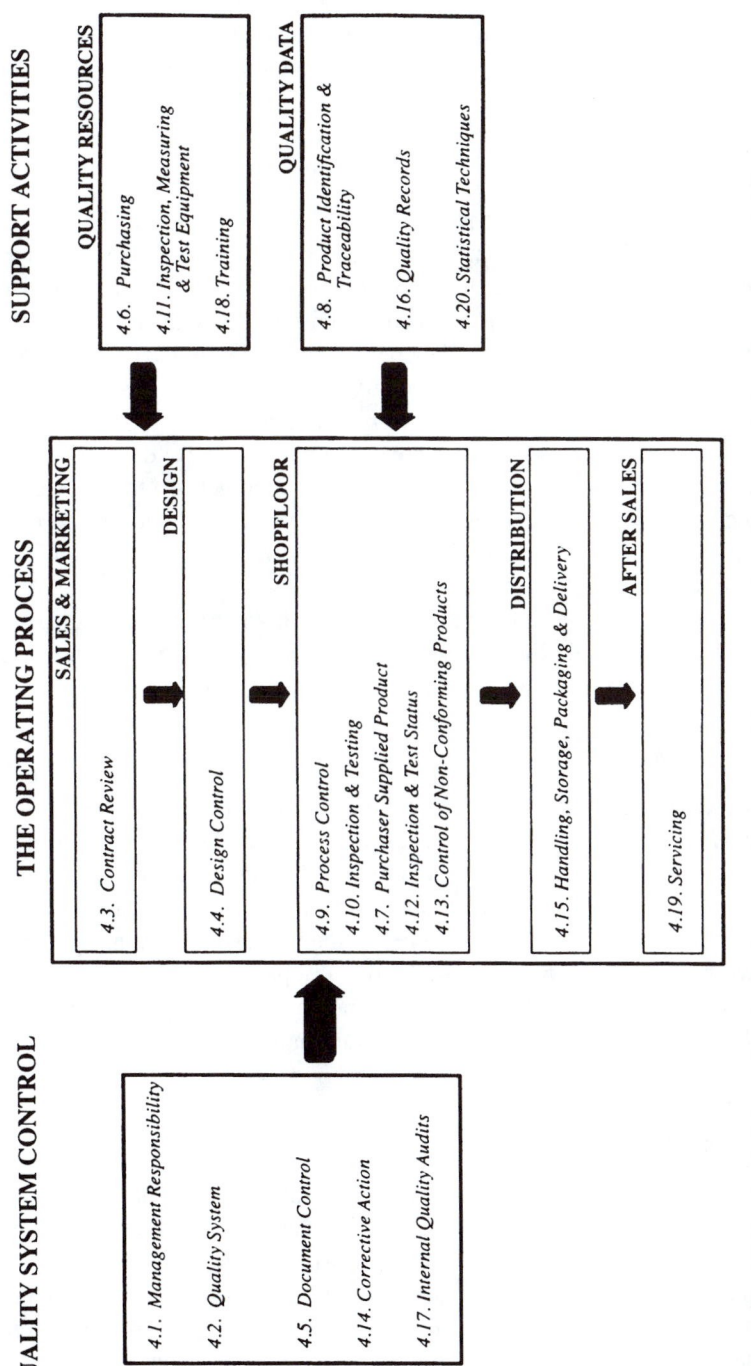

**Figure 12-1**  ISO 9000

have no quality dimension—clearly they have—but they are not formally addressed by the standard. In the assessment process for ISO 9000, a company is not evaluated in these areas.

### Design Control

Starting with an adequate definition of the requirements of the customer, design work must be carried out by qualified staff equipped with appropriate resources to produce a design that matches the requirements. The specific activities involved here will, as with all requirements of the standard, vary widely according to the type of business. The qualifications required to carry out design work on a nuclear reactor are obviously very different from the skills required to prepare a questionnaire in a market research company.

Design control requirements also cover the need to verify designs, establish criteria for verification, and control the output documents. Once a design is established, it is essential that this specific design be used and not an earlier, superseded draft. Ensuring this involves some form of document control and identification procedure.

The next four requirements are concerned with what happens at the service center or shop floor and cover the actual steps taken while making the product or providing the service to ensure that it meets requirements.

### Process Control

This requires that the work process be carried out in a controlled way. Included are documenting how the process is to be carried out, providing suitable written instructions for those doing so, and monitoring what happens during the process. For example, is the operating temperature of the furnace within the correct limits? Have the fire sensors been installed in the positions specified in the drawings? By what criteria is the output acceptable?

Special mention is made of the requirements of processes whose output cannot be adequately tested after manufacture and prior to customer delivery. Many service activities fall into this category.

### Inspection and Testing

Inspection and testing is concerned with establishing whether the input into the work process, the output, and the work at various stages in between meet defined requirements. The input may be third-party materials.

A special type of input is customer-supplied product (e.g., a component that is to be finished in some way in the supplier's factory). This is covered in Purchaser Supplied Product (4.7). In this case, the requirement includes appropriate inspection but also addresses the need to look after the customer's product, to make sure the correct one is processed and that its condition does not deteriorate while at the supplier. (In the wording of the standard, a "supplier" is the company registered for ISO 9000 and the "purchaser" is the customer.)

It is worth noting that inspection and testing of output is an explicit requirement of the standard, even though an effective system should not depend only on inspection and testing. The better the system, the less need for post-production inspection. The quality policeman should have a diminishing role and, in an ideal world, be eliminated.

### Inspection and Test Status/Control of Non-conformity

If testing is used to verify quality, it is essential to know which inputs, outputs, and in-process product have been tested and which tests and inspections have been applied. It must be established that the final product is up to standard prior to forwarding it to the customer and that the appropriate tests have been carried out. Stamps, labeling, location in the process area, and a variety of records are all suitable methods for meeting this requirement.

If, when testing products, some are identified that do not meet requirements, these should be separated from satisfactory products by, for example, marking and moving them to a special area prior to reworking or scrapping.

The last two requirements included under Operating Process concern the treatment of the product after it has been made.

### Handling, Storage, Packaging, and Delivery

This requirement addresses the need to keep the product in good condition after it leaves the shop floor and before it reaches the customer. It must be handled (moved within the manufacturer's premises), stored prior to forwarding, packed for delivery, and delivered so as to prevent either damage or deterioration. The latter may limit the shelf life of the product.

Appropriate methods to meet this requirement obviously depend on the product involved. Lifting by mechanical shovel is appropriate for builders' sand, but not for a mainframe computer. In the case of some services, certain requirements may not be applicable. Although *all* the requirements of the standard should be carefully considered in the context of a particular business, there may be a few that do not apply.

### Servicing

This is explicitly applicable in only some situations, despite the fact that one of the clauses that distinguishes ISO 9001 from 9002 is "where servicing is specified in the contract." If such servicing is specified, procedures are required to make sure that servicing work is carried out as required. If the contract with the customer does not specify servicing, then there is no requirement to meet. Some businesses may, however, choose to include in their quality system some form of servicing, even if it is not a contractual requirement. This may include various forms of customer follow-up. In addition to any formal requirements of ISO 9000, a company seeking registration should consider including in its quality system some safeguard for long-term customer satisfaction.

## Support Activities

The various requirements of the standard grouped as Support Activities are not integral to the production process, but they are needed if the quality system is to be successfully implemented. They fall into two subgroups: Quality Resources and Quality Data.

### Quality Resources

Three requirements—clauses 4.6, 4.11, and 4.18—ensure that the resources available within production are appropriate to quality needs. Purchasing (4.6) covers the development of procedures to ensure that supplies brought into the production process meet requirements. Specifics mentioned in this clause concern the selection and assessment of suppliers (the term "subcontractor" is used), documenting the supply process so that suppliers know precisely what is necessary to meet requirements, and verifying that what is supplied is what is required.

It is worth noting that the requirements of implementing a purchasing system do not require that previously satisfactory suppliers be minutely scrutinized. Those that have worked out well in the past should more than qualify for inclusion on an approved supplier list (which is commonly one element of an appropriate purchasing procedure). Nor do suppliers have to be ISO 9000 registered themselves. However, to ensure that their supplies are up to standard, suppliers may need to provide assurance of *their* quality systems, and ISO 9000 may be the most practical means for them to do this.

If inspection and testing is carried out within the production process, any instruments or equipment used in this activity must be capable of providing appropriate results (e.g., the micrometer is accurate enough to determine if the component is within the required range of tolerance). Inspection, Measuring and Test Equipment (4.11) is the requirement of the standard that meets this need. It covers procedures for selecting appropriate equipment for the test, calibrating and checking its accuracy, and ensuring that it is kept up to an appropriate standard. The application of this requirement in some service businesses may present problems.

The third class of quality resource included is people—Training (4.18). Even the most automated plant is dependent on staff being trained to meet the needs of the job. In some businesses, quality output is almost totally dependent on the skills of the people involved. Any business committed to quality must address and plan training needs.

### Quality Data

ISO 9000 requires records to demonstrate that quality activities are carried out. Throughout the clauses of the standard discussed above, the need for records is specifically mentioned. There are also requirements for quality data: identifying products and thereby tracing them through the production process, keeping records, and using statistical techniques to evaluate quality data.

There can only be quality records on a specific product (or product batch or, in the case of some services, project) if it can be identified. The requirements of Product Identification and Traceability (4.8) can certainly be met by physically labeling products (e.g., stamping the machine with a unique number). The quality records related to this specific product can then be examined. Other products (e.g., bulk deliveries of four) cannot be labeled in this way, but a batch of the product can nevertheless be linked, through records, to the specific processes carried out. For example, it can be determined that the flour delivered to the bakery on March 1 was part of a batch from a particular silo and was milled on February 12 during the third shift.

To be of use, quality records must be filed systematically, retained for an appropriate time (product life may be the criterion here), kept up to date, and maintained in a usable form. They do not have to be on paper; electronic data is an alternative. These requirements are specified in Quality Records (4.16).

## Quality System Control

A quality system includes the procedures carried out within and in support of the production processes. From another perspective, however, a quality system must be documented, reviewed, and updated in line with changes in the environment. Mechanisms are also needed to identify deficiencies in either the operation or the content of the system. This aspect of a quality system is covered in ISO 9000 Part I through five clauses that are grouped together under Quality System Control.

A quality system does not just happen. It is a major management task to both introduce an effective system and to maintain it. At the top level, a policy decision must be made in relation to quality, a *quality policy*. Typically, this is a one-page statement from which the system follows. The responsibilities for implementing each part of the quality system also must be defined. Usually one person is put in charge of coordinating them (the management representative). Special attention must also be given to responsibility for inspection and testing. Finally, the working of a quality system must be periodically considered and decisions made about necessary changes. All these requirements are covered in ISO 9000 Part 1 in Management Responsibility (4.1).

The clause of the standard Quality System (4.2) (so called even though the whole is a standard for quality systems) might be better titled if it included "documented." The requirement in this respect is twofold: the system must be documented and must describe how the system is to be implemented. Typically, *how* is covered by a procedure manual.

The document containing the quality system is also required to be controlled—Document Control (4.5). This includes an approval process for the contents, the availability of up-to-date copies to all concerned, and procedures for changing/updating the document or parts of it as changes in the system are agreed upon (again by some controlled method).

Unavoidably, things go wrong. No matter how rigorous the quality system, the standard of the plant, and the training and motivation of the work force, problems will occur. Such problems are reflected in the output: products do not conform to quality requirements. The standard's requirements for Corrective Action (4.14) cover procedures for the identification of such deficiencies, the actions taken to investigate their cause, and the prevention of recurrence. The latter may lead to a need for a change in the quality system, which might have to be considered by a management review (4.1) and brought about through the provisions for document control (4.5).

Lastly, it is a requirement that deficiencies identified are not only dealt with but are also actively sought through Internal Quality Audits (4.17). Such audits must be carried out systematically (to a schedule and method) and may lead to corrective actions and again to review and change. Internal audits mirror the work carried out by external assessors (the bodies whose reports lead to ISO 9000 registration) and are therefore essential as part of the process of approval. However, and more importantly, they can be a vital tool in quality enhancement and, consequently, commercial success.

## ISO Standards 9001, 9002, 9003, and 9004

The first three of these standards are the categories for which companies may apply for certification. The difference is simply one of scope.

**ISO 9001**, "Quality Systems—Model for Quality Assurance in Design/ Development, Production, Installation and Servicing," is the most comprehensive of all the standards. It confirms the conformance of processes from the primary stage of product development through production, shipping, installation, testing, and servicing.

**ISO 9002**, "Quality Systems—Model for Quality Assurance in Production and Installation," is the standard for an organization that does not carry out design and development; otherwise, the requirements are identical to ISO 9001. It deals with the procurement, production, installation, and servicing areas of organizations that are usually in the process industries.

**ISO 9003**, "Quality Systems—Model for Quality Assurance in Final Inspection and Test," is the appropriate standard for an organization whose business processes do not include design control, process control, purchasing, or servicing and which basically uses inspection and testing to ensure that final products and services meet specified requirements. Addressing only the detection and control of problems during final inspection, it is mainly designed for warehousing and distribution companies. The quality system would only be relevant for a fairly simple product or service.

**ISO 9004**, "Quality Management and Quality Systems Elements—Guidelines," is an advisory document, and although it is very helpful, implementation of its guidelines is not mandatory for certification.

## BENEFITS OF ISO 9000 CERTIFICATION

The benefits to the organization gained by improving quality in products and services were outlined in Chapter 1. To repeat:

1. Greater customer loyalty
2. Improvements in market share
3. Higher stock prices
4. Reduced service calls
5. Higher prices
6. Greater productivity and cost reduction

These same benefits would be achieved by ISO 9000 certification to the extent that actions leading to certification result in a quality management system. Moreover, certification provides the additional benefit of acceptance by EC customers and others whose criteria of acceptance include ISO 9000 certification.

In addition to the benefits that are common to both TQM and ISO 9000, the latter provides access to markets that might otherwise be denied. And, of course, for any quality system, be it TQM or ISO 9000, it just makes good sense.

Experience tends to confirm that companies do achieve these benefits. Consider the following examples:

■  A British government survey revealed that 89 percent of ISO 9000–registered companies reported greater operational efficiency: 48 percent reported increased profitability, 76 percent reported improvements in marketing, and 26 percent reported increased export sales.[21]

■  The British Standards Institution, a leading British registrar, estimates that registered firms reduce operating costs by 10 percent on average.[22]

■  Du Pont attributes the following results to the adoption of ISO standards in its plants:
  ■  On-time delivery at one plant increased to 90 percent from 70 percent.
  ■  Cycle time at one plant went from 15 days to 1½ days.
  ■  First-pass yield at one plant went from 72 percent to 92 percent.
  ■  Test procedures were reduced from 3000 to 1100.

■  A number of U.S. firms have reported benefits ranging from increased sales to improved communications.[23]

## GETTING CERTIFIED: THE PROCESS

Many managers will find that the requirements for certification are somewhat complex and that there is no shortage of books,[24] articles, and management consultants to assist them. Most sources suggest some form of the following five steps:

■  **Training for everyone from the CEO to hourly workers.**  Training should include an overall understanding of the vocabulary of ISO requirements, the role of the quality manual, and benefits that the system brings to a company. A second area for training is the actual day-to-day process of upgrading and improving procedures.

■  **Documentation of work instructions.**  New documentation is necessary for processes that have been improved or upgraded. The manual should outline every process undertaken by a company that affects the quality of the finished product.

■  **ISO 9000 assessment.**  The initial assessment is a detailed review of a company's quality systems and procedures compared to the requirements of

ISO 9000. The assessment process defines the scope of the ISO 9000 project.

- **The quality assurance manual** is a good way to get all the necessary documentation together in one place. The standards do not require a quality assurance and policy manual, but they do require a company to document everything it does and every system that affects the quality of the finished product.

- **The registration audit** is the final step in the ISO 9000 program. It is an audit by a registrar that is chosen by the company being audited. The purpose of the audit is to see that the system is working as described in the quality manual and that the system meets the requirements of ISO 9000.

## GETTING CERTIFIED: THE THIRD-PARTY AUDIT

Many managers perceive the thought of an audit of any kind as a necessary bureaucratic action that has a very low priority. This negative perception may increase when it is learned that preparation for ISO 9000 certification may take from 6 to 12 months and that the failure rate the first time around can be as high as two out of three. Nevertheless, a third-party audit is a prerequisite to certification. Speaking of certification, Deming noted, "You don't have to do this—survival is not compulsory!"

The traditional two-party quality audit system relies on the buyer–seller relationship, where the buyer (customer) "audits" the supplier. This puts a burden on both parties. Imagine a supplier with a hundred or more customers, each with their own specific requirements. From a customer's point of view, it would be beneficial if all suppliers could be judged by a single set of criteria.

The third-party audit places great importance on quality systems, a critical factor in the EC. The independent third-party *registrar* certifies that the quality system meets the requirements of ISO 9000.

What is the rationale for a third-party audit? Financial results are measured by financial statements, while product and service outputs are measured by quality. If the impartial third-party audit is required for financial systems, why not a similar check on quality systems? This is particularly important in helping to guarantee quality across international borders.

## DOCUMENTATION

There are three basic steps to the registration process:

1. Appraisal of the organization's quality manual

2. Evaluation of conformance to documented procedures

3. Presentation of findings, with recommendations for corrective action

A great deal of *documentation* is required. The justification is reflected in the management axiom, "If you haven't written it out, you haven't thought it out." Moreover, as people come and go, change jobs, and forget a procedure, documentation ensures that a record is maintained for continuity. The simple rule is that if all personnel involved in a given system or procedure were replaced, the new people could continue making the product at the same quality level.

The amount of documentation depends on the nature and complexity of the business. A hierarchical approach involving three levels is generally acceptable:

- **Level 1:** An overview type of quality manual consisting of policies that meet the requirements of the ISO standard for which certification is sought
- **Level 2:** Functional or departmental operating procedures in terms of "who does what"
- **Level 3:** Work instructions that explain how each task is to be accomplished

The criteria for approval are simple: Can you say what you do and do what you say? Questions such as the following may be asked: Is the process control system adequate for your needs? Is it understood by those who run the process? Are they properly trained to operate the process? Is the documentation up to date? Do you have an internal audit system that regularly assesses whether the control system is functioning as it should be?

## POST-CERTIFICATION

The third-party audit and subsequent certification, if achieved, should be viewed as a means, not an end to be achieved. The importance of preparation for certification lies not so much in the certification itself but in the quality system that results from the effort leading to it.

The customer is the ultimate beneficiary of the quality system, and any effort to obtain ISO 9000 certification without customer communication can be a waste of time and a compromise of any system that may result.

Certification is a beginning, not an end. Continuous evaluation, feedback, and fine-tuning are suggested. Who will perform this internal and continuing "audit" following certification? The responsibility, of course, is top management's. The role of the internal auditor, if any, is not clear. Should the role include getting ready for certification or maintaining post-certification requirements, or both?[25] The role is not clearly assigned and may represent an opportunity for internal auditors.

## CHOOSING AN ACCREDITED REGISTRATION SERVICE

Quality managers who decide to implement an ISO 9000 system are confronted by two related issues: how best to implement the new system and how to ensure that certification will be recognized by customers. This latter issue will normally be settled if certification is recognized by legitimate accreditation bodies.

U.S. firms located in Europe normally utilize one of the many accrediting bodies in those countries. Many are government sanctioned, such as Raad voor de Certificatie (RvC) in the Netherlands and the National Accreditation Council for Certification Bodies (NACCB) in the United Kingdom. IBM's Application Business Systems Division was the first American-based firm to be certified in all of its business lines. Certification was gained after an audit by Bureau Veritas Quality International.[26]

No single firmly established registrar-accredited authority is recognized in the United States, and confusion exists as to which auditors are accredited by whom. Two non-governmental groups, the Registrar Accreditation Board (RAB) (an offshoot of the ASQC) and ANSI, have carried out a joint effort to develop accreditation requirements for ISO 9000 auditing companies operating in the United States.[27] The creation of the ANSI/RAB accreditation program is the nearest source of credible U.S.-based registrars.

A number of criteria should affect the decision on the choice of a registrar, including knowledge in the specific industry and in the auditing of quality systems, how many similar firms a registrar has registered, turnaround time for audit results, the re-audit schedule should complement the business cycle of the firm being audited, and, most important, the registrar should be accredited.

As a general rule, it is probably not wise to shop around for the lowest price, because the cost of an audit is small compared to the overall cost of the registration effort.

## ISO 9000 AND SERVICES

The standards apply not only to the manufacturing process but to after-sale service and to service departments such as design within the manufacturing firm as well. Additionally, the standards also translate to the service sector. They specifically address quality systems for service as well as production. Indeed, ISO 9000-2, a separate guideline, was issued to explain ISO criteria in terms of selected service industries.

In the United Kingdom, standards are being used by educational institutions, banks, legal and architectural firms, and even trash collectors. At London's

Heathrow Airport, British Airways PLC adopted ISO standards to reduce complaints of lost cargo and damaged goods. In the United States, a growing number of transportation companies will not transport hazardous material unless the shipper is ISO certified.

There is some evidence that the ISO 9000 Series is receiving more interest from service organizations in the United States than in Europe. Service firms in consulting, purchasing, and materials management are expressing interest. It is believed by some that the greater interest by U.S. service firms is based on strategic considerations, as ISO 9000 is perceived as a "market differentiator."[28]

## THE COST OF CERTIFICATION

A frequently asked question is: How much does certification cost? This is a legitimate concern, although the question may be accompanied by another one: What is the payoff?

There is no set answer to how much it costs and how long it takes. Each company is different. The answer depends on such factors as company size, product lines, how far along the company's existing systems are on the quality continuum, whether consultants are used, and the implementation strategy adopted. It can cost a small company $2000 to $25,000 in consulting fees for advice on developing a quality system.[29] Employee time in creating the system is additional and can be the largest cost.

The major determinant is the firm's starting position. If the company has just won a Baldrige Award, registration of a plant or business might take just a few days. However, if the system must be created from the ground up, it can take a year and cost $100,000 or more.[30]

## ISO 9000 VS. THE BALDRIGE AWARD

The ASQC reports that one of the most frequently asked questions regarding the ISO Series is: "Aren't the Baldrige Award, the Deming Prize, etc. equivalent or better 'standards' than the ISO Series?" The answer, replies ASQC, is quite simple: "You can't hope to meet the expectations of any of these programs if you aren't already implementing the ISO 9000 (ANSI/ASQC Q-90) standards in your company. These standards provide the foundation on which you can build your quality management and quality assurance systems so you may ultimately achieve a high level of success. Moreover, the ISO 9000 Series is the only system accepted internationally."

The Baldrige is a much more comprehensive program than ISO 9000. It is truly a TQM system, whereas the ISO Series is much more limited in scope. It is a basic standard, a minimal requirement, and can be worth about 200 to 300 points in the Baldrige program. For example, it does not address the human resource dimension, as does the Baldrige. On the other hand, a company implementing the Baldrige criteria is in a much better position to implement the ISO standard.

The Baldrige criteria are much more specific. The guidelines spell out what is expected in detailed language. In contrast, the ISO Series is designed to be inclusive, not exclusive. It does not mandate that one approach be used over another. As long as you can say what you do and do what you say, you can get your system registered. This generic nature of the standards can be a source of frustration as well as liberation.

For those companies whose quality systems are on the low end of a TQM continuum, ISO may be a starting place on the road to eventually achieving a TQM system. Certification also has the advantage of putting the organization on a level playing field with the competition worldwide.

## IMPLEMENTING THE SYSTEM

Although the series provides guidance on the required attributes of the quality system, the standards do not spell out the means of implementation. Once a decision is made to adopt the standards and seek certification, the following major steps will facilitate successful change:

- Recognize the need for change and get the commitment of top management.
- Incorporate quality in the strategic plan as the linchpin of differentiation.
- Formulate and adopt a holistic quality policy statement adapted to ISO requirements. Get support and commitment from all managers.
- Determine the scope of the business to be certified. Will it be a particular process, related facilities, a geographical site, or the whole company?
- Determine the status of the current quality system through an internal audit. Define the *gap* between where you are and what it will take to close the gap.
- Estimate the cost in time and money and implement the plan by organizing the necessary action steps.

## THE FUTURE OF ISO 9000

Not all companies are pleased with the ISO 9000 process. There is substantial disagreement on the standards and the way they are administered. Compliance is said to be costly. Meeting regional and international standards and testing practices can cost even a small company hundreds of thousands of dollars annually. Multinational corporations, with hundreds of plants spread all over the globe, spend millions in the standards area.[31]

The most frequent complaint concerns the third-party registration process. (Third-party registration involves auditing and certification through independent sources rather than companies auditing their own supply bases or self-declaring that they are in conformity with a standard or testing practice.) Fifty-eight American and European multinationals met in Munich, Germany, in April 1998 and hammered out a 40-resolution manifesto that protests the high cost of international standardization and testing practices, not to mention the proliferation of standards that would require additional third-party registration.[32] These companies say they will abandon the third-party approach in seven years.

Many small and mid-sized companies will be tempted to throw up their hands and abandon overseas ventures. This is probably a mistake. Certification is a secondary goal; the primary goal is the maintenance of an effective quality management system. Even if third-party registration is eliminated (an unlikely event), the small or mid-sized company can use the guidelines and standards as a benchmark. ISO 9000 provides a good baseline quality assurance system, and regular audits can ensure that it is maintained.

## ISO 14000 ENVIRONMENTAL MANAGEMENT SYSTEM[33]

ISO 14000 grew out of discussions at the United Nations Conference on Environmental Development in Rio de Janeiro in 1992. ISO launched the new technical committee, ISO/TC 207, Environmental Management, in 1993. Today, delegations of business and government experts from 55 countries participate actively within TC 207. The very first two standards, ISO 14004 and ISO 14001, were published in 1996 and deal with environmental management systems. Published documents and ongoing work address the following areas:

- Environmental management systems
- Environmental auditing and related environmental investigations
- Environmental performance evaluation
- Environmental labeling
- Life cycle assessment
- Forest management
- Environmental aspects in product standards
- Terms and definitions

ISO 14000 Environmental Management System is an environmental management system based on the ISO 14000 standards and is a management tool that enables an organization of any size or type to control the impact of its activities, products, or services on the environment. ISO 14000 makes possible a structured approach to setting environmental objectives and targets, to achieving these, and to demonstrating that they have been achieved. ISO also has a wide portfolio of standards that are specific (e.g., air, water, or soil pollution). ISO 14000 provides the framework.

ISO 14004 provides guidelines on the elements of an environmental management system and its implementation and discusses principal issues involved.

ISO 14001 specifies the requirements for such an environmental management system. Fulfilling these requirements requires objective evidence that the environmental management system is operating effectively in conformance with the standard. It is a tool that can be used for internal purposes to provide assurance that a company is in control of its processes and activities that have an impact on the environment. It can also be used for external purposes to provide assurance to interested parties—customers, the community, regulatory agencies, and other stakeholders.

The benefits of ISO 14000 are several. There may have been a time when environmental responsibility was reactive, doing what was required by government regulations. This is no longer the case in today's environment-conscious world. The proactive manager knows that implementing a strategic approach can bring return on investment in environment-related measures. More specifically, complying with ISO 14000 standards can lead to benefits such as the following:

- Reduced cost of waste management
- Savings in consumption of energy and materials
- Lower distribution costs
- Improved corporate image among regulators, customers, and the public
- Framework for continuous improvement of environmental performance
- Employee satisfaction, by knowing one is working for an environmentally responsible organization

Consider also the opportunity cost of not achieving these benefits.

## QUESTIONS FOR DISCUSSION

**12-1**  Why is it important for U.S. firms to comply with ISO 9000?

**12-2**  Compare the standards of ISO 9000 with those of the Baldrige Award.

**12-3** Does ISO 9000 contain product standards or standards for operation of a quality management system? Explain the difference.

**12-4** Answer the criticisms that meeting ISO standards will add to production costs.

**12-5** What are the five sets of standards? Summarize each.

**12-6** What are the benefits of ISO 9000 certification?

## ENDNOTES

1. Benedicte Joubert, "ISO 9000: International Quality Standards," *Production & Inventory Management Journal,* Second Quarter 1998, pp. 60–65.
2. "Where ISO 9000 Came From and Who Is Behind It," taken from ISO Web site http://www.iso.ch/9000e/wherfrom.htm.
3. *ISO 9000 News* articles.
4. Gary Spizizen, "The ISO 9000 Standards: Creating a Level Playing Field for International Quality," *National Productivity Review,* Summer 1992, p. 332. This is an excellent summary of the provisions of ISO 9000.
5. The ANSI/ASQC Series is available from ASQC headquarters through the customer service department (tel. 800-248-1946). The ISO 9000 Series is available from ANSI (tel. 212-642-4900). Keep in mind that the ANSI/ASQC Q-90 Series is *identical* to the ISO 9000 Series.
6. Suzan L. Jackson, "What You Should Know about ISO 9000," *Training,* May 1992, p. 48. This is a good primer on ISO standards. ISO 9000 was adopted by the EC in 1990 as a global standard of quality. Its stringent requirements ensure that products manufactured along ISO 9000 are world-class. See Jack Cella, "ISO 9000 Is the Key to International Business," *Journal of Commerce and Commercial,* Jan. 25, 1993, p. 88. Even China is moving toward adoption of the standards according to Ed Haderer, "Setting Tough Standards," *The China Business Review,* Jan.–Feb., 1993, p. 34. The Shanghai-Foxboro Company Ltd., an affiliate of the U.S.-based Foxboro Company, became the first company in China to attain ISO 9000 certification.
7. "Want EC Business? You Have Two Choices," *Business Week,* Oct. 19, 1992, p. 58. In the United Kingdom, where the standards have become most widely embraced, over 80 percent of large employers with payrolls over 1000 are registered. See Kymberly K. Hockman and David A. Erdman, "Gearing Up for ISO 9000 Registration, *Chemical Engineering,* April 1993, p. 128.
8. Donald W. Marquardt, "ISO 9000: A Universal Standard of Quality," *Management Review,* Jan. 1992, p. 50.
9. "U.S. Firms Lag in Meeting Global Quality Standards," *Marketing News,* Feb. 15, 1993.
10. Jeffrey A. Tannenbaum, "Small Companies Are Finding It Pays to Think Global; Firms Win New Business by Adopting International Quality Standards," *Wall Street Journal,* Nov. 19, 1992, Section B, p. 2. See also *Marketing News,* Feb. 15, 1993, p. 1.

11. American Society for Quality Control, "ISO 9000," a brochure prepared by the Standards Development Department of ASQC, P.O. Box 3005, Milwaukee, WI 53201 (tel. 414-272-8575).

12. Milton G. Allimadi, "New Quality Standards Draw Fire from US Group," *Journal of Commerce and Commercial,* Jan. 4, 1993, p. 4.

13. Mark Morrow, "International Agreements Increase Clout of ISO 9000," *Chemical Week,* April 7, 1993, p. 32. This article attributes the success of ISO 9000 to its brevity (20 pages) and its simplicity. Since its inception, over 30,000 companies have registered.

14. Marjorie Coeyman, "ISO 9000 Gaining Ground in Asia/Pacific," *Chemical Week,* April 28, 1993, p. 54. In some parts of the Asia/Pacific region, the ISO 9000 quality standards have almost become domestic standards.

15. In a 1993 conference of the National Society of Professional Engineers, the topic of compliance with the EC's ISO 9000 quality control standards was discussed. See Jane C. Edmunds, "Engineers Want Quality," *ENR,* Feb. 8, 1993, p. 15. For Power Transmission Distributors (The Association), see Beate Halligan, "ISO Standards Prepare You to Compete," *Industrial Distribution,* May 1992, p. 100. The concern of the public utilities industry is reported in Greg Hutchins, "ISO Offers a Global Mark of Excellence," *Public Utilities Fortnightly,* April 15, 1993, p. 35. The computer industry's concern is reflected in Gary H. Anthes, "ISO Standard Attracts U.S. Interest," *Computerworld,* April 26, 1993, p. 109.

16. "Support Group Formed for Companies Seeking ISO 9000," *Industrial Engineering,* March 1993, p. 8. The National ISO 9000 Support Group will provide information, support, advice, and training at low cost to any American company interested in the ISO 9000 process. The goal of the group is to allow the free exchange of information and questions between companies seeking ISO registration.

17. Copies of the standards are available for a small fee from the American Society for Quality Control (tel. 414-272-8575) and the American National Standards Institute (tel. 212-642-4900).

18. Donald W. Marquardt, "ISO 9000: A Universal Standard of Quality," *Management Review,* Jan. 1992, p. 51. See also Kymberly K. Hockman, "The Last Barrier to the European Market," *Wall Street Journal,* Oct. 7, 1991, Section A, p. 14.

19. Michael E. Raynor, "ISO Certification," *Quality,* May 1993, pp. 44–45.

20. Figure 12-1 and the discussion of the three components are adapted with permission from Frank Voehl, Peter Jackson, and David Ashton, *ISO 9000: An Implementation Guide for Small to Mid-Sized Businesses,* Boca Raton, Fla.: St. Lucie Press, 1994.

21. Gary H. Anthes, "ISO Standard Attracts U.S. Interest," *Computerworld,* April 26, 1993, p. 109.

22. Donald W. Marquardt, "ISO 9000: A Universal Standard of Quality," *Management Review,* Jan. 1992, p. 52.

23. See Elisabeth Kirschner, "Nalco: Registration in Context," *Chemical Week,* April 28, 1993, p. 71. See also Marjorie Coeyman, "FMC: The Benefits of Documentation," *Chemical Week,* April 28, 1993, p. 69.

24. For example, see Barry Fisher, *How to Document ISO 9000 Quality Systems: Advice on What Documents to Write and How to Write Them,* Wiltshire, England: Marlborough, 1995. Also see Gurmeet Naroola and Robert MacConnel, *How to Achieve ISO 9000 Registration Economically and Efficiently,* New York: Marcel Dekker; Frank Voehl,

Peter Jackson, and David Ashton, *ISO 9000: An Implementation Guide for Small to Mid-Sized Businesses,* Boca Raton, Fla.: St. Lucie Press, 1994.

25. See Giovanni Grossi, "Quality Certifications," *Internal Auditor,* Oct. 1992, p. 33–35; Gary M. Stern, "Sailing to Europe: Can Auditing Play a Role in the New International Quality Standards?" *Internal Auditor,* Oct. 1992, pp. 29–33. Both of these authors, who are members of the internal auditing profession, argue for an expanded role for internal auditors in the certification and follow-on process.

26. "IBM, Help/Systems Receive ISO Certification," *Systems 3X-400,* Feb. 1993, p. 16.

27. Emily S. Plisher, "Seeking Recognition: U.S. Auditors Build Their Base," *Chemical Week,* Nov. 11, 1992, pp. 30–33. See also a special report entitled "Confusion Persists on Issue of Registrar Accreditation," *Chemical Week,* April 28, 1993, p. 42. As of April 1993, ANSI/RAB had accredited 27 quality system registrars. The "unofficial" list is contained in this endnote citation.

28. Gary Spizizen, "The ISO 9000 Standards: Creating a Level Playing Field for International Quality," *National Productivity Review,* Summer 1992, p. 335.

29. This is the estimate of OTS Registrars of Houston, an ISO 9000 registrar. "Small Companies Are Finding It Pays to Think Global; Firms Win New Business by Adopting International Quality Standards," *Wall Street Journal,* Nov. 19, 1992, Section B, p. 2.

30. Donald W. Marquardt, "ISO 9000: A Universal Standard of Quality," *Management Review,* Jan. 1992, p. 51. See also Ian Hendry, "ISO Standardizes Quality Efforts," *Pulp & Paper,* Jan. 1993, p. S4. Several of these firms report a cost of certification of about $112,000. Also, General Chemical's Green River plant achieved certification at an estimated cost of $150,000. Rick Mullin, "General Chemical's Green River Site: First ISO 9002 for Natural Soda Ash," *Chemical Week,* April 28, 1993, p. 59.

31. Amy Zuckerman, "How to Turn Standards Turmoil into Value-Added Strategic Advantage," *Quality Progress,* Sept. 1998, pp. 19–20.

32. Amy Zuckerman, "58 Multinationals Question ISO 9000 Registration; NIST Seeks Standards Summit," *Quality Progress,* Aug. 1998, pp. 16–21.

33. The descriptions in this section are adapted from material contained in the Web site of ISO, Geneva, Switzerland: www.iso.ch.

## EXAMPLE

## BALDRIGE WINNERS REGISTER FOR ISO CERTIFICATION

AT&T Network Systems Engineering Services joined a long list of AT&T organizations that have achieved registration to various ISO 9000 standards. These range from AT&T Bell Laboratories development groups and Network Systems manufacturing facilities to materials management locations and customer service organizations in the United States, Europe, and Asia.

AT&T is also one of several multinational Baldrige winners that have also begun to implement ISO 14000 (International Standards for Environmental Management Systems) standards. Other firms include IBM, Motorola, and Texas Instruments.

# MKS FITS ISO 9000
# INTO EXISTING SYSTEMS

### Nancy Chase

Achieving ISO 9000 certification doesn't require implementing a whole new quality system. At MKS Instruments, employees introduced ISO 9000 without losing the positive aspects of their existing system.

Although many companies preparing for ISO 9000 registration make drastic changes to their quality systems to try to get certified, or are forced to create a quality system from scratch, for MKS Instruments, an Andover, MA, manufacturer of gas-management instruments, integrating ISO 9000 procedures into the company was a process of evolution, not revolution. By treating ISO 9000 as simply one more step in the company's ongoing process of quality improvement, employees retained the positive aspects of their existing system, while reaping the additional benefits of ISO 9000.

Like most things that are worth achieving, an efficient quality system doesn't happen overnight. It takes time, flexibility, and a willingness to learn. When MKS was founded in 1961, it was a traditional U.S. manufacturer with a heavy emphasis on compartmentalized manufacturing. There was little employee ownership of, or responsibility for, the work processes. The quality-control program depended primarily on post-production inspection to find problems and mistakes.

Not content to remain static, in 1987 MKS adopted a total-customer-satisfaction program. Then in 1988, recognizing the importance of suppliers to its ability to manufacture and deliver its products, the company started a supply-base-management program. In 1990, it began integrating quality control into the manufacturing process. In 1992, the company's Kanban system with suppliers was launched.

"We are a company that is constantly involved in change, not a company of 'project-of-the-month.' It makes us more successful," explained Jerry Colella, director of corporate materials and logistics. At MKS, he said,

---

Reprinted with permission from *Quality*, April 1997, pp. 68–70.

new quality-improvement ideas, once introduced, are usually accepted and brought to fruition.

This is true in part because of the commitment and leadership of the company's management. As Frank Uttaro, director of corporate quality assurance, pointed out, "The company has a good track record of getting behind projects that make sense."

Like most companies, though, MKS had few resources to dabble in things that were not crucial to enhancing business, so the decision to implement ISO 9000 was not made lightly. "We got into it because there was a perceived benefit," said Colella. "We believed it made sense to do it. We had prior experience, had initiated systems at least this complex before."

This prior experience gave the company a head start when the time came to begin preparing for ISO 9000 certification. "The foundation was there," said Uttaro. "For a lot of departments there wasn't a big impact." Comparing the company's existing procedures with the ISO standard, Uttaro found that there were only five out of the standard's 20 requirements that weren't covered already. In meeting those five requirements, he said, "The biggest change by far was documenting the process side of the business, because we had a very good handle on the product. The key requirement that we had to fulfill was to get systems on paper. We were dealing with most of the requirements of the standard already."

In addition to creating better documentation, the company created a formal, consistent approval process with centralized control and automatic distribution. Other required changes were relatively minor. Uttaro said, "Our formal management review had to be changed slightly. The contract-review process had to be formalized, as did the design-control process. Service and purchasing, for TQM [total quality management] reasons, were ahead of the game."

Confident that they were already doing many things right, MKS employees were careful not to go overboard when making changes. "During the implementation we didn't try to reinvent the wheel. We just wrote [our existing procedure] down and went with it," said Doug Moran, mechanical sourcing engineer. "If what [we] did already met the spec, [we said,] 'Don't change it. Just write it down.'"

"We weren't asking [our employees] to take everything they were doing and throw it out and do it over again," said Uttaro. "You have the highest likelihood of success if you adapt [your process] as little as possible." Companies often make the mistake of adding non-value-added activities and contradicting their existing total-quality-management principles if they concentrate too much on the letter of the ISO "law" rather than the intent behind it.

"My concern was to have a system that was relatively user-friendly," said Colella, adding that a system doesn't have to be fancy to work. Each process should be easy to follow and easy to change when necessary. This makes it more palatable to the people using the process, because they realize that documenting something doesn't freeze it in place for eternity. If a system is too complex, Colella said, people would rather go around it. If you make a system simple, they will use it, and keep it current.

Achieving the desired level of simplicity was no easy task in itself. Uttaro said, "Overdocumenting was a big problem. People perceive the need to read into the standard what they think it means. But there are a lot of creative ways to adhere to the spirit of the things. There is a tendency in people to overcompensate for what they do." People should remember, he advised, that if the standard requires that a certain process be documented, "It can be a record that already exists. [ISO certification] doesn't require abandoning the existing system. People have a tendency to let the standard drive what they do. They should overlay the requirements on their business, not change their business to meet the requirements."

Although MKS had a history of continuous quality improvement, and the changes the company needed to make to implement ISO 9000 were relatively minor, no change is ever completely effortless. The company's long-term employees were used to doing things based on their own individual knowledge, not necessarily performing a task the same way each time or across departments. "There was definitely some push-back of people resisting being told to do things all the same way," said Uttaro. "People would say, 'I do it a different way because in my building it makes sense.' They didn't believe one system would work across the board."

To change that attitude, MKS made an effort to heighten the quality-system awareness of everybody in the company. The new system became part of the initial training for new employees, and Colella pointed out that the training itself was far easier once there was a single system that was written down, controlled, and kept current. The company converted some of the documentation into more visual formats to overcome the language barriers inherent in its diverse workforce.

With a documented, consistent system in place, employees began to have more accountability for their work, and gradually they accepted that there was a standard way to perform each process. That was one of the main benefits MKS experienced in relation to ISO 9000, Uttaro said. "It got people to do things consistently regardless of personal preference or how long they'd been with the company. It forced that discipline that every company really needs. Even though we make mistakes, we can track down the problem and fix it. Inconsistency doesn't allow you to go back and find the root cause of a problem."

Colella agreed with him, adding, "It gave us documentation to look at. It increased yield and reduced scrap because we had a way to measure things."

Employee accountability also resulted in workers taking more pride and ownership in their work. "When a customer would come in and tour the factory, they saw a lot of answers and involvement coming from people on the [production] line," Uttaro said. He also noticed an improvement in the company's warranty-return rate, since returns and field failures were treated as extensions of manufacturing problems.

For MKS, ISO 9000 was not treated as an end in itself, but as a means to that end, thus enabling the company to continue to improve the quality of its products and the efficiency of its processes. ISO was not the first step on that path, nor will it be the last. "The primary focus that drives all these things is focusing on the external customer, satisfying demand for high-quality, reasonable-cost products on time," said Colella. "How do we stay ahead of competition to satisfy the customer?"

Uttaro explained his basic philosophy this way: "We shouldn't make changes that will hurt our customer, but we should make any change that will help the customer. We're willing to change anything around, but it better not hurt quality and delivery."

# THINKING EXPORT?
# THINK ISO 9000

Davis Goodman

## Certification Serves as Seal of Approval

You've decided to begin selling to Europe, but no purchaser will place an order. You're well-known in the U.S. and have gone to Asia to introduce your product and company to top government officials there, but even after long meetings, they remain skeptical of your ability to perform. Your competitors are selling to South America but purchasers won't even meet with you.

Unlikely stories? Far from it. Each of these stories describes problems that are becoming increasingly common for companies without ISO 9000 registration.

Exactly what is ISO 9000 and why is it becoming so important? Which companies should think about registering? How long does it take and how expensive is it?

Most important, will the time and expense be worth it to your firm? The answer is simple: yes.

## The ISO 9000 Concept

ISO comes from the Greek, isos, which means equal. ISO 9000 and 9004 are actually guidelines for registration; the actual ISO standards are 9001, 9002, 9003, and 14001.

ISO makes up a globally recognized standard for management quality assurance systems within any industrial or service company (except for electrical and electronic product companies, which have their own standards). ISO certification doesn't guarantee quality, but rather consistency of procedures. Toronto-based R.N. Shaughnessy, former chairman of the ISO committee, who drafted the basics of the original ISO concept, says "the standards promote quality, reliability, sustainability, and predictability, which are important not only for the sake of purchasers but for the company's own efficiency and profitability."

## Global Standards for Global Players

All kinds of standards are playing an increasingly important role in world trade. Because many products now have a global marketplace, purchasers are increasingly being asked to deal with sellers whom they do not know by reputation. To make their supply chain more reliable, purchasers are using compliance with recognized standards as one means of determining a supplier's legitimacy or a product's quality. In addition, local laws often require that certain standards be met, particularly within the European Union. Not only can registration ease entrance to or growth in a foreign marketplace, it may be required just to get in the game.

According to Horst Stange, VP of global quality for Life Fitness Products, a global leader in the manufacture and sale of cardiovascular exercise equipment, "Almost every buyer we approach, from private companies to governments, wants to know that we are ISO 9000 certified. Not only have our sales dramatically increased around the world because of the certification, without it, we could not maintain our leadership position."

ISO 9000 started in the late 1970s, after the World Trade Organization began forming an international consensus to dismantle fiscal barriers to trade, such as duties and tariffs. Other barriers, such as technical requirements, could easily have replaced the fiscal ones. So the WTO set about devising a common standard to define product quality and product acceptability.

ISO 9000 is a voluntary certification; that is, there are no laws specifically requiring ISO 9000 registration. However, as with these other "voluntary" standards, ISO 9000 may often be required "in fact."

Conmed/Aspen Labs, Inc., a U.S. manufacturer of medical devices, based in Englewood, Colo., realized as early as 1992 that buyers would be demanding demonstrated compliance with some common standard, in addition to compliance with government regulations, and so the company became ISO 9000 registered in 1994. Now, reports Mike Hart, director of quality assurance and regulatory affairs, without ISO 9000 certification, Conmed/Aspen Labs would find it nearly impossible to sell to many markets around the world and at home, especially to the U.S. government. Even companies with global recognition are finding that purchasers are choosing suppliers based on quality—and they see ISO registration as a mark of merit. For example, the big three U.S. auto-makers require suppliers to meet QS 9000 standards—a more specialized version of ISO 9000.

Purchasers themselves may be ISO 9000 registered. To keep that registration, they must ensure that companies in their supply chain apply an adequate management quality assurance system as well—as evidenced by ISO 9000 registration. Finally, the U.S. and foreign governments have begun requiring internal audits or other forms of checking suppliers' quality assurance systems, and ISO 9000 registration usually meets this requirement. Nearly 60 countries have national standards virtually identical to the ISO 9000 series.

## Do I Care?

Any company may find that ISO 9000 registration becomes necessary, for any of the reasons discussed above. The process is not a simple or quick one, so determining whether to obtain ISO registration should be part of any strategic plan for overseas expansion.

ISO 9000 is most important for companies that deal with products for which there are safety or liability issues or which require exact measurements or calibration. Medical and engineering equipment, chemical products, computer equipment, industrial machines, exercise equipment, and the like are among the more obvious products affected by purchaser preference or government regulations requiring consistent processes and quality. But having adequate quality assurance systems is now a necessity in almost any industrial enterprise or service business. According to the *Quality Systems Update,* published by McGraw-Hill Companies, there are ISO 9000 registered companies for nearly every four-digit SIC code.

Lesley Swain, U.S. sports lab manager for TOV Product Service, an ISO compliance certifier in Boulder, Colo., says worldwide registration of companies meeting ISO 9000 standards increased nearly tenfold, from 1992 to 1997, to about 200,000 total. In the U.S., the increase has been even more dramatic, from about 500 companies with ISO 9000 registration in 1992 to about 18,000 at the end of 1997. Studies show that over half of all U.S. companies with ISO 9000 registration have fewer than 500 employees, and one quarter have fewer than 150.

Much of the push for registration is coming from European Union regulations. The adoption of ISO 9000 standards fosters some consistency across the EU's many borders. Downward pressure on suppliers results in more and more ISO 9000 registrations.

Recognition of the value of ISO 9000 is significant in many other areas of the world as well, including Asia. Companies serious about selling internationally should not be lulled into complacency by the lower level of interest shown for ISO 9000 in the U.S.

The ISO registration process and costs are different for every company. All employees should be involved, and obtaining the best results, as Mike Hart of Conmed/Aspen Labs has found, should "be only the start of the journey."

# FOR FURTHER READING

Abarca, Dennis, "Implementing ISO 9000 & ISO 14000 Concurrently," *Pollution Engineering,* Oct. 1998, pp. 46–48.

Arora, S. C., "Developing a Quality Management System," *International Trade Forum,* No. 1, 1998, pp. 22–27.

Boiral, Oliver, "ISO 14001: Against the Tide of Modern Management?" *Journal of General Management,* Autumn 1998, pp. 35–52.

Goodman, Davis, "Earning the ISO 9000 Seal of Approval. Part II. Balancing the Costs and Benefits of Certification," *World Trade,* Sept. 1998, pp. 46–49.

Olson, Roger E., "ISO 14000: The Business Manager's Complete Guide to Environmental Management," *Quality Progress,* Sept. 1998, p. 117.

Zuckerman, Amy, "How to Turn Standards Turmoil into Value-Added Strategic Advantage," *Quality Progress,* Sept. 1998, pp. 19–20.

# 13

# THEORY OF CONSTRAINTS

*The goal is not to save money but to make money.*
Eliyahu Goldratt, *The Goal*[1]

The theory is only in its adolescence, but few theories in the past have caught the imagination of managers as has the theory of constraints. Eliyahu Goldratt's revolutionary book *The Goal* began to appear in bookstores and corporate offices in 1986 and for the next eight years sold over one million copies. The primary method of distribution has been readers passing on copies to friends and colleagues.[2]

The book, written in the form of a novel, traces the thoughts and activities of plant manager Alex Rogo as he strives to save his plant from closure. He gradually realizes that traditional "keep busy" efficiency and utilization measures might lead only to increased stock and not to sales. The way to maximize sales and profit is to maximize bottleneck *throughput,* and a series of common-sense measures, first focusing on bottlenecks and later on reducing batch sizes, allow Alex to improve production performance. The plant is saved and Alex is promoted. Those ideas were codified by Goldratt into what has now become the emerging theory of constraints (TOC), which contends that every business has at least one resource that is preventing it from making infinite profits—infinite as each constraint is removed in turn in never-ending continuous improvement.[3]

> The core idea in the Theory of Constraints is that every real system such as a profit-making enterprise must have at least one constraint. If it were not

true, then the system would produce an infinite amount of whatever it strives for. In the case of a profit-making enterprise it would be infinite profits.[4]

For those managers who want more profits, Goldratt concludes that there is no choice; "either you manage constraints or they will manage you."

There are several innovative principles advanced by the TOC. One is the focus on **throughput**—the rate at which a system generates money. This focus is unlike total quality management and process control, which tend to focus on input and output. Equally important is the focus on throughput as a means of reducing time and cycle time to market. Time and speed have become critical concerns to most firms in the modern marketing environment that demands shorter lead times. Faster throughput will also reduce manufacturing and shipping time, and this results in higher revenues.

## THE GOAL[5]

Most for-profit companies believe their goal is related to money. Some would say that the goal is related to customers and others would argue that the goal is related to the work force. The TOC has no argument with any of these goals. No matter which one is chosen, the other two become necessary conditions (see Figure 13-1). A company whose goal is to make money now and in the future will find that it is not possible to do so unless it also satisfies customers and employees now and in the future. If the company does not seek to satisfy employees now and in the future, it will experience high employee defection, which will lead to high customer defections. If a company chooses satisfying customers now and in the future, it will find it is necessary to make money and to satisfy employees now

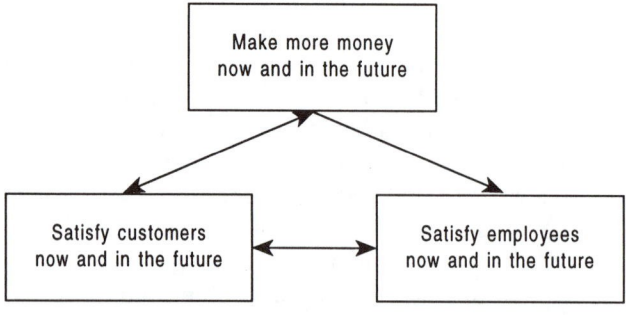

**Figure 13-1**  Integrated Goals of the Theory of Constraints

and in the future. This leads to the conclusion that in order to "make more money now and in the future," the goal of TOC, a company will also "satisfy customers and employees now and in the future."

## THE CHAIN ANALOGY

Rather than viewing the organization (system) as a collection of functions, activities, or processes, TOC treats it as a chain of interlinked links or a grid of interlinked chains. The performance of the whole chain is determined by the weakest link. Only after the weakest link has been strengthened will it be productive to concentrate on reinforcing other links. The weakest link is the **system constraint**.

The manufacturer in the example in Figure 13-2 produced products for resale. Marketing conducts research to determine customer needs. Design converts marketing inputs into product design. Manufacturing produces according to the market sales forecast and product specifications from design. Finished goods are warehoused and shipped as orders are received. Each function or activity is dependent on the preceding step. Moreover, the entire system (chain) is dependent on all of the others, and each link in the chain is a potential **constraint**. If marketing does not correctly judge customer needs or if design cannot adequately translate these into product specifications or prepares the wrong specifications, the product manufactured will not sell, and so forth and so on.

To reiterate, each link is a potential constraint. Of course, this illustration is a simple one and does not include other "links" in a company (e.g., finance, accounting, personnel).

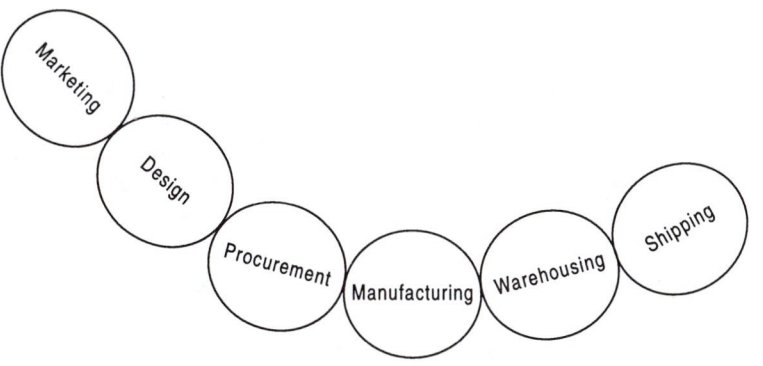

**Figure 13-2**   The Organization as a System of Interlinked Chains

# THE SYSTEMS APPROACH VS.
# CONVENTIONAL MANAGEMENT

The concept of an organization as a system was shown in Figure 6-1. The performance of the entire system is a function of the performance of each of its components. The same applies to subgroups (departments, activities, functions).

What Figure 6-1 does not demonstrate but what is basic to the TOC is that the sum of the optima is not the system optimum. In other words, if the performance of each part of the system (process) is individually maximized, the system as a whole will not behave as well as it could. Consider the conventional management advice:

- An improvement to any link in the chain is considered to be an improvement to the chain.

- System-wide or "global" improvement is believed to be the sum of all the "local" improvements made within each link.

This is analogous to saying that the primary measurement of success in managing the chain is the weight of the chain (e.g., if one manager beefs up his or her link, that makes the chain heavier and better).

What occurs is the situation depicted in Figure 13-3. The tendency is for each manager to compete for scarce resources and maximize the output of his or her link. The assumption is that maximizing each link is the way to maximize the effect of the entire organization. Emphasis is on improving individual links rather than "gluing" them together.

Dettmer[2] gives the example of an automobile. Most are designed to achieve a specific objective, such as luxury, economy, or speed. As a complex system, an automobile has to integrate the performance of many components to achieve its objective. If the objective is economy, it is counterproductive to "improve" the system by installing racing cams in the engine, even if they are the best-performing cams to be had. Likewise, inflating tires for maximum mileage efficiency improves their service life. A race car driver, however, is more concerned with how the car handles than the life of the tires. Overinflation might maximize tire life but compromises the overall performance of the car–driver system.

The following example is given by Ciras of Iowa State University.[6] In a printing company, members of a team from a press operation in the middle of their system came to management with a proposal for continuous improvement. (Think of them as being located in the manufacturing link above.) They had discovered that an improvement could be made to their press that would increase productivity by 25 percent! It would cost the company only $20,000. Conventional analysis showed that the payback period was relatively short. Would you authorize the investment?

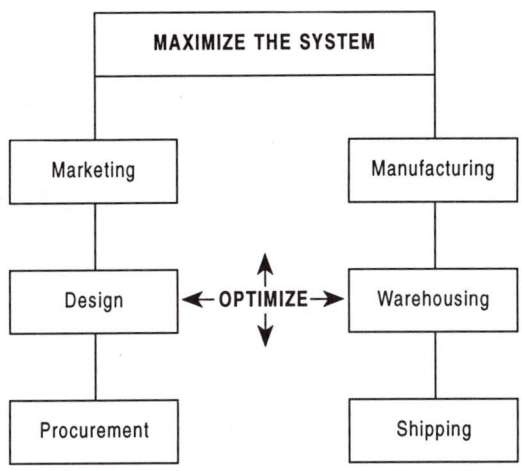

**Figure 13-3**    Traditional Organization Chart

Senior managers were about to sign the check when someone asked, "Where does the output of this press go? And what is the status of work in process at that next operation?" It turned out that work was already queued up at the next operation. In other words, the company almost spent $20,000 so that the output of the press in question could wait 25 percent longer at the next operation! Had the senior managers approved the expenditure, they may have had a false sense of success when viewing the 25 percent increase in the "productivity" figures of the press, but the actual bottom-line impact would have been a negative $20,000 because that money would have been spent without actually bringing any more money into the plant!

## PHYSICAL VS. POLICY CONSTRAINTS

Goldratt concludes that the vast majority of constraints are caused by policies—not physical constraints (e.g., machines, space, equipment, or other tangible resources). You should be able to easily identify policy constraints within and outside your organization. Take, for example, the current state of health care in the United States. Between the policies of Medicare, HMOs, and the insurance industry, how many people are pleased with their health care provider? Consider also the many company policies that constrain performance, such as policies concerning personnel, purchasing, warranty...the list goes on. Because these constraints are less visible, they are more difficult to identify and overcome. They foreclose many lines of inquiry as to possible solutions. A possible course of action can be stopped by the phrase "that's our policy." TOC provides the method whereby the process of continuous improvement can be institutionalized and the impact of absolute policies reduced.

## THE THEORY OF CONSTRAINTS AND THE PROCESS OF ONGOING IMPROVEMENT

To manage constraints (rather than be managed by them), and to ensure that emphasis remains on the system (chain) level rather than the component (link) level, Goldratt proposes a five-step process of ongoing improvement:

1. **"Identify the system's constraints [its weakest links]."** This link should be the first target of improvement.
2. **"Decide how to exploit the constraint."** Make the constraint, as it exists now, as effective as possible.
3. **"Subordinate everything else to the above decision."** Every other part of the system must be aligned and adjusted to support the maximum effectiveness of the constraint, even if it means "detuning" some non-constraints.
4. **"Elevate the system's constraint."** If steps 2 and 3 do not relieve the constraint to the extent that it ceases to be the weakest link, more rigorous action is necessary, such as formulating strategies to increase throughput across the constraint (e.g., offloading work to other sources or acquiring more capability).
5. **"If, in the previous steps, a constraint has been broken, go back to step 1, but do not allow inertia to cause a new constraint."** This is the feedback loop that makes TOC a continuous process. Implicit in this step (and the reason many organizations lose momentum in continuous improvement) is the caution to not become complacent. No solution is permanent. As the system's environment changes, a given solution will progressively deteriorate unless it is modified to account for those changes.[7]

Table 13-1 summarizes the use of this five-step process for general-purpose situations and for physical constraints. Reference to logic trees is addressed in the sections to follow.[8]

## THE THINKING PROCESS (LOGIC TREES)

Dr. Goldratt has developed his own expression of the scientific method of constraints management. The method is the structured logic-tree thinking pro-

**Table 13-1**   The TOC Five-Step Focusing Process: The Inherently Best Process of Ongoing Improvement

| Focusing steps | All situations (general purpose) | Physical constraints (simplified) |
|---|---|---|
| **Step 1.** Identify the constraint(s). | 1. Use TOC logic trees to sort facts (entities) into constraints, root causes, and core problems. | 1. Identify the resource or resources that are the primary obstacles to progress toward the goal. |
| **Step 2.** Decide how to exploit the constraint(s). | 2. Use TOC logic-tree process to decide how best to progress toward the goal within current constraints. | 2. Decide on a plan for the primary constraint that best supports the system's goal. |
| **Step 3.** Subordinate everything else to the above decision. | 3. Bring other factors in line with above decisions. Do not allow other improvement initiatives to interfere with the high priority of the above decisions. | 3. Alter or manage the system's policies, processes, and other resources to support the above decisions. |
| **Step 4.** Elevate (lift/ remove/break) the constraint(s). | 4. Use TOC logic-tree processes to select constraints for removal in the current iteration and to remove them. | 4. Add capacity or otherwise change the status of the original resource as dominating primary constraint. |
| **Step 5.** Return to step 1, but do not let inertia become the constraint. | 5. Go back to step 1, but do not allow previous decisions made in steps 1 to 4 to become unnecessary and damaging constraints now. | 5. Go back to step 1, but do not allow previous decisions made in steps 1 to 4 to become constraints. |
| **Comments** | This general-purpose process handles any combination of policy, process, and physical resource constraints. | This simplified process is the basis for TOC project management, logistics, and factory scheduling procedures. |

cess. The thinking processes involve the rigorous application of effect–cause–effect logic to answer the following questions:

1. What to change?
2. What to change to?
3. How to cause the change?

The answer to the first question—*what to change*—is equivalent to "identify the constraint." For this purpose, the "current-reality tree" (Figure 13-4) is a

- Current Situation

- Undesirable Effects

- Facts, Entities

- If... Then...

- Cause... Effect...

- And (linked)... Or...

- Root Causes

- Core Problems

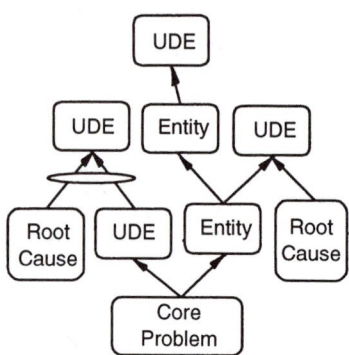

---

**Figure 13-4**   Current-Reality-Tree Management Process and Diagram

---

logical mapping structure to make the connections among a current situation's many symptoms, facts, root causes, and core problems. This may be confusing, but when completed, it answers the question: What to change?

The first step is to start with evidence of the negative effects that are apparent within the system. Examples might include such things as poor union relations, inventory turn going down, returns increasing, and orders late. These are called "undesirable effects" (UDEs) and are not the real problem but only an effect of the real or "core" problem. What is the interrelated web of cause and effect that links the undesirable effects together? Completion of this exercise should lead to the identification of the "core" problem.

Figure 13-4 is a simple diagram of a TOC reality logic tree. It is a generic diagram which indicates that core problems and root causes, typically shown at the bottom of a current-reality-tree diagram, are the causes of undesirable effects shown at the top.

## What to Change to?

Having determined the "what to change" from the current-reality logic tree, the next question is: What to change to? The answer should be obvious from the previous step, but two additional steps need to be taken:

1. Identify the breakthrough idea that will overcome the current constraint.

2. Ensure that the "cure" that is derived will not be worse than the "disease."

The "evaporating-cloud" (conflict) logic tree is an important aid in developing a breakthrough idea (known as an injection) that will resolve the conflict

- Conflict process
  and diagram

- Objective

- Needs

- Prerequisites

- Inherent conflict

- Examines assumptions

- Generates ideas

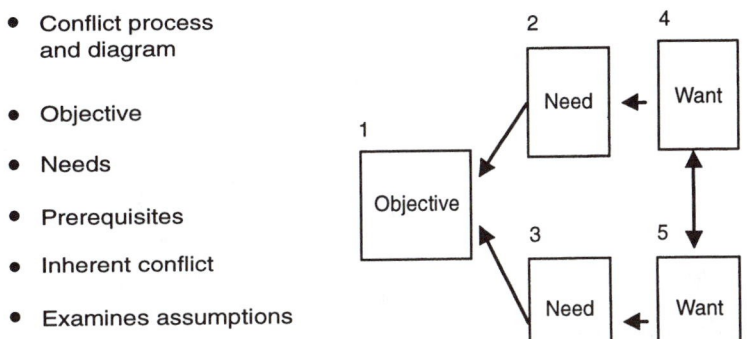

**Figure 13-5**   Evaporating-Cloud (Conflict) Logic Tree Management Process and Diagram

previously identified. The tool for doing this is the "evaporating cloud" illustrated in Figure 13-5.

Will the breakthrough idea have the desired impact on the system? In other words, would the breakthrough idea (injection) change the undesirable effects into desirable effects (DEs)? The tool for this step is the "future-reality tree." Return to the current-reality tree and insert the idea at the appropriate place. Then, redraw the logical connections and see whether implementing the idea would reverse the undesirable effects into desirable effects. If it works, you know what to change. The mapping tool is the future-reality tree. Figure 13-6 is a simple and generic future-tree diagram.

- Injections (Ideas)

- Intermediate Effects

- Desirable Effects (DE)

- "Trunk" of Tree

- Negative Branches

- "Tight" or "Loose"

- Strategies

- Vision Statements

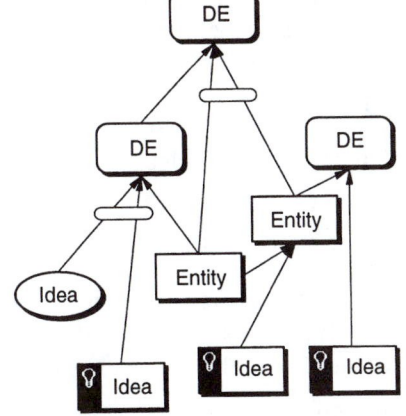

**Figure 13-6**   Future-Reality-Tree Management Process and Diagram

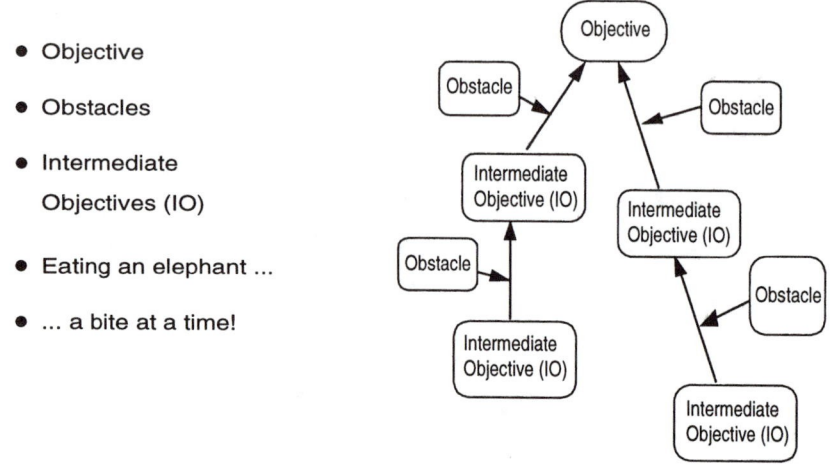

- Objective
- Obstacles
- Intermediate Objectives (IO)
- Eating an elephant ...
- ... a bite at a time!

**Figure 13-7**    Prerequisites-Tree Management Process and Diagram

## How to Cause the Change?

At this point, the core problem (constraint) is identified (from the current-reality tree), the breakthrough idea for improving the condition (from the evaporating cloud) is evident, and the future-reality tree has provided assurance that the idea will change the undesirable effects into desirable effects. The challenge now is to move from undesirable reality to desired future reality. The tool for this is the prerequisites tree (Figure 13-7).

A big advantage of this approach is that it involves people who should implement the change and those who may be resistant to it. The problem has probably existed for some time, and there is a significant conflict underlying the current behavior. Typical obstacles that might arise include:

- "We've tried that before."
- "It's not in the budget."
- "Too expensive."
- "The boss won't buy it."

By putting the problem of the necessary change on the table, participants who identify obstacles are asked to identify the conditions that would be necessary to overcome them. The process is straightforward:

1. Establish the objective; change undesirable effects into desirable effects.

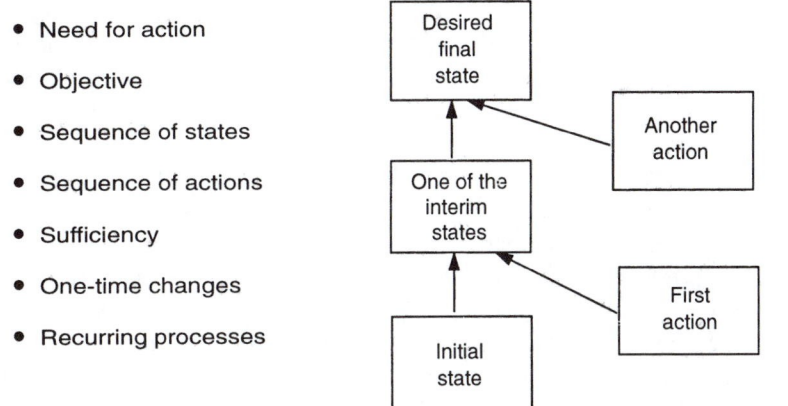

- Need for action
- Objective
- Sequence of states
- Sequence of actions
- Sufficiency
- One-time changes
- Recurring processes

**Figure 13-8**   TOC Transition-Tree Management Process and Diagram

2. Identify the obstacles to reaching the objective as well as intermediate objectives to overcome all the obstacles.
3. Arrange the intermediate objectives and obstacles into the structure and sequence of the prerequisites tree (Figure 13-7).

Once all additional ideas that are necessary to implement the original injection are known, a plan is mapped out that shows the actions necessary to achieve successful implementation. The tool used to accomplish this is the transition tree (Figure 13-8). This tool can be used to (1) document existing and new recurring processes (e.g., marketing processes, design processes, procurement, warehousing processes, shipping processes) and (2) accomplish one-time changes in circumstances (e.g., establish new facilities, improve processes, make strategic moves).

## THEORY OF CONSTRAINTS MEASUREMENT SYSTEM FOR DECISION MAKING

*If you can't measure it you can't manage it.*

Anonymous

Conventional accounting systems tend to focus on the cost factors that impact net profit, return on investment, and cash flow. Whereas these measures are required to satisfy certain requirements for financial reporting, they are not good for day-to-day *predictive* decisions. They are historical and of little use in feedforward control and providing proactive measures for management decisions, and certainly not for global decisions that impact the entire system. The answer eludes the manager who asks, "What do I think the impact of this decision will be on net profit at year end?"

The shortcomings of conventional accounting have led to the creation of "local" measurements that are believed to be connected to net profit or return on investment. For the most part, these measures are intended to determine the "cost" of producing a product or to calculate the cost variance, which is the difference between a "standard cost" and the calculated "actual cost." The result is a large number of "variance reports" that are after the fact and are micro measures based on faulty assumptions and which usually lead to poor management decisions. What is needed are "local" measurements that are linked directly to the long-term global measures of net profit, return on investment, and cash flow. Sometimes managers and executives lose sight of these shortcomings. As a result of their *cost-world* training, they are conditioned to focus on artificial targets, such as equipment payback periods and "paper" profits generated by internal money shuffling, rather than on the true goal of a business, which is to make money—real money, not accounting money. Today, many manufacturers are undergoing a paradigm shift in thinking—moving from the *cost world* to the *throughput world*. The result is the proliferation of programs to improve quality (total quality management), reduce inventories, shorten manufacturing cycle times, and improve response to the marketplace.

## What Measures to Use: Definitions

The essential components of the TOC measurement (decision-making) system are

1. Throughput
2. Inventory
3. Operating expense

which impact

- Net profit
- Return on investment
- Cash flow

**Throughput** is the rate at which the system generates money through sales, or the money coming into the system. Notice that throughput is a "global" measurement (i.e., the "system," not a department or a subsystem, generates throughput). Using a subsystem measure may optimize that unit but would move the company away from the true goal. Throughput cannot be measured in terms of units produced (e.g., pieces per hour); it must be measured in the same units as the goal: dollars. Building to stock is not throughput. Only dollars generated by the system get counted; raw material and purchased parts are not throughput.

**Inventory** is everything the system has invested in what it intends to sell, or all the money tied up inside the system. Under the TOC way of thinking, inventory is a liability, not an asset, as the balance sheet shows. There are two kinds of inventory:

- That which moves through the operation and ends up being sold to customers. The three types are raw material, work in process, and finished goods.

- The second type recognized by TOC does not move through the organization like materials do. It consists of all the items that are owned and are "being held" by the company because they are necessary to produce throughput. The building, machinery, computers, fixtures, etc. are common examples.

**Operating expense** is all the money the system spends in order to convert inventory into throughout, or all the money leaving the system. All employee time is operating expense. It makes no difference whether a person is performing "direct labor," "indirect labor," or is on vacation or sick leave. If a person gets paid the same amount at the end of the week regardless of how much throughput is generated, then his or her pay is operating expense.[9]

## THE THEORY OF CONSTRAINTS MANAGEMENT SYSTEM

The following symbols are used in this section:

- Throughout (T). Impact up
- Inventory (I). Impact level
- Operating expense (OE). Impact down
- Net profit (NP)
- Return on investment (ROI)
- Cash flow (CF)

**Question:** If we can increase T while maintaining level I and level OE, what is the impact on NP, ROI, and CF?

| If | T is up | I is level | OE is level |
|------|---------|------------|-------------|
| then | NP is up | ROI is up | CF is up |

**Question:** If we can decrease I while maintaining level T and level OE, what is the impact on NP, ROI, and CF?

| If | T is level | I is down | OE is level |
|---|---|---|---|
| then | NP is level | ROI is up | CF is up |

**Question:** If we can decrease OE while maintaining level T and level I, what will be the impact on NP, ROI, and CF?

| If | T is level | I is level | OE is down |
|---|---|---|---|
| then | NP is up | ROI is up | CF is up |

By determining **the impact that an action will have now on T, I, and OE**, we will know the future impact on NP, ROI, and CF.

**Question:** What about I? Because it has no direct impact on NP, it would seem to be less powerful in terms of impact on the bottom line. Even when I is down, there is no direct impact on NP. The answer lies in the reduction of OE. When I is down, carrying costs are down, and OE is down.

## Cost World vs. Throughput World

**Question:** Which is most important in terms of where to focus?

- Increase T
- Decrease I
- Decrease OE

| Cost world | Throughput world |
|---|---|
| Decreasing OE is #1 because we have relatively high control of our expenses. | Increasing T is unquestionably #1 because it has the greatest potential impact on the bottom line. |
| Increasing T is important but ranks #2 because we are at the mercy of the marketplace and have less control over sales. | Decreasing I is #2 because excess work in process and finished goods jeopardizes future T. |
| I is a "gray area" that we do not know what to do about; it is a "necessary evil" that must be lived with to protect sales. | Decreasing OE is #3 because significant reductions in work force usually jeopardize future T. |

## QUESTIONS FOR DISCUSSION

**13-1**  If an organization has three goals—making money, satisfying customers, and satisfying employees, explain how these goals reinforce each other.

**13-2**  What is the difference between the classical functional organization and the one suggested by the theory of constraints?

**13-3**  How would a management-by-objectives program or focus on individual activity results tend to reduce the potential output of the entire organization? Explain in terms of the "chain" analogy. Explain in terms of systems theory.

**13-4**  From the drawing in Figure 13-2, select one function and describe how one or more of the subactivities of the function become the system constraint.

**13-5**  Name a policy (Chapter 4) constraint that might exist in a function or activity and describe how it might be a constraint.

**13-6**  If we can maintain the level of operating expense and throughput while decreasing inventory, what is the impact on net profit, return on investment, and cash flow?

**13-7**  How might the classical cost-accounting focus tend to work against net profit, return on investment, and cash flow?

## ENDNOTES

1. Eliyahu Goldratt, *The Goal,* 2nd ed., New York: North River Press, 1992.
2. William Dettmer, "Quality and the Theory of Constraints," *Quality Progress,* April 1995, pp. 77–81.
3. Karen M. Kroll, "The Theory of Constraints Revisited," *Industry Week,* April 20, 1998.
4. Eric W. Noreen, *The Theory of Constraints and Its Implications for Management Accounting,* New York: North River Press, 1995.
5. Much of the content in this section and the thinking process to follow is suggested by Ciras at Iowa State University, who maintains a Web site on the topic of theory of constraints: http://www.ciras.iastate.edu/toc/WhatIsTheGoal.htm.
6. Ciras, Endnote 5.
7. Adapted from Dettmer, Endnote 2.
8. Used with permission from Thomas B. McMullen, Jr., *Theory of Constraints (TOC) Management System,* Boca Raton, Fla.: St. Lucie Press, 1998.
9. The implications of this definition are profound because most manufacturers' decisions on the production floor are highly influenced by measurements such as direct labor hours per unit, ratios of indirect to direct labor hours, etc. TOC exposes the erroneous actions that are often taken as a result and makes visible the real impact on the bottom line.

# MAKING PRODUCTION PREDICTABLE

Complex manufacturing involves more than getting bills and routings right, according to Ralph Carrell, production planner at Brenco Inc.'s Petersburg, VA, plant. "We produce a complex flow of parts; demand is volatile, and supply is not always reliable," he says. "Underuse of workcenters and people from time to time is followed by overtime expenses. While inventories climb, parts shortages can appear at critical assembly points." On-time deliveries can be jeopardized when these problems surface.

The plant, which manufactures transmission components for Ford Motor Co. and tapered roller bearings and remanufactured journal boxes for other customers, needed a predictable flow of parts, and that meant answering certain questions. How do you get a workcenter to produce subassemblies on time? What centers are feeding the bottlenecks? Are those bottlenecks really bottlenecks?

Five years ago, to identify and eliminate bottlenecks, Carrell began using Theory of Constraints software and Drum–Buffer–Rope practices. No matter how complex the manufacturing process, the DBR principle is simple. The slowest and most overloaded resource in any factory is the "Drum." The rest of the factory marches to its beat. "In a perfect world," says Carrell, "the right jobs arrive at a specified period of time before the Drum needs them. In the world of the plant floor, delays happen." If a nonconstraint does not support and feed the Drum with the right parts, the beat slows. Time buffers ensure that jobs will still arrive in time to keep the Drums beating. Plants could protect the shop floor's Drums by creating massive WIP inventory, of course, but Carrell says that's an expensive solution in Brenco's world of low-volume, high-product-mix manufacturing. What's more, unnecessary inventory clogs up the pipeline, impeding the flow of the material needed on the floor.

The DBR system with Theory of Constraints scheduling software worked well for Brenco. Inventories dropped, and on-time shipments rose to 95%. Still,

Reproduced, with permission, from *Manufacturing Engineering,* July 1998.

says Carrell, problems remained. "Although we identified our constraints, we weren't sure whether we were running the right parts, at the right time, in the right sequence, to feed our bearing assembly and constraint workcenters," he says. "We were spending too much time managing the nonconstraints."

DBR prescribes that the shop floor must work only on what it needs to support market requirements. The timing of job releases depends on what the Drums can support, offset by the Buffers. This ties the Rope from the Drum back to the starting operations in the shop. Carrel says that because the Rope was missing from the system, "material release was out of sync with the Drum and got jammed."

When he looked for software based on DBR, he found that a package called Resonance, from ThruPut Technologies (San Jose, CA), allowed him to identify constraints, subordinate the schedules of nonconstraints to the requirements of its Drum, and calculate the material required to support the shop floor and production plan. The nonconstraints' struggles for capacity ended, taking care of bottlenecks. The plant had been running two separate schedules, so that WIP got out of hand, tying up cash the company wanted for other projects. Synchronizing manufacturing with the new software produced a 17% drop in WIP over a nine-month period; Carrell expects another 18% drop in the next six months. Switching to a complete DBR system increased on-time delivery to 98%. Work that took Carrell and the other schedulers 12 hours to schedule now can be run in one hour. The startup process was pretty smooth, says Carrell, because plant employees understood Theory of Constraints theory and practices when the new software was introduced. Today, he says, "we have narrowed our field of vision to those items that prevent the manufacturing system from meeting customer ship dates. That means ensuring that gating operations do not release more product into the factory than needed to meet customer demand and that the correct parts in the correct quantities arrive at the Drum buffer and Assembly buffer at the right times. By managing fewer items, we achieve better results, faster."

**CASE**

# THE THEORY OF CONSTRAINTS: APPLICATION TO A SERVICE FIRM

### Christopher T. Olson

American Security & Alarm Co., located in Lubbock, Texas, has been in operation since 1978. Its owner and president, Leota Hinson, has built the company from a small service company to a major competitor in security services including guard service; residential, auto, and commercial burglar systems; and monitoring service contracts for alarm users. It employs approximately 30 security officers, three alarm technicians, two salespeople, and a manager.

Sales of burglar alarms are made through an on-site survey of the property, consultation with the prospect on his or her needs and goals and, finally, a recommendation accompanied by a bid. Included in the bid is an estimate of how long from the date of acceptance the alarm will be installed and completed. Once the sale is completed, immediate actions are taken to ensure prompt delivery of a high-quality product. All of the times included in this analysis are the direct result of the experience of employees as well as the manager of American Security & Alarm Co.

## Installation Process

Upon receiving an order for an alarm system, the technician must respond quickly to meet marketing's promises. The first step is to match the inventory to the purchase order. If all parts are available, they are loaded onto the installation truck. At this time, a supply depletion card is completed to account for the used

Reprinted with permission of APICS—The Educational Society for Resource Management, from *Production and Inventory Management Journal,* Second Quarter 1998, pp. 55–59. This is an edited version of the prize-winning full-time graduate submission in the 1997 International Student Awards Program sponsored by the APICS Educational and Research Foundation. Mr. Olson was enrolled in the graduate program in the Department of Management, Texas Tech University, Lubbock, Texas.

inventory. If all is working properly, this method of tracking inventory works well. However, if multiple sales are made of the same system, there is a potential for a shortage. Although there is an inventory of smaller parts readily available in the stockroom for such occurrences, rarely will there be more than two control panels which contain the computer required to run the system. Fortunately, American Security & Alarm Co. has a good relationship with its suppliers and can get products drop shipped at a relatively low cost. This process of gathering the inventory should take no longer than 90 minutes.

Upon completing the supply depletion card, the technician is ready to install the system. For both commercial and residential systems, the installation process is basically the same. It consists of nine additional processes at the installation site. For an example, I will describe the process of installing a system inside a three-bedroom home.

**Setup.** Upon entering the home, the technician would match the items on the purchase order to strategic locations inside the home. Ideally, the salesperson has created a map of the house with the designated locations clearly marked. If not, the technician must design the system himself. Theoretically, these locations should match the logic used by the salesperson during the consultation and recommendation stage. For our example, a location for the control panel must be identified, usually inside a closet or near the attic hatch. In addition, a sensor for each window and door and any motion detectors or ultrasonic sensors require a chosen position within the home. Finally, a siren, keypad, telephone line, power line, and any other accessories must be strategically placed. Our example of a three-bedroom home would average six windows, three doors, two motion detectors, one control panel, one siren, one keypad, one telephone line, and one power line, for a total of 16 items to be installed. This process of choosing locations should take no longer than 45 minutes.

**Drilling Holes.** After deciding where everything is to be installed, holes must be drilled to run the wires from the component to the control panel. These holes are usually at the top of a door or window frame for contact sensors. The holes for the motion detectors would be positioned at the joint between the wall and the ceiling. The remaining components are contained either in the attic or behind walls. All methods completely conceal the wires and give the greatest aesthetic appeal to the customer. This process should take no longer than five minutes per hole, or 80 minutes.

**Run Wires.** After a hole is drilled, a wire can be delivered through the hole with the use of the longer drill bits which are equipped with a wire hole on the non-drilling end, allowing the wire to pass through the rafters and insulation in the attic, making it easier to find the wire. Upon finding the wire in the attic, it must be run from the component to the control panel. This process should take no longer than 15 minutes per wire, or 225 minutes.

**Mount Components.** After one or all of the wires have been run, the sensors or components can be connected and mounted in place. Once a component has been mounted, it should be left so as to provide easy accessibility for adjustment. This process should take no longer than ten minutes for a motion sensor or a keypad and no longer than five minutes for each remaining component, with the exception of the control panel; in this case, 105 minutes.

**Connecting/Programming the Control Panel.** After identifying which wires lead to which component, the technician can begin to connect them to their respective terminals on the control panel. When all the wires are connected, the panel can be programmed. This identifies the sections of the house, called zones, to the computer inside of the panel. How it is programmed determines the operation and features available to the user. This process should take no longer than a base of 90 minutes plus five minutes for each wire; in this case, 180 minutes.

**Processing Client's Account Data.** In order for the alarm system to operate effectively, it must be able to communicate to some outside source that there has been an alarm. This outside source is called a monitoring station. Upon receiving the data, the station takes the appropriate actions to resolve the situation, whether that be to call the police, ambulance, fire department, or the customer. Although this process is quite simple, it is nonetheless slow, but should take no longer than 30 minutes.

**Product Testing.** One of the last steps in the installation process is the testing of the installed system. If all has been done correctly, this will take relatively little time. However, poor installation or poor equipment could result in this process taking several hours. Basically, each window, door or sensor is tripped. If all tripped sensors appear on the control panel and keypad, the system is ready for testing its communication capabilities. On the other hand, if a sensor did not report an alarm, the system must be checked for a broken wire, loose connection, improper installation, or a faulty component. Although troubleshooting times vary greatly with regard to the particular problem at hand, an average time of eight minutes per component would not be uncommon, resulting in a total of 112 minutes in this case.

Upon completion of the internal testing, external testing must be done, using the same procedure. After the alarm is reset, the monitoring station can be called and the results of the test obtained. If the report matches the test, the system is in peak performance. However, if the report was inaccurate, then either the control panel must be reprogrammed or the telephone line must be checked. This process should take no more than 30 minutes. Thus, the total testing process should take no longer than 142 minutes.

**User Instruction.** After testing has been completed, training must be given to the customer on use of the system. Although this is very basic, it should be done with care to provide the user the greatest satisfaction with the product. This process should take no longer than 30 minutes.

**Cleanup.** Finally, after the system and customer are working in harmony, a few things must be cleaned up around the house. For instance, curtains may need to be rehung, tools may need to be put back into the toolbox, sawdust may need to be vacuumed, and furniture may need to be moved back to its original location. This process should take the technician no longer than 30 minutes.

## The Problem: Total Capacity

As you can see from this example, a typical residential installation would take a total of 957 minutes for one technician to complete. This is equivalent to 15 hours and 57 minutes. In an eight-hour shift, a technician is able to work only seven hours at the site due to travel time to and from the site and lunch. Thus, a typical alarm system would take a technician 2.3 days to complete. This means that the three technicians employed at American Security & Alarm can complete approximately 26 installations in one month. Provided that the marketing department does not sell more than that, the capacity of the company is adequate. However, after reviewing sales records, it became evident that marketing was selling an average of eight systems per week (32 per month) and, as a result, the technicians were well behind schedule and not meeting marketing's promises.

This pattern of overdue orders created a problem called the hockey-stick phenomenon. At the end of each month, the company found itself having to rush to meet the performance quotas set by the company and the promises made by marketing. However, marketing was simply meeting the demands of the market. Nevertheless, the technicians were falling drastically behind at the end of each month. As a result, daily overtime, weekend work, and constant expediting all increased expenses and ultimately added to customer dissatisfaction.

### Analyzing the Company

In order to eliminate this hockey-stick phenomenon, some of the basic assumptions of the company needed to be challenged and affirmed or replaced. In addition, the goal of the company must be defined. According to Goldratt, the goal of a firm is to make money. With this in mind, it can be assumed that American Security & Alarm Co. was in business to make money. In order to achieve this goal, Goldratt states that a company must also be productive. He explains that the definition of productivity is not only to meet performance standards, but also to do anything that brings the company closer to its ultimate goal. To adequately measure a company's productivity, two sets of measurements must be used: one refers to the company's financial performance and the other to its operational performance. Financial performance is composed of:

- **Net profit**—an absolute measurement in dollars
- **Return on investment**—a relative measure based on investment
- **Cash flow**—a survival measurement

All three must be used together to have a clear understanding of the company's financial position. If, for example, the company appears to have a very high net profit, one would initially assume that the company is doing well. However, it is possible that the company had to invest a substantial amount of capital to make that net profit. As a result, the return on investment is quite low, implying a rather poor investment. Furthermore, the company could appear to be quite successful and still go bankrupt because of a lack of cash flow. It doesn't do the company any good to have money owed to it if it cannot meet its own bills with the cash on hand.

Operational performance includes:

- **Throughput**—the rate at which money is generated by the system through sales
- **Inventory**—all the money that the system has invested in purchasing things it intends to sell
- **Operational expenses**—all the money that the system spends to turn inventory into throughput

Throughput is essentially goods sold. Inventory is all of the goods that are considered either work in process or unsold finished goods. American Security & Alarm, however, does not ever experience unsold finished goods since its services are consumed at the same time the service is being performed, as with any service industry. Its only inventory includes work in process and raw materials (components) used in the alarm system. Operational expenses include the production costs such as labor, inventory carrying costs, materials and supplies, and the administrative costs associated with the production process.

In other words, throughput is the money coming in; inventory is the money currently inside the system; and operational expense is the money that is paid out to make throughput happen. Thus, from an operations standpoint, the goal of the firm is to increase throughput while simultaneously reducing inventory and operating expenses.

Whichever form of the goal is adopted, they both converge on the same result: increased profit for the company. However, a successful company is not run by the manager, but by the employees. Ideally, the employees will work together to make adjustments in the way they work and view the company, resulting in an increase in productivity. This, then, will be the goal used by the manager of American Security & Alarm Co. to motivate and inspire employees.

With this goal in mind, the company must change the way it thinks. Instead of examining each process within the company, the manager should instead review the installation process as a whole. During this examination process, problem areas should be identified. These can be called either constraints or bottlenecks, depending on their severity. Instead of trying to adjust the capacity of these constraints to match demand, the company should strive to balance the flow of its resources within the process with the demand from the market.

In this company, the technician is the bottleneck. When he is working alone, he is limited by the time required for each process separately. As a result, it is impossible for him to complete the installation any faster. Thus, marketing's demands cannot be met using this method of installation. On the other hand, if the three technicians were combined to form a team, the bottleneck will change from the technician to various processes within the installation. By having more than one technician, the team could be completing several tasks at the same time they are performing the bottleneck task(s). When the bottleneck changes, it will force the company to adjust its method of production in order to utilize the bottlenecks at full capacity.

## The Solution: Synchronous Manufacturing

### Existing System

It was determined that, in order to increase throughput in the company, the technicians' productivity would have to be increased. In order to do this, the installation process was redesigned. The main change was with the technicians' assignments each day. Previously, they were each assigned a separate job. This way, three different sales were being fulfilled at the same time. However, after reviewing their productivity, it was evident that a team structure could potentially be much more productive overall.

### Team Installation

Although it was necessary to do certain steps prior to others, there was nothing restricting a team from doing two or more things at once. For instance, an analysis of the installation process identified two processes that took an extremely long time to complete, namely the programming and connection of the control panel and the wiring of the house to support all of the components. After discussing the issue with American Security & Alarm Co.'s manager, it was realized that the wiring of the house was only a capacity-constrained resource and the connection and programming of the control panel was the bottleneck. When a team wires a house, they could potentially make it a bottleneck if they do not schedule it properly. However, the control panel takes a long time and there is very little savings that can be realized on it. As a result, its capacity is less than the demand placed upon it.

The process of installing an alarm system was identified as a T-plant in the VAT classification system. This is characterized by the fact that the components can be created into many different end products. This is true since each house or business is unique in some way whether it be the number of sensors, location of the control panel, or the needs of the customer. With this in mind, management can react to changing demands effectively by improving due-date delivery performance and reducing operating costs by:

1. Controlling the flow through the fabrication portion of the process
2. Reducing batch sizes to eliminate the wavelike motion
3. Stopping the "stealing" of parts and components at assembly

In our example, the fabrication process involves the drilling and wiring of the house. This can be effectively controlled through smaller batches. The stealing of parts refers to the tendency of a technician who completes his task early to skip ahead and work on another task to stay busy. However, this may cause a previous process to be incomplete and, therefore, slow down the overall installation time.

It became clear that the entire process could be cut from the original 957 minutes to 249 minutes using all three employed technicians. Therefore, the total installations completed per month as a team would be 33.7 units, compared to the 26.4 installations by the three individual technicians working independently. The additional 7.3 units of throughput were the result of the following changes to the installation procedure.

**Inventory.**  When the team arrived at the office at 8:00 a.m., they immediately selected the inventory required for the installation and loaded it onto the truck. While two people were loading the equipment at least twice as fast as one person could, the third person was completing the supply depletion card. This process was cut from 90 minutes to 20 minutes.

**Setup.**  Once the team arrived at the installation site, they were able to identify the locations for the components at the same time they carried the tools and components into the house. Since they were able to combine the time of the setup, they were able to cut the total time from 45 minutes to 10 minutes.

**Drilling, Wiring, and Control Panel.**  An individual technician must first drill, then install the wires and, finally, connect the control panel and components. A team, on the other hand, has somewhat of a choice as to which process to complete first. For optimum performance, the longest processes need to be started as soon as possible. As a result, one technician must begin to mount the control panel while the other two team members begin to drill and run the wires. The initial mounting of the control panel can take up to 15 minutes. During this time, one of the other two can drill a hole and pass the wire through the hole while the third one remains in the attic to grasp the wire and carry it to the control panel location. By "producing" only one wire at a time, thus reducing the batch size, the team effectively reduced the wavelike motion caused by larger batches arriving at the control panel at the same time. Since the control panel has been identified as the bottleneck, an hour saved here shaves an extra hour from the entire production system. As a result, the process of drilling, running the wires, and connecting the control panel can be cut from 485 minutes to 165 minutes.

**Mounting.** Once the control panel is completed, the two technicians can begin to test the internal operation of the system. For one technician, this process lasted 112 minutes because he had to walk to each sensor, trip it, and then walk to the keypad to identify whether or not it was working properly. When two technicians are testing the system, one can remain at the keypad while the other can trip all of the sensors throughout the house, one by one. This process will only take 14 minutes, approximately one minute per sensor.

**Data Transfer and Cleanup.** During the testing stage, the process of transferring data to the monitoring station will have been completed. In order to utilize all available time, the idle technician should begin to clean up as soon as he hangs up the phone.

**External Testing.** As soon as the internal testing process is completed, the communication system needs to be tested. A team is capable of completing this task in 10 minutes. The time saving is not as great as it potentially could be because this test requires the support of the monitoring station which will operate the same for both the individual and the team.

**Explanation of the System.** With testing completed for both the internal and external functions, the team can begin to wrap up the installation. Explaining the system to the user can take an individual up to 30 minutes since the explanation must include a demonstration which, as we have already seen, can take longer for one person. However, a team can run through the entire system and answer any questions in about 10 minutes.

**Cleanup.** The installation can be completed in an additional 10 minutes of cleaning by the team, as opposed to 30 minutes by an individual.

## Throughput Equals Profit

As previously mentioned, the throughput of American Security & Alarm has increased from 26.4 to 33.7 unit installations each month. The average gross margin on an alarm system of this size if $700. After paying wages and overhead, the net profit may be as low as $525. However, when the company was restructured into a team, throughput was increased by 7.3 units, or $5,110. Since wages did not increase, however, the increase in net profit is actually $5,000 after the overhead associated with the sale is paid rather than the $3,100 which would have resulted from paying employees overtime. Thus, throughput has increased. At the same time, inventory, including work in process since a system is now installed in just over four hours, has decreased. Operational costs have not increased. Rather, wages remained the same or even decreased since overtime is no longer required to meet current market demand.

As has been shown in this real-world example, Goldratt's theories can and do work. By viewing the company as a whole rather than several smaller processes, the accounting department was able to agree with the operational managers to achieve the company's ultimate goal—profitability. The theory of constraints has proven that throughput can be increased while inventory and operating expenses are decreased, even in a service industry.

# QUALITY AND
# THE THEORY OF CONSTRAINTS

### H. William Dettmer

The quality philosophy is straightforward, the tools to achieve it are available, and most people accept the need to improve. So why are so many organizations struggling to achieve and sustain gains in quality?

The answer to this question is critical to corporate survival because quality alone is no longer a competitive weapon. It is the price of admission just to play the game. Quality has become a necessary condition, not a discriminator.

There are many reasons why companies struggle to achieve quality, but a major contributor is their inability to think and act in terms of systems rather than components. It seems simple, but consider total quality management (TQM), for example. TQM focuses on process control and process improvement. In most TQM applications, the emphasis is on improving individual components or processes, then "gluing" the results together. Interaction between processes is usually limited to consideration of the immediate upstream supplier and down-stream customer. Synergetic effects of separate processes on the whole system are infrequently considered and almost never addressed.

W. Edwards Deming understood the need to maintain a systemic approach to continuous improvement. One of his four requirements for profound knowledge is appreciation of a system. Unfortunately many people don't really understand what Deming meant, even though they pay lip service to it. Because TQM focuses on improving processes, it doesn't address how to manage the system as a whole. The closest TQM seems to come to systemic guidance is the concept of concurrent engineering, which requires the cooperation of marketing, engineering, and production in product development. Effectively executed, concurrent engineering can do an excellent job of integrating the inputs of customers, designers, and producers.

From *Quality Progress,* April 1995. © 1995 American Society for Quality. Reprinted with permission.

But even concurrent engineering doesn't address the entire system. What about the finance, sales, supply, and distribution functions? They're all part of the system, too, and they have a major influence on corporate success.

## The Thinking Process

What is essential to ultimate success is a thinking process that enables a company to appreciate the effect of local actions and decisions on overall system performance. Ideally, a systemic thinking process would provide a context in which to place all of the diverse elements of quality, management, and organizational behavior. Try to visualize the thinking process as the setting of a mosaic, which holds together and integrates all of the tiles, producing an overall picture that is larger than the individual tiles. Such a thinking process should provide a means of determining what to change in the system, what it should change to, and how to effect the change.

To some degree, all of the quality philosophies and tools address the issue of identifying what to change, although they usually address it at the local, or process, level rather than the system level. Normally, little consideration is given to determining the overall effect of the change on the system as a whole, and virtually none to the collateral undesirable effects a change might have on other components or processes of the system. For example, how would a change in product X's production line affect company performance (the whole system) and the distribution or customer service functions (other system components)? TQM doesn't answer this question, but a systemic thinking process does.

## An Important Book

In 1986, a revolutionary book appeared in bookstores, corporate offices, and executive suites. Eliyahu M. Goldratt's *The Goal* has sold over 1 million copies during the last eight years with virtually no advertising or promotion. The primary method of propagation has been readers passing on copies to their friends and colleagues. Managers read this book and order it by the case for distribution within their companies.

What makes this book so unusual? After all, it's just a book on production control. Or is it? *The Goal* is not a textbook or a how-to guide; it's written, by design, as a novel. Much as a fable or allegory teaches a higher lesson through the context of an everyday situation, *The Goal* presents a thinking process, called the theory of constraints, in a way that readers can intuitively grasp. By following the story line, readers see the theory's logic clearly demonstrated and draw their own conclusions about its effectiveness and applicability.

*The Goal*'s purpose is to introduce readers to the thinking process that provides the context for a new continuous improvement approach. Its production control theme is merely one example, albeit a significant one, to which the thinking process can be applied. But, like an iceberg, only the tip of this thinking process shows above the waterline.

## The Theory

So, what is the theory of constraints (TOC)? TOC facilitates the examination of assumptions underlying traditional rules, policies, and measures. It focuses on the few critical constraints that limit the success of a system. It provides the methodology to define what to change, what it should be changed to, and how to effect change to continuously improve the performance of an entire system. Moreover, TOC precludes suboptimization, ensuring that solutions to complex problems are effective at the system level.

Look at it another way. *Webster's New Universal Unabridged Dictionary* defines a system as "a set or arrangement of things so related or connected as to form a unity or organic whole." Typically, in its simplest form, a system is depicted as an interrelated group of processes that receive inputs from the external environment, act on them in some way, and produce an output that is supposed to be of greater value than the sum of the inputs. Systems thinking is based on three principles:

- Systems principle No. 1: The performance of an entire system is affected by each of its components. In other words, every department influences the company's overall performance.

- Systems principle No. 2: The parts of a system are interdependent. How one part affects the whole system depends, to some extent, on what at least one other part is doing.

- Systems principle No. 3: If parts of a system are grouped together in any way, they form subgroups that are subject to the first two principles.

TOC goes a little further. Goldratt maintains that if the performance of each part of a system is individually maximized, the system as a whole will not behave as well as it could. Conversely, if a system is performing as well as it can, not more than one of its parts will be. If one considers this idea in the context of today's business world, it's somewhat revolutionary. Much effort and expense is devoted to maximizing efficiency at every level and in every sector of a company, without regard for the effect on the company's overall performance. In most cases, companies can't quantify what effect suboptimal decisions will have on the organization's overall performance, but they continue to make them anyway.

Consider an automobile, for example. Most are designed to achieve a specific objective, such as luxury, economy, or speed. As a complex system, an automobile has to integrate the performance of many components to achieve its objective. If the objective is economy, it's counterproductive to "improve" the system by installing racing cams in the engine, even if they're the best-performing cams to be had.

Likewise, inflating tires for maximum mileage efficiency certainly improves their service life. But an Indy car driver is more concerned with how the car handles than with the life of the tires. Overinflation might maximize tire life but compromise the overall performance of the car–driver system.

## Analytical vs. Systems Approach

What is the usual approach to system improvement? The tendency is to use an analytical one. Companies reduce a large problem to a set of manageable problems, solve these component problems, and then reassemble them into a "system" solution. TQM typically takes this approach by dividing the system into processes, then optimizing the quality of each process. This, of course, is preferable to chasing symptoms or discrete variations in individual steps of a process, but it can create new problems if the role of the individual process is not considered in concert with the other processes it affects (systems principle No. 2).

TOC addresses the larger systemic picture. Rather than viewing the system in terms of discrete processes, TOC treats it as a chain or a grid of interlinked chains. What determines the performance of a whole chain? The weakest link ultimately limits what the chain can do. Any effort to strengthen links other than the weakest one will do nothing to improve the chain's overall performance. Only after the weakest link has been reinforced will it be productive to concentrate on reinforcing other weak links.

TOC considers the weakest link to be the system constraint. By focusing exclusively on that constraint, any changes are immediately measurable in the system's output. Conversely, as long as the system constraint is not addressed, no effect on the global performance can be logically connected to actions or decisions elsewhere in the system. Once the single, overriding constraint is broken, some other weak link in the chain becomes the limiting constraint, which must subsequently be addressed.

TOC, like TQM, treats improvement as an ongoing process. But instead of focusing on localized improvements in all areas, it attacks the one constraint, or bottleneck, that limits overall system performance. By never losing sight of the system's performance, TOC maintains a systems, rather than an analytical, approach.

## The Five Focusing Steps

To ensure that emphasis remains at the system level rather than the component level, Goldratt has developed five steps to guide the improvement process:

1. **"Identify the system's constraints [its weakest links]."** There might be several weak links, but there is only one weakest link. This link should be the first target of improvement.

2. **"Decide how to exploit the constraint."** If the constraint is physical, make sure that no productivity is lost through inefficient use of the constraining resource. In other words, make the constraint, as it exists now, as effective as possible.

3. **"Subordinate everything else to the above decision."** Every other part of the system must be aligned and adjusted to support the maximum effectiveness of the constraint, even if this means "detuning" some nonconstraints.

4. **"Elevate the system's constraint."** If steps 2 and 3 don't relieve the constraint to the extent that it ceases to be the weakest link, more rigorous action is necessary, such as formulating strategies to increase throughput across the constraint (e.g., offloading work to other sources or acquiring more capability).

5. **"If, in the previous steps, a constraint has been broken, go back to step 1, but do not allow inertia to cause a new constraint."** This is the feedback loop that makes TOC a continuous process. Implicit in this step (and the reason so many organizations lose momentum in continuous improvement) is the caution to not become complacent. No solution is permanent. As the system's environment changes, a given solution will progressively deteriorate unless it is modified to account for those changes.

Moreover, changing a constraint usually changes the character of the system; it's not quite the same system it was before. Often the original system components don't interact in quite the same way because of system principle No. 2 described earlier. So, it's dangerous to believe that the improvement process can stop when the original constraint is broken.

## Physical vs. Policy Constraints

Throughout 12 years of developing and applying TOC, Goldratt has observed that very few constraints are physical (e.g., machines, people, facilities, or other tangible resources). By tracing undesirable effects to their root causes, Goldratt found that the vast majority of constraints are caused by policies—rules training, or other measures—that might have once been effective solutions but are now obsolete.

For example, the large proportion of freeways under repair (or needing repair) seems to be a physical constraint to the flow of traffic. But it's the federal acquisition policy mandating the award of contracts to the lowest bidder that has driven contractors to use lower-quality, shorter-life materials in an effort to keep costs down and remain competitive. Even if the physical constraint were removed (temporarily) by repairing all of the roads, the policy constraint would ensure a recurrence of the problem.

Why are policy constraints so much more insidious than physical constraints? Besides being less visible, policies set the rules for how things must be done. In so doing, they foreclose many lines of inquiry on possible solutions.

Most policies were put in place to solve a perceived problem. Contracts go to the lowest bidder because someone, at some time, saw a problem, such as: "We're paying too much for what we're getting." But the environment is continually changing, existing solutions are often not updated to keep pace, and few ongoing improvement processes are institutionalized to ensure that updates occur.

Herein lies a major strength of TOC. Direct observation and traditional TQM tools (such as statistical process control or design of experiments) work well at the process level, but they're ineffective in identifying policy constraints at the system level—constraints that can have the most dramatic effect on the entire system. In the TOC thinking process, Goldratt has provided a rigorous logical methodology that is well equipped to meet this challenge. Moreover, TOC provides a how-to vehicle for institutionalizing the process of continuous improvement, which is necessary to avoid having obsolete policies.

## Traditional vs. Systems Measurements

Traditional measurement systems are usually focused on improving local process efficiencies. A systems approach such as TOC requires a way to measure the effects of local decisions on global performance. Few traditional measurements offer this visibility.

TOC assesses the merit of local decisions by determining their effect on three dimensions of the system's performance in this order:

- **Throughput.** Throughput is the total sales revenues minus the total variable costs for producing a product or service.

- **Inventory.** Inventory is all of the money that a company invests in items it intends to sell.
- **Operating expense.** Operating expense is all of the money a company spends turning inventory into throughput.

All management actions, at any level, should be measurable against one of these interdependent, system-level scales. A change in one will result in a related change in one or both of the others. When the overall system is improving, throughput increases while inventory and operating expense decrease. Two major outcomes of TOC's focus on throughput, inventory, and operating expense have been the virtual invalidation of traditional management cost accounting and a simultaneous improvement in competitive price advantage. An important indirect benefit of TOC results from shedding the shackles of traditional cost accounting: Many companies are able to open doors to profitable new market segments.

TQM frequently drives people to measure everything. Organizations sometimes go "metric crazy." Many measurements are useless because nobody knows what to do with them. People often lose sight of the fact that the purpose of measurement is to gather data from which information can be derived. Information is the answer to a question asked about the system. TOC helps determine what questions should be asked and what important factors (constraints) should be measured to answer them.

Take the Pareto rule, for example, which is supposed to answer the question, "What should we work on first?" Conventional quality wisdom tells people to identify trouble spots, prioritize them by importance or value, draw a time/ resource limit line below the most important problems, and start to work on the No. 1 priority. This is a good analytical approach, but consider this: What if priorities 1, 3, and 4 are caused by a less noticeable core problem ranked No. 8, which happens to be below the time/resource limit line? Perhaps a well-placed bullet into the heart of No. 8 will solve problems 1, 3, and 4, with no additional expenditure of resources. But without the system-level, cause-and-effect examination TOC affords, how would one ever know? Moreover, solving problems 1, 3, and 4 without addressing the core problem (No. 8) almost ensures that either similar problems will appear again or other undesirable effects will arise to replace those eliminated.

It should be emphasized that TOC does not replace TQM, statistical process control, design of experiments, teamwork, or other tools and philosophies. Rather, TOC integrates and focuses these toward the organization's goal. It provides the means to know when each of these process tools is necessary and appropriate to improve overall system performance. Remember, the sum of local optima is not the system optimum.

## For Profit vs. Not for Profit

A typical reservation about TOC sounds like this: "It might be fine for profit-making companies, but we're a not-for-profit organization. How can TOC apply to us, when we don't measure our throughput in terms of dollars?" Nonfinancial measures are always more difficult to deal with, but throughput need not always be expressed in dollars. Instead, a measure of the product or service delivered can be substituted.

For example, a university or high school could express throughput as a function of the number of students graduated compared with the number who initially enrolled. The goal might be to shorten the time needed to turn inventory (students) into throughput (graduates) while meeting the necessary condition of quality. Throughput could typically be increased by reducing the dropout rate.

Just because profit is not an organization's goal doesn't mean that TOC can't be applied. It might merely require an adjustment by defining the goal, throughput, and inventory in terms other than dollars. Money can be, however, a suitable starting surrogate if a nonfinancial measure cannot initially be well defined.

## Company Struggling? Try TOC

TOC is firmly rooted in common sense. It allows for a structured, orderly, logical representation of intuition. It provides three powerful capabilities that can turbocharge a TQM effort:

1. It provides a way to model an entire system and expose constraints to improved performance.
2. It provides a means for identifying what to change, what to change it to, and how to execute the change for maximum system effectiveness.
3. It provides a way to measure the effects of daily management decisions on the performance of an entire system.

The theory is only in its adolescence. As it evolves, new ways to apply it will surface. Until now, for example, TOC has been used primarily to identify and manage constraints in existing systems. The role TOC could play in the up-front design of constraints in new or emerging systems has yet to be examined.

If your company's TQM efforts have succeeded and continue to produce improvements, you might be thinking, "These ideas are valid but obvious. There's nothing new here." It might be obvious to those who have made continuous improvement succeed because, as Deming points out, a system perspective is essential. But since so many organizations are struggling with TQM, it must not be obvious to everyone. If your organization is having a tough time making continuous improvement efforts show up in the bottom line, consider using the theory of constraints to help keep your system and its goal in perspective and to focus TQM where it will do the most good.

## TOC Basic Principles

Here are some basic principles of the theory of constraints:

- If a system is performing as well as it can, not more than one of its component parts will be. If all parts are performing as well as they can, the system as a whole will not be. The sum of the local optima is not the system's optimum.

- Systems thinking is preferable to analytical thinking in managing change and solving problems.

- An optimal system solution deteriorates over time as the system's environment changes. A process of ongoing improvement is required to update and maintain the efficacy of a solution.

- Knowing what to change requires a thorough understanding of the system's current reality, its goal, and the magnitude and direction of the difference between the two.

- Most of the undesirable effects within a system are caused by a few core problems, which are rarely superficially apparent. They manifest themselves through a number of undesirable effects linked by a cause-and-effect network.

- Elimination of individual undesirable effects gives a false sense of security while ignoring the underlying core problem. Solutions that do this are likely to be short-lived. Solving a core problem simultaneously eliminates all resulting undesirable effects.

- System constraints can be either physical or policy. Policy constraints are usually the most difficult to identify and break, but they normally result in a larger degree of system improvement than the elimination of a physical constraint.

- Inertia is the worst enemy of a continuous improvement process. Solutions tend to assume a mass of their own and resist further change.

- Ideas are not solutions.

# 14

# VARIFILM
# CASE STUDY

## OVERVIEW

**Business Description.** Varifilm provides $3 billion worth of specialty plastic films and recycled products each year to the food and industrial market segments. Film is used for food packaging, food sacks, product packaging, pallet wrapping, construction barrier film, electrical insulation, and a wide variety of industrial applications. The Varifilm product is not sold directly to consumers. In addition to the basic product research, development, and customer engineering, support is provided through operations and Research, Development and Engineering (RD&E). These activities are coordinated through sales and customer service. Varifilm works actively with industry councils and two leading universities to maintain its leadership role in the food and industrial packaging markets. Varifilm's Recyclables business uses its own and customer scrap to produce pallets, spools, and fence posts.

**Key Quality Requirements.** Our customers report five key requirements which are tracked to measure customer satisfaction. They are:

This case study is in the public domain. It has been abridged and modified to more nearly meet the instructional needs of the text. The source is the Malcolm Baldrige National Quality Award.

- Product Quality
- On-Time Delivery
- Ease of Access
- Price
- Knowledge of Coworkers

Product quality includes film properties such as stretch percent, gage (thickness), tear, seal strength, and burst strength.

**Organization Structure.** The company is organized into three strategic business units, each headed by a vice-president: (1) food packaging, (2) industrial films, and (3) recyclables. Varifilm is a functional organization with a matrix structure to drive major initiatives and the business process. Three cross-functional business teams, led by the marketing/sales leader, include Food Packaging, Industrial Film and Recycling. The three regional organizations (Europe, Latin America and the Far East) adopt and use the business team initiatives as appropriate.

**Customer Base.** The customer base includes construction insulation manufacturers, fabricated housing, hundreds of consumer goods manufacturers and food processors who utilize shrink and stretch film, and retail chains for sacks (plastic bags). The construction industry uses Varifilm's products in fence posts for road and farm applications.

**Markets.** Varifilm markets its products worldwide. The Recyclables operation currently provides products to North America only. Within the U.S., plants are strategically located so that all major market regions are viable. International plants have been strategically located near suppliers and market centers. In several cases, U.S. suppliers and customers are mirrored internationally. These partnerships have provided cost benefits to all concerned. Varifilm has been selective in the international markets it has chosen to participate in. Trade barrier changes in North America and Europe will be beneficial to Varifilm. Two additional sites in Eastern Europe and Asia are being considered.

| Market Share Region | Varifilm | Company A | Company B | JFC | Strongest Region Competitor |
|---|---|---|---|---|---|
| USA | 47% | 30% | 28% | 0% | 30% |
| Europe | 16% | 21% | 0% | 14% | 32% |
| Asia | 21% | 0% | 13% | 32% | 22% |
| South America | 26% | 22% | 15% | 0% | 28% |
| Japan | 0% | 0% | 14% | 48% | 30% |

**Position in Industry.** Varifilm competes directly with two other companies (Ref. Item 7.6) in the North American market. In Europe and Asia, there are regional competitors along with one of the U.S. competitors. The strongest threat competitively is a Japanese firm (JFC) who is currently building a plant in southern California. (Ref. Item 3.2.)

**Technology.** Primary resin received by rail car is processed by heating and extrusion. Chemicals are added to develop specific properties, and some products require multiple layers. In-line conversion equipment further processes (i.e., forming sacks) and packages the film. The recycling process is one of formulating and molding. Additives are used to stabilize the product and create proper color. Advanced computer process controls unique to the industry have been codesigned and developed with computer and equipment suppliers. This advanced technology has been responsible for the improved product uniformity and control. All film operations run continuously. The industry is capital intensive.

**Suppliers.** Resins, molds, dies, conversion equipment, inks, chemicals, and ideas are all critical elements to Varifilm's success. Supplier partnerships are developed not only with traditional suppliers but with Universities and Industry trade groups. The number of suppliers has been reduced by 33% over the past three years while supplier certification, supplier quality, and supplier satisfaction have all increased. (Ref. Items 5.4, 6.4.) While the products purchased by Varifilm are generally not unique, partnership programs with suppliers have led to special codeveloped formulations and equipment.

**Customer Partnerships.** Customer focus and customer partnerships targeted on value to the customer are key to Varifilm's increasing market share. Customer visits, coworker visits, customer product design teams, and product engineering support all have led to understanding and meeting present and future customer requirements. Electronic order entry and computer tracking of Just-In-Time delivery are examples of customer-partnership-directed service improvements.

**Regulatory Environment.** Varifilm operates in the world market and, as such, is committed to be a responsible citizen. In addition to normal FDA and OSHA regulations, there are a wide variety of Common Market and Asian regulations.

**Future.** There are four major issues facing Varifilm in the next ten years.

1. The nature of the market and the competitive threat from JFC in the United States.

2. Europe and Asia provide major expansion opportunities. Two new plants are under consideration.

3. Recyclables has created a major new product opportunity. Expansion of this business is limited by the availability of recyclable waste plastic. Fence post demand is expected to double in the next five years.

4. The Packaging Research Alliance project of formable plastic, while creating a major new product line, will exceed our ability to provide technical support.

**Union/Management Relationships.** All production coworkers are represented by the Film Workers United. The union has been a proactive force for quality. It participates in all quality training, has representatives on business leadership teams and site teams, and attends all quality leadership conferences.

## CATEGORY 1.0
## LEADERSHIP

### 1.1 Senior Executive Leadership

**1.1a** Our senior executives are effective at developing and maintaining a customer focus within Varifilm and at creating an environment for quality excellence because they have gone through a genuine and profound personal transformation.

Our senior executives are personally and visibly involved in quality, since it is Varifilm's model of doing business. Leadership has experienced first-hand the consequences of not being customer-focused and not having sufficiently shared quality values. Leadership works to create a shared quality vision and meet the needs of customers, suppliers, and coworkers. The new leadership model has shifted from telling coworkers what to do and "getting things done through people" to "meeting the needs of coworkers as they work to accomplish their jobs and achieve process supremacy and customer satisfaction."

**Phase I (1975–1982) Process Management.** The first phase of quality at Varifilm consisted of a detailed process management system along with a sophisticated statistical quality control system for continuous manufacturing.

**Phase II (1982–1989) Total Quality Management.** The year 1982 was an important turning point when John Romig, our President at that time, introduced and committed the company to Total Quality Management (TQM). This extended the quality process beyond manufacturing and introduced the quality principles through broad training and quality actions through team-based activity.

To firmly and consistently establish our commitment to this new approach over time, we hold Quality Leadership Conferences every other year, bringing together up to 150 top managers and selected participants from within their organizations to unite and consolidate Varifilm's leadership behind shared principles.

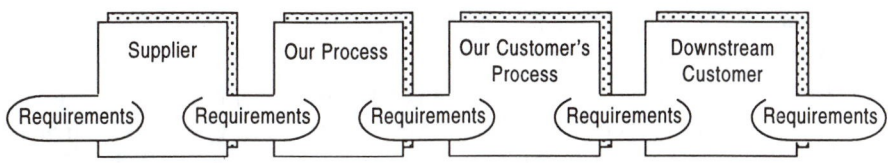

Customer Requirements Chain

At the end of the '80s, Total Quality Leadership began to move into its current and most exciting stage. We realized that we needed to more dynamically involve our people as individuals and team members in feeling personal responsibility for and ownership of the Varifilm quality environment and the values that support it.

As a definition of our quality aspirations, we adopted and implemented the Varifilm Continuous Improvement Criteria (VCIC). To revitalize and improve our quality process, fostering a more personal sense of ownership of the Varifilm quality environment, we implemented Self Managed Teams.

VCIC decides "what" we improve; the Self Managed Teams describe "how" we improve. Key measures are what we track.

**Phase III (1989– ) Quality Integration.** The third phase of quality at Varifilm builds on the first two phases and adds the strengths of recent teaching in Partnership/High Performance Work Systems (HPWS), Diversity, and Quality Leadership. Union management partnership teams now exist in all facilities, and HPWS teams are the result, with two plants regularly being benchmarked for their organization changes and quality achievement.

If there is a single moment when this third phase really began, it was May 1989, when our senior executives spent an intense week of transformation together at an Outward Climb facility working directly with Outward Climb staff and Mark Hurry, a well-known expert in organizational change, leadership, and empowerment. As a symbol of their shared realization that the pursuit of quality requires bold leadership, our senior executives renamed themselves the "Invincible Team" (I-Team).

With the experience they shared and the intense discussions they exchanged, the I-Team developed a foundation for improved Total Quality Leadership and culture change which included:

- Establishment of a new Purpose and Vision based on achieving success through meeting the needs of key partners in our business: the customer, the coworker, society, and the stockholder. (See Item 1.1b.)

- Adoption of the Baldrige Criteria as the improvement framework, naming it the Varifilm Continuous Improvement Criteria.

- Creation and adoption of the Self Managed Team process to deal with the human side of quality for all Varifilm coworkers.

- Recognition that we need to create an atmosphere characterized by valuing the individual, respect, trust, responsibility, teamwork, support and anticipation if we are to be successful in making the broad changes needed. These are focus areas in the Self Managed Team process.

Each member of the I-Team is committed to spending a minimum of one-third of his/her time on quality-related activities such as customer contacts, establishing values, and supporting coworkers.

1. Responsibilities include customer visits, communication, and participation in new product development. The I-Team also regularly hosts customer visits and opens all quarterly customer quality orientation sessions. Customer satisfaction is also one of the Key Indicators reviewed at each quarterly operations review.

2. Varifilm Quality Values (Goal, Policy, Definition) were established at the beginning of Phase I and reviewed and improved at the beginning of Phase II. These values were included in the original training, and the revised values have been rolled through the company using a large-scale model to gain acceptance and speed implementation.

3. The business planning process has, for the past two years, integrated quality, Key Indicators, customer requirements, satisfaction goals, and projections into the planning process. Unit goal measurement is ongoing. A formal review of Key Indicator (KI) progress is done quarterly with all 200 KIs being reviewed (Each unit has approximately ten KIs.). The I-Team's systematic review of each group allows for unit discussion of its measures and provides the opportunity to recognize improvements. This is an important regular feature of the I-Team meetings.

4. Although recognition is most often done at the unit level, the I-Team actively participates and hosts the biennial Quality Achievement Conference to recognize quality achievements.

5. I-Team members communicate quality values to customer contacts and outside organizations or groups of their choice. Each has also adopted one of the company's major initiatives (Key Indicators). I-Team member responsibility includes supporting teams as they work on their topic, participating in one work team or related educational or benchmarking experience, and being the advocate in I-Team meetings.

**1.1b** The purpose of Varifilm is to be committed to broad partnerships, and we strive to continuously improve our relationships.

| Item | Phase II | Phase III |
|---|---|---|
| **Values** | Quality | Quality |
| | The individual | The individual, respect |
| | Total Quality Management | Total Quality principles |
| | Integrity | Integrity, trust |
| | Leadership | Teamwork, support |
| | Customers | Partners, anticipation |
| **Goal** | Deliver error free products on time every time | Deliver error free products on time every time |
| **Principles** | Meet requirements | Meet requirements |
| | Error free work | Error free work |
| | Manage by prevention | Manage by prevention |
| | Continuous improvement | Continuous improvement |
| | | Knowledge through benchmarking |
| **Customer Objective** | Meet the requirements | Customer delight—be first in customer satisfaction and factors leading to customer satisfaction |
| **Coworkers** | Participation | Empowerment |
| **Suppliers** | Meet requirements | Partner in value |
| **Stockholders** | Provide return | Earn trust, respect needs |
| **Community** | Good citizen | Good citizen |
| **Environment** | Protect | Improve |

Historically, quality values go back to our founders' belief in "value and service for a fair price." This belief was rediscovered in Phase II and stated in the form of our quality Goal, Policy, Principles and Actions. Our "Quality Model" emphasized customer requirements and the importance of continuous improvement. In Phase III this quality foundation was expanded to include broader understanding of partnership, diversity, and quality leadership. The concept of partners included the customer, supplier, coworkers, stockholder/investor, the community and the environment. We are committed to meeting the needs of all partners with the customer being our main focus. All partners, however, must be satisfied.

These values are the basis for many kinds of consistent communication both within and outside the company. They are the foundation of strategic planning (Item 3.1) and our interactions with partners. These values are discussed in formal and informal interactions with members of the I-Team who were personally involved in developing and adopting them.

Our values are regularly reinforced in two ways: (1) annual reviews are included in the *Company News* sent to each coworker; and (2) each coworker team develops its own purpose and vision in support of the company values. In this way, coworkers actively participate in internalizing and putting into practice Varifilm values. This translation of values into the local environment and work group is a unique and highly effective approach that goes beyond normal communication. Most teams display Purpose and Vision statements in their work areas. For example, the following representative declaration is prominently displayed in an Illinois plant:

> *We are committed to meeting ALL customer requirements and supporting each other through teamwork, communication, dedication, ideas, respect, and support. We are committed to continuous improvement and striving to be the best!*

In addition to its annual issue dealing with our quality values, the monthly *Company News* recognizes teams as they "live" their purpose and vision.

**1.1c** Varifilm's values and customer focus are regularly communicated and reinforced through I-Team personal examples, the supervisor newsletter, and at the semi-annual, two-day leadership meeting of the Management Committee (top 150 managers). This meeting always focuses on quality, with an outside speaker and group discussion. Each leadership team member tracks quality activities such as talks, customer contact, recognition activity, seminars taught and attended, and time involved in Management By Walking Around (MBWA). Members have exceeded their goal of ten activities/month/person for the past three years.

**Cliff Bass,** *President & CEO.* Systematically visits major customers for improvement ideas and systematically visits each Varifilm site worldwide yearly.

**Mike Archer,** *Vice-President, Industrial Film.* Regularly participates in plant and RD&E recognition activities, participates on the Quality Council, co-teaches Module 3 (Process Improvement), and led the Order Entry Process Improvement Team.

**Carl Baker,** *Vice-President, Food Packaging.* Systematically visits one plant per quarter to listen to people, and routinely visits the plants of our three major customers to determine how we can assist them with their continuous improvement efforts.

**Leroy Jones,** *Vice-President, Recyclables.* In 1991, visited approximately 30 potential customers to understand how our new business venture can best meet long-term environmental issues, as well as meet short-term customer needs. Holds regular "Let's Talk" meetings.

**Art Axel,** *Vice-President, Quality.* Gives 15–20 Director's Awards per year to coworkers, suppliers, and/or customers in recognition of outstanding quality accomplishments. Leads efforts to achieve 100% ISO Certification of our facilities and our suppliers' facilities.

**Lisa Seavey,** *Vice-President, Human Resources.* Strategic leader of our people development processes. Manages and revises personnel systems and is the champion of the HPWS and Diversity programs. Transferred hiring responsibility to the individual units and teams.

**Terry Spade,** *Vice-President, Varifilm Far East.* Leads our culture change in the Far East. Personally leads the Self Managed Team training.

**1.1d** Our senior executives systematically and continuously improve their own processes. The I-Team is committed to continuous improvement in leading the quality effort. The I-Team utilizes surveys after talks and at its monthly meeting. Teams, presenters, and participants are surveyed. The I-Team reviews the results of their activities listed in 1.1c to improve.

Individually, our leaders read articles and books, and the team spends one week per year in group training and benchmarking activities. Members have attended the annual Malcolm Baldrige National Quality Award's Quest for Excellence Conference, and leaders of three Baldrige winners have spoken to the leadership team. Every two years a survey of coworkers is conducted. Several questions deal directly with senior leadership and are tracked by the I-Team.

## 1.2 Management for Quality

**1.2a** Each business unit or plant translates Varifilm's values into requirements for all levels of management and coworkers. Several specific processes are used:

**VCIC/Partnership Teams and Responsibilities.** During Phase II, each unit had a quality steering committee and teams based on the quality actions. With the use of Baldrige Assessment (VCIC), and since Phase III, each unit has a leadership team responsible for VCIC and a partnership team responsible for HPWS. The use of VCIC ensures continuous improvement and alignment of quality values and customer focus. Unit management is responsible for leading the processes and reporting annually to the I-Team.

**Strategic Planning.** The strategic planning process, which uses customer satisfaction data, customer requirements, and Key Indicators, defines responsibilities and promotes customer focus and quality values. (See Category 3.0.)

**Customer Requirements Model.** The Customer Requirements Model of Phase II established the internal and external supplier/customer model with requirements. This process is still used to develop inter-unit requirements.

**Cross-Functional Teams.** Varifilm's teams and partnerships (HPWS) define responsibilities and foster cooperation between units. Cross-functional teams run the various businesses.

**Management Committee Meetings.** These meetings are used to communicate values and responsibilities.

**1.2b** Our real objective is to create customer value and satisfaction, improve quality, and reduce costs by understanding and meeting customer requirements and living our values.

Varifilm's customer focus and quality values are communicated in a variety of ways. In addition to Purpose and Vision (see Area 1.1b), Key Indicators which align with customer requirements and are a part of the gain-sharing program are used to directly align coworkers with customer requirements. Basic benchmarking of manufacturing processes has been expanded to all organizations to determine how to accomplish each task more effectively with fewer people. The objective is to improve quality, reduce cost, and eliminate non-value-added work. We use a variety of analysis tools, including process flowcharting, and the seven old and new tools for identifying potential improvements. Visits to and from customers also solidify customer focus.

**1.2c** Each organizational unit regularly reviews the progress of its improvement efforts, key processes, and key indicators as an outcome of the VCIC.

The Leadership Team reviews Key Indicators quarterly, and each month one unit's Key Indicators are reviewed in detail. Key Indicators are displayed prominently as part of the HPWS and gain-sharing displays. To assist units not performing according to plans and goals, our objective is to ensure accountability, without encouraging improper actions, to meet a numerical goal. We, therefore, focus strongly on solving problems versus assigning blame. Frequent Leadership Team contact provides support as needed rather than waiting for reviews.

**1.2d** Three tools are used regularly to evaluate and develop improvement plans for awareness and integration of quality values.

1. The Baldrige Assessment, conducted every two years, provides unit assessment of the area along with action plans.

2. The Coworker Climate Survey (CCS), also done every other year, provides detailed information and comparisons between units and with leading companies through the Wheaton Group summaries.

3. Customer satisfaction surveys include questions related to this area. (See Category 7.0.) In addition to the formal survey process, interviews have been

used with all partners to better understand adopted values and to gain perspective on where improvements need to be made.

# CATEGORY 2.0
# INFORMATION AND ANALYSIS

## 2.1 Scope and Management of Quality and Performance Data and Information

**2.1a**   The scope and types of data and information we use are extensive. Figure 2.1 displays our key types of data and information and the computer systems on which they reside. How each supports quality improvement is evident from the data descriptions and from details given in other parts of this application.

Our quality and performance data meet the following criteria: related to customer satisfaction, required for performance analysis, consistent, quantifiable, objective and verifiable, meet industry standards, enable comparisons, meet government requirements, and can be transferred electronically between systems.

Each unit develops its own Key Indicators, which are measures of customer satisfaction, factors leading to customer satisfaction, and process measures. These indicators, along with financial measures, are reviewed by the I-Team quarterly and monthly, or more frequently by each unit.

**2.1b**   We ensure reliability, consistency, standardization, and rapid access to data and information through the use of computer systems and networks.

Our use of computer technology is one of our strengths. We are supported by a Corporate Information Systems Team of 100 people located in Norco, Whiting, and the plant sites. These resources keep abreast of changing technology, acquire and test appropriate software and hardware improvements, and maintain our systems. They employ systematic structured approaches to ensure software quality. Software development and modification are verified by user testing in a pilot-level environment before being put into full-scale use. The listing of systems in Figure 2.1 is an indication of the utility of our computer network.

Approaches used to ensure rapid and accurate data transfer include automated laboratory data entry at all manufacturing sites and Electronic Data Interchange (EDI) with customers and suppliers.

Update and review of quality and performance data are organized via our Process Management System (deals with information documentation; see Area 5.2a) and by site and business progress review approaches.

| Data | Information Systems |
|------|---------------------|

**Customer-Related**

| | |
|---|---|
| Order Entry | Electronic Data Interchange |
| Customer Complaints, Returns | Problem Report System |
| Customer Satisfaction Survey | Market Research Survey |
| Product Performance | Customer Data Interchange, Product Management System |
| On-Time Delivery | Distribution Management System |

**Internal Operations**

| | |
|---|---|
| Product Properties | Product Management System |
| Process Specifications | PMS and Plant Manufacturing Systems |
| Process Control | PMS |
| Yields | Plant Manufacturing Systems |
| Inventory Effectiveness | Finished Product Maintenance System |
| Preventive Maintenance | Preventive Maintenance Achievement System |
| ISO Certification | |

**Company Performance—Employee Related**

| | |
|---|---|
| Employment History | Coworker Information System |
| Personal Data | CIS |
| Coworker Views | Coworker Climate System |
| Career Development Plans | Coworker Promotion System |
| Community Participation | PC databases |
| Key Indicator Performance | PMS and Financial Information Analysis System |
| Training Activity | CIS |
| Suggestion Activity | CIS |

**Company Performance—Safety, Health and Environment**

| | |
|---|---|
| Safety Incidents | Plant Databases, Varifilm Safety Reporting System |
| Waste | Waste Information System |
| Materials Safety | Materials Safety Data Sheet |
| Environmental Incidents | Plant Databases, Corporate Prevent Incidents Systems |

**Company Performance—Quality Performance**

| | |
|---|---|
| Complaints | PRS |
| Competitive Comparisons | Competitive Databases |
| Market Share | MRS, Personal Computer Databases |
| Benchmarks | QUality Information System |
| Gain Share | Unit Records |
| Quality Survey Trends | QUIS, Plant Database |

**Supplier Performance**

| | |
|---|---|
| Material Specifications | PMS |
| Supplier Total Quality Trends | Supplier Database |

**Cost & Financial**

| | |
|---|---|
| Annual Budgets | Financial Information Analysis System |
| Customer Sales | DMS, FIAS |
| Sales & Earnings | FIAS |
| Capital Expenditures | Investment Management System |

**Figure 2.1**    Example of Varifilm Data

Computerized information transfer via electronic mail is highly used/deployed for communication within Varifilm. Every salaried coworker around the world has an account, and most hourly people have access to electronic mail. All cafeterias have E-mail desks for use by any coworker, and many customers and suppliers also have accounts. Messages can be easily sent to any account around the world. We also make extensive use of voice mail systems.

**2.1c**   Continuous improvement of the scope and management of data is essential in this information age. Continuous improvement processes used throughout Varifilm are also used to improve the scope and management of our data. The assessment process, customer input, and the Process Management System (PMS) are used to map, measure and improve our processes. The use of EDI, electronic mail and common databases has dramatically reduced cycle time. Voice mail wait time is monitored and managed at 15 seconds or less between 8 a.m. and 9 a.m., the busiest time of day. (Ref. Item 6.3.)

Methods to improve the scope and quality of data and information include:

| Process | Improvements |
| --- | --- |
| **Benchmarking** | Helped us see the power of cycle time as a measure |
| **Customer Input** | Measurements of our performance in meeting delivery time requests |
| | Measurement of response to request for information |
| **Computer Technology** | Improvements in data entry capability |
| **Key Indicators** | Improvements in reporting and identification processes |
| **User "Steering Teams"** | Expanded functionality of the Product Management System |

An indicator of data/information adequacy is audit results of our quality system.

## 2.2 Competitive Comparisons and Benchmarking

**2.2a**   Benchmarking and competitive comparisons are used extensively in Varifilm to address a business or function's critical success factors and priorities—importance for customer satisfaction, impact on success in the marketplace, operational performance, impact on strategic/industry needs, and competitive activities.

We select benchmarking partners from within the company and the industry and search for best practices wherever they can be found. We have had much success linking like functions and operations from different geographical locations.

Selection criteria include:

- International business
- Strong financial performance
- Capital intensive, manufacturing-based company
- A Baldrige winner or finalist
- Recognized leader in the industry
- Strong reputation in the function being studied
- Performance metrics

**2.2b** We have steadily increased the number and scope of our benchmark studies and competitive comparisons.

In 1989, Varifilm hired the T. A. Barns consulting firm to prepare functional excellence benchmarking studies of "Best of the Best" practices such as service, productivity and yield comparisons. Since then, Varifilm has developed its Benchmarking Team led by three internal experts. Ad hoc committees, marketing surveys, and customer and supplier contacts provide data for strategic planning and analysis of competitive practices. The three experts also act as coaches for business teams and HPWS teams who are interested in benchmarking.

Our benchmark studies have increased from 4 in 1989 to 20 in 1992. Figure 2.2 lists some of the studies conducted since 1990 and shows the scope and sources of competitive and benchmark data.

The Varifilm Finance and Planning Department collects and uses vendor comparative data as part of its supplier partnership program.

Competitive comparisons have always been a strong focus of our business teams. We use data from our global competitive intelligence databases to estimate indices of competition (sales, capacity, cost, etc.). Based on trends assessment, we use "competitive intelligence" to develop strategies for market, product, manufacturing, technical, environment, and resource developments which we document in the annual Business Plan (see Item 3.1). One innovative way to collect competitive intelligence is our trade show debrief process which is led by our benchmarking experts.

**2.2c** The Varifilm Benchmarking Process (Figure 2.3), resourced by our experts, helps us build synergy from numerous studies of best practices. Comparisons between our processes and best-in-class processes point out opportunities for improvement. This information is used by our business and/or functional teams to develop solutions to attain improved performance. Where possible, non-industry comparisons are also used. Much has been learned from the service and support sectors.

| Study Focus | Number of Participants | Study Application |
|---|---|---|
| **Product & Service Quality** | | |
| Customer Service | 4 companies<br>3 Baldrige winners | • One-Call-Quote System<br>• Cellular phone for each sales representative |
| Customer Focused | 4 companies | Introduced innovative design process and cycle time management (Omega/CTE process) |
| **Customer Satisfaction** | | |
| Recyclable Competitive Study | 6 companies | Decision to start up Recyclables business |
| Domestic Film Competitive Study | 7 companies | Reorganization of the Electrical business |
| Customer Satisfaction Survey | 25 top customers | Defined key success indicators for customers of Industrial Wrap; incorporated into business plans |
| **Internal Operations, Business Processes, Support Services, Coworkers** | | |
| Computer Systems | 5 companies, 1 supplier | Designed and implemented our global on-line interactive order entry system |
| High Performance Work System | 5 companies | Developed our HPWS |
| Child Care | 3 companies | Pilot program developed |
| Film Distribution | 1 educational institution<br>3 service companies | • Revised organization structure<br>• Decentralized decision-making |
| Plant Safety | 3 leading companies in safety | Developed safety training program |
| Maintenance | 2 airlines<br>3 industrial companies | Developed plans to improve craftsmen effectiveness and scheduling |
| **Suppliers** | | |
| Supplier Partnerships | 5 leading companies | • Revised certification process<br>• Improved recognition program |

**Figure 2.2**   Representative 1990s Benchmark Studies

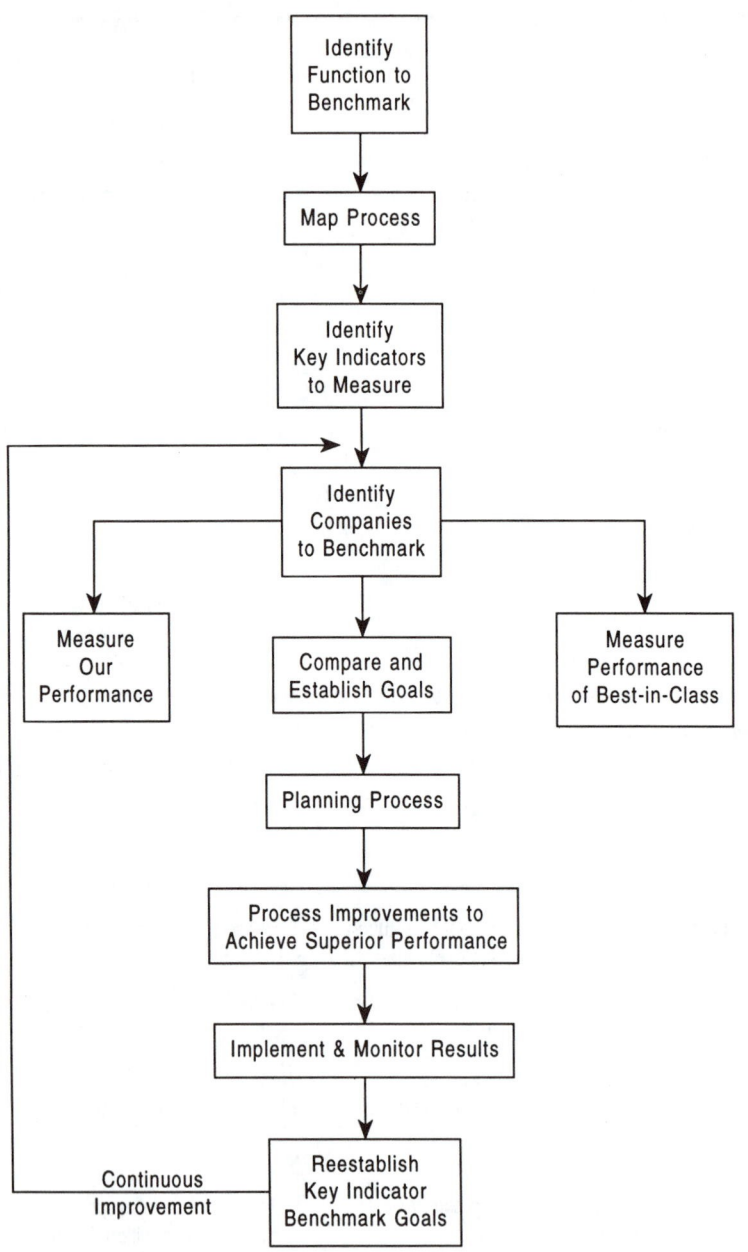

**Figure 2.3**   Varifilm Benchmark Process

**2.2d**  Varifilm has a Benchmarking Resource Center, comprised of a manager and three experts.

We actively participate in a network of professional benchmarkers and in professional associations such as the American Benchmarking Center and the Strategic Benchmarking Institute to evaluate new approaches for identifying best-in-class companies. We search computerized databases to identify companies recognized as leaders in specific areas. We also employ consultants to gather business information and metrics to identify companies that are "excellent" in specific functions.

## 2.3 Analysis and Uses of Company-Level Data

**2.3a**  We use a variety of approaches to collect customer data, which are routed to the specific groups for aggregation/analysis. For example, customer purchase information is directed to Marketing; complaint information goes to Technical Marketing and Manufacturing; new technology information goes to the Technical organization; and strategic information goes to business leadership. Most of the time, our customers communicate information directly to the appropriate group.

Problem information requiring immediate or near-term action is distributed, as quickly as possible, to people responsible for resolution (electronic mail is usually used). Customer-identified problems are automatically given top priority. Our Technical Marketing and Manufacturing people give these problems top priority until they are resolved. If a problem is not easily resolved or demands additional resources, business leadership gets involved to shift resources to ensure resolution.

Performance in each of our five key customer satisfaction requirements is tracked vs. customer satisfaction. This analysis has confirmed that what customers tell us is in fact a determinant of customer action as measured by market share. Representative summary charts are shown in Figure 2.4.

For service quality performance, our customer satisfaction survey points us to direct measures, such as percent of product meeting delivery time commitment. A corporate study has uncovered a correlation between non-management visits to customers and overall customer satisfaction. Customer satisfaction has led to long-term contracts and has improved market share, especially in a period of economic uncertainty such as 1992.

Each of our businesses is led by a leadership team comprised of the overall business leader, leaders for each major function (e.g., human resources, partnership team representative, manufacturing, marketing, technical) and others as appropriate. For purposes of overall planning and review, customer data are systematically organized and brought into team meetings. Marketing and Tech-

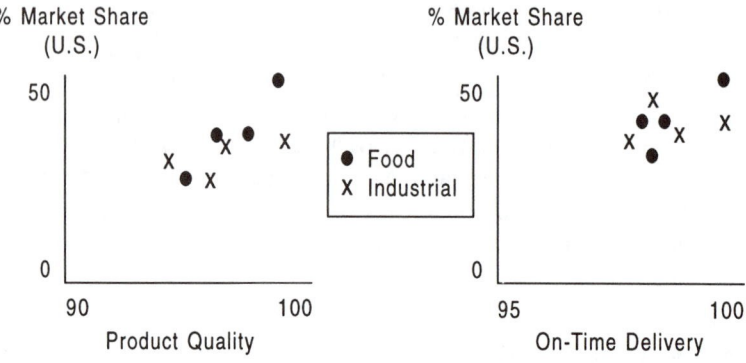

**Figure 2.4**    Varifilm Key Customers

nical Marketing are the key organizations for data analysis/aggregation and presentation. For the business planning process, described in Category 3.0, customer data brought into the process include satisfaction data, product and service performance data, new product information, strategic partnership factors, and competitive information.

**2.3b**    Manufacturing and Technical groups are responsible for performance data in manufacturing; however, every support function deals with its performance data (e.g., the Information Systems organization analyzes computer performance). Generic operational measures, commonly tracked at every level, are cycle time of key processes and defects important to internal or external customers.

Operational performance is systematically reviewed within each sub-unit of the business (e.g., plant site, Technical group, Information Systems group). When a problem is found, that sub-unit is responsible for correcting it. When resources and priorities are an issue, the I-Team or Business Team is involved. More often, operational data are used for continuous improvement. Teams analyze performance data using problem-solving skills to capitalize on performance that exceeded expectations as well as correcting poor performance.

The analysis and priority setting process includes:

1. Identify issues.
2. Determine revenue at risk.
3. Prioritize issues.

4. Identify performance measures.

5. Determine targets.

Each functional organization brings its operational analyses as input to the business plan development process. Key Indicators include First Pass Yield, inventory measures, environmental measures, safety measures, and functional performance measures.

**2.3c** Each business has financial analysts and market strategists who analyze and summarize financial and market trends.

We have corporate standards for the analysis of financial information [e.g., calculation of Return on Asset (ROA), After Tax Operating Income (ATOI), cash flow, profit margin, and fixed cost productivity]. Market trend analyses vary depending on the competitive environment. Data are reviewed regularly and summarized for use in the planning process.

**2.3d** Specific analysis cycle time is one key indicator (e.g., financial closing cycle). The basic key indicator is achievement of bottom line results (e.g., Do we have the "right" data at the right time to focus our efforts to achieve cost reduction and increases in revenue, market share, and profit?).

Past correlation studies have highlighted some issues important to both profitability and customer satisfaction. It is expected that further study in 1993 of VCIC item scores will uncover additional insight.

Customer surveys are leading indicators of purchase intent, lagging indicators of performance. In 1989, the top ten process issues were identified. Pre- and post- "Fix" purchase intent surveys were conducted. We have been able to track improved sales and now rank key product/process attributes.

Benchmarking gives us new ideas on analysis methods and key indicators. Cycle time reduction techniques include flowcharting and identification of "non-value-adding work." We used both of these methods in reducing the financial closing cycle by 70%. We benchmarked a leading Korean company's "Management By Planning" process to learn about integrating data for business planning. Approaches which help us integrate all analyses for effective decision-making include:

- Multifunctional business leadership team. Owners of each type of data are represented on the team.
- Our partnership focus ensures that all key bases are touched in the planning process.

## CATEGORY 3.0
## STRATEGIC QUALITY PLANNING

### 3.1 Strategic Quality and Company Performance Planning Process

**3.1a**   We have an integrated, systematic, and rigorous business planning process. In the late 1980s, we began integrating our quality and business plans. Today, all businesses have totally integrated their quality and business plans—*all* key quality factors impacting external customers and *all* key quality requirements impacting internal operations are included in the business plan. The Strategic Quality Planning Process (SQPP) model was developed in 1990 to ensure this integration. (See Figure 3.1.) The I-Team adopted SQPP for Varifilm strategic quality planning.

SQPP includes:

1. Analysis of the critical factors including VCIC assessment;
2. Planning: Strategic Business Intent; Alignment with Varifilm's Mission, Policy, Values; Business Operating Plans;

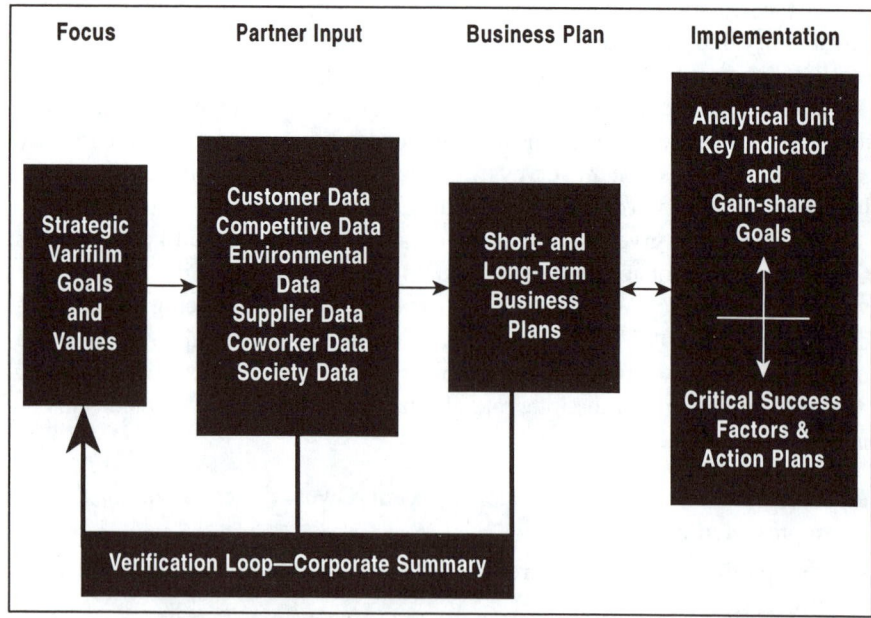

**Figure 3.1**   Strategic Quality Planning Process

3. Implementation: Deployment to the work units;

4. Input from coworkers across levels, sites, functions, suppliers, and customers;

5. Focus on our partners.

Business plans address customer requirements; competitive pressures; financial, market, and societal risks; our process and service capabilities; and our supplier capabilities. We use a variety of information sources from inside and outside Varifilm. (See Category 2.0, Figure 2.1.)

| | |
|---|---|
| **Customer Requirements** | Customer surveys, Product Specification Reviews, customer teams, focus groups, Fitness Reviews, and I-Team and coworker visits |
| **Competitive Environment** | Customer/supplier feedback, benchmark studies, trade assessments, reports of competitive intent, production capability, quality of products and services |
| **Risk Analysis** | Market team assessments, government requirements, societal concerns, corporate financial/market reports, global financial/market assessments, capital expenditure needs assessment, environmental cycles |
| **Our Capability** | Controlled Operating System (COS) updates, technology assessments, supplier technology developments, technical/engineering reports, Cpk |
| **Supplier Capabilities** | Supplier partnership, Cpk, Joint Specifications Development, certification audits, Material Specification Reviews, ISO 9000 |
| **Future Business Factors** | Customer surveys, Vision, and Mission |

Our businesses analyze their data to (1) assess where they are versus their quality goals, profit objectives, competitors, and industry trends; and (2) identify improvement opportunities.

To ensure that quality factors are included in the business plan, most businesses get feedback on customer-related and internal performance-related requirements from coworkers, customers, and suppliers via the Total Quality Fitness Review. VCIC is an integral part of the Total Quality Management (TQM) process.

All businesses develop a portfolio which includes an assessment of their financial performance and strategies, Key Indicators, and their total VCIC assessment score and goal. The I-Team reviews this information to (1) verify alignment with Varifilm's Vision, Mission, and continuous improvement strategies; and (2) authorize resource plans.

The calendar of planning processes is rigorously followed:

**March–April**     Business Customer Satisfaction Surveys completed.

**May–June**     Quality assessment complete (VCIC every two years).

**June–August**     Business strategy reviews are completed.

**September**     Costs and profit objectives are established.

**November**     Corporate alignment is achieved. Budget (one year) and Plan (five year) finalized. Key Indicators finalized.

**December**     Critical Operating Tasks for the coming year are established. Unit, team, and individual objectives set, aligned with goals.

Each business uses the aligned business plan to develop critical operating tasks, which are shared with all coworkers to enable them to stay focused on continuous improvement.

**3.1b**     Varifilm's strategic direction is guided by the Board of Directors and the I-Team. Business selection and emphasis follow the direction set during the annual planning process. Direction is discussed and reviewed with the board annually.

Realignment of the work processes has started with the introduction of process management concepts and the Phase III Partnership/HPWS work redesign. The partnership effort encourages process and analysis and process redesign.

The five-step partnership process is:

1. **Change event:**  Unit meets to hear from customers, suppliers, and leadership. Requirements, competitors, and vision are presented.

2. **Design team:**  A cross-functional design team is formed to develop and present a new structure which will meet the requirements of customers and coworkers. (Presentation and acceptance follow.)

3. **Work teams established:**  Work teams are established and develop their own process flow.

4. **Training:**  Cross-training occurs on redesigned process and job responsibilities.

5. **Implementation and continuous improvement.**

The same process analysis and improvement in Step 3 are now part of a course for HPWS teams. The teams use the process to improve and measure their own processes. Unit Key Indicators are aligned and improvement measured. Once the process is mapped, the ongoing team annually reviews its process for improvement. Several plants have hired JIT Associates to implement similar process improvement team training. Since 1990, six plants have implemented the process. (See Item 4.1.)

Unit and team activities, aligned with the strategic plan (see Item 3.1), are reviewed quarterly by the Invincible Team Key Indicator review and the annual unit review (see Item 1.2). Operational performance, energy and material utilization, waste reduction, productivity, product quality, and labor are all included.

**3.1c** Each work unit develops implementation action plans and schedules.

Business leaders communicate the critical operating tasks throughout their organizations. Presentations are made at each site, and they are available on videotape and electronic bulletin board systems at each site so everyone can become familiar with them. After the initial presentation, a cascading approach is used.

1. Supervision discusses strategies and plans applicable to their work units. Suppliers are also engaged in this process as appropriate.
2. Resources are committed to achieve the desired results outlined in the critical operating tasks and are based on scope and priority.
3. Business leaders "close the loop" by modifying the plan, as required, based on coworker and supplier input.

Our coworkers are empowered to update their systems and processes as part of their continuous improvement efforts. Graphs and charts of business measures (Key Indicators) are prominently displayed so everyone can track progress toward meeting strategic intent and gain-sharing goals.

Gain-sharing was negotiated in 1991. Each plant or unit has a gain-share committee, consisting of leadership, coworkers, and union representatives. The committee selects 3–5 customer-related goals that must include a customer service, product quality, and cost goal. These goals are submitted to and approved by the I-Team to assure fairness. Payout is targeted at 5% of annual salary if goals are achieved. The potential range is 0–10%. Gain-share aligns key indicators to each individual coworker. This is one tool used to align Varifilm's goals.

**3.1d** Our multifunctional teams coordinate business plans and facilitate alignment with Varifilm plans. (Ref. Area 2.3a.) Members of the planning group attend courses and seminars given by leading business schools to stay abreast of leading edge technologies. Based on their learnings, they identify improvement opportunities in our planning process and implement changes as needed.

## 3.2 Quality and Performance Plans

**3.2a**   Our businesses use customer requirements, competitive intelligence, and assessment of internal capabilities to define key quality factors and company performance requirements.

Key quality factors are based on customers' perceptions obtained from our customer partnership meetings and verified through our satisfaction surveys. Factors vary from business to business. However, those common to our main businesses include product quality; on-time delivery; commitment to the customer's industry; partnership; responsiveness to and understanding of customer requirements; and new product development. In addition to customer satisfaction and related directions, we also set goals for coworker and public responsibility.

Key company performance requirements are derived from the needs of our defined partners and are defined through the planning process. Major items are VCIC score, First Pass Yield, cost and revenue, profits, waste, EPA-related emission levels, safety, public perception (most admired), and coworker satisfaction.

**3.2b**   Varifilm's short-term quality and performance directions and goals focus on opportunities critical to our partners and utilize Key Indicators. (See Figures 3.2 and 3.3.)

Each business develops its short-term quality goals and objectives consistent with the five-year business plan. The goals focus on actionable results which address key customers' requirements and are aligned with Varifilm's goals and directions. These goals are documented in each business plan as well as in each business' critical operating tasks for the year. Short-term goals are most visible in the Key Indicator reporting and in each unit's gain-sharing objectives. As an example, Figure 3.3 shows some quality goals for three of our businesses.

**3.2c**   Varifilm long-term goals ensure our future! To achieve long-range goals, our businesses identify their global capital equipment, facilities, education and training, and personnel requirements for their plans and strategies.

Specific long-term goals include being the low cost producer of industrial and food packaging film and having the number one market share in those markets in which we compete.

Key Indicators are projected for five years. Generally, Varifilm's goal is to double or halve (as appropriate) the Key Indicator in four years. This goal creates a stretch approach, which has supported continuous improvement but also created a paradigm change mentality.

| | | Partners | | |
|---|---|---|---|---|
| Coworkers | Society | Stockholders | Customers | Suppliers |

**Short-Term Goals 1993**

| | | | | |
|---|---|---|---|---|
| Complete 20-hour SMT training Part time Work Option Coworker Satisfaction Gain-share Diversity training | Day Care Pilot 10x EPA requirements | ROA top quartile Make Most Admired Company List | Goals specific to business (see Figure 3.3) Customer | Reduce supplier base by 30% |

**Long-Term Goals 1996**

| | | | | |
|---|---|---|---|---|
| >95% work force in High Performance Work System Teams by 1993 | 20x EPA requirements | ROA top quartile Growth 12%/year Market share leader | Goals specific to businesses (See Figure 3.3) | 100% certified suppliers |

**Figure 3.2**   Varifilm Short- and Long-Term Goals

| Business | Goal | 1991 (Actual) | 1992 | 1993 | 1998 |
|---|---|---|---|---|---|
| **Food** | Product Change Cycle Time | 12 hrs. | 8 hrs. | 4 hrs. | 2 hrs. |
| **Packaging** | Product Introduction Cycle Time | 10 mos. | 6 mos. | 4 mos. | 2 mos. |
| | % Earnings from New Products | 14% | 23% | 25% | 25% |
| | On-Time Delivery | 90% | 99% | 99.9% | 6 Sigma |
| **Industrial Film** | On-Time Delivery (Request) | 85% | 95% | 99% | 100% |
| | First Pass Yield | 80% | 85% | 90% | 95% |
| | Customer Satisfaction Index | 80 | 85 | 90 | 95 |
| **Recyclables** | Customer Satisfaction Index | 85 | 90 | 95 | 97 |
| | Employee Satisfaction | 55% | 60% | 68% | 72% |
| | Broken Promises (On-Time Delivery) | 0.8% | 0.2% | 0% | 0% |
| | VCIC Score | 450 | 550 | 650 | 750 |

**Figure 3.3**   Examples of Business Quality Goals

**3.2d** All Varifilm businesses are keenly aware of market trends and competitive directions and develop their improvement plans so they can continue to perform well in the foreseeable future.

A clear example of this approach is illustrated by our Food Packaging business. This business is primarily domestic in focus and has tough domestic competitors. At this point in time, a leading Japanese film company (JFC) is building a state-of-the-art plant in southern California. We can project the selling price and product quality. In a dramatic display of commitment to the business, Varifilm committed $500 million to upgrade our equipment and laid out a plan to improve quality and hold or reduce cost in order to counter this strong competitive threat. We project our quality and price levels to be very competitive. Specifically, in Food Packaging's "Critical Operating Tasks," goals are identified for 1993 through 1998, and projected benchmarks are given for each.

# CATEGORY 4.0
# HUMAN RESOURCE DEVELOPMENT AND MANAGEMENT

## 4.1 Human Resource Planning and Management

**4.1a** Human Resource management has closely aligned itself with the businesses and goals of Varifilm. Since the implementation of Phase II and Phase III, Human Resources (HR) has been actively involved as a functional member of each business. As part of the business planning process, training and involvement requirements are defined. The focus has changed from phase to phase. During Phase I, HR focused on supervisor development, job descriptions, grievance procedures, process specification development, and negotiations. Phase II brought TQM training, statistics training, team training, participation, recognition, affirmative action, and coworker feedback systems. Phase III moved to coworker involvement, HPWS, coach training, diversity training and implementation, and coworker-developed skill training.

Our human resource management approach is a vital part of achieving coworker partnership. Our HR goals reflect a commitment to people development, from the constant goal of improving safety to the short- and long-term goals cited in Area 3.2c (Self Managed Teams, HPWS training, gain-sharing, diversity). We address these various goals through our efforts in education and training, recruitment, involvement, empowerment, and recognition. Long-term goals focus on the work team of the future, including the technical training that will be required.

Human Resources has its own set of Key Indicators which align and support business indicators. We envision an environment that truly and totally VALUES

PEOPLE. That means being caring enough, and conscientious enough, to place the needs of our people at the heart of everything we do, at the center of all our aspirations. It means HR management that translates our concern for people into the total fabric of all that we are.

1. **Education and Training.** Varifilm's "People Value"—"Value and Respect for the Individual"—We realize that only by achieving the growth and development of our people can we attain our quality and performance objectives. Education and training are important for developing Varifilm people, and we apply these methods to promote health and safety, coworker development, involvement, skill development, diversity, and greater customer focus. We respond to changing business and customer needs with our quality education programs.

   **Phase II:** With intensifying competition, we needed greater involvement with our customers. We implemented TQM training, customer requirement training, and quality skills training. These initiatives greatly increased customer contact for heightened coworker sensitivity to customer needs and continuous improvement.

   **Phase III:** SMT/HPWS process management, understanding the business, and creating work teams in a variety of learning experiences. This phase moves to a system of performing work in which all coworkers join together to drive the quality of the business results, and performance is valued over rank.

   **Empowerment:** Hundreds of ad hoc teams sprang up in the '80s for specific tasks and still function today. Currently, there are many self-directed (empowered) teams which operate and maintain the business processes.

2. **Mobility, Flexibility and Changes.** HPWS, emphasizing performance over rank, will further empower coworkers, and our gain-sharing for all coworkers is reducing artificial distinctions. We are proud of our progress and are determined that it continue.

3. **Recognition.** We enthusiastically recognize and reward individual and team contributions. That conscientiousness makes a difference. We recognized 23% of our work force in 1991 with monetary awards and have met our goal of 25% in 1992. (See Area 4.4b.) Highly effective, non-monetary coworker awards include plaques, mementos, tickets, merchandise, dinners, celebrations, donuts and coffee, and letters of recognition. Many of these are given by coworkers. HPWS, when fully deployed, will reward skills and performance, not seniority.

4. **Recruitment.** We are convinced that, to remain competitive, our work force must reflect an increasingly diverse society. That is why our proactive hiring goal requires that new hires at the management/professional level reflect the

diversity of our country which we need as a company to succeed. This recruitment requirement also stands for our non-U.S. units. We also have an upward mobility goal that stipulates parity by 1998 at all levels, including the executive payroll and Board of Directors.

**4.1b**   Our goal is a well-trained, diversified, empowered work force.

**Hiring Diversity.**   Since 1979, our goal for hiring women and people of color for management/professional positions is 45–50%. We have exceeded that goal in each of the last five years.

**Upward Mobility.**   Our goal is to achieve parity at every level of the professional and managerial group with the representation of women and people of color within the Varifilm work force. Thus, if 24% of professional and managerial coworkers are women (as is currently true at Varifilm), then women should be 24% of every level all the way up to the Board of Directors and CEO.

Currently, we have 24% women and 13% people of color at parity up to the manager level. Above that, the percentages fall off significantly. We have proactive programs to increase manager and above representation.

**Retention.**   Our goal is to retain all coworkers we hire.

**Diversity.**   Our goal is to value diversity and utilize the unique skills, abilities, and interests of each individual. We recognize that to be successful Varifilm coworkers must work in a quality way and that the skills and abilities of all coworkers are required. We offer seminars and workshops on racial and gender diversity. We have changed our perspective from expecting the individual to fit the organization to helping the organization accept and manage diverse and unique individuals.

| Item | 1988 | 1989 | 1990 | 1991 | 1992 |
|---|---|---|---|---|---|
| Minorities in Management as % of Total Hires | 35% | 39% | 58% | 60% | 55% |
| Salaried Females as % of Total Hires | 15% | 15% | 18% | 23% | 25% |
| Wage Roll Females as % of Total Hires | 45% | 45% | 46% | 47% | 49% |
| Salaried Blacks as % of Total Hires | 10% | 10% | 11% | 12% | 13% |
| Wage Roll Blacks as % of Total Hires | 15% | 15% | 15% | 15% | 15% |
| % Turnover Per Year | 8% | 6% | 5% | 6% | 4% |
| % Minority Turnover Per Year | 12% | 8% | 7% | 6% | 5% |

**Figure 4.1**   Hiring Diversity

**Affirmative Action.** Our diversity training and approach has replaced past affirmative action programs. While we are committed to affirmative action and measure and report as required by the government, our goals and objectives are much more aggressive. We offer affirmative action support for those seeking assistance in correcting any situation or in filing a complaint. The program has resulted in special training for several individuals. We support outstanding local minority students with scholarships and summer job programs.

**One Salary Roll by Year-End, 1995.** We are committed to an environment that genuinely values people. As an expression of that idea, we will achieve one salary roll by the end of 1995. Administratively, all coworkers will be on salary and will receive the same treatment regarding development and pay, while meeting legal requirements, without regard to type of position.

**Interviewing Process Improvements to Better Reflect Needs.** To ensure that we hire operating people with value for teamwork, risk-taking, and diversity, we have changed our hiring process to include three interview levels, job orientation including one three-hour team-building session, peer evaluation, and exercises to demonstrate problem-solving abilities, basic skills, and special technical skills. HPWS teams are now doing their own hiring using this documented process.

**4.1c** We use data from coworker surveys to improve the development and effectiveness of our work force and support processes. In the mid '80s we instituted the Coworker Climate Survey to measure coworker attitudes, understand the issues affecting coworkers, measure our progress and assess our future course. The survey monitors 11 Key Indicators among all coworkers such as well-being, satisfaction, and involvement.

Management compares survey results among sites, against the Corporate Leadership Survey (initiated in May 1991 and used throughout the Company at all levels) and against the Wheaton data (compares Varifilm to 13 other major companies). The Coworker Climate Survey (see Area 1.2d) and VCIC process are also used to measure changes and identify areas for proactive or corrective action.

Our turnover of all rolls is so low that it has ceased to be a reported measurement. We still track for diversity purposes. Historical data are only used for hiring and researching projections. We attribute this to pay and benefits, treatment of people, recognized opportunities for advancement, high ethical standards, and concern for doing the right thing.

What is more, when turnover is decreased and people are involved in continually improving their results together, it only makes sense that mutual loyalty and teamwork build. That is what seems to be happening more often at Varifilm.

## 4.2 Employee Involvement

**4.2a**    Our Self Managed Team (HPWS) process and opportunities for improvement suggestion systems actively seek and utilize coworker contributions.

The Team Training Process is a tremendous investment in our people. Its initial phase is a four-day seminar, "Encouraging Empowered Teams" (EET), for team leaders or a two-day seminar, "Self Managed Teams," for all coworkers.

In training, when a person learns that he/she can safely take more of a risk than he/she had believed, whether climbing a pole or jumping off a ledge—especially with the total and active support of the team cheering him/her on, that same coworker becomes more willing in the work place to handle the risk of a new idea, to offer feedback for improvement, or to push him/herself to make a change enhancing personal performance.

A series of four continuous development modules (one day each for team members and three days each for skill development, with one point person per team) are led by coworkers and follow the introductory piece. These modules integrate involvement and empowerment with a specific quality improvement project. (See Figure 4.2 for an overview of each module.)

We also share this training with our direct and downstream customers and suppliers. At our Whiting plant, for example, a cross-functional team of marketing and plant people participated in the two-day session with people from one of our largest customers. They shared their business concerns and needs. As a result of successful interchanges like these, we plan to share our process with more direct and downstream customers.

The training modules emphasize the success of synergy and enable teams to develop and empower themselves. Each natural work group team completes a meaningful quality project that improves some part of its actual work performance. Every coworker is a member of a team with which he/she interacts for an ongoing series of developmental experiential learning activities.

Most coworkers participate on or with several teams. We have natural self-directed work teams, task teams, design teams, customer partnership teams, supplier partnership teams, safety teams, quality teams, etc. Typically, these

| | |
|---|---|
| 1. **Team Organization Concepts** | Values, Vision, organization structure, recognition, participation |
| 2. **Work Redesign** | Concepts of work redesign, how to get started |
| 3. **Process Improvement** | How to map, measure, and improve a process |
| 4. **Problem-Solving Skills** | Varifilm's problem-solving approach and process |

**Figure 4.2**    Self Managed Team Modules

| | Open Line | | | | Suggestions | |
| | Wage Roll | | Salaried | | | |
| Year | Actual | Goal | Actual | Goal | Actual | Goal |
|---|---|---|---|---|---|---|
| 1988 | 100 | — | 10 | 20 | 550 | 500 |
| 1989 | 180 | 100 | 15 | 20 | 800 | 750 |
| 1990 | 111 | 100 | 20 | 20 | 1000 | 1000 |
| 1991 | 89 | 100 | 25 | 20 | 2000 | 1500 |
| 1992 | 37 | 50 | 19 | 20 | 3500 | 2500 |
| 1993 | — | 25 | — | 20 | — | 4000 |

**Figure 4.3**   Coworker Involvement in Open Line and Suggestion Systems

teams are cross-functional, spanning coworker levels to get the skills, knowledge, and abilities required to achieve the improvement objective.

**Suggestion Systems** traditionally offer opportunities for coworkers to contribute their ideas to improve safety, quality of product or service, the workplace, or other aspects of the business. Empowered learning teams have now taken over administration of the suggestion systems and brought about significant improvements in cycle time and quality of suggestion and time to implementation. Participants receive initial feedback within 3 days concerning the status of their suggestions and periodically thereafter regarding progress toward implementation. Monetary awards are given based on tangible savings or intangible value.

To promote a free flow of coworker communication, we have an open door policy and open line written process. Any coworker can discuss any suggestion, problem, concern or idea with any member of management and receive an immediate response. This is consistent with our move from a hierarchical management system to a teamwork/involvement culture, encouraged by OE and our SMT process. With the Open Line Process, a written question or suggestion receives the normal three-day written feedback. As teams have become a way of life, open line volume has significantly decreased.

**4.2b**   Our Self Managed Team process is synonymous with increased coworker empowerment, responsibility, and innovation.

SMT increases coworker responsibility in many self-directed work teams, cross-functional teams, and tasks teams—empowering all coworkers at all levels. Our training initiatives enable coworkers to interact successfully with customers and suppliers on scheduled customer plant trips, quality task teams, and problem-solving teams.

Wage roll coworkers now lead visits to customer plants and orientations of customers visiting our facilities. These visits by coworker teams to customer sites not only improve performance, they also enhance satisfaction. They help our people now realize that they are seen as more than just "bodies" to perform a task; they are thinking, creative members of the team who can achieve more if they have a chance to know and experience more. In addition, through these contacts, coworkers often generate a personal sense of loyalty to their customers—"Mary needs it this way. I know because I was there and she is counting on us!" The enthusiasm and perspective these customer contacts build are, frankly, nothing short of wonderful, and a critical part of understanding and meeting our customer requirements.

All categories of coworkers are linked to empowerment through the business objectives and key indicators. With clear goals, training, and encouragement to act, everyone is involved in continuous improvement activities. Management or leadership's role is to support teams as they do their job. Unit leadership is also empowered to redesign team activities and, when combined with HPWS activities, major improvements have occurred.

**4.2c** SMT participation, CCS data, participation in our suggestion systems, and use of tools are used to evaluate the extent and effectiveness of coworker involvement.

Coworker involvement, empowerment, and innovation are measured through the Coworker Climate Survey, tracking/assessing coworker suggestions and their results, and team participation. Our suggestion goal is for every coworker to make at least three suggestions per year. We ensure that all rolls participate.

**Self Managed Teams.** Participation was 96% for team leaders. Eighty-one percent of other team members, spanning all categories of coworkers, attended either the two-day or four-day training process.

**Suggestions** come from a broad cross-section of coworkers, with most submitted by wage roll coworkers. Salaried coworkers generally discuss their suggestions with their team, who can decide to adopt and implement them. (Ref. Area 4.2a.)

**Operational Linkage.** Key Indicators are reviewed by the I-Team once a quarter and each unit once a year. Coworker involvement data are not only reviewed but analyzed in context with all other unit data. (Ref. Item 3.1.)

**Coworker Climate Survey Results.** Figure 4.4 shows the percentage of favorable coworker responses by category, many of which measure some aspect of perceptions around involvement. Most categories have shown improvement during a time of change with HPWS, significant training and cultural redirection activities, and a national recession. We attribute this to our focus on the individual, team training, self managed teams, customer focus, and strong leadership involvement.

| Survey Index | Percent Favorable | | |
|---|---|---|---|
| | 1988 | 1990 | 1992 |
| Capacity to Act | 30 | 42 | 61 |
| Coworker Satisfaction | 48 | 55 | 65 |
| Coworker Involvement | 25 | 42 | 58 |
| Quality Leadership | 52 | 49 | 67 |
| Customer Focus | 32 | 43 | 62 |
| Commitment to Values | 65 | 68 | 72 |
| Communications | 68 | 68 | 68 |
| Training | 40 | 43 | 45 |
| Recognition | 47 | 51 | 67 |
| Valuing Diversity | 32 | 70 | 75 |
| Continuous Improvement | 35 | 68 | 76 |

**Figure 4.4**  Wage Roll Coworker Involvement

| Survey Index | Percent Favorable | | | Benchmark Top Quartile |
|---|---|---|---|---|
| | 1988 | 1990 | 1992 | |
| Capacity to Act | 40 | 45 | 50 | 48 |
| Coworker Satisfaction | 68 | 71 | 75 | 64 |
| Coworker Involvement | 45 | 48 | 59 | 51 |
| Quality Leadership | 71 | 74 | 75 | 62 |
| Customer Focus | 51 | 53 | 67 | 58 |
| Commitment to Values | 67 | 72 | 77 | 67 |
| Communications | 65 | 66 | 70 | 65 |
| Training | 55 | 45 | 49 | 57 |
| Recognition | 45 | 48 | 67 | 66 |
| Valuing Diversity | 32 | 40 | 55 | 60 |
| Continuous Improvement | 39 | 70 | 80 | 55 |

**Figure 4.5**  Salaried Coworker Involvement

## 4.3 Employee Education and Training

**4.3a**  Everything we do in Varifilm flows from our concepts of vision, our partners, and the business direction established by senior management.

1. It was in that context that the I-Team focused on Total Quality Leadership and training in areas of Organizational Effectiveness, Focus on the Customer, and Self Managed Teams.

   Most of our businesses decided to become global players and, therefore, need ISO 9002 certification. A natural result was the training given to coworkers who will be responsible for achieving ISO certification.

   At the site level, training programs are in place for all categories of coworkers. Programs include new coworker orientation (two days quality and two days values, unit goals, introduction to products), extensive general and job-specific safety training, step-by-step standard practices, equipment training, and Controlled Operating Procedure training.

   All coworkers learn basic quality skills of problem-solving and self-managed teams. At the job skills level, training needs are performance based. Qualification is determined by test results—for technicians, lab operators, environmental system operators—or by peer or supervisor follow-up.

   At the individual level, job training is jointly determined by task and personal developmental objectives. For example, as individuals and teams move toward greater self-management, they need the tools/skills to perform their present tasks or prepare for the next ones (e.g., Statistical Process Control, Pareto analysis, cycle time reduction, specific job skills and leadership).

   Courses on quality and continuous improvement are developed and presented by corporate resources in Logistics and Operations and Human Resources. They offer courses in Total Quality Management (Phase II), Statistical Process Control, Design of Experiments, Problem Solving, Data Collection and Display, Statistics, Leadership of Continuous Improvement, Principles of Coaching, Fundamentals of Continuous Improvement, etc. Corporate course catalogs are continually upgraded and made available to coworkers on-line.

2. The introduction of SMT training was delivered by an outside consulting group at the five special centers established for the purpose. Consultants then trained "trainers" on the four SMT modules. The trainers, in turn, trained all teams on these modules and the team point-people on the more detailed material.

   Additional methods of dissemination are:

   - Off-site training facilities and outside consultants/equipment vendors
   - Internally developed workshops and seminars
   - Experiential learning
   - Cascaded training (values)

- Individual and team training

- On-the-job training

- Self-training through access to training sections at sites which contain lending libraries and equipment that coworkers can check out for practice. The Corporation also offers an electronic catalog of course offerings and educational resources.

- Self-paced computer-aided training

- Traditional classroom approach

**4.3b**    Quality and related training has increased significantly.

A new plant coworker is trained for about 160 hours initially. About 25% (40 hours) is devoted to quality training. Training areas include: Quality orientation of policy, principles, values, SMT training, safety rules and procedures, equipment operation, dealing with hazardous materials, Process Management System, job procedures, Controlled Operating Procedures, quality checks, communicating quality issues, coordinating quality with internal suppliers and customers, terminology, Statistical Process Control, Product Quality Management, product specifications, product identification, and setting up equipment. When operators transfer from one area to another, they are trained on the equipment and standard practices for their new area of responsibility.

Average participation in SMT training in 1992 was 20.6 hours for every coworker in Varifilm. Our goal is to complete the processing with all coworkers by the end of 1993, which translates into another 28 hours/coworker.

Other job-related quality training available to our coworkers includes: Basic Statistics, Problem Solving, Statistical Process Control, Statistical Design of Experiments, Product Quality Management, Analysis of Variance, Strategy of Experimentation, Total Productive Maintenance, ISO 9000, Self Assessment–Malcolm Baldrige, Continuous Flow Manufacturing, Total Quality Management, Quality Circles, and Quality Function Deployment.

**4.3c**    Skill testing and participant feedback are used to evaluate and improve our training effectiveness. "Hard" skills (e.g., technician, laboratories, operator testing) are done in the classroom and laboratory to verify understanding of theory and practical application. Follow-up is done through job cycle checks. (See Area 4.3a.) "Soft" skills like empowerment and leadership are critiqued at the end of training so each participant can feedback learning and verify that training is adequate. Feedback forms are provided to instructors to enable them to improve their presentations. Coworker certification (first try) is tracked as a measure of course effectiveness.

**4.3d** Our coworker education and training trends show outstanding gains.

During the past four years, average hours of quality and related training per coworker per year for salaried people went from 15.0 to 111.0 ('88 to '92) and from 8.7 to 117.0 for wage roll. The forecast for '93 is 120 and 120, respectively.

## 4.4 Employee Performance and Recognition

**4.4a** Our recognition, promotion, compensation, reward, and feedback processes support quality and performance objectives.

In 1982, Varifilm tied its formal recognition policy to Quality Leadership as part of our quality principles to "Create an environment in which we value and recognize quality and innovation, increase individual involvement and teamwork, and seek full use of our talents to ensure that worldwide quality leadership is achieved and continually improved." In short, we intend that recognition should become the norm, rather than the exception.

Our processes recognize both business success and personal growth. Each unit has its own instant recognition program consisting of a thank-you card and small gift (less than $5 movie ticket, car wash, etc.). These can be used by any coworker and have averaged 2–3 per person per year over the past five years. Each unit also has a more formal unit quality award where individuals or teams submit a one-page write-up, and one (or more) is chosen for recognition each quarter. Both are considered non-monetary recognition vs. reward.

Recognition of personal growth for salaried coworkers is primarily driven by the Annual Progress Review process of annual discussion of contribution and development. This becomes the basis for promotion, salary, bonus, and other principal monetary rewards.

Wage coworkers discuss their contributions and needed improvements with team members and unit leaders as part of their training selection and gain-sharing reviews. Quality is an integral element in these discussions.

To support the recognition of personal growth and achievement, there are a number of specific awards that celebrate demonstrated success in Marketing (Customer Focus Award), Technology (Scientific Medal), Quality Leadership (Invincible Award), and Problem Solving (Root Cause Award). These Varifilm awards are augmented by business center awards recognizing functional and business excellence in creativity or a trait highly valued by the business center. At each site, newsletters, bulletin boards, flashing display boards, and video news recognize both team and individual success, allowing all to celebrate the success of their colleagues. Self Managed Teams encourage self-recognition among coworkers in work groups. Coworkers decide who should be recognized, and peer recognition is encouraged. As an example, in several areas at the Camden plant, the Suggestion System was revised by wage roll coworkers who now evaluate the suggestions.

We make a conscious effort to recognize teams as well as individuals. In some instances, we reward an entire business. One plant celebrated its business success by taking everyone on a one-day boat trip. This trip provided reward and recognition while reinforcing value for team building and encouraging even higher commitment to business excellence.

**4.4b** Our Coworker Climate Survey provides feedback on how well coworkers rate our recognition programs.

Our key method for evaluating recognition effectiveness is the CCS. Specific questions are included that focus on recognition. Improvement teams are established to take action on those items identified for improvement. We also use the Baldrige Assessment process to measure each business' effectiveness in recognizing coworkers and to recommend changes for further improvement.

**4.4c** Our coworker recognition and rewards have increased across all categories.

Before the end of 1982, fewer than 1% of coworkers received monetary awards. The Instant Recognition program provides thousands of instant recognition events each year. In addition all coworkers benefit from the gain-sharing program whose goals are tied to quality Key Indicator improvement and Varifilm performance. Gain-sharing has provided an annual payout to unit coworkers ranging from 1.4% to 9.7% of their annual salaries each year since 1991.

## 4.5 Employee Well-Being and Satisfaction

**4.5a** Safety and health are top priorities.

All of our quality improvement programs are conducted with this mind-set. We benchmark our safety performance and procedures against leading companies in safety. Varifilm believes that all safety and health incidents, injuries, and job-related illnesses are preventable. As such, each job-related incident, injury, or illness is thoroughly investigated for cause and remedy by a team of coworkers. Investigations are publicized at the site (and elsewhere, if appropriate) so that each coworker can benefit from the learning.

We also have Safety, Health, and Ergonomic Teams at each site. These teams are made up of coworkers from all job levels. They implement programs to increase awareness, improve the work environment, and reduce injuries or illness. The CCS shows a top quartile (77–80%) for favorable comments on safety and health.

Coworkers also can train for fire brigade, emergency squad, or career/education enhancement programs. A cross-functional team at our Norco plant conducted a work and family survey in 1991 to learn more about total coworker needs and how the company might better support them. This ongoing study was initiated by coworkers and received full management support.

**4.5b**   Developmental and job training are used extensively to support coworker development and/or accommodate change.

Developmental and job training are managed through our Tuition Credit Program, Job Training Programs, and Reassignment Programs. Our coworkers are encouraged to attend developmental and technical courses and seminars. Through our Promoting The Individual system, they are given opportunities to grow with their needs and interests. We also have a policy of promotion from within. Mentor programs are becoming increasingly prevalent as a way to improve communication and share career possibility ideas among coworkers.

Support for coworkers includes a variety of programs (complete health care programs):

- Holistic Health—our workplace health program
- Personal and family counseling programs
- Health club/YMCA membership support
- Alcohol & Chemical Dependence Rehabilitation
- Classes (family safety, boating safety, defensive driving, firearm safety, rape prevention, substance abuse awareness)

plus many other benefits (Coworker Assistance Program, site recreational areas, pre-tax savings plans, Child Care Locator, Flex Time, Parental Leave, Tuition Refund).

**4.5c**   Coworker satisfaction is determined by Coworker Climate Survey results and one-on-one meetings with coworkers and their supervision.

**4.5d**   On- and off-the-job safety and coworker satisfaction are indicators of coworker well-being and morale. Varifilm teaches and practices safety excellence, both on and off the job. Our safety performance is comparable to the best in the world. Our coworkers enjoy working conditions that are two times safer than the plastics industry average and ten times safer than all industry. Our sites compete for world safety records.

Our concerns for coworkers' on- and off-the-job safety inspired the development of the Individual Safety Program (ISP). ISP rape prevention and personal protection classes have received many awards and have been shared with our customers. Our coworker satisfaction is high. Our 1991 CCS data indicate 69% favorable response to the Business Success/Job Security category and 71% favorable response to the Like My Role category. The rate of coworker turnover is low, about 1% for salaried and 1.75% for wage roll (excluding retirements). These figures continue to be tracked for continuous improvement.

While about 80% of our wage roll coworkers are unionized, most belong to local, independent unions. Positive labor-management relations are most significantly demonstrated by the occurrence of no strikes in 18 years. Sensitivity to coworker needs has resulted in the fact that the union was asked to participate in the organization of all three U.S. Varifilm plants built since 1976.

We believe that we have been creating an environment within Varifilm—and our human resources are an important reason why—in which the continuous improvement approach becomes the limitless supply of fuel to keep the "pilot lights" burning when we ignite them in ourselves and our people. They will burn even more brightly in the years ahead, with even more satisfied and trained coworkers who even more fully help us meet the needs of the other partnerships to which we are so strongly committed. (Ref. Area 4.2d.)

# CATEGORY 5.0
# MANAGEMENT OF PROCESS QUALITY

## 5.1 Design and Introduction of Quality Products and Services

**5.1a** We have a long, successful history of product and service innovations. We began the Varifilm business based on our successful research into film-based products. Since then, we have developed thousands of variants to respond to changing market demands and specific customer needs.

Traditionally, most Varifilm products were designed by first envisioning a product concept, developing market test samples to assess customer receptivity, and scaling directly from a semi-works scale to full production. Varifilm's **Controlled Operating Procedures (COP)** detail the six stages of product design and introduction.

More recently, Varifilm has developed marketing structures which provide more direct intelligence on market trends, customer needs, and processing capabilities. Varifilm's Technical Marketing resources identify new product/process ideas through interactive discussions with direct and downstream customers. Customers' needs and processing changes are translated into engineering and product specifications.

Still, we needed to increase the success rate of our product development and accelerate our "time-to-market" to remain competitive. In 1989, Varifilm conducted a benchmark study, "Customer-Focused Product/Process Development" against "best-in-class" companies. The study showed us that we needed to make improvements in product design leadership, methodology, and supplier partnerships. The "Omega" and Cycle Time Excellence (CTE) approaches address these needs.

*"Omega" Process*, developed in 1990 by a Varifilm Self Managed Team, enhances the methodology, organization, and customer/supplier involvement of Varifilm's COP approach. (See Figure 5.1.) The Food Packaging, Electrical, and Construction businesses (about 80% of sales) have implemented "Omega."

*Cycle Time Excellence* (see Figure 5.1), a product management methodology licensed by Timeclock Associates for new product design, mandates leadership involvement in the process. CTE components include:

- A Program Approval Committee of a business' top leaders to authorize and direct the product development;
- A cross-functional Product Development Core Team to conduct development;
- Phase reviews to ensure organizational alignment to proceed, stop, or repeat; and
- Documented methodology in product development guidance.

| | COP | Omega Process | CTE |
|---|---|---|---|
| **Customer requirements translated into design** | Interactions with customer teams define define customer requirements. Requirements translated into design in Stage 1. | Customer partnership developed using QFD | Application of QFD using cross-functional teams assures translation into design |
| **Quality requirements early in process** | Product and process controls are established and tested to assure quality in Stage 3 | Cross-functional teams address quality requirements in Stage 2; product and process controls are tested | Quality requirements are addressed in Stage 2. Team monitors process until completion. |
| **Designs integrated to include all phases of production and delivery** | Supporting systems verified in Stage 5 | Supporting systems identified in Stage 4 | Supporting systems tested in Stage 5 |
| **Process control plan** | COP documentation in Stage 5 | COP documentation in Stage 5 | Documented Control Plan in Stage 4 |

**Figure 5.1**  Product Design Approaches

Recyclables adopted CTE in early 1991 and expanded to nine product development projects by year-end. Industrial plans to adopt it in 1993.

Customer requirement translation, addressing of quality requirements, production/delivery integration, and development of a process control plan are described in Figure 5.1.

**5.1b**   We identify product and service performance specifications during Stage 2, "Planning and Design" or "Feasibility," and we review them at the end of each test run and modify if necessary. Process specifications, developed during Stage 2, address process capability requirements.

**5.1c**   We conduct benchmark studies to identify improvement opportunities.

Our businesses pilot new practices they deem will add the greatest value and, based on their experience, expand and deploy to other sites and businesses. For example, as a result of our 1990 Customer Focused Product/Process Development benchmark study, we examined and tested the "Omega" and CTE processes. Our people are learning the QFD and robust design concepts imbedded in these processes. By year-end 1991, we completed our "Film Quality" benchmark study to identify further opportunities to improve our design processes.

## 5.2 Process Management: Product and Service Production and Delivery Processes

**5.2a**   Our overall system for manufacturing quality control is our Process Management System (PMS). PMS was developed in the mid-1970s by Food Packaging with our corporate statistical consulting group and deployed throughout Varifilm in the early 1980s. PMS is based on the concept of a "controlled process." We explicitly define a Controlled Process for each of our products through documentation and standard systems to ensure consistency each time we manufacture a given product. PMS includes the following components:

- A "Controlled Operating System" (COS), which documents equipment specifications, material specifications (for supply), production orders, Controlled Operations, Controlled Processing Procedures, Control Practices, measurement test methods and assessments, and plant tests and results for all production and measurement processes required for each product
- Routine variability analysis using process and measurement data
- Process control
- Measurement control
- Product release
- Management of change (modified processes, transfer of production between sites, etc.)

■  Product handling, packaging, and distribution

■  Supplier quality

■  Annual audits

We define our PMS in a set of Varifilm *Controlled Operating Procedures.* Over 15 (down from 30) full-time people administer PMS and keep COP up-to-date. Because of this fully deployed and refined approach, we have been able to achieve ISO 9002 registration in 90% of our units, generally in less than one year after starting. PMS is now a team responsibility.

Within PMS, we measure product properties which predict successful customer end-use requirements. A representative list of our product properties for Food Wrap is shown in Figure 5.2.

For all important properties, we use statistical methods to detect drifts from aim. We have used Statistical Process Control (SPC) since the mid-1970s. We have refined this method so that it calculates how far off-aim the process has drifted, highlights ineffective and control responses to signals, and provides automatic adjustments to minimal drifts as well as notifying the operator of the drift and adjustment.

As a final quality test, we release the product from our manufacturing operation based on a statistical sampling of a defined "lot" of product. This procedure ensures that all products routinely released for shipment meet all COS, On-Aim, and product property requirements, and conform to Product Release and Product Segregation System limits.

**5.2b**  We quickly move to understand and eliminate the root causes for any processes which are out of control. We have a rigorous system to handle out-

---

FDA Approved Materials for Direct Food Contact Surfaces

Gage (Film thickness)

Tear (Both machine and cross direction)

Sealing Temperature

Tack Temperature

Maximum Seal Strength (Both machine and cross direction)

Odor

Taste

Print Quality

Product Resistance

---

**Figure 5.2**   Representative Food Wrap Product Properties

of-control occurrences. Where the process is not automated, a manual adjustment is required, and a documented corrective action procedure is followed. This procedure is designed to identify and correct the root cause, and test for closure.

The Problem Solving Skills Module (Module 4) provides a structured approach for teams and individuals to determine and verify root cause. The problem analysis portion includes explaining the deviation, defining it, developing possible reasons, and testing and verifying reasons. As reported in Area 4.3b, 70% of all coworkers have been trained in this module.

If the measurement process is out of control, we suspend routine testing on the affected instrument and initiate diagnostic and corrective procedures immediately.

**5.2c** We aggressively pursue a variety of "world-class manufacturing technologies" to improve our manufacturing and delivery.

1. **Process Simplification.** All businesses use our PMS to reduce the variability of the manufacturing process. Electrical is using an expanded improvement process (Module 3) to optimize material and information flow from suppliers to customers and Continuous Flow Manufacturing to streamline the manufacturing process. Construction is piloting Advanced Process Control techniques to develop a process model which analyzes the ability of manufacturing technology to make products. Application of Continuous Flow Manufacturing at our Gary Construction Film Plant increased First Pass Yield by 8% and reduced work in progress and cycle time by 40%.

2. **Benchmark Information.** Benchmark studies have identified opportunities for improvement (see Item 2.2), and we continue to develop plans which address the areas in which we do not match or exceed "best of the best."

3. **Process Research and Testing.** Statistically designed experiments are widely used to optimize product and process quality. Statistical analysis of process data identifies sources of variation. Manufacturing technology committees representing each plant identify best practices, equipment, and approaches to be adopted.

4. **Information from Customers of the Processes.** Customer information is consistently evaluated with respect to how we can improve product quality, cycle time, and overall performance. Our Product Development Core Team (PDCT) reviews customer input monthly.

5. **Challenge Goals.** Challenge goals are set after extensive benchmarking of companies who have addressed the area under consideration and deemed to be "best in class." Varifilm has found that business teams and

HPWS work teams establish challenge goals using this methodology. Not only has credibility been given to the goal, but methods of achieving it are also learned.

## 5.3 Process Management: Business Processes and Support Services

**5.3a** The day-to-day management of support services and business processes is guided by our quality philosophy that taking immediate corrective action to determine and eliminate root causes of internal and external customer concerns and problems prevents defects.

We use one-on-one interactions, team meetings, and networks to assess procedures required to meet internal customer needs. The Self Managed Teams distribute How Are We Doing (HOW) questionnaires to their internal customers to identify opportunities for improving service. About 300 HOWs have been generated since mid-1990. This report solicits information on internal customer needs and expectations as well as assessment of the service performance. Interaction with the appropriate marketing and customer service organizations and coworkers is used to identify external customer requirements.

1. All businesses have adopted Varifilm quality tools to reduce business activity cycle times. A business group, working with its quality functional leader, defines (1) core activities, (2) cycle time for each activity, and (3) associated costs. A cost/time profile is created which shows costs per function and potential savings by reducing time required to perform activities within the function (Module 3, Figure 4.2).

2. The concept of "Key Indicators" has been adopted by manufacturing and support groups. Through defined Key Indicators, groups use process performance data to focus and measure improvement. All support groups use this approach.

3. Monthly and quarterly audits conducted by the functional leadership team measure compliance with key quality measures. Annual audits of Process Management Systems and Controlled Operating Procedures are conducted by another site's resources. ISO Registration forms a key assessment of on-site support functions and contract processing. Cycle time and defect reductions are part of the Total Quality Fitness Reviews.

**5.3b** Root cause elimination and process management in our business process are essential to meeting our customers' demands and expectations. People directly responsible for a given business process evaluate problems to identify and

| Function | Key Indicator | 1993–4 Goals | Frequency of Review |
|---|---|---|---|
| Info Systems | Up-time | 99.95% | Monthly |
| Procurement | Cost–Order processing | <$10 | Yearly |
| | % Orders EDI | 80% | Monthly |
| | Number of suppliers | –5% | Monthly |
| Warehousing | No. Quality/ Service Incidents | 0 | Monthly |
| Transportation | Variations/100 Loads | 0.5% | Monthly |
| | Carrier Quality | 99.5% | Monthly |
| Maintenance | Cost/Replacement Investment | 3.0% | Quarterly |

**Figure 5.3**    Support Service Key Indicators and Goals

eliminate the root cause. If a prompt solution is not possible, a team is assigned to solve the problem. (Ref. Area 5.2b.)

**5.3c**    All support organizations and teams are active in improving the effectiveness of their functions. Our Quality Leadership improvement focus is a strong driving force to make this happen.

The improvement processes described for manufacturing are used to improve support processes.

On a broad scale, the Self Managed Team process led groups through a structured process of improvement based on customer needs. This training is available throughout Varifilm. (See Area 4.2a.)

1. **Process Analysis/Simplification.** Process analysis/simplification and/or redefinition are pursued. We use flowcharting and benchmarking to help achieve more effective operations.

2. **Benchmark Information.** Benchmarking studies have identified opportunities for improvement (see Item 2.2), and we continue to develop plans which address the areas in which we do not match or exceed "best of the best."

3. **Process Research and Testing.** Statistically designed experiments are widely used to optimize business process quality. Statistical analysis of process data identifies sources of variation. Committees representing each business process identify best practices, equipment, and approaches to be adopted.

4. **Alternative Technologies.** We are accelerating the application of such leading edge technologies as cycle time reduction and SPC to our business processes.

5. **Information from Customers of the Processes.** Networks and cross-functional teams (including internal customers) are key for quality support activities across Varifilm. For example, Information Systems and Customer Service network in a Communications Excellence Team. Teams and networks are empowered to set requirements and improvement projects, but each is accountable for accomplishments.

## 5.4 Supplier Quality

**5.4a** We use the following key indicators to monitor and rate our supplier quality:

We formed the "Ingredients Quality Systems Committee" in January 1987 to "partner" with our suppliers to improve our raw materials. This self-directed, multi-site, cross-functional team developed, implemented, and manages systems to update material specifications, assess ingredient quality, rate supplier performance (see Item 6.3), eliminate problems, maintain an informational database, reward and recognize excellence, certify suppliers, and assist suppliers with their systems.

**5.4b** We certify suppliers for materials which meet a performance level judged to be in "full compliance with Varifilm's requirements" (see table).

**5.4c** We are constantly reviewing our procurement activities to ensure that we not only work with "state of the art" incoming materials, but also are viewed by our suppliers as a "preferred customer."

We annually review the performance of our Purchasing Department in selecting and describing to suppliers who are capable of supplying materials which consistently meet our standards and specifications. To this end, we have reduced the number of suppliers over the past three years by 33% while improving the view of Varifilm as a supplier by 53% of our customers.

**5.4d** We are encouraging ISO registration for our suppliers, and we are formally recognizing excellent performance. We benchmark Best-in-Class companies to improve our Supplier Quality Program processes and strategies. (See Area 6.4b.)

We recognize a supplier's successful attainment of our highest confidence in total quality partnering by Varifilm Certification and increased business where possible. Basic requirements for Varifilm Certification are:

- Proactively upgrade material specifications and ISO Certification
- Only conforming product was shipped within the last year
- Quality assurance as verified by ISO Certification or Varifilm on-site audits
- Evidence of continuous improvement
- Supplier Total Quality Rating (Scale 1–5)
- Use of statistical techniques

We also have a three-tiered, formal recognition system to acknowledge supplier successes:

- *Quality Leadership Award* for excellent ratings over time
- *Quality Progress Award* for a significant single event, or for significant improvement in overall rating
- *Partners Award* for good partnering, as determined by Varifilm sites working with the supplier.

Various levels of Varifilm management are involved in supplier recognition, appropriate to the level of recognition being given. There is a requirement to present the award to the supplier's *employee* at his/her location. To strengthen its responsiveness with suppliers, Varifilm has an annual "Supplier Day" as part of National Quality Month. Art Axel, Vice-President of Quality, gives awards to 10–15 suppliers whose quality contribution during the past year deserved recognition.

| Supplier Requirements | |
|---|---|
| **Product** | Conform to Material Specifications |
| **Quality** | Statistical Process Control<br>Quality Management System<br>Quality Plans and Improvement Goals |
| **Value-Added** | Total Pricing (including Varifilm process savings)<br>Inventory Management Support Provided |
| **Service** | Order Handling and Invoicing<br>On-Time Delivery<br>Safety<br>Environmental Responsibility |
| **Capability &<br>Technology** | Technical Service<br>RD&E Resources and Application |

| Method | What Is Assessed | Who Assesses | Frequency |
|---|---|---|---|
| Internal PMS Audit | Adherence to PMS by manufacturing sites | Corporate Quality Assurance | Every 6 months |
| ISO 9000 Audits | Quality Systems adherence | Wrights Register Quality | Every 6 months |
| Total Quality Fitness Reviews | Business performance vs. Baldrige criteria | Corporate Quality Resources | Every 24 months |
| Safety & Housekeeping Audits | Conditions, equipment, and practices comply with safety regulations | Site Environmental, Health & Safety | Monthly |
| Customer Surveys | Satisfaction with products & services | Varifilm Marketing 3rd Parties | Annually |
| Supplier Audits | Supplier quality mgmt. system capability | Division Quality Assurance coordinators | Every 12–24 months |
| Product Specification Review | Variability in product consistency & suitability | Cross-functional Product Teams | Annually |
| Mgf. Process Checks | Adherence of process to PMS specifications | Control Operators | Every 1–8 hours |
| Process Hazard Audits | Adequacy of process hazards safeguards | Site Environmental, Health & Safety | Every 2 years |
| Accounting Audits | Adherence to accounting procedure requirements | Independent Internal & 3rd-Party Auditors | Random, but at least annually |

**Figure 5.4**   Varifilm Assessment Strategies

## 5.5 Quality Assessment

**5.5a**   Across Varifilm's businesses and product lines, many approaches are used to assess systems, processes, practices, products, and services. (See Figure 5.4.)

The unique product assessment approach we use was briefly described in Area 5.2. Each quarter we input product and measurement variances, customer specifications, release limits, and the sampling plan. As output, we obtain the percent of product that complies with our customers' specifications. If this assessment tool indicates a degradation in compliance, we often make changes before customers detect the problem.

Our document system specifies what must be documented, when, and by whom; documentation standards; who can access the document; responsibility for maintenance and update; and security procedures (see listing of "Controlled Operating Process" documents in Area 5.2a). Products/sites which have achieved ISO Certification have demonstrated that their document control systems meet ISO standards.

We follow strict guidelines for review and retention requirements of written and computerized documents. Each organization or support group is responsible for updating its documents to reflect technology, practice, and quality improvements.

**5.5b**    Assessment findings are systematically presented to and reviewed and analyzed by appropriate business and plant teams to implement corrective actions. All audits require follow-up action to correct any deviations detected. Immediately following an audit, responsibility is assigned to achieve/restore conformance. Subsequent audits include examination of actions taken in response to previous audits. We train auditors to be competent in the subject they audit (e.g., PMS, process hazards) as well as the audit process.

# CATEGORY 6.0
# QUALITY AND OPERATIONAL RESULTS

## 6.1 Product and Service Quality Results

**6.1a & b**    Our key internal measure of product quality is the "Process Capability Index" (Cpk), and our measures of service quality are on-time delivery and order processing error rates.

For a given property, Cpk is the ratio of customer specifications to the range of our performance and directly compares our performance with our customers' needs.

Our immediate goal by year-end 1993 is to achieve a Cpk level of 1.33 (the benchmark level for process industries) for at least 65% of key processes. We have also set a longer range Cpk goal of 2.0 within five years to meet world-class benchmark standards.

In addition, Varifilm has shown improvement in product quality and performance through improvements in film stretchability (elongation), which results in thinness (gage) of films; the number of breaks per roll (film strength); and failures of film formed into bags (film sealing capability). In both measures we have exceeded Best-in-Class targets.

Our principal measures of on-time delivery are the percent of orders meeting committed shipment date (Shipments Reliability Index—SRI) and percent of orders meeting our customer's request date (Delivery Satisfaction Index—DSI).

Overall performance in SRI has improved from 79% in 1989 to 94% in 1992, while the DSI has improved from 77% to 86% over the same time period. Our current goal is 95% for both the SRI and DSI. Customer surveys indicate our direct competitors are not doing as well as Varifilm in either of these areas.

The improvement in on-time delivery, both SRI and DSI, is directly attributable to our ability to measure and improve the performance of the processes contributing to order fulfillment. Through the use of the Varifilm quality improvement process we learned that many orders were not shipped on time due to errors in the orders. As a result, we started to measure the **order processing error rate** and can now see a direct correlation between improvements in reducing the number of errors at order entry and on-time delivery, with an overall goal of reducing the number of errors at order entry to 0.01%.

The **percent of invoice errors** is another internal measure of our ability to deliver outstanding products and services which meet our customer's requirements and expectations. A longer range objective is to be equal to "world-class" companies which have 0.2% invoice errors.

## 6.2 Company Operational Results

**6.2a & b**  We monitor performance on operational measures of importance to our partners. Operational productivity, efficiency, and effectiveness of manpower, processes, and other resources impact all partners. Our two key drivers—reduced cycle time and reduced defects—continue to serve as cornerstones for all operational processes and are reflected in the indices used.

### Operational Measures Focused on the Customer Partner

**First Pass Yield.**  Since this performance measure was adopted in 1985, the average has steadily improved, and the range of performance among businesses has been reduced. Our benchmark studies reflect the industry leader's First Pass Yield to be about 94%. Our goal is 95%, with some of our businesses currently performing above that level.

**Nonconforming Product Shipped.**  Another operational measure we track is the percent of product shipped which did not fully conform to all specifications. We only ship nonconforming product after a full evaluation of potential customer impact, notifying the customer and securing agreement, and properly labeling as nonconforming. We have significantly reduced the nonconforming products we ship. To our knowledge, we are the only company in the film industry which tracks this index.

Varifilm's Total Quality Process also identified **manufacturing cycle time**, the time from order "to make" is received on the manufacturing floor to shipment to the distribution center, as a key driver to improved customer satisfaction. It also helps identify the major areas to manage our raw material, work in process, and finished goods inventory and correlates well with our progress in reducing them. Film manufactured product cycle time improved in 1992 to 2.8 days from 4.6 days in 1989.

Finally, we also measure the time it takes to enter an order. We achieved an improvement in the **order entry cycle time** from 53 hours in 1989 to 2 hours in 1992. Our goal is less than 30 minutes.

### Operational Measures Focused on the Society Partner

We have a rigorous program to control **air emissions** from our plants. Our environmental goals are consistent with federal and state environmental standards. Because of the success of this program, the original projection of 64% reduction of Superfund Amendments and Reauthorization Act (S.A.R.A.) Title 313 emissions ("right to know") by 1993 has been revised to 70% reduction.

Our plants are systematically reducing the amount of **process waste**. Varifilm's goal of 64% reduction by 1995 has been upgraded to 75%. In 1993, we expect to generate less than one ton per day (dry weight) of process waste compared to over 30 tons per day in the '87–'88 base period.

### Operational Measures Focused on the Stockholder

Our earnings also steadily increased throughout the end of the '80s and into the '90s. This also correlates well with sales per coworker, which shows a steady increase in sales per coworker since 1989.

## 6.3 Business Process and Support Service Results

**6.3a & b**  Our support functions have improved their performance versus goals. Our Business Support Services also focus on reduced cycle time and elimination of defects. A key improvement tool is the Varifilm Total Quality Process "Business Cycle Time." Teams of coworkers from all levels within these services identify non-value-adding activities which can be eliminated, thus reducing overall cycle time. Eight sites are deploying this process.

Each function developed continuous improvement goals, consistent with the Varifilm Continuous Improvement Criteria, and tracked its performance opposite these goals. Benchmark goals are used for Information Systems, Transportation, Maintenance, and Business Services. Product development processes have been benchmarked, and our business-specific cycle time goals are "stretch goals" based on past performance.

**Accounts Receivable Errors (ARE)** are calculated and reported monthly. After an overall increase in AREs in mid-1990, the rate was brought back to the 1989 levels by teams which used such tools as Pareto and cause-effect analyses to identify causes and corrective actions. Currently, business teams are conducting root cause analyses and planning corrective actions which address "pricing discrepancies."

**Information Systems** are another key business process at Varifilm. Since 1989, the percentage of **time the company's information systems have been operational** has increased from 93% to over 98%, the industry standard. These improvements are estimated to have saved Varifilm over $143 million by reducing hours lost by coworkers using these systems and increasing our ability to promptly interface with our customers at all times. Our current goal is 99.95%.

Information system improvements also enabled Varifilm to convert the number of **customers placing orders electronically through EDI** from 17% in 1989 to 63% in 1992, well above the industry standard.

Use of EDI also led to a reduction in the cost of processing a purchase order of $25 in 1989 to $18.10 in 1992. Our goal for 1993 is $10, or $2 below the industry standard.

We also measure the time it takes to introduce new products to our customers. Known in Varifilm as **New Product Cycle Time**, this measure calculates the time from commitment to a customer to provide a new product until delivery of production quantities. We achieved an improvement from 58 months in 1989 to 36 months in 1992. Our goal is to further reduce this to 30 months in 1993.

## 6.4 Supplier Quality Results

Our supplier program has progressed since 1987 toward meeting our goal of: "We will only purchase from suppliers who use quality management systems, including statistical techniques, meet all agreed-upon specifications, and continuously improve the quality and value of their products and services."

**6.4a & b**    Our suppliers are continuously improving the quality of their products and services. In 1989 we benchmarked supplier quality with five site-visited Baldrige companies. We selected these companies because our experience with them indicated they have superior supplier quality programs. The benchmarked companies have an active program to reduce their supplier base in order to leverage their resources and impact total quality of purchased materials. They achieved 20% to 70% reductions over a five-year period. Varifilm began to focus on reducing the number of suppliers in 1989. The goal is a 50% reduction in supplier base by the end of 1992. This study revealed our supplier systems (specifications, Total Quality requirements, auditing, SPC use, etc.) are excellent. However, we were impressed by the approach of these companies and adopted four key program performance metrics.

**Certified Suppliers** totaled 24 key suppliers by year-end 1992, down from 51 in 1989. These companies supply about 80% of our total raw material volume. Our goal is to certify all strategic materials suppliers using our supplier partnership process by the end of 1993.

**Total Quality Ratings of Key Suppliers.** We have rated 41 suppliers, accounting for over 90% of our raw materials volume. The current average score is 4.1 (Scale 1–5, 5 = "excellent"), with no supplier rated less than 3.0, "below satisfactory." Moreover, the percent now rated 4.6–5.0 is 26% compared with 2% during our 1989 rating. This represents an average rating increase of 0.5, exceeding the 1993 goal.

**% Out-of-Date Product Specifications** has decreased significantly. Our goal is to have no out-of-date specifications. We currently have a 5% level of out-of-date specifications compared to 3% average in the companies we benchmarked.

# CATEGORY 7.0
# CUSTOMER FOCUS AND SATISFACTION

## 7.1 Customer Expectations: Current and Future

**7.1a** We continuously review our methods of evaluating and improving our ability to meet the current and near-term customer requirements and make improvements when warranted.

1. Our customers are grouped by market—Food Packaging, Industrial Packaging, and Recyclables. In each grouping we constantly monitor customer requirements and expectations through surveys, partner feedback, complaints, gains and losses of customers, product performance, and trade literature. We review and prioritize these requirements to ensure that we are addressing our customers' most important requirements. Each business team or plant is responsible for prioritizing and tracking action.

2. We collect customer information by the methods described above. This information is directed to the appropriate product management teams who are responsible for managing our customer relationships. The information we collect includes: the product and service features most important to our customers, how Varifilm is doing, and how our competitors are performing. Priorities are based on (1) what is most important to our customers; and (2) differences between Varifilm's performance and our competitors in these areas. Our product management teams continuously receive and evaluate customer information.

Formal third-party telephone surveys are conducted annually of existing and potential customers. These data are formally reviewed by the business teams on a quarterly basis and verified by business team members' personal feedback from customer and market visits.

In addition, Varifilm exhibits at various trade shows including InterPak and the annual convention of the Institute of Food Technologists (IFT). The object of exhibiting is not only to sell products, but also to use a structured approach to gather customer-related information.

3. Once a year, our technical marketing and technical sales groups join our major customers' technical sales group in making their sales calls. This provides opportunities to learn about our indirect customers' problems and opportunities.

**7.1b**  Our continued success depends on our ability to understand and meet our customers' future needs.

1. Each of our businesses focuses on the time horizon which is most critical to its customers' future needs. While some of our Industrial and Food Packaging businesses realize they must focus on the critical time horizon of three–five years, Recyclables is often thinking 20 years ahead. All our businesses, however, are aware of trends that will affect the plastic film business into and beyond the year 2000.

2. We deal with technological, competitive, societal, and demographic factors which may impact customer requirements, expectations, or alternatives in three major ways:

- Varifilm has developed collaborative arrangements with the Total Quality Management, Food Science, Packaging Science, and Polymeric Chemistry Programs at a leading private and a leading state university. These partnerships provide an opportunity for undergraduate students to intern in our plants and laboratories, in support of basic research in food, packaging, and polymeric sciences. In addition, we have developed a mini-sabbatical program which allows for an exchange of university faculty and our scientists and engineers. This program provides us with information needed to determine future technologies.

- Each business tracks its specific global business environment factors. Our economists develop specific economic information relevant to each business, and resources within the business keep abreast of demographic and technical trends and forecasts.

- Our RD&E resources study basic trends affecting technology and consumer patterns. One model is "substitution." Recyclables substitution for metals is only about 10% underway in the U.S., and much less in other areas of the world. Substitution helps us understand consumer use patterns on a macro scale.

3. Through interaction with our customer partners and their customers, we collect information about our competitors' customers and other potential customers. We then interact with these potential customers directly at trade shows, trade association meetings, and indirectly through our interactions with equipment manufacturers to determine how we could best meet their needs.

4. We project the relative importance of our key product and service features into the future:

- Through discussions of future needs between our customers and our Marketing and Technical Marketing Representatives.

  Our I-Team members also hold formal meetings with our major customers' top leadership.

- Through our total customer partnership process we better understand future consumer needs. We frequently conduct focus group meetings with our customers' marketing representatives to identify consumer needs. When needs are clarified, we develop a value chain partnership, fully linking all customers from Varifilm to the retailer. This total partnership works to develop the new offering that will meet consumer needs.

- Recyclables uses the continuous improvement process to understand and meet new customer needs. It is based on the premise that the business exists to enable customers to design increasingly productive solutions to their own waste problems. The "iteration" step is where a Varifilm/ customer team jointly identifies better ways to meet customers' needs. Critical to this process are strong partnerships formed with strategic customers.

5. Each business segment within Varifilm quarterly reviews its market segments for changes which might either threaten the market for existing or new products or provide opportunities for new products or services.

**7.1c** Since understanding future customer requirements and expectations is so important to us, finding better ways to do it is built into all the approaches given above. Annually, a cross-functional team (Post Mortem Team) reviews the short- and long-term projections over the past five years, rationale for making these projections, and actual current events. Root cause analysis is conducted to determine why specific projects were not on target from either a positive or negative point of view. Strategies are then implemented to increase the accuracy of our projects.

Working with multiple companies throughout the value chain is perhaps the most important method for improving our ability to understand future marketplace needs. Vertical alliances are growing factors of our business.

## 7.2 Customer Relationship Management

Because we sell to over 2,500 customers, we develop relationship strategies to meet the needs of: (1) *Major Customers*—our partners; and (2) *All customers* from the small, independent businesses to Fortune 500 companies. Less than 10% of our total customers account for 80% of our sales volume. However, sales volume alone does not define our partners. Our criteria for customer partnerships include: customers whose market objectives are aligned with our marketing and technology capabilities; technology, product, or market leaders; and those with needs compatible with our knowledge and resources.

**7.2a & b**  Personal contact is the primary way we determine what is important to our customers. We understand the value chain for our products, and we place resources at various parts of the chain so we can better understand customers' needs.

Our primary customer contacts, their roles, their logistics, and/or technology support are shown in Figure 7.1. Standards are set by first researching issues important to the customer, such as knowledge and courtesy of coworkers or clarity of information. Key drivers are then identified, measures defined and then tested for accuracy.

Our End-Use Marketing, Marketing, Technical Marketing, and Customer Service Representatives (CSRs) build and maintain partnerships with strategic customers through regularly scheduled meetings and Total Quality Fitness Reviews. We also survey customers to verify our understanding of their needs and assess our performance in meeting them. In addition, Technical Marketing enhances our relationships with our customers through on-site assistance in solving problems, whatever the cause. This also helps us ensure realistic customer expectations.

**7.2c**  Our goal is easy access to knowledgeable, consistent contacts for all customers and regular follow-up through normal communication channels.

Our CSRs, the focal point of our day-to-day customer assistance and follow-up, are available by phone during normal working hours. We provide emergency access for our customers so they can reach us after hours and on weekends and holidays. If CSRs are unable to answer questions or address problems, they contact appropriate resources. Marketing personnel visit our strategic customers once a week and our smaller customers once a quarter. Technical Marketing representatives travel to our larger customers' plants 2–3 times per week, and

**Account Managers,** through customer relationships, develop business strategies for major customer accounts. Logistics/technology support: location near customer, electronic and voice mail, and computer access to order and sales data.

**Marketing,** through customer relationships, develops business strategies to fulfill all customer needs. Logistics/technology support: location near customer, electronic and voice mail, and computer access to sales, market, and product data.

**Technical Marketing,** working with customers, identifies key product and service features which meet customer needs, provides technical assistance, and seeks ways to improve our products. Logistics/ technology support: plant and laboratory investigative support, electronic and voice mail, and computer access to sales, customer, and product data.

**End-Use Marketing** services the "downstream" customer—captures key information and reflects consumers' likely market behavior relative to products made from our film. Logistics/technology support: location near industry decision makers (e.g., California, Florida and Texas for Food Wrap), electronic and voice mail, and computer access to sales data.

**Customer Service Representatives** receive, expedite, and track customer orders (key contacts for follow-up on recent transactions). Logistics/technology support: location within the business they support, electronic mail and computer access to sales and warehouse data, order entry and Problem Report System.

**Coworker visits** to customers define detailed requirements and establish joint commitments. (See Figure 7.2.)

**Figure 7.1**    Primary Customer Contacts

they visit smaller customers as needed to deal with quality and service concerns and new product implementation strategies.

Communication with our direct customers is not limited to our primary contacts; it occurs across organizational levels. In addition to our personal contact, our businesses maintain widely advertised 800 telephone numbers to offer specific product information. We also use this contact as a source of customer information including needs/requirements.

Each business ensures that customer assistance is available when needed through an 800 telephone number, product hotline, and voice mail systems available 24 hours/day, 7 days/week. Our major customers are also connected to our electronic mail systems. Our Electrical business utilizes a Call All Customers Program in which manufacturing operators at our plant phone small customers who normally would not have contact with a marketing representative.

We also maintain EDI systems which provide customers direct access to our Product Quality Management and order entry systems. (See Item 2.1.) Our customers choose the communication tools which work for them. Some routinely use electronic devices, such as voice mail and/or electronic mail, in their busi-

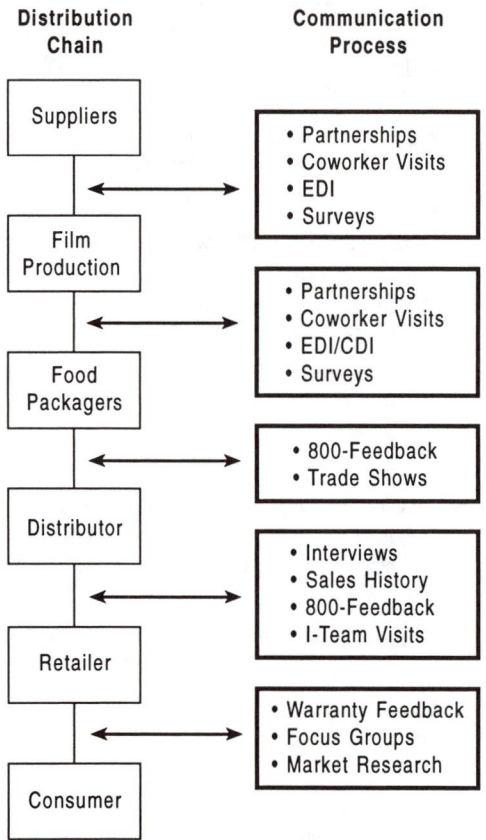

**Figure 7.2**  Food Packaging Distribution Chain with Communication Networks

nesses and therefore feel comfortable using automated devices in their dealings with us; however, smaller companies who have fewer electronic systems prefer the personalized "human" contact. Our customers make their preferences known through their daily contacts with us and in their survey responses.

For our largest customers, we send an electronic status report every morning to report the day's shipments, and we send additional status reports as needed throughout the day. When this report is received by the customer, it is reviewed. If a problem is spotted, a dialogue is initiated between the CSR and the customer to ensure that the supply will be uninterrupted.

We also use a variety of communication tools and strategies to reach customers at all levels in the distribution chain. The distribution chain and communica-

We will respond to customer inquiries as follows:

| | |
|---|---|
| Product delivery | 90% while on the phone; 100% within 24 hours |
| Price | 95% while on the phone; 100% within 24 hours |
| Product line | 90% while on the phone; 100% within 24 hours |
| Technical | Response within 24 hours |

**Figure 7.3**    Representative Customer Service Standards

tion networks shown in Figure 7.2 illustrate the use of different strategies to reach our "downstream" customers.

**7.2d**    Although we have always had service standards, in 1990, we identified the need for more quantitative, fully deployed service standards aligned with the Baldrige criteria. Cross-functional teams within each business were charged with upgrading their standards, reviewing them with customers, documenting them, deploying them throughout the business, measuring performance, and reporting results to the people who influence our ability to meet standards. By the end of 1993, all will have deployed improved service standards.

**7.2e**    Our businesses select qualified people for customer contact positions, provide training to ensure their success, and provide the support they need.

The primary method we use to ensure a common vision for guiding customer contact coworkers is their SMT experience. We continually reinforce this with our publications, including "Quality Reports."

1. The vast majority of our customer contact personnel are selected from within Varifilm. Each business identifies and selects its customer contact personnel with assistance from our human resource consultants.

2. Our customer contact career progression paths are not linear. A person may move from manufacturing to CSR or Technical Marketing to Marketing. Career options are defined in the booklet, *Your Personal Choices.*

3. Many courses are offered to assist people in improving their relationship management skills—"Business Communications" (which includes learning telephone styles), "Effective Negotiating," "Effective Product Management," and "Face-to-Face Selling." Our "Telephone Courtesy" course provides training in listening and talking to customers on the phone.

4. We increasingly empower our customer contact coworkers. Technical Marketing representatives can authorize up to $10,000 for an individual claim

settlement. The CSR can set up new customers, authorize less-than-truck-load shipments, initiate product returns, and authorize payments up to $2000 per incident to reimburse customers for out-of-pocket losses.

5. Coworker morale is assessed informally and formally. Daily interactions with management, customers, and peers provide opportunities to informally assess morale and attitude shifts and provide support. Coworker morale is tracked formally through the Coworker Satisfaction Survey. (See Area 4.2d.)

6. Customer contact coworkers are recognized and rewarded by peers, teams, managers, and corporate management. Every business and function has its own system of peer recognition for outstanding efforts.

7. Customer contact positions are highly valued. Although people are reassigned within the customer contact positions, turnover is low (<1%). The primary reason for leaving is promotion or career broadening.

**7.2f**    All businesses create Problem Reports (PRs) to track complaints, status, and resolutions.

1. When we receive a customer complaint, we strive to (1) satisfy the customer, and (2) resolve the problem.

    In 1990, we computerized PRs in our businesses to store and aggregate complaint information. We do not distinguish between formal and informal complaints. All are logged, and our Product Management representatives immediately begin investigation into the causes of the problems. Held accountable for resolving complaints, they solicit input from other marketing and manufacturing resources, including obtaining and analyzing samples. Solutions are documented in the Problem Report System (PRS). Our businesses track resolution cycle time for each reported trade problem to ensure minimal elapsed time from notification to problem resolution. Each business reviews its unresolved PRs to monitor progress, assign additional resources, if needed, and share learnings.

    Our computerized systems enable us to sort and aggregate complaints by business, customer, product, plant, and type of problem; and trade reports are used to share our learnings with other sites.

2. As part of the problem review described in (1) above, types and frequency of complaints are reviewed to determine the root cause and action necessary to eliminate them. In many cases, there is a direct correlation between complaints and input from customer requirements and expectations and the source of complaints received, which reinforces the priority given projects aimed at meeting customer requirements and expectations.

**7.2g** Varifilm Continuous Improvement Criteria biennial evaluations, Total Quality Fitness Reviews with customers and our own people, and our annual third-party customer satisfaction surveys are used to evaluate and improve our customer relationship management practices.

1. Methods used to gain customer feedback and confidence include direct contact with customers by our customer contact personnel who, through establishing strong personal relationships, are able to gain a better insight on how to improve their performance as well as Varifilm's overall performance.

2. Customer responses to specific survey questions are the key indicators we use to evaluate our customer relationship management practices.

   In our customer satisfaction survey, we ask our customers to evaluate the effectiveness of our relationship management and customer contact performance. For example, customers are asked, "How good is Varifilm Construction at working with customers as partners to improve their relationship?"

   Each business reviews this information annually to identify improvement opportunities. Goals and strategies are developed and prioritized based on the results. (See Item 3.2.)

## 7.3 Commitment to Customers

**7.3a** Our history of commitment to the film industry, our product innovations, the range and quality of products and services, and our responsiveness to new requirements build customer confidence in us; and we back this confidence with a range of implicit and explicit guarantees.

For all our products, we explicitly guarantee conformance to the Product Specifications Record, a formal document of all the product information needed for customer and/or end-use processing requirements. Many customers rely on this guarantee in lieu of their own materials testing. All businesses routinely update Product Specification Records during annual reviews for those product properties that reflect improvement.

Our commitments extend beyond our direct customers to the consumer. We test, certify, and warrant all products carrying the Varifilm certification mark. In Food Packaging, all new food wrap seeking certification is tested in our Olson laboratories. If the sample is not up to standard, our technicians work with the customers' technicians to identify and correct root causes. We document the certification status of our customers' products including all aliases (brand/style names). This information is used by our Consumer Warranty Team to quickly respond to consumer questions.

Although we only provide the film which goes into food wrap, our "Xtra Shelf Life" warranties include (1) Full warranty against flavor loss of foods and beverages wrapped in Xtra Shelf Life; and (2) Varifilm will replace any wrap that does not perform as warranted. Varifilm maintains a "1-800-NEWFILM" telephone number to provide information and resolve warranty issues.

Communication of these commitments is carefully drafted by "third-party" sources with the intent of bringing the customer's perspective into the interpretation of the commitment. These commitments use simple, universally understood words and phrases and are always printed using 12 point type or larger.

Before any commitment is transmitted to customers, the draft is reviewed with at least 3 customers to establish a clear understanding of content and meaning.

**7.3b**    We use the feedback from our customers and consumers to evaluate and improve our commitments.

In 1991, after reviewing the VCIC, Food Packaging decided to make its guarantee more explicit to ensure customer understanding. This guarantee, now found on all rolls of film and every order and invoice the customer receives, states:

> *"We are committed to meeting your requirements. If you are not completely satisfied with our film, we will replace it or credit your account for the cost. Please call us at 1-800-FIXIT4U. "*

This warranty does not change the existing implicit warranty; it avoids a gap between customer expectation and delivery by ensuring that all customers understand it.

## 7.4 Customer Satisfaction Determination

**7.4a**    We determine customer satisfaction through personal contacts, the third-party customer satisfaction surveys, and our Total Quality Fitness Reviews.

1. Our businesses are defined by product, geographic region (United States, Europe, Far East, Latin America), and market. We organize market segments within each business around end-use applications, which are characterized by similarities in customers, product requirements, and distribution channels. We currently serve over 40 major market segments. Market segments are also defined by customer groups with similar processing capabilities.

   Through personal contacts, our Marketing and Technical people provide information on how customers in each market segment think we are doing.

(See Area 7.1a.) Our customer surveys and Total Quality Fitness Reviews provide quantifiable information which help us verify this feedback. Survey results are grouped by product, key market segment, function in the customer's organization (RD&E, Purchasing), and by "sales" or "strategic customers." Key customer satisfaction requirements are:

1. Product Quality
2. On-Time Delivery
3. Ease of Access
4. Price
5. Knowledge of Coworkers

2. Our Customer Satisfaction Surveys assess what our customers value in a supplier; identify product quality, marketing support, customer service, and business effectiveness issues where improvements would increase customer satisfaction; and determine how our customers compare us with our competitors.

We interview key customer decision makers within the various functions (e.g., Research & Development, Purchasing and Business managers) who are knowledgeable about the use of our product in their operation. Because of their positions, their responses correlate directly to anticipated future market behavior.

Our businesses use a survey process developed in collaboration with and conducted by Customer Surveys Inc. (CSI). Respondents are asked early in the 20-minute interview to identify competitive suppliers. After rating the relative importance of a series of quality factors, customers are asked to rate Varifilm and each competitor on a 0–5 scale. (The scale is explained to each respondent, and a word anchor is provided for each number. For example, 5 is excellent, outstanding, the best; 4 is good, better than average.) CSI uses retired business executives, who are at ease talking with our external customers. The customers' narrative comments, including their views of our strengths and weaknesses, are documented for our use.

Use of a third-party firm to conduct the survey, customer anonymity, and the use of business executives as interviewers ensure objectivity. Survey design ensures validity—consultants have incorporated validation questions throughout the survey. After results have been tabulated, answers to these questions are compared to assure validity.

Since we began customer satisfaction surveys in 1989, we have completed 24 surveys, interviewing over 1600 customers, including customers in Korea and Europe. Each business conducts the survey annually. Electrical experimented with quarterly surveys; however, because customers reported this approach was too time-consuming, they now survey annually.

Businesses also use interviews with customers during the Total Quality Fitness Review process. (See Item 3.1.) These reviews are global and include customers outside the United States. Customer input on the Fitness Review and the customer survey showed a strong correlation in 1989 and 1990, so we now rely more on the customer satisfaction survey for customer input.

**7.4b** We compare customers' satisfaction with our performance versus our competitors.

1. At least twice a year, all businesses conduct an internal Trade Leader Assessment of Product Quality. Technical Marketing representatives ask our customers a series of questions to determine their level of satisfaction on product suitability and consistency. (See results in Item 6.2.)

2. Using customer survey data on in-kind competitors, we compute Indices of Relative Competitive Position for customer satisfaction. One index is the average rating gap between us and the average of all competitors for each quality factor, weighted for relative importance. The second index, used as a benchmark, is the rating gap between us and a "hypothetical" BEST competitor, created by the best score for each factor, weighted for relative importance. Customers also provide a "one-shot" overall satisfaction rating of Varifilm and our competitors using the 0–5 scale.

   Because of the limited number of in-kind competitors, our Recyclables' products businesses use a more generalized comparison in their surveys. Their customers compare us with other suppliers in the areas of product, customer service, market representative, and general business.

**7.4c** Our businesses use customer feedback and their experience to evaluate the survey process and recommend improvements. Business leaders review recommendations from the survey teams and make improvements before the survey is rerun. We annually upgrade our questions to improve clarity, understandability, and explicitness. We continue to revise our list of survey participants so we get the information we need.

We moved away from a quarterly frequency to an annual cycle based on customer feedback. Electrical upgraded its survey to use "paired comparisons" of importance and satisfaction to provide greater accuracy than the 0–5 scale.

Market teams use a variety of approaches to integrate survey feedback with other customer inputs. Comparisons are cross referenced with information from our direct personal contacts with customers. Food Packaging confirmed the assessment accuracy of its marketing personnel by including several of them as respondents to the customer satisfaction survey. Their responses closely matched the customers in both relative importance and satisfaction levels.

## 7.5  Customer Satisfaction Results

**7.5a**  Overall, we have maintained a consistently high level of customer satisfaction in the areas important to our customers.

The target measures (product quality, on-time delivery, ease of access, index-price) have been achieved in 1993 and in all cases have exceeded our best competitors.

Leadership reviewed the 1991 survey results and identified responsiveness and customer relationships as opportunities for improvement. Programs were initiated in 1992 to improve these areas. In 1992, customers reported improvements in customer partnerships, responsiveness, understanding of customer requirements, and sales representatives. These improvements are also reflected in our competitive comparison.

Each of our specialty products businesses asked customers to rate our year-to-year progress in overall performance in the areas of products, service, marketing representative, and general business. Ninety-four percent of the customers who rated us believe we are performing better than or the same as we were last year.

**7.5b**  Our customer dissatisfaction indicators support findings that our customers are satisfied with our products and services.

The number of complaints (Problem Reports) per million pounds shipped is extremely low (see Figure 7.4).

Our claim dollars and our returns (see Figures 7.5 and 7.6) are also small.

Varifilm has also received numerous awards from customers and government agencies. The number increased from 11 in 1980 to over 100 in 1992.

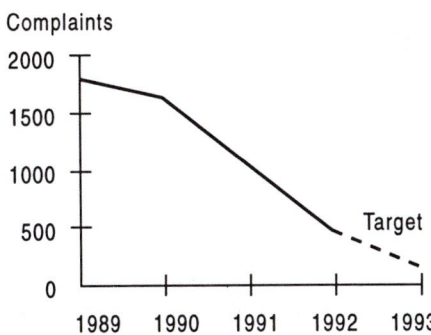

**Figure 7.4**  Customer Complaints per Year

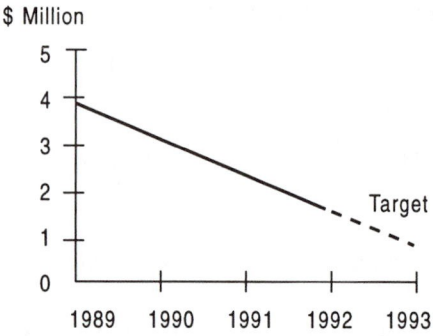

**Figure 7.5** Customer Claim Dollars

## 7.6 Customer Satisfaction Comparison

**7.6a** Varifilm businesses enjoy a competitive advantage in customer satisfaction. Our customers compared us with competing suppliers. They rated us higher than the average of all our competitors and comparable to the best-rated competitor in both 1991 and 1992.

**7.6b** We maintain long-term relationships with our strategic customers. Our businesses use sales history data to track sales by customers and by market segments quarterly. Given the nature of our businesses, analysis of trends in losing customers to competitors is not very insightful. For example, our Construction business sells to 95% of the existing plants—the number is decreasing as plants go out of business or companies merge. Strong end-use preference and

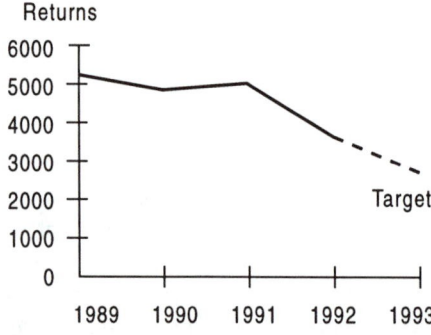

**Figure 7.6** Number of Customer Returns

performance warranties drive the majority of retailers to carry our products, which in turn exerts pressure on the plants.

**7.6c**   Our businesses are industry leaders, as demonstrated by our large market share. We have increased our market share during the past four years. Using data published by the Film Economic Bureau, an industry-supported association, we track market share for these businesses monthly. However, we do not view market share as the only indicator of customer satisfaction. Our businesses use these data and trends to better understand competitors' tactics, strategies, and intent regarding markets and capacity utilization.

Changes in market share of businesses do not surprise us; they usually reflect protracted negotiations for major programs in the industry or competitive consolidations.

Varifilm has itself developed unique long-term "value" contracts where quality improvements are shared with our customers. These aggressive partnerships assure future market share and growth

Our Recyclables business has few, if any, in-kind competitors. We generally measure their growth in new applications or substitution rates for functional competition. Where we have in-kind competition, Varifilm is the leading supplier, and we enjoy the largest market share.

# APPENDIX: QUALITY-RELATED INFORMATION ON THE INTERNET

### Quality Resources Online (www.quality.org)
Sometimes called "the mother of all quality pages," this site has links that are extensive, current, and organized alphabetically into major topics. This is probably the best jumping-off point for quality-related information.

### American Productivity and Quality Center (www.apqc.org)
The American Productivity and Quality Center in Houston has a primary focus on increasing competitiveness and productivity. It offers educational and training services, public seminars, and in-house training. It also houses the International Benchmarking Clearinghouse.

### American National Standards Institute (www.ansi.org)
This home page is a link to official and standards-related information. It provides access to the standards information database (SID), the national standards system network (NSSN), and other standards-related resources.

---

A good summary and description of additional resources can be found in Byron J. Finch, "An Overview of Quality-Oriented Resources on the Internet," *Production & Inventory Management Journal,* Vol. 37 No. 2, Second Quarter 1996, pp. 83–85. Also see Gary L. Parr, "Click into the World of Internet Quality," *Quality Magazine,* Dec. 1996, pp. 65–67. This source also contains an extensive list of sites for software, tools and equipment, and services.

### National Institute of Standards and Technology (www.nist.gov)

The National Institute of Standards and Technology (NIST) site contains basic information regarding the criteria, application, and administration of the Baldrige Award. It provides a link to the NIST pages devoted to each of the Baldrige Award winners, each of which presents a significant amount of information on its total quality management efforts. This is a large site with information on about anything that NIST, in Gaithersburg, Maryland, does.

### U.S. Department of Labor Best Practices Clearinghouse (www.saic.com/fed/uscompanies/labor/)

This site contains information related to best practices used by high-performance companies. It is a good site for benchmarking practices. It contains company profiles and detailed descriptions of practices in a number of areas.

### Best Manufacturing Practices Program (www.bmpcoe.org)

The Best Manufacturing Practices Program provides information on how more than 80 companies have solved manufacturing problems and improved processes. The site is administered by the Office of Naval Research.

### Clemson's Continuous Quality Improvement (gopher://deming.eng.clemson.edu/)

Clemson University's gopher provides a wide range of continuous-quality-improvement-related resources and allows key word searches among all of the files.

### Quality Standards—ISO 9000 (http://www.mep.nist.gov/resources/iso9000/iso9000.html)

### ISO Online (http://www.iso.ch/welcome.html)

### The ISO9000 Guide (http://www.ileaf.com/isoguide.html)

### ISO Certification Case Study (http://www.marinenetwork.com/~qualnet//.isocasel.html)

These sites contain the complete NIST resources on ISO 9000, a wide spectrum of educational resources related to ISO certification, an extensive guide to the process, and a detailed description of the case of a successful ISO certification.

### Quality Function Deployment (http://mijuno.larc.nasa.gov/dfc/qfd.html)

This NASA page provides an overview of quality function deployment processes with links to other important components, such as the voice of the customer.

### The QFD Institute (http://www.nauticom.net/www/qfdi/)

This site contains quality function deployment resources.

### The Quality Junction (http://www.cris.com/~Wcterry)

This is a comprehensive junction from which you can travel to a long list of quality-related sites. It is very functional and full of information.

### Quality Technology Page (http://mijuno.larc.nasa.gov/dfc/qtec.html)

This NASA page contains many of the tools and techniques of total quality management, such as design for quality, kaizen, the seven basic tools, the seven management tools, the seven new product planning tools, statistical quality control, and Taguchi methods.

### Science & Engineering Network News (SENN) (http://www.senn.com)

This site provides coverage of Internet resources for science and engineering disciplines. It covers Web sites, ftp and telnet sites, mailing lists, and news groups.

# INDEX